HANDLOADER'S DIGEST

NINTH EDITION

Edited by Ken Warner

DBI BOOKS, INC., NORTHFIELD, ILLINOIS

Our Cover

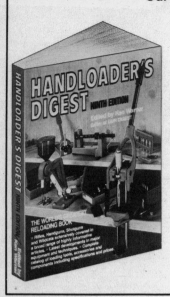

The cover of this edition of HANDLOADER'S DIGEST, our 9th, showcases the high quality Bonanza reloading products, with several new items. Making their debut this year are the "Blue Ribbon" reloader's scale which has a 511-grain capacity and three poises for greater accuracy. This model is the top of the Bonanza scale line. Also new is the Co-Ax "Blue Ribbon" priming device with the improved E-Z JUST shell holder jaws. The unique Co-Ax reloading press, Bench Rest powder measure and measure stand combine with Bonanza's full line of reloading dies and other equipment to give the reloader everything he needs to turn out precision handloaded ammunition. Photo by John Hanusin.

HANDLOADER'S DIGEST STAFF

EDITOR-IN-CHIEF
Ken Warner

ASSISTANT TO THE EDITOR
Lilo Anderson

SENIOR STAFF EDITOR
Harold A. Murtz

ASSOCIATE EDITOR
Robert S.L. Anderson

GRAPHICS
James P. Billy
Mary MacDonald

EDITOR EMERITUS
John T. Amber

PUBLISHER
Sheldon L. Factor

MEMBER OF THE
NATIONAL
SHOOTING
SPORTS
FOUNDATION
INC.

Manuscripts, contributions and inquiries, including first class return postage, should be sent to the Handloader's Digest Editorial Offices, One Northfield Plaza, Northfield, IL 60093. All material received will receive reasonable care, but we will not be responsible for its safe return. Material accepted is subject to our requirements for editing and revisions. Author payment covers all rights and title to the accepted material, including photos, drawings and other illustrations. Payment is at our current rates.

Arms and Armour Press, London, G.B., exclusive licensees and distributors in Britain and Europe; Australia; Nigeria, South Africa and Zimbabwe; India and Pakistan; Singapore, Hong Kong and Japan.

CAUTION: Technical data presented here, particularly technical data on handloading and on firearm adjustment and alteration, inevitably reflects individual experience with particular equipment and components under specific circumstances the reader cannot duplicate exactly. Such data presentations therefore should be used for guidance only and only with caution. DBI Books, Inc. accepts no responsibility for results obtained using this data.

ISBN 0-910676-33-X   **Library of Congress Catalog #62-15069**

CONTENTS

FEATURES

DEPARTMENTS

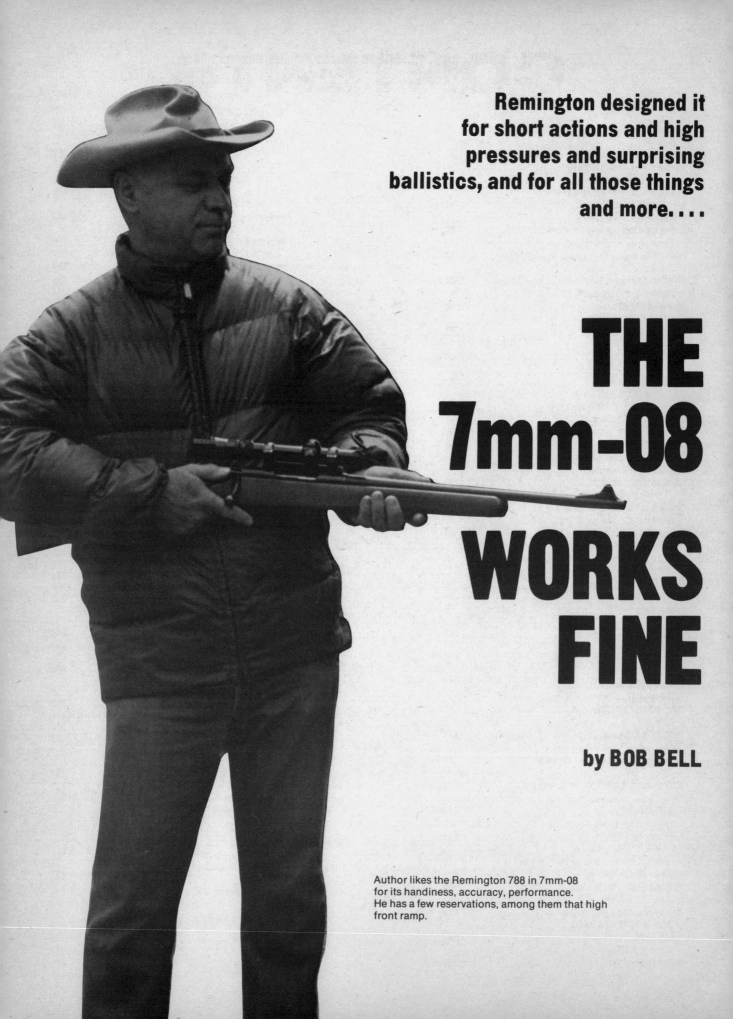

Remington designed it
for short actions and high
pressures and surprising
ballistics, and for all those things
and more....

THE
7mm-08
WORKS
FINE

by BOB BELL

Author likes the Remington 788 in 7mm-08
for its handiness, accuracy, performance.
He has a few reservations, among them that high
front ramp.

SIX INCHES of snow blanketed the ground, so it was easy to see the deer—three of them—drop out of the pines on the steep sidehill, moving ahead of the drivers. They slipped through a break in an old stone wall and disappeared in the high brown grass and alders of the frozen swamp that filled the bottom before me. I eased down behind a fencepost and waited, rifle ready, thumb on the safety. If they kept coming, they had to cross a powerline. It wouldn't take them long to do that, but at least they'd be in the open.

I waited, and watched. It was cold —8 degrees when we left the house that morning—but I didn't feel it now, even with my wool-clad butt buried in snow. Then I saw movement, brown among the tall brown grass. They'd reached the edge of the powerline and stopped, still in cover. Through the little Redfield variable, I could see one was a buck. Small, but good enough for the last day. I waited. Then, the deer was crossing the open stretch, maybe 70 yards away; then the buck was there and the crosswires were on him and the gun cracked sharply. In my solid position, the rifle couldn't recoil enough to make me lose him in the scope, so I saw him die. It looked as if every ligament in his body had been cut at once. In the blink of an eye he was motionless in the snow. The kill had been instantaneous.

An unusual incident? No. I've watched essentially the same thing dozens of times. You have, too. I describe it only because it was the first shot I fired at game using Remington's latest hunting cartridge, the 7mm/08. And because it was the first big game animal I've killed with a factory loaded round since the late '40s. And because that round went out of the new 788 Remington rifle—carbine would be a better word, considering its 18½-inch barrel—unaltered in any way except for the addition of a Redfield 1.7-5x scope.

It might seem strange to mention a factory round in a book devoted to handloading, but that's how it was. We'll get to the homegrown loads quickly. First let me say that this factory load hit the top of the shoulder and destroyed a fist-size section of spine, which explains the instantaneous kill. However, there's not the slightest doubt that this little 7mm/08 will do a fine job with conventional

New 7mm-08, left, with an assortment of Bell's pet 7mm's: 7x57 Mauser, 284 Winchester. 280 Remington, 7x61 Sharpe & Hart Magnum, 7mm Remington Magnum. All are outstanding cartridges, with ballistics that make them effective on a variety of game at most hunting ranges.

Bell's Model 700 7mm-308 wildcat got up by Al Wardrop has a 24″ barrel in this photo, and in all other respects is a vintage 700.

Bell's deer-killing 788 served well in wet and scrambling Pennsylvania deer hunts. Scope is a Redfield 1.7-5x variable.

A simple selection of your choice of 140-gr. 7mm bullets serves best in the 7mm-08, Bell has demonstrated.

Working up loads is familiar stuff to Bell. In the beginning stages, he gets up four round batches in baggies, shoots three and saves one, clearly labeled as shown.

Bell's early load work at the range is stripped to simplicity itself—3-shot groups and one-inch square orange aiming points.

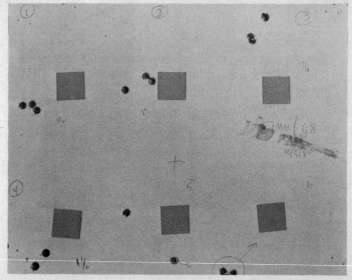

body shots also. It uses bullets of the same diameter, weight, shape and construction as numerous other 7mm's, at essentially the same velocity. Countless critters have been slain with those, so results with this new cartridge will have to be practically identical.

Interestingly, some Remington ammo, including the load we hunted with and chronographed, did not actually use a Remington bullet. Factory bullets were temporarily unavailable for that loading run, so the 139-gr. Hornady was utilized. As the nearby table shows, velocity according to the Oehler chronograph and Skyscreens was 2960 from a 24-inch barrel (exactly 100 fps higher than listed in published ballistics), and 2822 from the 18½-inch barrel. These are impressive results from such a small case. Truth is, they were so impressive we were skeptical about them, but repeated tests were consistent and velocities from several other cartridges tried at the same time were at their normal levels, so there was nothing wrong with the chronograph.

But good as these are, they're not significantly different from those of

range, say. That means they can get highly impressive ballistics out of this short case. If you don't think that's so, study the following table which compares the 7mm/08 with various highly regarded cartridges, all shown with the factory load which gives the highest remaining energy at 300 yards.

	300 Yd. V	300 Yd. E
25-06/120-gr. PSP	2360	1480
270/130-gr. PP	2400	1660
7mm/08/140-gr. SP	2189	1490
7x57/139-gr. SP	1910	1190
284/150-gr. PP	2160	1550
7mm Express/150-gr. PSP	2203	1616
7mm Magnum/150-gr. SP	2320	1990
308/150-gr. BP	2050	1400
30-06/150-gr. BP	2240	1670
30-06/200-gr. SPBT	2120	2000

Admittedly, the significantly larger cases using heavier bullets have more power (it would require rewriting the rules of ballistics to make it otherwise), but the little 7mm/08 equals or surpasses a surprising number of popular loads and is so close to the others that it makes one wonder if their edge is worth their attendant muzzle blast, recoil and rifle weight. So long as hunting is confined to the smaller species—deer, antelope,

and bullet release upon firing. That can increase chamber pressure dangerously.

Or reversing the situation, a necked-down 308 case might cause trouble if used in the factory 7mm/08 chamber. Not because it is slightly shorter, but because the neck will be thicker than the 7mm/08's. The brass from that larger neck diameter has to go somewhere when squeezed down, you know. The wildcat chamber, if reamed by a competent gunsmith, is cut to accommodate this, but the 7mm/08 chamber is not. So shooters should be leery of using 7mm-308 ammo in the factory 7mm/08 chamber, the neck diameter of which might not permit adequate case expansion to release the bullet easily.

Thus, the same problem might result from either switch—factory ammo in the wildcat chamber or wildcat ammo in the factory chamber—because in one situation the case neck is too long and in the other it's too thick.

I was particularly interested in all of this because for some seven or eight years I have been using a wildcat 7mm-308. In the early '70s I traded gunsmith Al Wardrop out of a short M700 action, originally barreled for the 308, intended to build a lightweight deer rifle. The 308 itself is a fine load, but I've never been fond of 30-caliber rifles, so I decided to go with some kind of 7mm. At first I was thinking in terms of a 284 Winchester, but I already had one of those, plus an assortment of other 7mm's, so I was in a bit of a quandary. I decided to be logical about it. I had an action engineered to handle the 308, so could easily try anything based on that case—from the 243, which didn't interest me, to the 358 Winchester, a real temptation. It would also be easy to neck down the case to 25 (remember the old 25 Souper?), 6.5mm, 270 or 7mm, or neck it up to 338—another real temptation. In the end, I decided to go with the 7mm. It wasn't an original idea. As mentioned, many wildcatters had done it years before. I even mentioned it in "Today's Wildcats," an article in GUN DIGEST 21 (1967).

P. O. Ackley's *Handbook for Shooters and Reloaders* suggested the 7mm-308 could give a 140-gr. bullet upwards of 3000 fps, thus there was no doubt it could handle deer and the like. I had Wardrop install a Douglas barrel chambered for this case. It was long enough to finish up at 27 inches, so we went with that length awhile to get some chronograph dope using bullets of 120 to 175 grains and a reasonable

---

7mm/08 Factory Numbers

Ballistics given for the 140-gr. factory load, the only one currently available, are as follows, from a 24-inch barrel:

	Muzzle	100 yds	200 yds	300 yds	400 yds	500 yds
Velocity (fps)	2860	2625	2402	2189	1988	1798
Energy (fp)	2542	2142	1793	1490	1228	1005
Trajectory (in)	—	+2.1	—0—	−8.1	−23.5	−47.7

---

previously established cartridges, so why offer the new one? Several reasons. Most important is the fact that this one fits neatly into a short action, a design that's gaining popularity constantly. Case length is 2.035″, compared with 2.540″ for the 7mm Express, 2.235″ for the 7x57mm, 2.500″ for the 7mm Remington Magnum. Even the squatty 284 Winchester case is longer, at 2.170″. Obviously such a cartridge had built-in appeal for Remington, a company which already was producing the M788 and a short M700. Also, by going to a new design for use in their strong bolt guns, Remington could load ammo to currently acceptable pressures without worrying about possible problems with ancient rifles, such as might occur if 7x57 loads were boosted to the 50,000+ psi

caribou, etc.—the 7mm/08 seems an extremely rational choice.

Let's look at some specifics. The 7mm/08 is basically the 7.62mm NATO cartridge, or 308 Winchester, necked down to 7mm. However, the two cases are not identical. According to SAAMI specs dated 4/21/80, maximum case length of the 7mm/08 is 2.035″, which is some 20 thousandths greater than the nominal length of the 308. This becomes important when it is realized that for many years experimenters have been necking down the NATO case to form a wildcat called the 7mm-308. Using the new factory cartridge in the wildcat chamber, which could well be shorter, might be dangerous. It can jam the case mouth into the chamber mouth, preventing normal neck expansion

A key measurement in managing the 7mm-08 Remington together with cases from 308 brass is the neck diameter of the loaded round.

assortment of powders. I had no intention of keeping the barrel at that length, but you don't often get a chance to check given loads at different lengths of the same barrel, so it seemed a good idea to take advantage of the opportunity. Looking back, I wish we had used more powders, but we weren't expecting the introduction of a near-twin factory load which has since given more interest to the whole situation.

As I was thinking in terms of a lightweight deer rifle, not an ex-

tremely accurate competition rig, the chamber was not cut unusually tight. I wanted it to readily accept necked-down 308 brass of any make, and there often are slight variations, particularly in neck length after a firing or two. To avoid the necessity for constant checking and trimming, the neck length of the chamber was made a bit longer than normal, giving an overall depth of 2.070" (a fortuitous happening in light of the extended neck length of the 7mm/08 when it appeared), and the neck area of the

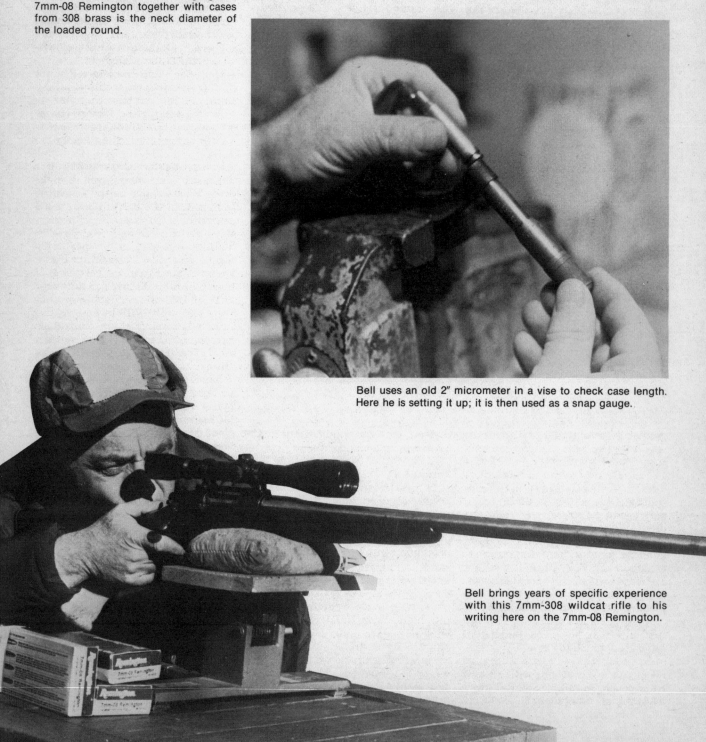

Bell uses an old 2″ micrometer in a vise to check case length. Here he is setting it up; it is then used as a snap gauge.

Bell brings years of specific experience with this 7mm-308 wildcat rifle to his writing here on the 7mm-08 Remington.

chamber was cut large enough to allow for the thicker-than-normal brass resulting from the necking-down operation.

In regard to this, it can be noted that with 7mm-308 ammo created by forming WRA 68 cases, the necks of loaded cartridges averaged .312″ just behind the case mouth and .314″+ near the juncture of the neck and shoulder. After firing, these measurements were .314″+ and .316″+ respectively. When I got the M788 7mm/08, measurements of Remington ammunition at the same reference points averaged .309″ and .312″ for loaded rounds, .315″ and .317″+ for fired cases.

RCBS dies were available for the 7mm-308 when I got my gun built, and were used for all my loading for it. However, when the 7mm/08 Remington brass appeared, with its normal-thickness neck, I found that these dies would not reduce the necks enough to grip the bullet firmly. I had a 7mm Lyman Tru-Line Jr. neck-sizing die with a 7/8-14 adapter, and it solved this problem, though it required an extra loading step.

There was nothing finicky about either the 7mm-308 or the 7mm/08. Both handled the normal range of powders which logically would be used in this size case, with no quirks or foibles to accommodate to. That was as expected, of course. The 7mm is a medium-size caliber and the case is of medium capacity if we consider deer cartridges as starting with the 243 and topping out with the '06. Cases in this range most often are loaded with bullets of medium weight propelled by powders of medium burning rate, and they work well without all the hype and hoopla that tend to accompany magnums.

Loading was straightforward. For the wildcat, I ran lubed 308 cases into the full-length RCBS sizing die, wiped them dry, dipped the necks into powdered graphite and ran them over the expander a few times to sort of smooth things up after the neck reduction. It's worth mentioning that a case formed in this way often has greater overall length than before forming. That is, a 7mm-308 is slightly longer than the 308 from which it was made. An old micrometer set up to use as a snap-gauge easily shows this, and it's something that should be allowed for when a chamber is being cut. Repeated firing lengthens necks even further, so that it's not unusual to find 7mm-308 cases which are longer than once-fired 7mm/08s, despite the longer original length of the latter. Except for the first full-length sizing of the 7mm-308s, cases were neck sized only. Case mouths were slightly chamfered after sizing.

I tried none of the varmint hunter's little accuracy tricks such as adjusting bullet seating depth to optimum relationship with the lands. In the first place, it wouldn't have been practicable; deer rifle loads have to work through a magazine, so bullets cannot be seated to give an over-all length significantly longer than normal. In the second place, it wasn't necessary; what's the good of a quarter-inch smaller group when all you have to do is hit a 12-inch circle?

All powder charges were thrown on a Bonanza measure, after being set up with my old Redding scale. I can't remember how long I've had it, but it still checks out with a comparatively new and much more expensive balance, so I go on using it. Remington 9½ primers were used for all handloads (and probably were the factory's choice in their ammo). Since the 7mm-308s used in testing were formed from Winchester brass, it would have theoreti-

7mm-08: Barrel Length Effect

Bullet	Load	27″	24″	22″	18½″
120 Hornady	40/4895				2500
	41/4895	2784			2553
	43/4895	3039			
	45/748	3165			
	47/760	2958	2816	2747	2625
	44/4064		3019	2963	2856
	48/4350	3012	2703	2618	2584
139 Hornady	41/4895	2784	2781	2734	2668
	42/4895		2824		
	43/4064	2942	2893	2832	2716
	45/760		2607	2582	2574
	45/4350	2590			
	46/4350	2721	2698		2433
	48/4350		2680	2638	2562
140 Remington factory*			2960	2915	2822
145 Speer	40/4895	2989			
	43/4350	2550			
	46/4831				2400
150 Remington CL	42/760	2491			
	44/760	2564	2538	2464	2343
	43/780	2525			
	44/4350				2285
	47/4350		2574	2534	2450
	47/4831				2482
154 Hornady RN	41/4064	2708	2667	2637	2566
	42/4350	2525			
160 Speer	45/780	2500			
	43/4350	2550			
160 Sierra	41/4064	2758	2678	2633	2566
	42/780				2089
	43/4350	2562	2421		
	45/4350		2511	2478	2418
162 Hornady Int.	41/4064	2758			
175 Speer	41/4350		2219		2066
	42/4350		2218		2153

*Early on, a small amount of factory ammo was loaded with the 139-gr. Hornady as Remington bullets of the desired weight were temporarily unavailable. The chronographing above was done with the Hornady-bullet ammo.

All testing was done with an Oehler chronograph and Skyscreens. Velocities shown are instrumentals taken at 7½ feet.

The above loads caused no problems in the rifles used, but should be regarded as general guides only and be approached with caution from below, using all due care. No responsibility arising from problems resulting from their use will be assumed by the author or this publication.

There's not a great deal of weight difference between Bell's two rifles in 7mm-08, but the 788 is lots handier in the woods.

Load development sometimes produces a problem that is not a problem in a good tight rifle, and this partial separation is an example.

cally been better to use Winchester primers, but decades of loading have convinced me that such quibbles are best allotted to the benchrest gang. Almost never can a difference be noted in a hunting rifle, so I don't get excited about such things anymore.

As mentioned, some early chronographing was done with a 27-inch barrel on the 7mm-308, although my intention always had been to wind up with a 22-inch tube for hunting. But it was a simple matter for Wardrop to cut it to 24 inches first, and he, Bob Wise and I did a fair amount of chronographing at that length. This should interest some shooters who are considering the 7mm/08 in the M700 Remington Varmint Special, which has this barrel length. Finally, Wardrop shortened my barrel to 22 inches and we chronographed most of the loads we'd tried earlier. These, too, have some application, as in December, 1980, Remington announced that the 7mm/08 would be available in the short action M700 BDL with 22-inch

barrel—which essentially duplicates the rig I've been using for years.

I was particularly interested in the 788 when it was announced in the 7mm/08 because it was a commercial version of a wildcat which had interested me for years, and because it would let me know how my loads worked in an even shorter barrel than my 22-incher.

Well, we shot 'em and the results from 27, 24, 22 and 18½-inch barrels are listed in the table. Unfortunately, there are some gaps, for reasons which I can't recall at the moment as some of this data was collected years ago. But I think things are complete enough to give a good idea of how things went with one wildcat and one factory load of nearly identical dimensions. You'll note that the factory load was shot in the wildcat version. Remington advises against this, and we do too, for we have no way of knowing how your 7mm-308 chamber compares with Remington 7mm-08 ammo. But as detailed earlier, various measurements

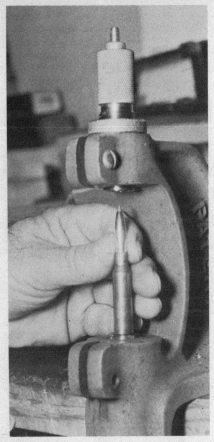

Managing the nicely medium 7mm-08 is no problem. In contrast with some others, for instance, there's plenty of room around a C-press.

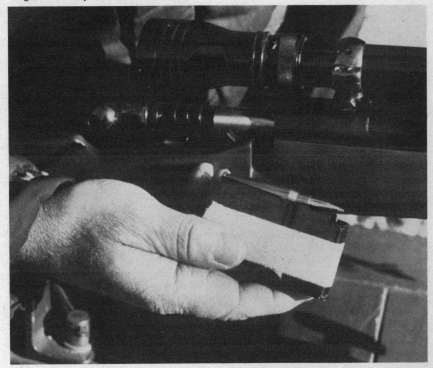

One wrinkle Bell worked out is the pure invention of a hunter—he taped his 788's magazine thusly so it wouldn't rattle.

indicated nearly identical dimensions for the two guns we were shooting, so we went ahead.

All loads were tested for accuracy as well as velocities, of course, the firing being done at 100 yards, in 3- or 5-shot groups, benchrest, with 10x and 12x Leupolds instead of big game scopes. Both factory ammo and handloads gave good to excellent accuracy. It was unusual to fire a group that went over 1½ inches, and some 3-shotters were as small as a half-inch. I feel that three shots is enough for a hunting rifle, especially when a number of groups is fired. One series fired with the 788, for instance, went 1, ½, ⅞ and 1½ inches. This might not excite a benchrester, but it will sure do the job on any critter this load is likely to be turned onto. I considered showing average group size with each load fired, but decided against it. Each gun is a law unto itself when it comes to handling a specific load, so such information has limited value. It seems enough to say that a wide variety of loads give good hunt-

ing accuracy. It won't be difficult to develop a good one in any normal rifle of this caliber.

An important reason for selecting the 7mm/08 is its availability in several fine rifles of different price ranges. When introduced in early 1980, the new cartridge was offered in an updated version of the no-frills M788, liked by cost-conscious hunters, and in the 24-inch M700 BDL Varmint Special for the metallic silhouette shooters who long have favored the wildcat 7mm-308 for their iron-critter bopping. It's now also available in a 22-inch M700. And, for that matter, in the Savage 99.

From the beginning, I was convinced a 22-inch barrel was the answer for this necked-down 308, and maybe it does make the most sense. But the 18½-incher is so handy I'm tempted to have Al chop my 700 one more time. Maybe I'll just compromise again . . . 20 inches oughta be about perfect, right? ●

Bell got lucky. His old RCBS 7mm-308 dies worked out fine with the 7mm-08, as did his original wildcat chamber. Not all do.

SPEER'S LATEST 7mm-08 DATA:

HERE, fired in a Remington Model 700 with 24-inch barrel, using Remington cases and CCI primers, are a number of useful loads developed by Speer's good old boys for the 7mm-08 Remington cartridge.

In the article immediately preceding this presentation, Bob Bell made the point that the 7mm-08 has a great deal of medium to it. That is, nothing about the cartridge is difficult, so long as you're not fooling around with a 7mm-308 wildcat as well. These charts absolutely bear him out.

Look at them: That's as wide a range of useful powders as you'll see listed for almost any modern cartridge. The 7mm-08 just isn't finicky.

It isn't bashful either. There are seven loads here to push a 130-gr. bullet over 3000 fps, and eight others to take it over 2900 fps. That's right up there with other great game cartridges.

Ken

Remington M700
24" Bbl.
Remington Cases   CCI 200, *CCI 250

.284-115 HP   C.O.A. 2.7"

Powder	Charge	Muzzle Velocity	Powder	Charge	Muzzle Velocity
IMR 4895	48.0	3230	IMR 3031	45.0	3187
	46.0	3084		43.0	3055
	44.0	2951		41.0	2947
760	*52.0	3224	H380	*52.0	3155
	*50.0	3101		*50.0	3038
	*48.0	2898		*48.0	2902
IMR 4320	47.0	3211	H450	*56.0	3112
	45.0	3076		*54.0	2898
	43.0	2961		*52.0	2763
IMR 4064	47.0	3211	785	*55.0	3060
	45.0	3061		*53.0	2957
	43.0	2921		*51.0	2861
N204	53.0	3203	IMR 4350	51.0	3049
	51.0	3091		49.0	2931
	49.0	2976		47.0	2837

.284-130 SP   C.O.A. 2.77"

Powder	Charge	Muzzle Velocity	Powder	Charge	Muzzle Velocity
760	*51.0	3086	H380	*49.0	3015
	*49.0	2980		*47.0	2887
	*47.0	2871		*45.0	2761
IMR 4350	50.0	3066	H450	*54.0	3008
	48.0	2936		*52.0	2905
	46.0	2841		*50.0	2881
IMR 4064	45.0	3052	IMR 3031	42.0	2938
	43.0	2905		40.0	2714
	41.0	2783		38.0	2531
N204	50.0	3046	785	*53.0	2926
	48.0	2916		*51.0	2828
	46.0	2797		*49.0	2711
IMR 4895	45.0	3023	IMR 4320	43.0	2905
	43.0	2894		41.0	2788
	41.0	2769		39.0	2655

Note: Maximum loads listed should be used with caution.

.284-145 SP & BT C.O.A. 2.8"

Powder	Charge	Muzzle Velocity	Powder	Charge	Muzzle Velocity
760	*49.0	2962	785	*52.0	2809
	*47.0	2832		*50.0	2701
	*45.0	2716		*48.0	2591
MRP	52.0	2901	H380	*46.0	2795
	50.0	2784		*44.0	2647
	48.0	2666		*42.0	2551
IMR 4350	48.0	2900	IMR 4320	41.0	2756
	46.0	2761		39.0	2635
	44.0	2643		37.0	2521
H450	*52.0	2889	IMR 4895	41.0	2751
	*50.0	2784		39.0	2628
	*48.0	2673		37.0	2517
H414	47.0	2854	748	*40.0	2712
	45.0	2723		*38.0	2564
	43.0	2598		*36.0	2423

.284-160 SP, BT, MT & GS C.O.A. 2.8"

Powder	Charge	Muzzle Velocity	Powder	Charge	Muzzle Velocity
MRP	52.0	2848	H414	*45.0	2684
	50.0	2746		*43.0	2571
	48.0	2651		*41.0	2468
IMR 4350	47.0	2810	IMR 4320	40.0	2612
	45.0	2697		38.0	2473
	43.0	2581		36.0	2351
760	*48.0	2789	IMR 4895	40.0	2590
	*46.0	2679		38.0	2465
	*44.0	2556		36.0	2341
785	*51.0	2750	H380	*44.0	2578
	*49.0	2656		*42.0	2463
	*47.0	2543		*40.0	2358
H450	*50.0	2733	748	*39.0	2516
	*48.0	2632		*37.0	2397
	*46.0	2541		*35.0	2281

.284-175 MT & GS C.O.A. 2.65"

Powder	Charge	Muzzle Velocity	Powder	Charge	Muzzle Velocity
MRP	51.0	2799	H414	*44.0	2666
	49.0	2717		*42.0	2576
	47.0	2645		*40.0	2481
IMR 4831	48.0	2734	IMR 4350	45.0	2648
	46.0	2660		43.0	2572
	44.0	2582		41.0	2509
785	*50.0	2706	H380	*43.0	2513
	*48.0	2605		*41.0	2411
	*46.0	2513		*39.0	2302
760	46.0	2678	IMR 4320	39.0	2513
	44.0	2606		37.0	2390
	42.0	2513		35.0	2271
H450	*49.0	2666	IMR 4895	38.0	2450
	*47.0	2599		36.0	2230
	*45.0	2551		34.0	2017

Note: Maximum loads listed should be used with caution.

NOTE: This data was developed in a pressure barrel of standard industry dimensional specifications. However, at the time of testing, industry reference ammunition was not available. Pressures of the maximum loads shown here are in line with those of Remington 7mm-08 factory loads fired under the same conditions as these data. Users should approach all maximum loads with caution.

He had to pay 2.9¢ per grain to get it, but this writer finds lots of good stuff in . . .

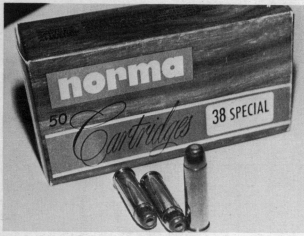

Norma claims a 200 fps advantage for this new 38 Special "Magnum" load, and gets it. The powder does it.

NORMA'S NEW HANDGUN POWDER

by **CLAUD S. HAMILTON**

MANY YEARS ago—more than I care to admit—I studied "Hayes' Elements of Ordnance" at the Military Academy in preparation for what was to become a career with Field Artillery. One of the things I remember best was the relationship between pressure and time that each individual propellant powder establishes when it is fired in a gun. Time, to a degree, can be equated in handguns to barrel length in inches. Most of our modern handgun powders give curves that look, in a general way, like this:

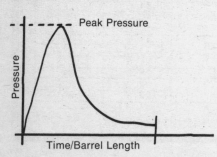

The sharp drop-off at the right indicates incomplete burning, and flash at the muzzle, another undesirable characteristic.

The challenge that has long faced chemical engineers in the powder business is three-fold. First, it is desirable to keep peak pressure low. Peak pressure determines how strong and heavy the gun tube must be. Next, the rapid fall off of combustion needs to be slowed and extended so as to enlarge the area under the curve; this area represents the useful work done by the powder, and the velocity imparted to the projectile. Finally, pressure ought to be made to drop to zero right at the muzzle so as to minimize blast and flash.

That's a tall order.

Back during World War II we experimented with ground aluminum oxide mixed into cannon powder to lessen the heat of combustion and eliminate flash. This was important since cannon are often located and fired upon by the enemy by their muzzle flash at night. The flash was pretty well eliminated but the result was that a dense cloud of black smoke covered the battery after each shot, and it was nearly as rough on the lungs as tear gas.

We have had some successes . . . During the war in Viet Nam we used Nitroguanadine as an additive to powders used with the 20mm gun with the same object in mind. These guns were much used on river craft operating against the Viet Cong at night, and their muzzle flash gave away their locations quickly. Nitroguanadine not only eliminated the flash but cooled combustion and reduced wear without cutting velocity or raising pressure. It is an excellent additive, and is not new. Ordnance has experimented with it since the early 1920s. The catch is that it comes only from Canada, and—you guessed it—is very costly.

There are other approaches used to control the speed and manner of burning so as to improve efficiency. Control of grain size and shape is one. Another is the use of coatings. What the chemical engineers are after, as a goal, is a time-pressure curve something like this:

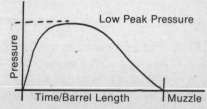

Norma's new powder—available only in loaded cartridges—is a very, very fine, grey ball powder unlike any powder the author has seen.

In no instance was hard extraction encountered. Note that the primers from these 38 Special loads are not excessively flattened.

Norma sold only 110-gr. loads with the new powder; the author decided to see how the powder might perform with bullets of 125, 140 and 158 grains and found it does splendidly, if somewhat expensively.

This Ruger Security Six 357 Magnum revolver provided no problem in the test of the new powder in the 357 case.

Norma of Sweden marketed and advertised a new 38 Special loading using their 110-grain JHP bullet for which they claim about 200 feet per second (fps) more velocity than U.S. commercial loads while retaining standard 38 Special peak pressures. It was, they stressed, *not* a "+P" load. This was not supported by tests by Hornady Manufacturing Company and others who recorded pressures in the "+P" range. Finally Norma decided to make their round a +P load officially.

Reading the advertisements, several questions came immediately to mind. First, of course, I asked "Why only the 110-grain load? Is the new powder they are obviously using not well suited to heavier bullet loads, or perhaps is it even dangerous? And how does it perform in other cartridges?"

So far as I know, Norma has not

These three revolvers were chosen to test the heavier 38 Special bullets: the K-38, the Model 15-2 Combat Masterpiece, and the Colt Detective Special.

Smith's 44 Magnum Model 29 sits in the Ransom Rest awaiting testing with Norma's new powder. The Norma powder performed only marginally better than U.S. powders, and seems to want a longer barrel in this large caliber.

offered their new powder in bulk for loaders. I had to get mine by buying the cartridges and cutting them up, not a very cheap way at $26 a box of fifty!

My first step was to pour the charges of ten cartridges into the tray on my powder scale and weigh them. Dividing that by ten I came up with a—surprising—charge of 17.7 grains. That's quite large compared to most powders we deal with in this country. This powder is as fine in granulation as any that I have ever seen, and is a ball powder. Spill a little on your bench and you'll be surprised at how everything you set down on it rolls about. It is also an unusual silvery color, and looks almost like finely ground metal.

Since there is no loading data published on this powder, I took the approach of computing my starting charges for heavier 38 Special bullets using the inverse ratios of their weights to that of the 110-grain bullet used in the Norma load. Rounded off, these gave me the following:

Speer 125-gr. JHP bullet 15.5 grains
Speer 140-gr. JHP bullet 14.0 grains
Speer 158-gr. JHP bullet 12.5 grains

I do not recommend this as a universal approach when working with unknown powders; in this case it worked well.

I used three revolvers to gauge the performance of this new powder with the heavy bullets: a Colt Detective

Special 2-inch, a Smith & Wesson Model 15 Combat Masterpiece 4-inch, and a K-38 6-inch. After I put up a series of loads using all three bullet weights, a friend and I went to the pistol range at Fairfax Rod & Gun Club and set up my Speed Meter II chronograph. I make it a habit to do all my handgun chronograph firing off the Ransom Rest and no longer shoot up skyscreens.

I have no pressure gun. My decisions on what was "maximum" were sub-

jective and based largely on the great muzzle blast and noise I got with my top loads. Primers did begin to show pressure signs but at no time did I ever see badly flattened primers and there was never any extraction difficulty with any of the three revolvers. I probably could have safely gone on a few tenths grain with each load, but as you will see, it wasn't necessary.

The Norma powder gives a clear advantage with all the heavier bullets. On averages it comes to +229 fps for the 2 inch, and +170 fps each for the 140- and 158-grain bullets. These, of course, are just my results with the limited number of rounds I could afford to shoot. It seems clear to me that the Norma powder has just about as much to offer for the heavier 38-cal. bullets as it does for the 100-grain load. I can see no evidence whatsoever of danger involved in its use with these bullets. There may be some, but not so far.

When it came to the matter of how this powder might perform in other cartridges, the first one to come to mind was the 357 Magnum. And, the problem once again was how to determine a starting load. This time I decided to keep things relatively simple and use the same 110-grain bullet Norma did. My charge, then, was based upon a volumetric comparison of the two cases. In this instance, I thought that the 357 could safely take a proportionally larger charge than the 38 Special because of the larger case volume. The ratio came out to be

BARREL LENGTHS AND VELOCITIES IN 38 SPECIAL

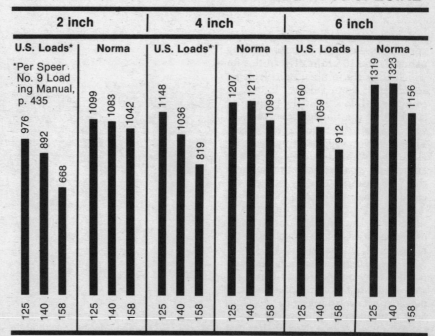

	2 inch			4 inch			6 inch	
U.S. Loads*		Norma	U.S. Loads*		Norma	U.S. Loads		Norma
*Per Speer No. 9 Loading Manual, p. 435								
976	892	668	1099	1083	1042	1148	1036	819	1207	1211	1099	1160	1059	912	1319	1323	1156
125	140	158	125	140	158	125	140	158	125	140	158	125	140	158	125	140	158

about 1.2 to 1.0 but I rounded off the starting charge for the 357 at 18.0 grains.

Next I decided to check out the 44 Magnum, which constituted a really big change in case volume. The big magnum, on a case volume to case volume basis, gave me a starting charge of 25.0 grains, and in this case I once again used the lightest bullet available to me, the 200-grain Speer JHP.

Finally, I made what for me seemed "the big leap." I chose the 9mm Parabellum as my final load, and it is quite a different breed of cat from the large revolver cases previously used. Here, if anywhere, I thought I might run into trouble, and so I went about the calculation of starting loads a little more carefully. First, I compared the case volumes as before. Then I "factored" that down still more by comparing the bullets to be used, the 90-grain Sierra JHP and the 115-grain R-P JHP, to a bullet which for the 9mm would be comparable to the 110-grain JHP. That bullet came out to weigh in at about 66 grains and so my starting charges were further reduced a bit. Say anything of me but that I don't believe in a bit of judicious "safe-siding" here and there when the occasion warrants. At any rate, my starting charges came out to be:

    90-gr. Sierra JHP   7.0 grains
    115-gr. R-P JHP   5.0 grains

Once again I headed for the range and set up the chronograph and Ransom Rest. The guns this time were a Ruger 6-inch Security Six in 357 Magnum, a 6½-inch S&W Model 29 in 44 Magnum, and my Model 59 S&W 9mm pistol.

Once again my determination of "maximum" charges came down to a subjective judgment based largely on blast, flash and recoil. With the Ruger 357 I stopped at 20.0 grains of Norma powder behind the 110-grain bullet which gave me 1680 fps. Primers were not excessively flattened nor was there any hard extraction. The 357, like the 38 Special, clearly can give 200 fps better velocities with the 110-grain bullet and this powder than U.S. commercial loads produce, and without excessive pressures.

The 44 Magnum turned out to be a real blaster and I have the feeling that this powder in so large a bore might do better in a longer barrel. I stopped at 27.0 grains when I got a very bright and large muzzle flash and the rest rotated all the way back to the pistol safety stop. Primers were beginning to flatten out but there was still no difficulty with extraction. With this bullet and barrel length, there was a gain of

only some 50 fps over what U.S. commercial loads give. Gun to gun variations can be larger than that, so Norma's powder had little to offer in this 44 Magnum. It might do better in the T/C Contender.

The 9mm Parabellum is another matter altogether. It is, to begin with, a relatively small, high intensity pistol cartridge, far more modern in design than the large revolver cartridges. As it turned out, the Norma powder is a very mild and forgiving powder and did not entrap me in a dangerous situation, as it might well have done. I found that I had "safe-sided" far too much in calculating starting loads for the two bullets I tried. The Model 59's slide did not begin to cycle properly until I had passed 8.0 grains.

Next I found myself in a funny sort of situation; I simply could not cram enough Norma powder into the 9mm case to give pressure signs! I pushed matters right on up to 11.5 grains at which point I was getting 1182 fps over the chronograph, and quit because it became hard to seat the bullets without spilling powder. At no time did I get any sort of excessive pressure sig-

nal or excess flash. The thing I did come away with was that this new Norma powder just does not have much to offer for the 9mm Parabellum cartridge. We can do just about as well with many U.S. commercial powders, and better with some, such as Herco. Norma's powder seems to be a real lover of the old fashioned big revolver cartridge case.

I hope that some shooter will soon invest the time and money to see what this fine new powder has to offer in the T/C Contender and in carbines. I certainly hope that Norma will see fit to make it available commercially to loaders. •

Readers are cautioned not to attempt to duplicate my loads. These worked safely for me in my guns but might not in yours. My pressure estimates were made subjectively, only, and not on the results of pressure gun measurements. This caution is reinforced by later findings that the Norma 110 grain 38 load does indeed develop pressure in the "+P" range.

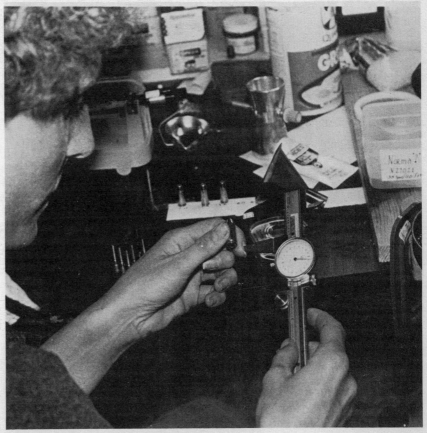

Carefully measured over-all length of 9mm ammunition loaded with Norma's new powder was only part of the cautious approach.

The Odd History and Bright Future of

PROGRESSIVE LOADERS

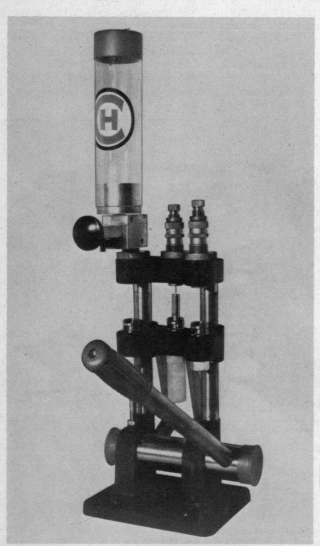

The origin of the first straightline progressive is a little unclear but they are thought to have developed from H-presses like this.

IN THE EARLY '30's in San Diego, California, an unusual thing happened. The members of a now-forgotten shooting club were having trouble loading enough 38 Special ammunition to keep up with their extensive practice. Their solution to the problem was an oddity: Not one, but several of the shooters went off and developed their own reloading presses! These presses, their odd history, and the possible future of their offspring constitute our subject.

Because these units may be the C-presses of the future, and since they are relatively unknown, let's define what they are: A "progressive" is a press that works at relatively high speed and with considerable uniformity on several shells simultaneously and does not require an operator to handle the shells individ-

It started 50 years ago in San Diego, and this writer thinks the progressive loader's time has come.

by KENNETH L. WALTERS

Ponsness-Warren has been developing a series of presses for metallic cartridges. This H-style unit would be a progessive unit if it worked on several shells simultaneously. Such units are known to be under consideration by this firm.

In 1937 and 1938 Star produced a very few straightlines. This picture, taken from Phil Sharpe's book, is apparently the only photographic record of that development.

ually between the various reloading stations. Units that have all their dies in a straight line and in clear view of the operator and that automatically index the shells between the die stations are called straightline progressives. Devices that are more like turret presses and that usually must have their shells manually indexed, though not individually, are called circulars. Models that can be converted to handle a variety of calibers are called universals, while machines that cannot be altered from their as-built calibers are simply called progressives. Finally, let's differentiate between hand-operated or manual units, the main emphasis here, and automatic or powered machines.

Exactly how progressives developed is a little unclear, but it would seem they were originally H-like units. If you compare the C-H three station H-press and the Ponsness-Warren H-style unit with an early Star straightline progressive, the resemblance is straightforward.

Star, as some of you probably know, is world famous for their circular progressive, a machine we'll discuss later. It is important to note, however, that a few years after the circulars were introduced (1930) Star produced a few straightlines (1937-8). Some of these extremely rare machines were sold and have recently been seen at California gun shows.

About the same time as Star was experimenting with their prototype circulars, two San Diego gentlemen, Harry Newcomb and a Mr. Cohn, developed a unit that later was to become known as the Buchanan. The picture nearby is admittedly poor, since it was copied from an old *American Rifleman* ad, but it is the only record we have of this early reloader. Even this, however, is a late Buchanan as the original ones didn't have the three legs. Note again how similar this design is to an H-press.

Shortly after this unit was developed and before it was commercially produced, the design was apparently acquired by Mr. J. D. Buchanan. He, in turn, produced it up to WW II. After the war, the Buchanan was manufactured by the Police Equipment Supply Company or PESCO. Production seems to have been short lived and few PESCO's are now known. I think the company, functioning in the late 40's out of Chicago, died not because of faulty design or lack of sales but rather because of quality control problems. It is believed, but not known for

This photograph, of a late model Buchanan, appeared in an ad. Early units did not have the three legs.

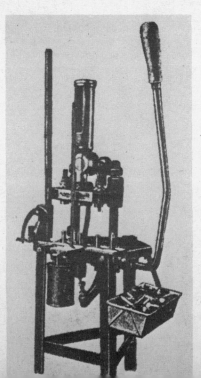

The Buchanan was sold to the Police Equipment Supply Company or PESCO. Production was limited and not many of these units are now known.

The Shockey, like the Ponsness-Warren, worked on only one shell at a time and hence wasn't really a progressive. The picture is from an ad.

Potter Engineering built a progressive-like press. Here several shells were in work but they had to be manually and individually moved between the various die stations.

sure, that the firm was sold and production resumed for a short time in the 50's, but if so the name and details have been lost. If you find a PESCO-like unit but with the name other than Buchanan or PESCO, you've found a truly rare unit.

A third press designed in the '30's in San Diego was the Shockey. Our picture, admittedly poor, is again based on an *American Rifleman* ad. This machine, you'll notice, is very much like the current Ponsness-Warren in that it had several die positions, one shell holder, and automatically moved the one shell between the stations. Since, however, it didn't have multiple shells to work on simultaneously, it and the current Ponsness-Warren, aren't true progressives.

Two other units also appeared, the Hill and Potter. The Hill was a

straightline, thought to have been made in prototype only. The Potter, again, was almost a progressive, but since it required manually moving the individual cases between its multiple shell holders, it doesn't quite qualify. The Potter firm, incidentally, still exists and while not heavily into reloading anymore, they will repair their old units.

You'll notice that all these straightline progressives, the Star, the Buchanan, and the pseudo-progressive Shockey, were developed in the thirties and in San Diego, all by one group of shooters, an unusual origin for an unusual series of units. It is odder still that each man who set out to design a press for his own reloading needs actually succeeded in producing a commercial product.

All these initial efforts were

straightlines, except for the circular version of the Star. Also, none of these straightlines lasted very long. San Diego, however, was not to be denied the honor of being the home of the first truly successful straightline. Starting in the late forties and ending in the early fifties, Joe Dircks made the so-called Dircks presses. Forty machines, fully automated and electrically powered units, were built initially as part of Joe's ammunition business and later as a business of their own. Large in size and capacity, these machines have been known to load over 100,000,000 rounds with little mechanical trouble. Only 40 units were produced and 12 of these were shipped to Japan. Thus only 28 machines were sold in this country, though several of these still exist. Eventually, probably around 1952, Joe sold his ammunition

The first really successful straightline was the very rare, fully automatic Dircks. These machines have been known to load over 100,000,000 rounds with little mechanical difficulty.

Joe Dircks also built the Tri-Standard including ten automated machines of the type pictured here. This and the straightline Star are the two rarest progressives known to exist.

About 90 manual Tri-Standards were built, most of which survive.

An original C-H Auto-Champion, Mark I, less dies.

business and with it the rights to his machine. None were ever produced again.

Later, between 1958 and 1962, Joe Dircks again produced presses, though this time they were the so-called Tri-Standards. Smaller than the original Dircks units, these machines were made in two configurations, about ten fully electric models, one of which is still known, and about 90 manuals, most of which survive.

All Joe's presses were for 38 Special only. No other caliber was ever produced, though some were independently converted. Also the true Dircks press, his first, was not a hand-operated unit. Although all the Dircks and Tri-Standard machines were fine reloaders, the truth is that they are certainly worth more to press collectors than reloaders.

After the Tri-Standard company was sold, production of straightlines again ceased. The next such unit had to wait well over ten years before C-H introduced the first Auto-Champ. Details on this initial machine are a little fuzzy but it was followed by three improved models, the Mark II, III, and IV. The Mark IV, from all accounts, is a nice, relatively inexpensive (under $500) machine capable of loading 38 Special, 357 Magnum, 9mm Luger and 45 ACP. I've personally used a MK II and have just bought, but not yet received a MK IV.

C-H, it should be noted, initially intended to produce a Tri-Standard copy. Production costs, however, prevented that, so a simplified, machine was made instead.

The next straightline was the Cougar & Hunter. Developed in conjunc-

tion with C-H, this unit was a lighter duty, smaller version with an improved priming mechanism and some other minor design changes. When C-H elected not to alter their production to accommodate this redesign, some of the C-H people started their own short-lived firm, the rights to which, complete with parts for 150 or so machines, were recently sold, though as yet production has not resumed. Only about 225 original Cougar & Hunters were sold.

Three more straightlines are known to be under development by Camdex, C'Arco, and RCBS. RCBS to date has built only prototypes, but plans to have a commercial product ready by early 1982. The RCBS is important because it is the first attempt at building such a device at a really low cost, now projected at about $400, and because it

Differences between the first Auto-Champ and the Mark II are unknown. The progression of these machines eventually lead to the Mark IV.

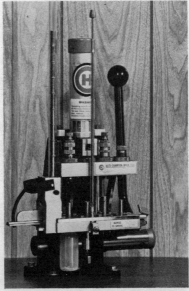

Auto-Champ Mark III. Note that the unit now has one additional die station.

The Auto-Champ Mark IV complete with the new cluster. Author reports difficulties with this, doesn't like it.

The Cougar & Hunter was designed by employees of C-H. When it was not produced as one of the then developing Auto-Champion series, independent production was commenced.

is the first such unit being designed by a giant in the reloading field.

The most important thing to note about straightlines is that to date none of these pistol presses, except for C-H's, has ever succeeded. Buchanan, PESCO, Shockey, and Cougar & Hunter could have been commercial successes, but for one reason or another weren't. Dircks was successful twice, but each time he sold out to a firm that didn't continue production. Only C-H has established themselves as a leader in this area.

Unlike straightlines, which have had a somewhat odd and erratic past, circulars have flourished from the beginning. Once Star developed the world-famous Star Universal (circular) Progressive, continuous production by the same maker/owner has continued uninterrupted. Flawless in construction and perfect in operation, Star now stands nearly two years behind in its orders. Star's success, attributed to high, constant quality, is what has been the incentive to so many other companies to enter the market.

Because Star was such an absolute success they got the highest form of praise, competitors who tried to copy their design literally. The first, appearing in the 1950's, was Phelps, which, with a relatively new owner, exists to this very day. Phelps units are slightly different from Stars in that anything that could be dropped as a non-essential construction detail was. Also Phelps offered a unit capable of reloading rifle rounds. This was a first, since Star and the straightline firms never ventured outside pistol cartridges for their mass-produced versions. Phelps units are advertised as being parts interchangeable with the Star but the maker admits this is true only after some handwork. Production is limited and availability is erratic. I know. I tried to buy Phelps loaders three times.

Another firm working on a so-called parts-interchangeable Star copy is the Seattle firm of Berdon. Their device, like Phelps, is supposed to be able to load both pistol and rifle rounds. Berdon went Phelps one better, however, by designing their presses to use regular dies instead of the special dies built only for Star and Phelps use. This, supposedly, would allow the reloader to use dies he already owned, though I doubt it would work because the dies would need extensive modification to handle the speed-related case positioning problems. Berdon's unit, inci-

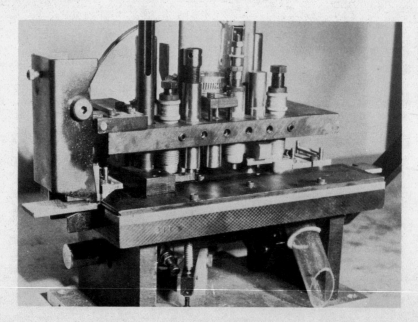

Camdex has experimented with a hand-operated straightline. This initial unit had repeated mechanical problems and it is not known if production of this unit is continuing.

The Ransom machine rest firm of C'Arco has recently introduced this straightline.

The all-time best is the Star Circular pictured here on a B&G base. These machines have been in continuous production since 1930 and are so popular that deliveries are now over two years behind. A rifle unit, larger than this, may materialize.

dentally, has been actively advertised for many years but only prototypes have been built to date.

Recently, no less than three non-parts interchangeable Star-like pistol presses were also planned, though only one firm, CPM, ever made it to production. CPM has had no less than three owners in just the last couple of years. The current ones, however, do seem actually to be able to produce.

The last and final Star-related press is the Dillon. During the early 60's, due to continuous requests, Star perfected and started making a few progressive rifle tools. The Dillon rifle/pistol press is based on one of these units although Dillon has made considerable improvements. Star's machine, incidentally, is still produced occasionally and production may expand if there is sufficient interest.

Dillon is planning three machines. His largest, already out, costs about $2400 (soon to hit $3000). His intermediate will cost about $1000 and there will be another for about $300. Details are lacking, but all will handle rifle and pistol cartridges. Mike Dillon hopes to be able to make his least expensive unit so appealing and inexpensive that it can actually compete with many uses for which C-presses are now bought. Of course, it will never completely replace the C-press but it, or others like it now on other companies' drawing boards, may greatly reduce C-press sales.

The real future of progressives lies in this potential to replace the C-press. Historically, progressives have been fast and highly uniform loaders priced out of the reach of most reloaders. With the drive by Dillon, RCBS and

others to put this equipment within the price range of most shooters, the market and applicability of this gear should greatly increase.

Normally, technological advances cause two types of improvements. The first is to provide a new unit of the old style but at a lower cost. Lyman's O-Mag is just such an inexpensive single station, as their recent advertisements claim. The second type of improvement is to provide more capacity at slightly higher cost. RCBS's straightline and Dillon's inexpensive circular are such challenges to existing C-presses. Remember, these machines will be under $400, or less than the cost of many current handguns.

Other firms known to be considering such equipment include Ponsness-Warren of shotgun-press fame. Others are rumored but no concrete data

The Clyde Products Manufacturing non-parts-interchangeable Star copy uses normal dies instead of the special ones found on Stars.

Derived from a Star rifle unit, this Dillon machine is a quality unit capable of loading both rifle and pistol rounds. It represents about the best rifle unit to date.

RCBS's straightline will be an extremely interesting venture because they are trying to build a complex design that is both easy to use and inexpensive to sell. If anyone can fill this tall order, RCBS can.

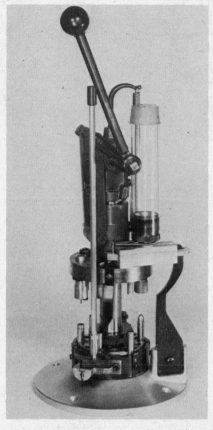

The Hollywood progressive is the only one ever built that could handle not only rifle and pistol rounds but shotgun loads as well. Then, too, it is about the only circular that isn't somehow related to the Star.

Phelps progressives, beginning in the '50's, return essentials of Star design, dispense with some details; they're also hard to buy, though still on the market.

exists at the time of this writing.

Finally, there is a unique circular built by Whitney on an old Hollywood Gun Shop design. This unit is the only progressive ever offered that can handle not only rifle and pistol cartridges but shotgun loads as well. Then, too, this seems to be the only circular ever made that wasn't in some sense related to the Star.

What started out as an exercise for the shooters of a San Diego gun club has expanded until this type of equipment might be the C-press of the future. Technology often improves products with time, and the time of the inexpensive universal progressive is just about upon us. •

This new Dillon unit is designed for simplicity and low cost. It appears to be a combination of a single station press's leverage system coupled with a four station H-press top. Dillon plans four units now.

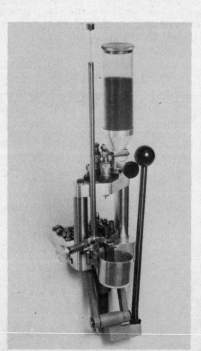

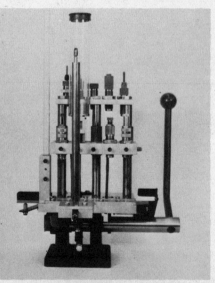

The newest straightline, the Jet. This unit is unique because it is the first straightline ever that was designed to handle both pistol and rifle rounds.

Living With PROGRESSIVE LOADERS

There's more than meets the eye, and the manual doesn't tell it all.

by KENNETH L. WALTERS

A HAND-OPERATED progressive reloader is a press that works on six or more cartridge cases simultaneously. During each operating cycle, cases are (1) fed into the machine, (2) resized and the old primer removed, (3) primed while the case mouth is being slightly flared, (4) charged with powder, (5) fitted with a bullet, (6) crimped, and (7) ejected. Because the presses are relatively complicated, special care is needed in their operation.

Machines that have their dies arranged in a row across the top of a platen are called straightline progressives. Such units usually advance cases automatically and have all the die stations in clear view of the operator. Operating wear can be high, however, because all the various dies apply pressure to the front of the platen tending to cause misalignment. Though several straightlines have been developed over the years, none has as yet enjoyed long-term production.

Circular progressives are essentially turret presses where each station works on a cartridge case. Because the dies are arranged around a central post, operating forces tend to be self-cancelling. The price for this design improvement, however, is that one or two of the die stations are not in clear operator view. Also case advancing mechanisms are much more difficult to design and not normally offered.

The first step any progressive does is to insert cases into the mechanism. If this is done manually, one needs to position the cases just to the left of the press, bottom down and within easy reach. Having a disorganized pile of brass noticeably slows down operations needlessly.

If automatic case feeders are used, one needs to ensure that both an adequate supply of brass is in the feeder tube and that the mechanism inputs the case correctly. Requiring nothing more than a quick glance once per operating cycle, this easily avoids having a machine stall due to a case cocking as it enters the shell plate. Though, perhaps, a little trouble because the cases must be visually in-

This contemporary straightline C-H progressive is an extension, adapted to current production technique and need, of the successful Dircks loader.

This is the standard—the Star circular progressive, in production for nearly 50 years, and now virtually mechanically flawless.

spected once per operating cycle, the speed gained by using these devices is substantial and well worth their nominal cost. Also, this is one of the few places speed can be gained with no sacrifice in safety.

Once the case is properly inserted, it is advanced to the station that does the full-length resizing and removal of the old primer. All progressives currently on the market use carbide sizing dies for pistol calibers and hence prior brass lubrication isn't necessary. The few units that can handle rifle shells, however, have to use steel resizing dies and hence *mild* lubrication must be done as a part of your brass preparation.

Because you can easily handle at least 300-plus cases per hour, lubrication buildup in the sizing die can occur rapidly. Thus every few hours this die should be inspected and, if necessary, cleaned.

Another item needs attention at the resizing station. It is possible to break off a decapping pin without knowing it. *Don't.* Always look at the die to ensure the pin is both present and straight. The worry isn't really that you'll break the pin off as it is that you'll eventually try to reprime a case that still has the old primer in it. That could cause, under unusual circumstances, a primer detonation. Although a primer detonation in any press can be dangerous and should be avoided, in a progressive they are particularly troublesome.

Primer detonation can occur in three areas: under the primer feeder tube, in the primer advancing mechanism, or in the case priming station. Usually 50 or so primers are stored in the machine in a primer tube much like that used on single-station tools. Below this is a small metal bar with a hole into which the primer is gravity fed. If the primer is cocked as it enters this bar and the operator applies excessive force, a primer can detonate causing the entire tube to explode. Documented cases of such mishaps are known. *(The U.S. Handgunner,* Vol. XXIX, No. 1, Jan.-Feb. 1978).

As the primer bar advances from the primer feeder tube towards the priming station, friction between the primer and the walls can also cause detonation. Here, however, only one primer is involved and it is enclosed within the guts of the mechanism. Such explosions are rare, and no known injuries have been reported. Still, I'm sure even one such incident would be very disconcerting.

A detonation at the priming station itself is also possible either due to dirt buildup at the primer pocket, trying to

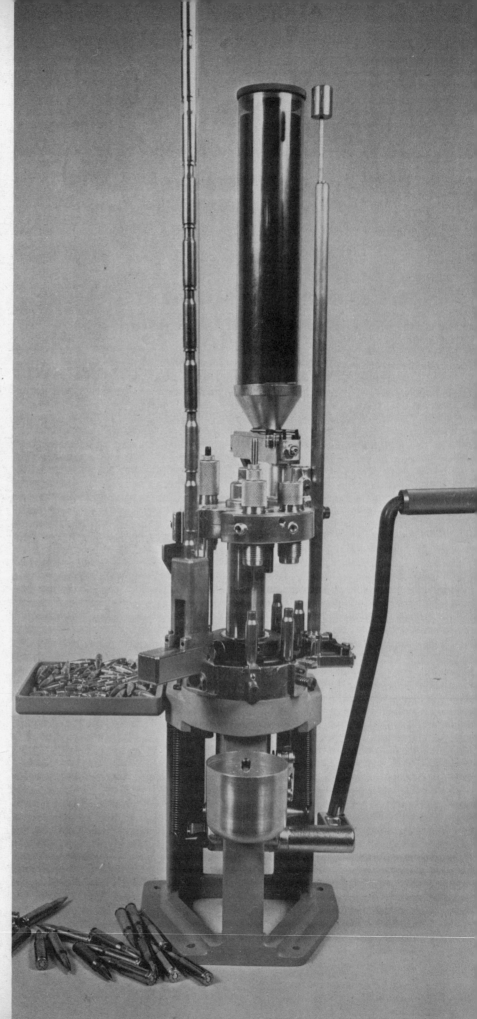

prime a case with the old, spent primer still in it, or a mechanism that tries to push the primer too far into the case.

There are several ways to overcome these primer related difficulties:

First, shield yourself from the primer feeder tube so that if a problem does develop you cannot be hurt. A good, stout piece of clear plastic securely anchored to your reloading bench works nicely.

Second, try several dry runs with only the primer mechanism and a single primer to insure that it feeds correctly. If there is a roughness, inspect the mechanism and remove any burrs. Also be sure the primer isn't pushed too far into the case. Adjust the lifting mechanism travel, if necessary. If this doesn't solve the problems, call the manufacturer and ask for help.

Third, use sorted cases of uniform, proper length. You need to have cases that offer uniform resistance to the resizing die so that if a case seems unusually resistant, it will be noticed. Winchester brass is preferred both for its ease in resizing and its uniform resistance.

Fourth, since increased pressure can result either from a primer jam or a stout case, you want to know which. Thus it is best to size and deprime your cases prior to running them thru the progressive. This is particularly true when using Remington brass since these cases seem to be much harder to resize and would thus hide a concurrent operating pressure increase due to a primer jam. Also, this independent depriming allows the primer pockets to be inspected and cleaned.

Fifth, don't let your concentration be broken by interruptions.

Most progressive operators, incidentally, neither independently size their brass nor inspect the primer pockets. This, however, should be recognized as a conscious tradeoff of safety for speed. If done (and I'm not recommending it), anytime there is any increase in the apparent force needed to operate the press, the case at the priming and full-length resizing stations should be removed and the machine inspected to insure no primer crushing was occurring.

If primer handling in progressives is so important, it is fair to ask why there are relatively few reported problems. Overlooking the possibility that this isn't the sort of thing most publishers like to print, the answer is quite simple. Until recently Star was the only manufacturer of such equipment. Though they did have problems in the late thirties and early forties, they solved their difficulties not by a press redesign but rather by truly craftsmanlike assembly. As newer firms enter this field, they will have to do the same or build in primer shielding. The latter seems to be the more common approach.

Some new progressives, like the Camdex, rely on the cartridge case itself to act as a shield at the primer station. This press will, by design, crush a primer if a case isn't present. As one who has had this happen, I can tell you from firsthand experience that it isn't comforting to know that you missed having a primer blow up in your face by pure luck.

Exact die layout varies between manufacturers but usually the next station charges the case with powder. Double charging is rare since all the units I've used (Camdex, C-H, and Star) have some sort of double charge prevention mechanism. Don't under any circumstance remove this from the machine.

Camdex guards against a double charging two ways. First, as is true of all straightlines, the case is automatically advanced away from the powder station. Second, as an independently purchasable option, powder height can be checked and an audible alarm sounded if an under or over charge is found. This option is well worth the nominal price.

Star checks by tripping a deliberate jam which doesn't allow recycling the press until the cases are manually advanced or the device deliberately overridden. If, however, a taper crimp die is used, this mechanism must be disabled. You'd be better off not to use such a crimp in these presses, since it negates an important safety mechanism. Also, the mechanism can simply become loose and inoperative. Since, however, the tripping makes a distinctive sound, listen for it to be sure it's working.

The next station feeds the bullet into the case either manually or automatically. If done manually, be sure the bullet is placed in the case firmly and sticking straight up. If this is done automatically, visually inspect for the same result. Automatic bullet feeders do jam. Don't use excessive force, however, because you can not be sure that a simultaneous primer jam isn't occurring.

Bullet feeders are, perhaps, the biggest area still needing manufacturer attention. Of the two I've used, one as part of a straightline and the other sold by an independent firm for use on the Star, neither worked. Though such devices should, in theory, be possible, they aren't yet a practical reality on the currently offered progressives.

Bullet seating and crimping comes next. Seating can be a real problem if either the case mouth wasn't properly flared or the bullet cocked in the case. Flaring can be easily corrected by just slightly lowering the corresponding die. Bullet cocking on a manual advancing unit is eliminated by carefully advancing the shell plate. Normally this is done by gently lifting the plate, by pulling upwards on a case, and then rotating it. On a unit with an automatic shell indexer, however, proper advancing requires a slow operation of the main press handle.

Incidentally, since many automatic advancers sold for use on circular press apply only a pushing motion to the case (they don't lift it first), excessive baseplate wear is common. If you use one of these devices, you should be aware that you are trading machine life for operating speed. Baseplate replacement under these circumstances will be necessary after 150,000 or so rounds. Without such a rig, if proper indexing is done, the baseplate would last indefinitely.

Crimping normally is only a problem if the cases aren't of uniform, proper length. Check to be sure the crimp looks even. Also take a completed cartridge, place it bullet down on your workbench and push hard. If the case was of the proper length but this caused the bullet to slip, readjust to give a harder crimp.

The final station ejects the case. Straightlines always do this automatically, as do some circulars. Stars, however, can eject only revolver cases and require manual removal of such rounds as the 45 ACP, 9mm Luger, and 380.

Stars, incidentally, are unique for another reason. If the unit is ordered directly from the factory and you specify the exact bullet to be used, they will tune the machine perfectly. This will eliminate the great majority of problems one might ever encounter as long as the factory settings are left undisturbed. No other manufacturer does this even though most cost more.

Progressive reloaders easily allow loading over 300 cases per hour and rates of 600-plus are possible. Safe operation, however, depends critically on continued operator attention. As the complexity of the tool increases, so must operator skill. •

Set up for rifle rounds, progressives work a little harder This is a Dillon, a sound derivative of the Star loader.

HIGH PERFORMANCE SLUG LOADINGS FOR 12-GAUGE

Only through firing the shotgun can the handloader test his slugs. This Mossberg 500 pump, in 12 gauge, rests on several of the targets it perforated in author's extensive tests.

Thousands of rounds at long range targets, through chronograph screens and a few whitetails have shown how it's done.

by JOE KRIEGER

OUT OF THE corner of my eye, I noticed the young chuck hunter watching from the green alfalfa hillside off to my left. The smoke had started to clear from the last of the handloads I had fired through the Oehler Skyscreen. These screens were fastened to an aluminum I-beam, positioned fifteen feet from the muzzle of my Remington Wingmaster. The sandbag rests cradled the scope-sighted pump as I retrieved the 12-gauge Federal empties lying about.

The chuck hunter walked toward me, his rifle slung over his shoulder.

"Sounded kind of funny," he said, referring to the booming resonance of the shotgun, for this was chuck season in Western New York where one expects the sharp crack of the centerfire on hot August days.

Jeffrey, the chuck hunter, was very much intrigued by the chronograph. I offered him a chance to try the instrument, and he fired three rounds from his 6mm rifle over the screens. I calculated the velocity of each round from the table provided by Oehler with the

chronograph, and complimented Jeffrey on the consistency of his handloads. The three rounds had only a 24 fps (feet per second) spread.

Jeffrey's questions were directed toward the chronograph's workings, and its accuracy as we walked to collect my targets. The targets were 150 yards downrange. His attention shifted from the chronograph as we approached the cardboard deer that served as my targets that day.

"Wow!," was his only remark, as he eyed the life-size deer target.

Ten shots were neatly patterned over the heart-lung area drawn on one of the targets.

"Not bad," was my reply, not out of some odd sense of humility, but from the knowledge that further load development could improve on this load, one of my first combinations using Federal cases with the Vitt Aerodynamic slug.

Jeffrey wondered aloud, why his own slug gun would not perform in similar fashion. I pointed out that the rounds fired were handloads, superior to anything available over the counter.

"You load your slugs?," he questioned, openly surprised.

I explained the ease of that task to Jeffrey over lunch in the Wyoming County village of Attica. Later that day we hunted chucks, and talked about shotguns and whitetails. I answered additional questions the young man had on slug-loading, but as we parted company, Jeffrey doubted that he would ever try to load slugs himself.

Jeffrey's reaction to my hobby was not the first such response I've noted, and I'd be extremely surprised if it was to be the last. I have known, perhaps, 50 handloaders, and have yet to run into another who loads slugs for his shotgun. There is a great deal of reluctance on the part of most handloaders to take on this task. The majority appear to feel very little can be gained by loading slugs. This opinion is in sad error for a great deal can be gained in loads for the shotgun.

At costs comparable to factory loads, the reloader can achieve the very best in range, power, and accuracy. If one concentrates his efforts, his shotgun can wield the single projectile every bit as usably well as a rifle. Cost comparisons and component prices are shown here:

Factory Loads, 100	$58.00
Vitt Slugs, 100	$36.00
Powder-100 rds.	4.50
Primers, 100	2.10
Remington SP cases, 100	1.50
	$44.10
Brenneke slugs, 100	$47.60
Powder-100 rds.	4.00
Primers, 100	2.10
Remington SP cases, 100	1.50
Wads	2.70
	$57.90

As you can see, the costs of the components are not prohibitive: using the Vitt projectile, one can even save a large percentage, when compared with factory loads.

Each year, articles appear between

The Lyman mould blocks pictured can provide the handloader with an adequate slug for practice. Some may use them for hunting, but the author likes the Brenneke and the Vitt much better.

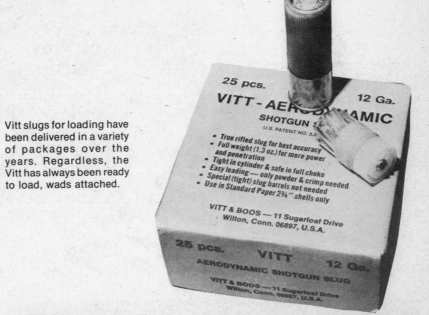

Vitt slugs for loading have been delivered in a variety of packages over the years. Regardless, the Vitt has always been ready to load, wads attached.

Brennekes imported by Stoeger have an over-the-slug spacer to be used when crimped with a star crimp. The cases are Remington All American target cases.

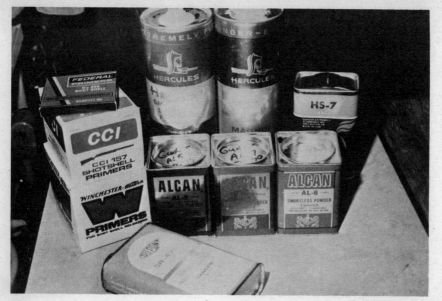

Due to the heavy weight of the Vitt and Brenneke slugs, a slow-burning powder is necessary to achieve high-velocity. In addition to the seven powders shown, SR7625, and HS6 were also used. A selection of primers is necessary to match the different recipes various manufacturers prescribe.

Once a load is selected, the Lee slide chart can be consulted, and the correct measure used to nearly obtain the charge needed. Here the 2nd edition of *Lyman's Shotshell Handbook* is used to determine a safe load.

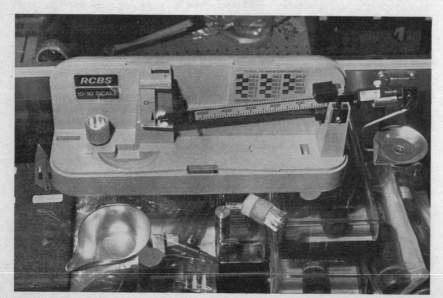

The RCBS 10-10 scale pictured is one of the best scales available today. It can provide the necessary sensitivity and accuracy, in addition to being able to handle up to 1010 grains.

July and November to aid the hundreds of thousands of hunters who must, by legislation, carry shotguns after whitetails and black bear. One seldom finds detailed information to aid the handloader in assembling slug shells. Factory ammunition, fired through "slug" or "buck" specials is covered, and that's usually all we find on the subject.

The slug loading process is not difficult, nor overly expensive. The reward may *only* be the inner satisfaction that comes from knowing you've done it, like tying trout flies. Then again, that reward may include the trophy buck that was just too far away last season.

We won't discuss the power the shotgun slug can transmit to the target, nor advise the hunter to hang up his rifle. In most respects, the rifle *can* out-perform the shotgun. I have seen a few slug-shooters who were far better prepared and more capable than a lot of rifle shooters, but that's different.

The following paragraphs detail information on components, tools, and the whole reloading process, from start to finish. I would like it quite clear that everything mentioned was obtained over the counter. I list them because they have worked for me, over many years, and for no other reason.

Slugs

Slugs for handloading will be much easier to obtain than some of the tools needed to load them. Of any slug available, the Vitt Aerodynamic is the best possible choice. Ray Boos, of Stratford, Connecticut, can provide a slug that puts the shotgun into an entirely new light, when judged for use on big game. Developed by George Vitt and Ray, more than 15 years ago, the slug's existence is still relatively unknown.

Those who have had the good fortune to use this slug will use no other, and for good reason. The Vitt slug can shoot flatter than any other; it can hit as accurately as the best; and it is the ultimate in power, when loaded to maximum velocity. This slug is an entirely self-contained unit, with its wad column attached with a screw. Like the older Brenneke slug, the lead carries a number of fins. The three-wad column, made up of an Alcan Airwedge, a .125″ card wad, and a ⅜″ waxed fiber wad, is all that should be used with this slug. This feature makes the Vitt the quickest and the easiest slug to handload.

The Brenneke slug is better known than the Vitt/Boos slug, and is sup-

plied in loaded rounds as well as components. This slug is at its best ballistically when handloaded to maximum velocity. While the Brenneke can easily be loaded to velocities exceeding the Vitt by nearly 100 fps at the muzzle, the Vitt, because of its greater sectional density, (.155 vs. .124), better ballistic co-efficient, (.125 vs. .097), and heavier weight, (575 grs. vs. 468 grs.), out-performs the speedier Brenneke projectile.

The non-handloading hunter should be aware of the fact that mild pressures of the factory-loaded Brennekes tend to keep it in the same category as the factory-loaded Foster slug: suitable and effective for big game, out to 125 to 150 yards. The handloading slug shooter can easily add at least 50 yards or more, by using the load recommendation given by the Hercules Powder Co., in their 1978 edition of their *Reloader's Guide for Hercules Smokeless Powders.* Other load recommendations can be found in the '75-76 edition of Du Pont's *Handloader's Guide,* but the Du Pont loads do not approach the velocity obtained by Hercules in their loads.

If the Brenneke slug in component form is not available locally, you may be able to talk a local dealer into ordering them for you from Buckeye Sports Supply, at 2655 Harrison Avenue, Canton, Ohio 44706, or Badger Shooters Supply, Inc., in Owens, Wisconsin 54460.

At 45 to 60 cents a shot, getting sufficient practice with the Vitts and Brennekes will get costly. It's well worth the money, but this cost may still deter some hunters from firing their shotguns prior to the season. A less costly means can be had, using slugs cast in a Lyman slug mold. These slugs shoot well as cast, so forget the tedious job of rifling the slug. The cost per shot should be less than 20 cents, depending on the price you'll have to pay for the lead. These slugs can be as effective as factory slugs, but with other, more efficient slugs available, I use Lyman slugs for practice only.

No matter what slug one uses for practice, be sure to sight the shotgun in with the slugs you plan to carry afield. Otherwise, you're bound to have problems hitting what you aim at.

Cases

A good supply of usable cases is an essential item for any reloader. Case selection for the slug-loader is rather uncomplicated, since a number of brands can immediately be eliminated. The Remington RXPs, Win-

chester's AAs and the Peter's Blue Magic, because of the inner taper of the walls, have not worked well for me, when used with the slugs having screw-attached wads. The wads used on the Vitts and the Brennekes are made for use in straight-walled cases, as are the plastic over-the-powder wads, and the fiber wads used in putting together loads with Foster slugs. When so loaded in these cases, the wads tend to move up the tapered walls of the case, and away from the powder charge. This leads to quite a variation in pressure and velocity for the individual rounds, and accuracy suffers. Though I have had no problems in regard to safety, the reason for handloading the slugs is to achieve the best possible combination, so I have decided to use other, more suitable shotshell cases for my slug loads, and reserve the three brands mentioned for shot loads.

The casual reloader may wonder why a deeper roll-crimp is not given to these shells, in order to keep the stubborn wads seated directly over the powder charge. While this will work to keep the wads seated in place, pressure rises beyond acceptable levels. A crimp that just holds the wads to the powder, without any excessive force, produces the best pressure-velocity relationship in these rounds, and the very best in accuracy.

For my slug loads, Remington SPs, and Federal Hi-Power cases have proven to be the best available cases in plastic. Case life has been good with both brands, when the cases have been reconditioned. The Remington cases can *usually* be reloaded 5 to 6 times, before any adverse change in accuracy can be noticed. The Federal cases give the same number of reloads, but they must be reconditioned, of which more below.

Both brands have individual aspects I consider to be troublesome:

The mouths of most Remingtons separate, that is, the layers that make up the shell tube separate, making the shell difficult to crimp a second time, unless reconditioned.

A significant number of Federal shells lose a portion of the case mouth on the first firing with my slug loads, making them useless. Yet, in spite of these two problems, the Remington SPs, and Federal HPs remain the best in plastic for slug loads.

From time to time, I have attempted to use paper shells in assembling slug loads, and these loads have worked very well. Paper cases do need additional care in keeping them in good condition. Re-waxing the case mouth,

The Lee measure is used to get near the charge desired. The powder is being dumped into the scale pan. The scale's beam has been locked in an ''up'' position to protect the knife edges from damage as the powder is added to the pan.

A powder trickler or spoon can add the last remaining grains of powder to the scale pan. After weighing the charge within 1/10th of a grain, the powder is dumped into the case.

approximately ⅜" from the end, works wonders for paper cases, and extends usable case life. A batch of Federal Monark cases have been re-waxed and reloaded 8 times, and continue to take an excellent crimp, and it is easier to turn over the crimp on paper cases than plastic. There is the additional care involved, and paper cases seem more difficult to obtain. The individual will have to decide for himself.

A person seldom realizes the difficulty involved in obtaining the needed shells for slug loads, until the task is upon him. It is not often that I have been able to find new, unfired shells in my area. I have had to look for other sources of usable shells.

Next best to new shells are shells that have been used in factory slug loads. Shells that have been fold-crimped will not take a roll-crimp. Slug loads and some buckshot rounds are factory loads still roll-crimped. Either type has been difficult for me to obtain.

I had some luck in '79, and was able to purchase several thousand cases that had been slug-loaded by the factory. At the time, I had hoped these would last for several years, eliminating the search for shells that would work. But a great deal of shooting will make it necessary to find another source by next summer.

A thought that will cause reloading

waterfowl and turkey hunters to cringe and beat the floor is to use 3-inch shells, trimmed back to the needed over-all length. Locally, I have had some luck in that regard and purchased about a thousand once-fired Remington SPs in that length.

I have found trimming advantageous, even when using the standard 2¾" shells. Both the Remington SPs, and the Federal HPs have a great deal of room internally. The very best roll-crimp, over a specific slug unit, can be applied when an optimum shell length has been determined. My own experience has shown the SPs at 2⅝", (66.9mm), and the HPs at 2⁹/₁₆", (65.1mm), take the best roll-crimp on my tools over the Vitts and the Brennekes. These lengths leave approximately 7/32" of shell tube over the nose of the slug.

Powders

I have based the selection of powder for slug loading on two factors—the barrel length and the weight of the projectile.

On barrel length, I have become fixed in my thinking: barrels from 24" to 28" produce the most acceptable results. This is true whether you are using the lightweight Foster slugs, (Lyman-cast slugs or Meyer's hollow-pointed slugs), or the heavy-weight Vitts or Brennekes. Factories load their ammunition as a compromise because they don't know what barrel length will be used by the consumer. The handloader on the other hand, can tailor his loads and use the slowest powder that will burn efficiently in his barrel to obtain the highest velocity attainable within safe pressure limits. This barrel choice eliminates a number of "slug" specials, but I base it on the results seen in firing more than 2500 rounds over the past four years. I believe it's a waste of expensive slugs to fire heavyweights out of a barrel under 24" long. If you still select the shorter barrel, Foster-type slugs will better fit your gun and your *apparent* needs.

With Foster slugs, powders with a burning rate of AL-5 and faster will perform admirably. The most successful powders in my own loads, using Lyman slugs, have been Green Dot, PB, Unique and SR 7625. The first three listed will work well even when coupled with barrels less than 24". SR 7625 works the best in my own loads, and produces the highest velocity in barrels 24" and longer (see load #2). If you should choose the Lyman slug for both hunting and your practice load, this is the powder to use.

The shotgun excels when loaded with heavy charges of slow powders under the Vitts and the Brennekes. Whether you're looking for long-range capability or sheer power, loads such as these can fill the bill.

Alcan powders are usually on the bench when I am putting together Vitt and Brenneke loads, because of the excellent results these powders have produced over the years, and good availability of Alcan powders in my area. The slowest Alcan, AL-8, has failed to burn completely in the 24" barrel of a Mossberg Slugster I carry. An excessive amount of unburned powder remains in the barrel, the point of impact is much lower than the

best loads using AL-5 and AL-7, and the accuracy is not very good, due, I think, to the excessive muzzle blast of this powder in that 24" barrel. When used in the 28" barrel of a Remington 870, accuracy returns, and the increased velocity adds to the power this load produces, (see load #8).

The fastest powder I have combined with heavy slugs is Alcan AL-120. Regardless of barrel length, this powder shoots some of the best groups I've been able to get and also produces one of the three most powerful loads I've used with the Vitts, (see load #4). AL-5 and AL-7 have also given very good results in my loads, with AL-7 standing out as the very best powder. This powder produces the smallest groups of any I've used, all the way out to 225 yards, and it is the fourth most powerful load I have put together. Alcan powders will continue to be the mainstay of my slug loading sessions as long as they are available.

I have used other powders, but found only two adequate for my requirements and needs: Herco and Blue Dot *almost* rival the Alcan powders. Neither has produced the accuracy given by the Alcan's for me. Blue Dot is the powder to use if you're looking for power (see load #1). At ranges under 100 yards, the differences in accuracy between Blue Dot and AL-7 are negligible on deer-size game, and should offer no handicap to the shooter.

I continue to shun ball powders in slug loads. I see an overwhelming disadvantage in them with no real advantage over the flake powders I have used. The density of ball powders, the thing that makes them so popular with the waterfowl shooter, works against them in the slug situation. They just do not take up enough room and without the necessary bulk, the slugs seat deeper in the shell, making the application of a good crimp impossible. With the Brenneke, it is possible to add to the wad column in order to fill in the space, but the Vitt slug is made to be used without the addition of any extra wads. Rather than play around, I'll continue to use flake powders.

One could solve this problem with a less capacious shotshell, with straight-sided tubes that could be roll-crimped. At present, such an alternative seems unlikely to appear. The possible use of Hodgdon's HS series, and Winchester's 540 and 571, has some appeal. I would think higher velocities *might* be attainable with several of these slow burners and that thought fascinates me.

Primers

The shotshell reloader who uses both flake and ball powders should take care to choose the correct primer for each powder type. Ball powder *can* find its way into the unprotected flash hole of certain primers, and cause excessive pressure there. Many new to the sport, may not be aware of that possibility. I find it easier to use only primers with covered flashholes, though I deviate at times.

When using published loads, it is best to follow the entire recipe as published, including the primer selection; you'll be less inclined to run into problems that way.

In my own loads, I have found Winchester 209 and Federal 209 primers to perform very well in cases using that primer size. Both primers produce a spark hot enough to ignite large powder charges. Remington SP's take a 57 primer, so the selection here is limited. Only the CCI 157 and Remington's own 57 can be used. From time to time, I have noticed an Alcan G57F primer recommended for use with Alcan powders, but I have been unable to find any dealer that stocks this primer, so it seems we are still limited to the two primers in that size.

I have had some trouble with the CCI 157's in some of the loads using heavy charges of the Alcan powders. A large number of misfires have occurred when using 39.5 grains of AL-7, and the CCI primer, though it works fine in other loads. I would find it quite upsetting to have one of these loads in the chamber, at a time when a whitetail might offer a shot. To eliminate that possibility, I strayed from my previously stated rule, and am now using Remington primers in this load. Since AL-7 is a flake powder, the use of this primer is not hazardous. The Remington primer shows an increase in the velocity in this load, while showing no apparent increase in pressure. It is obvious that there must be some increase in the pressure produced by this load, but it is still within the safe limits.

Of the two 209 size primers, the Federal primer produces in my loads higher velocity with the same powder charge than the Winchester primer. A maximum load for a Winchester primer could be dangerous, I believe, should the loader make a thoughtless primer substitution.

Tools

Many of the tools you need may already be on your bench. When I first started loading slugs, reloading was totally new to me. In fact, slugs were the first loads I assembled. With only a press and a scale, I did very well. My first season using loads with Lyman slugs was a success. It is possible, with only a small inventory of tools and without any magic for the handloader to put together a combination of primer-powder-and-slug, that will put venison on the table.

As I got more involved with reloading, I found additional pieces of equipment handy to the point of becoming nearly indispensable. I had originally planned to break down the tools here into two categories: one group of those I felt was indispensable, and a second list that might be useful, but not indispensable. If I were now asked to eliminate the equipment I really don't need, I would balk. Each and every piece of equipment has its place in the steps necessary.

The following break-down on the tools and the steps they perform follows no set order of importance.

The Press

Some means of applying the crimp to the case is needed. Because of the lack of interest in loads that use roll-crimps, usable tools for this task are few.

My original tool is the only "regular" reloading press that can be used to roll-crimp a shotshell—Lyman's Easy Shotshell Loader. This press is the very best for this chore, and probably the most versatile shotshell loader ever produced. With additional die sets, the press can load anything from 2½" .410's to 3½" 10-gauge shells. While not as quick as the progressive machines available, it will do what is asked of it. The Easy has not been advertised for several years, but large numbers are still available at sporting goods stores and some mail order houses. In the summer of 1980, I purchased a second Easy press for less than the first one cost me in 1967. Follow the comprehensive instruction sheets packed with the press and the die sets.

Lyman produced another fine tool for roll-crimping, their Star Crimping Tool. The tool's only function was crimping, and it was excellent. It could be motor driven, or fitted with a hand crank. This tool has not been manufactured for more than 15 years, probably longer than that, yet the tool I have is like new, though years old and much used.

The next alternative is a drill-press setup, using one of the roll-crimping heads available from several manu-

facturers, Lyman included. This setup will prove most viable if you load other gauges, since you have only to change the rotating head. The outlay for this setup will vary, but I put together a tool using a Black & Decker shop drill, and an inexpensive drill press fixture. I already had two tools to do the crimping, but I wanted to be sure the drill press idea would work before suggesting its use to anyone.

I'll advise you early that drill speed in excess of 600 rpm, will cause you some problems. Case tubes tend to get hot, and twisting will result. After ruining several dozen cases, I found

that reducing the rotation by connecting the drill motor to a Dremel tool speed-control worked. With that control at 3 or 4, on a scale of 6, the shell can be crimped as well as on either of the Lyman tools. More could hardly be asked of a tool that costs less than 25 dollars to put together.

The over-all length and the crimp depth remain constant when using this setup, if I take care to snug up the depth-stop adjustment, and tighten the U-shaped bolt that holds the motor to the fixture. An oak block is fastened to the bed of the fixture, and a hole bored out to accommodate the base of the shell. Care should be taken to see

that this hole is aligned correctly with the stroke of the press. This can be done easily, by squaring a drill bit to the block of wood, before fitting the crimp head into the jaws of the motor.

Of the three alternatives, two will provide only a means of closing the mouth of the shell. Only the Easy press can seat primers and apply the necessary wad pressure to the slug/wad unit. With the other two, the handloader will have to have another means at his disposal, for the other steps. If you already load shot loads, your present tool will do the other steps. If you're just getting started,

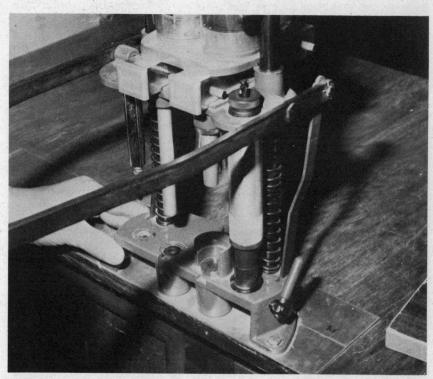

Lyman's Easy Shotshell Loader was used exclusively in carrying out the steps necessary to load the Brenneke and the Vitt slugs. It performed flawlessly, using the steps suggested by the Lyman Technical Staff.

you will not have to go to too much expense, to obtain the needed tools. Lee's Load-All shotshell press can do an excellent job, and the outlay for this press is small by today's standards.

This press, and Lee's Load-All Junior, provide the handloader with a means of seating the slugs, something the other, more expensive presses cannot do. In every instance, the wad seating units on *all* other presses, including the Easy press, are totally useless for seating the slugs; if you try it, you're bound to destroy the chamber used on these presses. The wad guide on the Lee press will allow for the oversize slugs to pass smoothly into the shell without any hang-ups. By using the Lee wad guide to seat the Vitt slugs, any damage to the attached OP wad can be eliminated.

Another Lee product that you might find useful on the bench is that company's powder measure kit. Whether you're assembling slugs, shot or brass cases for rifle or pistol, this measure set can be a real time saver. Loads, once selected, can be assembled quickly, by using the correct measure to *nearly* obtain the weight needed. A chart supplied with the kit makes this simple to do. The remaining amount of powder can be added to the scale pan

racy of the load on the target, but also for your personal safety. Under no circumstances should you trust a powder bushing to meter the required charge of powder. Pressures in these loads are just too high to "come close" to the weight needed. I have always believed the scale to be the most important piece of equipment on the reloader's bench.

My own choice is RCBS's 10-10 scale. This scale can provide the needed sensitivity and accuracy, and it also has the capacity to weigh the Vitts, at 575 grains, and the Brennekes, at 468 grains. If you choose not

the copper pipe with a Stanley razor knife. The shells were then all the same length. Different lengths can easily be made up.

When trimming paper shells, insert a dowel of the correct diameter first. Without it paper shells will usually crush, rather than cut.

It should be noted that the shell length that works for me in my loads may not work on your tools if you are using a crimping head without the recess for the rounded nose of the slug. The flat-faced crimping head, used to roll-crimp shot loads, *may* require a slightly longer shell to get the rolled-over edge of the shell tube onto the slugs. Experimentation will come up with the right length. The crimp should *just* come in contact with the slug for best results.

Reconditioning Cases

Availability or, more correctly, unavailability sometimes makes it necessary to re-use cases. My own preference, is to use only new or once-fired cases, but that is not always possible.

For reconditioning, I use the Therm-O-Matic Shot Shell Former, marketed by Forster Products. This tool is still manufactured, and can be ordered from a number of mail-order houses, if it is unavailable in your area.

Paper cases should be re-waxed to get the best results. Different wax mixtures have been tried, and all achieve about the same results. To uncomplicate the job, I use pure candle wax, available at many hobby shops. The wax is melted, and heated to 300°; each case is dipped mouth first into the wax, to a point just above the crimped section, and held there for 3 to 5 seconds. The case is then positioned on the mandrel of the Forster case former. With the temperature at the highest setting, the wax will sizzle, and is forced into the layers of the paper tube, bonding these layers together. The shell will again perform adequately for continued use.

Plastic cases do not require the waxing. A heat setting of 3 on my tool will smooth out the wrinkles and puckered mouths. Inserting a tapered wooden dowel into the case immediately after removing it from the case former will "bell" the shell slightly; this allows for easy entry of the slug-unit when loading the shell. The heat also bonds the separated plastic layers together, extending the life of plastic cases like Remington SP's.

Failure to recondition every shell after each firing is a waste of valuable components and the time it takes you

As evident here, the Easy Loader produced excellent reloads. Length remained consistent throughout a loading session that saw more than 300 rounds assembled. The accuracy produced by these handloads attests to the excellence of the Lyman press.

using a powder trickler, though I continue to use a "baby" spoon to add the last few tenths.

The Scale

One will never have to weigh 500 grains of powder, but if you choose to segregate slugs by weight, you may find that your present scale is unable to handle the heavy Brenneke and Vitt slugs. In this situation, a large capacity scale *might* be an item you may wish to add to your tool inventory.

When working with the near-maximum pressures developed by many of the loads used for slugs, accuracy is important, not only to the accu-

to segregate slugs, then any good quality scale will do.

Shell Trimming

To obtain the correct shell length, you can use one of the prefabricated tools available from Lyman. I have used another method which does just as good a job on the shells.

When my need to trim shells came, the city of Buffalo was buried under four feet of snow. I had to use what was available at home or wait until spring. I took a length of ⅞-in. copper tubing, and cut a piece to correct length, which left ¼-in. of a Remington shell sticking out. I cut this off along the rim of

to assemble them. No amount of care will produce satisfactory results if this step has not been completed. Frayed, wrinkled mouths give against the upward pressure of the slug-units, seated at 50 to 100 pounds of wad pressure. You'll find crimps opening up after a short time, a condition not conducive to accuracy.

The mouths of the cases take a great deal of abuse on firing, as the sharp, squared fins push violently against the crimp. If the slug has not ripped away a portion of the mouth, careful reconditioning *can* make the case usable. At best, any case that can be used 4 times with slugs should be considered exceptional. As cases deteriorate, they perform less like new cases, resulting in greater shot-to-shot variation, and less accuracy. You'll have to determine for yourself when a case is no longer adequate, but slugs cost about 40 cents apiece, and it seems inappropriate to reuse a case costing only 7 or 8 cents too many times.

Reloading Procedures

The individual steps that lead to a complete round are not difficult. True, it takes a little more work and time than turning out a box of shot loads, but persevere and the results will astound you.

After cases are deprimed, the next step will depend on whether you will use 2¾" shells or the shorter length I have used. The reason I use the shorter lengths is to get a perfect crimp. If one uses the full length shell, the roll-over will be ¹/₁₆-in. to ³/₃₂-in. deeper than my loads, depending on the shell brand. It has always been my belief that deeper crimps bring higher pressure without a corresponding increase in velocity.

If you have trimmed the hulls, plastic shells can now be primed and charged; paper shells should be waxed and reconditioned on the Forster case former before proceeding. This additonal step will assure the firmness needed at the shell mouth for a good turn-over. As with any reload, primers should be seated flush with the case head.

Each charge should be carefully weighed, not metered. A good measure, such as the Pacific rifle measure or Lyman's 55, can accurately throw a charge, but the loader must be absolutely sure of the weight; only a scale will do here. The measure or the Lee dippers can speed-up the task of charging.

When a load calls for additional wads, as in the case of the Brenneke slug loads, it is best to seat these wads

Lyman Slug Loads

	Case	Primer	Powder/grs.	Wad	Vel./fps
1.	Fed. Monark pap.	Fed. 209	Unique/28.0	PGS, ⅜" fiber,[1] + .125" card + .200" card	1510
2.	Rem. Low Br. slug	Rem. 57*	SR 7625/38.0	PGS, ⅜" fiber + .200" card	1550
3.	Rem. SP slug	Rem. 57*	Green Dot/27.5	Herter's OP, + .250" fiber + 2 .070" cards	1430
4.	Rem. SP slug	CCI 157[2]	Win. 571/47.0	Herter's OP, + ⅜" fiber + .070" card	1500
5.	Fed. HP pl.	Win. 209	PB/32	Herter's OP, ¼" fiber + 2 .135" cards	1460

[1]All fiber and card wads used are Herter's brand.
[2]No. 4 is a Ball Powder load, be sure to use CCI 157 primer.

Pap. = paper; pl. = plastic; OP = over-powder.

WARNING: These loads were carefully worked up by the author, but reflect one man's experience and are not recommendations by HANDLOADER'S DIGEST.

Vitt Slug Loads

	Case	Primer	Powder/grs.	Vel./fps
1.	Fed. HP pl.	Fed. 209	Blue Dot/48.5[1]	1530
2.	Fed. HP pl.	Fed. 209	SR 4756/41.0[1]	1470
3.	Fed. Monark pap.	Fed. 209	Herco/36.0	NA
4.	Fed. HP pl.	Fed. 209	AL-120/31.0[2]	1505
5.	Rem. SP slug	Rem. 57*	AL-7/39.5	1490
6.	Alcan Field pap.	Alc. 220 MF	AL-5/37.0[3]	1460
7.	Alcan Hi-Br. pap.	Alc. 220 MF	AL-7/40.0	1470
8.	Rem. SP slug	Rem. 57*	AL-8/45.0[4]	NA

Pl. = plastic; pap. = paper; NA = not available.

[1]Nos. 1 and 2 are similar to Lyman loads from 2nd, except for primers.
[2]No. 4—I feel this load approaches maximum pressures
[3]No. 6 definitely a maximum load, do not exceed.
[4]No. 8 load best used in 28" barrel for best results.

WARNING: These loads were carefully worked up by the author, but reflect one man's experience and are not recommendations by HANDLOADER'S DIGEST.

Brenneke Slug Loads

	Case	Primer	Powder/grs.	Wad	Vel./fps
1.	Fed. HP pl.	Fed. 209	Herco/37.0	½" fiber + .135" card	1570
2.	Rem. SP slug	Rem. 57*	AL-5/36.0	Herter's OP + .070" card	1510
3.	Rem. SP slug	Rem. 57*	SR 4756/37.0	Herter's OP + .070" card	1470

Pap. = paper; pl. = plastic; OP = over-powder.

WARNING: These loads were carefully worked up by the author, but reflect one man's experience and are not recommendations by HANDLOADER's DIGEST.

Approximate Tool Costs

Lee Load-All Shotshell Press	$35.00
Lee Powder Measure Kit	4.98
Lyman Roll Crimp Head	11.95
Drill Press Unit	26.95
Total for the minimum tools needed	$68.88

If you're just getting started, you can expect to spend less than $70.00, much less if you're a good shopper, since the prices listed are retail. A shotshell case former will be needed if you use other than once-fired cases, adding about $20.00 to the total. Additional items will be purchased, I'm sure, as you find a need for them.

lightly over the powder, prior to seating the slug/wad unit. Wad pressure is then applied to the nose of the slug. On my Easy loader, the ram used to apply the wad pressure is a hollow aluminum tube. George Vitt fabricated another ram from bar stock to prevent marring the slug nose, but, not the mechanic Mr. Vitt was, I use a copper washer, placed over the slug. Be sure you remove that washer before crimping the shell.

I suppose wad pressure could be another source of experimentation for the slug-loader, with different amounts of pressure producing varying degrees of accuracy in a specific load. I was fortunate in that my first loads produced excellent accuracy in my shotguns. I have yet to come up with a more accurate combination, so I see no reason to vary wad pressure from my original loads. The amount used with Alcan AL-5 and AL-7 is 45 to 50 lbs. of pressure, due in part to Vitt's recommendations, and also because all the components, and the case length used were compatible with that amount of wad pressure. Everything fit neatly!

I felt that since AL-8, Herco and Blue Dot were slower than the first two Alcan's, more wad pressure might aid in combustion. Further research showed 100 lbs. to be the usual recommendation for Herco, when using the built-up wad columns, rather than the usual one-piece plastic unit; so 100 lbs. has been used with these propellants. I hope to do some chronographing to see what effects wad pressure might have on the velocity a given load might produce at some time in the future. For now, I feel that the amounts listed give very good accuracy, and suit the components used.

Once the slug has been seated, and the wad pressure applied, I immediately crimp that round, rather than letting uncrimped rounds accumulate. If you let the shell remain uncrimped for too long a time, the filler wads will start to expand to their original thickness, lessening the pressure over the powder, and filling more of the case. This changes the depth of the crimp, from shell to shell, depending on the expansion of the wads, and gives just one more source of variation to be avoided.

After adjusting the Star tool to the proper shell length, the operator can crimp the shells in just one pass, and have a beautifully crimped round. With the Easy loader, and the drill press setup, I have found it necessary to apply the crimp in at least two passes, preferably three, to get the best results. The first pass should just begin to turn-over the mouth of the case. After raising the crimping head, a second pass can complete the crimp, without the twisting of the shell tube that will occur if attempted in one pass.

If different loads are assembled for testing. I have found it easier to mark each individual round with a felt-tipped, permanent marker, rather than separating the groups assembled with different components. I note the powder type, and weight, and the primer used on the tube. Black ink seems to work the best, on both the red Federal cases, and the green Remingtons.

When a load is fired for grouping, the target is noted with the load fired, and the measurements later taken in the warmth of my gun room. Index cards are kept on each load, and the results noted on the back of the card. I don't want to reload a combination that does not produce the required accuracy more than once, so these records become important as new combinations are tried. One need not get so involved with record keeping as I have, but it can prove very useful as time goes on, and an increasing number of loads are put together.

With all the work behind you, I'm sure you'll agree it was not as difficult as you had anticipated. The satisfaction comes when you see the results on paper, and even more so, when one of your handloads drops your next whitetail. Be assured, it will be more than luck that leads to your success. ●

The Lee Junior Load-All press is an inexpensive unit/tool that can do about all that the more expensive progressive loaders, can though the steps take a bit longer. Here the handloader is depriming and sizing.

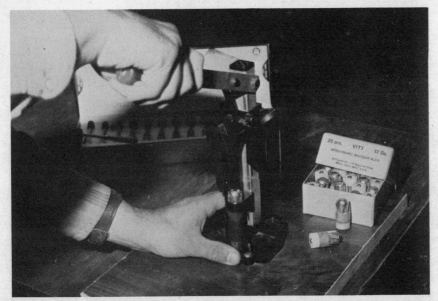

A Vitt slug is being seated into the Remington case using the Lee wad-guide found on the Lee Junior Load-All. Do not try to do this using your MEC or Pacific shotshell loader, or any other for that matter. Damage is bound to result to the wad seating station of any but the Lee.

Author finds these two the best bullets in his Marlin Carbine in 357 Magnum. Left, 158-gr. soft-nose; right, 160-gr. half-jacket.

These are the hollow points wrung out for the 357 Carbine loadings here, from left: 125-gr., 140-gr., 146-gr., 158-gr.

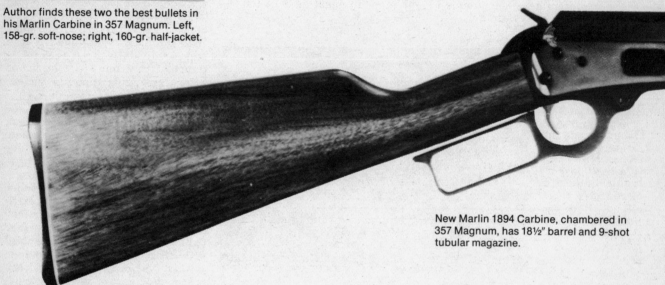

New Marlin 1894 Carbine, chambered in 357 Magnum, has 18½" barrel and 9-shot tubular magazine.

These eight Speer bullets tested in the Carbine are, from left: 125-gr. JHP, 140-gr. JHP, 146-gr. HJHP, 158-gr. JHP, 158-gr. JSP, 158-gr. LSWC, 158-gr. LRN, 160-gr. HJ.

Combination Loads
for the Marlin
357 Carbine

by ROBERT K. SHERWOOD

THE CYCLIC phenomenon is evident in shooter tastes as well as biology, and in the past 100 years a wheel has come full circle. In 1873 there appeared to be a wide demand for rifles and revolvers which used the same load, and for this reason Colt and a number of others chambered revolvers for shells used in the Winchester rifle of 1873.

In a frontier time this was not too hard to understand. Ammunition supply was a problem; while the rifle was the more efficient arm, a revolver was always at hand, and men needed to be armed at all times in many professions.

It was only logical to avoid the complication of two sizes of ammunition when one wouldn't do much more than the other in a rifle. Certainly there were rifles chambered for cartridges that no pistol could conceivably handle, but the greater range and power of these was often sacrificed for portability and handiness, and that meant carrying a rifle chambered for a short stubby pistol cartridge, such as the '73 was chambered for.

As the century progressed, light repeating rifles were developed for more effective cartridges. Revolvers had mechanical limitations that limited them; they do today. Rifles did not; they could improve by means of cartridge dimension and design. The stockhand of the turn of the century was likely to carry a 45 or 44 on his belt and a 30-30 or 30-40 in his saddle scabbard. By the mid-1930s, pistol-cartridge rifles faded from the scene, with the obvious exception of the 22 rimfire.

The whole idea was largely forgotten and might have stayed that way, but here and there people began rebarreling or reboring old Winchester Model 1892s for the 357 and 44 Magnum revolver rounds. In 1962, Ruger noted the trend and began marketing a 44 Magnum auto carbine, and by 1968 Winchester, Marlin and Remington all produced rifles for the largest practical pistol cartridge. The 357 escaped attention for a while longer, but it was only logical that the governing trends which established the 44 as a rifle cartridge created the same demand for a 357 rifle. In 1978 Marlin began chambering their 1894 carbine for the 357 Magnum shell.

The cycle is complete and a percentage of the shooting crew is back to interchangeable rifle and revolver cartridges, though I am not entirely sure why. One may see a cycle and study it; to say that he fully understands it is, in the words of Aldo Leopold, a moment's voice in the derisive silence of eternity.

The carbine is here, and the fact that it sells like reasonably priced gasoline indicates the demand is big and continuous, regardless of reasons. It is a pretty little carbine, having no peer as a light and handy rifled shoulder arm.

The barrel is a scant 18½ inches in length and mine weighs about 5.5 pounds empty. It feeds without malfunction all 38 and 357 cartridges except for wadcutters and magnums with the bullet seated too far out. It's a fun and reliable gun, within its limits.

There is yet one professional class of person who might need a rifle that handles the same shell as his revolver —the policeman. He may want a rifle as a secondary arm that handles a factory 357 revolver shell; he is required by regulation to carry these. He may want a shoulder arm with more range capabilities than a shotgun and less danger space than, say, a 30-30, for the protection of innocents in the area of a fire fight. The little Marlin carbine meets all these requirements with the right factory load. Thus the case for the only practical professional use of the arm that I can see.

The sporting purchaser of the 357 Marlin 1894C will put it to a multitude of uses, and most of them will load for it. Not nearly all the loads that work to satisfaction in the 357 revolver will do so in the rifle, and such a rifle has many limitations, regardless of the load used in it.

It does have some advantages. It is entirely adequate for Coues deer, Florida Key deer, wild turkey and javelina. All of these are mostly hunted in close cover and the range limitation is not a serious handicap. A

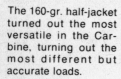

The 160-gr. half-jacket turned out the most versatile in the Carbine, turning out the most different but accurate loads.

Chronographed with an Oehler 33, Sherwood's good loads may be found in a chart nearby.

The difference between the handgun and the carbine with the same load is plain to see: In sand, the carbine simply blew up the 160-gr. half-jacket; the handgun didn't.

Crony George Hartwell helped with shooting chores, which burned up 800 bullets and quite a bit of time.

deep woods trapper might well use it for occasional shots at bobcat, lynx, coyotes and badgers at the close ranges afforded in such country. Its weight and handling values appeal to the brush and timber hunter. It might work for the hunter of larger subspecies of whitetail or for a mule deer hunter in close-range country; shot placement would be of paramount importance. Nothing will make it the equivalent of the 25-35; this caliber or equivalent has always been my bottom line for the taking of mule deer. I'd not advocate that anyone, regardless of ability, use it on bear or elk. It is a lot of fun to plink ground squirrels and rockchucks with, and it works well with certain loads for this sport, up to

dard. Those giving acceptable 5-shot groups at 100 yards were chronographed with an Oehler 33 and the shocking power was calculated using Speer's bullet energy tables on page 424 of their *Reloading Manual Number 10*. Group spread of three inches was used as an accuracy limit. All firing was accomplished from a solid bench with sandbag rests for forearm and butt.

A few general problems came to light in the firing. The little rifle started walking its zero on the fourth or fifth shot. This was probably due to the fact that the front barrel band hogtied the barrel so tightly to the magazine. Not much one can do about that; the barrel band pin also secures the

have a slight edge in terms of a tenth of an inch or so.

Much further shooting was accomplished with the rifle; little of it could be summarized quantitatively. Identical loads were fired into wet sand from the Marlin and from a Blackhawk revolver with a 4.8-inch barrel. The rifle burst and shattered the bullets while the revolver nicely mushroomed them. This proved little except to demonstrate an obvious difference in power. Sand is very resistant; a sandbag will stop a military rifle bullet, and a bullet that would not mushroom in flesh or on an occasional bone will do so in sand. A bullet that would merely mushroom well in the body of an animal will often shatter or separate in sand.

The best loads found were fired at gallon containers of molasses through a half-inch pine shield. This spread a lot of syrup on sagebrush and totally wrecked some heavy plastic containers. The 158- and 160-grain bullets did maintain a straight line of flight through the wood, plastic, molasses and sagebrush behind. This told me that if I held on the lung or heart of a small deer I would hit it, and the bullet would not be deflected if it hit a rib. Further, such a deer would be rendered worse than uncomfortable by the wallop, to judge by the ten-foot splatter of molasses.

Certain conclusions resulted from shooting and recording 800 rounds. They are summarized as follows:

● The most versatile powder checked was 2400. It supplied a qualifying load with all the jacketed Speer bullets used.

● The bullet demonstrating the greatest versatility in the 357 rifle was the 160-grain half-jacket. More accurate loads were found for it than any other bullet tested.

● Ball powder 296 gave the highest velocities in accurate loads of any powder tried.

● The 158- and 160-grain bullets seemed better suited to the twist of the Marlin than lighter bullets; more accurate loads were obtained with their use.

● Lead and alloy bullet accuracy was difficult to obtain from my Marlin.

● All loads tested are usable in 357 Magnum revolvers.

In conclusion, I realize these are not all the possible working loads for this rifle. Each owner will have to experiment to find the best for his rifle-revolver combination, if he desires others. It is hoped that the foregoing will save some steps for those who do not wish to fire 800 rounds testing. ●

TABLE I

Load #	Speer bullet (grs.)	Powder	Weight grains	Inches Best Group	Velocity feet/ second	Energy foot/ pounds	Recommended use
1.	125 gr. JHP	2400	18.3	3.0	1871	869	chucks and such
2.	140 gr. JHP	680	18.0	2.5	1529	727	chuck, fox
3.	140 gr. JHP	2400	17.2	2.5	1767	966	coyote, bobcat
4.	158 gr. JSN	296	16.0	3.0	1702	1013	small deer, pig
5.	158 gr. JSN	2400	15.0	1.8	1542	831	javelina
6.	158 gr. JSN	680	17.6	2.4	1441	727	turkey
7.	158 gr. LSWC	N1010	3.5	3.0	861	261	ground squirrel
8.	160 gr. HJ	H-110	17.0	2.8	1620	931	small deer, pig
9.	160 gr. HJ	2400	15.0	2.0	1586	893	coyote, b-cat
10.	160 gr. HJ	680	17.6	3.0	1501	800	javelina
11.	160 gr. HJ	4227	15.0	2.5	1453	747	turkey
12.	160 gr. HJ	296	16.6	2.8	1701	1027	deer, pig

Note: JHP = Jacketed Hollow Point; JSN = Jacketed Soft Nose;
LSWC = Lead Semi-Wadcutter; HJ = Half Jacket.

Note: Chronograph screens were set five feet apart, nearest screen ten feet from muzzle.

ranges of about 120 meters.

In all use the load used will be of great importance. Not all loads giving adequate revolver accuracy will give acceptable accuracy in the rifle. In the interest of safety, those who use both a rifle and a revolver in the same caliber should limit his rifle loads to those his sixgun can handle.

I recently fired over 800 rounds through my Marlin 1894C 357 to classify and categorize loads, starting with some I had used in the revolver for many years, and staying with those safe in my revolver. Ten powders were used with Speer's line of jacketed and swaged 357 bullets. (I omitted the 180-grain silhouette bullet; it would not feed with a normal crimp.) All tests were fired using a CCI #550 primer. Loads were fired first to determine the best bullet-powder combinations possible for each bullet type and weight, using accuracy as a stan-

magazine, and said magazine comes out if you remove it.

Lead and lead alloy bullets did not do well in the rifle, at least those tried. Proven pistol powders, such as Bullseye and Unique were no more accurate than FFFg black; 630 did nothing spectacular with any bullet.

Those loads furnishing acceptable hunting accuracy are listed and summarized in Table 1. All powders were tried with all bullets tested, but it would be pointless to list a page or more of loads that did not work.

It might be well to add that no appreciable difference in accuracy was noted between the 158-grain jacketed hollow point and the 158-grain jacketed soft nose; loads for one will do for the other. The soft-nose had a slight edge. For practical purposes the same loads for the 140-grain jacketed hollow point apply to the 146-grain half-jacket hollow point; the first seemed to

How Much ZAP?

How much, that is, do you need; how much do you get? Here are records on 51 kills to tell you.

by **JOHN A REESE, Jr.**

This 24¼-inch waterbuck was taken with 8x68S Mauser at 60 yards. It's shot number 45 in Table 1.

Photos by Buck Burns

THERE is probably less known or understood and more curiosity about the actual effect of bullets on game than any other single factor in the shooting/hunting game.

Nearly all the name gun writers and many noted hunters have had a go at it from one angle or another in the past 100 years. But long months of careful research by this writer did not turn up much comprehensive or—more to the point—conclusive information on the subject. On the other hand, it is hard to find a big game hunter who doesn't have a few theories on the subject and some will defend them loud and long on what appears to be a pretty narrow base of experience and observation.

Well, anybody who hopes he will read all of the secrets here that he has been seeking on what cartridge zaps game the best, had better think more conservatively. This article won't give anything more than a few more answers in the myriad of mysteries surrounding what happens when the bullet hits.

Before we get into the details, let me lay out for you what the basis of experience was and what the guns were.

Because it all took place in the late winter of 1970 in Kenya, you may have to do a bit of interpolation to draw conclusions on what to expect if you are hunting in Maine, Idaho, Texas, Virginia or Alberta. However, I discount in great measure the claims that African mammals are so much harder to kill than North American ones. Or even European game. I have hunted in Europe, Africa, North America, and Asia for some 40 years and do not find such a great difference in tenacity to life as has been touted in many articles and books on African hunting. This is only opinion based on my experience, and again I don't know of any way this comparison can be measured. For example I have seen a puny little 40-pound roebuck, a splendid and courageous little animal in most of Europe's hunting fields, go much farther with a heart-lung shot, than a number of impala, apparently with the same shot, although the impala might weigh twice as much. Not always, but sometimes.

Now, the guns: A representative battery was deliberately selected for the purposes of this limited study. They were a Czech Brno 308 Winchester, a 7mm Weatherby Magnum, a Winchester Model 70 375 H&H Magnum, two Mauser 8x68S Model 60s, a superbly accurate 458 Winchester built on a Mauser action with a Douglas premium barrel, a 404 H&H Enfield and a couple of rental Winchester African 458s for backup and finishers. We'll leave the shotguns out of this.

Then, the ammunition: The 308 was fed on 200 carefully run-up handloads of 1964 once-fired arsenal match cases stuffed with 40 grains of 4895 and CCI primers behind 180-grain bullets. Some 100 loads with Brennecke TUG bullets were used in addition to 100 SP

Two party members with impala taken early in the hunt. The 150-pound animals were taken with 8x68 Mauser and a 308 Winchester. Reese found little difference between this size African game and equal American animals.

Left to right—7mm Norma 160-grain; 308 Nosler 180-grain; 308 DWM-TUG 180-grain; 8mm (323) RWS 224-grain; 375 DWM-TUG; 458 Winchester 500-grain solid: All are reported on here.

ABOUT THESE TABLES:

The accompanying article and tables discuss and disclose the effect of medium caliber rifle bullets in killing some 50 game animals at ranges from 35 to 325 yards. The animals ranging in live weight from 30 to 1900 pounds. All bullets performed well. Carefully kept records disclose that half of the bullets exited. Of the remainder, some 17 bullets were recovered, and 9 bullets were not found.

Of the bullets not found, some lodged in animals shot at sunset; in the hasty field dressing that then took place the bullets could not be located, or in the case of large game careful and painstaking search failed to turn up the spent bullet in what was often hundreds of pounds of damaged tissue. It will be noted in Tables 1, 2 and 3 that the 375 or 458 were sometimes used as a finisher, these bullets were used as needed to quickly dispatch game and are not included as photographic exhibits nor were they weighed.

The medium class bullets used were selected by the hunters as their first choice for the rifle that they used and the class of game hunted. Although, as previously stated, all bullets performed well, it was found that the Norma 160-grain softpoint, semi-pointed boattail bullet and the Nosler 180 grain pointed bullet gave the best results. The 8mm RWS 223-grain hollow spire point, and the 308 DWM Brenneke TUG softpointed bullet in 180 grains did their job well but in several instances lost their lead cores. Examination of bullet jackets from these bullets discloses that they were not sufficiently bonded to the bullet cores that they carried. (See Table 4 for weights of fragments).

In summary it appears evident that the most important factor in the hunt is that the bullet must be properly placed. If you don't hit the animal in a vital spot the bullet can't do much to make up for poor shooting. To this end a bullet designed to kill game should be accurate, so that it can be placed where the shooter intends by use of the rifle's sighting equipment. This same bullet should open up or expand on thin skinned game and it should have enough terminal energy when it strikes to penetrate to the vital spot which has been selected, then it should preferably punch on through and exit. The bullet should not shed its jacket or blow up, if by doing so it will make a superficial wound, nor

should it shed its jacket, as it will often permit the bullet's core to markedly wander from its intended path or axis. This means that some poorly designed bullets on the market today do not do the job required of them to

successfully culminate a hunting trip. High quality factory or handloaded cartridges may cost more, but ammunition selection is a poor place to effect economy on a costly, and infrequent hunt.

TABLE 1

Weapon & Cartridge: 8x68S Mauser; Factory Load, 223-Grain Spire, Hollow Point Zeiss Diavari 1.5-6x scope

Animal & Estimated Live Weight	Paced off Range (Yds.)	Point of Impact	Reaction	Remarks
2 Thomson's Gazelle 40	180	Paunch	Fell in place, slowly	Bullet not recovered.
3 Zebra 700	60	Lower neck	Ran until hit in rump from rear at 180 yds. w/308. Fell	Small fragment of one bullet recovered, not identifiable.
5 Impala 165	150	Shoulder at 90° angle	Fell in place	Bullet, well mushroomed recovered under hide on opposite shoulder.
9 Thomson's Gazelle 45	120	Left hip	Fell in place	Bullet exited at opposite groin large exit hole. Bullet not recovered.
10 Zebra 650	160	Rib cage behind diaphragm	Ran several hundred yards	Bullet recovered under hide on opposite side.
12 Zebra 700	120	Rib cage, high	Spun in tight circle, ran 30-40 yards, fell	No exit hole. Bullet not recovered.
13 Oryx 450	70	Base of left foreleg	Faltered, went to knees recovered, ran 30 yds. Fell dead	Bullet penetrated both forelegs, cut forward top portion of heart. 2" exit hole. Bullet not recovered.
15 Grant's Gazelle 75	200, 1st 240, 2nd	Rump, 1st shot paunch, from rear, 2nd shot	Ran after 1st hit; pitched forward on second hit	Second shot, fired as as animal was quartering away. Bullet exited at lower neck on opposite side. Exit hole 4-5" in diameter. Neither bullet recovered.
18 Zebra 700	340, 1st 300, 2nd 40, 3rd	Middle of both forelegs Rump Neck	Ran to left Turned back toward gun. Went down, not dead, 3rd shot finisher in neck	3rd shot left 2½" exit hole. 2nd bullet recovered in off ham.
19 Steinbuck 35	80	Top of rump	Ran 85-100 yds, dropped	Animal facing shooter, head down. Bullet broke on hip, damaged rear of spine. Bullet not recovered.
20 Impala 150	70	Center neck from side	Dropped in place	One in. exit on far side. Bullet not recovered.
21 Wart hog 180	300	Just forward of hip	Dropped in tracks	Animal standing quartering away from gun. Bullet raked through entire body—recovered under hide at neck.
25 Oryx 450	120	1st shot hit far back in rib cage.	Animal ran 50-60 yds.	Finished by shot in shoulder w/375 H&H.
26 Grant's Gazelle 65	300	1st shot in paunch. 2nd forward of hip	Ran on 1st shot Fell on second	Second shot exited causing 2" hole just behind off foreleg. Heart & lungs damaged.
27 Bush Buck 400	100	Neck	Dropped in place	Bullet severed spine, exited through 1" hole. Not recovered.

TABLE 1 (continued)

Animal & Estimated Live Weight	Paced off Range (Yds.)	Point of Impact	Reaction	Remarks
28 Impala 170	200	Shoulder	Ran 20 yds., piled up dead	Bullet exited through off shoulder, 1″ exit hole; not recovered.
29 Water Buck 525	100	Behind shoulder center of body	Dropped in place	Perfectly mushroomed bullet recovered under hide of off shoulder. Narrow wound channel through both lungs.
30 Thomsons's 40	200	Center of body just ahead of diaphragm	Fell in place	Liver & diaphragm damaged. Bullet not recovered.
36 Bush Buck 350	80	Middle of back	Fell in place	Hand-size chunk of tissue blown out of back, spine severed. Bullet not recovered.
38 Reed Buck 180	120	Low in shoulder 1st shot	Bucked, ran unsteadily	1st shot exited opposite shoulder making 3-4″ hole.
		Behind shoulder, 2nd shot.	Collapsed slowly, died	Second did not exit. Neither recovered.
39 Bush Buck 400	140	Base of neck at shoulder	Dropped in place	Bullet severed spine, making 1″ hole. Not recovered.
40 Reed Buck 200	100	Center of neck	Fell in place	3″ exit hole.
43 Eland 1950	60	Rear center of neck	Dropped in tracks	Massive spine fracture, small fragments of bullet recovered in neck. Prof. hunter put in back-up shot in shoulder as animal fell. 458 solid went through both shoulders; not recovered.
44 Impala 170	25	Hit in rump from rear	Fell in place	Well mushroomed bullet recovered under hide of right shoulder.
45 Water Buck	60	Rib cage at diaphragm, 1st shot Front of chest, 2nd shot	Humped back ran 50 yards, faltered, went down slowly. Died instantly.	2nd shot was coup de grace; animal would have died quickly from 1st shot.
46 Impala 160	50	Hit head-on in chest.	Fell in place	No exit.
49 Eland 1700	120	Rear portion of paunch	Humped back, ran 75-85 yds.	Finished w/458 solid in chest.
50 Zebra 700	120-150	1st shot in rump 2nd shot behind shoulders; 3rd shot into ribs	Bucked, ran 10 yds., fell; recovered and stood. Went down on 2nd shot but recovered feet again. Fell 3rd time, but not yet dead	1st bullet recovered from rump. Finisher put into chest from front (4th shot)

Note: Numbers appearing at extreme left are bullet reference numbers, hence do not appear in order in Tables 1-4 as they do in Table 5.

TABLE 2

Weapon & Cartridge: 308 Brno; Mauser; 40 gr./4895 — 180gr. Nosler sp pointed, part. & 180-gr. Brennecke TUG (DWM)

Animal & Estimated Live Weight	Paced Off Range (yds.)	Point of Impact	Reaction	Remarks
1 Thomson's Gazelle 35	135	High on back behind shoulders	Collapsed instantly	Nosler bullet not recovered. Took out u-shaped chunk of tissue, hand-sized.

pointed 180-grain Nosler Partition bullets. These both proved to be excellent reloads, shooting into slightly over one minute of angle. The Weatherby did its stuff on once-fired factory cases (presumably from Dynamit-Nobel) filled with 68 grains of Norma 205 under Norma's 160-grain softpoint, semi-pointed boattail bullet. Norma large rifle primers were used. The two Mausers performed well on a diet of RWS factory loads topped off with 223-grain hollow, spire point bullets. This bullet has a hard lead core running through it nearly to the hollow pointed tip.

Not that it has much bearing on what we are after, but some readers would like to know about the sights. On the 308 was a 3-9x Kahles. The Weatherby wore a Pecar 3-7x and the two Mausers were equipped with Zeiss Diavari 1.5-6x tubes. All other rifles were fired with open iron sights, and were used mostly at relatively short ranges.

It will be of some interest to mention here that both Model 60 Mausers cost their shooters several trophies when a small stop lug on the bolt sleeve became battered and bent, which resulted in several failures to fire. Mauser has corrected this defect, and on-the-spot repairs were made halfway through the safari and both rifles resumed delivering good accuracy. The 8x68S cartridges proved to be entirely satisfactory, although the recoil was a bit stiff.

Elsewhere on these pages is a tabular summary of what each rifle/cartridge combination did to some 50 pieces of game. The four hunters were all experienced and proven marksmen of wide experience, each of them having shot over 200 big game animals in the preceding 25 to 40 year span. The hunting party was guided by Kenyan professional hunters Pete Smith, and Dan Shaw. The experience and tables accompanying this article include shots fired, when taken, by the professional hunters as well.

Any effects on such heavy game as rhinoceros or elephant are not included here, in the thought that there will be nothing comparable for American hunters to consider. The largest animals taken and effects observed were Cape buffalo and eland, either of which approach the one-ton mark in weight. That's bigger and tougher (presumably) than the biggest elk or moose. Because there are no bears in Kenya, we couldn't do much in comparison here. Big game hunters in North America are mostly concerned with the various ungulates, so nearly

TABLE 2 (continued)

Animal & Estimated Live Weight	Paced Off Range (yds.)	Point of Impact	Reaction	Remarks
4 Impala 175	125	Right shoulder point	Fell in place	Nosler bullet exited middle of back, leaving 1¾" hole not recovered.
14 Zebra 700	40	Right side of front neck	Sank to ground, rolled over, feet in air. Dead	DWM bullet broke spine, severed carotid artery, penetrated into body. No exit; not recovered.
16 Grant's Gazelle 80	120	Right shoulder	Fell in place	Nosler bullet exited through opposite shoulder leaving 1" hole.
17 Bush Buck 425	50	Base of throat	Fell in place	Nosler bullet exited above hips leaving cigar-shaped exit hole.
23 Oryx 425	150	Behind left shoulder	Jumped straight up, fell w/o taking a step	DWM bullet recovered under hide of right shoulder extensive damage to lungs and heart.
24 Eland 1800	115	Behind right shoulder	Ran until hit by 458 solid	Required 3 458 solids to finish. Lungs & heart damaged by first shot (Nosler)
42 Steinbuck 35	80	Left shoulder	Fell in place	Nosler bullet exited right shoulder; 5" wound.
47 Water Buck 575	60	Hit in ribs over lungs	Ran 60-70 yds. went down	Finished w/shot in chest. DWM-TUG bullet recovered.

TABLE 3

Weapon & Cartridge: 7mm Weatherby Mag.; 68 gr. Norma 205/160-gr. Norma Soft Point Boattail

Animal & Estimated Live Weight	Paced Off Range (yds.)	Point of Impact	Reaction	Remarks
6 Impala 140	100	Neck	Dropped in place	2" exit hole; bullet not recovered.
7 Impala 150	125	Neck	Dropped in place	2" exit hole; bullet not recovered.
8 Impala 140	100	Right shoulder	Dropped in place	2½" exit hole left shoulder. Not recovered.
11 Zebra (common) 700	140-150	Center left shoulder	Ran 60 yds., fell dead	Bullet not recovered, although it did not exit.
22 Impala 160	100	Rib cage behind diaphragm	Ran 20 yds., dropped dead	Bullet jacket and small portion of core recovered under hide on off shoulder.
31 Grevy's Zebra 800	250	Rib cage left side behind diaphragm, 1st shot.	Humped back and ran 300-400 yds.	Animal was trailed for 1000 yds. before being finally dispatched.
		Rump, going away w/375 H & H 2nd.	None observed, animal continued moving.	Only a few small fragments of 375 bullet(s) recovered. No exit holes found.
		Spine w/375 H & H 3rd shot	Went down to stay	
32 Zebra (common) 700	320	Point of right shoulder	Bucked once, then spun in tight circles 3 or 4 times, fell heavily on side	No exit; bullet not recovered.

everyone in North America can find a near parallel to his favorite quarry.

Before examining in detail what appears in the tables, some general—not final—conclusions suggest themselves.

For so-called plains game—the antelopes and gazelles, which largely correspond in size to and length of shots taken on North American game, (deer, sheep, bears)—the 308 and the 7mm Weatherby were best. And if you must pick between the two, the 7mm had a good edge, because it could reach out farther and flatter and deliver just as much zap when it arrived, even though the bullet was 20 grains lighter. This suggests that the 284 with similar bullets would do as well. The 8x68S Mauser is also a fine cartridge, but the 223-grain bullet might have had to give away a little velocity for weight that probably wasn't needed. Still, it hit like a ton of bricks, the bullet stayed together and mushroomed well, better than the 160-grain Norma bullet, which tended to break up more. The Nosler bullet also seemed to hold up well and punch through.

Now to the heavier calibers, if you still think you will need them on North American game. The venerable and fully proven 375 H&H is just fine and has the respect of nearly every professional African hunter I met. Among their ranks are the over-kill advocates, just as you can find them in the States. This segment of the shooting fraternity favors the 404, 458, 470 or even the 500 Jeffrey double.

The 404 does not have enough zap for really big game but it is mildly popular because it offers a low cost conversion for the action of the British Enfield. The rifle is issued to game scouts and is often bought by farmers for pest control.

There can be little doubt that there is a certain comfort factor in a 470 or 500 double rifle. They are surer and quicker for the second shot than the bolt-action 458s, but they are becoming scarcer and scarcer in East Africa. The Winchester 458, because it is rugged, reliable and principally one hell of a lot cheaper, has pretty much pushed the double cannons to the edge of the big game scene.

But that is not what we are talking about. The point is that most professional African hunters, who, we must concede, know the most about zapping heavy, dangerous game there, have switched to the 458 with factory solids as the combination to keep them alive and their customers doing a repeat business.

Apart from the politics and regu-

Buck Burns with 43-inch Cape Buffalo. The 1900 pound animal was hit at the base of the throat with one 500-gr. 458 solid which tore the length of his body cavity. It took two more 458 hits and a 375 H&H bullet, all at 20 yards. The party tried the big ones, too.

Writer John Reese with a fine Grevy zebra stallion. The animal weighing 800 pounds was downed with one shot from the 7mm Weatherby Magnum using a 160-grain Norma steel jacket soft point bullet.

TABLE 3 (continued)

Animal & Estimated Live Weight	Paced Off Range (yds.)	Point of Impact	Reaction	Remarks
34 Impala 140	100	Broke both fore-legs, cut chunk out of lower chest.	Fell in place, but required finisher shot in neck	No bullet recovered.
41 Thomson's Gazelle 45	120	Through center of neck just ahead of shoulder.	Fell in place	Bullet exited far side of neck, leaving hand-sized hole. Spine severed.
48 Wart Hog 200	120	Front, center chest.	Fell in place	Jacket fragments recovered in region of stomach.

TABLE 3A

Weapon & Cartridge: Winchester 458 African; Factory Load w/500-gr. solid.

—Note: Other effects of this combination used to back up lighter rifles appear elsewhere in these tables.

Animal & Estimated Live Weight	Paced Off Range (yds.)	Point of Impact	Reaction	Remarks
35 Cape Buffalo 1900	20	Front, center chest	1st shot hit head on, low, at the base of the throat. Buffalo then whirled and ran 40 yds. to flank through thick brush. Hit 2nd time with 375 H&H in shoulder and went down. Recovered and took another 458 and a 375 in shoulder area. Went down to stay.	Two 308 DWM finisher bullets were recovered from neck. One finisher 458 recovered. Other bullets not recovered. Turkana tracker and Masai skinner spent 45 minutes looking through entrails with massive tissue damage but were unable to find any other bullets.
37 Steinbuck 30	100	Right shoulder	Dropped in place	¾" exit hole left shoulder. (Obviously too much gun for this animal. But was taken on return from stalk of Buffalo w/heavy rifle.)

TABLE 4

Bullet No.	Caliber & Diameter	Bullet Mfr.	Original Weight In Grains	Recovered Bullet Wt. In Grains	Est. Wt. of Animal From which Recovered	Remarks on Recovered Portions of Bullets
2	8mm (S)	RWS	223	96	40	Core of 8x68S
5	8mm (S)	RWS	223	147	165	Whole jacket & core
10	8mm (S)	RWS	223	173	650	Base & core
18	8mm (S)	RWS	223	72	700	Jacket & core fragment recovered
21	8mm (S)	RWS	223	178	180	Nearly whole jacket & core
22	7mm	Norma	160	74	160	Case base & core
23	308	Nosler	180	127	425	Over 2/3's of partition and base recovered
29	8mm (S)	RWS	223	182	525	Nearly whole jacket & core
31	7mm	Norma	160	9	800	Two small steel jacket fragments
35A	308	DWM-TUG	180	55	1900	35A fragments of two Brenneke TUG's fired into base of neck
35A	308	DWM-TUG	180	95		
35B	458 Win.	Winchester	510			510-grain Winchester bullet largely intact
47	308	DWM-TUG	180	54	575	Fragments of core
48	7mm	Norma	160	26	200	Steel jacket splinters
49	8mm (S)	RWS	223	152	1700	Jacket & core
50	8mm (S)	RWS	223	179	650	Nearly perfect mushroom
51	8mm (S)	RWS	223	54	165	Jacket only

Bullets largely zapped on through animals weighing 150 to 180 lbs. or less.

lations in the matter, the simple fact is that in Kenya, then, the 375 H&H Magnum, and the 458 Winchester killed most of the big game shot by professional hunters, either on safari or in game control. This may be over-kill but they are the cartridges most frequently used by professional hunters.

Now let's take a comparative look at how the North American big game hunter can come out of this welter of figures and conjectures with something to apply at his loading bench or at his favorite gun store in preparation for next hunting season. That need not leave out the lucky guys planning to go to Africa for a safari some time soon. Maybe there's something here in this experience for everybody.

There is nothing here to tout you off tried-and-true Betsy. If Betsy has been putting venison in the freezer regularly, stick with her. But if you have a load that you seem to shoot pretty well, but still lose a buck or two from time to time, maybe you better switch to something in the 30-caliber class at not-too-hot velocity (say, 2,500-2,600 fps) with a soft point. That's particularly if you hunt in country where most of your shots are within 200 yards. On the other hand, if you are going where the country is open and the shots are long, might be you should go for something in the flatshooting 7mm Magnum or 280 class with a soft-point boattail in a load which leaves the muzzle at 3,100 or thereabouts.

Except for Kodiak or Brown bear, where you might want just a tetch more zap, I honestly believe with the aforementioned loads you've got all the big medicine you'll ever need in North America. That means from moose on down to a scrubby California coast deer. Place the shot right and you'll get him without spoiling much meat.

Now just one more word. There is no such thing as a sure thing when you are hunting. Especially with ungulates. You can put down with one shot a 1,500-pound moose cold stone dead in the blueberries—sometimes. Other times, you can blow half the heart and lungs out of a scrawny little old whitetail, shoot twice more, and lose him. So, pardner, there just isn't any pat solution. But I hope that some of the data offered here will give you more one-shot kills and less traipsing the rough brush cussing your choice of rifle and cartridge. ●

MORE DATA NEXT PAGES

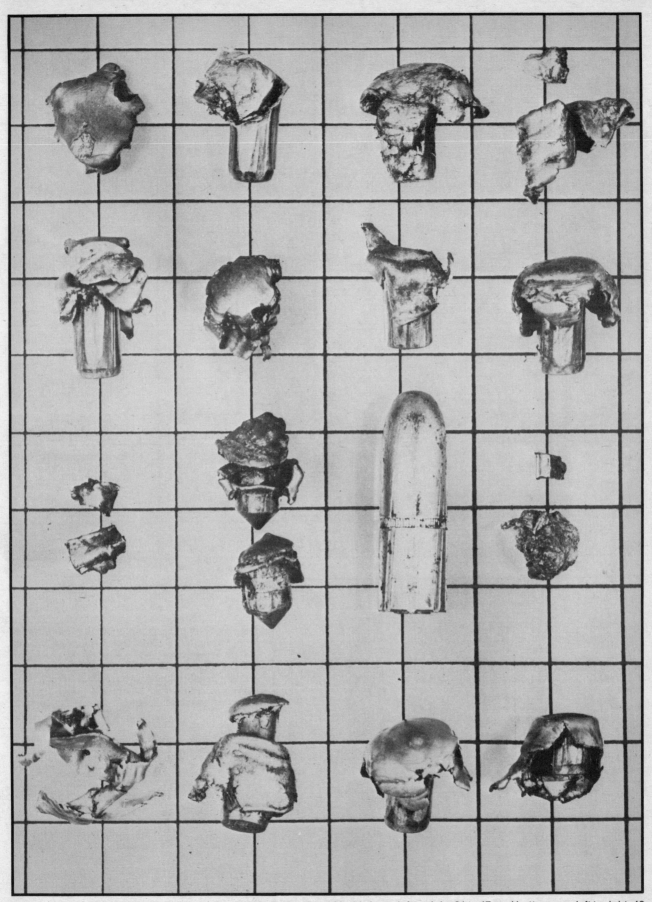

Top row, left to right: Bullets 2 to 18; second row, left to right: 21 to 29; third row, left to right: 31 to 47; and bottom row, left to right: 48 to 51. See Table 4 for details.

Before and after. Bottom row (left to right)—unfired 7mm Norma 160-gr. steel jacket soft point boattail; 308 DWM Brenneke TUG; Nosler 308 180-gr. Nosler; 224-gr. 8mm (323) RWS hollow point steel jacket; 458 Winchester 500-gr. solid. Top row left to right of same bullets showing typical performance on game. Left: Cartridges as loaded.

TABLE 5
Reese-Burns Safari Game List

		Hunter	1970 Date	Professional Hunter	Caliber*	Yards	Trophy Field Measurement (in.)	Est. Weight
1.	Thomson's Gaz.	Burns	25 Feb	Pete Smith	308	135-200	11½	35
2.	Thomson's Gaz.	Vollman/Schipper	25 Feb	Pete Smith	8x68*	180-200	12⅛	40
3.	Zebra	Vollman/Schipper	26 Feb	Pete Smith	8x68/308	60-200		700
4.	Impala	Burns	27 Feb	Pete Smith	308	125	25	175
5.	Impala	Vollman/Schipper	27 Feb	Pete Smith	8x68*	150	23½	165
6.	Impala	Reese	27 Feb	Dan Shaw	7mm Wea.	100		140
7.	Impala	Reese	29 Feb	Dan Shaw	7mm Wea.	125		150
8.	Impala	Reese	27 Feb	Dan Shaw	7mm Wea.	100		140
9.	Thomson's Gaz.	Appel	26 Feb	Dan Shaw	8x68	120	12⅞#	45
10.	Zebra	Appel	28 Feb	Dan Shaw	8x68*	130-160		650
11.	Zebra	Reese	28 Feb	Dan Shaw	7mm	140-150		700
12.	Zebra	Appel	28 Feb	Dan Shaw	8x68	120		700
13.	Oryx	Vollman/Schipper	1 Mar	Pete Smith	8x68	70	27⅛	450
14.	Zebra	Burns	1 Mar	Pete Smith	308	40		700
15.	Grant's Gaz.	Appel	1 Mar	Dan Shaw	8x68	200	20	75
16.	Grant's Gaz.	Burns	2 Mar	Pete Smith	308	120	20¾#	80
17.	Bush Buck*	Burns	2 Mar	Pete Smith	308	50	14½#	425
18.	Zebra	Vollman/Schipper	2 Mar	Pete Smith	8x68*	340		700
19.	Steinbuck	Appel	1 Mar	Dan Shaw	8x68	80-85	4¼#	35
20.	Impala	Appel	1 Mar	Dan Shaw	8x68	70	26	150
21.	Wart Hog	Vollman/Schipper	3 Mar	Pete Smith	8x68*	300		180
22.	Impala	Reese	3 Mar	Dan Shaw	7mm Wea.*	100		160
23.	Oryx	Burns	4 Mar	Pete Smith	308*	150	27½	425
24.	Eland	Burns	4 Mar	Pete Smith	308	115	23½	1800
25.	Oryx	Appel	4 Mar	Pete Smith	8x68	120	28¼#	450
26.	Grant's Gaz.	Vollman/Schipper	4 Mar	Pete Smith	8x68	300	18¹/₁₆	65
27.	Bush Buck	Vollman/Schipper	5 Mar	Dan Shaw	8x68	100	12½	400
28.	Impala	Vollman/Schipper	6 Mar	Dan Shaw	8x68	200	(1 horn)	170
29.	Water Buck	Appel	5 Mar	Pete Smith	8x68*	100	19½	525
30.	Thomson's Gaz.	Ericka	5 Mar	Pete Smith	8x68	200	12¼	40
31.	Grevy Z.	Reese	7 Mar	Pete Smith	7mm*	250	#	800
32.	Zebra	Reese	7 Mar	Pete Smith	7mm Wea.	320		700
33.	Zebra	Burns	7 Mar	Pete Smith	7mm Wea.	175		700
34.	Impala	Reese	8 Mar	Dan Shaw	7mm Wea.	100		140
35.	Buffalo	Burns	8 Mar	Pete Smith	458*	20	43/41/13#	1900
36.	Bush Buck	Appel	8 Mar	Pete Smith	8x68	80	10	350
37.	Steinbuck	Vollman/Schipper	8 Mar	Dan Shaw	458	100	4⅛	30
38.	Reedbuck	Appel	9 Mar	Dan Shaw	8x68	120	8¼	180
39.	Bush Buck	Appel	9 Mar	Dan Shaw	8x68	140	13¾	400
40.	Reedbuck	Vollman/Schipper	9 Mar	Dan Shaw	8x68	100	9¼#	200
41.	Thomson's Gaz.	Reese	9 Mar	Pete Smith	7mm	120	12⅞#	45
42.	Steinbuck	Burns	9 Mar	Pete Smith	308	80	4¼#	35
43.	Eland	Vollman/Schipper	10 Mar	Dan Shaw	8x68	60	24½#	1950
44.	Impala	Vollman/Schipper	11 Mar	Dan Shaw	8x68	25	24½	170
45.	Waterbuck	Vollman/Schipper	11 Mar	Dan Shaw	8x68	60	24¼#	600
46.	Impala	Ericka	12 Mar	Pete Smith	8x68	50	29#	190
47.	Waterbuck	Burns	13 Mar	Dan Shaw	308*	60	24	575
48.	Wart Hog	Reese	13 Mar	Dan Shaw	7mm*	120		200
49.	Eland	Appel	13 Mar	Pete Smith	8x68*	60	21½	1700
50.	Zebra	Appel	13 Mar	Pete Smith	8x68*	120-150		650
51.	Impala	Burns	13 Mar	Pete Smith	8x68*	160		165

*connotes bullet recovered
#best trophy of type

GOOD OLD cartridges may suffer occasional setbacks. Ultimately they seem to endure and continue to gather in followers from each new generation of shooters. Rifle cartridges like the 257 Roberts, 220 Swift and 7x57 are presently benefitting from a revival that is more nostalgic than a rediscovery of qualities that are matched or bettered by cartridges of more recent lineage. Not so with one particular handgun cartridge—the 32 S&W Long and other 32 caliber handgun cartridges, as well.

After almost disappearing from catalogs for 25 years, with the exception of one or two small police revolvers, the 32 has come from the edge of extinction to become *the* contending centerfire handgun cartridge for serious competition work in matches where no power rating is placed on the cartridge. In the tough world of International pistol competition, the 32 has completely obliterated the long-standard 38 Special from the winners circle. The practical pistol events have also revealed the superiority of the 32 in competition and in Australia all National records for ISU Centerfire and Service Pistol events are held by 32 caliber pistols.

In 1974, Walther unveiled a 32 S&W Long version of their GSP series 22 target auto pistol. This pistol won the Centerfire event at the World Shooting Championships in Switzerland in 1974 on its first appearance. From that time, continual development of pistols, loads and projectiles has moved the 32 from virtual obscurity to a pre-eminent position with serious target handgunners throughout the shooting world.

Following on from Walther's GSP 32 which was a straight blowback design, high performance 32 target autoloaders have been introduced by Hammerli and Sako. The French Manurhin MR73 is the first target revolver to be introduced in 32 S&W Long since the K32 S&W.

Stimulus for development of a 32 target cartridge by Western European gunmakers came from the Soviet Union. The 7.62 Nagant target revolver, the TOZ 36, was introduced by the Russians in the late 1960s. These unusual gas-seal revolvers loaded with deeply seated (½″ below case neck) wadcutter projectiles proved their competitive performance with a target load that essentially reproduced the ballistics of the 32 S&W Long.

Both S&W and Colt have produced

THE 32 COMES BACK

From Australia, where they have both handloaders and ISU shooting, comes a realistic appraisal of the virtues of the .32-inch bore.

by JOHN ROBINSON

32-cal. bullets tested (left to right): cast Saeco 98-gr; cast RCBS 98-gr.; cast AVS 95-gr.; cast RCBS 85-gr.; RWS 100-gr.; Alberts, Bullzi, Lapua and Sako.

32 S&W Long target revolvers although only small numbers of Colt Officers Model 32s were made and they are now highly desirable collector's items. The S&W K32 has also achieved that status.

Are the advantages of the 32 over the 38 Special real or imaginary?

In a pistol built around the 32 cartridge, the benefits *are* significant. The relatively low power of the 32 allows it to be used in blowback operated autoloaders, and this immediately solves the accurizing problems inherent in the Browning swinging link system or one of its modern derivatives.

The smaller physical size of the flush seated wadcutter cartridges allows magazine dimensions to be reduced and thus in pistols where the magazine is located in the grip, the

constraints on grip angle and shape imposed by 38 Special cartridges are greatly minimized. This allows the handling characteristics of the pistol to be improved.

Along with the reduction in mass of cycling parts and the low recoil of the 98-grain target loading, it all adds up to a package that is a superior performer.

All current series 32 auto target pistols—Walther GSP, Hammerli P240 and Sako—have low barrel axes in relation to the shooters hand. This minimizes vertical stringing due to grip variations and generally improves recovery characteristics of the pistol in rapid fire events.

The Russian TOZ 36 revolver and its successor, the TOZ 49, both exhibit similar handling characteristics to the autoloaders.

Steve Jenkins demonstrates the low line of the Walther 32 GSP.

Accuracy of the 32 cartridges is no better or worse than 38 Special loads. Good quality factory target loads and handloads will perform to the same standard as their 38 counterparts. The 32 S&W Long target loading as produced both by Lapua and Sako of Finland and RWS/Geco in West Germany use 98-grain hollow based wadcutter projectiles which have all been chronographed in my Walther GSP (115mm barrel) at up to 800 feet per second. The 32 S&W Long seems thus the *only* cartridge where the target loadings exceed the velocity of the standard defense loads which list a 98-grain round nose bullet with a muzzle velocity of 750 feet per second.

The 32 S&W Long is almost a scaled-down version of the 38 Special and projectiles used in the 32 follow the form of their 38 counterparts very closely. No 32 target projectiles were available until 1974 when Lapua produced 98-grain hollow based wadcutters and Sako subsequently added their version in the same weight. Both these projectiles departed radically from convention. Both projectiles, instead of having annular lube grooves, used longitudinal grooves (Lapua) and ridges (Sako). In Australia, several manufacturers have started making 32 wadcutter target bullets.

Testing of most available projectiles by the author has established that swaged, dry lubricated 32 projectiles produce most consistent performance. Locally made Bullzi, Finnish Lapua and Sako and the recently introduced US-made Taurus (now Alberts) 32 projectiles perform very well, as do the new RWS/Geco hollow base wadcutters from West Germany.

Because of the early shortage and high cost of 32-cal. projectiles, casting of target bullets has been widely practiced Down Under. RCBS, Saeco and Hensley & Gibbs list 32 caliber wadcutter bullet moulds in weights ranging from 85 to 100 grains.

The normal bullet diameter for the 32 is .312″. As in 38s, variations in bullet diameter occur and I have found variations ranging from .311″ to .3145″ in individual pistols. Obviously, undersized bullets won't work well in oversize barrels and moulds and sizing dies have to be matched to bore diameter for good results with solid base cast bullets. Hollow base wadcutters, with their flexible skirts, can more easily accommodate these barrel variations.

Any of the fast pistol or shotgun powders will work in the 32 but some special care needs to be taken for consistency with handloaded ammunition. DuPont 700X, Hercules Bullseye, Winchester 231 and Norma 1010

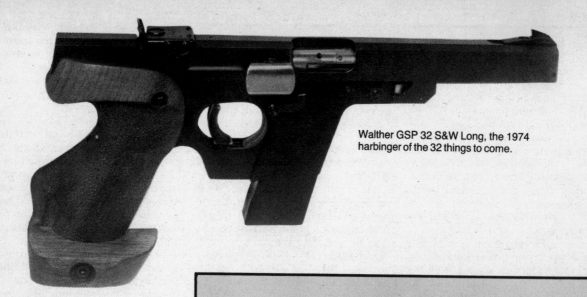

Walther GSP 32 S&W Long, the 1974 harbinger of the 32 things to come.

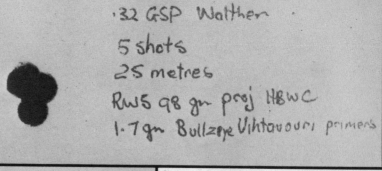

.32 GSP Walther
5 shots
25 metres
RWS 98 gn proj HBWC
1.7 gn Bullzeye Vihtavouri primers

They can shoot! This exceptional group measures only ¼″ on centers and was fired from a Ransom Rest.

Cartridge comparison: 45 ACP, 32 S&W Long, 7.62 Nagant Short and 7.62 Nagant.

Problems with blowback autos: these cases have started to bulge around the unsupported head area with loads that would be quite safe in even old revolvers chambered for the 32 S&W Long.

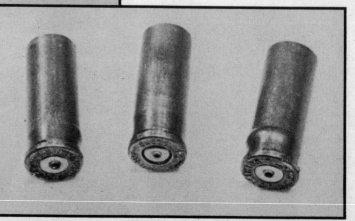

Two very rare K32's. These pistols are now bringing high prices because of the shortage of such good quality 32-cal. revolvers.

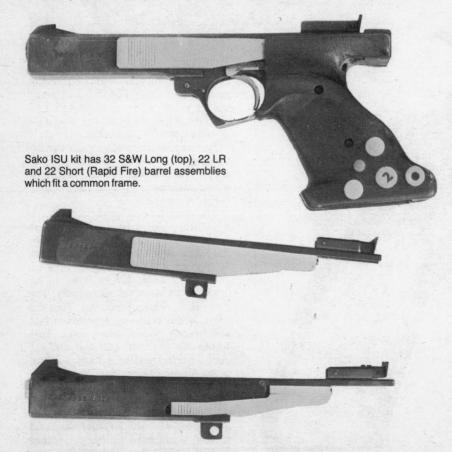

Sako ISU kit has 32 S&W Long (top), 22 LR and 22 Short (Rapid Fire) barrel assemblies which fit a common frame.

will work satisfactorily. One of the preferred powders not on the above list is Winchester's 452AA target shotgun powder. Experiments by the writer and others in Australia have shown 452AA to be particularly well suited to the 32 S&W Long and the Nagant 7.62 in target loadings.

With the powders listed above, charges used can vary from 1.4 grains to 1.8 grains. Over 1.8 grains, velocities and pressures may become too high for target loads in some blowback autoloaders. With such light loads, charge weights must be very uniform and 0.1-grain variation is unacceptable as it will significantly affect average velocity.

The burning characteristics of 452AA and the extremely good flow characteristics through the powder thrower have made it a very popular powder which is also being used increasingly in the 38 Special and 45 ACP for target work.

Care must be taken to keep the bullet base clean when loading cast or other grease lubed bullets. Powder contacting the lubricant may be deactivated, especially in hot weather. In the small 32 case, 0.2 grains of powder in a 1.5-grain load is a substantial percentage if it is contaminated by bullet lube.

Slower burning powders like Unique, which allow larger powder charges of 2.0 to 2.4 grains to be used, are worthy of consideration because they are less sensitive to minor powder charge variations purely on a percentage basis. Unfortunately, those loading manuals listing the 32 S&W Long are not a reliable source of loading data for target shooters and the loads listed in most manuals are too hot for target loads, especially in blowback autoloaders. All target loads use flush seated wadcutter projectiles which occupy a large percentage of the available airspace in the case, and this jumps pressure up substantially, compared with conventionally seated round nose bullets.

Recommended loads and velocities are listed in a nearby table.

Another phenomenon that is peculiar to blowback autoloaders is primer setback. Soft primers such as Federal 100 small pistol primers do not grip the primer pocket as tightly as Remington 1½ or equivalent Winchester primers. While the case is held in the chamber by friction on the chamber walls, a soft primer can push the bolt back against the relatively weak recoil spring. This poses no safety hazards but makes fired cases a nuisance to reload as they will not slide

Russian TOZ 36 (top) in 7.62 Naganthas has been replaced by the TOZ 49 which uses a shortened version of the 7.62 Nagant case.

TOZ 49 cylinder shows the correct relationship of the loaded round in the chamber compared to the original 7.62 Nagant case used in its predecessor.

Inside the TOZ 49: pistol's trigger is fully adjustable for weight, sear engagement and backlash. Added to the Nagant gas sealing system which ensures perfect barrel/cylinder alignment, this makes for a very accurate pistol even though finish in non-critical areas is rough.

into the shellholder with their primer protruding. Only Federal 100 small pistol primers have exhibited this characteristic out of all the available brands tried by the author.

Because of its influence on the development of the 32 as a target cartridge, the Nagant 7.62 round and its associated development is particularly relevant.

The long (1.53") Nagant cartridge is a military development of the late 19th Century. This unique cartridge has its projectile seated *below* the neck of the case. When a Nagant type revolver is cocked, the cylinder is indexed forward as well as radially. The case neck, which protrudes from the front of the cylinder, is inserted into the breech end of the barrel. This forms the so-called gas seal and ensures perfect cylinder/barrel alignment for every chamber.

The TOZ 36 target revolver utilizes the 7.62 Nagant case and was loaded with 100 grain wadcutter projectiles at reduced velocity (750 fps) compared to the roundnosed military loadings which are credited with 1100 fps. The popularity of the TOZ 36 in Australia led to the local manufacture of Boxer primed 7.62 Nagant cases and a regular supply of new brass has been available here for ten years.

The TOZ 36 revolver has several interesting features:

Front and rear sight elements are interchangable.

The trigger is fully adjustable for backlash, sear engagement and weight of pull.

The gate-loaded single action revolver has no ejector and the cylinder is removed for unloading by taking out the cylinder axle.

In 1980, an improved version of the TOZ 36 appeared, designated the TOZ 49. In the absence of any information on the pistol's origins from the USSR, it can only be assumed that the changes were brought about by the fact that the front ½" of the Nagant case was wasted in the target loadings,

so the case was shortened nearly ½" (to 1.020") and the cylinder and frame modified to suit the shorter case. A vestigial ejector was also incorporated which acts on the section of the rim of the case neck protruding from the right side of the cylinder and backs the fired cases out just far enough to be extracted with the fingernail.

Demand for these Russian revolvers is strong and demand always exceeds the somewhat erratic supply from the Soviet Union. Each pistol is test fired at the factory and the group size for five groups, each of ten shots, is recorded, along with the series' aggregate. These aggregates are generally around the 1" mark at 25 meters. The author has substantiated this performance with machine rest testing of several of these revolvers.

From old magazines, I gather that the reason for the 38's initial popularity over the 32 was reputed to be its ability to buck the wind better at 50

yards over the NRA course. The Service Pistol Match, as shot in Australia, is similar, but more difficult than the PPC revolver course. It calls for one series to be shot at 50 yards on an ISU Silhouette target. Other series are shot at 25, 10 and 7 yards.

The course of fire for the program is for 90 shots/900 points. In all major competitions at State and National level, the 32 has consistently outscored the 38 in each section of the course. The demand for 32-caliber revolvers for this event is understandably high. No malfunctions are allowed and any malfunctions or misfires can mean the loss of the entire string of shots. The 100% reliability of most revolvers therefore makes them highly desirable.

Until the introduction of the Manurhin MR73, no competitive revolvers have been readily available in 32 caliber. This has resulted in local innovators using such revolvers as those

Russian TOZ 49 is designed for competition with appropriate low barrel axis and fully adjustable trigger and sights with interchangeable elements.

32-Cal. Target Loads

(Pistol: Walther GSP 32. Barrel Length: 115mm

32 S&W Long

Bullet (grs.)	Powder Charge (grs.)	Velocity (fps)
98 HBWC	1.2/DuPont 700X	525
98 HBWC	1.4/DuPont 700X	610
98 HBWC	1.6/DuPont 700X	665
98 HBWC	1.8/DuPont 700X	735
98 HBWC	1.6/Win. 452AA	605
98 HBWC	1.8/Win. 452AA	643
98 HBWC	1.6/Win. 231	582
98 HBWC	1.8/Win. 231	635
85 RCBS cast	1.8/Win. 452AA	655
98 SAECO cast	1.7/Win. 231	603
98 SAECO cast	2.0/Win. 452AA	745
98 SAECO cast	2.0/DuPont 700X	788

Factory Load Data		
Lapua 98 Hollow Base WC*		799
Sako 98 Hollow Base WC		805
Geco/RWS 100 HBWC		765

*WC—wadcutter

Hammerli P240 32 S&W Long is doubtless a finely accurate target arm, but at over $1000, not many try it.

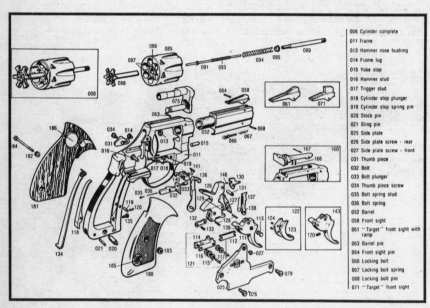

008	Cylinder complete
011	Frame
013	Hammer nose bushing
014	Frame lug
015	Yoke stop
016	Hammer stud
017	Trigger stud
018	Cylinder stop plunger
019	Cylinder stop spring pin
020	Stock pin
021	Sling pin
025	Side plate
026	Side plate screw - rear
027	Side plate screw - front
031	Thumb piece
032	Bolt
033	Bolt plunger
034	Thumb piece screw
035	Bolt spring stud
036	Bolt spring
052	Barrel
058	Front sight
061	"Target" front sight with ramp
063	Barrel pin
064	Front sight pin
066	Locking bolt
067	Locking bolt spring
068	Locking bolt pin
071	"Target" front sight

Exploded view of the Manurhin MR73 32-cal. revolver.

made by Dan Wesson as a basis for conversion to 32 by sleeving the cylinders and installing 32 barrel tubes.

More recently, shooters have been snapping up Colt New Police 32 revolvers and if the original 4″ barrel tests out as accurate (some are very good), then a heavy rib with adjustable sights is attached, and the barrel shrouded to add weight. A trigger job and a set of oversize grips adds up to a reasonable and inexpensive 32 target handgun.

The cost of most 32s is a sore point. The 32 target pistols from Western Europe are very expensive, with prices starting at around $600 and easily breaking the $1000 mark for the Swiss-made autos.

Recent rumors have Smith & Wesson working on a 32-caliber version of their Model 41 rimfire target auto. The introduction of such a handgun would be warmly welcomed worldwide if such a pistol has price and performance on a par with the S&W K38. Perhaps S&W might be persuaded to bring back the long lost K32.

The developments surrounding the 32 may also have influenced the demise of the 38 Special as the pre-eminent cartridge in serious International competition. With the exception of Hammerli's P240, no new target pistols designed around the 38 Special have appeared since S&W introduced the Model 52 in 1962. Three completely new 32 autos, two revolvers and two more autos on the drawing boards (Britarms in the UK, AG Domino in Italy) are in prospect. *Revival* is exactly the word. •

This shows the unique action of the Manurhin M73 revolver double-action mechanism.

ACTION MECHANISM

When the weapon is in rest position (Fig. 1), the trigger spring (118) is exerting on the rebound slide roller (116) an axial horizontal force P. When firing in double action, the pull on the trigger pushes the slide (114) rearward and compresses spring (118). During this motion and due to the shape, position and articulation of the spring, the fulcrum of the spring on the roller is progressively displaced upwards.

The compression load P1 on the spring is thus not directly opposed to the pull force on the trigger. Only the component P2 is still acting - if the frictions of the slide mounted on 4 rollers are left out of consideration.

The force P2 is constant. It is smaller than P1 and, according to the design, tends to be practically equal to the initial force P.

This particular working method of the MANURHIN MR 73 revolver is being protected by patent.

fig. 1

This experienced experimental handloader and gunsmith knows a lot about, but can't explain, the vagaries of.....

CASE HEAD THRUST

Everything else equal, the big ones just can't operate as hot as the little ones.

by J. D. JONES

CASE HEAD thrust is one of the least understood facets of ballistics. We are inundated with information and misinformation regarding "pressure." We are not, however, told anything vaguely informative regarding case head thrust which I will simply define as a force exerted by the head of a case during the period of cartridge ignition until the rearward thrust, if any, of the case is exhausted.

Case head thrust is recognized by many and discussed by few. In my opinion that is because very little is known about it.

During the period of weapons development between World Wars I and II, some attempts were made to produce primer-activated unlocking systems with some degree of success. The systems were generally unnecessarily complicated, required excessively close tolerances in manufacture, were subject to fouling problems, suffered from parts delicacy, and were obviously not quite suitable for military usage. The point that the rearward thrust of a primer could be made to open or at least initiate the opening of a rifle or machine gun action is signifi-

cant in itself. Sometimes evidence of this primer thrust can be found in well-worn guns by simply examining the area around the firing pin hole to see if the metal has been pushed back.

In case preparation for wax bullet loads, it's necessary to drill out primer flash holes to neutralize primer set-back which sometimes interferes with cylinder rotation. To demonstrate this, simply fire six primed cases in a revolver. Unless it is headspaced very tightly, the primers will protrude from the case after firing. When a normal load is fired in a revolver, the primer

In rolling blocks, case head thrust in 45-70 ties up the very strong action with loads nowhere yet near blow-up.

Author believes case head thrust accomplishes most of the work that makes this a semi-automatic.

In Thompson-Center Contender barrels, the 223 is reasonable at 50,000+ CPU pressure, but not the 30-40 case. Hot-loaded, it will stretch frames.

backs out and then the rearward thrust of the case causes the case to move back against the recoil plate of the revolver, reseating the primer flush with the head of the case. Revolvers with excessive headspace can give the appearance of excessively flattened primers with normal "magnum" loads.

At this point we can look at several other concepts. One is that possibly "recoil operated" as applied to a method of gun operations may not be the most accurate terminology. The other is that "headspace" can be a very important factor in case head thrust, resulting action stress and rate of fire in machine guns. Another is that since the force of an explosion is exerted equally in all directions and since the shaped charge principle certainly works, case shape may have an effect in case head thrust.

The pressure of the case against the chamber walls may affect, and at some point in the process of increasing and decreasing pressures, even lessen case head thrust. It follows that a chamber with a mirror finish would probably increase rearward thrust compared to a rough chamber bearing tool marks which would allow the case to "grip" the chamber walls.

Case head size also affects thrust as does the pressure inside the case. For example, the 221 Fireball is commonly operated at pressures of 55,000 CUP. For purposes of simplicity, let's assume CUP translates to pounds per square inch and, disregarding any other factors, let's assume the case head area of the 221-cal. case is one square inch. Under these circumstances the head of the 221 case could be expected to exert a pressure of 55,000 pounds against the bolt face. Following the same set of assumptions of 55,000 PSI inside the cartridge case, assume the case head size of a 308-cal. is two square inches. The twice-as-large case head of the 308 exerts, in this case, 110,000 pounds against the bolt face.

Such assumptions are probably realistic assuming cartridges fit the chambers exactly. But what happens if the cartridge is undersize for the chamber, the classic example of excessive headspace? During ignition a combination of firing pin blow and primer action probably forces the cartridge all the way to the front of the chamber. As pressures build during powder burning the case starts moving rearward at quite high velocity and slams into the bolt face at some considerable velocity. Assuming zero friction and equal case and bullet weight both the case and bullet should be moving at the same velocity. If the bullet has engaged the rifling, case velocity may be greater than bullet velocity. I don't know if anyone is ready to try to measure the case head thrust under that set of circumstances.

Case head thrust certainly isn't all bad. Without it and a few other factors thrown in we wouldn't have the many blowback or recoil operated guns we now have, such as all 22-cal. semi-auto rifles and pistols, the workhorse military semi-auto pistols, submachine guns and a great number of machine guns such as the 30 and 50-caliber Brownings.

A self-loading action is easy to use in a demonstration of the effect of case adhesion, or friction on chamber walls. In the machine guns, simply wetting the ammunition results in a higher rate of fire. Water is noticeable. Oil is very noticeable. Oiled ammo in a straight blowback such as the many 25, 32, and 380 autos gives excessively violent operation with increased felt recoil and ejection. It isn't a good idea to oil ammo or shoot reloaded ammo without removing case lube. In a bolt action rifle, oiled cases when fired with normal loads may give the appearance of a very high pressure round and are strictly not recommended.

At one point I was very interested in developing a high velocity round for the 45 ACP and shot several guns to excessive looseness pursuing that goal. I found the 45 with mild loads to eject fired cases very mildly. As the powder charge went up ejection became more positive, and then went to what could be considered violent. As the powder charge continued upward the cycling of the guns slowed. Extractor marks on the rim became more pronounced. In some cases ejection was reduced to equal that of very mild loads. High pressures simply kept the case firmly affixed to the chamber wall, greatly modifying case head thrust and its effects. (For information purposes, in case you might be tempted to try it for yourself, some cases blew out at the unsupported area in the chamber and at least one chamber was bulged. This was strictly an experimental thing.)

The Auto Mag behaves the same way. I've actually pulled extractors through the case rim and left the case in the chamber only to find it fall out at the mere touch of a ramrod. I must assume that in some cartridges that it is possible that if the pressure is high enough and the case strong enough that at the point of maximum pressure inside the cartridge that case head

In these relatively mild loadings, designers need not lock pistol breeches, but as they get bigger, they get tougher to hold together.

The 1911 has proven to the author that case adhesion to the chamber walls alters thrust effects, sometimes usefully.

The 9mm operates easily at higher pressures than the 45 ACP not only because of the lighter bullets, but because of its lesser case head thrust.

thrust may drop to practically zero due to chamber wall friction. If this is true, case thrust would, from the point of ignition, raise very rapidly, suddenly fall off and then return at or near maximum thrust.

Having worked extensively with the Thompson/Center Contender for about ten years, as well as quite a number of other handguns, I've formed some opinions that are contrary to some accepted opinions. Case shape is number one. I've heard and read experts opinions that "case shape doesn't make any difference," usually referring to velocity as generally nothing else is referred to in that concept.

In my opinion, case shape makes a difference in three areas—velocity, pressure and case head thrust. I've developed a series of wildcat cartridges for handguns based on the Contender action. I'd be hard pressed to guess at the number of rounds fired in testing. Some things were apparent prior to this testing.

For example, the 25-35 case has a very great amount of taper from rear to front and produces only mediocre velocities before the cases stick compared to the basic 30-30 case which does not have as much taper. I've run into case sticking with the 25-35 in one lot of brass with six grains of powder less than another lot.

Brass construction also rears its head. The 22 Jet delivers poor velocity compared to the smaller 22K Hornet or 218 Ackley Bee. In fact, the Jet actually lost velocity with many powders as the charge was increased. Its problems in revolvers, due in large part to case head thrust is legendary, as is its ridiculous shape.

Interestingly, I found that the 7mm JDJ delivered higher velocities with the same powder charge and bullet weight with formed cases than it did while fire forming. The 7 JDJ is based on the 225 Winchester case which is quite strong. This version has almost straight walls and a 40° shoulder and short neck. It is truly maximized for case capacity. The standard 225 simply opened to 7mm has quite a bit of taper and resembles the 30-30 considerably. I *think* that during the fire forming process the excessively tapered case simply funnels powder down the bore and after firing the formed case retards powder movement, aiding powder burning, increasing both pressure and velocity and apparently not increasing case head thrust appreciably. The velocity increase has, on occasion, exceeded 100 FPS. That's significant. I've received reports that the 30-30 and 30-40

Ackley Improved velocity increases behave in the same manner. This may be more significant in the short 14" Contender barrels than in long rifle barrels. I haven't checked it but feel that longer barrel time may level out powder burning and velocities.

In any event, in working with a series of wildcats and factory rounds from 17 through 50 caliber in the T/C, it's obvious that case head thrust is a significant factor. Excessive pressure is only one facet of overstressing the T/C—or any other firearm. I get sick of hearing and reading "I don't have any signs of pressure with X load." If the bullet has moved out of the case, that is a sign of pressure. Pressure is necessary to obtain velocity. In a properly headspaced rifle, good brass, and modern primers, there is usually no visual sign of *excessive* pressure at 50,000 + CUP if you can believe DuPont data, and I do.

The Contender, for example is perfectly happy at 50,000 + CUP in 222 case head diameter. I wouldn't even guess how many rounds the gun would digest before any frame stretching is apparent. I think it would go through several barrels and sets of internal parts. However, at that same 50,000+ CUP pressure, I do not believe you can increase case head size without stretching the frame due to excessive case head thrust. As case head size goes up, pressures must be reduced to control case head thrust.

I feel my wildcat cartridges based on the 444 Marlin case (.358-.375-.411-.430) must be kept at moderate pressure levels to maintain case head thrust at acceptable levels. The 45-70 and 50-70 must be kept at low pressure levels or permissible thrust will be exceeded. In this sense, these large capacity cases operate on the same principle as the old British express cartridges. They use a large amount of powder at relatively low pressure to attain desired velocity. Smaller, shorter cases would have to operate at higher pressures, with faster burning powder, to attain the same velocity and would give correspondingly greater case head thrust.

It's true that small cartridges are more efficient than large ones. But for maximum power, there just isn't any substitute for case capacity. All of these large wildcats, including the 45-70, and 50-70, are capable of producing a great amount of power and all have straight or nearly straight case walls.

When you hear of a bolt or lever action gun getting "sticky," opening with some difficulty, this is a result of

a load producing case head thrust that is excessive for the action. In essence, regardless of the pressure developed by a particular cartridge in one gun, its head thrust may make it unsuitable for another action. The large modern rolling block actions are, in my opinion, very strong. I really think it would be quite difficult to blow one up with anything resembling any commercial cartridge properly loaded. However, if in 45-70 you load progressively heavier, case head thrust makes the action "sticky" and I assume would probably lock it up at pressures that are nowhere near the "blow up" point. Case head thrust makes the gun completely useless if ammunition produces enough case head thrust to lock up the action.

As far as I know, no one has done much in the way of studying case head thrust and its various applications and problem areas. One manufacturer is now attempting to come up with something meaningful as a way to accurately measure case head thrust. Many months into the project, results remain at zero.

I feel quite sure many mathematicians will feel they can produce formulas to accurately determine C.H.T. I distrust those formulas and will only accept them when I see them proven by hardware to measure what actually happens when a round is fired. Numbers only go so far. Sometimes when the firing pin hits the primer an entirely different story is told.

I don't pretend to have the answers, only the questions. Here you see only opinion reached through the process of firing many thousands of rounds with unscientific equipment. I may change my mind about much of it tomorrow if something else looks better. How did I prove the acceptability of the Contender action to the series of cartridges and loads developed for it? Simple. Keep pressures moderate or low and fire several thousand through a few guns and then examine them for stress. Use the same frames in "proofing" barrels developing loads and just plain shooting.

I know of no way to "prove" any new concept, caliber, part, or design except by using it and watching for problems to develop. Some years ago I was told that a very reputable manufacturer made 28 changes in a shotgun the first year it was in production due to reports of failure in the field. This manufacturer is large and certainly has design engineers, computers, and excellent testing facilities. The "proof" is still in the pudding. •

**Perhaps they should have
said it couldn't be done,
but now you can make . . . .**

41 MAGNUM SHORTS

by JAMES P. COWGILL

THE 41 MAGNUM is a powerful, accurate cartridge which produces heavy, but manageable recoil. Handguns in this caliber can today be found and afforded, probably because no Hollywood star or fictional secret agent has yet carried one.

Why not shoot a 41 Magnum? Well it's not *the* most powerful handgun cartridge in the world, if that makes a difference. The 41 Magnum is probably second behind the 44 Magnum but only by about ten percent in muzzle energy from factory loads. The typical

41-45 cartridges. From left—Sierra 170-gr. JHP, Speer 200-gr. JHP, and Speer 220-gr. JSP.

41 cal. bullet has a better sectional density and ballistic coefficient than the 44, thus shoots a little flatter and gives more down-range energy.

Compared with the many 44 or 357 Magnum loads available, only 210-grain Jacketed Soft Point and Lead Round Nose bullets are loaded by Remington for the 41. For the reloader, an adequate variety of bullet types is available, and only the independently wealthy or the subsidized can afford to fire great quantities of factory ammo.

There is no standard reduced load cartridge for the 41 Magnum, as there is for the 44 Magnum (44 Special) and the 357 Magnum (38 Special). What about the old 41 Long Colt? Don't try it, it's too loose. However, it is possible to form 41-caliber brass from 45 ACP cases, creating 41-45s which can be loaded, fired, and extracted from the 41 Magnum chamber.

The re-formed cases might be called

Dies and cases involved in successive steps forming 41-45s. From left—45 ACP sizer and case; 44 Magnum/Special sizer with sized-down case; 41 Magnum bullet seater die and neck-tapered case; 41 Magnum sizer and resized case; 45 expander and belled case ready for bullet.

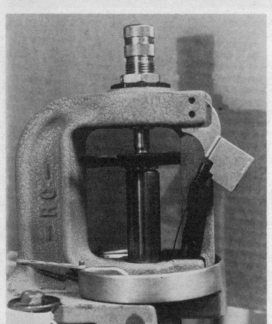

45 ACP case on its way to a smaller caliber. Shell holder is not used because case must be sized all the way to its head to fit revolver chamber. Steel plate on ram head permits necessary penetration in die, resulting in "stuck" case.

Great force is required to make a 41 out of a 45, so press is worked at bottom of lever stroke to gain maximum mechanical advantage. Die is lowered after each stroke until desired case penetration is obtained.

How to remove "stuck" 45 ACP case from 44 or 41 sizing die. Hardwood dowel and hammer work well when shell holder is not usable in sizing operation.

From left—45 ACP case; Federal 185-gr. 45 ACP JHP round; 41-45 round loaded with Speer 220-gr. JSP bullet; Speer bullet, 41 Magnum handload; and Remington 41 Magnum factory round with 220-gr. JSP bullet.

41-45 Loads And Velocities

Bullet/grs.	Charge (grains)/Powder	Velocity (fps)
170 JHP	5.6/Bullseye	754
170 JHP	5.5/Red Dot	990
170 JHP	10.0/Unique	1370
200 JHP	3.5/Bullseye	643
200 JHP	5.2/Red Dot	880
220 JSP	3.5/Bullseye	642
220 JSP	8.0/Red Dot	848

All rounds fired from Smith & Wesson Model 57 Revolver, 4-inch Barrel. Instrumentation: Oehler Model 33 Chronograph, 5-foot screen spacing, 15-feet downrange.

Smith & Wesson Model 57 revolver extracts cylinder full of 41-45 loads. Heads of reformed 45 ACP cases fit 41 Magnum extractor and eject with no problem.

41 Short, as they are only two-thirds the length of the 41 Magnum. In the tradition of the great wildcatters, I would modestly submit my own name to the cartridge (41 Cowgill?) except that the re-forming process is probably more trouble than it is worth, and I sincerely doubt the round will achieve the success and acceptance of such variants as the Ackley and the Gibbs.

The price paid for 41-45s is effort, not money, because 45 ACP brass is much more plentiful and affordable than 41 Magnum cases. Production may be justified if 41 Magnum ammunition is unavailable locally, or, heaven forbid, discontinued for lack of interest and made obsolete.

Except for the healthily curious, I do not recommend the process of re-forming 45 ACP brass to fit the 41 Magnum. Hard work is involved and stresses that tax both the limits of reloading equipment strength and the loader's patience.

Nevertheless, to make the load 41-45s you need:

- New or once-fired 45 ACP cases (preferably brass instead of plated).

- Large Pistol primers, 41 cal. bullets, powder, case lubricant.
- Heavy-duty reloading press, 45 ACP and 41 Magnum shell holder heads, steel plate (to cover ram for some operations—a Lyman die wrench, stamped from sheet steel, worked well).
- The following dies (use steel rather than carbide sizing dies—force involved will likely shatter carbide rings):
  — 45 ACP sizer, expander
  — 44 Magnum/Special sizer
  — 41 Magnum sizer, seater
- A hammer and ⅜-inch diameter dowel or rod (to eject "stuck" cases from sizing dies).

Fired cases should be de-primed, lubricated and sized with the 45 ACP sizer die. New cases need only be lubed.

In the first step, the 44 Magnum/Special sizer die is installed in the press and a steel plate is placed over the ram. The plate is necessary to force the case fully into the die, right up to the extraction groove. The base of the shell must be worked down and this cannot be done with the shell holder head gripping the base of the case. Leave the shell holder head in the press ram and cover it with the steel plate. The shell holder base will prevent the ram groove from closing under pressure, a condition which makes later insertion and removal of shell holders difficult.

Balance a 45 ACP case on the steel plate and adjust the 44 sizing die so that the case just begins to penetrate the die at full stroke of the press handle and ram. *Great force* is required to swage down the case, so it is necessary to operate at the end of the press stroke where the leverage of the operating handle is at its greatest multiplication. Repeatedly stroke the press fully and withdraw the ram. Rotate the die slightly with each stroke so that the die descends and sizes the case more fully each time the press cycles. Continue until the case is thoroughly "stuck" in the die, that is, until it penetrates to the extraction groove. Insert the dowel or rod in the die and tap with the hammer to eject the case which, incidentally, could now be loaded and fired in a 44 Magnum or Special chamber.

The case is still too large in diameter to fit a 41 Magnum sizing die and its mouth must be tapered first. Replace the 44 sizer with the 41 Magnum seating die, whose mouth will just accommodate the re-worked case. Back out the seating plug and use this die to taper the case for a quarter inch.

Replace the seater/crimper die with the 41 Magnum sizer, lubricate the case and size it as before, that is, by repeatedly working the press handle at the end of the stroke as the die is rotated downward into the press. Continue sizing until the case is again "stuck" up to the extraction groove and eject with hammer and dowel or rod. The steel plate can be set aside and a 41 Magnum shell holder used for all further reloading operations.

The case mouth must be belled to accept a .41 caliber bullet. Install a .45 ACP expander die with plug. A .41 Magnum expander cannot be used because the decapping pin collet is too

Sizing down a 45 ACP case this way requires a rugged press, a sturdy table, a good hammer, and a good eye. Die is upside-down in press and wood block protects case head.

Alternate way to eject "stuck" 45 ACP case from 44 or 41 Magnum sizing die. Die is inserted upside-down in press and dowel is forced into the die with press stroke.

long to allow penetration in the .41-45 case to the expanding shoulder. *Caution:* Expand only the lip of the case ever so slightly. Anything more and the 45 expander will split the 41-45 case, wasting the effort required to reach this point.

After expanding, the case may be primed, charged with powder, and fitted with its bullet, seated with the 41 Magnum seater die and plug. Choose a seating depth you would use in reloading a 41 Magnum cartridge, and crimp with the mouth of the 41 Magnum sizing die because the crimping shoulder of the seater/crimper will not reach the mouth of the 41-45 case.

Obvious alternatives to 45 ACP brass for the 41-caliber resizing operation are rifle cases which can be sized and cut off to the desired length. Candidates must be sizable down to .434-inch in diameter. Rims should not exceed .494-inch across, or they must be turned down to fit 41 extractor and cylinder rebates. The rim or head should not be appreciably thicker than .060-inch to permit easy cylinder closing and rotation, and correct headspace. Checking cartridge dimensions in reloading manuals, the 30-06, 308, 35 Remington, and the 220 Swift all look promising. *But:* the test is found in resizing the case webs. The necks can sometimes be resized with ease, but the virtually solid brass webs may seem next to impossible. Go easy if you want to experiment in this direction—don't break your tools.

How were the 41-45 loads chosen? The object of the project is to produce a tame kitty, not a wildcat in the usual sense of the word. Wildcats usually are intended to surpass the ballistic performance of conventional combinations. The 41-45 will do a lot less than

the 41 Magnum, but that is the object of the project—to develop alternative cases and reduced loads. Assuming the 41-45 and the 45 ACP case have similar strength limitations, only loads approximating those published in reloading manuals for the 45 ACP were tested. Powder types and charges for popular target loadings and one "maximum" load were tried. Federal Large Pistol primers were used throughout.

How does the 41-45 shoot? All the loads were accurate, shooting to approximate point of aim of full-up commercial ammo (4-inch barrel at 25 yards). Recoil and muzzle blast were not uncomfortable, and very similar (predictably) to those of 45 ACP target loads in a heavy-framed revolver. One load, 170-grain Sierra JHP over 10 grains of Unique, shows considerable promise as a defense-hunting load. Its muzzle velocity of 1370 feet per second and respectable 700 foot-pounds of muzzle energy produce no over-pressure signs. If you wish to work up hotter loads, be conservative, because the 41-45 case has been stretched .020-inch from the resizing operation alone. Each case has been through a lot even before firing. In any circumstance, there is no way a re-worked 45 ACP case can contain the pressures encompassed in 41 Magnum case design.

The 41-45 extracts smoothly from my 41 Magnum cylinders. The Magnum's rim diameter is .494-inch, while the 45 ACP head is .480″ across, leaving plenty of surface for the 41 ejector to readily shuck the empties. Fired 41-45s can be handily reloaded with a single operation required with the 41 Magnum sizing die.

If you have the dies and 45 ACP cases you can make 41-45s with only elbow grease and time required as we have shown. If you are certain you have all the 41 Magnum brass you will ever need in your entire lifetime, don't bother! •

Editor's Note:

Many years ago, I wrote something for John Amber in HANDLOADER'S DIGEST, and he couldn't make it work in his guns, and when he printed the article, he said so in an editor's note.

It is with greatly mixed feelings therefore that I note here I have seen Mr. Cowgill shooting his loads in S&W revolvers, and even in a third S&W I brought along, but that, in general, 41-45s of his manufacture do not fit in the chambers of either of two Ruger 41 Magnum single-actions I own.

Ken Warner

Give Us This Day Our Daily Lead . . .

by C. RODNEY JAMES

SINCE THE DAY William Lyman began marketing his tools to stuff new bullets into used cartridges, an increasing number of Americans have been rolling their own ammunition. Of late, this practice has been touted as the means to get the best performance out of one's rifle or handgun, and rightly so, but one must not lose sight of the original purpose of reloading—*economy*.

Unfortunately, about the only place one can fight rising ammunition and component costs is in the bullet department. A number of loading guides offer suggestions for the use of scrap materials to make bullets, but nearly all of this metal turns out to be *for sale!* Tin, in particular is not a cheap item. Philip Sharpe's suggestions in his *Complete Guide to Handloading* offer more nostalgia than anything else when he advises reloaders to melt down toothpaste tubes and scrap tin piping used to tap beer kegs. I have never seen a tin beer keg tap in my life and toothpaste tubes all seem to be made of plastic or aluminum.

There *are* bargains to be found, and the best are obtained for nothing but a smile and a grateful "thanks." The great untapped resource: friends and acquaintances who are not reloaders. Now if one plans to take this path a few friends might drop by the wayside; with tact, however, many things are possible.

That I made my own bullets was met with reactions of curiosity and a bit of awe around the university where I taught. It did not require much in the way of questioning for me to launch into a brief lecture on bullet casting which always included a wistful description of how quickly the lead pot was emptied by casting 500-grain 45-70 bullets. Somewhere near the end of the talk the question was put to the listener of whether he or she might happen to know of any lead, tin or lead alloy that was just lying around waiting to be recycled. Many did.

This scouting went on around the neighborhood as well. I managed to locate a gas station, not too far from home, that did not reuse or resell the wheel weights they collected. Each oil and lube time, I was duly presented with one or more quart cans of embryonic bullets. Such throwbacks to the good old days must be well patronized, not to mention jealously guarded against poachers.

Sometimes, lead beat a path to *my* door as in the instance of the happy day the telephone company paid a visit to do some pole work in the back yard. When they finished their labors, I engaged the linemen in conversation and soon became the owner of several short lengths of lead sheathed cable. By peeling the sheathing back from one end, then clamping the wire firmly in a vise, the sheathing could be pulled off with relative ease.

To keep my office from looking like a scrap yard, I put a cardboard carton under the desk. Wheel weights, plucked from gutter and street, piled up. One of these, a particularly fine specimen of the truck tire variety was rescued from a busy intersection by no less than the head of a department. Sheets of pure lead, from France yet, had been used by an artist to shape her plexiglass sculpture. After it had been cut into small and odd shaped pieces, the sheet was no longer of any use to her. Office maintenance involving wall work produced several pounds of screw wall anchors. Bits of solder, old fishing sinkers, the odd chunk of plumbing pipe and type metal were received with effusive thanks.

Then there were exotics. Moldings from leaded glass windows, the glass smashed in the process of demolition, contained tin in the soldered joints. Lead piping from the innards of a defunct player piano and the tin pipes from an equally dead pipe organ were combined to play a new tune as they passed down the barrel of my Springfield. Finally, there was a lead diver's weight, purported to have been worn on a treasure hunt, now no longer needed for scuba work.

These diverse materials were blended into bullet metal which produced some five to six hundred rounds of ammunition that provided target shooting for a number of very pleasant summer afternoons. With the coming of autumn, while others saw *only* new students and faculty, I welcomed in a whole new source of supply. Now I cannot state for a fact that these bullets shot one whit straighter than the store bought kind, but they most certainly shot sweeter. •

Roll Your

Tight chokes don't have to mean tight patterns. Spreader loads are the answer.

by TOM TURPIN

Selected by your Editor, this article "Roll Your Own Spreader Loads," is from DBI Books' *Reloading For Shotgunners,* edited by Robert S. L. Anderson. In recent years, there has been little written on the subject of shotshell reloading; however, *Reloading For Shotgunners* has filled that gap. Of course, in compiling the fourteen articles in that book, some of the best known authors on the subject of shotshell reloading were commissioned. They include Tom Roster, Don Zutz, Frank Petrini, Ed Matunas, Art Blatt, Dick Eades, Tom Turpin and Dean Grennell. The subject matter ran from "Wildcatting the 12 Gauge," by Ed Matunas, to "The Psychology of Skeet and Trap Reloading," by Art Blatt. Ed Matunas did an outstanding job of providing over 70 pages of load tables for all of the popular gauges. There is also a section of the book devoted completely to the operation of the MEC 700, the P-W Du-O-Matic 375 and the Pacific 366 Auto Reloader. The article at hand was included in this edition of HANDLOADER'S DIGEST for two separate and distinct reasons: First, and most importantly, it rounds out HANDLOADER'S DIGEST by providing you, our reader/reloader, with some valuable "how-to" information on the subject of spreader loads. Secondly, and we're not embarrassed to say it, we're proud of what *Reloading For Shotgunners* has accomplished. We felt we should share that accomplishment with the readers of HANDLOADER'S DIGEST.

Reloading For Shotgunners is available from DBI Books, Inc., 1 Northfield Plaza, Northfield, IL 60093. At $7.95 a copy, the shotshell reloader will find himself armed with a book that provides answers essential to turning out quality reloads.

AMONG SHOOTERS and hunters, the mystical pot of gold at the end of the rainbow seems to be the "all around" gun. Literally volumes of material have been published on the subject, not to mention hours of conversation around the campfire devoted to the issue. Although many different methods have been tried, nothing has materialized that is totally satisfactory. In all probability, a totally satisfactory solution will never be developed.

In the field of shotgunning, many ideas have been pursued to provide the one-gun shooter with a suitable firearm for all the scattergun games. Perhaps the closest that we have come to the attainment of that goal is the adjustable choke device, of which there are several types on the market. One type uses an adjustable collet at the muzzle which can be adjusted by simply turning the device. Turning in one direction increases the constriction at the muzzle—turning in the other

Own Spreader Loads

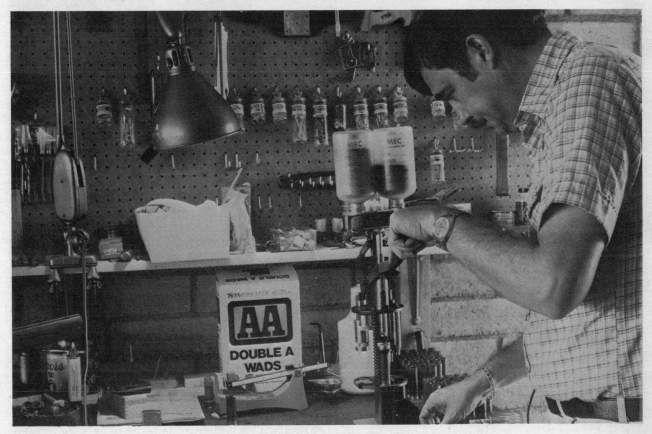

An elaborate reloading setup is not needed for making your own spreader loads. Here, the author is using his MEC 600 Jr.

direction decreases the constriction. In effect, one can change the choke of his gun with a twist of the wrist! Another type that enjoys some success uses removable tubes to change the choke. While this type is not as fast as the collet type, it seems to be equally successful in the marketplace.

I even recall a few years ago, perhaps it was even more than a few, there was a collet type adjustable choke on the market that changed settings automatically. It was started with the first shot set at improved cylinder choke; and, when it was fired, the device automatically switched to modified choke for the second shot and to full choke for the third.

Even though both the collet and the removable tube-type choke gizmos work quite well, there is an extremely large segment of the shooting population that does not like them. I suspect the primary reason for the dislike is cosmetic, and

not a lack of efficiency. I recall one of my shooting friends making the statement that these choke devices reminded him of " . . . shooting with a beer can attached to the muzzle of his gun." It's safe to say that many of the adjustable chokes currently on the market are not attractive to a lot of shooters.

There is, however, another method of changing the performance of the shotgun without resorting to the addition of choke tubes, adjustable collets and the like. It has long been known that a given gun will perform differently with changes in ammunition. Even though a gun might be marked full choke, there is certainly no guarantee that it will provide full-choke patterns with all ammunition. In fact, it is not unusual for a given gun to provide improved-cylinder patterns with one load, and full-choke patterns with another. Regardless of what might be stamped on the barrel, the only true indication of the performance of the

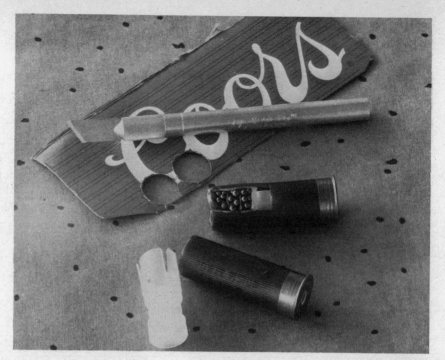

The round-wad type of spreader loading is illustrated here. Note that the cardboard dividers separate the shot into three compartments.

gun is determined at the patterning board. I highly recommend that anyone who is interested in the performance of his scattergun, take it to a patterning board with various loads, and try them all. That alone might very well solve some of the "one gun" problems. (In fact, I highly recommend you see the article on patterning by Don Zutz elsewhere in this book.)

If patterning your gun with various loads does not result in a load that provides sufficient spread for upland hunting, Skeet shooting, or other shotgunning needs requiring more open boring, do not despair! There is something else that can be done to open up the gun's performance. You can turn out your own tailored spreader loads!

Spreader loads are not new. The Belgians at one time loaded a shotshell with square shot! The principle involved was that the square shot would not "lump" together as tightly when traveling down the bore, and when exiting the bore, would have considerably more wind resistance, causing the shot to spread over a wider area (more quickly) than did the traditional round shot. I think there was also an Italian load that utilized a flattened type of shot, on the order of tiny discs rather than round shot. I have never used them, and cannot comment on their effectiveness.

In the absence of square shot and lead discs, there is another approach to convert the tightly-choked scattergun for situations requiring more

open chokes. This approach involves adjourning to the reloading bench, and loading up a batch of spreader loads. Manufacturing your own spreader loads is neither difficult, nor does it require any specialized equipment other than a standard shotshell reloader. My own particular reloading tool is a MEC 600 Jr., but any of the tools will work fine.

There are basically two methods of making spreader loads. The first involves the construction of a cardboard "X" to insert in the shotshell, dividing the shot column into four sections. This separation of the shot column facilitates the spreading of the shot column once it leaves the muzzle. The other method also separates the shot column, but does it through the use of small cardboard circles which are alternated with layers of shot in the shell. Both methods work very well, and either will get the job done. I personally prefer to use the "X" method, but only because I find it easier to do. As far as effectiveness goes, I have been unable to detect any significant differences between the two methods.

I recommend trying both methods and selecting the one that best suits your reloading style. With your own particular load and components, it may be that one method will prove to be more effective—in *your* gun—than the other. Again, with my loads, I have been unable to detect any significant differences. Both of these methods are rather simple to do, and require no special tools or equipment. Some thin cardboard, a straight-edge, and a sharp knife or scissors are all that will be needed.

Any thin cardboard stock can be used to make the separators. As an astute observer will note in the accompanying photos, a 6-pack container which originally held a popular brand of beer was the source of my cardboard stock. It has the added advantage of being free, provided you intended to buy the beer anyway! Another excellent material is business card stock. As long as the stock is stiff and not too thick, it will work fine.

Using the base of the wad column as a template, the cylindrical spreader wads can be easily made from a six-pack beer container.

Although a bit counterproductive for spreader loads, I use the one-piece plastic shot cup/wad column in all my shotshell reloading. It is well known that the plastic shot cups tend to tighten patterns. I guess I have just gotten lazy in my old age, as I take the easy route. The pattern board shows clearly that the spreader loads do their job quite well, regardless of the use of the plastic shot cups.

To make the cardboard "X," simply measure the length and width of the shot cup, and cut strips of cardboard slightly undersize from the width of the shotcup. Once that is done, cut the strips to the exact depth of the shot cup. Then, measure the width of each strip to find the center. Using a sharp knife, cut a slit in each strip at the center line, to slightly more than half its length. After that, it is a simple matter to fit the two strips together, forming the "X" cardboard shot separator.

Once the "X's" are made, load the shells in the normal manner until the step is reached where the shot is dropped. At that point, insert one of the "Xs" into the wad before dropping the shot. This will divide the shot cup into four separate compartments; and, since the cardboard takes up some of the volume capacity of the shot cup, it may be necessary to remove a small amount of the shot prior to crimping. Once the crimping operation is completed, set the shell aside or place it in a box marked for spreader loads. Don't get the spreader loads mixed up with your regular loads.

The other method of making spreader loads is almost as simple to do. Instead of cutting the cardboard stock into strips, it is cut into circles. The base of a one-piece wad can be used as a pattern to draw the circles on the cardboard, and scissors used to cut them out. Make two of these circles for each shell to be loaded.

Again, as with the "X" method, load the shell normally until the shot dropping stage. At this point, I drop the shot into the small pan that comes with a RCBS powder scale. Most any other container can be used however. I pour

The "X"-type of spreader load is made by forming a cardboard "X" which serves to separate the shot charge into four compartments.

The right barrel of the author's Parker trap gun produced 79 percent patterns without the spreader load, and 57 percent patterns with it. Bear in mind the only difference between the two loads was the addition of the cardboard "X" in the shot column. Spreader loads are ideal on close flushing game in dense cover.

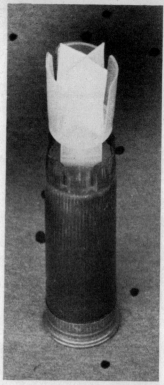

This shotshell has the cardboard "X" fitted into the one-piece plastic wad, and is ready to be filled with shot. The spreader itself may displace some shot, so be sure to hand-fill each wad with shot.

about ⅓ of the charge into the shot cup, and place one of the cardboard dividers on top of it. Another ⅓ of the shot is then poured in and topped with the second divider. Finally, the remaining ⅓ (or slightly less), is poured in and the shell crimped. This completes the load.

All that remains to be done is to adjourn to the patterning board to check the results. To prove emphatically how well the spreader load works, I like to make up identical loads, with and without the cardboard partitions for the patterning session. I think you will be surprised at just how well this simple addition to the shot column will "open up" a tightly choked gun. My own Parker double trap gun has 32-inch barrels choked "full-and-fuller!" A light game load that I often shoot in this gun uses 17½ grains of 700X powder and 1 ounce of No. 4 shot. Without the cardboard partitions, this load patterns 78-79 percent in the gun. By merely adding the partitions, I am able to achieve patterns in the 58 to 59 percent range. Effectively, the old Parker can be instantly changed from a shotgun that delivers very tight full choke patterns to one producing wide modified patterns.

Making up a batch of spreader loads is not as good as acquiring a new gun or a new barrel choked in more open borings. Of course, it doesn't cost nearly as much either! If you are one of those gun nuts that is only looking for an excuse to acquire another gun, then by all means hide this article from the better half, and go ahead and buy one. On the other hand, if you need a more open bored gun to improve your upland game shooting percentages, then I recommend you investigate spreader loads—they are not a panacea, but they are a big step in the right direction.

Stoking a Model 70 Target 30-06 with carefully constructed reduced loads in an accurate way to go. Shooter is Dennis Lundmark.

The state of riflery and the state of the economy both call for a . . .

REDUCED LOAD ROUNDUP

by PAUL G. WILKINSON

THE INTRODUCTION of the Alberts Schuetzenplinker 30-caliber lead bullet has got to be the best news to hit handloading since the Lee Loader. Squibb loads are back in style, jacketed bullets and powders are more expensive than ever, and more shooters are realizing, again, that "light is right."

The Alberts Schuetzenplinker is a thoroughly modern rendition of an old, but sound concept. It offers superb accuracy potential for light loads powerful enough for small game and varmints. The Schuetzenplinker with a typical load in most 30 caliber rifles compares with the old blackpowder 32-40 Winchester. The bullet is a smooth, dry-lubed 154-gr. round-nosed design, ready to load and shoot out of the box and to be sold at about half the price of jacketed bullets.

Cast bullet shooters have used reduced loads for generations, but swaged lead rifle bullets have not been readily available for about 50 years.

Many a shooter of that era cut his teeth on 30-06 gallery practice cartridges, which were loaded by the arsenals for use in Springfield and Krag rifles. These were meant for indoor practice, or short-range use on outdoor ranges that didn't have adequate safety zones to permit the use of standard service ammunition.

Shooters of the pre-war era also often shot 32-20 revolver bullets in 30-cal. rifles with light charges of pistol powder. Some 35-cal. rifle shooters today do the same thing, using 38 Special lead bullets. Soft lead buckshot or cast round balls can, and have been used for minimum loads, but they sometimes leave a lot to be desired for accuracy. There are some tricks to this, about which there will be more nearby.

For minimum-load plinking a charge of 3 grs. of Bullseye, Red Dot, or 700-X works well with the 154-gr. Schuetzenplinker in any rifle case from 30-30 to 30-06 size. This gives

about 700-750 fps (feet per second) and 1″ groups at 25 yards from typical hunting rifles. Accuracy with these very light charges is actually better in some rifles when you load the bullet backwards! Better accuracy is obtained nose forward in somewhat higher velocity loads at 1050-1250 fps. Much above 1250 fps, accuracy deteriorates, as it will with any soft, plain-based bullet.

Schuetzenplinkers are strictly for low velocity loads. Everything has to be perfect for 1250-1350 fps loads to work, so they cannot be recommended for general use. Keeping velocities below 1250 fps avoids potential leading problems and you can shoot to your heart's content with little need for your cleaning rod.

When all else fails, in short, follow the directions: Alberts has clear instructions and tested loads all worked out. Why experiment? Follow the formula.

The method for loading Schuet-

All of these will make accurate convenient reduced loads in 30-caliber rifles. From left: O Buck; Alberts 100-gr. 32 WC; Schuetzenplinker; Speer 110-gr. varminter; Sierra 150-gr. FP; Lyman #3118 120-gr. 32-20 bullet; Lyman #308241 154-gr. plain base; Lyman #311291 170-gr. gas check design.

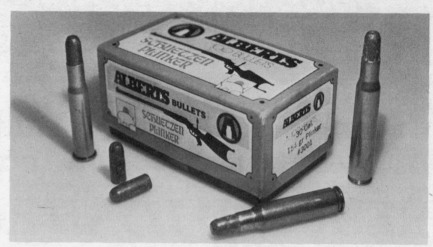

The new thing is the deceptively plain Alberts Schuetzenplinker—it's all sized and lubed and ready for 30-calibers from 30-30 to 30-06 and bigger.

zenplinkers is nothing new to the cast bullet shooter. It varies a bit from normal procedures with jacketed loads, so I'll go into some detail: It is very important to chamfer the inside of the case mouth well, and to expand or "bell" it slightly so the bullet can be seated without shaving lead or the dry bullet lubricant which covers the bullet. Otherwise, bare lead will contact the bore. Accuracy goes right out the window with that shot and those following until the bore is scrubbed clean again.

There are several suitable neck expanders which will do the job. One of the best is the Lyman "M" die, long a standard piece of equipment among cast bullet devotees. RCBS has a similar die which has interchangeable tapered expanding plugs in various calibers which also work well. The Mequon Unitized Loader (formerly Lee Custom) contains a cast bullet neck expander. These all work. Lacking any of them, you may improvise with a 30 Carbine or 32-20 expander die.

You must still deburr cases even when using the stepped expander. Otherwise, they may still shave some lead, which is no good. Once the case has been chamfered, you don't have to do it again unless the case is trimmed.

Rimless cases used for plinker loads should be kept separate from those used for full loads. Primer blast drives the case forward in the chamber, setting the shoulder back and gradually increasing headspace. Rimmed cases

such as the 30-30 don't suffer this problem since their forward motion is stopped by the rim. Set-back of rimless cases is reduced or eliminated if flashholes are enlarged with a No. 40 (.098″) drill, but then, obviously, any such case must never be fired with a full charge because of possible primer leakage.

I mark plinker load cases for identification by filing a notch across the rim. This was standard practice before WW II when National Guard units used to reload the 30-cal. Gallery Practice Cartridge, M1919, for the Springfield, using a 140-gr. swaged lead bullet and 10½ grains of DuPont SR-80 or 6 grains of Bullseye.

The Schuetzenplinker accomplishes the same result in the 30-06, but with a slightly heavier bullet which gives better accuracy. The 30-06 M1919 gallery practice load would hold the bull of the Rifle "A" 1000-Inch Range target at 28 yards. The Schuetzen-

plinker will keep them in a ragged hole from a good rifle at that distance, and will nearly stay in that 1½″ black at 100 yards. You can expect 2″-2½″ groups from accurate hunting rifles at 100 yards, which is sure useful accuracy for small game or target practice.

For best results seating depth should be tailored to the individual rifle. The bullet should be pressed gently against the leade of the rifling when the cartridge is chambered. If the bullet is allowed to "jump" into the rifling, as usually happens with a short pistol-type bullet in a rifle, accuracy suffers. The relatively long nose of the Schuetzenplinker is thoughtful. It permits the correct seating in most standard chambers, without pushing the base below the neck in cartridges such as the 308 Winchester. The nose diameter is large enough so the front of the two-diameter bullet rides the lands for best accuracy.

At first I was a bit skeptical, but

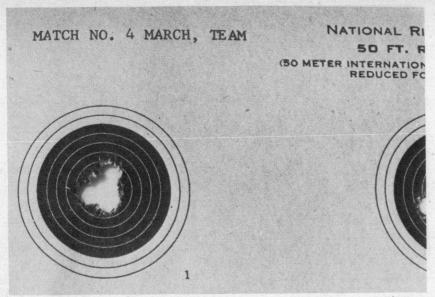

MATCH NO. 4 MARCH, TEAM

This is fine plinking from 25 yards fired on the 50-ft. reduced International smallbore target from a Model 70 in 30-06.

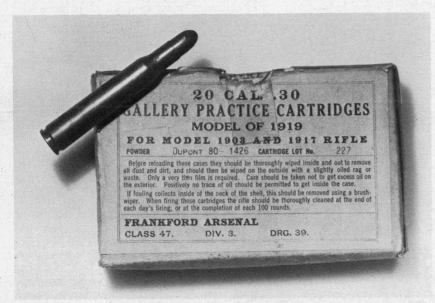

20 CAL .30
GALLERY PRACTICE CARTRIDGES
MODEL OF 1919
FOR MODEL 1903 AND 1917 RIFLE

Old military gallery practice cartridges were about the last time 30-caliber shooters saw swaged lead bullets. Then and now, they work fine at low velocities.

shooting proved Alberts right. I prefer Hercules RL-7 for my cast bullet loads and tried it, but I found that at suitable velocities, RL-7 didn't burn efficiently, causing excessive fouling and erratic velocities. Somewhat faster powders such as 2400 and IMR-4227 were tried. Hercules 2400 was also unsuitable, due to leading, though IMR-4227 did fine in suitable light charges, giving 1100-1300 fps.

It turns out the best powders for loading the Schuetzenplinker are relatively fast pistol and shotgun powders, such as Bullseye, Red Dot, 700-X and Unique. These were the only ones

I tried, but Green Dot, W-W 231, and similar powders in this range should also work OK. The basics should be followed as for the recommended powders in the manufacturer's data:

- Do not attempt to load below 700 fps or 3 grains of Unique as you may lodge a bullet in the bore.
- Best accuracy will probably be obtained at velocities from 1050-1250 fps.
- Do not attempt to exceed 1300 fps. The Schuetzenplinker isn't intended for that.
- Be extremely careful to check the powder level in every case to insure against double charges or rounds with no powder in them.
- Follow the instructions.

In my experience the best "standard" load for cartridges from 30-30 to 30-06 size was 7.3 grains of Unique, giving about 1250 fps in the 30-30, 1200 fps in the 308 and about 1080 in the 30-06. A charge of 6 grains of Bullseye or 700-X was nearly as good for a "universal" load, though velocities were somewhat lower.

Some potentially promising applications of the 154-gr. Schuetzenplinker are in the 30 M1 Carbine, and in certain handguns. A charge of 11 grains of IMR-4227 gives the Schuetzenplinker about 1450 fps in the M1 carbine. When seated to fit into the magazine it feeds like a champ and operates the action semiautomatically. Its velocity is really too much for top accuracy, but with lighter loads this long bullet tips somewhat—it isn't stable in the carbines' 20″ twist. Accuracy is "minute of beer can" at 50 yards. Most M1 carbines don't do a lot better than that with GI ammo anyway.

The charges of Unique listed for the 30-30 work reasonably well in the Contender pistol, though for the 30 Herrett you must back off a full grain. Velocities are about 100-150 fps less than in a rifle. A charge of 11 grains of IMR-4227 works well in the 30 Herrett for a plinker, giving about 950 fps.

The most unlikely application of this bullet is in the 32 S&W revolver. Alberts tells of an intrepid young man in Virginia who insisted on shooting them with 3.5 grains of Unique in his Colt Police Positive built for the 32 Colt New Police load. Velocity was about 750 fps and the load significantly more potent than the normal load. I wouldn't recommend such a load except in 38-framed guns such as the Police Positive Special or S&W K-32. Bullets are seated to the shoulder on the bullet and heavily roll crimped. According to Alberts, accuracy was on the order of 3″ at 25 yards.

The Schuetzenplinker's adaptability to extreme minimum loads has value. It isn't a good idea to attempt to load jacketed bullets below about 1050 fps, since there is a real risk of lodging a bullet in the barrel. If a lead bullet sticks, it can be removed easily by tapping it out with a cleaning rod. Don't try that with a lodged jacketed bullet. That's a job for a gunsmith, and even done right there is some risk of damaging the barrel. You should never, by the way, try to shoot an obstruction out, even with a blank charge, since you may ring the barrel.

For the ultra-light minimum load,

Charge/Velocity Data for Hercules Bullseye with Alberts Schuetzenplinker

Rifle/Caliber	Charge (grains)								
	3.0	4.0	5.0	5.5	6.0	6.5	7.0	7.5	8.0
30-30 Win. Rem. 788 22" bbl.	787 8Sd	933 23Sd	1070 6Sd	1128 11Sd	1181 12Sd	1236 9 Sd	NR	NR	NR
308 Win. Springfield Armory M1A 22" bbl.	766 13Sd	913 25Sd	1034 12Sd	1053 30Sd	1106 22Sd	1205 10Sd	1248 10Sd	NR	NR
30-'06 Win. M70 Target 26" bbl.	685 27Sd	834 20Sd	956 11Sd	1006 10Sd	1030 30Sd	1118 10Sd	1164 18Sd	1204 27Sd	1257 8Sd

Charge/Velocity Data for Hercules Unique with Alberts Schuetzenplinker

Rifle/Caliber	Charge (Grains)							
	3.0	4.0	5.0	6.0	7.0	7.5	8.0	9.0
30-30 Win. Rem. 788 22" bbl.	701 18Sd	831 15Sd	990 16Sd	1090 15Sd	1212 8Sd	1257 11Sd	NR	NR
308 Win. Springfield Armory M1A 22" bbl.	687 13Sd	829 26Sd	955 24Sd	1056 12Sd	1163 13Sd	1259 15Sd	NR	
30-06 Win. M70 Target 26" bbl.	623 18Sd	765 13Sd	865 15Sd	960 30Sd	1055 25Sd		1152 8Sd	1249 30Sd

If the muzzle of your rifle looks like this, you know your lube is lasting the course and if there's a problem, that's not it.

Charge/Velocity Data for DuPont 700-X Powder with Alberts 154-gr. Lead Schuetzenplinker

Rifle/Caliber	Charge (grains)							
	3.0	4.0	5.0	6.0	6.5	7.0	7.5	8.0
Rem. 788 30-30 22" bbl.	746Av 18Sd	905Av 17Sd	1028Av 13Sd	1150Av 12Sd	1224Av 12Sd	NR	NR	
308 Win. Springfield Armory M1A 22" bbl.	750 13Sd	902 18Sd	1017 20Sd	1134 11Sd	1179 9Sd	1242 22Sd	NR	
30-06 Win. M70 26" bbl.	651Av 23Sd	801Av 16Sd	934 13Sd	1039 23Sd		1154 8Sd		1246 8Sd

the 154-gr. Schuetzenplinker works best in a 10″ twist rifle, such as the 30-06. In a 12″ twist, as in the 308 Winchester, bullets may yaw or "tip" a little at velocities below 1000 fps. At the lower velocities obtained in the Contender pistol, they may also yaw. In these guns, Alberts suggests a highly accurate alternative—Alberts 32 S&W Long, 100-gr. hollow-based wadcutter. This bullet shoots extremely well with light charges giving about 1000-1200 fps. Heavier loads than those indicated, however, must not be used with this bullet. This is because the hollow base might separate and be left in the bore as an obstruction. The 32 wadcutter makes a nice clean hole in target paper, and is a deadly squirrel load. It is very wind sensitive, however, and for ranges much beyond 25 yards the 154-gr. Schuetzenplinker is far superior.

My impressions of the Alberts Schuetzenplinker are so favorable, I hope he brings them out in other calibers. I think 45-70 would be, for instance, a natural.

Alternatives For Reduced Rifle and Handgun Loads

The cast bullet is still king of the economy plinkers. The velocity of most small game or plinking loads is seldom over 1400 fps, so the casting alloy need not be hard, strong or expensive. Wheelweights or salvaged backstop lead work fine. At low velocities, plain-based bullets work OK, so you can save $7 per thousand by not buying gaschecks. For cast bullet plinking loads, pistol and shotgun powders are best and you can usually get 800-1000 rounds from one $8-10 pound of powder.

You can use cast gascheck designs for light loads without the gascheck. The ring of lube left around the base does no harm if the loads are used soon. Indeed, the additonal grease actually improves accuracy. However, if you store the loads for a long time, or shoot them in hot weather, that lube where the gascheck isn't may melt and attack the powder.

Probably the best 30-caliber plinking bullet is the Lyman 311241, which weighed 154 grs. when cast of wheelweight metal. Another great reduced-load bullet is the blunt-nosed gascheck 311440. The Lyman catalog doesn't list either of these bullets anymore, but moulds can sometimes be found secondhand. Moulds for similar designs can be had from NEI in El Paso.

Of the Lyman designs, the plain-based 3118 32-20 rifle bullet and the gaschecked 311466 are probably the

Reduced Rifle Loads

You must chamfer and bell cases to get Schuetzenplinker benefit—if you scrape one, you get naked lead in the bore.

Handgunners can round-ball it, too. Here's the 44 Magnum and Speer's .433-in. ball, and the 38/357 with buckshot. Easily loaded, they group well up close.

At left, the 311291 cast gas check design will exploit virtually the full range of 30-30 potential; the Schuetzenplinker at right is for low velocities only, but it's simple.

Caliber	Bullet		Powder	Grs.	Approx. Velocity
22 Hornet	40-45	Cast	Unique	3.0	1300
	40-45	Jacketed	Unique	4.0	1450
222 Rem.	40-45	Cast	Unique	4.0	1300
	50-55	Jacketed	Unique	7.0	2000
223 Rem.	45	Jacketed	Unique	6.0	1900
	50	Jacketed	Unique	7.0	2000
	55	Jacketed	Unique	8.0	2100
22-250	55	Jacketed	Unique	9.0	2000
220 Swift	55	Jacketed	Unique	10.0	2050
243 Win.	#3	buckshot	Bullseye	3.5	1100
	#3	buckshot	Unique	5.0	1300
	87	Jacketed	Unique	10.0	1700
6mm Rem.	#3	buckshot	Bullseye	4.0	1200
	#3	buckshot	Unique	5.5	1300
	100	Jacketed	Unique	10.0	1600
	100	Jacketed	IMR-4198	18.0	1700
250 Sav.	87	Jacketed	SR-4759	12.0	1600[1]
	87	Jacketed	Unique	8.0	1450[1]
	100-117	Jacketed	Unique	8.0	1400[2]
257 Robt.	87	Jacketed	Unique	8.5	1450[1]
	100-117	Jacketed	Unique	10.0	1400[2]
25-06	100-117	Jacketed	Unique	12.0	1650[2]
270 Win.	130	Jacketed	Unique	12.0	1500
7mm-08	140	Jacketed	Unique	10.0	1300
7x57	140	Jacketed	Unique	12.0	1450
280 Rem.	140	Jacketed	Unique	14.0	1500
30-30 Win.	#0	buckshot	Bullseye	3.5	1100
	100	lead WC	Bullseye	3.5	900
	154	lead	Bullseye	6.0	1200
	110	Jacketed	Unique	9.0	1600
	150	Jacketed	Unique	8.0	1300[3]
308 Win.	#0	buckshot	Bullseye	4.0	1100
	100	lead WC	Bullseye	4.0	900
	154	lead	Unique	7.6	1200
	150	Jacketed	Unique	8.5	1100[3]
	150	Jacketed	Bullseye	6.5	1050
30-06	#0	buckshot	Bullseye	5.0	1200
	100	lead WC	Bullseye	5.0	1000
	154	lead	Bullseye	8.0	1250
	154	lead	Unique	8.0	1150
	150	Jacketed	Unique	12.0	1350[3]
8x57	#00	buckshot	Bullseye	5.0	1150
	#00	buckshot	Unique	6.0	1100
	170	Jacketed	Unique	12.0	1600
35 Rem.	#000	buckshot	Bullseye	5.0	1100
	148	lead WC	Bullseye	5.0	900
	148	lead WC	Unique	6.0	875
	158	lead SWC	Unique	8.0	1200
	158	Jacketed	Unique	10.0	1500
375 H&H	220	Jacketed	SR-4759	34.0	2000[4]
	220	Jacketed	Unique	14.0	1400[4]
	255	cast	Unique	14.0	1300[5]
444 Marlin	.433″	ball	Bullseye	5.0	1000
	.433″	ball	Unique	6.0	900
	240	jacketed	Unique	15.0	1400
44 Magnum	.433″	ball	Bullseye	5.0	1100
	.433″	ball	Unique	6.0	950
45-70	.460″	ball	Bullseye	5.0	900
	.460″	ball	Unique	7.0	1000
	300	Jacketed	Unique	14.0	1350
	405	Jacketed	Unique	14.0	1250
458 Win.	.460″	ball	Bullseye	6.0	950
	.460″	ball	Unique	8.0	1000
	405	Jacketed	Unique	18.0	1250

NOTES:
[1] 25-20 flatnosed bullet works better than spitzers.
[2] 25-35 flatnosed or roundnosed bullets work better than spitzers.
[3] 30-30 flatnosed or roundnosed bullets work better than spitzers.
[4] Hornady bullet for 375 Win. is preferred, but 235 Speer can be substituted.
[5] Use 38-55 bullet.

With something like 3 gr. of a fast-burning powder inside—out of a Lee dipper is fine—this 30-30 case needs just the buckshot stuffed in the neck and some Crisco wiped in to be ready.

Firing Table for Alberts Schuetzenplinkers: 1300 fps

Ballistic Coefficient (C1):			.184		Bullet weight (grs): 154	
			Standard Metro			
Range Yards	Rem Vel.	Rem Energy	Total Drop	Elev-ation	Max. Height	Defl. In 10MPH Wind
0	1300	578	0	0	−1.5	0
50	1178	474	2.7	8.5	.1	1
100	1085	403	11.7	13.2	2.5	4.1
150	1017	354	28.1	19.7	7.1	9
200	963	317	52.7	27.1	14	15.3

Range Yards	Bullet Path From Sight Line	
	MOA	Inches
25	4.6	1.2
50	4.8	2.4
75	2.7	2
100	0	0
125	−3.1	−3.9
150	−6.5	−9.7
175	−10.1	−17.6
200	−13.9	−27.7

Firing Table for Alberts Schuetzenplinkers: 1000 fps

Ballistic Coefficient (C1): .184				Bullet Weight (grs.): 154		
			Standard Metro			
Range Yards	Rem Vel.	Rem Energy	Total Drop	Elev-ation	Max. Height	Defl. In 10MPH Wind
0	1000	342	0	0	−1.5	0
50	950	308	4.5	12	.6	.7
100	907	282	18.6	20.1	4.2	2.8
150	870	259	43.3	29.8	10.8	6
200	836	239	79.4	40.5	20.6	10.7

Range Yards	Bullet Path From Sight Line	
	MOA	Inches
25	9.7	2.4
50	8.1	4.1
75	4.4	3.3
100	0	0
125	−4.7	−5.9
150	−9.7	−14.6
175	−14.9	−26.1
200	−20.3	−40.7

best choices. The 311291 170-gr. gas-check bullet also merits consideration. The 311291 bullet is the best choice if you wish to get into 30-caliber bullet casting, and want one mould to cover everything from grouse through deer. The starting loads listed in the *Lyman Cast Bullet Handbook* are fine, but with plainbased bullets I'd use the even lighter Alberts Schuetzenplinker data.

The best cast bullet designs for reduced loads are blunt, flat, or round-nosed bullets of standard weight which can be seated close to the rifling to minimize jump. In minimum velocity loads standard weight bullets may not be adequately stabilized, so you may have to consider lighter weights. For powder-puff loads with light bullets, semi-wadcutter or full wadcutter designs are best.

"Collar button" bullets were once common in blackpowder days for indoor shooting, but few of these mould designs are available anymore. You can get similar moulds for your 30-caliber rifle by using 30 carbine or 32 revolver bullets. You can also use 38 Special bullets in 35-caliber rifles. Some 45 pistol bullets do fairly well in the 45-70 or 458 if they are cast soft and if the mould is somewhat oversize, as many are.

Lacking these, the lowly round ball can be made to work very well. The secret is to have the ball somewhat larger than groove diameter. A groove-sized ball doesn't hold the rifling well because of its short bearing length, particularly if it's a soft lead buckshot. A fatter ball squeezes down and has a short cylindrical section.

A somewhat oversized ball, such as Single-O (.32) buckshot in a 30-caliber rifle, can be pressed snugly into the mouth of an unsized fired case, which has been reprimed and charged with 3 grains of Bullseye and wiped with a little Crisco or bullet lube over the case mouth to lubricate the ball and seal the round. You would be amazed how well these can shoot. A Double-O buckshot works well in the 32-40, 32 Special or 8mm Mauser, and Triple-O works fine in the 35 Remington or in 38 Special revolvers. A .460″ round ball and 5 grains of Bullseye shoots well in the 45-70. Still larger balls work OK if you size them first, making a short cylindrical "bullet."

Round balls work well in handguns too. The *Speer No. 10 Manual* gives tested loads in most calibers. I shoot a lot of roundballs with 5 grains of Bullseye in my 44 Magnum. While they shoot a bit low, they are as accurate out to 25 yards as my full power loads, and they are a lot less punishing to shoot.

You can load pipsqueak handgun loads with regular cast bullets too. The light, collar-button styles are still available here, as short full wadcutters, typically shot for 50-ft. gallery targets in 38 Special with 1.0-1.5 grains of Bullseye. You can also get good results with similar charges and a standard 148-gr. lead wadcutter. Don't ever try to load these light loads with jacketed slugs, however, since you'll lodge one in the bore. In the 45 ACP as little as 1 grain of Bullseye will let a lead wadcutter bullet clear the barrel every time, though it will shoot low and won't work the 1911 action. In a 44 or 45 revolver you must use at least 1½ grains of Bullseye, since some pressure is lost through cylinder gap.

You may want sometimes to make a low-powered load with jacketed bullets. Provided you have a velocity of at least 750 fps, you can do it in handguns. In rifles, you need at least 1050 fps to avoid lodging a bullet in the bore. In 22 centerfires use the 40-45-gr. Hornet bullets. Use 25-20 or 25-35 bullets in the 25-06, and so on. In most 30-caliber rifles the 150-gr. flatnosed 30-30 bullets work best. They jump less going into the rifling than the 110-gr. bullets often used for reduced loads, and they have much better accuracy.

During my military service I had to load some sub-sonic rifle ammunition which could be used in a silenced sniper rifle. I found the 150-gr. 30-30 bullet with 6.5 grains of Bullseye or 8.5 grains of Unique worked very well in the 7.62mm NATO, giving about 1050 fps and 3 minutes of angle (MOA). I have since used these charges for small game loads with good results. For the 30-06 you should increase these charges a full grain.

For heavier reduced loads for varmint shooting and the like, there is a good deal of data in the Speer manual. Most of the Speer loads use SR-4759 powder which isn't available except in 4-lb. caddies and lots of stores don't carry it. You can use 4227 or 4198 with good results also. Unique is available almost everywhere and is the ideal reduced load powder, in my opinion.

The overriding consideration which makes reduced load shooting worthwhile is the fact a firearm doesn't need to be run at full power all the time, anymore than any other machine. Using your guns with less than full loads will let you shoot more and enjoy it more, and make you a better shot.

Think about that. ●

The full range of centerfires can be served with reduced loads. From left: 223 with soft point bullet and low charge; 308 Winchester with the Speer 110-gr. varminter; another 308 with a 30-30 flat-point; the 35 Remington with a jacketed revolver bullet; the 375 H&H Magnum with a Hornady 220-gr. 375 Winchester bullet; the 458 with a 45-70 jacketed bullet.

Charge Table for Alberts Schuetzenplinkers

Caliber	Mequon Measure Number	Powder Charge (grs.)	Powder Type	Velocity (fps)	Remarks
30 M1 Carbine	052	11.0	IMR-4227	1450	Feeds from magazine semi-auto
30-30 Winchester	039	5.8	Bullseye	1200	
	039	4.8	700-X	1000*	
	039	5.1	Unique	1100*	
	052	7.3	Unique	1250	accuracy load
	052	6.4	700-X	1200	
	052	11.0	IMR-4227	1150	
	065	13.5	IMR-4198	1300	
	065	13.9	RL-7	1280	
	069	10.6	SR-4759	1160	
308 Winchester	039	5.8	Bullseye	1100	
	039	5.1	Unique	950*	
	052	7.3	Unique	1200	accuracy load
	052	6.4	700-X	1150	
	052	11.0	IMR-4227	1080	
	065	13.5	IMR-4198	1250	accuracy load
	069	10.6	SR-4759	1100	
30-06 Springfield	039	5.8	Bullseye	1025*	
	052	7.8	Bullseye	1250	accuracy load
	052	7.3	Unique	1080	
	065	7.9	700-X	1200	
	065	8.8	Unique	1200	accuracy load
	069	14.5	IMR-4227	1250	
	069	13.9	IMR-4198	1180	accuracy load

*Powder charges marked with asterisk (*) are also suitable for use in the indicated caliber with the 32-cal. Alberts 32 S&W 100-gr. hollow-base wadcutter bullet #2901. Heavier charges must not be used with these HBWC bullets due to base deformation which might result in gun damage.

The 30-06 case still makes fine

Despite the fact that all are several decades old, the 8mm-06, 338-06, (or 338 OKH) and 35 Whelen are very practical big game cartridges—perhaps more so today than when they were designed—especially for hunting heavy game in timber.

WILDCAT MEDIUMS

by **JOHN BARSNESS**

To THE average hunter, the old rifle in the sporting goods store might have appeared junk: an '03 Springfield with half the blueing gone, somewhat sloppily fitted into a finishless, clublike stock with no buttplate. What I noticed (aside from an asking price of $120) was that the rifle's serial number indicated it was a nickel-steel action, the most desirable Springfield action, that the bolt handle and safety

him, and I cackled all the way out of the store.

Though I did some quicky gunsmithing on the rifle, enough to hunt—and take a Rocky Mountain whitetail—with it that fall since, amazingly, the somewhat pitted bore would put three 200-grain Noslers into an inch at 100 yards, I had bigger plans for the Springfield. That winter I sent the action off to be rebored to 338-06, the "modern" version of Elmer Keith's beloved 333 OKH, and began

6.5/06 really do anything a 25-06 or 270 won't? I don't think, however, such calibers as the 8mm Remington Magnum, the 338 Winchester and 340 Weatherby have really done away with the over-30 '06 wildcats.

Admittedly, the 333 OKH and its cousins, the 8mm-06 and 35 Whelen, were born back in the days when there were almost no "high velocity" cartridges above 30 caliber available to the American public. Prior to 1950 most larger-bore rounds were meant

Very few of the reloading headaches that wildcats can create are encountered when loading '06 wildcats. Simple necking up—which an RCBS special expansion die makes even easier—is the only case-forming operation needed.

Most 200-grain bullets in 30 caliber are designed for heavy game, such as the Nosler on the left. In larger calibers the 200-grain bullets are almost all designed for deer-sized game.

were already adapted for scope use and the action was drilled and tapped, apparently correctly, for scope-mount bases, and that the stock was eminently retrievable, an oversized "stockmaker's special" that someone hadn't had the smarts to cut down to size. There was too much powder fouling in the barrel to tell much about the bore's condition, but I didn't really care about that. I told the young clerk that if he threw in a Pachmayr recoil pad I'd give him a hundred bucks for the gun. He said it sounded all right to

serious retrieval work on the stock.

Conventional wisdom has it that the need for wildcats—and especially wildcats based on that most-altered case of all, the 30-06—are pretty needless with today's array of factory rounds. The intensive factory cartridge development since World War II has indeed just about done away with any need for a sub-30 '06 wildcat. With the 240 Weatherby (essentially a belted '06 case), 25-06, 270 and 280/7mm Express, the only reasonable caliber not available is 6.5mm; will a

for lever, pump and semi-auto rifles, and hence were of modest velocity and normally loaded with flat- or round-nosed bullets. In fact, there was only one really powerful over-30 factory round available in the 1930s and '40s: the 375 H&H Magnum, which had a reputation as an "elephant rifle," scaring away most of the customers. The 35 Whelen was born in the 1920s; the 333 and 8mm-06 in the 1940s; all ostensibly to create more power from a bolt-actioned rifle than the 30-06 yet not quite as scary as a 375. By today's

The necked-up '06 wildcats are especially practical for the timber hunter, who often has to shoot running or badly angling game. Heavy, moderate-velocity bullets also waste less meat at timber ranges than do high-velocity magnums.

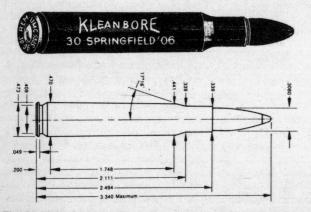

The 30-06 basic case offers medium-bore wildcatters the ideal base, and 30-06 rifles normally need only the bigger bore—no other change.

A wildcat rifle based on a factory 30-06 is very versatile: powerful enough for heavy game, but still short and light enough for practical use on woodland whitetails.

standards, all three are fairly modest rounds. Why then was I so overjoyed at the prospect of a 338-06 when I could pluck a 338 Winchester Magnum, ready-to-shoot, from the nearest store's gun rack?

There was one big reason, and a host of smaller ones. The biggie was that there is *still* a gap in factory cartridges available in this country, a gap in rounds above 30 and below 40 caliber, what the British so fondly call the "mediums." They've never been particularly popular in America, however, so we're limited to three basic types: the anemics in 32 Winchester Special, 32 and 35 Remingtons, and 375 Winchester; the brutes in 8mm Remington, 338 Winchester, 340 Weatherby, 358 Norma, 375 H&H, and 378 Weatherby Magnums; and the semi-obsolescents in 358 Winchester and 350 Remington, though both have revived somewhat lately due to their re-chambering in a few arms.

There is *no* factory offering available in America that drives 32 to 375 caliber bullets of good sectional density to moderate (2500-2800 fps) muzzle velocities. The 358 Winchester and 350 Remington *almost* qualify, but not quite. If a hunter wants a rifle of more power than the '06, he's limited essentially to the same 150-180 grain bullets driven by more powder (the 7mm and 300 Magnum), or bigger bullets *and* more powder (the above-30 magnums). There's nothing in a third possible category: the same powder capacity and heavier bullets.

What would be the advantages of such a rifle? For one, it could drive 200-250-grain bullets fast enough to be usable for most hunting, even in open country, and be built light and short enough for use in thick cover, and not kick like angry packhorses. All the factory-available magnums are 24"-barreled, fairly heavy guns, not particularly handy for the "black timber" much western big game is pursued in these days.

Timber hunting is the kind I find myself doing more and more of in Montana, because that's where the game is, and the timber is behind my yearning for a reasonably compact rifle with a bit more punch than the 270 or 30-06. I grew up, like millions of post-war hunters, a fan of both cartridges mainly due to my reading of Jack O'Connor, I eventually found them both merely "adequate," but not ideal, for timber hunting in the west. After finally going to the 200-grain Nosler in the 30-06, I found the Elmer Keith viewpoint better and better. Big, moderate-velocity bullets *do* pen-

etrate better, more consistently leave a blood trail—always desirable in thick cover — shoot up less meat—a blessing with today's beef prices—and if necessary, punch through bigger bones than do lighter, higher-velocity bullets, no matter how well-constructed. Now don't go screaming about the 270 and Noslers because I've used said rifle and bullet for years—still do, for most deer hunting and open-country elk—and use the 243 for pronghorn and some deer. I'm not a big-bore fanatic, just a practical hunter.

Another realization came about the same time. The necked-up '06 wildcats, once hampered by a lack of suitable bullets, are suddenly improved in that department. The 8mm-06, long handicapped by bullets designed for the 8x57's loaded-down factory velocities, was vastly aided by the new bullets designed for the 8mm Remington Magnum. The 338-06 has an enormous number of 200-300-grain projectiles waiting for it. Even the 35 Whelen was improved, with 200-grain Hornady and Remington spitzers putting a low end on the array of 250-grain bullets always available in 35. Most of the new bullets in all three calibers were getting spitzer or semi-spitzer points, improving their long-range capabilities, probably because hunters were finally shucking the myth of woods rifles (read "medium bores") always needing round-nosed bullets to "buck brush."

It seemed reasonable that all those new bullets could be driven efficiently by an '06-capacity case in 22" or shorter barrels, considering that the 270, 280/7mm Express and 30-06 are usually factory-chambered in 22"-barreled arms. In theory they'd be even more efficient in short barrels than the standard '06, because of the improved expansion ratio. So any factory 270 or 30-06 could be rebored or rebarreled to any of the calibers, leaving me with my ideal rifle. Recoil would be heavier, of course, but another myth I'd long ago dispelled for myself was the one of the 30-06 (or 270 or 7mm Magnum) being the stoutest round the "average hunter" can handle accurately. Some can, some can't—but most can if they shoot more than a box of shells a year.

One summer I spent a week in Glacier Park, doing an article on the "bear rangers" who keep track of the park's often-dangerous grizzlies. The rangers are all required to be adept, if not expert, with 44 Magnum revolvers, short and light 12-gauge riot guns, and scoped 300 magnums. Some

of them had never fired any sort of firearm before; I witnessed one of these doing a Dirty Harry imitation on the range one afternoon with his 44. He fired 200 full-power rounds that day, rapidly and accurately. His lone comment was: "You get used to it."

If he could handle that, I figured I could handle slightly more recoil than the '06.

Now came the moment of truth: actually obtaining a wildcat rifle. For years I'd heard all the standard horror stories concerning wildcats. They are hard to reload; shells aren't available if you forget or lose yours; wildcats are more expensive in the long run than factory rifles. In essence, wildcats are an all-round pain in the nether regions.

Most of these problems, I soon found, were non-problems. Since the decision was for an '06-based 'cat, the rifle itself would be no problem or major expense. One thing there is no dearth of in Montana come early fall is good, used '06s. Contrary to popular belief, the month or two before hunting season is a fine time to find a cheap hunting rifle, at least in the West. Everybody's trading in the old deer-whanger—a bolt-actioned 30-06, at least 50% of the time—for a shiny magnum. They're everywhere, at reasonable prices. That's a particular advantage of a bored-up '06 wildcat; the aspiring medium-bore hunter has anything but a lever action to use in conversion, from the bolt (even left-handed), to the pump, semi-auto and single shot.

As for not being able to buy factory ammo—well, every real gun nut deserves at least one wildcat in his life, and I realized I'd been hunting with handloads for 15 years and never forgotten or misplaced my custom shells. I reflected a bit more, after finding an almost-new 350 Remington Magnum Model 700 in a sporting goods store, as close a factory offering as I could imagine to my dream rifle, for the low, low price of $375, and realized I wouldn't be any more apt to find a spare box of 350 shells in a backwoods store than some 35 Whelens. So much for the expense and factory-availability angle.

So I did it. The only thing left was to decide what caliber.

The 8mm-06 seemed a very good choice for all-round hunting; a 150-grain Sierra (ballistic coefficient .400) at 3100 fps would do for long-range pronghorn and deer hunting; a 220-grain Remington Core-Lokt or Hornady Interlock at 2600 would serve on bigger game. There was even the 125-grain Hornady for varmints, or the 250-grain Barnes for black timber elk. But I had my 270 for plains hunting, and there isn't any better caliber going for that purpose; my 243 takes care of jackrabbit shooting; and the 250-grain Barnes can also be loaded in the standard '06. The 8mm-06, I concluded, would perhaps be the perfect gun for the one-rifle wildcatter—have you seen any lately?

The 35 Whelen was very attractive, with the most tradition behind it, and a good array of heavier bullets, especially 250-grain spitzers, which could be driven to 2500 fps for a fairly flat-shooting heavy bullet load. There were also the 200-grain Hornady and Remington spitzers and Barnes semi-spitzer for flat, lighter long-range loads; these can be driven at around 2800 fps. I knew the 250-grain Remington and Hornady were tough, reliable big game bullets, and the 250, 275 and 300-grain Bitterroots (if available) would work on anything short of a freight train. I also briefly considered the 375 Whelen, or 375-06, but rejected it because the lightest bullet available is the 235-grain; I was looking for a better light-end load. The 375 offers bullets up to 350 grain, however, so anyone really mad about excess avoirdupois might consider one.

Finally, the decision came down to bullet selection, especially Noslers. I believe there are bullets as tough as the Nosler, and as accurate, and as available, but none that are all three. The 338 is the only caliber of the three '06 wildcats I seriously considered in which the nonpareil Nosler is made. The two weights offered, a 210-grain spitzer and 250-grain round-nose (actually a semi-spitzer, with a ballistic coefficient of .364) seemed about ideal for the two loads I had in mind: a reasonably flat-shooting load for open country where the 210 at 2700 fps would do nicely and a heavy, close-range load that could still reach out a bit and the 250-grain at 2500 fps, when sighted 3″ high at 100 yards, is about 10″ low at 300, an easy top-of-the-shoulder hold on elk and mule deer. There were also the 250-grain Hornady solid, in case I ever wanted to run a Cape buffalo out of my corn patch and the super-streamlined 250-grain Sierra boattail spitzer. The bullet selection in 338 isn't any greater than in 8mm, but many of the .323″ bullets are designed for the 8x57, and the heavy bullet selection is much better in 338 than either 8mm or 35. That was the key, though a hunter couldn't go seriously wrong with any one of the three.

Total cost tallied up this way: 30-06 Springfield—$100; reboring—$55;

The hunter contemplating an '06-based wildcat has an enormous choice of rifles and actions available—even the left-handed bolt, such as this Remington 700. The lever action is the only type not currently available in 30-06.

Timney trigger—$20. I did all the stock work and reblueing myself, so add a little for finishing materials and sling-swivel bases, say ten bucks. The loading dies from RCBS run $38, since they aren't a standard catalogued item. That's $15.50 more than a set of 338 Winchester dies, and $8.50 more than a set of 8mm-06 or 35 Whelen dies, which are standard items in the RCBS wildcat line.

I also ordered an additional tapered expansion die, which runs $18; this opens up case mouths and isn't absolutely necessary, as the expander ball does the same trick, but it's a lot easier on brass. I'd really recommend it for the 35 Whelen. These were all early 1980 prices; things, naturally, have probably gone up by now. Even adding the additional $33.50 paid for the necessary loading dies, however, the whole shebang only ran $218.50 a pretty low price for a medium-bore dream rifle in today's economy. Complete with K3 Weaver in Leupold bridge mounts, sling, and magazine full of 210 Nosler handloads, the Springfield weighs slightly more than 8½ pounds.

What more can I say? Wildcatting the 30-06 for the '80's has been definitely worthwhile. Now I just have to find one of those darned elk. •

For the average American hunter feeling a need for more power than the 30-06 (center) the usual choice has been to go to a cartridge with more powder capacity and using the same 150-180-gr. bullet weight range, such as the 7mm Remington and 308 Norma Magnums (left). A more practical solution for some hunting is the same powder capacity with more bullet, as provided by the 338-06 and 35 Whelen (right).

An advantage the '06's larger offspring have over the parent cartridge is heavier spitzer or semi-spitzer bullets of good ballistic coefficient. The 200-gr. 308 bullet (left) is the heaviest bullet normally given a point in that caliber, while the 35 offers the 250-gr. spitzer (center) and the 338 the 275-gr. semi-spitzer (right).

Notes On The Loads

There was an incredible dearth of information for bullets lighter than 250 grains in the 338; what I have here are loads worked up with the aid of a Powley computer, most chronographed over a Custom Chronograph M500 and its M600 Light Screens. Safe working pressure was arrived at by the fairly standard method of primer pocket tightness; the pockets stayed tight with these loads for as long as I kept re-stuffing the brass, which was Remington 06, used with CCI 200 primers. By the way, if anybody wants to be really oddball and traditional (not always mutually exclusive) Colorado Custom Bullets markets the Barnes line in 333 caliber, so an honest-to-God 333 OKH is still theoretically possible. I don't know who'd rebore to that caliber, however, and even Elmer Keith thinks the 338 version is better.

SUGGESTED LOADS
(all maximum unless otherwise noted)

Bullet/ Weight (grs.)	Maker, style	Load	Velocity (fps)	Barrel length (in.)	Load Source
338-06/ 200	Barnes SS Bitterroot SS Herter RN Hornady Spire Speer SZ	60-4320	2737	22	Author
210	Nosler SZ	**59-4320	2695	22	Author
225	Bitterroot SS	**56-4320	2613	22	Author
250	Barnes SS	**57-4064	2635	—	Ackley* (also attributed to Elmer Keith)
	Bitterroot SS Hornady RN, Solid Nosler RN Sierra SZBT Speer Grand Slam SZ	**54.5-4320	2470	22	Author

RN—Round Nose   **SS**—Semi-spitzer   **SZ**—Spitzer   **SZBT**—Spitzer boattail
* P. O. Ackley's *Handbook for Shooters and Reloaders,* and correspondence with Elmer Keith.
**Maximum Loads—start 10 percent *below* the loads listed and work up a tenth of a grain at a time.

Anybody wishing to reload Berdan primed cartridge cases is faced with removing the spent primers. Various methods of removal have been tried over the years and several tools have been produced commercially. These various methods are slow and risk damaging the anvil of the case, and if the anvil of a Berdan case is deformed in any way the newly loaded round may not fire. In addition, these commercial tools are unsatisfactory for use on military cases where the primers have been crimped into the primer pockets.

Hydraulic decapping does not risk damage to the anvil and over the years I have used this method on 303 and 7.62 cases. The idea is to screw the body of a full-length sizing die into a reloading press. Put a lubricated case fully into the die and fill it with water through the open top of the die. A steel rod that has been turned and polished to be a neat fit in the mouth of the sized case is inserted into the neck of the case and struck smartly with a hammer.

The first problem with this method is getting a good fit between the punch and the neck of the case if the thickness of the neck walls varies much in the batches of cases you get. The second problem is the water. When the primer comes out so does the water and you, your loading bench and most things round about will get soaked.

Experimenting with hydraulic decapping has led me to develop a system which allows the decapping of crimped-in Berdan primers at a rate of 600 per hour without any risk of damage to any part of the case. The key to the system is to enclose the case in a cylinder and apply the hydraulic pressure both to the inside and outside of the case, thus avoiding expanding the case as happens when pressure is created only inside the case. The plunger is made to be a good fit in the cylinder and thus avoids the problem of fit between the plunger and case which, as we have seen, is one of the drawbacks of decapping in a full-length sizing die.

The two accompanying drawings should convey the idea well enough to enable it to be built in a few hours. Exact dimensions have not been included on the drawings as most measurements are not critical. Notes on the drawings point out important dimensions and the following explanation will cover critical points.

Weight is a virtue to aid stability in use. The base should be mild steel plate an inch to two inches thick and

DECAP BERDAN CASES QUICKLY

by GRAHAM C. HENRY

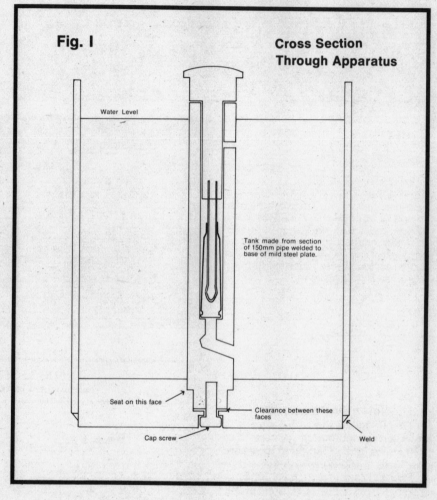

Fig. I

Cross Section Through Apparatus

Water Level

Tank made from section of 150mm pipe welded to base of mild steel plate.

Seat on this face

Clearance between these faces

Cap screw

Weld

should be welded to a section of 6-inch steel pipe. Before welding the tank together the base should be machined to accept the cylinder and counter bored for a capscrew.

The cylinder should be made from a suitable tool steel, not mild steel. The bottom end should be carefully machined for a snug fit in the base and it should be seated on the outer diameter for strength. Clearance should be left between the end of the cylinder and the bottom of the hole in the base to ensure a good seat on the outer diameter (see drawing).

The bore of the cylinder should be a reamed hole of ½-inch or 13mm depending on the availability of material for the plunger. If the bore is made larger than the case, the case may move laterally and may not always be correctly centered over the 7mm (5/16-in.) hole under the primer. This 7mm hole is required to leave the primer and the crimped area of the base of the case unsupported against the water pressure. The bottom of the bore hole must be flat to prevent loss of pressure between itself and the base of the case. This is the most critical point to the functioning of the apparatus.

The plunger must be made from tool steel and hardened and ground to be a sliding fit in the reamed bore of the cylinder. The best idea is to use a nitrided ejector pin and so avoid most of the work involved in making the plunger. These pins are used by tool and die makers and are available from engineering suppliers. The collar to stop the downward travel of the plunger must stop it just short of the mouth of the case being processed.

very solid support. Any spring or resilience in the support will cushion the force applied. Fill the tank with water to the level indicated and add a small amount of liquid detergent. This lessens the surface tension of the water and enables it to fill the case more quickly. If this is not done some air bubbles may stay in the case after it has been dropped down the bore and the presence of any air at all will prevent the build up of enough pressure to expel the primer. With a case down the

If many cases are to be processed two ancillary pieces of equipment are needed. You can prefill cases in a square plastic container fitted with a sheet of metal an inch off the bottom. This sheet should have holes drilled through it in the pattern of a hand-loader's loading block. Cases can then be stood upright in the container and the container filled with water. With two such containers a helper can keep the operator going with a constant supply of cases.

The second aid to speedy operation is a strip of heavy gauge sheet metal in which is cut a slot about 9 to 10mm wide and 50mm deep. This piece of sheet metal is clamped on the flat above an empty container with the slot toward the operator. When the plunger is withdrawn from the apparatus with the decapped case hanging from the extractor, pass the extractor into the slot and then lift vertically. The shoulder of the case will not be able to pass up through the slot and the case will fall off the extractor and into the container below. With the plunger still held in the hand, the extractor can now be pushed into the neck of the next case in the supply container alongside and this case, already full of water, can be lifted clear and lowered into the cylinder of the decapper. In this way the hammer and the plunger need not be put down between operations and a rate of six hundred cases an hour can be sustained.

Before the deprimed cases can be reloaded the crimp around the primer pocket must be removed. A cutting tool to be run in a drill press can be made. I prefer to swage the edge of the primer pockets. A swage can be made to fit in a loading press instead of the shell holder. To support the case during swaging, a rod should be made which will thread into a bullet seating die in place of the seating punch. The body of the rod should be just small enough to pass through the neck of the case and the lower end of the rod should be formed to provide good support to the inside of the head of the case. With the die body locked in the press the support rod can be screwed down until the swage forms the edge of the primer pocket to the desired radius. Berdan primers are not the same diameter as Boxer primers and special tools must be made. These tools must be counterbored to clear the anvil in the case.

Mark the heads of the cases which have been processed as once the crimp has been removed, decapping after subsequent firings is much easier. ●

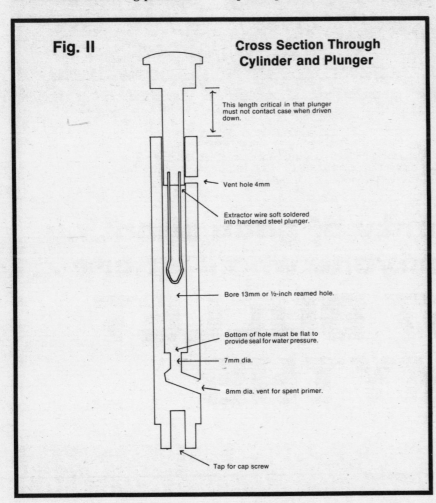

Fig. II

Cross Section Through Cylinder and Plunger

This length critical in that plunger must not contact case when driven down.

Vent hole 4mm

Extractor wire soft soldered into hardened steel plunger.

Bore 13mm or ½-inch reamed hole.

Bottom of hole must be flat to provide seal for water pressure.

7mm dia.

8mm dia. vent for spent primer.

Tap for cap screw

The key to the speedy operation of the apparatus is the extractor of brass or stainless wire which is bent to shape and soldered into the end of the plunger. Use soft solder as the heat required will not affect the heat treatment of the plunger. The extractor wire must be of a shape such as to pass easily through the neck of the case and then spring back enough inside so as to lift the case out when the plunger is withdrawn.

There are several points important to the effective operation of the tool. Firstly it must be placed firmly on a

bore, insert the plunger and slide it down until it just blocks off the vent hole in the side of the cylinder. The plunger needs to be this far into the cylinder to ensure alignment and support. With the plunger so positioned strike it squarely and sharply with a two to three-pound hammer. With a little practice the correct amount of force will be found and even heavily crimped primers will be expelled with one blow. Any problems at this point will be caused by entrapped air, too light a hammer or inadequate support for the tool.

by MICHAEL VENTURINO

Three jacketed bullets at left are Hornady 357, 158 JHP; Speer 9mm, 125 JSP; and Sierra 44, 180 JHC. Cast bullets on right are 357, 150 HP; 9mm, 121 RN; and 44, 185 SWC. The cast bullets are just as useful as the jacketed, and cheaper.

There's plenty of good shooting available to anyone who'll ignore . . .
CAST BULLET MYTHS

Round-nose cast bullets make excellent small game bullets. These range in caliber from 32-20 to 45 Colt. From left, they are Lyman Nos. 311257, 358242, 410426, 429383, 452374, and 454190.

BROWSING IN gun stores is one of my favorite rainy day pastimes and recently, while doing that, I met another handloader. In our ensuing conversation he revealed that he loads for about a dozen different calibers.

When I asked what style bullet moulds he uses, he said, "None. All the calibers I load need jacketed bullets so I just buy them."

I asked what calibers *need* jacketed bullets?

"Oh," he replied, "I load for the 357 Magnum, 41 Magnum, 44 Magnum, 45 Colt, 30 Carbine, and 30-30 among others.

Maybe I should have been flabbergasted at that but I wasn't. I have heard such things too many times before.

tremely simple to use. Bullet alloys may be blended for better results in some instances but often a simple and easily obtained alloy such as wheelweights will do as well. Linotype is also an excellent bullet alloy but is getting very difficult to find. I have, at this writing, about 1,000 pounds of wheelweight alloy and only one 22-pound bar of linotype.

Bullet casting tools are uncomplicated. All that is required is a pot to melt the alloy in, a lead dipper, bullet mould, and a means for lubing and sizing the new bullets.

Lubricating and sizing can be done by the Kake Kutter and hand-sizing die method or with the vastly faster and less messy bench-mounted machine. Either way, you squeeze the raw bullet through a proper diameter

and set the scale for .5 grain under that for handguns and .025 gr. for rifle bullets.

With bullets from Lyman mould No. 429421 cast of linotype, the heaviest bullets from my mould do not go over 240.0 grains. Therefore, I set the scale for 239.5 grains and use any which weigh that or more. Bullets that scale less are set aside for plinking.

Cast bullets are often said to be inaccurate. I say that's rubbish. I have worked with many handguns using a Lee Pistol Machine Rest as a testing device, and have been amazed at the accuracy they will give with cast bullets.

The two most recent sixguns I have tested are a Smith & Wesson Model 29 in 44 Magnum and a Smith & Wesson Model 27 in 357 Magnum. Both revol-

Line-up of semi-wadcutters that are good for hunting, from 358 to 454: From left—RCBS 38-150 KT, Lyman No. 348429, Ohaus No. 41-210 K, Lyman Nos. 410459, 429360, 429421, 452460, 452423, and 454424.

Probably more misconceptions are spread about cast bullets than any other facet of the handloading game. They are often said to be: (1) hard to make; (2) inaccurate; (3) barrel leaders; (4) poor for hunting; and, (5) most disgusting of all, obsolete.

These things simply are not so.

As one who has cast over 100,000 bullets in the past 10 years and who owns 35 bullet moulds, you might say I go for cast bullets in a big way, and know something about these misconceptions, at least.

Cast bullets are not hard to make. They need not be of sophisticated alloy, and the tools required are ex-

sizing die, and then get lube into the grooves provided.

As for the actual pouring, anyone who can hold a lead dipper steady enough to pour a quantity of molten lead into a bullet mould can turn out good bullets. As long as the alloy fills out all corners of the mould and the sprue is not cut before the alloy hardens sufficiently, the bullet is usually good.

The bullets should be inspected. For accuracy, some people weigh each bullet. Mostly I feel this isn't necessary, but occasionally do it when striving solely for accuracy. I weigh a few bullets to find the heaviest any will go,

vers have 5-inch barrels. I have been searching for a good target load to put in those long 357 Magnum cases, and I found it. My last 18 five-shot groups at 25 yards using 4.0 grains of Bullseye and semiwadcutters cast of wheelweight alloy in RCBS mould 38-150 KT averaged 1.21 inches. In the Model 29, a charge of 21.0 grains of 2400, and a gas check wheelweight bullet from Lyman mould No. 429244 averaged 1.32 for 4 five-shot groups at 1320 fps. Changing the bullet to Lyman No. 429421 gave a 4 five-shot group average of 2.06 inches. That is still very respectable accuracy.

With rifles, cast bullet accuracy is

Author bench tests cast bullet loads in Model 54 Winchester in 257 Roberts, and lots more calibers.

more difficult to obtain but is by no means impossible. Cast bullets may never take the place of jacketed bullets in modern, high velocity rifles but they do have a place of their own.

I use cast bullets regularly in a 257 Roberts Model 54 Winchester (to save wear on an already old barrel) and a Remington Model 700 30-06 (using light loads to save some wear on my rapidly aging shoulder). For gopher shooting, a 90-grain cast bullet (Lyman No. 257312) and 5.0 grains of Unique in the 257 Roberts or 112-grain cast slug (Lyman No. 311316) and 8.0 grains of Unique in the 30-06 give wonderful accuracy at 25 yards. For longer ranges out to 100 yards, I change to 2400 and use 14.0 grains in the 257 and 21.0 grains in the 30-06.

With the 25 yard loads both rifles group one-half inch or less, and the more powerful 100 yard loads usually go into 1½ inches. The lighter loads are also great for grouse shooting when out for big game as the noise levels are very low, about on a par with a 22 Long Rifle.

Lead alloy bullets are often accused of being terrible barrel leaders, and at times this is a correct accusation. Cast bullets can lead barrels badly and, of course, jacketed bullets never do.

Bullets cast hard enough for the velocity they will be used at and lubricated with a modern lube such as the various Alox/beeswax blends give minimum leading if they give it at all. Gas checks can sometimes help stop leading, and should always be used on bullets designed for them to obtain best accuracy.

Some of my favorite 44 Magnum loads do lead very slightly but it

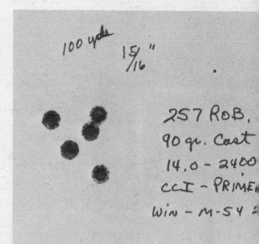

This 100-yard group with the Model 54 257 Roberts and cast loads shows top results.

These cast rifle bullets will give excellent results with a little experimentation. From left, they are Lyman Nos. 257312, 287221, 311316, 311291, 31141, 311284, 457124, and 457406.

Lyman mould 358156 HP shown with hollow point pin. Note size of hollow point in bullet. This bullet with the right alloy will expand.

From left, Sierra 30, 165-grain boattail; Lyman No. 31141, 170-grain flat nose; Sierra 25, 100-grain spitzer; and Lyman 25-caliber No. 257312, 90-grain flat nose—all are useful rifle bullets.

A wide assortment of shapes and weights have been worked out in cast bullet designs over the years. One or the other will meet most shooting needs at short ranges.

brushes out with a dry bristle brush. I have fired up to 50 rounds in either of my Smith & Wesson 44s in the Lee Rest with the last five shots giving as good accuracy as the first five. So it seems the slight leading I get with those loads hurts nothing. With most of my loads I get no leading at all.

Cast bullets are often said to be poor for hunting because they will not expand if cast hard enough to resist leading.

This is basically true.

However, it is debatable if expansion is needed if a semi-wadcutter, especially a 44 or 45 is used. Because of their sharp shoulders, flat noses, and large diameters these handgun bullets are good killers without expansion.

If penetration is needed as when hunting elk or bear, the hard cast semi-wadcutters may be in a class of their own. It takes a lot to expand a bullet cast of linotype.

Contrary to their reputations, round nose, cast bullets are not all that worthless for hunting. They do have their place when hunting small game such as rabbits or grouse because they don't tear up as much meat. Lyman bullet No. 429383 is a round nose 44 bullet of about 245 grains depending on alloy. Over 5.0 grains of Bullseye in the 44 Magnum it is very accurate and deadly on small game. Velocity is about 725 fps from my five-inch Smith & Wesson.

If a shooter insists on expansion from cast bullets, the gas-checked, hollow-point designs can be used. I have used Lyman No. 358156 H.P. with good results, but never on large animals.

As for the charge they are obsolete, the dictionary gives this definition—"Gone into disuse; disused; neglected; out of fashion; imperfectly developed, or abortive."

If the way the number of bullet mould manufacturers has grown in recent years is indicative of the growing popularity of bullet casting, then certainly the cast bullet is not obsolete. As for "imperfectly developed," then what bullet is perfect? And, if cast bullets will do everything jacketed bullets will do and do it cheaper, who can call them obsolete and jacketed bullets modern?

"Out of fashion" is the only part of the above definition by which anyone can term cast bullets obsolete. Lightweight jacketed handgun bullets are the current vogue.

What is in fashion has never interested me. I wear boots, jeans, and drive a pick-up truck. ●

The author's Number One, in 375 H&H, dropped this nine pointer on a hunt in Pennsylvania's McKean County during the 1980 season

Use The 375 H&H Magnum On Whitetails?

Sure. With handloads, you can make it do the job without overkill.

by **JOSEPH S. KRIEGER**

IT WAS MY third visit to the small gun shop in ten days and the rifle laying there on the green velvet pad was already mine though the salesclerk seemed unsure. With two Ruger single shots in my gun rack and a Mark X 375 barreled action just waiting to be stocked in my basement shop, there was little need for this rifle. But there was also hand checkering on figured, oiled walnut fitted to polished blue metal. When the owner cut the price $50 I no longer had any choice. In 375 H&H, the Ruger Number One represents an even better value than the shooter has come to expect. One need only compare the prices of other rifles available in that caliber to see that:

Ruger Number 1, 375 $405.00
Remington 700 Safari, 375 $649.95
Winchester 70, 375 $652.00
Whitworth Express, 375 $560.00
Sako Standard
  Sporter, 375 $692.00

(suggested retail prices from the 1981 GUN DIGEST, 36th ed.)

Even so, friends asked, ". . . but what will you do with it now?"

A scheduled moose hunt was more than a year away, and trips to British Columbia and Alberta were only notes on a yellow pad, unless . . . why not whitetails?

A dim November sky found me sitting quietly in a stand of pines near Coryville, Pennsylvania, with the Ruger across my legs. My stand overlooked a narrow valley with thick overgrown orchards on the hillside below me and the hillside across the valley. Between the orchards ran a noisy brook strong with the run-off from melting snow. Gray squirrels scampered around my stand as the sun climbed higher through gray clouds. I held the urge to follow the grays' quick movement in check, I did not want to give away my position to any whitetails that might be moving about in either orchard.

Less than an hour after sunrise the buck appeared—he was just there. I never saw any movement until he crossed a wide opening in the orchard across the valley. The nine-pointer had probably been bedded down when I first came to my stand and the wet muffled any sound I made.

For a few minutes I watched the animal move among the apple trees, nipping at the underbrush and the apples that littered the ground. Turning the variable scope up to 5x, I searched the thicket for other movement. More

minutes passed and I saw nothing. Moving back to the buck, I slid the tang safety forward and steadied my right hand and the forearm of the Ruger over my knee. The shot, accurate as expected, caught the buck squarely in the heart. For an instant he tried to shake off the effects of the bullet, then he went down. He never took a step after the shot.

A spectator watching the situation develop that warm November morning might have thought it quite easy to get a buck. But that spectator would fail to realize the planning and the work that went into the preparations for the hunt. The load work-ups and the prehunt scouting in that one area amounted to more time than most hunters spend afield, so the hunt wasn't all that easy.

The first range session with the 375 showed that factory ammunition was all too powerful for use on an animal as fragile as a whitetail. The majority of the 80 bullets fired penetrated 18 to 24 inches into the hard dirt backstop. These bullets could hardly be expected to expand in the chest cavity of a whitetail. This was true for both Winchester 300-grain Silver Tips, and Remington 270-grain soft points.

Lead bullets *seemed* the most promising alternative to factory loads. At 1700 to 2000 fps, these bullets equal the energy of a number of muzzleloaders I've used for whitetails.

I hoped careful handloading would provide a suitable load, give the accuracy required and reduce the recoil, so I got a Lyman #375248 mould.

After casting, Hodgdon Alox lube was applied to the bullets using the melt-and-pour technique. When the lube cooled, the bullets were cut from the cake using the Lee cutter provided in the kit. Since the #375248 required no gas check, the bullets were forced through a Lee sizer die nose first.

The cast bullet results on paper were a disaster. A number of shots missed the 2' by 4' cardboard backing completely. I used two alloys but both performed badly.

A second mold, a Lyman #375449, was purchased and I went back to my workshop to try again. This mold dropped bullets which weighed 264 grains and used gas checks. Bullets from both molds were again segregated by weight and sized using the Lee kit. The #375449 bullet was forced through the Lee die base first. This crimped the gas check onto the bullet base. I hoped the use of this bullet with the gas check would give better accuracy than the earlier results.

Twelve loads were assembled, six

using Bullet Master lube and six with Alox. The results of this second range session were no better than the first. Shots were scattered over the paper. The rifle showed no liking for either bullet or lube used during that test firing. At that point I'd had almost enough. I could have tried another mould, but the desire to continue burning my hands and arms in an attempt to get lead bullets to work in the Ruger was diminishing.

In all fairness, I should add that I used only one bullet diameter in my tests. Another diameter sizing die might bring accuracy to these loads, but I chose to look elsewhere for a suitable load after a friend purchased a Marlin 336 in Winchester's 375 Big Bore. Being a handloader, John soon had a supply of the two lightweight bullets available in 375 on hand. These, I thought, may offer an easy way out for me.

Hornady's 220-grain flat-point was purposely designed for the Big Bore carbine and for North American big game. Speer's 235-grain semi-spitzer was made for the higher velocities that come with the magnum case. The trick was now to load down the big rifle using these two bullets and still maintain accuracy.

In most of the manuals checked, velocities approached 3000 fps with the 235-grain Speer. Only a few loads fell at or near 2500 fps, the velocity I considered maximum for whitetails, and all these used slow burning powder, slower than IMR 4350. H4831 and H450 filled the big case to the neck and eliminated unwanted air space.

The actual loading process for this cartridge is no more difficult than for any other for the experienced or well-read handloader. After loading the 243 Winchester, and the 22/250 Remington for more than ten years, however, the 80 to 90 grain powder charges in the pan of the old Herter's powder scale had me double and triple-checking both manual and scale more than once. You'll never have to worry about powder aging or deteriorating with a 375 H&H in your rack. Full cans just seem to vanish when the rifle is fired often.

As with *all* belted cases, the handloader should not thread the full-length sizing die down to the shell holder. Adjustment should be made to allow the rifle action to close snugly against the case. Too much sizing overworks the brass and can lead to case separation, a situation that could be disastrous in the field.

Too little sizing is also a problem when loading for a Ruger Number

The 375 H&H is a handful. Here the shooter is about to chamber a 300-grain Sierra boattail handload. Recoil is something the shooter can learn to accept with adequate practice.

The 375 H&H case is massive. It just does fit into the stroke of the Lyman Spartan press that did all the work keeping the big rifle booming. Lyman AA dies were also used.

I turned to Hornady's 220-grain flat-point after getting poor accuracy with lead slugs. Sierra's 300-grain boattail gave the very best in accuracy, but the Hornady was not that far behind. The Hornady was a much better choice for lighter game. In the foreground are Lyman #375248 bullets, which proved inaccurate in my rifle.

One. It is an extremely strong action, but does not have the camming power of a bolt action. Remove the stem and the expander ball from the sizing die if you want to adjust the sizing. Start with a fired and lubed case, bring down the die a little at a time and try the case in the gun until the breech block clears the head of the case. A little drag as the breechblock and lever are locked in place is a sure sign the adjustment is correct.

Lyman dies and a Spartan press were used to assemble all the rounds loaded for the Ruger. With the bullets seated, the cartridges had to be tilted to retrieve them from the press. In spite of the close quarters, the press performed perfectly. The only other problem I had was a sharp shoulder on the sizing die that scraped a ring of brass from the lower body of the fired cases when the case was sized. Additional lube did little to stop the scraping. Finally, I put a gentle radius on that shoulder and the scraping ceased.

The 375 has an affinity with accuracy, according to reports, and the tradition continued with my Ruger and jacketed bullets. Of the 18 loads fired and chronographed, only two failed to cut two inches at 110 yards with three-shot groups. The best loads measured an average 1.75″. A second firing of the top four loads using five-shot groups gave equal accuracy.

The Hornady bullet was the more accurate of the two when loaded with the slower powders. It wasn't until I loaded IMR 4064 and IMR 4895 under the Speer semi-spitzer, and the velocity exceeded 2500 fps that it gave accuracy equal to the Hornady. With 80 grains of H4831, the Speer bullet had a flyer in almost every group I fired. There were also signs of yaw on the targets, (unround holes in the paper), though not a single keyhole was had with the 25 rounds fired.

I seated bullets to miss the rifling by ¹/₁₆″. I've always found this to allow for all the accuracy the bullet can give. With the Ruger, over-all length is not restricted by a magazine, therefore the entire internal capacity is usable. If an individual were looking for maximum velocity and still wanted to maintain proper functioning, I believe the Ruger Number One to be the answer. This was not a consideration when loading the lightweight bullets for whitetails, but when teamed up with a Sierra 300-grain boattail or a Speer 285-grain Grand Slam, the rifle will literally stop anything that walks, and give unexpected accuracy with an assortment of loads.

I finally came to the conclusion that the Hornady 220-grain flat-point was the bullet to use for whitetails in the fall. It proved to be the most accurate of the two used at the velocity needed, though on deer-size game both bullets would work equally well. The Hornady performed very well at the lower velocities and I felt the necessary expansion would come without the bullet being overly destructive.

All my expectations were fulfilled that dreary November morning. Both

the rifle and bullet did a superb job. Well, honestly, my 35 Remington or one of my slug-shooting shotguns could have performed as well over the 155 yards, but there was something special about that morning. As I dragged the buck out of the woods with the Ruger slung over my shoulder, I almost expected to see a Land Rover parked on a dusty road, but there was my Plymouth sitting in the snow as I came over the last hill. ●

375 Holland & Holland Magnum
Loads For Smaller North American Game

	Bullet/Wgt./Type	Powder/grs.	Velocity** (fps)
1.	Hornady 220 Flat-Point	H4831/80.0	2491
2.	Hornady 220 Flat-Point	H450/82.2	2510
3.	Speer 235 Semi-Spitzer	IMR4895/66.4	2568
4.	Speer 235 Semi-Spitzer	IMR4064/67.5	2546
5.*	Sierra 300 Spitzer-Boattail	MR3100/76.0	2428
6.*	Sierra 300 Spitzer-Boattail	MR3100/78.0	2472
7.*	Sierra 300 Spitzer-Boattail	MR3100/79.0	2506

Primer used **CCI 250.**
*Loads given for comparison; bullet construction too heavy for smaller big game.
**Velocity measured 10 feet from the muzzle, using an Oehler Model 12 and Skyscreens. Velocity average of not less than 16 rounds per load.
Temperature at the time of firing: 30°F.

Energy Comparison

	Caliber	Bullet/grs.	Velocity (fps)	Energy[1]	Momentum[2]
1.	375 H&H	Speer/235	2550	3394	86
2.	375 H&H	Hornady/220	2500	3054	79
3.	35 Remington	Hornady/200	2000	1777	57
4.	12-gauge	Brenneke/468	1570	2562	105
5.	30-06	Sp. Pt./150	2850	2706	61
6.	270 Winchester	Sp. Pt./130	3000	2599	56

[1]—Energy = (weight × velocity^2) ÷ 450240.
[2]—Momentum = (weight × velocity) ÷ 7000.

Lead Bullet Loads: 375 H&H

	Bullet	Powder/grs.	Velocity* (fps)
1.	Lyman #375248	IMR3031/47.0	2037
2.	Lyman #375248	IMR4895/50.0	2075
3.	Lyman #375248	SR4756/25.0	1780
4.	Lyman #375248	Unique/17.5	1525
5.	Lyman #375296	IMR3031/40.0	1750
6.	Lyman #375296	IMR3031/44.0	1860
7.	Lyman #375296	IMR4895/48.0	1920

Primer used **Remington 9½**
*Velocity measured 10 feet from the muzzle, using an Oehler Model 12 and Skyscreens.
Temperature at time of firing: 45°F.

UPGRADING The 30-30

Woefully retarded as ready rolled, no cartridge responds more readily to the reload route than the all-time renegade favorite 30-30.

THE GREATEST rewards resulting from reloading are improved performance and a four-for-one cost saving. It is ironic coincidence that the cartridge most in need of the reload benefit is also the most widely used sporting, general utility and Social Security round fondly known as the 30-30 by millions of users.

The 30-30 is not widely reloaded because it is the cartridge choice of the average low profile sport, who generally is not the "gun club gunny" but the once-a-year deer hunter and year-round king of his castle. He is the essence of that silent majority sportsman and salt-of-the-earth American consumer, worker, citizen.

With sky-high costs now a factor of increasing concern to the regular 30-30 man and woman along with a desire by many to become more proficient, by way of more shooting, the 30-30 reloader has come on strong of late. There's a good reason.

The usual 30-30 reload manual data excludes the spitzer high performance bullets because the pointed spitzer bullet in contact with the primer of the cartridge ahead of it in a tubular magazine might fire that cartridge due to inertia from recoil. Those of us who

Frank Marshall testing. Note method of holding rifle simulates the hold as in hunting. This can be significant.

enjoy reload upgrade benefits of such bullets in our 30-30 bolt, over-under combo, drillings and single-shot rifles, realize a fantastic ballistic advantage of 100% energy increase at 200 yards along with 100% improvement in the hittability factor due to a lowered trajectory curve along with the considerable accuracy improvement.

In total gain, the use of a modern spitzer boattail ball approximating normal weight and velocity of 30-30 loads actually results in a 109% improved cartridge to 300 yards. In perspective, this simple expedient makes the 30-30 better to 300 yards than the normal flat-point load to 150 yards. All the usually voiced objection is eliminated with none of its many good points forfeit; i.e. lightweight rifles, low recoil, etc.

Many lever gun reloaders avail themselves this benefit by simply loading *one* in the magazine and one chambered for a two-shot sporting rifle which eliminates the primer contact hazard.

Doing it this way requires particular attention to seating depth in order that the one in the magazine will function up through the action. It is also advised to lower the powder charge two to three grains because of that increased seating depth. Ballistics advantage is so evident that lower velocity of approximately 100 fps (feet per second) at muzzle is of no concern.

I found I could load to lower pressure with this high-coefficient ball concept with no noticeable forfeit of performance but with a highly favorable increase in case life, a factor of importance in lever type rifles.

A bullet is available today, very accurate, and not as critical in the seating depth for action clearance as a true spitzer—the 165-gr. Sierra hollow point boattail acclaimed as a close contender to the famous 168-gr. Match bullet. Due to the considerably shorter ogive nose section of this hollow point *hunting* bullet it is ideally suited to

as the magazine was depleted. The most consistent practical performance resulted from the one-chambered, one-in-magazine idea, regardless of bullet used. The idea presents a very satisfactory upgrade in these rifles from that standpoint alone.

Seldom does flushed game allow two shots. I have personally never fired more than two shots at one such target in a half century of ridge prowling.

In order to better evaluate the advantage of the Sierra 165 HPBT ball over the normal 170-gr. flat point bullet and also to shoot factory loads as a standard of performance, I bought a second hand, as new, Model 340 Savage bolt action. It has a quick detachable three-shot box magazine.

This rifle, I soon learned at the bench, was conspicuous by its ability to shoot the common 30-30 cartridge to that load's fine inherent capability. The upgraded process was assisted by a low and central-mounted 3x scope.

I verified, to 300 yards, the ballistics book figures when high-coefficient bullets are substituted for flat or round nosed bullets at *equal* MV. A highly significant factor apparent in this field test and not normally consid-

ered from the ballistics-only standpoint, was the "hittability" factor improvement with a scope sight assist. This particular M340 is the only current bolt rifle system in 30-30 and unique in this practical tight-locking design by being the lowest priced centerfire repeating rifle on today's market. It should have great appeal to the normal 30-30 user not hung on the old lever cranker image sustained by movie magic.

The 30-30 is here to stay and will be a big reload favorite since the benefits are much more rewarding than with any current factory cartridge because it lends itself to the upgrade process so readily and is most in need of a boost. Most spectacular is with the scope and bolt gun accuracy combination, utilizing the high performance bullet. Next are the more common lever or pump tubular magazine rifles with the streamlined balls, one chambered and one in the magazine.

With these options of various degrees of upgrade, the 30-30 can be as practical as it is popular. Reloading this way takes a minimal output for a maximum return from the performance and economy standpoint. •

With HANDLOADS

by FRANK MARSHALL, JR.

the 30-30 upgrade procedure. The one-in-magazine, one-in-chamber rule must still be observed. Over-all cartridge length is 2.550″.

When testing factory loads, a very interesting oddity became apparent in tubular magazine rifles. Rifles sighted in, as is usually done, with one round loaded in chamber only are, in fact, not sighted in when the magazine is full. The difference varied from rifle to rifle in many checked, but the variation in impact was considerable with all rifles, absent in none, and enough in some to cause a miss on a less than perfect close-in shot.

More interesting were the poor groups resulting from shooting a magazine full with the gradual variations in magazine spring tension, rifle balance and heat, all affecting the group

Bullet: 170-gr. F.P. Sierra at 2100 MV

Range	Muzzle	100	200	300
Velocity (fps)	2100	1700	1300	1000
Trajectory (from sight line)	− 0.75-in.	On	− 11-in.	− 42-in.
Accuracy	.308	3-in.	8-in.	20-in.
Retained energy (ft. lbs.)	1700	1100	680	445

Bullet: 165-gr. Sierra at 2100 MV

Range	Muzzle	100	200	300
Velocity (fps)	2100	1900	1760	1625
Trajectory (from sight line)	− 1.75-in.	+ 3.60-in.	On	14-in.
Accuracy	.308	1.25-in.	3-in.	5-in.
Retained energy (ft. lbs.)	1680	1460	1200	1000

IT SEEMS ALMOST impractical to consider any improved cartridge these days, but for a fan of the Winchester Model 94 carbine for hunting the hills of Virginia, there just ain't nothing else beyond the 30-30 and the 375 Winchester. That's all the reason I needed to try the 30-30 Ackley Improved.

In discussing my plans with several friends, I'm afraid I got little encouragement. I agreed with them that in a lot of cases, the "improved" cartridge ends up burning more powder with little or no increase in velocity. Even Parker Ackley, who worked up dozens of improved cartridges over the years, said, "Save your money" when ques-

tioned about improved cartridges at a recent NRA convention.

I persisted, but I set a goal or two as well: For the 30-30 conversion to be worthwhile to me, I'd want at least a 200-fps increase over factory loads, which means a cartridge equalling some factory loads in 30-40 Krag or 300 Savage. I didn't know if this could be done safely, but I was sure gonna try.

Chambering reamer and RCBS reloading dies, at hand, Ben Toxvard of Shenandoah Guns in Berryville, VA, and I completed the conversion of the Model 94 in less than an hour. All that was required was to unscrew the barrel from the receiver, chuck the

barrel in the lathe, align it and cut the new chamber in about three or four passes. After a slight polishing and reassembly, the rifle was ready to fire without further modification. It even fed perfectly.

As with most "improved" cartridges, the shape is obtained by firing conventional factory loads in the improved chamber. I bought 100 Remington 170-grain factory loads and squeezed off 20 or so daily until I had 100 fire-formed cases for the 30-30 Ackley Improved.

I also had a number of older fired 30-30 cases on hand, so I loaded these up with 7.5 grains of Unique powder behind a 150-grain bullet, and this

There remains a time-honored option involving a bigger chamber, which is what this author did to . . .

IMPROVE THE 30-30

BY JOHN E. TRAISTER

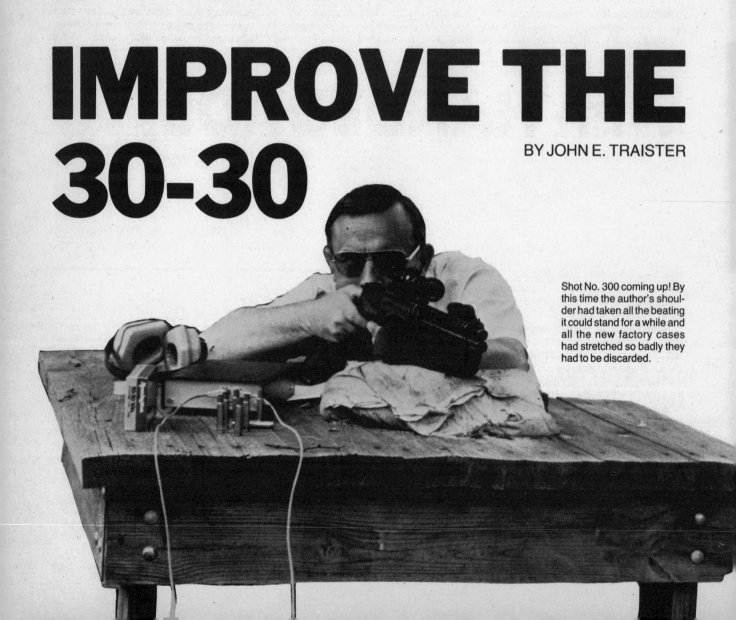

Shot No. 300 coming up! By this time the author's shoulder had taken all the beating it could stand for a while and all the new factory cases had stretched so badly they had to be discarded.

load did the trick in all cases except those manufactured by Federal. The brass must have been thicker in the Federal cases and it took a full charge load in these to obtain the sharp shoulders of the Ackley design.

During the fire-forming process, I had only one case neck split and this was an old Winchester-Western case which could have been 10 years old or so. I had planned to use only the factory new cartridges for working up loads, but I thought perhaps I'd use some of the old cases I had lying around for reduced loads. It's a good idea never to use any but new cases when working up loads to get a fair and accurate comparison of the loads.

An old case may split and it may not be due to the load; on the other hand it could be, so use only new cases in good condition when working up loads.

Parker Ackley's book *Handbook For Shooters & Reloaders Vol. 1,* lists loads for the 30-30 Ackley Improved up to and including 150-grain bullets, so I decided to start with the 150-grain bullet. One of Ackley's top loads for the 150-grain bullet uses 34 grains of 4198 powder for a velocity of 2700 fps. I had a can of H4198 and started off with 31 grains behind a 150-grain Sierra Flat Nose Bullet. My Oehler Research Model 33 Chronograph showed an average velocity of 2330 fps; pressure signs showed low pressure. These

loads were increased, ½-grain at a time, until I reached 32.5 grains of H4198 for a velocity of 2557 fps. I went all the way up to 33.5 grains of H4198, but primers started to flatten, so I settled for the most accurate load of 32.5 grains. Here are the results of the string:

150-grain Sierra Flat Nose Bullet

31 grains H4198	2330 fps	poor accuracy
31.5 grains H4198	2420 fps	
32 grains H4198	2460 fps	good accuracy
32.5 grains H4198	2557 fps	excellent accuracy

The 130-grain Speer flat nose bullet came next. A load of 34 grains of H4198 was my starting load and gave exactly 2700 fps at 15 feet from the muzzle—the distance my screens were

Four fired 30-30 Ackley Improved cases and one ready to go. A standard 30-30 Winchester case is shown for comparison. Author found he had an oversize chamber.

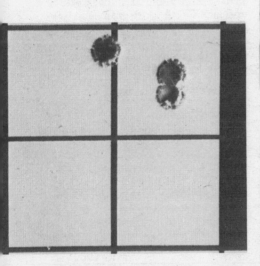

The first three shots for accuracy tests with the 170-grain bullet produced (above) this ¾-inch group slightly low and to the right of the aiming point.

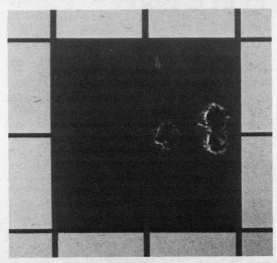

The Leupold 4x E.R. scope was adjusted and (at right) the next three shots turned out to be a very similar group—two touching and one out.

View looking down author's 50-yard range. Note author's arrangement of Oehler Skyscreens. The holder is made from PVC pipe with cardboard frames to make sure bullet is aligned over Skyscreens.

This is, the author thinks, the non-pareil hunting gun. He likes the Model 94—here the Model 94 Antique—so well he wants it improved, but can only do that by tinkering the cartridge.

set up. I went to 35 grains of H4198, but the primer showed signs of high pressure, and I backed off to 34.5 grains of H4198 for a velocity of 2755 fps. This load was so accurate, I settled for it and tried no further loads with this weight.

Over the next three days I touched off over three hundred rounds working up loads for the 170-grain and 180-grain bullets. By this time my shoulder was feeling the action, and I had to quit for a few days. Here are the results for the 170- and 180-grain loads:

170-grain Sierra Flat Nose Bullet

29 grains H4198	2190 fps	low pressure
31 grains H4198	2335 fps	
31.5 grains H4198	2353 fps	good accuracy
32 grains	2383 fps	

180-grain Sierra Round Nose Bullet (no crimp)

31 grains 3031	1942 fps	low pressure
32 grains 3031	2071	low pressure
33 grains 3031	2113	low pressure
33.5 grains 3031	2217	Mod. pressure
34 grains 3031	2190	Powder compressed, no crimp to hold bullet in place; kept popping out of its seat!

During those first three days of testing, I had completely used up my 100 new cartridge cases. The hotter loads stretched and each case was good for only two loads. The rear end of the chamber on this particular Model 94 seemed a little loose and perhaps a tighter chamber might help the problem, but in the meantime I had to find some more cases if I was to continue. While I was scrounging around for new cases, I did pick out some of the better cases and loaded some reduced loads for plinking and small game.

A few years back I had loaded the Speer Plinker® bullets in conventional 30-30 cases and this combination did

SUMMARY

30-30 Improved		30-30 Win.	Gain in fps
130-grain	2755	2450	305
150-grain	2557	2340	217
170-grain	2353	2140	213

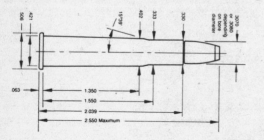

offer a fairly good reduced load, but these plinkers could not be crimped satisfactorily and therefore couldn't be fed through the tubular magazine. Many times I'd push the bullet back into the case as I fed them through the loading gate. Then, you don't want those half-jacket bullets going much slower than 1200 fps or they may lose their jackets in the bore.

I then tried the Speer .308″ flat-nose Varminter in the 30-30 which were much better for loading and gave excellent accuracy, but they still had a little too much oomph for some of my situations.

The obvious thing to do would be to purchase a bullet casting outfit and use lead bullets of any size or velocity that I wanted. However, what little time I have any more to hunt, I don't want to waste on setting up and casting 10 or 15 lead bullets.

Then as I was looking through some back issues of the *American Rifleman,* I came across an ad showing a Marble auxiliary cartridge for the 30-30 that utilized 32 S&W cartridges (in the neck of the case). This gave me an idea. I checked with my supplier the following day and sure enough, he had plenty of Remington 32-caliber, 88-grain, .314″ diameter, lead bullets in stock. This was almost the exact weight I was looking for.

After some experimenting, I came up with a load of 4.5 grains of Unique powder behind this 88-grain bullet—giving a velocity of 925 fps at 15 feet. I could keep all rounds in a 1-inch square at 25 yards with open sights —just about the average range for squirrel around my neck of the woods.

The load has less penetration than a 22 LR cartridge, but more "knockdown" power. A 22 Long Rifle will shoot completely through a Wards catalog at 25 yards; the 30-30 with reduced loads only shot about ¾ the way through. The bullet, however, expanded excellently and it will expend most of its energy within a squirrel's body without tearing up meat any more than a 22 Long Rifle.

The only trouble I've had with the load was in seating the bullet. The slightly oversized (.314″ dia.) bullets didn't want to seat in the neck of the 30-30 cases—resulting in damaged cases and/or bullets. I used the neck of one of my center punches which had a smooth taper to slightly expand the mouth of the cases before putting them through the seating die. This worked perfectly and I've had very few damaged bullets or cases since.

A load of 5 grains of Unique powder behind the 88-grain lead bullet in the Ackley Improved case gave identical results—except accuracy seemed a little better. Three shots touched each other at 25 yards.

I was able to obtain about 100 more 30-30 cases and after fire-forming them as discussed previously, I decided to go back to the 170-grain bullet for more tests, as this would be the bullet used for most of my hunting.

This time I started out with 33 grains of 3031 powder and worked all the way up to 39 grains of powder for a velocity of 2600 fps, but I don't recommend going over 35.2 grains behind the 170-grain flat-nose bullet. Although the velocity at 15 feet was only about 2300 fps, this load gave me the best accuracy of any load tested in my field . . . and besides, primers began to flatten at 35.5 grains of powder.

Next came the 110-grain Speer flat-nose bullets—the ones I'd planned to use on groundhogs around my home during the summer. Ackley shows a load in his book of 30 grains of 4227 behind the 110-grain bullet for 3280 fps. I tried this full-charged load in my rifle and didn't come anywhere near that velocity. Of course, I'm using the 20-inch carbine barrel and perhaps Ackley (or the person furnishing the data) used a 32-inch test barrel, this could have accounted for the difference.

The next powder tried was Reloader 7, and the results follow:

110-Grain Speer Varminter Bullet

32.5 grains R7	2554 fps
33.5 grains R7	2627 fps
34.5 grains R7	2695 fps
35.5 grains R7	2792 fps

The old standby H4198 was the next powder used and 35 grains of H4198 give an average velocity of 2888 fps. I increased this charge to 35.8 grains for an average velocity of 2901, but things happened on this load! First of all, primers indicated high pressure. Then when I examined the target, I found that some of the bullets had keyholed and I had more holes in the paper than shots fired! The bullets could have disintegrated or some of the jacket or lead could have ricocheted from the backstop. Who knows? Anyway, I started reducing the load until I arrived at 34.5 grains of H4198 for an average velocity of 2863 fps along with superb accuracy. Just this morning a groundhog that had been feeding on my garden peas caught one of these Speer bullets through the head at approximately 75 yards.

Over-all accuracy with the rifle is surprisingly good. At 50 yards, all groups with the most accurate loads were within ¾-inch. The 130-grain bullet backed with 34.5 grains of H4198 powder had three shots touching almost every time at 50 yards, using a Leupold 4x E.R. scope mounted ahead of the receiver. At 100 yards, I was shooting right along with a friend using a Winchester 670 rifle chambered for 243 Winchester.

I called H.P. White Lab at Bel Air, Md., to inquire about pressure tests. They said they'd be happy to work me in, but they didn't have a barrel for their pressure gun chambered for the 30-30 Ackley Improved; if I could send the barrel along, though, they would do the tests for me. The cheapest price I found was $375 for the barrel so the pressure tests will have to wait for a while. However, for every load listed, I personally fired several rounds somewhat above the ones listed and am quite confident that the ones fired are "safe" in my rifle. Yours may be different, so always start a little low before working up to the maximum loads listed. All of the recommended loads are below the maximum loads listed in P.O. Ackley's Handbook.

The tests are by no means complete, and I'll probably be playing around with the rifle and loads for the next year or so, but I'm quite happy with the conversion and plan to use the rifle for varmints during the summer and big deer in the fall.

Incidentally, for all practical purposes, the 30-30 Ackley Improved did reach actual chronographed velocities of 30-40 Krag factory loads—and all in a little, compact carbine. ●

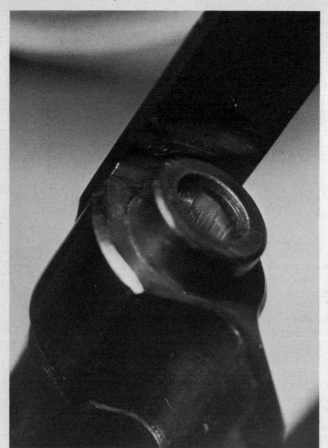

Revolver with rough, tight factory forcing cone will tend to split lead and foul more rapidly, causing unpleasant shooting and a decline in accuracy.

The cleaned forcing cone can make a happy difference in both shooting and in leading. Lead-splitting will be gone as well.

It's simple: FORCING CONES CAN BE FIXED . . . if you have the right tools

by **WILL G. PAUL**

REVOLVER shooters rarely pay any attention to the rear ends of the barrels, but they should. The forcing cone of a revolver is analogous to the leade of a rifle barrel, and has a significant effect upon accuracy. Its purpose is to help the bullet get from the cylinder into the rifling with minimum deformation. And bullet deformation is the primary cause of inaccuracy in all rifled firearms, regardless of the mechanism by which it occurs.

Revolver shooters are a trusting lot and assume much on faith which just isn't in the cards. If a revolver and its cylinder were absolutely perfect and indexed precisely on every chamber, so the chamber throats lined up with the barrel axis the same way each time, you could do without a forcing cone at all. However, that isn't the case. Even in the best revolvers timing may vary from chamber to chamber, depending on the state of wear, how accurately the cylinder was bored, and whether it is fired single-action or double-action. Faced with these inherent and induced sources of misalignment, the forcing cone is hard pressed to help the bullet without its getting scraped, upset, or knocked off balance.

In most cases the revolver enthusiast will find the original factory forcing cone works OK, but there are times when it won't. A gunsmith friend of mine once obtained a batch of Rossi 38 Special revolvers which spit lead horribly. Their timing was OK, but the forcing cones were minimal, rough, and sharp-edged. A few minutes time spent with a forcing cone reamer on each gun not only cured the lead spitting problems, but turned the rather ordinary guns into highly

useful ones with a minimum of effort. A friend had a Charter Arms 38 he liked, but it had a tendency to lead, and didn't shoot as well as he'd hoped. A minor reaming job to clean up the tight, rough forcing cone in this gun helped a great deal, as it has in many others of various brands I have known.

Expensive guns aren't immune from the occasional rough forcing cone, characterized by circumferential tool marks which indicate a dull reamer, applied in a hurry by a tired worker late on Friday afternoon. I recently saw a new Colt Python with a forcing cone that looked like it had been made with a cast iron cockleburr. Other favorites such as Ruger or Smith & Wesson make rough ones occasionally, when reamers get dull or Lady Luck lets a metal chip drag under a cutting edge.

What's the harm of a scratch, you ask? Any tool marks in the forcing cone run *across* the direction of bullet travel, and tend to scrape lead from the bullet. Once a particle of lead is scraped off and smeared around, it provides a base on which more will adhere, and more lead build up, eventually migrating down the bore, leading it, often severely.

Jacketed bullets are not affected by leading, but they are still subject to damaging deformation depending upon jacket thickness, core hardness and gas pressure. The primary cause of all revolver bullet deformation is base upset. This is significant even with light target loads with very soft hollow-based bullets and fast powders, as in 38 Special wadcutters. However, jacketed bullet shooters will also experience it when shooting full loads in cartridges like the 357 Magnum or 44 Magnum. Hard jacketed bullets in

moderate loads, such as the 45 ACP or 38 Special are least affected.

With soft lead bullets, base upset usually starts in the chamber throat, between the case mouth and the front of the cylinder. If the bullet fits this throat tightly, it won't upset appreciably, for it is held in alignment by the cylinder, and guided straight into the barrel with minimum damage. But if the bullet is undersize and soft enough to deform under the pressure of discharge, it will upset to fill the throat. This always causes some distortion either from base upset or gas cutting. If the forcing cone is excessively large the bullet base can continue to upset as it jumps the cylinder gap into the barrel. This condition is aggravated in high pressure loads if the forcing cone angle is too steep, and of large diameter, giving the bullet base plenty of room to upset into, so it must be squeezed down again to enter the barrel. This excessive deformation of the bullet knocks it off balance. With jacketed bullets used in hot loads, this can cause the core to loosen from the jacket, really raising hob with accuracy.

While conventional rifleman's logic would suggest that the short, steep angle would reduce bullet jump and probably help, that isn't really the case in revolvers, since the front of the bullet would start to slow up as it engraves while its base is unsupported, giving it someplace to flow under pressure. The potential damage done to a bullet by base upset greatly exceeds that caused by any additional "skidding" resulting from a few hundredths of an inch greater jump. The most accurate revolvers I've used all have long gradual forcing cones, which weren't excessively large at the

Brownell's forcing cone set consists of a reamer, extension rod, handle and muzzle bushing. Optional items shown here include reamers for other calibers, brass rod bushings, and 82° chamfer tool. Still other items not shown are brass laps, and a facing cutter.

rear, permitting the bullet to ease gradually into the rifling. Recently I had a chance to start from scratch with a new revolver barrel, starting from no forcing cone at all, reaming it in stages, and I came to the same conclusion. This holds true whether you are shooting wadcutters or magnum loads.

The benefits are most obvious in target guns, but it is possible to get a noticeable level of improvement even in ordinary field and service guns. First you should examine the forcing cone in your revolver. If it is smooth, concentric, not prone to lead, and has no sharp edges, you should LEAVE IT ALONE. But if you see tool marks and leading, there's a simple cure. A great many ordinary revolvers I've used were serviceable working guns, but could be made to lead less and group more consistently after a bit of careful adjustment. You can't expect any real miracles here, but I've found that if done right, this never hurts, and usually helps, even if just a little.

It used to be that forcing cone reamers weren't a readily available item, as most revolver 'smiths ground their own. Now, Brownells has available to the trade and hobbyist alike a professional quality forcing cone reamer set which is useful for trouble-shooting standard guns as well as cutting cones in new custom barrels. When cleaning up the original factory forcing cone only a light cut should be taken to clean up the cone, insure it is round, and remove existing tool marks, no more. After this is done, you can also break the sharp edge of the cone where it meets the barrel face, using an optional 82° cutter.

The basic kit has a standard 18° reamer for one caliber, with a handle, extension rod and muzzle bushing. You can add optional things like the 82° chamfer tool, a barrel facing cutter, reamers for different calibers, or a special 11° shallow angle cutter, which is available in 38/357 caliber only. This is intended for use with 38 Special wadcutter ammunition, but it also works well with 357 Magnum ammunition with either lead or jacketed bullets.

A new item recently added to the options for this set is a facing cutter. This is used to true up an out-of-square barrel face without having to pull the barrel and turn it in a lathe. It is also useful when fitting new barrels to get correct cylinder clearance. Too tight a gap causes lead buildup on the cylinder face which impedes free rotation. When fitting new barrels the cylinder gap should be adjusted to pass a .004" feeler gauge, but not .006". For guns already in service as much as .008" does no harm if not accompanied by a lot of cylinder endshake. The facing cutter works like an endmill and requires considerable care in use to avoid chattering. It is more an item for the professional gunsmith than the amateur gun hobbyist.

If you decide to ream the forcing cone of your revolver, you should do so carefully, for if you blow it, you'll be out the cost of a new barrel! Only in very rare instances when the original cone is too tight will you ever have to enlarge its basic diameter. Therefore, you should use the 11° reamer for working on original 38 or 357 factory barrels so you can clean up the existing cone without enlarging it. If in

doubt, measure the cone opening at the barrel face. A rule of thumb is not to enlarge the cone opening to exceed 1.05 times the basic bullet diameter. This comes out to .376" for 38/357, .430" for 41 Mag., .450" for 44 Mag., and .475" for 45 Colt.

Remove the cylinder from your revolver, clean the bore thoroughly and swab the forcing cone with machinist's dye so you can see just where the cutter is working. With the revolver frame held solidly in a padded vise, insert the extension rod and handle through the muzzle, and position the conical muzzle bushing, and if desired, the optional cylindrical bushing at the rear end of the barrel, before you put on the reamer. Brush the reamer flutes with oil, and tighten it on the handle before starting. Now grasp the handle, hold the muzzle bushing in place and pull back firmly as you rotate the handle one-half turn to make that first cut. Back the reamer out after each cut, brush away any metal chips, and reoil the cutting edges. Usually it will take only a cut or two to clean up the original cone. If you proceed carefully, backing off the cutter each time, you should have a smooth cone which requires no polishing. It doesn't hurt to polish it with a bit of 320 grit on one of the optional brass laps, though careful wrapping of wet-or-dry paper around the reamer, well oiled, works just as well. The final touch, if you wish, is to break the sharp edge where the cone meets the barrel face, using the optional 82° chamfer tool. *Don't* overdo this, since doing so will increase base upset. You only need to make one light cut about .010" deep. That's it. ●

Muzzle bushing helps keep the cutter and rod centered in the bore, so the cleanup cut is kept concentric.

The 82° chamfer tool is used only to break the sharp edge of the forcing cone slightly. It is run in only about .010"; don't overdo this.

Frederick Courtenay Selous of Africa tested the Velopexes and said he liked them.

By 1905, WHEN the cordite nitro-express, from small to large bore had firmly taken root and most British big game hunters had sold or retired their beloved black powder rifles, there occurred a repetition of the light bullet "express" fad. This time it occurred with the new nitro-expresses, which more often than not were based on popular blackpowder cases but loaded with cordite to give cupro-nickel jacketed bullets high velocity.

Such nitro-express cartridges included the 500 3-inch and 3¼-inch, the 500/450 3¼-inch, the 450/400, the various 360s and the like. They were not merely the cordite "L. C." loadings to simulate original blackpowder ballistics, or "Light Cordite" loads with lead bullets, but heavy loads of cordite using heavy cupro-nickel jacketed bullets. Most such full-powered cordite loads achieved velocities from 2,000 to 2,200 fps which in Rigby's straight 450 3¼-inch nitro-express, for example, produced an unprecedented near-5,000 ft. lbs. of energy with a 480-grain bullet at 2,150 fps.

Previous to 1897, the blackpowder ancestor of Rigby's 450 nitro-express had been merely a stag and boar rifle, or a "small-bore" to use the Victorian terminology, based on a "large-bore" being anything *over* a 577! In those pre-cordite days of the blackpowder express, "high-velocity" was obtained by using light for caliber lead bullets with huge hollow points or copper tube nose caps to increase expansion. Special rifles were produced regulated for these light loads and made much lighter than identical chambered rifles, double and single, which was confusing to those unfamiliar with such differences, all but indistinguishable at a glance.

Tested by Selous, there were great hopes for the . . .

HOLLAND VELOPEX . . .

but it didn't last.

by JACK LOTT

Left: a 465 Velopex bullet of 365 grains, showing typical double cannelures. Right: a hollow-pointed 465 soft nose of unknown weight.

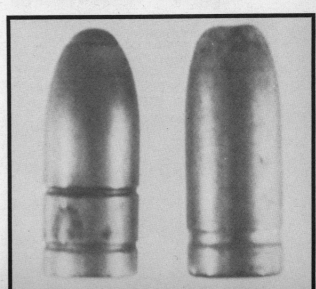

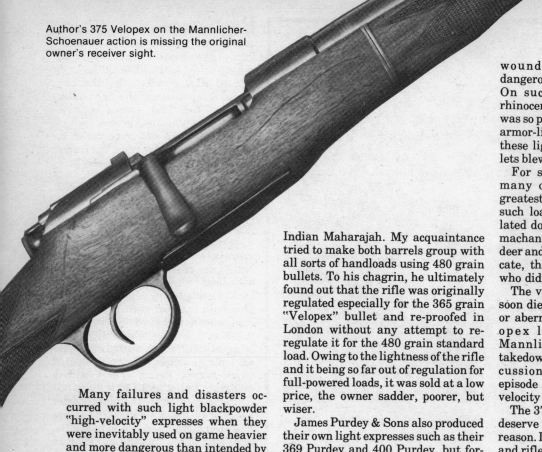

Author's 375 Velopex on the Mannlicher-Schoenauer action is missing the original owner's receiver sight.

Many failures and disasters occurred with such light blackpowder "high-velocity" expresses when they were inevitably used on game heavier and more dangerous than intended by the maker. As a result, such authorities as Sir Samuel Baker condemned the light expresses and they more or less died out at the end of the century.

Grotesquely, within ten years after the advent of the cordite nitro-express the same phenomenon arose with the new look-alikes of the blackpowder expresses, the nitro-expresses: a new race of light bullet "high velocity" creations in most popular calibers from the 375 Express to the 465. To complicate matters for today's purchaser of large-bore double rifles, some 465s and other large bore doubles by British makers were made solely for light bullet loads such as Holland's 465 "Velopex" load of 75 grains of cordite and a 365 grain "Velopex" bullet at 2,282 fps, as opposed to the full-power load of 75 grains of cordite and a 480 grain bullet at 2,141 fps. I know of an unfortunate purchaser of such a Holland "Velopex" 465 as made for an

Indian Maharajah. My acquaintance tried to make both barrels group with all sorts of handloads using 480 grain bullets. To his chagrin, he ultimately found out that the rifle was originally regulated especially for the 365 grain "Velopex" bullet and re-proofed in London without any attempt to re-regulate it for the 480 grain standard load. Owing to the lightness of the rifle and it being so far out of regulation for full-powered loads, it was sold at a low price, the owner sadder, poorer, but wiser.

James Purdey & Sons also produced their own light expresses such as their 369 Purdey and 400 Purdey, but fortunately these were distinct cartridges and not merely standard nitro-expresses with lighter bullets. Despite such shortcomings, the fad of light-bulleted nitro-expresses enchanted the susceptible and impressionable among the then-new generation of shooters unfamiliar with the previous failure of blackpowder light expresses. Magazine rifle cartridges such as Westley Richards' 425 Magnum and W. J. Jeffery's 404 both sported optional 300 grain "high-velocity," low sectional density loadings which were useless except as selling attractions.

And attract they did, shamelessly encouraged by sometimes lurid testimonials in proprietary catalogs. Unfortunately some purchasers didn't know the difference and purchased such rifles and loadings and then proceeded to Africa or India and there

wounded large and sometimes dangerous game with horrible results. On such thick-skinned game as rhinoceros and buffalo the penetration was so poor as to barely get beyond the armor-like skin. On charging lions, these light and highly frangible bullets blew up in massive chest muscles.

For sophisticated gun buffs like many of the Indian Princes, the greatest purchasers of double rifles, such loads and their specially regulated double rifles were excellent for machans or shooting from a howdah at deer and boar. For every such sophisticate, though, there were a hundred who didn't know.

The vogue for such big-bore freaks soon died out. Still, this phenomenon or aberration as typified by the Velopex line of bullets and the Mannlicher-Schoenauer-actioned takedown 375 Velopex rifle merit discussion as a brief but historical episode in the development of high-velocity ammunition.

The 375 Velopex cartridge and rifle deserve special mention for another reason. It was the first belted cartridge and rifle combo on the market and the lesser forerunner of today's plethora of belted magnums. The story of Holland & Holland's Velopex cartridge (400/ 375 Express) begins in 1904 when Mr. Henry W. Holland applied for a British patent on his "belted" case. According to Austrian patent records, the Austrian inventor Roth also obtained a patent for a belted case, but Holland is generally credited with originating it.

The belt was conceived as a means to eliminate the feeding problems of rimmed cases in Mauser magazines, which also reduced the amount of modification of receivers, magazines, bolt faces and extractors to handle the large diameter rims. This applies to the original 375 Velopex round but naturally not to today's H&H-type

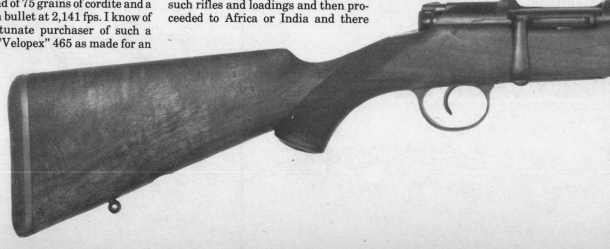

Westley Richards trunk case with 425 W.R. Magnum and 375 H&H Velopex takedowns used by American hunter and Rhodesian pioneer, John C. Blick, Major F.R. Burnham's brother-in-law.

"belted" magnum cases with their larger-than-standard base diameters. In those days, the belt was not at all regarded as something *avant garde,* but rather a means of reverting to the old reliable rimmed or flanged case in view of the then-considerable trouble with maintaining headspace with the modern rimless cases. In short, the 375 Velopex case with its belt was a new means of reverting to an old system so that a sort of rimmed case could function in the then-new Mausers.

Although the London firm of John Rigby & Son used slanted box magazines on their rimmed 400/350 nitro-express Magnum Mausers, Holland's belted 375 Velopex would function in an ordinary Mauser or Mannlicher-Schoenauer action.

Left to right—400/375 H&H Nitro-Express, the first cartridge with a belted case and identical to 375 "Velopex" excepting standard 270-grain semi-pointed expanding bullet. Next, 375 H&H Magnum and 378 Weatherby.

John C. Blick's favorite rifle when used with 320-grain bullet—a Holland-Schoenauer 400/375 Belted Nitro-Express rifle, originally called the "Velopex" rifle.

No. 27,912 A.D. 1904

Date of Application, 20th Dec., 1904-- Accepted, 26th Jan., 1905

COMPLETE SPECIFICATION

"Improvements in Small Arms and in Cartridge Cases therefor."

I, HENRY WILLIAM HOLLAND, of 98, New Bond Street, in the County of Middlesex, Gunmaker, do hereby declare the nature of this invention and in what manner the same is to be performed to be particularly described and ascertained in and by the following statement:

This invention relates to cartridge cases especially for small arms.

The flange at the rear end of the cartridge with which the extractor engages was formerly usually made to project beyond the body but as this arrangement makes if difficult to pack the cartridges in a magazine this flange is now often made of the same diameter as the body and the bottle shape of cartridge alone is relied on as a stop but in such cases difficulty is often experienced in preventing the cartridge from entering too far into the bore of the gun and thus causing mis-fires.

According to this invention I form a small ridge just in advance of the groove for the extractor and I form a corresponding shoulder in the chamber of the gun. By these means I effectually prevent the cartridge from entering too far.

The drawing is a section to an enlarged scale of a cartridge made according to this invention.

a is the body of the cartridge and b is the usual flange at its rear. c is the ridge forming the subject of the present invention.

Having now particularly described and ascertained the nature of my said invention and in what manner the same is to be performed, I declare that what I claim is:

Small arms and cartridges substantially as described and illustrated in the drawing.

Dated this 19th day of December 1904.

HENRY W. HOLLAND.

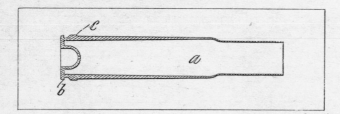

Holland's patent for that first belted case is shown above; the catalog page below shows what a variety of bullets, including the Velopex, the firm offered in 1910.

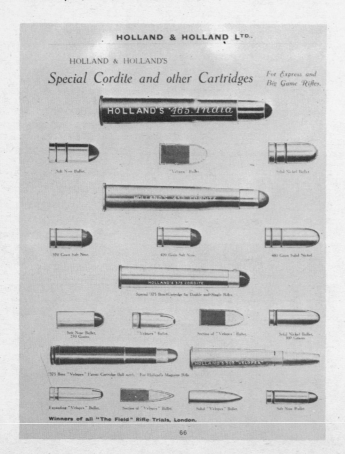

The 1905 Model Mannlicher-Schoenauer rifle was selected by Holland & Holland as the basis for the new 375 Velopex rifle. The standard Velopex was produced as a takedown by incorporating a detachable forearm with Deeley & Edge release and lapped, slip-fit threads and a pin lock for fixing and detaching the barrel. When such work was performed by highly skilled craftsmen such as employed by Holland's, a detachable barrel takedown was quite accurate enough, but not when such a design is produced on a production basis.

Frederick Courtenay Selous was presented a 375 Velopex rifle for field testing around 1907 when he took the Mannlicher-Schoenauer-Holland rifle to Norway on a reindeer hunt with the world-famous big game hunter P. B. Vanderbyl. Selous wrote but little about this trip other than in testimonials produced in Holland's catalogs, but Vanderbyl recorded some comments in letters to Selous' biographer, J. G. Millais. Selous obtained a remarkable seven stags in five days.

"Although Selous and I were friends of many years standing we only did one shooting trip together, and that was after reindeer in Norway. We sailed from Hull to Stavanger in August 1907, and marched with pack ponies a few miles from the head of Stavanger Fjord to Lyseheien where a small shooting-box (hunting block) had been erected. Owing to a five year closed season which had just terminated, we found the reindeer fairly numerous, and not too difficult to approach, but as they always feed upwind, and cover a lot of ground, we had some days to walk long distances before spying any.

"We were quite successful on this trip, and secured thirteen stags between us, with some good heads among them. When not hunting, we beguiled the time with some French novels which Selous produced, and I never knew of his liking of this kind of literature before."

After his Norway reindeer hunt, Selous tried the 375 Velopex on red deer stags in Scotland's Highlands, taking five. I am unable to find out what rifles Selous took on his rather short 1909 East African safari, during which he rendezvoused with Teddy Roosevelt, whose safari Selous arranged. Selous did give Holland & Holland a favorable testimonial on his Norway and Scotland hunting trips where he tested the 375 Velopex on game, but nothing was said about using it in East Africa.

Selous was too knowledgeable to

rely on such a trick bullet for such heavy game as the eland and other large and tough African antelopes. In Norway and the Scottish Highlands, the game was relatively tame and confined to private hunting preserves with no large predators other than man, and of course, the game is at closer ranges than on the East African plains. With true flat-shooting, long-range cartridges just appearing, such as the 30-06 with its 150 grain spitzer at 2,700 fps, Selous, typically progressive, favored the new developments.

Holland & Holland must have placed a lot of faith in the Velopex design to give its name to their new rifle, but the rifle didn't die along with the cartridge, since conventional bullets kept up its popularity for decades after the name Velopex was forgotten. With its poor ballistic coefficient and rapid loss of velocity, the 375 Velopex performed adequately up to 200 yards on game up to the size of red deer, but would have been a poor penetrator of anything much larger. It was a typically Victorian approach to high-velocity, and similar to the earlier method of obtaining high-velocity with light, copper-capped blackpowder bullets.

When the appeal and availability of the Velopex ammo died away, the 400/375 H&H Belted Nitro-Express continued as a fairly popular round for years, even just after WW II. The conventional loadings included a 270 grain bullet and a 320 grain bullet, both before 40 grains of cordite with the first producing some 2,000 fps and the latter 1,900. To this day the 400/375 H&H Belted Nitro-Express and its flanged (rimmed) brother cause confusion to rifle buyers as their low-priced "375 H&H Belted Magnum" or "375 H&H Flanged Magnum" double rifle, turns out to be a 400/375 Belted or Flanged rifle for obsolete ammo and far below the Magnums in power.

Pre-War Holland catalogs listed the 375 Velopex velocity at 2,500 fps, but not bullet weight, which must have been around 200 grains. I can also find no bullet weights for their 303 Velopex loading at 2,800 fps. Despite such mediocre ballistics, the 400/375s and their metric relative the 9.5 Mannlicher-Schoenauer rimless, persisted as popular meat rifles in Africa and Southeast Asia.

My own original 375 Velopex rifle belonged to John C. Blick, who lived and died in Visalia, California. Blick, the brother-in-law of the great scout, Major Frederick Russell Burnham, D.S.O., used this rifle as his mainstay

The clue was convenience. With takedown rifles and bullets for all seasons, Holland's tried to convince one and all that the technical problems were all solved. Above: The handy 375 "equally serviceable in the jungle or on the hills" rifle. Below: Those seven shots are really in about 1¾".

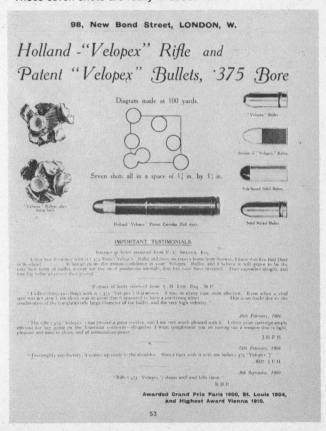

Velopex worked for everything in any bore. Above is Holland's boast for flanged 303 cartridges in double rifles; below, you could do just as well, of course, with a flanged 375.

for general game during a 1912-1913 East African expedition. Financed and accompanied by Childs Frick, son of Henry Clay Frick of the U.S. Steel fortune, with some 200 camels, the pair went up the Nile, into Uganda and Kenya where they took many animal specimens for American museums such as the Field Museum, the Smithsonian Institution, the Carnegie Museum and the Museum of Natural History.

After Kenya they climbed the Ethiopian escarpment into that one-time forbidden territory of King Menelik, who had defeated the Italians at Adowa over a decade previously. Menelik, like most Ethiopians, loved rifles and had never seen a 375 Velopex rifle or its case mate, Blick's 425 Westley Richards takedown. Menelik "requested" Blick to make a gift to him of both rifles, but Blick, wise to the ways of African chiefs and kings, refused. Both he and Childs Frick were then compelled to be Menelik's "guest" in a villa used for just such occasions. Every conceivable variety of food, "dancing girls" and entertainment was employed by Menelik to pry the rifles from Blick's grasp, but when he proved adamant, Menelik became grandiosely friendly and permitted the Americans to proceed under his protection.

As a veteran of Rhodesia's 1896 Matabele Rebellion, Blick, like his famous brother-in-law, was a fellow scout along with F. C. Selous. Selous' recommendations were accepted by Blick and his patron Childs Frick in obtaining the two rifles, both of which had been tested by Selous. To my knowledge, and according to cartridges remaining with the rifle, Blick only used the 320 grain load, which would have been quite effective on medium to large antelope.

In the case is a note which says "This is Mr. Blick's Lyman sight.", but no such sight accompanied the rifle, so I assume it is lost forever. It had to be the earliest Lyman bolt release sight for the Mannlicher-Schoenauer, one which replaced the original bolt stop and not the later Lyman Model 36 which screws down onto the original later form of M.S. bolt release. Anyone having such a *pre*-Model 36 Lyman peep sight for the Mannlicher-Schoenauer available: I would appreciate hearing from you.

According to Stoeger's 1940 catalog, the then latest ballistics for the Holland 400/375 nitro-express were a 270 gr. bullet and 43 grains of cordite at 2,175 fps and 2,840 ft. lbs. of muzzle energy.

As it was for Holland's famous belted magnums, the 375 Velopex case was the basis of an advanced innovation, Holland's 240 Apex, the ancestor of today's popular 6mm cartridges, and unlike the 375 Velopex, a truly efficient cartridge for its caliber on light game such as small deer.

R.C.B.S. made me up a set of dies to load and form 375 H&H Belted-Express cases out of 30-06 brass, which it does very neatly.

Since there are undoubtedly many hundreds of rifles for Holland's 400/375 Belted Nitro-Express or 375 Velopex still floating around the country at gun shows or in gun shops, it is useful to know that one can produce modern Boxer-primed ammo, using R.C.B.S. dies and 30-06 cases reformed with belts. I have no recommended loads, but one is safe to use. 375-inch diameter 270 gr. jacketed bullets such as produced by Hornady, and beginning with IMR powders such as 3031 and slower-burning, start ten percent under 43 grains. Increase slowly while inspecting primers for cratering and cases for head expansion with a micrometer. If as much as one half thousandth of an inch expansion (.0005″) results, reduce load by at least one grain.

If possible, chronograph your results so as to equal factory ballistics. I would not advocate using 300 grain bullets with their much lower velocity and higher trajectory. Stay with 270 grain bullets and velocities of around 2,000 fps and you have a nice mild deer and black bear load for woods ranges. You will be surprised at the accuracy of your handloaded 400/375, if my experience with factory ammo is any indication. Properly loaded with factory or handloaded 270 grain ammo, the 400/375 produces more energy and velocity per bullet weight than Winchester's new 375 in the Big Bore Model '94.

Velopex bullets were usually the same length as full-weight-per-caliber bullets, therefore stabilized with the same twist. Their light weight was achieved by keeping the lead core well to the rear and installing a fibre core forward in the nose. This principle worked well as far as it went, but it is good that a previous generation got the Velopex and other light bullet high-velocity trick bullet freaks out of their system. We enlightened sophisticates of the super-sonic magnum age have enough problems choosing correct bullets from our bewildering repertoire of miracle bullets that do everything for us but gut and skin the game, so I am told. ●

You could Velopex with big bores, too, in the Holland line, and, further, you could expect to hit a postage stamp seven times in a row at 100 yards using a double rifle, open sights, and, of course, the special 365-gr. Velopex load. It is harmless enough, so long as you didn't buy something exclusively regulated for Velopex.

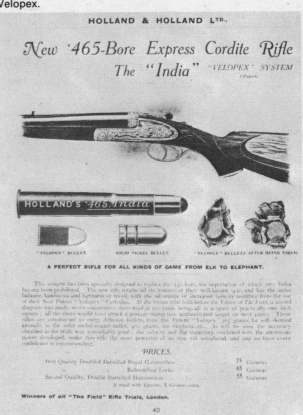

From top: Marlin Model 1893, caliber 32-40; Enfield Mark I commercial, caliber 303 British; Savage Model 99A, caliber 308; Remington Model 760, caliber 30-06; Remington Model 8, caliber 35 Remington; Remington Model 14, caliber 35 Remington; Marlin Model 1895, caliber 45-70.

PRIMARILY A handgun collector with a penchant for automatics, I still find enjoyment in other arms. I find in many collectors today a sort of intolerance for those not in their specialties. I have been for years telling new collectors to specialize just for the sake of making their money go as far as it can, but I certainly never meant anyone should drop other gun interests.

When I, very young, first started to collect guns, I was only allowed to have non-shooters, which in those days meant antiques. I specialized in Civil War guns, buying from Bannerman in New York and from antique shops all over. Before World War II, I had discovered that some of my

more crowded and the prices started to climb. Books, rare in the early days, came out every month on some new facet of collecting. I drifted from all autos to just U.S. pocket automatic pistols and sold off most of my earlier collections of Civil War and Remington arms to pay for my growing interest and to acquire more U.S. autos. So one could say that I am a collector going way back, but that I have also been shooting for a good many years, too.

In the late '50s and early '60s when surplus military ammunition started coming up on the American market, I started to shoot anything and everything I had in my collection. I bought a

World War II, I got a Pacific "C" loading press, a powder scale and some dies for 30-40 Krag and 22 Savage Hi-Power—all for $10, I might add. I had no interest in reloading because ammo was so cheap, so this reloading bonanza sat on a shelf. One of my tin canning buddies did reload and I guess watching him shooting up 38 Specials like BBs finally got to me and I became a reloader starting with 38 Specials, and going to 9mm Luger and 303 British and 8x57mm Mauser and 7.65 Argentine and I don't know if it will ever stop, considering today's prices for commercial ammo.

The cost of dies and a bullet mould don't amount to much if you do any

A noted firearms collector and authority shoots tin cans with these guns? Yes, and he knows about. . . .

Reloading for Fun

by DONALD M. SIMMONS

antiques could be shot, and I kept this a secret from my family. I bought Spencer carbine ammunition from Bannerman and shot my Spencers. I discovered a special bulk powder called Kings Semi-Smokeless which could be used in my muzzle-loading rifles, my Sharps rifles and my Colt and Remington revolvers.

There weren't many other people in my home town in Pennsylvania who collected guns and none I knew shot old wall hangers, so I learned slowly how to determine the necessary charge of powder using the old cover-the-ball-in-the-palm rule at first and then I used the measuring spouts on antique powder horns as a more accurate measure.

Just before World War II, I branched into Remingtons, collecting any arms ever made by them and shooting many of their derringers and revolvers. I had bought up boxes of obsolete 38 and 32 rimfire cartridges as well as 41 rimfire for these various arms.

When I returned from the Okinawa campaign with a Model 38 Arisaka rifle, my sole trophy, my collecting interest took a new direction—modern automatic pistols. I collected Luger, Walther, Mauser, Nambu, and Glisenti and all the many pistols which were used in World War II. Over the years this field became more and

case of Italian 9mm ammo meant for their Beretta submachine gun. Though green and mottled, it would shoot perfectly in the stronger German 9mm Luger caliber pistols. This ammo was about as cheap as shooting 22 Long Rifle and a hell of a lot more fun.

By now, I suppose some of you are wondering what this great shooter is trying to hit. Well, let me confess—I shoot at tin cans, old bottles and clay pigeons and I still am not sure what a Minute of Angle means and I am not sure I really care. If you put a piece of paper with a bunch of rings on it out in front of my sights, I develop a sort of palsy. I can't hit a bull in the butt with a bass fiddle, but let a wounded can start to roll toward me and I can't miss.

For many years, back then, three overgrown boys used to meet weekly and go to one dump near us and shoot everything in the way of guns we could legally fire. We didn't limit ourselves in any way to only automatics, we used revolvers, single-shot pistols, rifles and even shotguns occasionally and we had a ball! Today, I have moved away and one of our trio is dead and our favorite dump shooting range is now intersected by an Interstate highway, but I still like tin canning with high powered arms.

In one of my gun deals just after

amount of shooting. I also got a MEC shotgun reloading outfit from a friend who decided to stop shooting his 12 gauge—this led to adding 16 gauge and finally 410. Reloading really makes tin canning possible and while I shoot clay pigeons with my shotguns, it is still just an advanced form of tin canning.

Living as I do now in Arizona in the winter and Pennsylvania in the summer, I must decide each year what long arms particularly to take with me when decamping. It is these long guns that are my dirty dozen—they haven't drawn blood from anything but a beer can for years but they are my great friends and I would like to introduce them to you!

The Rifles

My oldest rifle, in design at least, is a 32-40 Marlin Model 93, which replaced a Model 93 Marlin 32-40 bought in Tucson in 1936 and shot with commercial ammo over the years until it became too expensive. I found this much better example at a gun show and sold the old one because its bore was too pitted to shoot lead bullets.

The Marlin with its octagonal barrel and a tang peep sight is just my kind of rifle. The action is very easy to work on

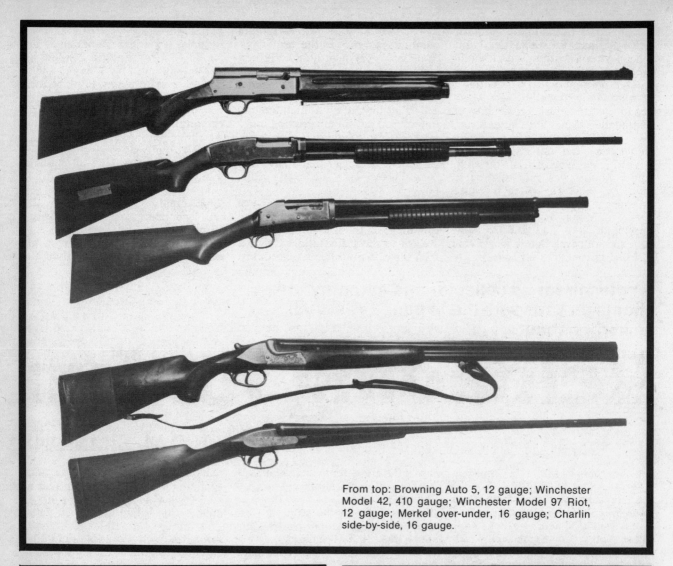

From top: Browning Auto 5, 12 gauge; Winchester Model 42, 410 gauge; Winchester Model 97 Riot, 12 gauge; Merkel over-under, 16 gauge; Charlin side-by-side, 16 gauge.

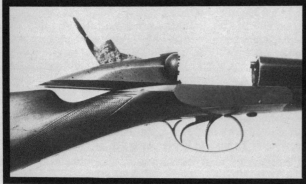

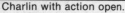
Charlin with action open.

Merkel closeup showing the engraving.

and this one is very smooth. Some may laugh at my choice of caliber, but I am not after moose, I am after a battered V-8 can so caliber is unimportant. My reloads for this 32-40 use an Ideal #321297 with a gas check at a weight of 184 grains with 6 grains of Unique to drive same. As I ran out of 32-40 brass some time ago, I just use 30-30 brass in my sizing die with excellent results.

Next is my commercial Mark I En-field. I bought my first Enfield right after World War II. It was a Mark III used by the Austrian police for post war duties, and over the years I have had nearly 30 different Enfields pass through my hands, but I never found a real keeper until I saw this one at a small gun show. The bolt cover is engraved "Army & Navy Co. Operative Society Ltd" over "105 Victoria St. London S.W." The action is engraved with a scroll all over and the beautiful

walnut stock is hand checkered. The rear sight is a typical British three-leaf for one, two, and three hundred yards with a large adjustable leaf for up to 2000 yards. The typical awk-ward Enfield cut-off is still intact.

All in all, it's one of my favorite rifles, ready to drop anything from an aspirin tin to a garbage can. I re-load for 303 using a 205-gr. Lyman #311299 with a gas check and backed by 12 grains of Unique. I also have several thousand military ball rounds.

I currently have six Remington Model 8 or 81 autoloading rifles. I like them all, but my shooter is a 35 Remington. My first Model 8 was given to me in 1939 by a retired Army General—it is 25 Remington and turned out to be a rare Army-modified rifle that was too good for shooting. My 35 shooter has such a nice action that it will operate using hand cast bullets with complete reliability. I use an Ideal #358430 backed by 12 grains of Unique. Being an autoloader, the Remington Model 8 is great on shooting a rolling #10 can. I have just a semi-buckhorn rear sight to make for quick shots.

This Model 8 was bought at a Tucson gun show several years ago. When I borelighted it, it appeared to have a badly pitted barrel. I got it home and worked on it with Hoppe's #9 and brass bristle brushes but the pits were still there. So I took it to the dump anyway and fired it with great success and when I came to clean it again, I found the bore like new. Apparently, someone years before had used a heavy oil or light grease to protect the barrel and the mess all shot out leaving a brand new bore. You lose a few; you win a few!

As a companion piece to my Model 8, I have newly acquired a 35-caliber Remington Model 14, designed by Mr. J.D. Pedersen who also designed Remington's famous pocket automatic pistol—the Model 51. Like anything designed by Pedersen, it is beautifully constructed and a great pleasure to shoot.

For some reason, unknown even to me, I never owned a Savage 99 until this year when I decided I would like one and bought a new one in 308 Winchester. Mine is a 99A and now all I wonder is—why did it take me so long? Currently, I don't have a mould to cast bullets for 308 so I am reloading with 165-gr. spire point bullets and use 38.5 grains of 3031. My brass is from 30-06 run through the 308 sizing die and then neck trimmed to size. I am very pleased with my Savage 99 and find it highly accurate at my tin can range of 100 yards.

My next rifle is also new to me and like my Remington 14, it is a pump, a Remington Model 760 in 30-06. The Model 760 is a lot easier to load than the Model 14 because of its detachable magazine, and it is really smooth. I don't reload for 30-06 because I still have so much military surplus ammo. The 30-06 760 makes a very good long range canning gun.

I have had a good many rifles in 45-70—Springfields, Remington Roll-ing Blocks, and even a Peabody—but never a repeating lever-action rifle. So last spring I bought a Marlin Model 1895. I have only shot a few commercial rounds through it so far, but what I have seen I've liked. When I get around to reloading for the Marlin, I will naturally be shooting it more.

My last rifle was a gift from my uncle and I have always treasured it. It is a German sporting Mauser, made up from surplus Mauser '98s after World War I, restocked and equipped with a 4-power telescope. The rifle has a double set trigger and the scope is the typical German quick detachable. All in all, a very nice gun to shoot and it can range out with its 8x57mm cartridge.

I have always liked Mauser rifles but this sporting model is my favorite. When large quantities of Canadian ammo were available, I bought two cases and, of course, the 8x57mm is reloadable. For tin canning, I use the Ideal #323378 at 246 grains with gas check and propel it with 13 grains of Unique.

These eight rifles form my shooting battery and each one is a pet of mine, even the new ones like the Marlin 1895 and the Savage 99. They are just great for my kind of shooting.

The Shotguns

Now, my kind of shotgun shooting is a good bit less formal than regular Skeet or trap but we have great fun with a sit-down Trius trap and a backup second Trius which can shoot off delayed doubles or for those who want the real challenge, a triple or even a quadruple. I reload for all my shotguns and that is, to my mind, the only way to go. You, of course, can shoot tin cans from a Trius trap but clay pigeons are much more satisfying. I consider my kind of shotgunning just tin canning with pigeons.

Way before World War II, I had a Damascus, double-barreled, hammered shotgun and I got my rabbit before I learned a Damascus barrel was unsafe to shoot. About 1948, I decided to go into shotgun hunting seriously and dropped into my favorite New York dealer, Bob Abels, to see what he might have. Well, Bob had just got in a beautifully engraved German Merkel 16-gauge over-under. The guy who had sold it had been told its chambers were too short, and neither Bob nor I knew whether this problem existed, but we decided it could be my problem for $125. That was one of the best ways I ever spent $125. The gun took standard 2¾" shells and while I no longer hunt, I do shoot a lot of clay pigeons.

In 1951, I decided to make my wife-to-be a partner in hunting as well. I bought her a well-used Winchester Model 42 410 pump, one of the great ones for my money. I even had a silver plate engraved with her name and the date of her birthday attached to the stock. I don't think she has run a box of ammo through the gun but it sure has been used. Anytime I think I am getting too good at clay busting, I just try a few with the 410 and then you see if you are really on or just think you are.

The same uncle who gave me my favorite Mauser rifle also posthumously gave me one of my favorite shotguns. This is not the gun of the clubhouse or the after the hunt drink, but it's my kind of gun. It is a Model 97 Winchester 12 gauge riot gun. Here is a pump gun that is just fun to shoot. One time on a bet I shot a bird with it without even bringing the gun to my shoulder. I was immediately asked to do it again and I have been declining ever since. The shotgun I used was my riot Model 97 which says something for its inherent pointing qualities and something for the luck of the Irish.

I tried very unsuccessfully to shoot Skeet one day with this same Winchester. I used #5s in factory loads and a wave of concussion issued to both sides of me. They were brave men who shot with me that fateful round of Skeet. I got 13 birds and succeeded in lowering the average of all my companion shooters.

I had been reading, five years ago, about a French shotgun called a Darne. What I found in a gun show was really a forerunner to the Darne, a Charlin Automatique made also at St. Etienne, France, using the same principle. The breech is opened by pulling on two ears just behind the breech block; a steel knee is broken, and the action slides backwards. My Charlin is in 16 gauge and is a very fast acting shotgun. I have learned to open the breech as I take the gun from my shoulder. To someone standing by, it almost looks like the breech opens itself! The Charlin is a plain Jane with very little engraving and most of the finish on the action is gone but it still shoots great and has a neat uncluttered appearance.

That's my dirty dozen, actually a dirty bakers dozen. I have not regaled you about hunting bears in the Yukon; there have been no charges of wounded buffalo in the African veldt; I even spared you hearing about pheasant hunting in the Dakotas. What I have told you is my great secret—I shoot tin cans and clay birds and I love it!!

•

In history and for this shooter,
the 220 Swift and the 17 Remington
make a great . . .

UNMATCHED PAIR

by LONNY H. WEAVER

Photos: Jerry L. Weaver

ONLY TWO cartridges have reached the magical figure of 4,000 fps (feet per second) commercially, the 220 Swift and the 17 Remington. The 220 Swift made its debut in 1935, in the Winchester 54. Listed at a sizzling 4,140 fps at first, the figure was later reduced slightly to what has become the standard 220 Swift factory load—a 48-grain soft point bullet at 4,110 fps.

The Swift completely changed the sport of varmint hunting.

Remington, over 30 years later in 1971, introduced the 17 Remington which zipped a tiny 25-grain .172″ hollow point bullet at a sizzling 4,020 fps. Remington chambered its smallest caliber in their 700 BDL, fitted with a 24-inch sporter weight barrel, and Harrington & Richardson soon announced their H&R Ultra 317 rifle in 17 Remington.

The 17 Remington did not change the sport of varmint hunting, but it repeated the Swift's history, in a way.

Both cartridges have been surrounded with an unfair share of controversy. Critics claim they both erode barrels far too soon, that they are very sensitive to slight load variations, that they are wind sensitive, and that they are not very accurate, to name just a few of the alleged faults. Admirers claim excellent accuracy, flat trajectory, low recoil, complete and dependable bullet blowup, etc., etc.

The 220 Swift, moribund in the '60s was resurrected in 1973 by Sturm, Ruger. Where Winchester had offered the Swift in sporter weight and varmint weight, Ruger made it available only in varmint weight. The temptation was thus, to a degree, removed from those who would against better judgment try the "new" Swift on deer.

Almost as soon as Winchester introduced the Swift cartridge, 1930s shooters had used it on big game. With well-aimed shots at the heart-lung area, the Swift is a very impressive killer on deer, but the type of once-a-year deer hunter we encounter the most is just not that precise.

The idea of a 17-caliber cartridge is not a new one. P. O. Ackley in his *Handbook For Shooters And Reloaders*, gives credit to the 17 Pee Wee, which was a 30 Carbine case necked down to 17 caliber, as the first 17 caliber. Before World War II there was a wildcat called the Landis Woodsman which was a 22-3000 case necked down to 17 caliber, which supposedly hit the 3,600 fps mark.

Ackley pioneered such wildcats as the 17 Hornet and the 17 Bee. Both these cartridges reportedly zipped along between 3,400 and 3,700 fps. The 17 Javelina, developed by Bill Atkinson and Paul Marquart of Arizona, proved to be one of the more popular 17 versions, based on a shortened 222 case and capable of pushing a 25-grain bullet along at 3,800 fps and up. Like the 220 Swift, the Javelina was tried on deer-sized game and like the Swift, produced the same results. Like the Swift, the 17-calibers began to get a bad name because they failed in a field in which they were not intended. Like the 220 Swift, the 17-caliber is a varmint cartridge *period*.

As soon as the 17 Remington appeared on the scene, history began to repeat itself once again. With the exception of the name of the cartridge, the stories were almost exact repeats

Opposite: A steady rest helps the author make the most of the 220 Swift's flat trajectory and explosive hitting power on small targets at distant ranges.
Below: Author prefers the 8 pound Remington 17 to the heavier 220 Swift for long summer treks and fast offhand shots.

of those we read about the 220—"totally worthless," "erratic performance," etc., etc.

It's been my experience and the experience of others whom I have read or spoken to, that the 220 is perhaps the most complete and satisfying *varmint* cartridge I have ever had the pleasure of owning. If I had to thin out my gun rack, the very last to go would be my Ruger 77V chambered for the 220 Swift.

If my experience and that of others has been good in the recent years, then what was all the fuss about before 1972? That's a fair question and I think that I have a few of the answers.

In the years preceding the introduction of the Swift, a cartridge capable of 4,000 feet per second was simply a dream. A dream very few expected to come true for 50 years. Then Joe Dreamer got out of bed one day and there it was, by Winchester! And then:

• Our hero, naturally, first stuffed it with as much powder as he could get in the case and see if he could make it go faster. BLAM—the rifle blows up.

• Next, if it will scatter a woodchuck about in a 50-foot radius, then it's got to be death on deer. The bullet hits bone and a deer with an ugly wound gallops off to die a slow death.

• Next, he has found a real tack driver, so, off to run two or three boxes through it before supper time. After the 46th round in 15 minutes, eggs could be fried on the barrel and the worthless piece of steel and wood won't keep a bullet on the paper.

• So the 220 Swift is difficult to load for, is an unpredictable killer, wears out barrels like his kid wears out shoes, and it's one of the most inaccurate cartridges he has ever had the misfortune of being acquainted with!

Two of the above incidents actually did happen. And history has repeated itself with the 17.

I bought my 17 Remington and two boxes of ammo from a fellow who couldn't wait to "get rid of the damn thing" for the small sum of $125. Hearing a laugh behind my back, I left and went straight to the local gunshop and purchased a cleaning rod and powder solvent, a Weaver K6 scope, a set of RCBS dies, some Remington No. 7½ primers and a box of 25-grain Hornady bullets. Not only had that fellow not

Author's pair of varminters match velocities and proper holds, but not weight and bulk. The shorter ranged 17 Remington Model 700 is right for walk-up shooting; the Swift for sitting.

topped this Remington 700 BDL with a scope, he apparently had never touched the bore with a cleaning rod and brass brush! By the next morning, the bore was shining and I had the scope installed.

I was zeroed in in no time and settled down to fire some record groups using the Remington ammo. Five 3-shot groups measured as follows: .69, .52, .75, .70, and .52-inch. Did I say something about history repeating itself? The next day, reloads—19 grains of IMR 4198—produced consistent groups hovering around the half-inch mark and churning up a muzzle velocity in the neighborhood of 3,900 fps. I bet the guy who sold me this "damn thing" eats catsup on roast pheasant.

Just about any rifleman who considers himself a varmint hunter is a reloader. Varmint hunting requires gilt edge accuracy and both the 220 Swift and the 17 Remington are capable of producing it. However, you may have to "pay the price" when it comes to these two super hot rounds. No, I'm not contradicting myself and saying that these two cartridges are difficult to load for, in my experience they've been quite the opposite. I make it a practice to weigh each load individually, to check the over-all case length after each loading, and to check for any thickening of case necks on a regular basis.

The 220 Swift is based on the old 6mm Lee Navy round. It's a very strong case. It has an over-all length of 2.205 inches and a 21 degree shoulder. That 21 degree shoulder as compared to the sharper 28 degree shoulder on the 22-250, has accounted for some reports of case neck thickening which results in the loader having to periodically check and ream the case neck. Whether you'll have to ream your cases or not, I do not know, but for what it's worth, I've never had to ream a Swift case yet and I usually get from six to eight loadings from each case before I discard it. New unprimed cases are available from Winchester, Norma and Frontier. I've never had any difficulty in finding brass.

IMR 4064 and 4320 are two of the powders that have worked best for me. My standard load consists of a CCI-200 primer, a Winchester, Norma or Frontier case, 38 grains of 4064 and a Speer 52-grain hollow point bullet, which, when put together, gives me an average muzzle velocity of 3,800 fps and groups that stay around the half-inch mark.

One of the past criticisms of the Swift was that it was only accurate with full power loads. This certainly

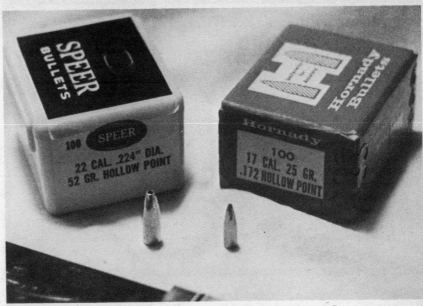

The 25-grain 17-cal. bullet is less than half the size of a 22-cal. 52-grain hollow point, yet when pushed to velocities approaching 4000 fps, the explosive effect is completely out of proportion to its size.

A Harris Bipod, 17 Remington and 22 Swift ammo, a pair of binoculars and a broad brimmed hat when combined with the 700 BDL and 77V rifles make for a pleasant day afield.

17 Remington

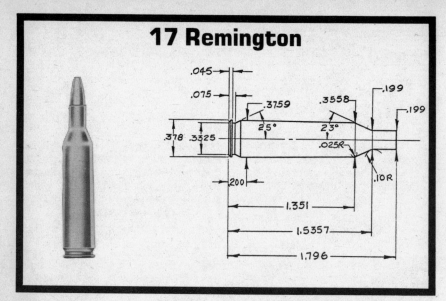

Suggested Loads for the 17 Remington*

Powder/grains	Muzzle Velocity
4198/17	3479
4198/19	3887
3031/20	3576
3031/21	3815
3031/22	3975
4895/21	3585
4895/24	4110
4320/22	3631
4320/24	4050

*All loads are for a 25-grain bullet. Only Remington 7½ or CFI-BR-4 primers should be used. The author or publisher assume no responsibility for the use of these loads by readers of this article.

220 Swift

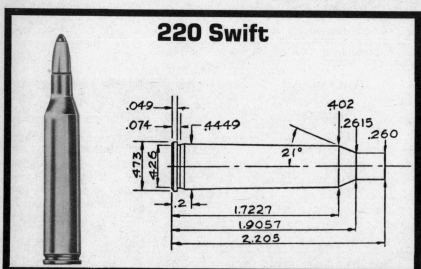

Suggested Loads for the 220 Swift*

Bullet (grs.)	Powder/grains	Muzzle Velocity
52	4064/35	3440
52	4064/38	3800
55	4064/38	3700
70	4320/34	3100
70	4831/39	3160

* The author or publisher assume no responsibility for the use of these loads by the readers of this article.

Author preparing to introduce a distant groundhog to the 220 Swift/Ruger 77V combo.

has not been the case with my 220, which has shown its best accuracy around the 3,700 and 3,800 fps mark. I have to believe that this was another of those Swift myths.

Another real winning combination in my Ruger has turned out to be the 70-grain Speer semi-spitzer in front of 40 grains of IMR 4350 which results in an average muzzle velocity of 3,250 fps and shoots into a consistent .75-inch at one hundred yards. It's interesting to note that this 70-grain Speer sports a ballistic coefficient of .214 as compared to .213 for the 75-grain Speer 6mm hollow point.

The 17 Remington is based on the 223 Remington, but with the neck reduced and the shoulder moved back slightly. The wildcat 17/223 has achieved some popularity but the 17 Remington is not the same creature as this wildcat as evidenced by the Remington's 23 degree shoulder versus the sharper 30 degree shoulder of the non-factory number.

If new or once-fired 17 Remington brass is difficult for you to come across, then you may reform 223 or 222 Magnum cases very easily. Case forming involves forming, trimming, and reaming. Any loads used with 223 military cases as well as the 222 Magnum cases should be reduced by at least 5%. New Remington cases have a length of 1.796″ whereas 223 Military cases may size as short as 1.770″.

The only real problem I experienced when I initially began loading for the 17 Remington was adjusting to the small diameter of the case neck and bullets. You'll need, in addition to a good set of dies, a powder funnel capable of dropping powder down that small neck and a 17-caliber case neck brush, all of which are available from RCBS. Remington and Hornady make excellent 25-grain 17-caliber bullets and I use them both with equally good results. My favorite powders are IMR 4198 and IMR 3031. My standard load consists of 19.0 grains of 4198, a Remington 7½ primer and the Hornady or Remington hollow point bullet. This load manages to give me .50 to .75-inch groups all day long.

A word of caution about primers is in order. Remington strongly recommends that their 7½ primers be used for best results. CCI-BR-4 primers, I've been hearing, provide good results in this 17 Remington case.

When I started putting my battery together, I always tried to match two rifles as close as it was ballistically possible. My pet deer rifle is a Ruger 77 chambered for the 30-06 and it's matched with a like model chambered for 308. The loads for these two rifles are very close. I've done the same thing with my pet varmint rifles also. The 17 and 220 with factory ammo shoot to almost identical points of impact at 100 and 200 yards. That is a big plus. More than once in the past I caught myself aiming at a 300-yard chuck with a 222 hold and a 220 Swift rifle.

At a little over 8 pounds, the Remington 700 BDL is a welcome companion on long summer walks after the tricky woodchuck. It's a 250-yard rifle. My 10-pound Ruger is a 300 to 350-yard varminter of the first order, but any 10-pound rifle gains a few pounds per hour with the temperature at 90° a long way from the car.

These cartridges are both about as safe as you can use because the bullets blow up so easily. The 17 Remington does have the edge on noise, and is noticeably easier on the ears in more densely populated areas.

If sighted to print ¾-inch high at 200 yards, the 17 drops only 5 inches at 300 yards. The little 17-cal. bullets have been accused of excessive wind drift but I don't think they blow off course much more than the popular 222 in the same wind. I sometimes feel this "excessive wind" drift is a bit overplayed anyway. When someone tells you that a certain cartridge is no good because when the wind is blowing at a 40-mile-per-hour clip, it "drifts" 14 inches, ask him how many people he knows who actually varmint hunt, squirrel hunt, etc., when the wind is blowing that hard.

The 17 Remington and the 220 Swift are interesting. Both rifles serve a definite purpose in the varmint hunting world. They are accurate, safe, and perhaps most important of all—they are fun. Don't believe everything you've read. •

I've tried inside and I've tried outside and for fixing cartridge case necks...

OUTSIDE IS BETTER

by **NORMAN E. JOHNSON**

A major reason for case neck turning or reaming is shown here by the excessively flattened and partially blown primer on a 257 Improved case sized down from a military surplus case resulting in an overly thick case neck. Bullet gripping by the case mouth during chambering can lead to serious results—even rifle blowups—and almost always some loss of accuracy.

THERE EXISTS some controversy with regard to the choice of procedures involving case mouth reaming versus outside neck turning as a means of reducing neck wall thickness, or, in general, improving uniformity of case neck walls where eccentricity is present.

There are two important reasons why case necks are reamed or turned, requiring, of course, some removal of case neck metal during the process from either the inside or the outside of the case neck. The usual reason for neck wall thickness reduction is to prevent excessive, and sometimes dangerous, bullet gripping by the case mouth during chambering. The second major reason involves improving case neck wall uniformity as a way of producing better rifle accuracy. This is particularly important in bench rest shooting or any shooting where accuracy under 3/4 MOA (minute of angle) is expected.

A little closer look at the difference between case neck reaming or turning will indicate which method may satisfy a specific need based on the type of shooting one does and the result preferred. There are some obvious advantages and also disadvantages noted when these methods are compared.

Repeated firing of high intensity cartridges, especially those having a steep shoulder, causes brass to flow forward into the case neck area thereby causing the neck wall to thicken. Repeated use of such brass cases can cause problems. Thickened case necks may also arise as a result of sizing down larger caliber cases as is common. Here again, neck walls thicken and should be restored to normal industry specifications. In some situations, new cases with maximum wall thickness, loaded with maximum diameter bullets but chambered in a rifle having minimum chamber neck dimensions can present problems after the first or second firing. The problem here, of course, is bullet gripping during chambering—a condition which must obviously be avoided from a safety standpoint.

On the accuracy side, variation in case neck wall thickness is a major cause of poor case/bullet alignment, a condition which usually contributes to some degree of inaccuracy on target. The bullet, when seated, becomes eccentric to the body of the case, contributing to noticeable runout and corresponding loss of accuracy. I pointed this out in my article in the Sixth Edition of HANDLOADER'S DIGEST, entitled "Bullet Alignment Vs. Accuracy," and also in the 1966 GUN DIGEST in "Case Neck Variations and Their Effect on Accuracy." These articles pretty much summed up the degree of variation in neck wall thickness one can tolerate, depending on the level of accuracy expected, as well as case-bullet runout variance relative to expected accuracy levels. In general, then, the levels of excellence one must try for with respect to case bullet runout and case neck wall variation can be seen in the table.

A point worth mentioning here entails eccentricity of case necks attributed to internal malalignment of sizing dies and bullet seating dies, per se. While sizing and seating dies can be checked for accuracy, little can be done to correct them if found defective. The fact remains, however, that even perfectly aligned and uniform case necks can result in malaligned ammunition if sizing and seating dies are of poor quality.

While average hunting performance may not show the significant ill effects of case-bullet runout resulting from thickened, non-uniform or badly aligned case necks, the benchrest shooter and serious varmint hunter will surely note such performance defects, usually produced as erratic performance. On the other hand, thickened case necks that stretch out to as little as .003" over maximum industry standards, can present a hazard to the

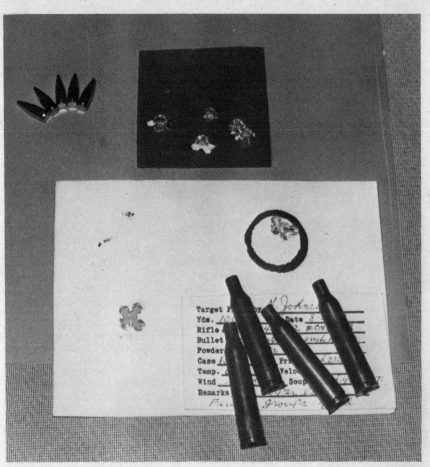

Normally the 220 Swift cartridge is not considered a benchrest performer, yet careful attention to case neck wall concentricity, including careful outside neck turning, enabled author's rifle to shoot 100-yard groups under ½ MOA and 400-yard groups under 2 inches.

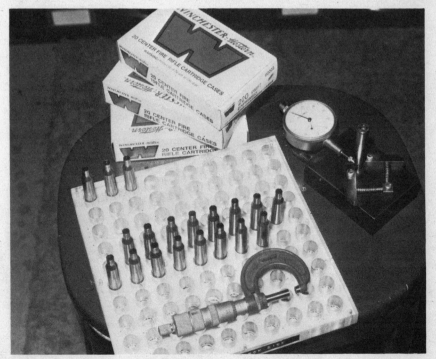

Author has determined through extensive testing that where serious accuracy is demanded, case necks should be checked and outside turned to within .00025" or less variation in thickness, if possible.

Special case neck wall thickness gauge with dial indicator designed and used by author to check neck wall thickness variation.

Case head expansion is frequently the result of excessive pressure generated by thick case neck "bullet gripping." Micrometer measurements before and after firing help shooter monitor pressure signs.

Performance Related Neck Wall Thickness Variation

Bench Rest Under 1/2 MOA Accuracy	Long Range Varmint Under .75 MOA	General Hunting
.00025"	.0015"	up to .008"

Performance Related Case-bullet Runout
as taken at bullet ogive 1/3 way proximal to bullet tip

Bench Rest 1/2 MOA or under	Long Range Varmint Under .75 MOA	General Hunting
.00025"	.001 - .0015"	.005 - .006"

Case-bullet runout gauge designed and used by author in special accuracy tests in connection with case neck wall thickness variation.

shooter as chambered bullets become restricted during firing.

Thus, having established two basic reasons for changing case neck wall dimensions, we can proceed to evaluate the merits or drawbacks of inside neck reaming versus outside neck turning.

Riflemen go to great lengths to evaluate methods and techniques in producing top grade accuracy. My experience in working with case necks goes back many years and grew from a twofold concern affecting both shooter's safety as well as accuracy.

Inside Neck Reaming

For some years I was quite satisfied to reduce case neck thickness by the quickest and simplest method at my disposal. This usually involved a basic shell holder and inside reamer for each specific caliber. My first real concern for the ineffectiveness of this method came about in 1964 while working with a target grade Model 70 Winchester in caliber 243 Winchester. It had routinely produced excellent accuracy until I chose to ream out the case necks using the standard inside reaming method. Immediately my accuracy worsened to the point where I became very concerned. Groups using match grade bullets which were previously averaging around 1/2 MOA opened up to near an inch at 100 yards, and several flyers were noted. I then set out on various experiments working with case necks, which has been an ongoing process for a number of years.

One of my first experiments included the evaluation of various techniques used to ream the inside of case necks to reduce neck wall thickness. My efforts proved less than optimistic using this method as I monitored my results using the following criteria: (1) Actual measurement of case neck wall variation around the periphery of case mouth using special case neck gauge. (2) Case-bullet runout tests taken before and after reaming, using a special dial indicator bullet alignment gauge. (3) Accuracy tests on target comparing performance both before and after inside neck reaming using more than a dozen bench rest rifles.

The ensuing test results led to my

eventual discontinuance of inside case neck reaming except for use in accuracy levels where pure bench rest accuracy wasn't demanded. Two benefits do present themselves in this type of case neck alteration, namely cost effectiveness and ease of operation. A hundred cases can be inside reamed in less than half an hour.

Before I leave this method of case neck wall thinning, I should like to point out another most discouraging result which I had encountered using this technique. I had one lot of 100 caliber 220 Swift cases which had gradually but symmetrically thickened to a neck wall thickness averaging about .021". I was seeing a few mild pressure signs but accuracy was good. Case-bullet runout was under .001" at the time. I elected to inside ream the entire lot of 100 cases which had all been alternately fired around six times prior to the reaming operation. Accuracy immediately fell off as a result. Case neck walls varied by as much as .007" after reaming and case-bullet runout jumped to a discouraging average between .002" to .008". In short, I had ruined my cases. This particular experience is quite indicative of my results with other cartridges too, and pretty much sums up my poor recommendation for using this method. The primary problem associated with inside reaming arises from the reaming process doing nothing more than enlarging a hole in a case mouth having non-uniform wall thickness. It does nothing to correct eccentricity. Metal is usually removed unevenly and only in isolated cases will a good result occur, even with symmetric cases. Of course, such neck reaming is sufficient to provide the necessary .002"-.003" clearance between case and chamber neck where accuracy is not a primary consideration.

Outside Case Neck Turning

My experience using outside case neck turning involves a variety of techniques. These include the use of commercially available, hand-operated neck turning devices manufactured by such companies as Marquart Precision and Forster Products, and these do a very satisfactory job. I also use a precision turning lathe using a collet-held case mouth mandrel or a special motor driven case neck lathe which I designed and built for the job. The job of outside case neck turning usually costs more and requires somewhat more time than inside reaming but produces an outstandingly accurate result if performed correctly.

The principle involved using any of

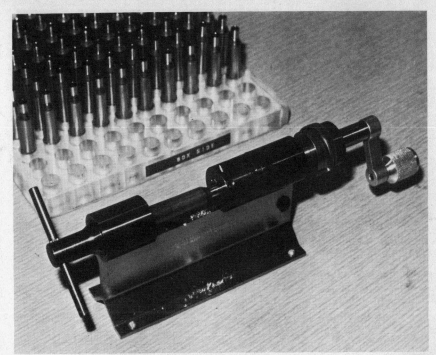

Outside case neck turning tool manufactured by Forster does good job of restoring neck wall thickness to uniformity.

By using a special collet-held spindle to hold case mouth friction tight and primer pocket in lathe live center, author produces near perfect case neck wall thickness uniformity during outside neck turning.

Closeup view of lathe performing precision outside neck turning operation. Case necks can be quickly outside turned to any desired wall thickness. Uniformity to less than .0001″ is possible in this way.

these three outside neck turning devices requires the use of a mandrel or guide inside the case mouth as a locating point. The commercially produced outside neck turning units usually use a hand turned cutting edge which revolves around the case neck aligned by a pilot, thereby reducing case wall thickness. The lathe principle involves a rotating case held in true alignment as a carefully positioned cutting edge moves along the axis of the case neck. My experiences with the lathe type principle have given outstanding results producing near perfect neck thickness measurements. The degree of accuracy in using the lathe method of reducing wall thickness is easily maintained at under .0002″ and any subsequent measurable bullet runout is primarily a contribution of the bullet seating operation and not that of poor case neck wall uniformity.

The lathe method, then, is the most accurate I have found to produce uniformity of case neck walls and requires the careful production and use of a case mouth mandrel cut to exact size in a lathe collet and left in the collet until all cases are sized. Cases are later outside turned to a desired uniform thickness at a rate of about 100 cases per hour in this way.

To make the mandrel I simply cut a stainless steel rod, held in the lathe collet, to a diameter .0005″ over the size of the sizing die expander plug. The case is then sized with a good quality sizing die and the .0005″ friction fit holds it securely in place on the lathe as I butt the lathe live center gently into the primer pocket to align and hold the case head. I use a good, sharp carbide cutting tool to shave off the required brass from the neck in one smooth pass of the lathe carriage. As the lathe tailstock releases the live center from the primer pocket, the case rotates in perfect alignment and can be removed from the mandrel by grasping it firmly with the fingers.

There is one caution I should like to point out here involving the use of outside neck turning or reaming in conjunction with poorly aligned neck or full-length sizing dies. Any attempt to turn or ream poorly aligned case necks as a result of bad sizing operation spells trouble. Turning or reaming such necks will result in a non-uniform tapered neck, a direct opposite of the result we are trying to obtain.

For serious shooting I run a routine check on all new cases and if correction is required, on even a small percentage of them, I go through the usual

The basic lathe collet and spindle principle puts the lathe live center in primer pocket. System is used by author to outside turn necks.

case sizing procedure and outside turn the entire lot.

A helpful case sizing procedure which I have used involves a two stage or single, somewhat larger, expander plug when performing the case neck sizing operation. This, of course, can be used either with full-length or neck sizing only. My reasoning behind this is based on the tests which I have performed which convincingly indicate that a lighter, more uniform bullet pull from the loaded case mouth produces better accuracy. This is particularly true for those shooters in the envied bracket—near or under half MOA. The larger expander plug also promotes an easier and less upsetting bullet seating operation. Too firm a bullet seating pressure can totally destroy fine accuracy, and many shooters are quite unaware of this. Some bullet seating operations actually shave copper from the side of the bullet, usually on one side, and cause considerable case-bullet runout as well as case bending.

I usually change to an expander plug in the range just .0005" under actual bullet size. The normal range here is around .001" under or less, and is altogether too firm a seating pressure for most serious accuracy needs. My first experience with bullet pull effects was written up in the July 1967 *American Rifleman* and was based on some accuracy problem which I encountered with bullet pull variation.

Bullet pull variance is largely attributed to case neck wall thickness differences from case to case, providing another good reason for turning case necks to as uniform a thickness as possible. I now outside turn case necks to within .0002" or less and a desired bilateral clearance between case neck and chamber neck of around .002". My experiments have shown, however, that reducing neck walls decidedly more, even to a neck chamber clearance as much as .008" doesn't appear to noticeably affect accuracy so long as case-bullet alignment remains good and bullet seating depth is just short of the lands. This is assuming that the case, per se, is the primary aligning factor of the chambered cartridge and not the case neck itself.

When we consider that a lot of 100 cases, when repeatedly reloaded and fired, will likely be sufficient to wear out the average rifle barrel, the amount of time devoted to proper case preparation and maintenance seems a relatively small contribution for the benefits we derive. I, for one, require no further justification for doing so. ●

Special motor-driven mini-lathe designed and built by author to outside turn case necks. Here a 220 Swift is seen in place.

Closeup view of case in special lathe. Case neck mouth fits special spindle as a precision carbide cutting tool removes metal during outside turning operation to a neck wall thickness of less than .0001" variation.

The Forty-One: All-Around Magnum

by **RUSS GAERTNER**

Handgunners soak up controversy, and I'm no exception. A long-standing argument centers around the .41 Magnum, introduced by Remington in 1964 as the ideal police caliber. Smith & Wesson chambered two revolvers for the new cartridge, and Ruger followed with the Blackhawk, but the guns and the round have not prospered in competition with the widely accepted .357 and .44 Magnums. I think handgunners are passing up a good bet.

Experts tend to discourage shooters from trying a .41 with such remarks as: "If you can manage a .41 Magnum, you can handle a .44." I can personally disprove that.

Other writers base their verdict on the .41's failure to displace .38 Special and .357 Magnum police guns. I reject that one because such factors as use in snubbies and ease of control in fast double action by inexpert officers come into play.

Some who turn thumbs down complain that no short, cheap loads can be fired in .41 Magnum guns, but .38 and .44 Specials are usable in .357 and .44 Mags. This is trivial because factory .44 Specials are expensive and too weak to be useful, and only the mildest .38 Specials should be fired in .357 chambers. Full .38 loads can erode chamber walls ahead of the case mouth, as I discovered to my sorrow.

The unanswerable argument is that top .41 Magnum power falls short of the heaviest .44 levels. Various tricks have been tried by .41 fans to "disprove" this fact. One writer even measured velocities of very hot .41 handloads from a 10-inch Contender barrel. He failed to mention that his loads were probably too hot for revolvers.

Yes, .44 Magnum revolvers are certainly more powerful than .41s, *but* the .41 can be handloaded for more power than *factory-loaded* .44s. A handloaded .41 Magnum revolver can produce 1,000-1,100 ft.-lbs., and do so safely. I will detail special methods, components and equipment to do the job.

Author's careful work leads to very hot loads revealed here. To let him prove his point, cut 20% to start.

Personally, I shoot and like all of the brothers Magnum. They're all great! Having recently tackled the .41 in depth, I can now make a solid case for the caliber as *our best all-around magnum revolver cartridge.* By that I mean that you can do virtually everything with a good .41 that you can with *both* a .357 and a .44, if you handload. And that includes the gamut of tough handgunning.

Coming from a shooter whose favorite guns were .44 Magnums until a couple of years ago, and who has written ten articles extolling the virtues of both the .357 and .44 Maggies, that is quite a mouthful. My reasons for trying the .41 were personal, but the facts speak for themselves.

First, let's look at the .41 revolvers, because you can't separate a cartridge from the guns chambered for it. I worked with two guns: the Smith & Wesson Model 57 and the New Model Blackhawk. Both are great guns but they are quite unalike.

The Smith M57 is a beautiful double-action revolver with premium features, including target grips, sights, trigger and hammer. It's hefty, the 6-inch gun topping 48 ounces, an ounce heavier than the 6½-inch Model 29 .44 Magnum, with which it is otherwise identical. The outside cylinder and barrel diameters are the same, but .41 chambers and bore are smaller, so the M57 carries more steel and is actually stronger. The extra strength is unnecessary but the weight helps to moderate recoil, so this may be a gun for the recoil-sensitive shooter. The Model 57 is not cheap (about $420 list price), and you will pay a premium to get one promptly, though the M57 is said to be in better supply than the M29.

More readily available is the Ruger Blackhawk single-action in .41 Magnum. Not a premium gun, it certainly qualifies as a fine value, probably the "best buy" (about $200 list.) It has a durable blue on the strong steel cylinder, receiver frame and barrel, though it is not highly polished. The grip frame is a dull black-finished aluminum alloy, which keeps the gun's weight down to a handy 40 ounces. Some object to this grip frame, but it is serviceable and strong.

The essential difference between the two guns is in their actions. I like to do some double-action shooting, and the Smith is a great DA gun. Whether the general shooter needs DA is another matter. The SA Ruger is more than adequate for all-around use, and it is tougher than the double-action Smith for field carrying. The Smith may be slightly faster for a second shot than the Ruger, but a good SA shooter can get off an accurate second shot in 2-3 seconds, less than a second slower than a good DA shooter. It's a matter of personal preference.

Both guns benefit from some careful

work to deliver their best performance. The Smith has a fine single-action trigger pull as delivered, but the DA pull is heavy and needs smoothing. I do this work myself, but if you are not familiar with it, leave the job to a good 'smith. I strongly recommend Mag-na-porting of the big magnums and Mag-na-port Arms (30016 S. River Rd., Mount Clemens, Michigan 48045) can do a tuning job on guns they are porting. I have this package on several Smiths and it has been excellent.

Practical grips are a must for me. Usually I make my own, but a set of Pachmayr's Presentation grips on the Model 57 has given me the most secure hold I've had on any handgun, and they're a comfortable fit, too.

The Ruger needs a good tuning to smooth and lighten the action and remove the creep in the trigger pull. Simply installing a Bullseye trigger return spring will lighten the pull weight (Trapper Gun, 28019 Harper, St. Clair Shores, Mich. 48043), and it is well worth the $6.95 price. Ruger grips are usable out of the box, but I wanted a longer set with a filler behind the trigger guard. I made them out of smooth walnut, but Herrett and others have good models.

Smith & Wesson offered the Model 58 Military and Police, a 4-inch DA revolver with fixed sights. Though handier to carry than a 6-inch gun, the M58 still weighs 41 ounces. The .41 Magnum loses too much, I think, from a 4-inch barrel and I believe any handgun for general use needs adjustable sights.

A low-cost route to a .41 is to have a used large-cylinder .357 Magnum rechambered and the barrel rebored The S & W Model 28 Highway Patrolman (N frame) or a Ruger Blackhawk can be converted for something over $50. The job should be done by a well-equipped specialist. David Woodruff (Box 5, Bear, Delaware 19701) works in this field and will not touch a poorly suited gun. This conversion makes better sense to me than the popular change to .45 Colt, in terms of greater strength and better performance.

To compare the three magnum cartridges, I collected the data in Table I by firing Remington full loads from standard revolvers with 6-6½ inch barrels. All had cylinder/barrel gaps of .004-.005 inch, on the tight side for maximum velocities.

There is a sizable difference between factory published data and that found from standard revolvers, due to the factory's use of solid test barrels

with no gaps. Others have found similar results, but we need to compare these loads with top handloads.

Percentages make the differences clearer. The factory-loaded .41 Magnum is actually 52% more powerful than the .357 and only 16% less powerful than the .44. With other barrel lengths, bullet weights, and makes of ammo, these numbers will vary some. But the relative rankings will remain similar.

How do these numbers translate into practical needs? Experts tell us that 1,000 ft.-lbs. is the minimum power for humane hunting of big game. The .44 just passes that test, the .41 falls about 150 ft.-lbs. short, and the .357 manages just above half.

Others claim that the .357 Magnum is adequate for big game. I've never hunted with a .357, but I think that even with perfect bullet placement the cartridge is underpowered for any-

Heavy 41 Magnum handloads kick plenty, but not as punishingly as a fullhouse 44. The author now easily manages the heaviest reasonable loads in a Model 57 Smith. A recovering rheumatoid arthritic, Gaertner argues that the 41 is controllable by the average serious handgunner, while the 44 may not be.

thing larger or tougher or more dangerous than small deer.

My experience has been limited entirely to the .44 Magnum for actual hunting. Let me briefly describe just the results of two hunts with the .44 single-action revolver.

My first shot at a prime, male Colorado black bear from about 10 yards over a pack of hounds was good. The 225-grain Speer JHP dropped him almost instantly and he was dead in less than half a minute, although three follow-shots were taken. This was a clean, humane kill due to plenty of power and perfect bullet placement in the lung/spine area.

Another time, however, I took three shots with a .44, spread out over several minutes, to finish a Tennessee wild boar. The first two shots seemed to have no effect on the big Rooshian, as they call them, even though the hits missed vital organs by just a few inches. It was bad bullet placement by definition. The boar never was knocked off of his feet, until the final brain shot. Not a clean or humane kill, despite pretty fair shooting and sufficient power. If we had not been using dogs, we might have lost that boar,

Two great 41 Magnum handguns, the Ruger Blackhawk single-action and the Smith & Wesson Model 57 revolvers. The author's Ruger wears a homemade set of smooth walnut grips, while the M57 carries Pachmayr rubber stocks. Logo and legends are gold-filled.

and he would have died painfully and slowly from his wounds.

My point is that even a .44 Magnum has none too much power, not enough to make up for poor bullet placement, but the more power the better, if you can handle it under field conditions. In my opinion, the .41 Magnum is the least powerful handgun which should be used on big game, and that only by good marksmen who will pass up doubtful shots.

With this data in mind, it's obvious that the .41 Magnum has power, but how versatile is it? There is a factory 210-grain lead load at a claimed 1050 fps (515 ft.-lbs.), about equal to a full .357 load in power. This is the police load, suitable for well controlled double-action fire. From 6-inch revolvers it produces 980 fps or 447 ft.-lbs. The loading is good for general use but

it is easily duplicated by more economical handloads. Nearby there is a complete discussion of my handloads.

The .357 Magnum was once believed to be as heavy-recoiling as a man could reasonably manage and still hit accurately. When the .44 Magnum appeared, we were assured that only steel-fisted 300-pound wrestlers could bear its jarring recoil. We were even warned that an ordinary mortal could expect to have a wrist broken or all of the skin torn from his palm! Hogwash!

When the overblown rhetoric was discounted, the .44 was not a Superman's gun. Any normal adult can shoot it safely. Few shooters *enjoy* the fullhouse .44. I was one of them, however, liking nothing better than a range session in which I fired three or more boxes of heavier-than-factory loads from the Smith & Wesson Model

29 or a single action such as my Ruger Super Blackhawk, or the old scoped Herter, practicing before a hunt or testing loads.

Several years ago my handgunning skills evaporated almost overnight. I was hit in the summer of 1977 by rheumatoid arthritis, RA for short, the crippling kind, which caused so much pain and weakness in swollen joints that shooting was out of the question. After several months I was still so weak and my hands so painful that I could barely hold a .22 auto up to eye level, and unsteadiness prevented my hitting anything. As for DA shooting, I could not pull a lightened double action more than a few times. Any physical activity had to be paid for with stiffness and pain.

I don't need the reader's sympathy. The point is that illness gave me a chance to learn just how much recoil a weakened, or normally weak, person could handle. About a year ago, medical treatment began to take effect. Soon I could shoot target handguns, including the .45 auto and a .357 Magnum Dan Wesson with medium handloads, though not accurately. I tried others but a .44 Maggie was too much for me with any loads heavier than mild. At that time I estimate my general strength at 35-40% of normal.

I had been thinking about .41 Magnum revolvers, and it seemed to offer a good test of the caliber to try shooting these guns. If I, a partially recovered RA victim, could manage .41 recoil, then any normal adult could surely do the same, with practice.

Table I

Remington Factory Loads

Caliber/ Bullet	Factory Data From Test Barrels			From Revolvers*	
	Velocity, fps	Energy, ft.-lbs.	Recoil, ft.-lbs.	Velocity, fps	Energy, ft.-lbs.
.44 Mag. 240 JSP	1470	1150	16	1380	1013
.41 Mag. 210 JSP	1500	1050	12	1352	851
.357 Mag. 158 JSP	1550	842	6	1270	566

*Measured with the Oehler Models 11 and 33 chronographs with Skyscreens; average instrumental velocities 5 feet from the muzzles of the following revolvers: .44, 6½-inch Herter; .41 Ruger 6¼-inch Blackhawk; .357, 6-inch Dan Wesson.

Smith & Wesson barrels and cylinders in the big magnums are identical except for the smaller-diameter chambers and bores in the 41 Model 57 (left), resulting in its slightly thicker and stronger walls and webs, compared to 44 Magnum Model 29 on right.

Author habitually uses Lee Rest in shooting long test strings, found the practice very helpful as he recuperated from arthritis.

Nine different 41 Magnum near-maximum jacketed handloads fired one-handed, offhand by the author at 25 yards from S&W Model 57. Four different bullets (170, 200, 210 and 220 grains) were fired and no two loads were the same, showing the 41 Magnum's tendency to shoot to the same zero. The group was one of the author's first proving that even a recovering rheumatoid arthritic can manage a heavily loaded 41.

Ruger Blackhawk mounted in the Lee rest and ready to fire over the Oehler Chronotach Skyscreens and group on a target downrange, giving simultaneous accuracy and average velocity of handloads. The S&W M57 awaits its turn.

Nine loads from the Ruger Blackhawk in the Lee rest, grouped on the back of a standard target. Several measures less than one inch center-to-center of widest hits, fired at 25 yards through chronograph screens.

At first the .41s made my weak wrists and hands sore, even using the Lee rest, but I was still improving week by week. After another two months I tackled longer sessions with heavy loads from the Lee rest, or I fired these using a two-hand hold for fair accuracy and speed. Double action fire was still too much.

It was about three months longer before I could shoot a .41 Magnum with one hand, offhand, and keep most of my hits in the black of a rapid-fire 25-yard target. This was slow fire, of course, but I felt real pride at my first target in that category, and it happened that the loads were nine different ones with four different bullets, left over from a session with the Lee rest which I had just finished. All were heavier than factory! Quite an improvement for an arthritic barely able to lift a .22 a few months before!

As this is written my shooting has improved to include pretty accurate DA control of the Smith M57 with full loads. Naturally I have periodically tested myself with a .44 Magnum. My Mag-na-ported Smith Model 29 is still too rough with heavy loads, but I can handle a dozen or so heavy handloads in the Ruger Super Blackhawk, also Mag-na-ported. These loads carry about 80% of full power.

This experience proved to me that a person with perhaps 50-60% of normal adult strength and some RA-damaged joints in his hands and arms can shoot a full-power .41 Magnum, but that such a person cannot withstand full .44 recoil. Of course, I didn't have to learn any of these guns, because I have fired the .44s for years. I have also proved that heavy handgunning does no harm to a recovering RA victim. I have enjoyed the .41s and credit some of my recovery to the interest and exercise of regular handloading and trips to the range.

Sure, the .41 is a big step up from the .357, but my experience says that any normal adult *can* handle a .41 with the heaviest safe handloads, which are heavier than factory loads. So, load the .41 down to .357 levels, if you like, then begin to work up as you learn the gun and caliber. Before long you can be shooting .44 Magnum power accurately in the more manageable .41.

The .41 Magnum is capable of the entire range of useful power for any need from plinking to hunting dangerous big game. Handload the .41, and you don't need either a .357 or a .44!

I believe, with all these good reasons, that .41 Magnum is our best all-around magnum caliber.

How Gaertner Loads His Forty-Ones

For 90% or more of any shooter's needs, cast bullets are ideal. They are easy on the gun and inexpensive. One or two bullet designs will do almost any job in the right loads. Only the heaviest loads require jacketed bullets; they will be covered later.

I don't cast my own slugs, devoting my efforts to load development and testing. For years I have tried cast bullets by various makers, but most of them are too soft, including some newer swaged types, even for velocities below 1,000 fps.

The products of Taylor Bullets (327 E. Hutchins, San Antonio, TX 78221) are cast hard enough for all kinds of shooting in calibers from 9mm to .45. Their 215-grain SWC is my favorite for .41 Magnum. It is accurate well beyond 100 yards and can be pushed to 1100-1200 fps with little leading in the right loads. It will not expand much, but is useful for small or medium-sized game or less serious uses, and I like it for double-action practice.

Note added in proof. The author learned recently that Taylor Bullets, producer of the 215-grain SWC used in loads for this article, has discontinued bullet casting. However, other good .410″ 210-215 grain SWCs can be substituted for the Taylor bullet.

Shooters who want a heavier bullet for silhouettes, for example, might try the 225-grain SWC by Ohio Shooters Supply, 7532 Tyler Blvd., Mentor, OH 44060. Their bullets are machine-cast and wax-lubed. They are not target quality and some have poorly filled, rough bases. Bullets selected for good bases were nicely accurate from my Ruger in the Lee rest.

Several loads were developed with the 225-grain SWC. A fine general purpose load was 7.0 grains of Unique for 893 fps (398 ft-lbs.) and tight 1.2″ 5-shot 25-yd. groups. My warmest good load used 8.5 grains of Unique to give 1050 fps (551 ft-lbs.) and 1.3″ groups with allowable leading. Hotter loads leaded too much and were less accurate. Herco (7.0 grains) gave a good light load (825 fps) with 1.5″ groups.

Author's careful work leads to very hot loads revealed here. To let him prove his point, cut 20% to start.

For target shooting, plinking, or general shooting at ranges out to 50 yards, a full wadcutter is accurate and effective. The Green Bay 210-grain WC is usable up to 1100 fps without excessive leading. I consider leading bad if two dozen shots deposit enough metal to affect accuracy and begin to raise pressures.

If you do much experimenting with the warmer cast bullet loads, you will need to delead whenever visible deposits build up. The usual method is to fire several jacketed loads and clean promptly. This works, but such loads are not cheap, and heavy loads should not be fired in a leaded barrel. The best lead remover I've used is sold by Big 45 Frontier Gun Shop (Valley Springs, SD 57068) at less than a dollar. It looks like stainless steel turnings but is softer, and a few strands wrapped around a brass brush will break up leading quickly and harmlessly.

Table II lists loads with these two bullets which fill almost any bill, except those which can only be met with the heaviest jacketed loadings.

Either Unique or Herco covers the most useful range of loads. Eight grains of Unique behind the Green Bay WC gave 1080 fps (Load 5) and the same charge of Herco, 1066 fps (Load 6); both are good loads grouping into about 2 inches. A more accurate load is the WC over 7.5 grains of 231 for 1086 fps. These groups and velocities are for my guns, of course, but the loads are not critical and should apply to other guns of the same makes fairly generally.

Switching to the Taylor bullet, 8.0 grains of Unique gave me 1024 fps and 1.5 inch groups. The same weight of Herco, 1035 fps in Load 14. Dropping down to 7.0 grains of either powder and bullet made the mild Loads 4, 10, and 13 with velocities in the 927-1000 fps range. I call these "mild" but a perusal of ammunition tables shows that they are still pretty stiff handgun loadings, as hot as top .45 auto rounds, for instance.

For hotter loads, I like the Taylor 215 SWC with 9.0 grains of Unique or Herco. The latter powder gave my most accurate cast bullet combination, Load 15 averaging 1.2 inch groups at 25 yards. That is as good as factory ammo from my guns, or my better jacketed bullet rounds. I don't guarantee that other guns can match that, but the load should be very accurate in any sound gun. Ten grains of Herco or Unique was too hot and leaded badly; even 9.5 grains was too much.

My hottest practical load was made with the Taylor bullet over 10.0 grains of SR 4756, for 1206 fps and 694 ft.-lbs. That combination is the closest thing to a jacketed hot load which I developed, with fine 1.5 inch groups and just light leading. Load 16 is a good candidate for hunting and silhouette shooting, or serious defensive shooting.

Bullseye (5.0 grains, Loads 1 and 9) gave good target loads with either bullet, shooting into 1.3-1.5 inches, or 6.0 grains of 231 gave similar results with fair accuracy (Load 2). Velocities ran 872-888 fps, which may seem high for paper punching, but lighter charges did not match the uniformity of these from my guns. They are also good beginning double-action practice rounds.

My handloading methods for cast bullet loads were conventional. I use a

These six bullets, in the right loads, can handle any 41 Magnum need from plinking to big game hunting. All are a true .410-inch in diameter: (left to right) Green Bay 210-gr. wadcutter; Taylor 215-gr. semi-wadcutter; Sierra 170-gr. jacketed hollow cavity; Speer 200-gr. jacketed hollow point; Sierra 210-gr. jacketed hollow cavity; Speer 220-gr. jacketed soft point.

regular RCBS die set with one addition, the RCBS carbide sizer, which actually polishes the brass as it resizes. No need to lubricate or remove grease later, either. Well worth the price, but be sure to get a die with a *tapered* insert to avoid the unsightly "squeeze ring" produced by some straight sizers.

After resizing I decapped and expanded, belling the mouth just enough to start a bullet by hand. If primer pockets are caked with primer residues, I clean them or tumble the brass for general polishing with ground nut hull medium. Repriming was with CCI No. 300 regular large pistol primers, seated fully in a separate RCBS priming tool.

For velocity and accuracy work, I weighed each powder charge on a Lyman/Ohaus scale. Bullet seating and crimping were done in one step with the punch set to seat the bullet down to its crimping groove. This worked with the Taylor bullet, but if loads with the Green Bay WC were to be fired in the Ruger I had to seat them about a sixteenth of an inch deeper, otherwise the rounds could not be fully chambered in the Ruger. To match velocities with the regular seating, I cut powder charges 0.5 grain, since shorter seating raises pressures and velocities.

Crimping was not critical, and I used a mild crimp which is easy on the brass. With the short-seated WC, the crimper was adjusted to barely remove the belling at the mouth.

Other guns, components and methods will give somewhat different results. The largest source of varying velocities in other revolvers is variation in cylinder/barrel gap size, I believe. As received, my Smith M57 had a gap of .008 inch, at the long end of the usually preferred range, .004-.008 inch The .008-inch gap is fine for double-action work, where residue buildup on the cylinder face can hang up the rotation, and for most other shooting. But top performance with hot loads is harder to get with a wide gap, and loads developed in such a gun would be overpressured in many guns with tighter gaps. So I adjusted the Smith gap to .005 inch to match the Ruger Blackhawk's gap. I was lucky to do it right first try, but amateur gunsmiths would do well to leave their guns as is and develop loads suited to them.

Cast bullets serve well for 90% or more of the .41 Magnum shooter's needs, but hunting big game or knocking down heavy metal silhouettes at long ranges calls for well-designed jacketed bullets pushed to higher velocities. To put it another way, we need to make the .41 shoot as much like a .44 Magnum as possible.

Pushing the .41 up to and over 1,000 ft.-lbs. of muzzle energy, even with the right powders and bullets, required higher efficiencies than I could get with usual methods and dies.

The theory of high performance (H-P) handloading is to use heavy charges of slower powders, ignite them uniformly and burn them efficiently at high-normal pressures. This is possible only in handloads made up with a heavy bullet pull, not just a hard crimp. To get uniformly heavy bullet pulls, the brass must be resized in a "tight" sizing die and expanded with an undersized expander.

I ordered these from RCBS (P. O. Box 1919, Oroville, Ca 95965), to be made so the sizer would reduce the case mouth inside diameter to .404 inch and the stem to open the neck to .405 inch. These dimensions are only .002-.003 inch smaller than you get from standard die sets, but they make all the difference.

For H-P loading I picked new, or once- or twice-fired, clean R-P brass, resized it first in the RCBS carbide die, then lubed lightly and resized full-length in the RCBS tight sizer. Next I degreased it in a tumbler with thinner-moistened cloth scraps.

I trimmed the brass on a Lyman Universal trimmer to 1.275 inches; even new brass may vary enough to prevent a uniform crimp from being applied. Then came expansion with the .405 stem and light belling at the mouth, followed by light chamfering if necessary. At this stage, the brass should be inspected for possible splits around the mouth; primer pockets may need cleaning.

Repriming is done with CCI No. 350 magnum large pistol primers. (Never use large *rifle* primers in handgun calibers.) Powders suited to H-P loads are hard to ignite; some of them work well with regular primers of some brands, but I use magnums for uniformity in all heavy H-P work. I use a separate RCBS priming tool to "feel" them to the bottom of the pockets.

Powder charges for these loads were weighed individually. However, a good measure such as my Ohaus Du-O-Measure, is faster for larger batches and almost as accurate as weighing.

Bullets were seated, then crimped in a separate step. The Sierra bullets were seated to be crimped into their cannelures, and the Speers, which have no cannelure, are seated with the front edge of the jackets about .05 inch below the mouths, then crimped over the jackets. I try to match the factory crimp, but it is not critical if resizing is correct.

There is my procedure for H-P handloads. It works well, and it is certainly safer than careless target handloading, because a double charge of fast target powder, such as Bullseye, can blow up a gun. H-P charges fill the cases, so it is impossible to stuff double charges into the cases; heavy charges must be compressed during bullet seating, in some cases.

With that procedure under our belts, let's turn to results. Then we will consider how to get a handle on pressures. First, a word of caution: my components were from different batches and lots from those which a reader might use. Hodgdon's H110, for example, is a great powder and one of the best for .41, but "old" H110 was hotter and lighter charges were required than more recently marketed powder (which I used here). Bullets also vary; I found one box of a certain bullet which measured closer to .411 inch in diameter than the correct .410 inches. It's a good idea to mike bullets, because even .001 inch oversize can raise pressures in heavy loads.

Second, no two guns are exactly identical. Minimum chambers raise pressures; a tight gap has the same effect. Weak or badly timed guns are bad news for H-P handloading. If in doubt, ask a pistolsmith to check your gun, before you start pushing for top loads.

What it comes down to is that true H-P loads must be worked up carefully for each gun. *My* loads are safe in *my* guns, but they may be too hot for *your* guns. They are meant to show what can be done with the caliber and components which are widely available, *not* to be used directly in your guns. If I were going to develop a load for another .41 Magnum handgun I would start with charges 3 or 4 grains below my maximum charges for the same bullet and powder, then work up in .5 grain increments, watching for pressure signs.

Are H-P results worth all the trouble? If you need top performance, the answer is "Yes," because there is no other way to get it. Only the individual shooter can decide whether to push his gun and himself this hard.

I developed top loads for four jacketed bullets, one each of 170, 200, 210 and 220 grains. All were .410 inch in diameter, and two were designed for rapid expansion, while the other two were able to penetrate deeper with less expansion. Other makes may be equally good, but these bullets proved to be capable of both fine accuracy and exceptional power. I'll discuss the results listed in Table III in order of increasing bullet weight.

1. *Sierra 170-grain JHC*. This little jacketed hollow cavity design is the high velocity champ in .41 Magnum. It will give the mildest recoiling H-P loads and the greatest expansion, when fired at comparable muzzle energies. These points in its favor mean that it is the true H-P bullet for the caliber. However, remember that higher velocities tend to be less uniform and light bullets do not penetrate well.

The only excellent propellant I've found for the 170 is Hodgdon's H110. The most accurate load was 24.0 grains for 1569 fps or 928 ft.-lbs., which gave me 1.2 inch groups from the Lee Machine Rest at 25 yards. That's a fine load for coyote, antelope, small deer and other lightly built animals. Shock at that velocity would be explosive on such game.

Good as Load A was, both Loads B and C topped it, at least for power. B with 25.0 grains of H110 edged over 1,000 ft.-lbs., still with 1.5 inch accuracy. My maximum was 26.0 grains H110 (Load C), which did not show excessive pressures in my guns, and this is as much H110 as can be stuffed in the case and compressed during bullet seating. 1074 ft.-lbs. and 1.4 inch groups, too! The only drawback is a lot of muzzle blast and flash, but that is characteristic of most H-P loads.

The hollow cavity design with dead soft lead core expands to a saucer-shaped disc over an inch in diameter when fired into Duxseal. Expansion is less explosive on game, and the slug is

Table II

.41 Magnum Cast Bullet Handloads

Load	Bullet/grs.	Powder Type	Weight, grains	Velocity, fps	Remarks
1	Green Bay WC/210	Bullseye	5.0	872	Good target load; 1.3 inch groups.
2	"	231	6.0	888	Mild; 2.0 inch groups.
3	"	231	7.5	1086	Good general load; 1.4 inch groups.
4	"	Unique	7.0	1000	Medium Load.
5	"	"	8.0	1080	General load; 1.7 inch groups.
6	"	Herco	8.0	1066	Good Load.
7	"	"	9.0	1193	OK, but too much leading.
8	"	"	9.0	1240	Short seated (see text); too much leading.
9	Taylor SWC/215	Bullseye	5.0	885	Target load; 1.5 inch groups.
10	"	Unique	7.0	930	Mild; DA practice; 1.5 inch groups.
11	"	"	8.0	1024	Good load; 1.5 inch groups.
12	"	"	9.0	1161	Fair load; 2.7 inch groups.
13	"	Herco	7.0	927	Good mild load.
14	"	"	8.0	1035	General load.
15	"	"	9.0	1109	Most accurate warm load; 1.2 inch groups.
16	"	SR 4756	10.0	1206	Best hot load; 1.5 inch groups.

Notes: All loads made in old fired R-P brass with CCI No. 300 regular large pistol primers. Velocities are instrumental 5 feet from the muzzle, using the Oehler Model 33 Chronotach with Skyscreens II. Test guns: Smith & Wesson Model 57, 6 inch barrel, for loads 1-7; Ruger Blackhawk, 6½ inch barrel, for loads 8-16. Average group sizes are for 4-shot groups at 25 yards, measured center-to-center of widest hits.

41 Magnum handloads from matched components cover the entire gamut of handgunning needs. All of these fine bullets are a true .410-inch in diameter: (left to right) Sierra 170-gr. JHC; Speer 200-gr JHP; Sierra 210-gr. JHP; Speer 220-gr. JSP; Green Bay 210-gr. WC; Taylor 215-gr. SWC. Powders and charges are discussed in the text, as well as special methods; these loads were in Remington R-P brass.

a fine choice for coyote, antelope, small deer, and the like. Shock effects at these velocities are deadly on such targets.

Both 2400 and W-W 296 are a bit too slow for the light 170, but Loads D and E are in the good category. The Hercules powder is somewhat erratic, and Winchester-Western's 296 *requires* heavy bullet pulls, so do not use either with this bullet and standard dies. With the sizer/expander, results are more uniform and very acceptable, but neither will match H110. Other powders (630, H4227, etc.) are touchier and less efficient.

2. *Speer 200-grain JHP*. This fine hollow-point is similar to the 225-grain .44 Magnum slug which I have handloaded and hunted with for years. It expands well in Duxseal but will hold together in tough game and penetrate deeply. It would be my bullet of choice for somewhat longer ranges than the 170, where fairly high velocity and good shock are still needed, a top choice for dangerous game at all handgun ranges, and equally good for other game.

H110 was still a top powder and my maximum 24.0 grain charge pushed the Speer 200 to a sizzling 1534 fps for 1044 ft.-lbs. with good 1.8 inch groups; this is Load H. 2400 was good with this bullet, but Load K, 23.0 grains, just topped 1,000 ft.-lbs., while groups spread out to 2.2 inches, and that was maximum.

W-W 296 came into its own with the 200 (again only with tight cases) and maximum Load M was 25.0 grains,

Table III
Gaertner's High-Performance .41 Magnum Experiments

CAUTION: ALL LOADS TOO HOT UNLESS WORKED UP FROM 20% BELOW

Load	Bullet/grs.	Powder Type	Weight, grains	Velocity, fps	Muzzle Energy ft.-lbs.	Remarks
A	Sierra JHC/170	H110	24.0	1569	928	1.2-inch groups; excellent.
B	"	H110	25.0	1636	1010	1.5-inch; most uniform.
C	"	H110	26.0	1687	1074	1.4-inch; *maximum*.
D	"	2400	24.0	1603	969	1.9-inch; *maximum*.
E	"	W-W296	25.0	1529	877	2.9-inch; fair load.
F	Speer JHP/200	H110	22.0	1430	908	1.3-inch; very good.
G	"	H110	23.0	1470	958	1.5-inch; most uniform.
H	"	H110	24.0	1534	1044	1.8-inch; *maximum*.
I	"	2400	21.0	1444	924	1.3-inch; good load.
J	"	2400	22.0	1475	965	1.8-inch; okay.
K	"	2400	23.0	1514	1018	2.2-inch; *maximum*.
L	"	W-W296	24.0	1449	930	2.1-inch; good load.
M	"	W-W296	25.0	1558	1078	1.2-inch; *maximum; best load*
N	Sierra JHC/210	H110	22.0	1381	888	1.7-inch; factory load equiv.
O	"	H110	23.5	1476	1014	1.5-inch; *maximum*; excellent.
P	"	2400	20.0	1304	792	1.9-inch; okay.
Q	"	2400	21.0	1445	972	2.1-inch; *maximum*; fair.
R	"	W-W296	23.0	1407	923	1.4-inch; good load.
S	"	W-W296	24.0	1512	1065	1.0-inch; *maximum*; excellent.
T	Speer JSP/220	H110	21.0	1334	867	2.0-inch; okay.
U	"	H110	23.0	1491	1087	2.1-inch; *maximum*; good.
V	"	2400	20.0	1318	840	Okay.
W	"	2400	21.0	1379	926	1.9-inch; *maximum*.
X	"	W-W296	21.0	1271	790	1.8-inch; okay.
Y	"	W-W296	22.0	1471	1056	1.6-inch; *maximum*; excellent.

Notes: These loads and results are safe in the author's guns, but they are *not to be used directly* in other firearms. H-P handloads must be worked up carefully, starting with at least *20 percent lighter charges than the lightest weight* given for the same powder, and watching for signs of excessive pressures. Velocities are instrumental averages (Oehler M33) five feet from the muzzle.

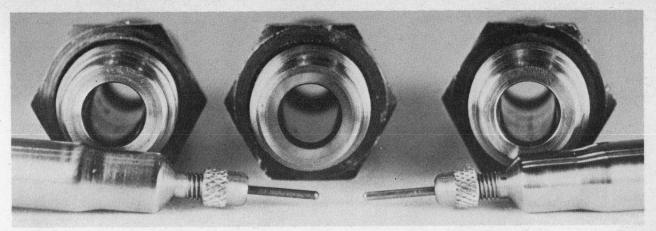

Good 41 Magnum handloads can be made with either the standard resizing die on the left or the carbide sizer (center) and regular expander. High-performance jacketed-bullet handloads, however, require a special-order "tight" sizer and expander. The dies shown are from RCBS.

giving 1558 fps and 1078 ft.-lbs. with *1.2-inch* groups. That was the most powerful load I developed and one of the most accurate—quite a combination! I don't know whether other guns will handle it as well; W-W 296 is certainly one of the two best .41 powders, H110 being the other. The 296 consistently gave very uniform loads, by which I mean that velocities are within 10-30 fps of the average, leading to better accuracy.

3. *Sierra 210-grain JHC.* This bullet is the longer version of the Sierra 170, and it behaves similarly, expanding almost as explosively in Duxseal. It will hold its power better at longer ranges but cannot be driven as fast, of course. A fine choice for any hunting, or for silhouette shooting, out to long ranges.

With the Sierra 210, W-W 296 displaced H110 as the best powder. Load S, 24.0 grains of 296 gave over 1500 fps and 1065 ft.-lbs. and my best groups— 1.0 inch at 25 yards! That is better than I have ever been able to do with factory loads, and at 27% more power! A great load for any serious purpose.

H110 was also very good with the 210, Load O at 23.5 grains yielding 1475 fps and 1014 ft.-lbs. I try to stay away from fractional weights, because they usually are not different enough from even-grain charges to be worth listing. In this case, 23.5 grains was a true maximum in my guns; 24.0 grains was definitely too hot. For all loads marked *maximum*, I made several batches in different sets of cases, as well as loads even heavier (*not* recommended) before making a final judgment.

4. *Speer 220-grain JSP.* This heavy soft-point is the penetration star of the common .41 bullets, but it does expand pretty well in Duxseal.

Again the best loads were made with W-W 296, my *maximum* 22.0 grains producing 1471 fps. This was hot Load Y, for 1056 ft.-lbs. and good 1.6-inch groups, and it would be effective on the largest, toughest game, such as elk, moose, big bear, or long-range heavy silhouettes.

Unfortunately, the best powders are pretty critical with the heavy 220, one grain more or less making the difference between just good and hot loads. It's easy to push charges too high, and I would recommend being very careful in load development with this bullet. The 220 with its heavy recoil in hot loads kicks almost like .44 Magnum factory loads.

To determine how high to push powder charges, we need a standard of reference for chamber pressures. Factories use special solid test barrels with copper crushers or handguns fitted with crystal transducers and complex electronics. Their results are

S&W Model 57 mounted in the Lee rest, which is bolted to the bench. Velocities are being clocked with the Oehler Chronotach Model 33 as shots are grouped on a 25-yard target.

Larry Caruso, a silhouette match winner and hunter, fires the author's third 41 Magnum revolver, a converted Smith & Wesson Model 28. Gaertner will describe the gun and its conversion in a GUN DIGEST article.

the original measurements.

That has to count as an added advantage of the .41 Magnum over the .44 Magnum. I have shot loose .44 Magnum and .44 Special revolvers with such H-P handloading and shooting. Those guns had to be tightened, a costly job for a good pistolsmith.

Compared to fired factory R-P loads, I permit a bit more primer cratering and brass expansion before I call a load "maximum." Primer cups are the first component to show pressure effects; even the Remington load shows slight cratering, but the crater does not protrude and the cup does not flatten, in my guns. To check for a protruding crater, I scrape a fingernail slowly over the fired primer. If the nail tends to hang up, pressures may be too high.

Primer cup flattening is allowed in my hottest loads, but I stop before the edge begins to sharpen and widen, leaving just a hairline against the edge of the pocket. This is easily seen by decapping and noting whether the cup is wider at the bottom than at the open top. But the best pressure indicator is the fired brass case itself.

Any load which sticks fired cases in the chambers is too hot. My maximum loads did not stick cases and all brass ejected easily with one finger, even in the Smith, where one case can hang up the whole cylinderful.

If you have a micrometer, "pressure ring" measurements can help to predict when loads are approaching maximum. The pressure ring is the section of case wall just in front of the web, where the most expansion occurs. I clean the gun well, mark one chamber, and fire several loads from that chamber. I mike three diameters around the pressure ring, average them, then average several cases. From my Smith M57, the average for Remington jacketed loads was .4355 inch.

Heavy loads run up to .0010 inch larger, but cases over .4365 inch may stick in the chambers. The difference may not seem large, but remember that the brass cannot expand more and this is the point beyond which brass begins to flow, thus it will not spring back away from the chamber walls.

Some experts instruct handloaders to raise charges until cases stick in the chambers then back off 1-2 grains. With pressure ring measurements, I simply raise charges until miking indicates that cases are close to sticking, then stop. The results are about the same, but no excessive strain on the gun is involved. ●

useful as industry standards, but such data does not duplicate actual pressures developed in your gun, even by factory loads. Factory pressures for .41 Magnum are said to be around 40,000 psi, but proof charges run up to 50% higher, so quality guns are very strong.

The handloader's best standard is a full-power factory load with the headstamp. I use the Remington 210-grain jacketed load in R-P brass. The danger in excessive pressures is that your guns can loosen over months or years of shooting. After firing hundreds of handloads heavier than factory during this work, my guns show no looseness and cylinder/barrel gaps and headspaces—the most likely points to get sloppy first—still have

RIFLE CARTRIDGE POWER:

Stopping?
Killing?
Shocking?

Which is the one you want?

by GUY G. GERMANO

EVERY BUYER of a hunting rifle seems to be primarily interested in its power—*killing power* or *shocking power* or *stopping power*. Unfortunately, in the jargon of the hunting-shooting fraternity these terms are frequently confused or abused by many of the brethren; they're certainly, often enough, so carelessly and interchangeably used to be almost meaningless. Let's examine them and see if we can clear things up.

Killing Power

All calibers have *killing power*—that is their purpose in the scheme of gunnery—but some have more killing power, or faster killing power, or surer killing power than others, if placed on the same spot, on the same animal, under similar conditions. Take the lowest-powered caliber, the modest 22 rimfire; there are many recorded instances of the 22 Long Rifle having killed deer, wolf, and even bear; there's at least one authenticated case of the 40-gr. bullet reaching the brain cavity of a threatening African lioness, causing instant death. Further, there are numerous cases of the 22 spelling disaster to fox, wildcat, coyote, even to puma, wild boar, and an occasional elk. But as every hunter knows, or should know, the 22 rimfire is not legal nor intended for the larger critters. It is generally considered ideal or "adequate" only for small birds or pests, small furred animals at short range—say, to 75-100 yards. To be sure, the 22 rimfire has "killing power" even against man, as attested to by the charge that pocket-size 22 pistols and revolvers are among the most frequent homicide weapons in use today, and by the ammunition makers printing the caution "Dangerous within one mile" on their 22 cartridge boxes. But that is not to say that the 22 *rimfire* has consistent, dependable killing power "up to man." If that were so, the military of many nations would have rushed to adopt it because of its economy, compactness, and light weight.

The term "killing power" does not refer to the mere potential, the occasional, or the lucky chance destruction of animals at close range, but to the generally adequate capability of a certain caliber/bullet under normal, average hunting conditions, and for a single projectile only—not a magazine full pumped pointblank at a few feet. For this reason, some ammunition companies have published lists of certain calibers and bullet weights generally considered suitable for specified game classifications and situations, such as: 1) small birds, animals, and pests; 2) varmints; 3) such medium game as deer and black bear; 4) long-range trophy game for plains and mountain shooting; 5) dangerous or extra-large game, usually at short range. The term "killing power," therefore, should be understood to mean the consistent, quick destruction of specified game under normal hunting conditions. But it should be noted that even the recommendations of reliable ammunition manufacturers may change from time to time. I'm sure that most of them no longer consider the 300 H&H 220-gr. bullet or the 300-gr. 405 as adequate for the largest game on earth "in the hands of a skilled hunter," as they did some 30 years ago.

Caliber Ranges

Generally speaking, the 22 calibers, rim- and centerfire, with bullet weights up to 60 grains and a muzzle energy to about 1,700 ft.-lbs., are regarded as humane and sufficient for animals not exceeding 75 pounds or so. The 24 to 26 caliber group, with bullet weights to 140 grains and a muzzle energy to 3,100 ft. lbs., are deemed sufficient for deer, sheep, goats, bear, and game of similar vitality. The 26 to 35 caliber group, with bullet weights up to 300 grains and a muzzle energy to 4,000 ft. lbs., are listed for the heavier big game: caribou, elk, moose and, in the larger calibers, for grizzly and Alaska brownie. The magnums, from 7mm to 375, are thought powerful enough for anything in North America, and for most of the soft-skinned plains game of Africa if used with bullets of correct construction and in weights of 160 to 300 grains and muzzle energies of 3,500 to 4,500 ft. lbs. Finally, calibers of 40 or over, with a bullet weight of 400 grains or more, and a muzzle energy to about 5,000 ft. lbs. or more are designated as the right ticket for the 5 largest and most dangerous animals on earth: lion, tiger, Cape Buffalo, rhino, and old Tembo, the elephant. But even these heavy bullets must be well-placed; even a cannon ball can do no more than frighten if it merely goes over the quarry's head.

There are, however, two schools of thought with reference to adequate "killing power" and "stopping power" for large, dangerous game—the big-bore boys, and the high-velocity crowd. The large bore clan is represented by many of Africa's professional hunters, plus Elmer Keith and other stalwarts in this country; the

Shocking Power

Generally, "shocking power" refers to the ability of a bullet of a given caliber and weight to render helpless large or dangerous game with a well-placed shot, and to do so, I feel, consistently. This is done, presumably, through a large wound channel, destruction of viscera and lesser organs, and disabling paralysis and hydrostatic effect generated by extensive damage of tissue and blood vessels—all this via the explosive impact of an ultra high-speed, partially disintegrating bullet, usually placed well forward in the chest cavity. Small and medium game are more subject to this phenomenon than the larger animals. In fact, the African big-bore disciples don't believe that the "big 5" can be killed or stopped by shock alone—or certainly not always.

The high-velocity crowd, on the other hand, places great faith in the hydrostatic effect of super-speed projectiles, contending that even if there is no instant kill, there is at least sufficient paralysis and immobility to enable the hunter to put in a second or third finishing shot. It is generally believed that a velocity of 2,700 fps (feet per second) or higher at the moment of impact is required formula to reduce the critter to near-absolute im-

clearly demonstrates the expansive, explosive, jarring effect of super velocity. Given the right combination of speed and bullet construction, there is no question that "shock" is a prime factor in rendering an animal *hors de combat*.

Velocity, however, is not the only factor in "shocking power." The weight, diameter, and disintegrating qualities of the projectile can contribute to the lethal effects, as is demonstrated by the mushrooming of soft point and hollow point bullets, the soft-lead impact of the rifled slug, and the multiple thrusts and damage of several buck-shot pellets hitting simultaneously. The 12-ga. rifled slug, for instance, although leaving the muzzle at only 1,600 feet per second, or less, mushrooms to the size of a quarter-dollar or larger on soft flesh, creates a terrific wound channel, may disintegrate or zig-zag erratically in the heart-lung area, and results in surprising shock and destructiveness. In fact, some regard it as a companion round to 00 buckshot in a 12 ga. double barrel as top insurance against lion, tiger, or leopard in face-to-face situations in thick cover. It may also be said of the heavier big-bore projectiles—especially the solids—that they plow straight through flesh and are less subject to deflection by bone and

latter is espoused by Roy Weatherby, the champion of high-velocity, and an increasing number of modern ballisticians and gun editors. Although my sympathies are with the high-velocity group—to a certain degree—I'm not going to duel with my typewriter against the big bore crowd, at least not until I've had further convincing experience. However, this perennial argument may well become purely academic unless strong conservation steps are taken, because there'll be no large, dangerous game left to prove whether one or the other faction was right.

mobility. Many ordnance experiments seem to indicate that velocity, rather than bullet weight or hard projectile construction, determines penetration of armor plate. Roy Weatherby offers the classic argument that a light touring car traveling at high speed can shatter a stone wall with greater destruction than a large heavy truck at slow speed. It is also known that blades of grass or straws have been found sticking into—or through—trees and telephone poles as a result of the terrific velocity-pressure of tornados. Further, experiments on gelatin blocks and simulated animal flesh

brush. But, whether because of large bore or super velocity, shock *does* take place, and it is especially effective on medium-sized game. It does, of course, take more shocking power to affect a larger animal. Finally, heavy, broad, soft-lead revolver bullets are generally regarded as having greater "shocking" and "stopping" power than do the faster, lighter metal-jacketed projectiles.

Stopping Power

Stopping power is usually taken to be the striking force that will halt, turn, or put down a charging animal.

This is an ambiguous term, with little or no scientific data to differentiate it from "killing power" and "shocking power." Most shooters roughly regard it as a force sufficient to put the animal down and prevent it from charging or running away. Whether a large game animal can actually be *knocked down* by a bullet's energy, as such, is highly questionable. Adventure movies, TV, and hunter's tales frequently give the impression that when a man or a dangerous animal is squarely struck by a bullet from the front, that it invariably knocks him down or somersaults him backwards. Such terms as he "fell as if pole-axed," "knocked him off his haunches," or "stopped him cold," or the like, convey the impression of great stopping power. In actual practice, however, a man or large animal is rarely, if ever, "stopped in mid-air" or "sent reeling backward." When struck by a bullet, even a very powerful one, a man or animal usually appears stunned, may stagger or slump drunkenly, or runs erratically before toppling over. Invariably, he falls forward, carried by his own momentum in the same direction he was running.

Warren Page covered this subject thoroughly in "Knock Down Nothing" (GUN DIGEST, 16th ed., 1962), his long experience in hunting the world over

by the impact of a heavy bullet. When such turning takes place, and it does happen, it is probably caused by a combination of factors, one of which no doubt is bullet striking force. But bullet *striking* force is not necessarily the major contributing factor. The animal doesn't react only to the pain and impact of the bullet, but also to the sudden crack of the rifle shot, the sight or smell of man at close range, and any irregularity in the terrain, as well as the general weakening of his system resulting from shock, pain and sudden loss of blood, oxygen, and shattered bone structure. All of these factors probably contribute to the turning, stopping or falling of the animal. Theoretically, an animal is toppled more easily from a broadside or quartering shot, than from a frontal shot during an assumed charge, which must counteract its forward momentum—assuming all shots are well placed with equal energy at moment of impact.

Penetration

"Stopping power" would take place faster if the bullet did not penetrate, in which case the full thrust of the bullet's energy would be expended on the surface of the animal, truly knocking it down or away. But that, of course,

tion which paralyzes, "turns," or "drops" the quarry.

It is not my intention to conclude with all of the intricacies of interior and exterior ballistics and their relationship to bullet power and performance. Suffice it to say that many factors determine the rifle and bullet's capabilities aside from the bullet itself—barrel length and rifling twist; length, drop, pitch, shape of the stock (which may affect your speed, accuracy, and recoil recovery), and type of sights used, and so on. Cartridge components can vary within the same caliber, as can the ballistic coefficient of the projectile, its metallic composition, etc., all of which affect bullet performance on game.

Recent years have seen tremendous strides in cartridge efficiency and specialization, as well as in powders and bullets. There is no denying that bullet power—killing, shocking, or stopping—is improving. In fact, all calibers and cartridges are excellent and reasonably deadly in the range of use for which they are intended. But it should be remembered that the most important element in hunting is man himself—his familiarity with his rifle and loads, the practice that has taught him where to place his bullet, his judgment of distance, of when to shoot and when not to, his personal compo-

convincing him that knocking an animal *off* its feet or knocking it *over* was impossible. Dropping it in its tracks, of course, did occur, and fairly frequently.

In my opinion, it would require a muzzle energy of at least 40 times a man's weight to make him reel backward from a frontal shot. In the case of a man weighing 170 pounds, say, it would take a striking energy of 6,800 ft.-lbs., and there aren't currently many such shoulder arms, nor men who can fire them.

We frequently read of a charging bear, buffalo or rhino being "turned"

doesn't happen.

It is the full force of the injury itself—because of the penetration—that stops the animal, not the impact force of the bullet. To be sure, some animals are stopped in their tracks, seemingly by the bullet. Bears are sometimes so-stopped, even when the shot is not really well placed, but they're usually soon on their feet again and running!

It is probable that the stabbing shock of the bullet tearing a wound channel, splintering bones, rupturing blood vessels, and mushing up nerves and organs form the actual *combina-*

sure, his ability to discover and stalk game (or to follow his guide's directions intelligently), and to take best advantage of cover and firing position. These and other factors govern good bullet placement and account for meat in the freezer or a trophy in the den. In short, maximum bullet power is no substitute for good shooting. The golden rule in hunting is to use as powerful a caliber—with an adequate bullet—as you *can handle* comfortably, accurately, and with maximum confidence. That goes for small game and large, but it applies especially if you're after the big ones! •

HANDGUN CARTRIDGES

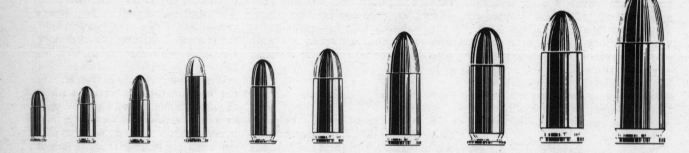

How do they really measure up?
Here are solid energy deposit measurements.

by **JAMES CLYDE GATES**

FIREARMS AND ballistics have been discussed and argued since man first put gun powder in the early bombards and propelled a stone toward a wall somewhere. We have known for centuries that all moving projectiles develop a force called Kinetic Energy. The *American Heritage Dictionary of the English Language* (copyright 1969) defines the word "kinetic" thus: " . . . of or relating to the motion (velocity) of material bodies (mass) and

the forces and energy associated therewith." The energy in foot pounds of factory loads is easily and often calculated and published. Such figures show the amount of energy stored in a moving bullet, but they rarely show how much of this energy was *deposited in the target*.

In order for KE figures to be correct, it is plain, the bullet must stop (come to zero velocity) in the target. If that happens all of the bullet's *energy* is released in the target. These energy figures, computed while the bullet is in flight and at the moment of impact, are considered to be Impact Energy.

What happens as the bullet decelerates while passing through the target or stopping therein is an entirely different matter, and that phase is what will be discussed here.

We have explained "Impact Energy," but after penetrating the target a bullet still retains velocity (however decelerated) and mass. This being so, the bullet still has energy, although reduced. This remaining energy is labelled Exit Energy. The difference between Exit Energy and Impact Energy is the amount of energy absorbed

by the target or Energy Deposit.

This Energy Deposit is only recently being explored and related to killing power, knockdown, or whatever the term that might be used.

Let's, for the moment, use some well known rifle loads to further explain how the differences in Energy Deposit work. As an example, we have:

(1.) 30-06 Springfield with a 180-gr. soft point bullet, velocity at 100 yards —2670 feet per second (fps); and,

(2.) 30-06 Springfield with a military 172-gr. full metal jacket (FMJ) bullet, velocity at 100 yards—2330 fps.

The Impact Energy of each of these cartridges at 100 yards would be, in foot pounds: For No. 1.—2370 fp; for No. 2—2170 fp.

Now, let's say each of these bullets hit and penetrated 12 inches of flesh-like material weighing 25 pounds (about the size of a large woodchuck). The results—for discussion—in Exit Energy are: No. 1—500 fp.; and No. 2—1100 fp.

We now see that the 30-06's 180-gr. SP bullet expanded and decelerated more than the unexpanded 172-gr. FMJ bullet, thus giving us the following Energy Deposit: No. 1.—1870 fp or 79%; No. 2—1070 fp or 49%.

Those percentage figures show how much the Impact Energy of each load was converted into Energy Deposit.

Now, since this article has been written to show handgun cartridge effectiveness, let's proceed to demonstrate that it's the amount of Energy Deposit that determines where the killing power comes from.

The faster we can slow down or stop the bullet in the target, the more energy

we deposit in the target. The foremost factor in slowing down or stopping the bullet is its construction and shape.

The results you will be seeing show the Energy Deposit of various handgun cartridges strictly from a ballistic viewpoint. I make no recommendations on the use of one cartridge over the other for hunting, police use or military use. I do, of course, have my opinions based on these findings and field tests, but I leave it to you to form your own opinion as to which suits your needs. I am trying to show the fallacy in using published "paper" energy as criteria in your cartridge selection, and to cast some new light on bullet performance.

Energy Deposit

What, in fact, happens when a bullet travelling at supersonic speed strikes? To answer this question, even partially, we must use Energy Deposit because this is the only method that takes into consideration the bullet's shape and construction as part of the test. Unless one considers these factors, calculations become wholly theoretical.

Killing power cannot be established by calculations alone. There must be a test medium, one conforming as closely as possible to living tissue and body fluids. Experiments have shown that nerve damage (shock) and tissue damage (bleeding) are the base of killing power.

A supersonic bullet has a shock wave that is transmitted to tissue and body fluids. Tissue and nerve damage, thus killing power, are related to the amount of energy deposited and the shock wave. Body tissue is somewhat elastic, but body fluid will not compress. When the bullet enters the target three things happen simultaneously:

1. A wound channel of pulverized tissue appears.

2. A shock wave causes body fluids to be put in motion . .

3. The destruction of large and small blood vessels and nerves accompanies this shock wave.

Most wound channels are more or less the same for bullets of near-matching calibers regardless of their velocity. It appears that elastic body tissue returns to its normal position after the initial shock wave except for the wound channel. If the shock wave causes the tissue to expand beyond its elastic limits, the tissue tears apart. If the shock wave is great enough, it will explode the target, much as a crow explodes when hit with a high velocity varmint bullet.

ENERGY DEPOSIT TABLE

Caliber	Bullet/grs.	Type	Make	Bbl./ins.	Impact V.	Impact/fp.	ED/fp	(A) %	(B) %
22 LRHP	37	LHP	W-W	3½	994	77	77	100	46[a]
22 LRHP	36	LHP	R-P	3½	985	71	71	100	42[a]
25 Auto.	50	FMJ	W-W	2	789	69	43	62	26
25 Auto.	50	FMJ	R-P	2	774	66	47	71	28
32 Auto.	71	FMJ	W-W	3½	880	122	53	43	32
32 Auto.	71	FMJ	S&W	3½	911	130	64	49	39
32 Auto.	71	FMJ	R-P	3½	912	130	66	51	40
380 Auto.	95	FMJ	R-P	3½	786	131	67	51	40
380 Auto.	95	FMJ	W-W	3½	866	158	74	47	45
380 Auto.	88	JHP	S.Vel	3½	1080	228	133	58	80
380 Auto.	84	JHP	S&W	3½	922	157	140	89	84[b]
9mm	115	FMJ	W-W	4	1162	345	113	33	68
9mm	125	JSP	Spcl.	4	1085	494	127	26	77
9mm	115	FMJ	W-W	4	1223	381	104	27	63
9mm	90	JHP	S.Vel	4	1414	397	377	95	227[b]
9mm	115	FMJ	R-P	4	1189	360	117	33	71
9mm	115	FMJ	CIL	4	1202	370	104	28	63
9mm	115	FMC-SWC	S&W	4	1160	349	176	50	106
9mm	100	SP	W-W	4	1305	378	274	73	165
9mm	115	JHP	S&W	4	1156	340	323	95	195[b]
9mm	115	JHP	R-P	4	1196	364	330	91	199
38 Super	130	FMJ	W-W	5	1208	423	138	33	83
38 Super	107	JHP	S.Vel	5	1281	388	376	97	227[b]
357 Mag.	158	Lead	R-P	4	1191	496	166	33	100[c]
357 Mag.	158	SP	R-P	4	1285	574	237	41	143
357 Mag.	110	JSP	S.Vel	4	1366	460	271	59	163
357 Mag.	110	JHP	S.Vel	4	1369	465	344	74	207
38 Spcl.	158	Lead	W-W	4	754	200	62	31	37
38 Spcl.	110	JSP	S.Vel	4	1200	352	167	47	101
38 Spcl.	110	JHP	S.Vel	4	1200	352	271	77	163
38 Spcl.	130	FMJ	R-P	4	796	184	63	34	38
45 ACP	230	FMJ	R-P	5	812	334	117	35	70
45 ACP[d]	230	JHP	Norma	5	812	334	170	51	102
45 ACP	185	JHP	R-P	5	914	342	272	80	164
45 ACP	190	JHP	S.Vel	5	1053	466	349	75	210
41 Mag.	210	SWC	R-P	4	961	416	188	45	113
41 Mag.	210	JSP	R-P	4	1259	739	523	71	315
44 Spcl.	246	Lead	R-P	4	660	236	69	29	42
44 Mag.	240	JSP	R-P	4	1251	833	545	65	328
44 Mag.	180	JHP	S.Vel.	4	1442	828	565	68	340
44 Mag.	240	JHP	W-W	4	1263	845	621	74	374
44 Mag.	240	JHP	R-P	4	1221	792	639	81	385

Note: Remember that the energy figures shown are for barrel lengths listed. Longer or shorter barrels will change the velocity, thus also the Impact Energy. For example, the 357 Mag. appears in factory charts as fired from an 8⅜" barrel. The barrels listed here are those in common use.

(A) This shows the percentage of Impact Energy deposited by the bullet in the test medium. The higher the percentage the better the bullet has expanded. These figures are found by dividing the Energy Deposit by the Impact Energy.

(B) This is the most important column because it shows the percentage of efficiency on one cartridge compared to the Standard of Comparison. These figures are found by dividing the Energy Deposit by the Standard of Comparison (166 fp).

FMJ—Full Metal jacket, JHP—Jacketed Hollow Point. JSP—Jacketed Soft Point. SWC—Semi-Wadcutter. SP—Soft Point. RN—Round Nose.

[a]—All test shots (5) stopped in test medium.
[b]—1 or more test shots (5 per test) stopped in test medium.
[c]—Standard for comparison. See text for details.
[d]—This Norma load does not expand in gelatin or flesh unless a bone is hit. However, because of its flat nose it deposits more energy than does the standard 230-gr. RN FMJ.

It is here that the fallacy of using wet clay, etc., to test bullets appears. Clay, having no elastic return, shows the extreme edges of the fluid movement. We never see the degree of cavitation or expansion in tissue equal to the results found in clay when a particular bullet is used. There is, of course, cavitation as the bullet passes through tissue, but unlike clay it snaps back unless pulverized.

The ideal situation for quick kills with rifle and handgun bullets can be summed up as follows: *A bullet so-constructed that, when fired at its maximum velocity, it deposits all its energy within the target to be killed*. A bullet with twice the energy of another which deposits just half its energy in the target is no *more* effective than that other if that other deposits all its energy in the target.

Establishing Energy Deposit

We have explained the terms Impact Energy, Exit Energy and Energy Deposit. By showing how these terms and figures were arrived at you will better understand their values.

Two Oehler chronographs, using Skyscreens, were used. The first pair of Skyscreens were set up 10 feet from the firing point. The test material was located 5 feet from the down-range Skyscreen. Ten feet beyond the test medium the second chronograph and its Skyscreens were set up. This arrangement permits velocity to be read before the bullet enters the test medium and after it passes through. The bullet is recovered from a 6 ft. by 6 ft. by 6 ft. heavy cardboard bin filled with styrofoam "peanuts," the type used in packing.

Five shots in each caliber and bullet weight were fired. If either chronograph showed more than 5% variation the shot was fired again. The 5-shot velocity averages gave us the needed figures to make the calculations.

Velocity readings from the first chronograph and the bullet's weight gave Impact Energy. Readings from the second chronograph and the recovered bullet's weight gave the Exit Energy. The difference in these figures is the Energy Deposit; that is, the amount of kinetic energy (KE) deposited in the test medium.

Our test medium consisted of ½-lb. of pure gelatin plus ½-lb. of shredded newspaper pulp mixed with enough water to permit stirring. The mix was then poured into 12" cube boxes, with water added to fill and the top taped shut. The mix was held until the cardboard became damp. A thermometer was then inserted and the mix chilled. When we were ready for the test shooting the mix was brought out and held until the temperature reached 50° F. At this point the test shots were fired. All figures in the Table derive from this 12" of material.

I did not include wildcat loads and handloads; at this time I wanted to test and report on the most popular and readily obtainable factory calibers. The barrel lengths of the test firearms are those in common use. Longer barrels would give increased velocity and, thereby, an increase in Energy Deposit. Shorter barrels than those used would show similar decreases.

One problem in testing factory ammunition arises because of the changes in such cartridges that occur from time to time—velocities are fairly stable, though often not conforming to company specs, but alterations in bullet jackets or core hardness can change the expansion characteristics, thus affecting the bullet's performance in tissue or in test materials. For example, tests we've made have shown some small differences between the original Super Vel bullets and those now offered.

In the tests described here various bullets and brands of ammunition were used and mixed as fairly as possible. All ammunition—bought and paid for—functioned well in the guns designed for it. Tests for accuracy were not made since different firearms tend to shoot different loads more or less accurately.

Efficiency Ratio Percentage

Two columns were included to permit comparisons. Column A shows what percentage of Impact Energy was converted to Energy Deposit. These figures show how efficient a bullet design is in decelerating its velocity. The higher the percentage the more you're getting out of the load.

Column B shows a percentage comparison to the popular 357 Magnum 158-gr. standard loading, one familiar to most handgunners and used for that reason.

Here is a good example of the importance of bullet design (nose shape and construction): look at the Table and compare the standard Remington 115-gr. 9mm at 1189 feet per second (fps) with 117 fp of Energy Deposit, against the Smith & Wesson 115-gr. 9mm at 1160 fps with 176 fp of ED. Both cartridges have full metal jacket bullets, so there is little or no expansion. Both have the same weight and similar velocities. The only real difference is in the shape of the bullet nose.

The S&W semi-wadcutter causes more movement in body fluids, thus causing more shock.

Those few loads which did not penetrate the test medium are footnoted.

Conclusion

It seems clear from our tests that full-jacketed loads at safe velocities fall short when compared with the effectiveness of soft point bullets at the same velocities. Such calibers as the 30 Mauser, 30 Luger, et al, show a significant increase in Energy Deposit when loaded with expanding bullets. Both equaled or surpassed most other loadings under the 41 Magnum. The most balanced loads seem to occur in the 9mm Luger class for ease of hitting, recoil, and killing power.

A lot of pre-conceived ideas about killing power appear to have been unfounded. These beliefs were swept away by the introduction of expanding bullets in such calibers as 9mm and 380. The radical difference between the 45 automatic with a FMJ bullet but depositing only 117 fp of energy and the new and hot 380 automatic load punching in with 140 fp makes one think. The 41 and 44 Magnums hit like bombs, as did some 357 Magnums and 9mm Lugers in the 300 fp class.

Most surprising to me was the round-nose factory load in 44 Special with only 69 fp. Of the various round-nose FMJ loads, all performed poorly except one. The S&W full-jacketed semi-wadcutter outperformed all other 9mm Luger round-nose loadings, producing up to 176 fp of Energy Deposit. This result can be attributed to its bullet-nose shape and, as I've said, should suggest to the commercial manufacturers the need for some changes in nose design.

The 22 Long Rifle hollow point outclassed the 25 automatic badly. It also outclassed those 32 and 380 automatic loads with round-nose FMJ loadings.

In all cases except one, hollow-point construction outclassed the soft points. The hollow points also did better on the feed ramps of some automatics than did the soft points. In many cases soft points showed some nose deformation through hitting the feed ramps.

The single most important factor in energy deposit is bullet construction and nose shape. It's not the size of the cartridge but how its bullet works that counts and that reminds me of an old saying:

"It's not the size of the dog in the fight,
It's the size of the fight in the dog!" ●

There isn't much of a trick to SPENDING LESS AND GETTING MORE if you <u>know</u>. . . ■ by KENNETH L. WALTERS

There's only one buy in chronographs, and it's not the high-priced spread, says this author who ought to know.

Walters keeps and uses about all the presses there are, partly because he loads a lot; partly because he likes machinery.

IT SEEMS TO be a deep-seated belief that if something costs more it has to be better. A more expensive home or a more costly car should somehow be better than a cheaper one. No doubt there is truth to some of this, but it isn't always the case. When you spend more in some shooting circles you can get decidedly less. Let's see if we can identify some of these areas.

Years ago when I was still working as a chemist, I was involved in equipping a large, multimillion dollar laboratory. One of the things that we had to buy quite a number of was balances. Since the order was big enough to seriously interest all the balance makers, we got each of them to come and show us their products. Obviously, I thought, a good scientific balance had to be better than the cheap little ones used in reloading so my goal was to find the best, relatively inexpensive balance and get one for myself. After several months of looking, I selected a Torsion Model DWL2 which at the time cost $400.

Now, I thought, I've got just about the finest reloading balance anyone could ever get. Clearly the Torsion line was the best possible scientific instrument and this model coupled the advantages of this unique line with a rather nominal cost. Certainly my $400 investment had to be better than what the average reloader could get for from $20 to $125. To say that I was pleased with myself was putting it mildly.

After I had gloated a bit about my super balance, a fellow reloader said: "How do you know your balance is better than mine? Have you ever tested the two?"

No, I hadn't. But certainly a scientific instrument had to be better than a reloading balance and besides mine cost more. I did, however, decide to prove my point by testing. By the time my little study of balances was complete (*American Rifleman,* October, 1979), I had tested an even dozen reloading balances and my Torsion.

My studies uncovered two interesting conclusions. First, the errors that occur in reloading balances are small (± 0.2 grain normally) and unimportant. Second, all units performed essentially identically, differing only in cost and convenience.

When you buy a balance, you should first note what weight range it will cover. Some have an upper limit of about 300 grains while others go far higher. Pick a unit that can handle the projectiles and powder charges you have in mind. Second, remember that as you spend more for a balance you may get a slightly more convenient model or one that looks prettier but you will not get one that somehow works better. A $20 C-H scale will be as adequate for your purposes as my $400 scientific model.

Another place where I've spent considerable time and effort studying what's available is in chronographs (1977 GUN DIGEST; March, 1978, *The U.S. Handgunner;* July, 1980, *Rifle magazine*). Although building a balance is a basic, established art, making a chronograph is something that is undergoing change because electronics is a field where costs are constantly dropping and circuits are getting more versatile.

Basically there are two types of chronographs, one that uses some sort of physical screen that the bullet breaks and another, called a photoelectric, that works by detecting the bullet's shadow. Until recently the latter type was quite expensive and a little trouble prone.

Chronographs also differ in the type of data they display to the user. Some output rather meaningless numbers, octal codes actually, that have to be looked up in a table to translate them into velocities. Others display the time it took a projectile to fly between the two sensors. Finally, there are machines that output the desired velocity directly. Truth is that today any of these options are possible and there shouldn't be any great cost difference between them. If there is, you are being suckered.

When photoelectric machines were first coming out, they were, reasonably enough, expensive. Also until good output displays were perfected, they, too, cost a bit. Now, however, it is possible to get good direct velocity machines with adequate displays and photoelectric detectors for quite reasonable prices.

More expensive machines exist for two reasons. First, in the case of the Oehler M33, you can get a scientific instrument that does range statistics via a microcomputer. The unit costs about $300 and is truly worth the money *if* you want and know how to use the statistics it provides. Other machines appearing over the last several years in this price range and beyond don't do anything more than the Oehler, sometimes considerably less, and still have a high price. This is either just older, less versatile tech-

nologies that cost more to do less or a manufacturer that's bleeding you. Such things happen in the chronograph business.

In buying a chronograph then, get a direct velocity output photoelectric machine that is either the least expensive or the most versatile. Nothing else is worth considering. You can, incidentally, buy units that simply cost a lot and, to varying degrees, don't work (March, 1978, *The U.S. Handgunner*).

Another area where spending more just wastes money is in lead thermometers. Such devices are of considerable utility in analyzing pure lead for blackpowder shooting (*American Rifleman*, August, 1980). Such devices are available from a couple of reloading firms plus chemical supply companies. I have used them all. The $20 Brownell unit worked. The $100 scientific pyrometer didn't. Spend less and get something that works.

Single station reloading presses are another area where this principle works. Currently the major designs are the C press and two versions of the O, a simple O and a compound O. C presses are quite adequate for reloading ammunition but not really strong enough for bullet swaging nor case forming. A simple O press will do all these things with no problem and normally costs only a few dollars more

than a C. A compound O does these same chores but does them much easier because it has better leverage. The price increase one pays for this, however, is nearly double that of a simple O press.

Within these three designs then, as you spend more you get more. Seems fair.

There are, however, other single station reloading presses that cost more but do less. One nice little H-press that I have and like works beautifully on reloading ammunition but isn't well suited to case forming. Another unit, a columnar press, costs over twice what an O costs but does little that the O can not handle. These aren't really bad presses, at least as far as I know, but they are bad buys.

Multiple stage presses have variations of the same problem. Currently there are several types of machines that are meant to speed up reloading for a nominal increase in price compared to the O designs. These include the turret presses, both simple and columnar; H-presses, three and four-holers; and a couple of unusual designs that are meant to index the shell holder through several die stations. These I call manual indexers.

The point is that all this equipment works about equally well and at the same relative speeds but the prices

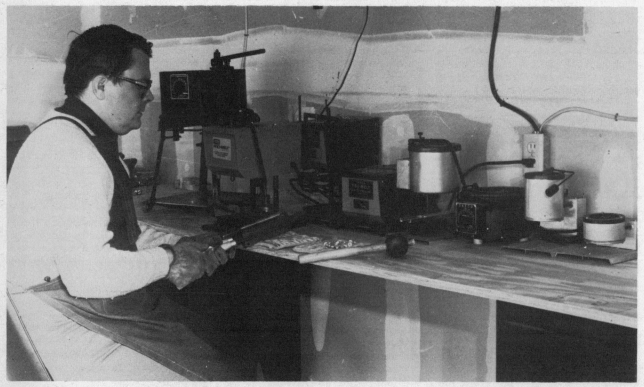

Not many of us own eight lead pots like Walters, but those of us who do are also entitled to an opinion.

There's no substitute for knowing, Walters says, and this is how he finds out—working at it.

involved range from $130 to $440. It may not always be true that a good simple turret press, like that made by Lyman and Redding, will be more price attractive than the rest, but it is certainly true today. What happens, then, if you spend $440 for a manual indexer instead of $130 for a Lyman turret? You get a machine that can handle only four die stations instead of six and that costs more than $200 too much compared to a machine that in every way is at least its equal. The more expensive machine will work, of course, but it is like me investing $400 in a balance when $20 would have done the job.

There are two more examples of this sort of thing of which I'm aware. The first is casting furnaces and the second is guns.

Casting furnaces come in four sizes, namely 4, 10, 20, and 95 pounders. Having used them all, some observations seem appropriate. First, the four-pound size is really too small to do much with. Also, 95 pounds is too much. Unless you're making *really* large batches of ingots, furnaces of this size are not worth their high cost, not to mention the possible house rewiring necessary to accommodate the darn things. The ideal size in furnaces is 20

pounds. It is big enough to handle any job, including the use of eight and ten-cavity moulds and economical—a modern 20-pounder costs what an older style 10-pounder used to, and is well worth having.

Up to and including the twenty-pound styles, as you pay more you get more. Above this size, however, more money only gets you a bigger furnace which doesn't work as well as a smaller one, costs more to run, and is more difficult to operate because they aren't very well made. I own eight furnaces—one four, one ten, five twenties, and a ninety five—and I'm convinced that a good twenty pounder can do it all. Both the Lyman and RCBS are good but I think the RCBS is, perhaps, the better of the two.

The final topic we are going to consider is guns. It is true, I think, that there is a brand or two on the market that the world would be better off without. But even within the ranks of the very best pistols, for instance, it is possible to spend more and get less. Consider a comparison between the Beretta 92 series and the newest member of the Walther P38 family, the P-5. The Beretta in U.S. military testing has been shown to be the best 9mm automatic available. From per-

sonal experience (1979 *GUN DIGEST*) I can tell you that the Beretta performs flawlessly, handles any kind of ammunition from round nose, hollow points, or cast truncated cones, and is, by current standards, relatively inexpensive, costing somewhere between $400 and $500, I think. The Walther P-5 also works very well but only with round nose ammunition, has a smaller magazine capacity, and costs twice as much. Either gun is very well made, of course, and there are undoubtedly a few applications where the Walther's smaller size would be attractive, but the Beretta is clearly the better all-round buy.

What then does this all boil down to? Simply that in a wide spectrum of shooting equipment it is possible to spend less and get more. In some cases this is because of technological changes, as, for instance, in chronographs. At other times, building something fancier, like balances, or bigger, like furnaces, just doesn't allow the basic task to be better accomplished. Finally, sometimes world economics makes it possible for a firm like Beretta to build a better gun less expensively than Walther can.

Regrettably, there is no substitute for knowing. ●

PATCHED
for the

BULLETS
458
WORK WELL WITHOUT LEADING

by **JOHN D. SOUTH**

WITH THE USE of the hard alloys to adapt cast bullets to modern smokeless powder rifles, one of the foremost advantages of these bullets is lost— their ability to expand like the formidable hunting projectiles of black powder rifles. This is especially lamentable in rifles of large caliber where moderate velocities suitable for cast bullets still come up with plenty of power. Large heavy bullets produce considerable energy even at lower velocities.

Or so it has always seemed to me. As any cast bullet shooter well knows, the problem of excessive barrel leading arrives immediately when smokeless powder and soft alloys are mated together. Of all the expedients I have tried to overcome this problem, the best revives the old paper patch, somewhat modified.

Several years ago I tried patched bullets in the 43 Spanish Remington. Bullets were from an adjustable mould I had made up. It cast a bullet with a straight cylindrical body capped with a short truncated nose-end. The body of the bullet could be cast to any length desired, while the nose-end retained the same configuration regardless of that length. This configuration—a cone with its end cut off—was used on all of the bullets discussed in this article. It provides no bearing surface. We'll call it the nose-end.

The body of the bullet casts to bore diameter—equal to the diameter across the top of the grooves in the barrel of the rifle. The patch, tightly wrapped around the bullet, filled the grooves of the rifling when the bullet entered the bore as it was fired.

The patch was .002-inch thick bond paper of 100% rag content. It was cut so two wraps encircled the bullet, the edges butted but not overlapped. The ends are cut at an angle so the butt runs diagonally. The patch projects slightly below the base of the bullet; this projection is turned in and pressed flat against the base of the bullet, serving to hold the patch in place. With the patch covering the full length of the bullet's body it has no nose bearing section, after the fashion of a wadcutter bullet. To prevent the hot gases of the smokeless powder charge from burning the patch at its base and fusing the lead, I loaded thick wax wads under the base of the bullet. These served effectively as gas checks.

This fully patched bullet is the shorter one depicted in the accompanying sketch. The patch is intended to come off of the bullet as it leaves the muzzle when fired.

When I first tried these bullets in the 43, a difficulty was encountered. They gave some leading in the barrel, and recovered patches indicated they had been scraped and torn in passage through the barrel. The old barrel had a few rough spots in the bore, and these apparently were the cause of the damage to the patches. I tried lubricating the patches and the leading ceased.

Recovered patches showed that the lubricant was most effective in preventing scraping and tearing of the patch. The lubricant which I found to be most satisfactory was molybdenum disulphide powder, known as Molykote type Z. This was rubbed over the surface of the patch, after wrapping it on the bullet.

I tried these bullets patched in this manner in various lengths giving weights of from 325 grains to 400 grains, seating them out of the case to fill the length of the throat ahead of the chamber in the rifle. Various charges of different powders compatible with the strength of the old rifle were tried, along with different alloys of the bullets. They gave no barrel-leading, but accuracy was not satisfactory. Although some shot fairly well, flyers made poor targets.

With another idea in mind, the mould was set so as to cast a very long bullet weighing over 500 grains. This bullet was patched somewhat differently. The patch covered the bullet from the base about ⅜-inch back of the truncated nose-end. As shown in the sketch of the longer 43-cal. bullet, this bare section effected a nose of land diameter. In the rifle, the bullet extended from the case so that the patched section filled the throat of the chamber, while the bare nose-section extended into the bore on the lands of the rifling.

Patched thus, these bullets gave fair accuracy consistently. The nose-section was both bare and soft lead, but there was no leading.

Having had that 43-caliber experience, I decided to have a mould made up for my 458. I am indebted to Art Dolat of Canoga Park, California for making the moulds and other accessories. The mould was made to cast a bullet having a diameter of .450-inch when a soft alloy is used. Otherwise, it was of the same configuration as the 43 bullet.

A few trials showed the .002-inch thick bond paper to be too thin for use in the 458, and rifling cut through the paper. I resorted to .003-inch thick paper, two wraps of which brought the bullet's diameter to .461-inch. This paper resisted cutting fairly well; and chamber dimensions would not permit a still thicker paper, so I used the .003-inch in these tests.

As before, I first tried bullets patched the full length of the body in various lengths running from 340 grains to 400 grains. And as with this manner of loading in the 43 Spanish, the bullets were too temperamental to give consistent accuracy, although some good targets were produced.

Naturally, the next step was to try a long bullet with a pilot-nose. With a bullet of 500 grains, the patch wrapping started back about ⅜-inch from the forward edge of the body, after the same fashion that the long bullets were loaded in the 43 Spanish.

A few short trials were enough to

 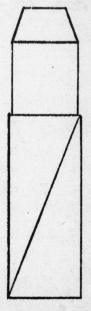

The author's earlier patched bullet successes were with the 43 Spanish, and resulted in bullets patterned like these.

dispel any hope of success for these bullets—they leaded the barrel immediately. Nor did reduced powder charges with a harder alloy help. Evidently the narrow rifling lands of the 8-grooved barrel would not support the nose of the bullet like the wider lands in the old Remington barrel had done. At any rate, this bullet was ruled out.

I felt that if the nose could be patched to the diameter of the rifling lands rather than left bare, there might be possibilities. This, of course, would necessitate a nose section of smaller diameter to accommodate the patch. Accordingly, another mould was made up, with the bullet stepped down to smaller diameter to form a nose section. I intended to use .004-inch thick paper so the mould was made to cast a bullet of diameters suitable for this thicker paper when an alloy of 1 part tin to 24 parts lead is used. The body of the bullet is ⅝-inch long, joining the stepped down nose-section which is ⅜-inch long and capped with the nose-end which is ¼-inch long. This makes a bullet 1¼-inch in length and weighs within 3 grains of 500 grains in the soft alloy. These dimensions are shown in the sketch of the 458 bullet.

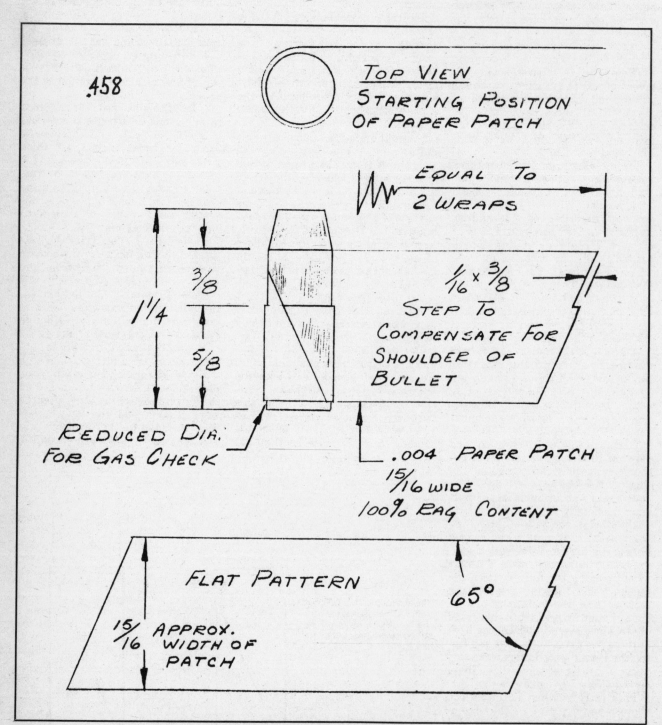

Author's mode of dealing with patching the relatively complex two-diameter bullet is plain to see here.

I felt that the regular 45-caliber copper gas-check cup would be an advantage over the wax wads I had been using, so a tool was made to cut the recess after the bullet had been cast. It's a block of metal with a hole for the base of the bullet. A slot milled across the block intersects the hole and a cutting blade is set in the slot. The bullet is held by the nose, the base inserted in the hole, and rotating the bullet cuts a recess in its base. The gas check is put on after the bullet has been patched.

The patch is bond paper, 100% rag content, .004-inch thick. It makes two wraps, again with a diagonal joint. The patch does not turn over the base, but covers the entire bullet up to the nose-end. The outside edge is pasted its entire length to the inner wrap. The patch is rolled on so it won't unroll should the bullet, or the entire cartridge, be rotated to the right by the bolt. The sketch shows the direction that the patch is rolled on the bullet.

The body casts to a diameter of .4435-inch; with wrapping, it is increased to .460-inch. The nose casts to a diameter of .4345" and when patched is about .452-inch. These diameters are reduced slightly by sizing later. After the paste on the outer edge of the patch has dried, it is ready for lubrication.

The paper patch is rather fragile. Should it get scraped in the process of loading, it may be torn or scuffed. The belt recess, for example, presents an edge over which the bullet must pass as it is chambered. So I employ a lubricant that will strengthen the outer wrap of the patch as well as provide lubrication. With a liquid wax called Johnson Bravo Wax, which sets as a hard thin coat when it dries, I mix enough Molykote powder to make a thick paste. Only a small amount is mixed at a time as the wax sets up rather quickly. I wipe a coating of the mixture over the entire outer surface of the patch. The bullet is then left to set till the lubricant dries.

Now the bullet is ready to have the gas check cup pressed on its base, and to be sized down in sizing dies. The sizing down is only a slight amount, affecting only the heavily lubricated patch which is smoothed to a neat uniform diameter. I use an Ideal lubricating and sizing press with a die of .459-inch diameter. The die has holes for regular lubricating use, but I plug them up with a cement compound so that the edges of the holes will not catch on the patch on the bullet. Then the press is used in the regular manner, both for sizing and gas-checking.

This process does not affect the nose of the bullet, so I use a die specially made up for sizing the nose. In a block, a .450-inch bore, slightly beveled, takes the patched nose. The bullet is merely rotated in the bore and the lubricated patch on the nose comes out to a smooth diameter of .450-inch, sized to ride on the lands of the rifling.

The patch, now strengthened by the hard lubricant and paste, is resistant to deformation. It lacks one very necessary feature—it must present surface to the air so that it will be torn off the bullet. To provide a means for the patch to shed itself, I cut slits along its length. Using the point of a sharp knife or razor-blade, five slits are cut, spaced around the circumference. They start about 1/16-inch back from

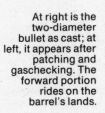

At right is the two-diameter bullet as cast; at left, it appears after patching and gaschecking. The forward portion rides on the barrel's lands.

the nose and stop 1/16-inch from the base. This works well.

These bullets fit rather snugly in fired cases, so I don't size cases. A slow-burning powder seems to be best for these soft bullets. After a series of trials with various charges and brands of primers I worked up a load which I could not better, if equal, with any other combination. So I am content to stick with this one load.

With CCI No. 250 magnum primer, the charge is 68.5 grains of DuPont 4350 powder. A card wad is placed on top of the powder and a pinch of dacron on top of the wad fills the remaining space, regulating the seating depth of the bullet. The bullet body fills the length of the chamber. The nose of

.450-inch diameter extends into the bore, resting on the lands of the rifling.

My rifle is a custom Mauser with a heavy 22-inch barrel. It is equipped with a Lyman No. 48 receiver sight and a blade front sight. All tests were made at 100 yards range, bench rest; group measurements are center to center of the bullet holes. I usually shoot groups of 6 shots. My best groups run from 1⅛-inch to 2 inches. These are subject to change to a predictable 3 inches, usually caused by one flyer, although the rest of the shots may also have greater dispersion than the better targets show. I have not been able to eliminate this unpredictable poorer grouping.

In an Oehler Model 10 Chronograph, three rounds gave readings of 1846 fs (foot seconds), 1803 fs and 1831 fs. The bullets give a light minimum of leading that is not hard to remove. Cleaning it out with a brass brush after the day's shooting eliminates build-up of any consequence. The cartridges so loaded function well enough through the magazine. They are, of course, quite powerful, and with accuracy not impossible for use in the brush.

They are certainly not for the handloader who is interested in production. But with equipment on hand, and with practice acquired, for the cast bullet devotee who goes for this sort of thing, they are not so tedious to make up as it may sound. In fact, the steps probably go quicker than it takes to tell. ●

HATCHER NUMBERS MADE EASY ÷ + x

by MARSHALL R. WILLIAMS

GENERAL Julian S. Hatcher is not so well known today as he was a few years back. For many years he was one of the two or three foremost authorities on small arms in the United States. He was the author of several books including what was probably the first authoritative treatise on machine guns in about 1917, two, now dated, but for their time definitive, books on pistols and revolvers, and two forensic ballistics books. His best known work now is *Hatcher's Notebook* a somewhat random compendium of useful information on a variety of small arms related subjects. At different times during his life General Hatcher was a technical editor for the *American Rifleman,* the official publication of the National Rifle Association (N.R.A.).

Among knowledgeable pistol shooters General Hatcher is best known for what are now generally referred to as Hatcher numbers. The Hatcher numbers refer to an early effort to evaluate pistol cartridges according to their relative effectiveness or stopping power. The General was a small arms ordnance expert early in his career and had access to records now generally referred to as the Thompson-La Garde reports. The U.S. Army, after its disastrous experience with the 38 Long Colt revolver cartridge during the Moro uprising in the Philippines at the turn of century, formed a committee to investigate the effectiveness of available pistol cartridges and recommend a cartridge for the Army's adoption. The committee was headed by Col. John T. Thompson, later the designer of the Thompson submachine gun, and Col. Louis A. La Garde, an Army physician.

The committee experimented with the 7.65mm Luger, the 9mm Luger, 38 Colt's Automatic, 38 Long Colt revolver cartridge, the 45 Colt, the 476 Webley and possibly others.

The experiments covered two areas. The first involved shooting live beef animals, about to be slaughtered, in the abdomen with the various cartridges to determine how many shots were required to put the animal down. No more than ten shots were fired into each animal. The animals were then poleaxed and butchered immediately in an effort to be as humane as possible. The results showed that ten shots from the 30-caliber pistols did not always get the animals down, five to seven shots were generally required with the various 38s, while the 44s and 45s would put the animals down in about three shots.

The other part of the experiment involved shooting human cadavers with the various cartridges in such a manner as to provide comparative data on the effects of the various bullets on different parts of the anatomy and having the medical men determine the probable disabling effect of the wound on a living person. The cadavers were x-rayed and dissected.

While the experiment was macabre, it was certainly as objective a study of the comparative effectiveness of available pistol cartridges as could be made.

So far as I know the complete report has never been made public. At least I do not know of any reference source for the whole report. However, Hatcher's second book, *Textbook of Pistols and Revolvers* published 1935, contains a resumé of the experiments and results.

The Committee recommended that no cartridge less effective than the then current 45 Army cartridge be adopted. The Army cartridge to which they referred was a version of the 45 Colt which was shortened so it could be used in the Smith & Wesson Schofield revolver. It shot a 230-grain lead bullet propelled by 28 grains of black powder at a velocity of 770 feet per second (fps). This is the origin of the performance specifications for the 45 ACP. The jacketed bullet and increased velocity came later to improve reliability in the Colt Model 1911 45 ACP.

General Hatcher studied the results of the tests and came up with a formula which he thought correctly rated

TABLE I

Cartridge	Bullet Wt./Type/Vel.	H. Number
22 Short	29 gr. RNL at 1050 fps	2.6
22 L.R.	40-gr. RNL at 1150 fps	3.95
25 ACP	50-gr. RNJ at 810 fps	3.96
30 Luger	93-gr. RNJ at 1220 fps	17
32 ACP	71-gr. RNJ at 960 fps	10.2
380 ACP	95-gr. RNJ at 955 fps	18
9mm Luger	115-gr. RNJ at 1160 fps	26.6
38 Super	130-gr. RNJ at 1280 fps	33.26
38 Spl.	148-gr. W.C. at 770 fps	31.6
38 Spl.	158-gr. RNL at 855 fps	30
38 Spl.	158-gr. SWC at 855 fps	37.5
357 Mag.	158-gr. SWC at 1410 fps	61.8
41 Mag.	210-gr. SWC at 1050 fps	80
44 Spl.	246-gr. RNL at 755 fps	60
44 Mag.	240-gr. SWC at 1470 fps	142
45 ACP	230-gr. RNJ at 850 fps	62.5
45 L.C.	250-gr. F.P. RNL at 860 fps	80

the effectiveness of the cartridges in relation to each other. His first efforts were in 1927 and he tried to relate the kinetic energy of the bullet, its cross sectional area, and a factor for the shape and material of the bullet called the form factor. In 1935 he published his revised formula and substituted the momentum of the bullet for the energy of the bullet.

The later formula is the one now widely accepted as being useful in comparing the effectiveness of various pistol cartridges. Mathematically the formula is as follows:

$$H = \frac{M \times A \times F}{2}$$

where
M = Momentum in pounds
A = Cross-section area of bullet in inches
F = form factor
H = Hatcher Number

The form factor is an effort to account for the differences in effectiveness of different shapes and types of bullet. General Hatcher used the typical round nose lead bullet as the unit of comparison. When the round nose lead bullet is 1, the round nose full jacket bullet is .9, i.e. only ninety percent as effective. The full wadcutter and semi-wadcutter were much more effective and rate a 1.25 or twenty-five percent more effective. Very blunt round nose lead bullets such as the 41 Long Colt and bullets with a small flat nose were slightly superior and got a 1.05.

Because the numbers involved in the momentum and areas were so small General Hatcher multiplied the form factor by 1000 to get numbers which were not just small decimals. Hence form factors are:

RNJ = 900
RNL = 1000
WC or SWC = 1250
Blunt = 1050

The reason for dividing by 2 is that if you don't, the above formula will give numbers which are exactly twice the number published by Hatcher for the given cartridges. It has been suggested that Hatcher got his momentum figures by working backwards from energy figures and either neglected or did not bother to account for the fact that Kinetic energy is one-half mass times velocity squared. ie. $E = \frac{MV_2}{2}$. At any rate the result of the Hatcher equation must be divided by two to get the published Hatcher number.

An example of the Hatcher equation for the standard 38 Special load looks like this, assuming a 158-gr. RNL bullet at 855 feet per second:

$$M \times A \times F \div 2 = H$$
$$\left(\frac{158}{7000} \div 32.16 \times 855\right) \times \left(3.14 \times \left[\frac{.375}{2}\right]^2\right) \times 1000 \div 2 = 30$$

Where:
Momentum = weight in pounds divided by constant of gravity times velocity

$M = \frac{158}{7000}$ (bullet in pounds) $\div$ 32.16 (K of gravity) $\times$ 855 (Velocity)

Area = pi $\times$ radius $\frac{(diameter)}{2}$ squared

$A = \pi \,[pi\,]\, R^2$
$\pi = 3.14$
$R = \frac{.375''}{2}$ or .1785
$A = .100$ sq. in.
$F = 1000$ (round nose lead bullet)

If the round nose lead bullet were replaced with a semi-wadcutter or wadcutter of the same weight, the Hatcher number would be 37.5 or exactly 25% greater. If it were replaced with a jacketed round nose the number would be 27 or 10% less.

The Hatcher number for the cartridge recommended by the Thompson-La Garde committee is figured as follows:
230-gr. 45 RNL at 770 fps.
$\frac{230}{7000} \div 32.16 \times 770 \times .160 \times 1000 \div 2 = 62.9$

And curiously, the Hatcher number for the 45 ACP with its 230-gr. RNJ at 850 fps is:
$\frac{230}{7000} \div 32.16 \times 850 \times .160 \times 900 \div 2 = 62.5$

If you have a pocket calculator, the calculations are relatively simple. However, there is a table of Hatcher numbers for the more common pistol calibers based on published specifications for factory cartridges here in Table I.

Since the charted numbers are for factory cartridges they are of little help to the reloader or experimenter who works with cartridges giving other velocities than standard. For a given bullet all factors in the equation are constants except the velocity, so it is relatively easy to figure a Hatcher factor (not a form factor) for a given bullet which can be multiplied by the velocity of the experimental cartridge to determine the Hatcher number for a different velocity. If a Hatcher number is known for a given load, the Hatcher number is divided by the velocity for that load and the resulting number is the Hatcher Factor. The Hatcher Factor may be multiplied by a new velocity to obtain the new Hatcher number. For example, in Table I above the Hatcher number for 38-cal. 158-gr. SWC at 855 fps is 37.5. To get the Hatcher Factor for this bullet divide 37.5 by 855 which gives us .0438596 which rounds off to .044.

Since this is the same bullet used in the 357 Magnum load listed we may check our answer by multiplying .044 by 1410 which gives us 62.04 which is within a fraction of the figure in Table I for the 357 Magnum.

To save the reader the effort of getting out his calculator and figuring these, Table II contains the Hatcher factors for some of the more common bullets.

TABLE II

Caliber	Bullet	Factor
9mm/38 auto	.355 115-gr. RNJ	.023
	.355 130-gr. RNJ	.026
38 Spl.	.357 148-gr. WC	.041
	.357 158-gr. RNL	.035
	.357 158-gr. SWC	.044
41 Mag.	.410 210-gr. SWC	.076
44 Mag.	.429 240-gr. SWC	.097
45 ACP	.451 230-gr. RNJ	.074
45 Colt	.452 250-gr. FP RNL	.093
	.452 250-gr. SWC	.116

In order to determine the Hatcher number for a load using any of the above bullets one simply multiplies the velocity times the Hatcher factor listed above. For example, to obtain the Hatcher number for the 45 ACP standard load with 230-gr. RNJ .451″ dia. at 850 fps, we take the Hatcher factor shown in Table II for the 230-gr. .451″ RNJ bullet which is .074 and multiply times 850 which gives 62.9.

To determine what velocity is required of a bullet to produce a given Hatcher number you simply divide the desired Hatcher number by the Hatcher factor. If you want a Hatcher number of 45 using a 357 158-gr. SWC which has a Hatcher factor of .044, simply divide 45 by .044 and get a velocity of 1022 fps.

Another trick using Hatcher numbers is to keep in mind that the number varies with the type and style of bullet used. Thus a 38 Special with the standard round nose bullet and police load rates a Hatcher number of 30. Change the bullet to a semi-

bores. While I am willing to believe, and I have even read figures to make me think there is empirical evidence, that the 45 ACP is twice as effective as a 38 Special (i.e. 62.4 vs. 30) I do not believe a 38 Special is seven and one-half times as effective as a 22 L.R. (30 vs. 3.96).

I have had occasion to be in court as defense attorney and Juvenile Judge when shooting cases were being tried. Most involved 22 cal. pistols, generally of the cheap pot-metal junk variety with short barrels and consequently low velocities. Frankly, in most of the cases in which the shootings were fatal they were also immediately disabling. Two cases stand out in my memory, both involving drunken assailants: In one the Blood Alcohol Content (B.A.C.) of the assailant was .33% (in Virginia, .10% raises the presumption of DWI) and he was angrily attacking the man who shot

slows down at a faster rate than a medium speed round nose does. Consequently, at ranges where most game is shot with a pistol the Hatcher number may be different from those shown in Table I. If we look at the Hatcher numbers for the 357 Magnum, the 44 S&W Special, and the 45 ACP, we find they are all three practically the same, around 60 - 62. Because its velocity drops at a faster rate, however, at fifty yards the 357 drops behind the other two and at 100 yards it drops even farther back. Table III gives comparative data.

It might be worthwhile noting that the relative stopping power of the 45 ACP can be increased nearly 39% by simply changing the bullet from a RNJ to a Lead Semi Wadcutter:

$$\frac{230}{7000} \div 32.16 \times 850 \times .160 \times 1250 \div 2 = 86.8$$

Since the 44 Special uses a RNL bullet it can only be increased by 25% by changing to a Lead Semi Wadcutter. The 357 Magnum can not be improved on with ordinary bullets because it starts with the best form.

If you are interested in the lowest velocity and therefore, lightest recoil in the 45 ACP using the 230-gr. Lead SWC, which will give a Hatcher number of 62.5, you can work the equation substituting an X for velocity and using 62.5 for your Hatcher number:

$$\frac{230}{7000} - 32.16 \times [X] \times .160 \times 1250 - 2 = 62.5$$

Divide both sides by

$$\frac{.102125X}{.102125} = \frac{62.5}{.102125}$$

The required velocity is

$$X = 612 \text{ fps}$$

TABLE III

	45 ACP 230-gr. RNJ		44 Spl. 246-gr. RNL		357 Mag. 158-gr. SMC	
	Vel.	H. Number	Vel.	H. Number	Vel.	H. Number
Muzzle	850	62.4	755	59.4	1410	62.0
50 yds.	810	59.5	725	57.0	1240	54.5
100 yds.	775	56.0	695	54.7	1120	49.3

wadcutter and the rating jumps 25% to 37.5. If a 158-gr. 357 RNJ bullet were used, the Hatcher number would drop by 10% to 27. Thus if we know the Hatcher number for a given load and bullet we can rapidly calculate the effect of a change of bullet style provided weight and velocity remain the same.

The chief complaint about the Hatcher numbers is that Hatcher didn't figure a bullet form factor for expanding bullets of the type now commonly used in modern high velocity ammunition, nor has anyone come up with a satisfactory approach. There is an inherent problem in these bullets; to be more effective than lead bullets they must expand, but their expansion is unpredictable. Probably the correct way to figure them is to average the frontal area of the unexpanded bullet with the frontal area after expansion and use the form factor for a very blunt bullet since this is the classic mushroom shape.

I further believe that Hatcher's Formula is more effective in comparing medium bores to large bores than in comparing small bores to medium

him. According to all testimony, the assailant fell over backwards and never moved once he hit the floor. The bullet hit him in the front of the chest, touched his heart and lodged in his spine.

In the other case I do not remember the exact B.A.C. but I believe it was about .25%. At the moment he was shot, the assailant was attempting to beat his brother-in-law's head in by alternately hitting said head against the ground and yanking it up against a car bumper. He was shot through the chest from side to side. Although he lived about twenty to thirty minutes he too hit the ground and never moved.

I could go on but these two cases clearly illustrate the point. All pistol cartridges are dangerous. We would do well to remember that no caliber smaller than 30 was used in the Thompson-La Garde tests and no comparable data are available. Remember, then, that the Hatcher formula is more reliable in comparing medium bores to large bores.

An interesting thing happens when you compare Hatcher numbers downrange. A high speed semi-wadcutter

There are two points frequently considered by more modern methods of comparison with which Hatcher's formula does not concern itself. The first is the effect of recoil on the ability to deliver aimed fire and the other is hard target (body armor) penetration. Of the cartridges shown in Table III, the 357 Magnum will have more recoil than the other two in guns of equal weight. It will also have greater penetration at all ranges shown.

Hatcher numbers are fun to conjure with. I think for comparing lead bullet loads and jacketed bullet loads it is probably still a useful tool. I believe it can be adapted to cover expanding bullets within limitations by averaging the frontal area of the bullet before and after expansion. The calculations involved, while cumbersome to do with paper and pencil, are a snap with a pocket calculator.

●

Squib loads work well for close-range shooting at gophers. Holstered handgun is loaded with shot for snakes.

Retire your 22s.
Use ... SQUIB
LOADS

by **BRANDON WOLF**

WHILE MOST riflemen-handloaders prepare their ammunition in order to get optimum velocity and/or accuracy, some few of us find great satisfaction in loading a more specialized type of rifle ammo—the low velocity squib load, usually lead (cast) bullets and light charges of handgun powders.

"Squib" is a very informal term generally taken to refer to both rifle and handgun loads of sub-standard velocities for a particular caliber. It is a relative term with no fixed limits which means that what may be squib to me may not be squib to you.

A cast 30-06 load at 1,500 fps (feet per second) could be considered a squib load while a cast bullet in 45-70 at the same velocity could certainly never be called squib. To my personal way of thinking a squib is generally about one-half the velocity of a full powder load with approximately the same bullet weight. Again this is not a hard and fast rule, but my general guideline.

I have fired hundreds and thousands of this variety of handload through an assortment of rifles in the past ten years ranging from a Ruger Mini-14 223 through various 6mm's, 257 Roberts, 7mm's, 30-06s, and even one 458 Magnum. I came to rely on them so much, in fact, that I do not even own a rifle chambered for the 22 rimfires any more. I can count on my big bore rifles doing that work.

The best bullets for squib loads are cast bullets. This is true for several reasons, chief among them is the fact that at very low velocities (say no more than 1,000 fps) a jacketed bullet is apt to stick in a rifle's barrel. Another rea-

Author's favorite squibs are 223 Remington, 257 Roberts, and 30-06. All shoot well enough for gophers.

son is the scarcity of commercially available plain, lead rifle bullets. Unless a shooter can find a custom bullet caster he must rely on his own cast rifle bullets to top his squib loads. Personally, I have been a bullet caster since my teens so it is only logical to use that type of bullet whenever possible.

Cast bullets for squib loads need be no different than for any other type of load. And, because velocities are so low, most any type of castable lead alloy is suitable.

Most rifle bullets are long in relation to their diameters and are usually difficult to cast unless the alloy contains a fair amount of tin such as linotype. Linotype contains enough tin to cause lead to flow very easily which makes it ideal for cast bullets. However, it is expensive, so for this informal variety of handload I prefer to use wheelweight alloy with just enough linotype (or tin when available) to make the alloy cast easily.

As a general rule bullets above 25 caliber cast OK from these blends, while those below 25 caliber give more difficulty. Below that point it takes a little experience and experimentation to get a good casting alloy. Using wheelweight based alloys does cause a higher percentage of culls, but on the other hand, the cost per bullet is very, very small.

Whenever possible I try to use a light bullet for the caliber in my squibs. For example, in 30-06 and other 30 calibers I prefer Lyman mould No. 311316 in both hollowpoint and solid form. These bullets weigh about 105 to 115 grains depending on alloy, and have proven to be exceptionally accurate even in a friend's 300 Weatherby Magnum. He has taken a coyote and a deer using the solid bullet over 16.0 grains of 2400—the little bullets were placed just right, of course.

In some rifles the lightest bullets will not be sufficiently accurate, and in those I have gone to the medium weight bullets. A case in point is my Winchester Model 54 in 257 Roberts. I first tried Lyman's No. 257420 (65 grains) in it but groups ran around three inches at 25 yards. Moving up the scale a bit to Lyman No. 257312 (89 grains) gave me accuracy of ½ to one inch at the same range. By the way, these slow moving lead bullets, especially the longer ones, are prone to ricochet, and should only be used with a safe backstop.

One thing I have found about squib load rifle bullets is that if they are designed to wear gas checks, then they

A target gopher is, under author's conditions, at most a 50-yard try.

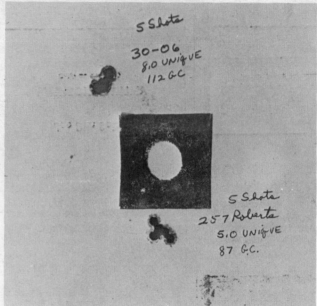

Squib loads are capable of excellent 25-yard groups such as these made by 30-06 and 257 Roberts.

Unique powder is the all-around favorite for squib loads in a great many rifle cartridges.

Author prefers these cast bullets for squibs in 22, 24, 25 and 30 calibers. From left they are 225415 H.P., 245496, 257312 and 311316 H.P., all by Lyman.

A cast bullet about to be seated in a belled 257 Roberts case shows good squib technique that gets good loads quick.

should always have them. At these velocities a gas check bullet is not really necessary, and if a plain base bullet mould is all that is available, then by all means use it. The results will probably be fine. *But,* if your mould is for a gas check bullet then put the gas check on it. I have found that if the gas check is omitted about 30% of the shots will be flyers from the group.

As for bullet lubes, I rely on the various types containing Alox for most cast bullet shooting. Lately I have been trying Bullet Master Lube, a liquid, which is applied by dipping the bullets in it. So far it has been very effective.

For appropriate powders for these loads, I will say that nearly any fast handgun-type powder will do. I have tried Bullseye, Unique, SR-4756, Red Dot, 2400, and SR-4759. Of these, my all-round favorite is Unique.

With cast rifle loads Unique burns well, gives fine accuracy for the most part, and it measures easily. SR-4759 is another very good powder for cast loads in that it is very bulky for the charge weights being used. However, that bulkiness does not lend itself to being measured with any great accuracy.

One would think that squib loads would not be sensitive to the amount of powder being used, but they most certainly are. For example, in a 30-06 Remington Model 700 I once owned, a charge of five to six grains of Unique gave groups of two to three inches at 25 yards. I thought the rifle was just not going to be a cast bullet shooter. Nevertheless, I moved the powder charge to seven grains and the groups shrank to one inch; moving the charge weight up one more grain rewarded me with very consistent ½-inch five-shot groups.

Bullet for that load was a flat-nose 105-gr. cast 32-20 and the load's velocity of 1,377 fps made it the equal of a 32-20 carbine.

In almost any dissertation on cast bullet loads, one must eventually get to the subject of fillers. Right off the bat with this variety of cast bullet load, I will say, "Do not use fillers!"

They have never helped accuracy at all in my loads, and they take too long to prepare. When you are substituting these squib loads for 22 rimfire as I am, it must not take overly long to prepare them, or you will not get much shooting done. When the gophers are out, I want to be out also!

Primers for squib loads can be nearly any brand or type, ranging from pistol primers through the hotter magnum rifle types. It takes a little

Whenever possible, use a short bullet instead of the longer ones. Shorter bullets use less lead and are less prone to ricochet.

When a bullet design calls for gas checks they should always be used. Top group used bullets with gas checks, which were omitted to shoot the lower group.

Author has had very good results using squib loads even in this Ruger Mini-14 in 223-cal., operating the action manually.

experimentation, but I have used them all with good results.

One other beautiful fact about these very low pressure loads is case life. It is forever! I use cases for full charge loads until they begin to show some amount of wear such as loose primer pockets. I then transfer them to squib load use and I have never had to discard one.

One word of caution: mark your squib load brass in some manner so it will not get mixed with brass intended for full charge loads. Sometimes, the firing-pin blow can shorten the case measurement from its shoulder to the head, which gives the same effect as excess headspace. Firing that case with a full charge could possibly be dangerous.

Don't try to make squib loads to match the accuracy at 100 yards of your full charge loads. First of all, they will rarely do it, and secondly, such accuracy is just not necessary.

I like my squibs to group right around one inch at 25 yards which translates to about 4 MOA. Now, some readers might think that is lousy accuracy, but it lets me head-shoot gophers out to 25 yards, and past that I am not good enough for more than body shots anyhow. My maximum range is about 50 yards, or the same as with a 22 rimfire.

Currently, my handloading project is developing squib loads for my 223 Ruger Mini-14, and I have been having some fine results. I am using Lyman bullet No. 225415 HP, lubed with Alox or Bullet Master, over 3.0 to 5.0 grains of Unique. Accuracy has been around one inch or less at 25 yards, which is just about what this semi-auto is capable of in my hands with jacketed military ammo.

Of course, these light loads do not function the action which is exactly what I want. When walking the gopher fields, I do not want to be hunting for each and every case used. Therefore, with these light 223 loads I work the action manually for each shot. It may not be a semi-auto that way, but with the 30-round magazine, I can sure carry a lot of ammo in a handy place. I have a Weaver 2½x scope on the Ruger and I mean to be hell on the gophers.

Some shooters might think I am nuts for going to all the trouble of loading these squib loads when I can buy 22 rimfires and do the same job. I thoroughly enjoy my hobbies of bullet casting and handloading and I would much rather load ammo—of any variety—than buy it, so I wonder why they shoot store-bought 22s. ●

SOON OR LATE, anyone who handloads will need to remove bullets from loaded cartridges. The reasons may be one or more of several; a couple of examples come immediately to mind —occasionally a quantity of military cartridges is available, and you may want to make them over into hunting loads by replacing the original bullets with commercial bullets of equal or lesser weight. This way you can have a shooting supply ready in a few minutes without the chore of depriming, sizing, repriming, and charging with powder. This can be done with calibers such as the 223 (5.56mm), 7mm Mauser, 7.62mm NATO, 7.62mm Soviet, 7.65mm Mauser, 30-06, and 8mm Mauser, and even a few pistol cartridges. (I understand the Army Marksmanship Team at Fort Benning pulls the GI bullets from 7.62mm Match ammo, and replaces them with Sierra 168-gr. match bullets.) Another reason for pulling bullets is to reduce the powder charge. If you've loaded a batch of cartridges and find, after firing a couple of rounds, that they're slightly hot, you can salvage them by pulling the bullets and reducing the powder charge. (Better yet, of course, is to load only one or two cartridges with a particular powder charge, until you find the weight that works with the bullet you're using, rather than loading a batch with a powder charge you've never tried before.)

One other reason for pulling bullets is to examine the bullet, or to examine and weigh the powder charge. This is usually done to only one or two cartridges of a particular caliber, such as when a new cartridge comes on the market, or when a collector wishes to know more about a cartridge.

Basically, bullet pullers or extractors come in two types—the inertia type and the collet or chuck type, with modifications. Which type is better for you depends on what you want to do with it, or how you foresee it being used.

Inertial Types

The best all-round bullet puller for general use is the inertia type, if you only intend to pull a few bullets of various calibers for examination. It is possible to make such a puller in the home shop with simple tools, and Harold MacFarland illustrates and describes one of these in *Gunsmithing Simplified*. A few years after the book was published, a lightweight inertia puller was offered commercially. Originally named the Guns Inertia Bullet Puller, it is now called the Kexplore, and consists of a hard plastic (Tenite) head bored out to take cartridges up to 45-70, a polyethylene plastic cap with slot, and a hardwood handle. It weighs 4 ounces, empty, and originally came with three clips for common caliber cartridges, plus a universal clip with tapered hole that will accept cases ranging in size from the 25 ACP to the 458 Win. Magnum. The puller will pull rimmed and rimless cases up through the 45-70, but the last cartridge has a large enough rim to sit directly on top of the plastic head, without need of a clip. I've used one of these pullers since they came out and have pulled hundreds of different bullets for examination, in almost every caliber manufactured today, plus a number that have not been available for many years. It has never failed, that I can recall, although there have been times when it took a good many swings before the bullet broke loose. It is best to make sure the puller is used against a good solid surface— I like a large block of oak, or a block of 1″ steel—and use it like a hammer, striking the surface at a 90-degree angle. According to Newton's Laws of Motion, a body in motion tends to remain in motion...and when the case is suddenly stopped by impact of the puller with the solid surface, the weight of the bullet tends to keep it moving forward, much the same way a drunk driver has a tendency to go through the windshield when his car strikes a tree. When the bullet finally drops out, the powder follows, and both can be recovered for weighing and examination. There is a tendency for a few granules of powder to be lost around the head of the case on impact, at least with some powders, but usually it retains the majority.

A few years ago, the Quinetics Corp. in Texas, brought out a modified inertia puller called the Kinetic Bullet Puller. It has a similar plastic head but a hexagonal metal shaft for a handle and a ribbed plastic grip. The unique part is the 3-piece chuck which will accept most cases from the 32 ACP up through the 45-70. The chuck isn't needed with the 45-70, but a 12 gauge top wad should be placed over the head of the case before the cap is tightened down, as the hole in the cap is larger than the 45-70 rim. In use, the cartridge is pushed down into the

Bullet Pullers

For one reason or other every handloader will eventually feel the need to remove seated bullets. The types available today are described and their use explained.

by LARRY S. STERETT

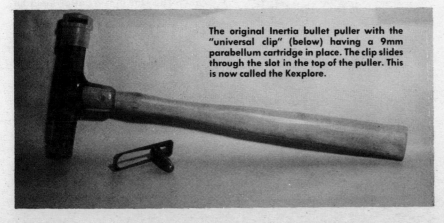

The original Inertia bullet puller with the "universal clip" (below) having a 9mm parabellum cartridge in place. The clip slides through the slot in the top of the puller. This is now called the Kexplore.

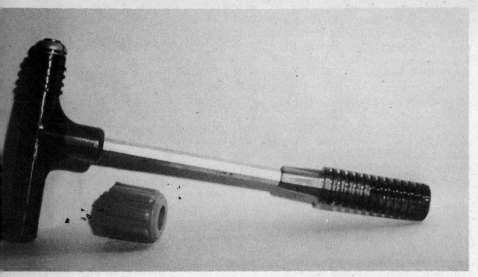

The Quinetics kinetic bullet puller with a shell in the collet chuck; the cap has been removed.

The Bonanza "B" type bullet puller for standard ⅞"x14 presses; the "A" type, not threaded, is used in the Co-Ax press. Note the bullet is gripped in four areas around most of its circumference, much the same as with the collet pullers.

chuck, bullet first, until the rim or extractor groove catches securely. Then tighten the cap, and strike a solid surface with the puller, bullet end down. After the bullet is pulled, the case, bullet and powder can be removed. Quinetics says it is not necessary to remove the puller cap for this, but I've found it is a lot less messy if the cap is removed, the case extracted, and then the bullet and powder gently poured out—when that bullet slides out, the powder granules can come spilling with it, so have a suitable container ready. The Quinetics model weighs 5 ounces, comes with an extra chuck assembly spring, and sells for $11, or $3.30 more than the Kexplore.

There used to be an inertia puller on the market called the Three V X-15, which sold for about half of the Quinetics' price, but I haven't seen it advertised for at least a couple of years.

Recently another inertia type has appeared. Priced at $16.95, and called the "Tap-It Bullet Extractor," this model is advertised as weighing ¾-pound. An advertising sketch of the "Tap-It" appears interesting, but two letters to the Arizona firm making it failed to even gain a reply, so no comments can be given.

The inertia puller, as is true of some others, is to be used only on centerfire cartridges, since the pressure exerted on a rimfire cartridge base could cause it to fire. This isn't to say you couldn't use a puller on a rimfire cartridge and get away with it, but why take unnecessary chances?

Collet Pullers

The collet-type bullet puller appears

similar to a loading die in being threaded to fit standard loading presses having a ⅞" by 14 thread. The puller uses a split chuck, or collet, which will pull one specific bullet caliber, and the chucks are usually available in calibers ranging from 22 to 375 caliber. The chucks do not mar the bullets, making them suitable for reloading, and after some practice the procedure is fairly rapid. It consists of unscrewing the chuck from the puller body and putting in the correct size chuck, after which the puller is threaded into the loading press. With a cartridge in the tool shellholder, and the ram in the up position, the puller body is adjusted so the chuck will grip the bullet just above the case neck; then run the puller lock nut down and tighten. The chuck is tightened on the bullet by turning the handle on the head, and as the ram is

A representative collect-type of bullet puller, along with one of the collets. Turning the handle clockwise tightens the collet on the bullet.

lowered the bullet is pulled, usually with little effort due to the press leverage. With a hand cupped under the puller, the tension on the chuck is released and the bullet drops down. The powder remains in the case, which can then be placed in a loading block if you intend to load the cartridge with a different bullet of the same or lesser weight.

At the present time, there are at least 10 collet-type bullet pullers on the market. These include models by Bair, C-H, Eagle, Forster, Herter's, MSS, Lachmiller, Pacific, RCBS, and Texan. They range in price from just under $4 for the Herter's (two models which resemble the Forster and RCBS design), up to just over $10 for the Eagle which will pull all bullets from 22 to 45, using three special collets. The collets, as previously mentioned, are usually for one caliber only, and range in price from just over $1 up to just under $4, depending on specific brand. The basic types of collets used in the pullers are A) the Forster-style, which uses short collets and a single arm on the side of the puller head for leverage, or B) the long collet RCBS-style with a T-handle on the puller head, although some of the most recent RCBS pullers have only the single arm in place of the T-handle. Brands of the Forster-style include Forster, Herter's F, Pacific and the Texan, while the Bair, Herter's H, Lachmiller, MSS, and RCBS are the RCBS-style.

Miscellaneous Forms

There are also a few miscellaneous types of bullet pullers, or extractors, including some that are semi-automatic in use. The simplest of these

From left—Forster collet, complete Forster bullet puller, and the discontinued Brian bullet puller with a 30-cal. FMJ bullet protruding from the top.

Shooters Accessory Supply bullet puller, made with 4 holes, the calibers of your choice.

is the nutcracker type, such as the Shooters Accessory Supply and Lac-Cum. The Shooters AS model is a spring-steel block joined at the end but split down the middle, and with a pair of handles. The block contains 4 holes, each of a different bullet diameter, and 6 different blocks are available. (For example, No. 5 has holes for 22, 243, 7mm and 30 caliber bullets.) To use, a cartridge is inserted in the shellholder of a loading press from which the die has been removed, and the ram raised until the bullet protrudes above the threads of the press. The correct diameter aperture is dropped over the bullet, the handles squeezed together, and the ram of the press lowered to pull the bullet. The bullets are not damaged, and may be used for reloading later. With a little practice use of this type of puller can be quite rapid, and the powder stays in the case. Too, the current price is only $5.95.

A somewhat similar puller is the Lac-Cum, except it comes only with one collet and a wrench, for $7.49, and collets for another caliber are $3.25. The Lac-Cum is used the same way as the S.A.A., but the collet (a 4-cut type similar to the Forster-RCBS form) is at the tip of the puller. Like the S.A.S., the Lac-Cum doesn't mark the bullets, and it is said to pull the toughest military bullets.

The semi-automatic bullet pullers have to be used with a regular loading press having standard ⅞"x14 threads, except for the Bonanza "A," which is designed for use with the Bonanza Co-Ax press. The first such puller I can recall was the Brian. It was on the market for only a short time,

looked exactly like a loading die, and was for 30-cal. bullets only. It had an aluminum body with steel lock nut, and inside were 8 evenly-spaced spring-powered steel balls. The puller was adjusted until the balls were just above the case neck when the tool ram was completely up, and lowering the ram pulled the bullet. After removing the case with powder intact, and inserting a fresh cartridge in the shellholder, the ram was raised and lowered, and the process repeated. The pulled bullets would keep popping out of the top of the puller like lubed bullets out of a "kake kutter." It was fast, and very economical at the time it was on the market, but it did leave 8 small indentations around the bullet.

Semi-Auto Types

Currently there are only two semi-automatic pullers on the market—the Bonanza A (the "B" is threaded for standard loading presses), and the Redco M800. The Bonanza models are simple, with 4 flexible jaws that automatically close on the bullet as it is raised up through them, in the same

basic procedure as with the old Brian model. Each puller will pull only one caliber, and they are available for 8 calibers from 22 to 32, with the "B" at $3.50 costing $1 more than the "A", and the pulled bullets are reusable.

The Redco has the appearance of a loading die, and will pull all calibers from 22 to 35, in somewhat the same manner as the Brian. Like the Brian model it does mar the bullets slightly.

If you have the need to pull any bullets (and what handloader doesn't) there are plenty of bullet puller/extractors available. You just pays your money and makes your choice. One word of caution should be heeded, if your choice is one of the collet or semi-automatic types. Be sure the pullers are adjusted so they are in contact with the bullet only, and not the case neck. Otherwise you could damage the case and possibly even the puller, and at least a couple of the pullers could yank the neck right off a thin-necked case. ●

We learned at press time that the Redco puller is no longer available.

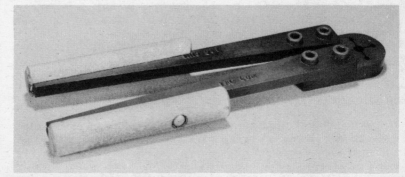

The Lac-Cum bullet puller, a collet type in rather unusual form, has interchangeable collet heads, thus letting one set of handles serve for a wide range of calibers.

The 264 Winchester Magnum– how

by Bob Hagel

The 264 is at its best as a long range rifle for such game as deer, sheep and goats. Andy Hagel, Salmon, Idaho taxidermist, shot this bighorn ram at nearly 400 yards with a 264 and 125-gr. Nosler bullets.

Few modern cartridges have ever kicked up the storm of controversy that followed the appearance of the 264 Winchester Magnum in 1960. It was hailed by some as the ultimate long range cartridge for everything from woodchucks to moose. Others strongly condemned it as being far over-bore in capacity, and felt that it showed no advantage over the 270 as a big game cartridge, and was certainly not as good an ultra-long range varmint cartridge as the 270.

Like any other cartridge that had made the scene, especially one that is such a radical departure from conventional notions of what a cartridge should be, many hunters decided it was adequate for any big game this continent had to offer, and immediately set out to prove it. Much game was killed

with it, small and large, in fact, everything from woodchucks to moose, and some of the big bears were clobbered as well. As is usually the case with a new cartridge, some of its fans told and wrote glowing tales of how it killed just a little better than any cartridge before or that was likely to follow; that it made such cartridges as the 270 Winchester and 280 Remington look like 25-35s by comparison.

Then the bubble broke, and it became obvious that while it was a good long range cartridge for the smaller big game animals, it left something to be desired for the heavy stuff. Even though the 140-gr. bullet did boast good sectional density, it often blew up on heavy animals at close-to-medium range, and failed to penetrate the big

bones and heavy muscle and get inside on shots fired into animals quartering to or away from the rifle. When loaded with bullets that did hold together, giving deep penetration, internal damage was not as great as larger caliber bullets because of the smaller frontal area of the expanded bullet. It would do the job under good conditions, but it was not ideal for the big stuff.

Of course as a varmint rifle it soon lost favor with most hunters because of the cost of shooting it, the recoil, and the fact that it was harder on barrels than the 6mm cartridges and the 270.

For antelope, sheep, goats and long-range deer shooting it delivered the goods very well, and it won many fans who used it for this

As definitive a testing of this controversial cartridge as
you're likely to get. The author, a veteran hunter-
handloader, fired hundreds of rounds — under carefully
controlled conditions — in preparing this important material.
It's filled with fresh and original information that no
264 shooter will want to miss.

good is it?

kind of shooting, with occasional use on heavier game. But was it actually superior to other small-bore cartridges like the 270? Was there much real advantage as a hunting cartridge? If there was any advantage, was it outweighed by some disadvantages found at the loading bench? Actually, did it have anything to offer that other cartridges lacked?

A dozen years later, and after the advent of several new cartridges, many riflemen are still wondering the same thing. One thing for sure, the advent of the 7mm Remington Magnum, built on the same case but expanded to .284", just about put the finishing touches on the downward popularity slide of the 264. As a big game cartridge the big 7 will do anything the 264 will do and add a lot to it, especially when you go to heavy bullets and heavy animals. As a varmint cartridge neither one is ideal except under very specialized conditions.

The 264 has many peculiarities that are not generally recognized by the average gun buff—strangely enough, even by those who have loaded for it quite extensively. For one thing, while I've never bought the idea advanced by some knowledgeable experts that nearly all of the big belted cases are far over bore capacity, I will agree that it is true in the case of the 264, even with the slowest powders available today.

264 Over Bore

This over-bore capacity bit doesn't necessarily stem from the fact that it takes a lot more powder to produce more velocity than one can get with the 30-06 case necked to 6.5, but that when you do reach the pressures it takes to get enough more velocity to be realistically useful, pressures become very touchy. This is especially true of some of the ball powders. If you hold velocity down everything goes along quite well, but then you are getting the kind of velocity the 270 will give with approximately the same bullet weight. This is not to say that you can't surpass 270 ballistics with the 264, but it serves to drive home the point that when you do reach the higher velocity the cartridge is capable of with the *right* powders, be pretty cautious about what powders you use and how you use them. Any little variable can cause trouble, and there are many of them. We'll get back to powders later.

Perhaps the greatest variable the handloader has to contend with in the 264 is in the bullet designs made by the various bullet companies. The reason for this is that the Model 70 Winchester, the rifle originally chambered for the cartridge, and the chambering procedure followed by most other manufacturers and gunsmiths, is throated very short. This short throat caused no problems as far as W-W factory ammunition is concerned, as the long 140-gr. bullet is of two-diameter design. The bullet shank from base to cannelure mikes out at a full .264", but about ⅛" forward of the cannelure it drops to about .255", and continues to taper slightly on out to where the

spire point starts. This allows the bullet to be seated out about as far as the M70 magazine will allow proper functioning of the cartridge. It also places the bullet base only about halfway down the case shoulder. This does not greatly interfere with the powder capacity of the case, and yet the bullet does not bump tight against the lands.

The story is far different when the handloader goes to work with the various makes of bullets normally used. Some of these bullets are made in two-diameter form, some are not, and there are some that do have some taper forward, but not enough to keep them from jamming into the lands if seated to factory over-all cartridge length. This situation causes no end of trouble for those who are not aware of it, or do not take the trouble or know how to check it with every bullet they use. It does two things that can and do raise pressures excessively with full throttle loads. If the bullet is jammed tight into the lands pressures skyrocket, and if the bullet is seated deep enough in the case to relieve this situation, the powder capacity of the case is cut enough to increase pressure above bullets of the same weight and diameter that are seated farther out.

Obviously, bullets that are wedged hard into the lands cannot be used anyway because of the danger of pulling the bullet from a round that is extracted without firing. This has ruined more than one hunt when there's nothing on hand to push the jammed bullet out of the throat.

Bullets Compared

To give you some idea of bullet diameters and tapers from the various bulletmakers, here is a run-down: Hornady bullets are similar to the W-W 140-gr., but not as much difference in the two-diameter setup. Both the 140- and 129-gr. bullets mike .264″ on the shank, to the cannelure, then drop off to .259″ about ⅛″ forward of that point and taper slightly more out to the start of the spire. These bullets can be seated out to the crimping cannelure. The 160-gr. is entirely a different matter. While it has a .264″ shank it tapers only .001″ ⅛″ ahead of the crimping groove, and only .002″ in the first ¼″ forward of the cannelure. If you seat this bullet at the cannelure in a Model 70 with standard factory throating (the late rifles at least) you push it far into the lands.

Sierra bullets in weights from 85-gr. to 140-gr. mike an average of .2637″ on the shank on my caliper. They have no two-diameter dimension and carry the full diameter out in a fairly long bearing surface to where the ogive starts; shape is the same as their other

calibers. This requires them to be seated very deep to avoid pressing against the lands. This is especially true of the 140-gr. boat-tail.

The Speer 140 gr. mikes only .263″ on the shank for about ⅜″ forward of the base, then drops off in a gradual taper. This design, while not two-diameter, does allow the bullet to be seated well out with about the same amount of bullet inside the case as the 140-gr. Hornady. The smaller full diameter also serves to relieve pressures further. The 120-gr. is similar with, of course, less bearing surface. The 87- and 100-gr. Speer bullets are built along conventional lines, but all Speer 264 bullets are actually only .263″. In my testing this seemed like a good idea.

Nosler, the bullet that would make the 264 Winchester into a cartridge for heavy game if any bullet could, was at one time made in true two-diameter form, similar to their 338 bullets of the same design. This design was dropped in favor of the normal design, where the jacket diameter is reduced over the partition to relieve pressure. John Nosler told me that he was not happy with the accuracy re-

ceived with the former design and dropped it. The newer bullets average out at .2638″ on the shank and measure .263″ from the pressure relief groove forward to where the ogive begins. This is true of both the 140- and 125-gr. bullets. They require deep seating to avoid hitting the lands and kicking pressures upward.

We also tried some of the Barnes 150-gr. and 165-gr. bullets (now made by Colorado Custom Bullets), but found that they did not produce acceptable accuracy, with even the 150-gr. tipping badly at times at 100 yards. The 165-gr. could not be used at all because of the high pressures it produced even with light powder charges. This arises probably because the 165-gr. measures .265″ at the base and carries a diameter of a full .264″ for nearly half of its 1¹⁵/₁₆″ length. This is coupled with a soft copper tubing jacket, which could conceivably cause some slugging in the bore.

The photo of the cutaway cases shows the various seating depths which must be used in new Model 70 rifles so that the different makes and weights of bullets used

These bullets, of various weights and brands, are seated in the cutaway cases exactly as they have to be seated in the Model 70 Winchester rifle to clear the lands. This photo shows clearly what the handloader is up against if he is not aware of the differences in bullet design. From left: Sierra 85-gr., Speer 100-gr., Speer 120-gr., Nosler 125-gr., Hornady 129-gr., Hornady 140-gr., Speer 140-gr., Nosler 140-gr., Sierra 140-gr., and Hornady 160-gr. How this seating affects case capacity is readily visible.

will clear the lands by about 1/16". Few bullets could be seated deeper than this and still hold tightly in the case neck. To seat them longer will raise pressures beyond safe limits with maximum loads for this seating. By looking closely at this photo it is not difficult to understand what the average handloader is up against when he is not aware of the great difference in the design of the various makes of 264 bullets. There are other 264 bullets that were not used in the tests, but those described are the most popular.

There is no cut and tried way of knowing at what depth the various weights, styles and brands of bullets must be seated to prevent contact with the lands. That is, how much of the bullet must be seated within the case, or how much can protrude. Over-all lengths are worthless unless you have them for *every* bullet, and know that you have a standard throat. But even standard throat length is not quite enough. Different makes of barrels have different land heights, as well as different taper angles in the lead.

The simplest way I know of to check this is to seat a bullet in the case at least 1/8" longer than a factory-loaded round. Light a common kitchen match or candle and smoke the seated bullet evenly all the way around, from the case mouth to well onto the ogive. Insert the round carefully into the chamber and close the bolt. (If the bolt closes hard you'll know the bullet is jamming into the lands, and you can withdraw the cartridge and seat the bullet deeper.) Extract the cartridge gently so as not to smear the smoked area. If you seated the bullet out far enough the marks left by the lands will be plain in the smoked area. Measure the length of shorter marks (some may drag against the lands on one side as the case is extracted) and add 1/16". Now turn the seating stem in the die upward while keeping the lock ring in its original place on the stem. When the clearance between the lock ring and the top of the die indicates the same distance you just measured (bullet marks plus 1/16"), hold the stem tight and set lock ring down tight. Now those bullets will seat to miss land contact by about 1/16".

Which Powders?

As for powders that will give the highest velocity, only the slowest

Cast of 264 chamber in new Model 70 rifle shows short throating for this cartridge. Bullets must be seated very deep to avoid jamming into lands if not of two-diameter design. Land marks have been darkened for better visibility.

burning will do the trick. This is true even with the lightest bullets. However, with the very slowest powders available such as H-870 and H-570, you run out of room in the case with 85- to 100-gr. bullets. Here, such powders as 4350, 4831 and Norma's old 205 do best. Norma 204 would probably do well, but it wasn't tried.

With all bullet weights from the 120-gr. up, H-870 the out-of-print H-570 gave consistently higher velocities than anything else used. Accuracy was also very good with both powders, but on an average the log or rod type H-570 held the edge. This discontinued powder gave very uniform velocities with nearly all bullets, regardless of the charge or the amount of compression. Velocities were quite uniform with most powders in spite of high pressures.

Strangely enough, H-450 ball, a powder that has apparently been used extensively in this cartridge gave no end of trouble in the test rifle, a new Model 70 with a 24" barrel. The first lot tried gave such high pressures, with velocities running much below other powders, that I picked up a can of a differ-

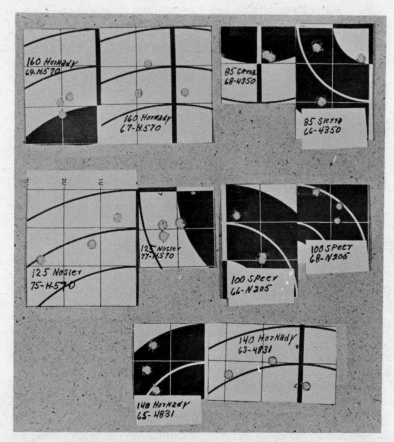

These 10 targets (5 pair) fired at 100 yards show that maximum loads gave greater accuracy than when cut by two grains. Targets are shown as fired, not selected.

140-gr. Sierra bullet (left) and 140-gr. Hornady. Both have been smoked and chambered in the 264 rifle to show where lands contact both bullets. Note that contact is farther forward on two-diameter Hornady even though it is seated much farther out. The Sierra bullet bumps solidly at start of ogive, cannot be seated farther out without bullet pulling from unfired cartridge extracted from chamber.

make this test I used the same case that had been used with other H-450 test loads and got the same results. In this 264 cartridge both lots of H-450 were extremely touchy. A load could be worked up to the point of .001" belt expansion, then the load backed off to where there was none, and a couple of rounds fired to check, with the results normal. But when a batch of the same no-belt-expansion loads were run for velocity and accuracy tests, a primer would blow right in the middle of things. Most cases had been fired several times before with stiff loads, and some were only once-fired, and all of them checked before and after firing, so it didn't lie here. Primers were, of course, the same, and bullets from the same box as with other powders; powder was from the same can, and weighed on the same scale without changing anything. I don't have the answer and neither does Bruce Hodgdon. Maybe it is just the circumstance of a powder being touchy in a case of this capacity and bore. Anyway, I can't recommend it in the 264 Winchester.

Another unusual circumstance that comes to mind is contained in an article by Ken Waters that appeared in *The Handloader* for July-August, 1971. Ken reported that he ran into excessive pressures with a load of 66/Norma 205 behind the 120-gr. Sierra bullet; excessive to the point of locking the rifle bolt. While my top load, and one with which I fired many rounds, was 65/Norma 205 (my lot was not the same as Waters used) behind the 120-gr. Speer, I did use 66 grains as a test load with no trouble whatever—just a little hot and up 1 grain from what was a full throttle load in my rifle. Of course the Sierra bullet does set up a little more pressure because of its longer bearing surface and larger diameter, but there *shouldn't* be that much difference. My load gave an MV of 3267 fps and only 20 fps variation between high and low readings.

Knowing Ken Waters' ability as a handloader and his desire to stay on the safe side, I think this is a strong indication that the 264 is very touchy when top pressure levels are approached, and that a slight variation like a different powder lot can raise pressures beyond the danger level.

My own results with Norma 205 were very good with all bullet weights. I could not go as high (with most bullet weights) as the maximum loads listed in the *Speer Manual No. 8*, with the exception of

ent lot to check with. With the second lot of H-450 I was able to use an average of 2 grains more with all bullets weights tried, but velocities were still not what they should have been for the pressures involved. Accuracy was better with the second lot, and pressures more uniform (they had varied as much

as 180 fps between shots with the first lot), but my charges were still below those recommended in most of the manuals. With other powders my top loads contained charges as heavy or heavier than those shown in the manuals, proving that the rifle or other components were not the cause. Just to

264 Winchester Magnums (center) compared to the 270 Winchesters at left and 7mm Remington Magnums, right. Loads are standard for factory round with 130-gr. and 150-gr. in 270, 100- and 140-gr. in 264, and 150- and 175-gr. in 7mm Rem. Mag. These are the two cartridges that form the best base of comparison for the 264 cartridge as a hunting round.

the 87-gr. bullet. Velocities also ran somewhat lower, about the amount one would expect between their test rifle with its 26″ barrel and mine with a 24″ tube. Also, unlike many other cartridges where N205 gives better velocities with most bullet weights, in no case could I reach the velocity that some other powders gave with the various bullet weights. All loads, though, showed uniform velocities and accuracy was good.

To go back to the many makes and weights of bullets used in my testing, as might be expected, it is possible to use more powder with two-diameter bullets like Hornady's than it is with Nosler and Sierra bullets. As an example of this, I found that I could consistently use at least 2 grains more powder behind the Hornady 140-gr. than with the Nosler of the same weight. The charge had to be cut another grain (3 in all) for the Sierra 140-gr. BT, while the Speer 140-gr. required only 1 grain less than the Hornady. These notes are based on 4831 but they're about right with most other powders also.

Accuracy and Pressures

Here is something that may upset those who deplore high pressures and who strongly advocate mild loads for top accuracy in all cartridges. It is a fact that with *every bullet and powder used*, with the exception of H-450, the best accuracy was obtained from the hottest loads that could be used. No great attempt was made to work out the most accurate load for any bullet and powder combination, but several loads were cut by 2 or 3 grains to check velocity and accuracy. Not one single group with charges reduced below maximum showed accuracy as good as the top charge! (True, H-450 did give tighter groups at reduced velocity, but this powder was so erratic that little work was done with it. After you blow a couple of primers and have to drive the bolt open, you sit back, lick your wounds and do some deep thinking before further experimenting with that powder in that caliber!)

As far as accuracy goes, certainly I have no complaint where this particular 264 rifle—or any other 264 I have used—is concerned. The rifle used for all of the testing reported was a new Model 70 acquired in 1971. With its 24″ sporter barrel the average 3-shot group with all bullets and powders tested ran about 1¼″ at 100 yards. Some of these groups ran as big as 2″, but some went below ½″. One group with

264 WINCHESTER TEST LOADS

264 Winchester Magnum Model 70 Win., 24″ bbl. W-W cases, weight 246 grs. Federal 215 primers. Oehler 20 chronograph w/Oehler 50 electronic screens spaced 10′ apart and 10′ from muzzle to start screen. Average temp. 75° F. All velocities are MV converted from instrumental at 15′.

Bullet/grs.	Powder	Charge/grs.	MV	Avg. group/remarks
W-W factory 140	——	67.5	3035	1½″
W-W factory 100	——	71.5	3525	2″ (MV erratic)
Hornady 160	H-870	71	2947	1⅛″
Hornady 160	H-570*	65 (max)	2931	½″
Hornady 160	H-4831	59	2808	½″
Speer 140	N-205*	64	3113	2½″
Nosler 140	4350	57	2976	⅞″
Nosler 140	H-4831	63	3097	2″
Nosler 140	H-570*	72	3184	1¾″
Nosler 140	H-870	73	3139	1½″
Nosler 140	H-450	59	2915	1⅛″
Hornady 140	H-4831	65	3163	1⅛″ (hot)
Hornady 129	N-205*	65	3213	1¼″
Hornady 129	H-570*	74.5	3318	1¼″
Hornady 129	H-450[1]	61	3065	3¼″
Hornady 129	H-870	76	3314	1¼″
Hornady 129	H-4831	67	3289	1½″
Hornady 129	4350	60	3157	1¾″
Hornady 129	H-450[2]	63	3202	1″
Speer 120	N-205*	65	3316	1½″
Speer 120	H-870[3]	76	3378	1″ limit of compression
Speer 120	H-570[3]*	74.5	3382	1⅝″ limit of compression
Speer 120	H-4831	68	3377	1⅝″
Speer 100	N-205*	68	3492	1″
Speer 100	H-4831	70	3455	1⅛″
Speer 100	4350	65	3512	1⅛″
Speer 87	N-205*	72	3761	1″
Sierra 85	H-4831	73	3815	1″ (little hot)
Sierra 85	4350[4]	68	3809	

Under no circumstances should any of these loads be used in other rifles without working up from at least 2 to 3 grs. below. While some manuals list several more grains of H-450 than the loads given here, these were maximum working loads in this rifle. Hotter loads were tried and became very erratic to the point of blowing primers.

[1]First lot of H-450 very erratic. [2]Second lot of H-450; see text. [3]Limit of compression (compressed load). [4]Most accurate load tested; ⅛″ to ½″. *Discontinued, but still popular propellant.

the 85-gr. Sierra, backed by 68/4350, and clocking 3809 MV, went into one hole measuring ⅛″ center-to-center. Other groups with this same bullet averaged ⅜″ to ¾″! Oddly enough, maybe bullets at the other end of the scale did almost as well. The Hornady 160-gr. produced groups consistently under one inch with full throttle loads. None of the 140-gr. bullets made especially tight groups in this rifle, although they were certainly not bad with stiff charges of most powders. The W-W factory 140-gr. load did about as well as any other.

During the trials of this one M70 264 rifle, 40 different loads, plus factory ammo, were tested for both velocity and accuracy. In addition to this, hundreds of rounds were fired in working up loads and in checking combinations that did not give satisfactory results. A partial list of these loads, given in the

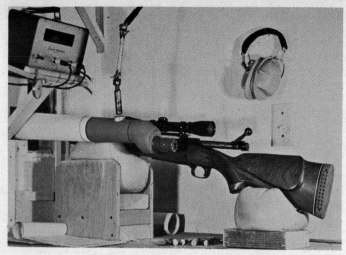

All test shooting was done from this room with temperature held at 74-76 degrees F. Oehler 20 chronograph was used with Model 50 electronic screens set up in room beyond firing port. Accuracy testing was done at the same time, the target set up outside at 100 yards.

chart, shows those that will prove most useful, and gives a comparison between bullets and powders. It is NOT SUGGESTED that anyone use any of these loads in his rifle. All loads listed were safe in the test rifle with the components used, but because this cartridge is so touchy at high pressures, any slight variation could give trouble.

To check load pressure levels and case life, one case was marked

Manual and Loads

Anyone who checks the 264 Winchester Magnum loads in the many reloading manuals will be highly confused; they vary so much that it would almost seem that they are talking about different cartridges. Two of the manuals do not show loads for the powders that gave me the highest velocities at all. In my

Only Lyman and Hodgdon use bullets put out by various makers, but in only one brand for each weight. The fact that the cartridge is touchy and erratic, when loaded to high pressures, accounts for much of the variation, I suspect. A blown primer caused by some slight variation will make most test shooters cautious!

To stay as nearly as possible to laboratory standards, and to keep everything as uniform as possible, test shooting was conducted from inside a shooting room. Temperature was held at 74-76 degrees for all loads. The chronograph was an Oehler #20 using #50 electronic screens set up in another room beyond the shooting port. The screens were spaced 10' apart with the start screen 10' from muzzle. Instrumental velocity at 15' was converted to muzzle velocity for the various bullets. Accuracy was checked at the same time on a 100-yard target in the open beyond the shooting building.

In summing up, we might use the 270 Winchester as a base of comparison on one side, and the 7mm Remington Magnum on the other. In doing this we find that it is possible to get more velocity from the same bullet weight with a 24" barrel—which most 264 rifles now have—from the 264 than from the 270. You can also squeeze a little more velocity from the 264 with the 140-gr. bullet, using the right powders, than you'll get with the 130-gr. load in the 270 with similar pressures.

But when working with maximum pressures in both cartridges the 264 is much more temperamental, making the 270 a lot nicer cartridge to work with. The 264, however, with bullets of the same style, is just a little flatter at long range with bullets of the same weight because of their better sectional density and ballistic coefficient. If you use the heavier bullets for heavy game you find the difference becomes even less between the 270 and 264 because you are overloading the 264 bore even more. With the 160-gr. bullet velocity is just over 2900 for the 264, and just under for the 270—all top loads. For this kind of bullet weight the 7mm Rem. Mag. will beat this by some 250 fps with similar pressures.

Everything considered, and while the 264 Winchester Magnum is quite a good cartridge, it seems to be something of a misfit. ●

These are the various weights of bullets tried in the 264. From left: 85-gr. Sierra, 87-gr. Speer, 100-gr. Speer, 120-gr. Speer, 125-gr. Nosler, 129-gr. Hornady, 140-gr. Nosler, 150-gr. Barnes, 160-gr. Hornady, and 165-gr. Barnes. Several other bullets of the same weights were tested but are not shown here.

after it had been fired several times in working up a test load to pressures where the charge was backed off for chronographing. It was then mixed in with other cases and repeatedly used when it was picked up. At the end of the testing it has been used more than 20 times and still held the primer tight enough for further firing. This shows that while pressures were in all loads high, they were not excessive in *this rifle.*

own loading I found that my top charges ran quite closely with the *Speer Manual No. 8,* maximum loads. In most cases I was not able to use the charges listed in the Hornady manual, especially with H-450. I consistently used more powder than either Lyman or Sierra show as maximum.

Some of this variation, of course, comes from the different rifles involved. Much of it is caused by the use of only the bullets made by the company that puts out the manual.

a couple of

25s
25s

A rifle duo, both in 25-06, and how they perform. Good load data plus drop and group figures to 500 yards— not computed!

by FRANK BAKER

THE 25-06 cartridge has long intrigued many rifle enthusiasts, me for one since 1943 when I was a 13-year-old and newly bitten by the gun bug. I pored through my father's old copies of *The American Rifleman* and *Arms and the Man,* drooling over illustrations of Griffin and Howe's custom Springfields and Mauser rifles stocked in French walnut and fitted with Zeiss scopes in Noske mounts. G&H called the 25-06 the 25 Special. Bud Dalrymple's articles in the late '20s and early '30s referred to it as the 25 Niedner, Dalymple's 1903 Springfield having been barreled and chambered for it in Adolph Niedner's shop at Dowagiac, Michigan. In those naive days, of course, I didn't realize that the 30-06 case necked down to 25 caliber—the 25-06—was overbore with contemporary powders and that it needed slower ones for optimum velocity.

As a young adult I frittered away the 1950s and 1960s with 30-06s, 308s, my sporterized 30-40 Krag, several 30-cal. belted magnums, a 348 lever gun, and even a couple of 375 H&Hs—but nary a 25-06. Early in 1970, however, my old double-heat-treated 1903 Springfield action, made in 1926 as part of an NRA sporter, needed a new barrel. A local gunsmith had a No. 4 Douglas premium barrel in 25 caliber and 1:10″ twist. This was quickly fitted, chambered for the 25-

06 and blued. I glassed the receiver ring and rearmost 2 inches of the barrel in a straight-grained European (French?) walnut, and free-floated the rest of the barrel. A now-discontinued but optically first-rate Leupold 7.5x scope was mounted in the high Echo side mount that Dad had installed on this action in the early '50s. The issue trigger had long been retired in favor of a standard Canjar, set to about 2½ pounds. In the interest of safety and the ability of this action to vent powder gases from a split case I drilled a ³⁄₁₆″ gas port in the left receiver ring (where 1903-A3 Springfields have

Author's first 25-06 1903 Springfield has old (1955) high Echo mount and older (1926) Lyman 48 receiver sight.

them) and another in the bolt body facing downward into the magazine (where Mausers are ported). This Springfield also has its original Lyman 48 receiver sight, as well as a spare 3x Weaver scope and a Lyman 17 aperture front sight.

First loads

A batch of once-fired Frankford Arsenal 1960 Match cases was necked down in RCBS dies and trimmed to 2.490″ in a Wilson trimmer—most '06 cases need trimming after sizing to 25-06. After digging into my Lyman, Speer and Hornady loading manuals and fiddling with the Powley computer I started out with loads some 2 to 4 grains under handbook maxima. Both 4350 and old surplus 4831 were used with Hornady 87-gr., Sierra 100-gr. spitzer, Sierra 117-gr. spitzer boat-tail, and Hornady 120-gr. hollow point bullets. Such loads, I thought in my innocence as an old 30-cal. hull-stuffer, should be safe. They really were not. Several gave markedly stiff extraction, as indicated by the strength needed to lift the bolt handle. None of these sticky-extracting loads, however, loosened the primer pockets. But these near-max and obviously slightly over-max loads *did shoot!* H-4831 gave about a minute of angle with the Sierra 100-gr. spitzer and 1" to 1½" with the other bullets, but 4350 really came up a winner. The hot load, 51 grains of 4350, put five 100-gr. Sierras into 9/16" at 100 yards, as pictured. The 117 Sierra boat-tail easily gave ½"-⅝" groups. The long 120-gr. Hornady hollowpoints went under 1" with H-4831, but unlike the Sierras, did no better with 4350. Bullets of 100-120 grains shot better than the 87s in the 10-inch twist. Bullets of all weights showed very nearly the same centers of impact at 100 yards, good news indeed.

My Avtron T973 chronograph, though, had bad news. My outfit wasn't showing any decent 25-06 velocities—at least with loads that extracted easily from the chamber. After about 300 rounds had been run through the barrel some near-max loads giving gilt-edge accuracy chronographed as follows, all with W-W 120 primers (instrumental velocities corrected to muzzle velocities and rounded off to the nearest 5fps).

48/IMR 4350/100 Sierra/3,125 fps
49/IMR 4350/100 Hornady/3,125 fps
45/IMR 4350/117 Sierra BT/2,825 fps

So I had a 257 Roberts in a 25-06 case! The throat of this rifle allowed most spitzer bullets to be seated to 3.20" over-all length. Grasping at straws, I thought that maybe more velocity could be obtained if the throat were lengthened. The gunsmith reamed it so that over-all cartridge length could be 3.35" and the case could hold about 2 more grains of powder. A new series of loads showed that the throat job left accuracy unaffected—see the photo of ⅜" group with 45/4350/117 Sierra BT—but velocities were about the same. After some 150 more rounds were fired the optimum loads and 100-yard 5 shot

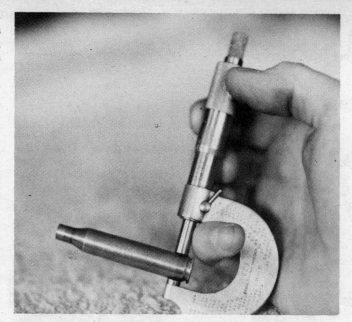

Case expansion, measured ⅛"-3/16" forward of extractor groove, is a sensitive indicator of safe handloads.

groups were:

52/IMR 4350/87 Sierra/Rem.
　9½ primer/3,180 fps, ⅞-1¼"
49.5/IMR 4350/100 Sierra/Rem.
　9½ primer/3,040 fps, 9/16-¾"
54/old 4831/100 Hornady/CCI 250/Rem.
　9½ primer/3,100 fps, ⅞-1⅜"
46/IMR 4350/117 Sierra BT/Rem.
　9½ primer/2,780 fps, ⅜-⅝"
54/old 4831/115 Nosler/CCI
　250 primer 2,975 fps, ¾-1"

So the final evaluation of this rifle was that it is much like a very accurate 257 Roberts. Presumably the low velocities are due to a tight barrel. Neck-reaming and trimming cases to as much as 0.020" under normal length had no noticeable effect on pressures.

In October of 1974 I took the Springfield out to Diamond peak in the northwestern corner of Colorado for deer. The load used was 46.5/4350/117 Sierra BT. A small 3-point buck was hit in the jugular vein at about 365 yards, a lucky shot and an instant kill. The load was sighted 3" high at 100 yards and I had to hold about 12" high on the buck. This obviously isn't a 270-type trajectory, so the 25-06 Springfield-Douglas was retired.

Second 25-06 Rifle

Because the 25-06 still seemed to be an optimum rockchuck-big game cartridge, in spite of the sub-par velocities out of the Springfield, in the summer of 1975 I bought a Ruger Model

The Avtron T973 chronograph, here set up for operation, reveals the awful truth about the author's earlier velocities!

77 in this caliber. This rifle's 24" barrel is stiff, close to Douglas' No. 4 contour, about 0.700" muzzle diameter. Total weight of the rifle with my 7.5x Leupold scope or the old Redfield 6x, carrying sling, and full magazine came to 9 lb., 6 oz. No featherweight, but I hoped it would give varmint accuracy. The trigger on this rifle, incidentally, works well as set to 2¾ lbs—contrary to reports of poor triggers in some M77s.

A hundred Frankford Arsenal match cases were prepared, along with 20 Remington cases of recent manufacture, and development of loads was begun. The Remington cases held essentially the same amounts of powder as the FA match cases, and heavy loads gave both makes just about the same expansion, as measured ⅛" forward of the extractor groove. Several features about loading the Ruger rifle soon came to light. It has a short throat; maximum

swell, some 0.0002"-0.0003" greater than the other 4 or 3 cases. The *maximum* diameter, measured from these sample 5 cases, was used to determine the maximum load for a particular bullet and powder charge. As this maximum diameter reached 0.7100" bolt life and extraction from this Ruger M77 became a bit stiff, as just mentioned. The expansion to 0.7100" *did not* produce loose primer pockets— these remained tight. Maximum

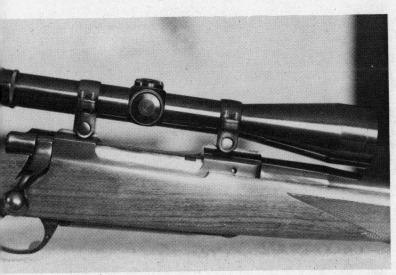

Some excellent 25-cal. bullets. From left—Sierra in 87, 100, and 117 grains; Nosler (new style) of 100 and 115 grains; Speer 120-gr. and Hornady 120-gr. hollow points.

M77 Ruger's scope rings are just high enough for the bell of the 6x Redfield scope to clear the barrel.

sort of pressure yardstick for that particular rifle. This critical expansion diameter, as we might term it, might be appreciably less for your rifle than for my Ruger, or it might be a little greater, depending on chamber and bore dimensions and hardness of your cases. Let's remember, too, that Ruger M77s and No. 1 rifles, as well as Remington M700s, post-64 Winchester M70s, and others of modern design can handle the gas vented back at

over-all length for spitzer bullets is about 3.14"-3.16". Maximum loads typically were 1 grain *less* than those listed in the 1970 *Lyman Reloading Handbook*. Bolt lift on fired cases became a bit heavy when the body of the case measured ⅛"-³⁄₁₆" forward of the tractor groove (as pictured) miked 0.7100" or greater. Expansion of the case at the slight swelling just forward of the case web is, in my opinion, the best indicator of pressures and thereby in the determination of maximum loads. In practice the cases from this chamber ran 0.0003"-0.0004" out of round—as determined by a micrometer that reads 1/10,000". Series of 5 rounds for each load showed one or two cases with a diameter, at this

working loads were set at 1 or 2 grains of powder below those giving case expansion to 0.7100". One grain of powder less was used for loads that gave small variations in case expansion (and presumably small pressure variations) from shot to shot. Two grains less was used for loads giving greater pressure variations. Alternatively, any load giving less than 0.7000" was accepted as safe *for this particular rifle*.

Use of this method for other rifles involves first finding the case diameter at the swelling region forward of the extractor groove for a load, really any load, that gives appreciably heavy bolt lift or extraction. Once this diameter is reached you use it as a

50,000 or more psi from a blown primer or ruptured case head much better than do Springfields, pre-64 Winchester M70s, and all other Mauser designs or Mauser derivatives. Using the latter types of rifles I would set the maximum working loads at 2 to 4 grains below the point of stiff extraction.

After about 200 test rounds had gone through the Ruger M77, chronographed velocities of acceptable maximum loads turned out as follows:

57/H4831/87 Sierra/Rem. 9½ primer, 3,370 fps
53/IMR4350/87 Sierra/Rem. 9½ primer, 3,420 fps
48/IMR4064/87 Sierra/Rem. 9½ primer, 3,360 fps
49/H380/87 Sierra/CCI #250 primer, 3,340 fps
52/IMR4350/100 Sierra/Rem. 9½ primer, 3,255 fps
56/H4831/100 Sierra/Rem. 9½ primer, 3,190 fps
56/H4831/100 Nosler/Rem. 9½ primer, 3,350 fps
54/H4831/115 Nosler/Rem. 9½ primer, 3,140 fps
53/H4831/117 Sierra BT/Rem. 9½ primer, 3,020 fps
53/H4831/120 Speer/Rem. 9½ primer, 3,020 fps
53/H4831/120 Horn. HP/Rem. 9½ primer, 3,070 fps

WARNING: In *this* table the "H4831" is Hodgdon's 4831 of new manufacture. As most handloaders realize, IMR4831 is *not* equivalent to the new H4831. Loads of IMR4831 must be reduced 1 to 3 grains from those listed for H4831.

These loads in the Ruger, in contrast to those considered safe in the custom Springfield, were well in the 25-06 ballpark and were most welcome. The most obvious results were the relatively high velocities of both Nosler bullets: the 100-gr. projectile at 3,350 fps and the 115-gr. at 3,140 fps. Both are superb loads.

Fired Drop Figures

I could have used the chronographed velocities and ballistic coefficients found in loading manuals to work out a drop table. Date in the excellent *Sierra Bullets Reloading Manual* enable the shooter to do this for various altitudes and temperatures. However, I chose the direct route, went to a 500-yard range at 7,900 feet elevation, and ran drop tests by actual

Bullet	MV	Drop (in inches) at Yardage					MOA
		0	100	200	300	500	
87 Sierra	3,420	−1.5	0	−2	−6.5	−35	1.4
100 Sierra	3,255	−1.5	−0.2	−2.5	−8.5	−40	1.25
115 Nosler	3,140	−1.5	−0.5	−3.5	−10	−36	0.7

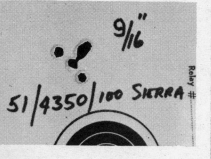

100-yard group shot with hot load from 1903 Springfield 25-06.

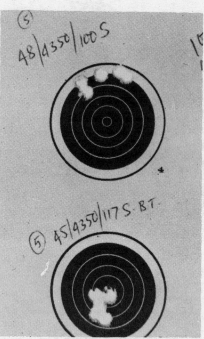

Two 5-shot groups of near-maximum loads from 25-06 Springfield at 100 yards, using Sierra bullets of 100- and 117-gr. weights. Lower group measures about 3/8″.

shooting. Three loads from the above table were used: 53/4350/87 Sierra, 52/4350/100 Sierra, and 54/H4831/115 Nosler. In the interests of components cost and barrel life I fired 3-shot groups only at 100, 200, and 500 yards with each of the three loads. The results, of course, are only approximate in that determination of centers of impact of 3-shot groups is not precise. But trajectories determined this way are certainly good enough for the big game hunter.

The drop figures and average group size tell two important things about this particular M77 Ruger: 1) it's an outstanding long range rifle for medium game (deer-sheep-goat, etc.) with the 115-gr. Nosler bullet in terms of accuracy and flatness of trajectory; 2) its accuracy with those 87-gr. and 100-gr. bullets suitable for varmints is not quite good enough to make it a

Rocky Mountain chuck rifle. For chucks at or above timberline and at distances of 250 yards or more a rifle that shots minute of angle is marginal; ¾-to ½-minute is needed.

Some would use the 25-06 for elk; many hunters would not. I consider the 115 Nosler load at 3,140 a good load for cow elk and spike bulls. It will take trophy bulls if they can be hit well in the rib cage or other vital areas. Much of the passionate argument in the outdoor press about what's-a-good-elk-rifle has been largely pointless, because of 95% of the elk harvested each Fall are cows and young bulls that are easily dispatched with garden variety 270-308-30-06 cartridges. Perhaps 5% of the animals taken are big bulls, which may be more neatly killed with magnum cartridges—if the hunter can shoot these well, of course.

No cartridge, no matter how big or fast its bullet goes, is reliable on rear end shots. In the 1972 season in the White River country of Colorado I had a shot at a trotting spike bull. Headed west, all I could see was his east end as he angled down a steep draw. My 375 H&H Ruger No. 1 single shot came up easily, I held the post of the Lyman 2½x scope square on the center of his rear end, eased off the trigger (as I had done with cast bullets on a running boar range), and sent the 270 Hornady spire-point on its way. A solid hit was made, but about 3″ to the left of center. The bullet thus did not hit the spine as I'd hoped; however, it did break the left hip and the bull went down after about 80 yards and was finished there. As Jack O'Connor and other widely experienced hunters have emphasized over the years, a good 270 or 30-06 load into the chest cavity is vastly more reliable than a 375 or 458 into the rear end. Angling shots, starting through the flank or paunch and extending into the lungs or heart may be made with strongly constructed bullets, those that penetrate deeply and used in favorable circumstances by good shots—preferably where the hunter will also have the opportunity for a second or third shot.

Conclusion

But to get back on the 25-06 track: there are the results on my two 25-06 rifles. The Springfield-Douglas shows outstanding accuracy but its velocities are not quite up to par either for deer at long range or rock chucks. The Ruger M77 and Nosler bullets make a nearly unbeatable combination for open shooting at much North American big game. The M77, though, can't hack it as a chuck rifle with bullets of lighter construction or cheap enough for much varmint shooting. Where to now? Say…remember what Bob said at the range? That Shilen's stainless barrels keep half the bench rest boys happy. And Remington makes their 40XB in 25-06. Hmmm! Wife, dear, we're getting a refund on the Income Tax, aren't we? "Hello, operator, give me Mr. Ed Shilen please…" "Hello, I'd like information for Ilion, New York; yes the Remington Arms Company…"

The 1886 Winchester Rifle
—and how to load for it today

The ten different calibers of the '86 Winchester require five different bullet diameters and nine different cases, but they're all either available or readily convertible from 45/70 or 348 brass, or by using RCBS or B.E.L.L. basic cases.

by ALLAN WILSON

TEN YEARS after introducing their famous Centennial rifle of '76, Winchester brought out the Model 1886. Almost immediately a popular success, over 158,000 had been made at its end in 1935. Indeed it was to continue, to all intents, as the Model 71. Unlike some others, nearly all 86s went to big game hunters. Although it is often said that the Winchester Model 94 has accounted for more whitetail deer than any other rifle, certainly the 86 seems a likely contender for the title of taking more species of big game on the North American continent—from the turn of the century to the 1930s—than any other. In the opinion of many it represents the finest lever action hunting rifle ever produced.*

Today the Model 86, besides being avidly sought for by collectors, is, more and more, again appearing in big game country. Too, it's more than just nostalgia, I think, that accounts for this renewed interest. It is the rare hunting enthusiast who fails to be impressed with the 86's silk-smooth action, excellent balance and the superb choice of calibers. Its reliability and durability can be sensed from the very first handling in both the feel and the sound as the action is cycled.

Fortunately, these exceptional design characteristics, developed and patented by John Browning, are responsible in good part for a high Model 86 survival rate. With the exception of 4 calibers 86s can readily be found in most of the original chamberings at gun dealers around the country. The prices asked are competitive with the cost of any high quality centerfire rifle manufactured today. Naturally the engraved specimens, the rifles in mint condition, and such scarcer variations as sling-ring carbines, extra long barrel lengths and deluxe models bring substantially higher prices from the advanced collector. Better leave those to him!

*For an interesting and illustrated report on the 1886 Winchester—and its successor, the Model 71—see *The Winchester Book* by George Madis (1st ed., Dallas, Texas, 1961). The Model 1886 was John Browning's second patent which Winchester bought from the great inventor.

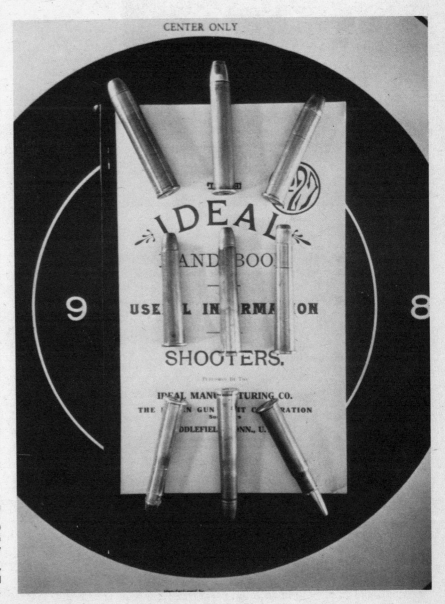

Nine of the Model 86 calibers. Top, from left—a C.C.C. 50/110; an original WRA 45/90 handloaded with a Hornady bullet, and a modern 45/70 case, also Hornady loaded. Center, from left—an original U.M.C. 40/65; a custom 40/70 loaded by Sailer, and an original 40/82 WCF handloaded. Bottom, from left—a custom 38/56 handloaded by Pomeroy; another Sailer custom load in 38/70, and an original WRA 33 case holding a Hornady bullet.

Three all-time favorite Winchester 86s; from left—an octagon-barrel full magazine 45/90 rifle; a light-weight carbine in 45/70 and the 33 Winchester. Owned by the author, he uses all three for hunting in northern New England.

Doing that should help the shooter-hunter to economically acquire one, or several, of the existing thousands of "plain Jane" 86s, most of them surprisingly wear-free even after many years of use, save for blue wear and the odd dents and scratches in the wood.

Model 86 Calibers

The 86 was offered in ten calibers during its lifetime, as the table below shows. Although it is well known that the 50/100 and 50/110 were produced in small numbers, two other calibers, the 38/70 and the 40/70, are much harder to locate today. However, the latter two rarely go at premium prices, for most dealers seem unaware of their scarcity.

As for shooting the 86s the only cartridge available commercially from major manufacturers is the 45/70. All of the others require custom-ammo or handloading; in fact 45/70 owners often reload for better results than the low-performance factory round offers.

All 86s can also be used with cast lead bullets, of course. In fact, all of the original calibers were introduced using lead bullets, except for the 33; this last caliber of the series appeared in 1902. However, lead bullets rarely seem to shoot as well as jacketed types unless the bore is in near-new condition, absolutely free of any roughness. But if you can't resist the challenge to experiment with cast bullets, go to it. Lyman and RCBS offer suitable moulds for most 86 calibers, and ready-to-shoot cast lead bullets are available from various suppliers.

Finding Cartridge Cases

Original cartridge cases are often difficult to locate, but usable cases can be managed easily, one way or another. As Table 2 shows, all 86 cases (except the two 50s) have nearly identical dimensions, these conforming closely to the standard 45/70 dimensions; however, variations from .595″ to .605″ will be found on samples from different manufacturers and from different production lots and production time periods. Thus all calibers can be made from 45/70 brass, apart from the 50s. Happily, the 45/70 case is exactly the right length for three of the other calibers and can also be used as a "short case" for the 2.40″ length 38/70, 40/70, 40/82 and 45/90.

If such short cases (2.10″) are used, just seat the bullet out farther, which will eliminate, usually, any feeding and functioning problems. The over-all loaded-cartridge lengths in Table 2 should be used as a rough guide; much will depend on the dimensions of the bullet you use. If the full diameter of the bullet is not reached until relatively near its base then you can load to the lengths in Table 2; if the diameter is reached sooner (higher on the bullet), then it may be necessary to load to a slightly *shorter* over-all length. In other words, a long-tapering ogive or nose form permits loading to maximum length, whereas a blunter-shaped bullet requires deeper seating in the case. The best technique is to assemble several dummy rounds (no propellant, no primer), at max length initially, then cycle these from the magazine tube through the receiver and in and out of the chamber. Progressively seat the bullet deeper for each trial until the correct length is determined. The dummy rounds can then be used to adjust the seating die correctly.

The over-all length/bullet-diameter problem may arise even with the "short" 45/70 cases. However, most reloaders prefer to use cartridges of original length, and we can give thanks that the case supply problem has been solved—not only for all cases of 45/70 dimensions, but for the various 50s as well, not to mention the big British cases.

Case Procurement Solved

Our benefactors are Fred Huntington of RCBS and Jim Bell of Brass Extrusion Labs., Ltd., or B.E.L.L. The 45 Basic Case from RCBS is a slightly tapered "straight" case, nominally 3.25″ long, and with 45/70 rim/head dimensions. These cases, which can be used to form every caliber for the 86 Winchester except the 50s, require the use of RCBS case-forming and trim dies in addition to the regular reloading dies. Charles Huntington of RCBS has put together an excellent case-forming instruction booklet, using this new case, including details on all of the 86 calibers from 33 to 45/90.

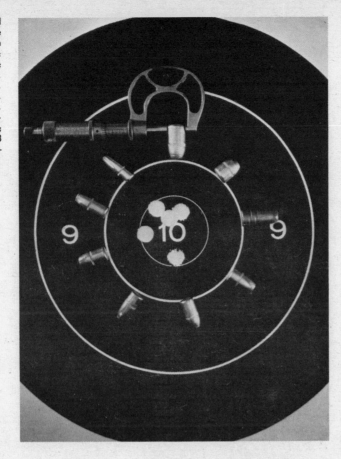

Some of the jacketed bullets available for the 86 Winchester. From the top, clockwise: Barnes 450-gr. 50 cal.; next, Barnes 300-gr. 50; Remington 405-gr. 45; Hornady 300-gr. 45; McCallum's 260-gr. and 300-gr. 40s; Sailer's 260-gr. 40; McCallum's 255-gr. 38 and the Hornady 200-gr. 33.

Jim Bell makes several different cartridge cases for obsolete British and U.S. chambers, among which is the 50 Sharps 3¼". I'll describe this big case later on.

Table 1—Bullet Diameters and Weights

Cal.	Dia., ins.	Wgt., grs.	Source of Jacketed Bullets
33	.338	200	Excellent results with 200-gr. Hornady.
38/56	.375	255	Available from custom makers only.
38/70	.375	255	Same as 38/56.
40/65	.406	260	Available from custom makers only.
40/70	.406	330	Use 250- or 260-gr. custom bullets.
40/82	.406	260	Sames as 40/65.
45/70	.458	405	Widely available commercially.
45/90	.458	300	Excellent results with 300-gr. Hornady HP; works well in 45/70 also.
50/100	.510	450	Limited availability from custom makers.
50/110	.510	300	Same as 50/100; the 300-gr. bullet is best choice in 50/100 or 50/110.

Note: Names and address of custom bullet makers are listed later.

Notes on the M86 Calibers

33 Winchester Although 33 Winchester ammunition was not put back into production when World War II ended in 1945, this bottle-necked rimmed cartridge was produced up to 1940 and can still be found in limited quantity at many dealers. In addition, boxes of 33s are commonly offered at gun shows around the country.

Cases can also be formed from 45/70 brass; run the 45/70 cases through a 33W full-length sizing die, trim to 2.10" if necessary, and fireform. However, this one-step operation may not be successful; the cases may not chamber. If this happens, order a case-forming die from RCBS, then use it as an intermediate sizing die. This may or may not hold true with other 45/70 conversions. I suggest you try the one-step operation first and see.

One other reloading "trick" may occasionally be required. Cases may begin to swell after several firings just forward of the rim in the area not normally in contact with the sizing die. To correct this use a 45/90 die body only, no matter which caliber is giving difficulty and, using a bench vise, press the lubed cases into the die nearly up to the rim. Knock the cases

out with a steel or brass pin. This works with all but the 50 calibers and rarely has to be repeated.

38/56 Though the 38/56—another rimmed bottle-neck—was produced in great numbers into the mid-1930s, you are not likely to find a box of these around except at relatively high cartridge-collector prices. However, you can find single unboxed samples quite readily, usually at gun shows, and if you don't object to mixing brands this is a good low-cost source. Lacking originals, cases can be formed for the 38/56 in the same manner as for the 33. Full-length size 45/70s in a 38/56 die, trim to 2.10" if required, and fire-form.

38/70 This cartridge, never popular, was produced for only a few years. If you are lucky enough to find an 86 in this caliber your luck probably won't hold in finding original cases. In converting available factory cartridge cases to the 38/70 you have two choices. The simplest is to use 45/70 brass and full-length size. It is then necessary to seat the bullet farther out to compensate for the shorter brass. If you use this method ask your custom jacketed-bullet maker to position the crimping cannelure accordingly, thus permitting loading to the proper length. A better solution is to use the RCBS cases or 45/90 brass; the latter is the correct length, 2.40".

40/65 Of the three 40-cal. sizes chambered in the 86 Winchester, only the 40/65 is based on the 45-70 standard length, 2.10". The other two, 40/70 and 40/82, are 2.4" long. The 40/65 is not easy to locate, and the best solution is to full-length size 45/70 cases.

40/70 These cases are virtually impossible to find; substitutes are usually made from 45/70 or 45/90 cases, but the easier-to-find 40/82 cases can also be used. In either instance the over-all cartridge length must be about 2.75".

40/82 These case dimensions are nearly the same as for the 40/70, and substitute cases can be made in the same way. The major dimensional difference occurs at the shoulder; the 40/82 is smaller at .445" than the 40/70, which is .495".

45/70 and 45/90 No big problem here with cases. Though 45/70 brass often works well in the 45/90, the full length cases, using the RCBS basic cases, are much preferred.

50/100 and 50/110 Both cases are identical as are the rifle chambers. Until the advent of the B.E.L.L. cases some shooters used the British 450/ 3¼" Express cartridges or cases.

TABLE 2—Cartridge Case Dimensions

Cal.	Rim diam. a	Body diam. b	Case Lgth.	Over-all Lgth. c
33	.597	.495	2.10	2.78
38/56	.600	.501	2.10	2.57
38/70	.595	.503	2.34	2.81
40/65	.602	.496	2.10	2.49
40/70	.595	.502	2.40	2.80
40/82	.604	.504	2.39	2.78
45/70	.599	.503	2.10	2.70
45/90	.605	.505	2.43	2.93
50/100	.603	.550	2.40	2.74
50/110	.605	.551	2.40	2.74

a. Actual measurements on different samples will vary as shown.

b. Measurements made immediately forward of the rim.

c. Over-all length can vary substantially depending on the bullet used; see text.

After trimming to 2.40″ they can be fire-formed. Another solution was to use 348 Winchester cases. Stand the deprimed cases, base down, in a pan of water a half-inch deep. Heat the neck and shoulder of each until it starts to show red, then tip the case over in the water. Cases so-annealed can be loaded with 15 grains of Bullseye and then topped off with Cream of Wheat. DO NOT use any bullet. The 348 case can then be fire-formed to 50 caliber. With some lots of 348s you

New brass for all M86 calibers is still available. From the top, clockwise: RCBS 45 Basic cases; 38/56 cases made by Pomeroy; factory 45/70 cases; 50/110s by Pomeroy and 45/90s by Godfrey. The Godfrey and RCBS cases can be reformed to any of the 86 Winchester calibers except the big 50s—which is where the 50 Sharps case made by Jim Bell comes in.

may do this successfully without annealing; with others case splits will often occur. Jim Bell's 50 Sharps 3¼″ case is the easiest way to go, though a mite expensive at $1.25 each. This case, by the way, also makes all of the big Sharps cases, the 50-70 Gov't., the 45-75 and others.

One other tip: Some years ago the Connecticut Cartridge Company offered many remanufactured obsolete cartridges for a while, the 50/110 included. It is not uncommon to find C.C.C. ammo at gun shows and at a few dealers. Cartridge collectors haven't yet run the prices up for C.C.C. ammunition, so they are still reasonable.

Summary

In summary then, various options exist by which the obsolete cartridge-case problem can be solved for the 86 Winchester. My personal preference, more nostalgic than logical, is to buy original cartridges which, for most calibers, run $20 to $25 per box of 20. This avoids the cost of special case-forming dies. Their disadvantage is that such cases may be age-weakened or be of the less durable balloon-head case design. This is only a minor problem if black

Here are some of the B.E.L.L. cases, unformed or reformed, plus several original cartridges. Jim Bell's modern drawn-brass cases can be converted to virtually any of the old medium-to-big calibers.

Table 3—Source List

Barnes Bullets
P.O. Box 215
American Fork, UT 84003

Jacketed bullets in .338″, .348″, .375″, .406″, 458″ and .510″ diameter; specify for original "short" length cases.

Brass Extrusion Labs., Ltd.
800 W. Maple Lane
Bensenville, IL 60106

Variety of new basic cases, one type usable for Model 86 calibers 50/100 and 50/110. Write for information.

Godfrey Reloading Supply
Box 668
Brighton, IL 62012

Bullets, dies, cases for most 86 calibers.

Dick Griffith
6000 Chandler
Bakersfield, CA 93307

Custom cases.

Hornady Mfg. Co.
P.O. Box 1848
Grand Island, NE 68801

Jacketed bullets in 33, 375 and 458 calibers.

Old West Gun Room
3509 Carlson Blvd.
El Cerrito, CA 94530

Sometimes has original 86 cartridges.

Robert Pomeroy
Morison Ave.
E. Corinth, ME 04427

Custom ammunition and/or cases for all 86 calibers.

RCBS/Omark
Box 1919
Oroville, CA 95965

45 Basic cases, reloading and case-forming dies for all calibers.

Anthony Sailer
Box L
Owen, WI 54460

Custom ammo for all 86 calibers smokeless or black powder; also jacketed 40-cal. bullets.

NOTE: Ammunition can only be shipped to holders of a current signed Federal Firearms License; see your local dealer.

---

powder or Pyrodex is used, but a balloon-head case rupture can be a disaster if a modern propellant is used. I should also note that, in 20 years of shooting jacketed bullets in the old soft steel barrels, I have never detected any barrel wear or erosion *as long as black powder was used.*

However, if you want long case life, such as the old Ideal Everlasting cases gave, then buy RCBS Basic 45 or B.E.L.L. cases and the required forming dies. These modern cases offer the utmost security and performance, including the use of smokeless powders.

Here are a few loads, given in grains weight, for several Model 86 calibers, these taken from Hodgdon's new 48-page publication, *Pyrodex/Black Powder Data Manual* ($1).

Cal.	Bullet, grs.	Pyrodex CTG, grs.	MV
38/55	270	42	1354
38/56	270	45	1375
40/56	245	52	1460
45/70	350	56	1449
45/90	350	67	1495

This new Hodgdon manual is highly recommended. It's full of lab-tested load data for muzzle-loading arms of all types, using Pyrodex or black powder, plus good reading by George C. Nonte, Dr. Sam Fadala (on black powder hunting), and a worthwhile "Case Interchangeability Chart" compiled by Nonte.

The final option, the one taken by most shooters, is probably the easiest, the least expensive and the fastest way to get on the firing line. This entails buying fully loaded ammunition from a custom handloader. Whatever way you go, Table 3 lists some of the better known and reliable suppliers, firms which offer custom cartridge cases, bullets and ammunition. •

Loaded ammunition for the 86s can come from a variety of sources such as the still-to-be-found Connecticut Cartridge Company (top left). Winchester 33s remain on some dealers shelves and new factory brass in 45/70 continues in production. Such custom handloaders as Anthony Sailer (top right) are an excellent source and original factory ammo such as Peters 38/56 (lower right) is often on sale at gun shows at moderate costs.

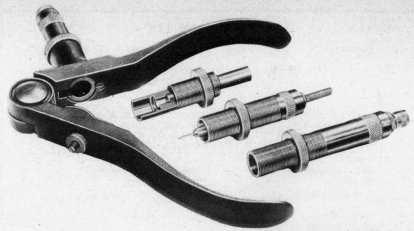

The current version of our oldest hand-loading tool, the Lyman 310, makes excellent reloads—if a bit slowly.

MOST HANDLOADERS have a loading room or solid bench which serves as a base of operations, but there are times when many shooters find it necessary to leave that loading bench behind. These traveling shooters generally fall into two broad categories. First there are the short-timers—fellows who may be gone for only a few days or weeks. This group includes the weekend varmint hunter and the vacationer who takes a favorite gun along just in case he finds a good shooting area. Others in this fraternity are shooters who live in urban areas. Nowadays, many of these must make a minor hegira just to locate shooting room for experimentation or good varmint hunting. Some are finding it more practicable to just camp in a favorite spot and make a weekend of it.

The second group includes the fellow who may be away from home for many months—the student attending college in another state or the wanderer who wants to see some of the country while still young and free.

In either situation, it usually takes only one occasion of being where the shooting is good and the ammo short to convince the traveler/shooter he should become a traveler/handloader.

A traveling handloader's needs could range from an extra hundred loads for the weekend varmint hunter to several thousand for the battery of guns the wanderer may have.

If a traveler is going to handload he must have portable loading tools—and know how to use them. Such tools are not new. The frontiersmen, the buffalo hunters who roamed our West, were intimately familiar with them, as proven by the number of pre-1900 loading tools displayed in our Western museums.

When a traveler rode a horse or wagon, or walked, weight and space were limiting factors. He either had light, compact loading gear or he didn't have any. It was that simple. Such tools are exemplified by the old Ideal tong tool, which in some versions included a bullet mould as an integral part.

Compact Hand Tools

Even in today's motorized era compactness is an asset, and many in need of totable tools turn to those made by Lyman, Lee, English, and perhaps others.

Riflemen, especially those who use jacketed bullets exclusively, suffer the least inconvenience when handloading away from home. Most riflemen load their shells in lots of 20, and

Handloading and the Traveling Man

The traveler who wants to handload en route needs portable loading tools. This report covers the Lee tools, the Lyman 310 and the Bill English Pak-Tool—plus instructive notes on a semi-portable outfit as well.

by MICHAEL VENTURINO

Author has loaded thousands of cartridges with hand tools while away from home. Most of it has been in (from left) 38 Spl., 357 Mag., 44 Mag., 45 Colt and 30-06.

to *carefully* load a box of rifle ammo with hand tools takes only a few minutes longer than to do just that with bench-mounted equipment.

While hand tools load good ammo when used properly, none I've tried is better equipped to turn out precision ammo than the Lee Target Model Loader. This little outfit, which includes a case-neck reamer, case trimmer, adjustable straight-line bullet-seating tool, primer-seating tool, and more, is ideal for the varmint hunter who expects MOA (minute of angle) accuracy.

The Lee tool, delivered in a flat compact box can be stored—along with a can of powder, a box of bullets and primers—in such a small kit that even the most space-conscious traveler won't find it a nuisance. The only extra needed is a hardwood or plastic mallet.

The cast bullet shooter may not find the Lee outfit useful because it doesn't permit belling the case mouth, a necessity when trying to seat cast bullets without shaving them.

However, a belling tool can be easily made—a shorter section of hardwood dowel rod can be turned to a taper, as can a piece of round hard plastic or metal. A handle can be made from a ball or a drawer knob, using wood, metal, porcelain or whatever.

The Cast Bullet Loader

The cast bullet shooter will find the Lyman 310 tool a better choice, perhaps. A neck-expanding and mouth-belling die are supplied with each tool. For those who don't mind the cost, and want real cast bullet accura-cy, buy and use the Lee and 310 tools together.

If ammo of less than bench-rest precision is all that's needed, the 310, the regular Lee Loader, or the English tool meet all requirements.

In my last semester in college I used a 310 tool to load over 1,000 rounds of cast bullet 30-06s because I couldn't afford regular dies for my press. The 310 tool treated me so well then that I still prefer it when loading '06s.

Powder Measuring

The powder dippers often recommended for use with the various portable tools are a handicap when trying to develop accurate ammo. This is *not* to say they're useless, because they are accurate when used properly, but they offer little flexibility for the experimenter. Also, most of us have a few pet loads, and I have yet to see a dipper that would give exactly the charge I wanted—unless homemade.

A logical solution—at the cost of a little space—is to carry along a powder scale. It requires only a level surface in a draft-free room, and it lets the loader pick exactly the charge he needs.

I still use a dipper to throw the near-basic charge into the scale pan and then dribble the remainder in with a powder trickler.

As long as the shooter doesn't try to load for a variety of rifles in the same caliber, he seldom needs to full-length size his cases. However, Lyman can supply full-length sizers, the type used in a vise. True, few travelers carry a vise, but most gas stations have them and their operators will often permit their use. How-ever, it is much easier and faster to sort cases before loading, thus making sure they will chamber in the rifle they will be used in.

Handgunners are the shooters who will be inconvenienced most by hand tools, as their sport usually calls for more ammo. Where loading 20 rounds by hand can be pleasant and relaxing, loading 50 or 100 can be tedious.

I had several problems when using Lyman 310 tools to supply my handgun fodder. Most annoying was trying to size nickel-plated 38 Special and 357 Magnum cases.

Lyman 310 Problems

Nickeled cases are harder—or seem to be—than plain brass cases, and the effort required to size them will wear out even the most muscular handloader. I've raised blisters on my hands by sizing 200 nickeled cases at one sitting.

Solution? Use plain brass cases only for 38s and 357s. I have 1,000 military 38 Special brass cases, headstamped WCC 66, which I've been using for a year and a half. They slide into the 310 tool's dies very easily, and most of the time do not even need lubrication. Thus far only two have been discarded because of splits. For 357 Magnum, the brass cases sold by Speer give equal results.

Crimping on some jacketed bullets can also be a problem with the 310 tool. Jacketed bullets having a true crimping groove work okay, but those with a mere cannelure give trouble. I loaded up a batch of 44 Magnums for my Ruger Super Blackhawk using the Sierra 240 JHC, which has such a cannelure. I could not generate enough pressure by hand to turn the case mouth into the cannelure, so the bullet in the fourth or fifth round in every cylinderful moved far enough forward to tie up the gun. Running the remainder of these 44s through the crimping die in my press when I got home solved the problem. Where such ammunition may be used for personal defense against man or beast, this could be dangerous. Moral: use crimp-grooved bullets.

Loading for the 45 rimmed Colt with the "nutcracker" tool is a pleasure, except for primer-seating. The thin rims don't have a strong surface for the shell holder to grasp, and often the force to seat the primers causes the rim to slip past its groove. This soon turns the case rim into a mass of burrs, which often bind against the recoil shield of the sixgun. It helps somewhat to press the case mouth against a block of wood during primer seating.

The portable Pak-Tool, designed and marketed by W. M. English, does full-length sizing of handgun cases, crimps rifle and handgun cases, offers good leverage for all operations.

The Lee Target Model Loader performs functions not possible with other portable tools—inside case-neck reaming, case-mouth trimming and primer-pocket cleaning.

The compact and handy Bair (now Bear) pistol measure may be bench mounted or used in the hand to charge cases rapidly via a fixed-cavity rotor. Rotors for different charges are available.

Full Length Sizing

Full-length sizing is more important in loading for handguns than rifles (except as noted), and the lack of a practical way to full-length size cases is a serious handicap with some hand tools.

One summer, working in the West, I was pleased to discover that five of the six fellows I was working with owned 357 Magnum revolvers. We spent many evenings in informal shooting matches, burning up quite a bit of ammo. It didn't take us long to discover that we had to sort ammo for each gun if it had been loaded with the 310 tools. Cases fired in a Smith & Wesson 27 would chamber only in it and a Smith & Wesson 19, and vice versa. Cases fired in a Colt SAA copy would chamber in both S&Ws but not in two Ruger Blackhawks or a real Colt SAA, and cases used in the Colt would work in all sixguns except the two Rugers.

These problems should be solved by using the Pak Tool, which does full-length size handgun cases, and crimps the case mouth as well.

When loading for sixguns it's impractical to weigh every powder charge, so a powder measure is necessary if you want to avoid dippers. For standard charges I use a fixed powder measure, these made with different

This is the Pakit, a hand-operated loading tool once offered by Pacific. No longer made, but it might be found in used stocks.

rotors or inserts for various powders and charges. Bear and Bonanza make these, as did Pacific. When experimenting, the Lyman 55 adjustable measure is used in conjunction with a powder scale.

As odd as it may sound, some of my most pleasant handloading was done in a bunkhouse in Yellowstone National Park, while working as a horse wrangler. Yes, guns are illegal in the Park, but handloading gear is not. My guns were kept by friends outside the Park, where we went to shoot.

In the evenings I used to sit on the porch, a few hundred yards from the Grand Canyon of the Yellowstone River, with a view of natural wilderness unexcelled anywhere, and do my loading while watching the horses feed. If I sat there long enough, a few deer and, occasionally, a moose, elk, or buffalo would wander by. I wish every handloader could experience that.

Beware of Shortages

The traveler's reloading outfit must be self-sufficient. If his pet load depends on a certain make and weight of bullet, then he should carry a sufficient supply of that projectile. If he is a cast-bullet shooter, he should cast, size, lube, and box enough bullets at home to last during his travels. The same goes for powder, primers, or any other components.

He should never count on gun stores in the areas he passes through to supply his special needs, for they'll invariably be fresh out of whatever it is he wants. Once I failed to find even one can of Bullseye powder in all of Bozeman, Montana. Also, many stores carry only certain brands of components, so if your pet load depends on Remington primers, Hornady bullets and Norma powder, you'll be out of luck if the store you stop at carries only CCI primers, Speer bullets, and Du Pont powders.

The man who may be gone for months at a time can survive with hand tools, but he may find it hard to satisfy his needs over lengthy periods. Sometimes, when away from home for an entire summer, I relied entirely on hand tools, but at times, when it came to a choice between handloading and my summer social life, I socialized! Therefore, I often had an urge to shoot and nothing loaded up to shoot with. For that reason, and because of the problems associated with loading for handguns, a *semi*-portable rig is a good idea for those away from home for several months.

Semi-Portable Rigs

Any of the smaller "C" presses can meet this need. I now use an RCBS Jr. for this job, but whatever press is used, it can be mounted on any available surface with inexpensive C-clamps. I've used picnic tables and even the plywood platform which serves as a bed in my camper.

In handgun calibers it is a good idea to use the tungsten carbide sizing dies whenever possible. They make case sizing so easy that the press doesn't need sturdy mounting. Full length sizing of bottleneck rifle cases does require a strong press mounting, but if a well-anchored table can't be found, have a friend sit on the table being used. Of course, neck sizing is all that is usually necessary, but it's nice to be able to full-length size when you want to.

With a semi-portable outfit such as this, it is more productive to set aside one day to load ammunition, and then assemble big lots, up to 500 or so rounds.

Cast bullet shooters, gone for many months, would be wise to bring their bullet moulds and sizing-lubricating gear with them. The first time I traveled west with my loading tools, I left my bullet moulds at home, intending to rely on store-bought bullets. The nearest gun store turned out to be over 100 miles away from where I was working! The next summer I took along bullet moulds, a lead pot, kake kutters and sizing chambers for the 310 tools.

Bullet Lubing

The kake kutter method of lubricating bullets is slow and messy, and wastes much lubricant. I tried smearing it on with my fingers and found this to be a little faster but *unbelievably* messy! Lubricant usually ended up on bullet bases, bullet noses, bullet sides, my shirt, jeans, hands, face, and hair.*

Also, the sizing chambers for the 310 tools would not work with the Hornady crimp-on checks. They simply would not start through the die. Other than this minor fault, the sizing chambers worked fine.

A kake kutter lubricating and sizing kit is also put out by the Lee company. This unit even has a tray for holding the melted lube.

I've now decided to go the whole route and use a regular lubricator and sizer—when I'm going to process a lot of bullets—such as the Lyman 450, also mounting it with C-clamps.

---

*A worthwhile tool, made for use with a Kake Kutter, is Stanley's Helper. This device "captures" up to 100 or more lubed bullets in a plastic reservoir, avoiding the multiple handling of the greasy bullets. Available from Stanley Co., Box 323, Arvin, CA 93203; price $5.95 plus 50¢ postage, when I bought mine.

This Bonanza form of powder measure is reasonably compact, may also be disassembled for easier packing.

The new RCBS sizer-luber should work equally well.

A cigar box of accessories such as a primer flipper, de-burring tools, micrometer, primer pocket cleaner, case lube pad, screwdrivers, and allen wrenches will come in handy. Several sets of loading dies and an assortment of moulds completes my kit.

A "semi-portable" outfit as outlined is certainly not for the weekend varmint hunter. It is a scaled-down version of the equipment found on most handloading benches, and it's capable of making as good ammunition as found anywhere.

I haven't done it yet, but I could load shells right in the back of my truck while camped in a remote location. Still, I have yet to end up anywhere that I couldn't, with a little imagination, find surfaces suitable for mounting a reloading press.

No, I haven't discarded my hand tools, I still use them in certain situations. When I leave again for long periods of time they will be along to "assist" my semi-portable gear. I just don't want to be limited entirely to hand tools the next time my loading bench is 2,000 miles away. On the other hand, I don't want to be without them in case I find another porch to watch the sunset from!

Traveling in itself is fascinating, but a hull stuffer who combines it with handloading gets a unique and satisfying experience. He is as independent in his shooting needs in, say, the Montana badlands, as he is at his own loading bench at home. ●

The Stanley device reduces the handling of greasy bullets as they emerge from the top of Kake Kutters, so called. A useful small tool.

AMERICAN BULLETED CARTRIDGES

A detailed and comprehensive review of newly developed and introduced metallic cartridges and components.

by KEN WATERS

Latest Developments In Metallic Cartridges

A strange year filled with unpredictable events lies behind us. Not even the most confident soothsayer could have been expected to foresee its unusual happenings.

How, for instance, does one react to almost simultaneous announcements of the emergence of an exciting new version of a world famous rifle and an apparent going-out-of-business notice, both from the same company!?

Or that a pair of old cartridges are given new life through improved modern factory loadings, while another of equal merit is discontinued?

This all may be symptomatic of the uncertainty of our times. What seems pretty evident however, despite such news and inflationary high prices, is the continuing vitality of the shooting industry. It's a reassuring spectacle, one segment of which we're about to subject to our annual appraisal:

Winchester-Western

At the most recent Winchester Seminar held at Nilo Farms late in 1980, the key announcement from this writer's point of view was the introduction of a new Featherweight version of the time-honored Winchester Model 70 rifle, and the companion disclosure that the new rifle would be chambered for the 257 Roberts and 7x57 Mauser cartridges in addition to the usual—243, 270, 308 and 30-06. That was distinctly interesting to us since it seemingly heralded a re-birth of popularity for that pair of old but still excellent cartridges.

Actually, the 257 Roberts is not as old as the 270, and the 7x57 is only about ten years older than the 30-03, parent cartridge of the 30-06, so age of origin is obviously irrelevant. What counts here, as with any cartridge, is performance and both these rounds have legitimate claim to plenty of that.

With admirable foresight, Winchester has continued to offer 257 Roberts cartridges in a trio of loadings throughout the years during which no rifles were being chambered in that caliber, with bullet weights of 87-, 100- and 117-grains

at muzzle velocities listed as 3170, 2900 and 2650 fps respectively. Thus, purchasers of the new Model 70 Featherweight in this caliber will have a good selection of available factory ammo from which to choose.

Unfortunately, the same can't be said for the 7x57 where only a single loading with 175-grain bullet is to be had. Badly needed is a factory loading with 139- or 140-grain, or even 150-grain spitzer, bullets at higher velocity with flatter trajectory. In the meantime, Winchester could utilize the 125-grain Power Point or 150-grain 7mm bullets currently being made. Loaded in 7x57 cases, these bullets could readily provide muzzle velocities in excess of 2700 and 2800 fps.

Coupled with that excitingly good news however, came a release that is so astounding I still have trouble believing it. To avoid any chance that I might have misconstrued their intentions, I will quote parts of the Olin public relations release:

"The board of directors of Olin Corporation authorized the disposal of the company's Winchester sporting arms business in the United States, as part of a major restructuring of the Winchester Group to better focus Olin's resources on the Group's successful sporting and defense ammunition business, domestically and internationally. . . . This concentration on our ammunition business insures that those operations will receive the necessary resources and corporate support to be more successful."

It has all the earmarks of a return to the time some of us are old enough to remember when the Winchester Repeating Arms Company of New Haven, Connecticut, and the Western Cartrige Company of East Alton, Illinois, were separate entities. It appears there will be ammunition, and there are even new things this year.

Latest in the Winchester-Western cartridge line-up is an item of importance primarily to owners, present and prospective, of small self-defense pistols. An old favorite due to its compact size has been the 25 Automatic. Increasing numbers of the little pistols are being sold, and Winchester-Western has paid new attention.

Traditionally, the 25 Automatic has been loaded with

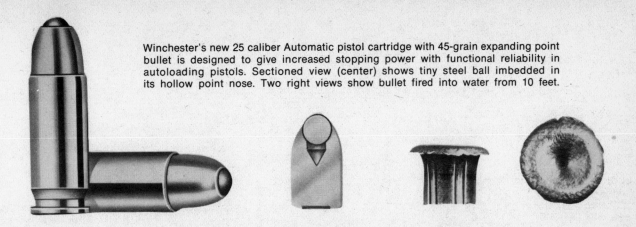

Winchester's new 25 caliber Automatic pistol cartridge with 45-grain expanding point bullet is designed to give increased stopping power with functional reliability in autoloading pistols. Sectioned view (center) shows tiny steel ball imbedded in its hollow point nose. Two right views show bullet fired into water from 10 feet.

50-grain round-nose full-metal-cased bullets to insure absolute reliability in feeding from magazine to chamber. W-W's solution to the challenge of providing a more sophisticated bullet is ingenious. Starting with a lead bullet with Lubaloy plating providing a construction with less stiffness than the old metal jackets yet one which would insure dependable feeding and at the same time prevent barrel leading, they next incorporated a hollow nose cavity in which a tiny steel ball is inserted. The entire assembly weighs 45 grains, and this 10% decrease in bullet weight has permitted an increase in muzzle velocity to 835 fps from a 2″ barrel.

As the accompanying photo of one of these bullets that was fired into water at a range of ten feet shows, a significant improvement has been achieved over the old bullets which gave virtually no expansion. While the small increase in velocity may have helped slightly, the new design combining a softer construction with that expanding nose feature is due the major credit for this superior bullet performance.

Interestingly, this construction is very closely similar to that of the old Hoxie bullets which were applied to Winchester cartridges away back in 1907, which likewise utilized a small round ball placed in the nose of a bullet, the ball being driven back into an air-filled cavity to produce increased mushrooming.

Ballistics in 2″ Barrel:
Winchester 25 Automatic

Bullet		Velocity (fps)		Energy (ft. lbs.)	
Wt. Grs.	Type	Muzzle	50-yds.	Muzzle	50-yds.
45	Expanding Pt.	835	740	70	55

Another oldie to receive Winchester-Western's revitalizing treatment was the great old 45-70 Government cartridge, introduction of which in a 300-grain bullet loading was reported in this column last year before we'd had an opportunity to try them out. Now we can tell you more about them.

In a modern scope-sighted Marlin Model 1895 these new W-W loads with 300-gr. hollow-point bullets chronographed 1763 fps MV and made five shot groups at 100 yards as small as 1½″. I consider this excellent performance. In an H&R replica of the Officer's Model Springfield Trap Door rifle, the 26″ barrel of this rifle produced increased velocities averaging 1805 fps, yet with case expansion measurements only slightly more than standard 405-grain Winchester loads show in this same rifle. The H&R handled and ejected fired cases without difficulty and with no apparent strain. And an 1886 Winchester 45-70 with 26″ octagon barrel and plain open sights put five rounds of this

ammo in 3″ at 100 yards, chronographing 1808 fps, and producing no problems.

Finally, we want to report briefly on Winchester's 225-grain bullet loading for their 338 Magnum, received too late for a test report last year. Muzzle velocity averaging 2763 fps comes close to W-W's predicted 2780 fps, and accuracy is at least as good as with 250-gr. loads in our 338 Model 70, and better than the 200-grain factories.

Federal

Increasingly, it seems, we look to the Federal Cartridge Corporation for some of the practical and therefore useful metallic cartridge loadings that other ammunition makers pass over or ignore. In recent years they have become particularly adept at bringing out new loadings with superior ballistics in certain of the old but still viable calibers.

Past examples of this were the first modern Express load for the 45-70 wherein bullet weight was decreased to 300-grains and velocity *increased* to 1880 fps, combined with a hollow-point for quicker expansion. And a new load for the venerable 30-30 with 125-grain hollow-point at 2570 fps MV.

Both cartridges have proven excellent as to accuracy in several test rifles of those calibers, and although the 45-70-300 loading requires a barrel longer than 24″ to reach its advertised velocity, the 30-30 125-grain rounds chronographed an average 2551 fps MV from a standard Model 336 Marlin *rifle* barrel.

Now Federal ballisticians have directed their talents toward that old but revered revolver cartridge, the 44 Special. Following the same principles, a 200-grain lead hollow-point semi-waddcutter bullet has been substituted for the traditional 246-grain round-nose lead bullet, enabling muzzle velocities to be increased to a claimed 900 fps from 6½″ barrel revolvers according to the 1981 Federal catalog. The old 246-grain factory standard specifications called for a MV of only 755 fps from 6½″ barrels.

The new ammo arrived just in time for a series of trials over chronograph screens. From our Colt Single Action with 5½″ barrel, velocities averaged 830 fps taken at 10-ft. from the muzzle. In a Ruger "Redhawk" with 7½″ barrel, velocity climbed to an even 900 fps. That's not too different from advertised velocities considering that we used a revolver whereas Federal probably fired them from a closed test barrel; also, that our velocity readings were taken at 10-ft. rather than muzzle.

But increased velocity accounts for only part of the heightened effectiveness of the new round. The square shoulder and hollow nose cavity contribute considerably to an increase in stopping power—something the 44 Special has long needed. It is, in fact, the only *factory* load in this

New Federal cartridge for 44 Smith & Wesson Special revolver has 200-grain semi-wadcutter hollow point bullet.

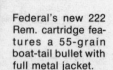

Federal's new 222 Rem. cartridge features a 55-grain boat-tail bullet with full metal jacket.

caliber from any maker with an expanding bullet, and almost certainly the best of all loads in this caliber.

As always, accuracy is an important consideration, and the new 44 Special rounds are plenty good in that department also, grouping nicely even from a fixed sight gun. I'm happy when an out-of-the-box service revolver will group five consecutive shots in 1½" at 20 yards and 5" at 50 yards, and especially on a windy day.

Federal's other addition to the centerfire metallic line in 1981 is a special purpose loading for the 222 Remington, consisting of a 55-grain boat-tail bullet with full metal jacket intended to *prevent* bullet expansion. The primary purpose of these rounds is to provide hunters of fur bearing animals with a flat shooting load that will reach out and yet not damage pelts unduly. Long range shooting must have been contemplated judging from the stress Federal has placed on the boat-tail feature of these bullets. Velocities are listed as 3020 fps at muzzle, 2480 fps at 200 yards, and 1780 fps way out at 500 yards.

Remington-Peters

After last year's blitz, when Remington introduced two new cartridges, a new cartridge case and three new loadings for existing cartridges, they could hardly be expected to make additions to this year's metallic line-up. It appears, rather, there's to be some pruning of old wood.

According to the most recent Remington cartridge chart, four cartridges have been designated "Subject to stock on hand," meaning an end to production. When they're gone, there won't be anymore. Two are old numbers sure to be sorely missed by traditionalists—the 25-35 Winchester and 38-40 Winchester. The other two marked are the 100-grain PSP Corelokt in 264 Winchester Magnum caliber and, surprisingly, the 90-grain PSP Corelokt loading for the 6mm Remington.

Last year, we reported Remington's introduction of a third member of their unique Accelerator family of cartridges, this time in 308 Winchester caliber, and a new higher velocity lighter recoiling load for 44 Magnums with 180-gr. semi-jacketed hollow-point bullet. Now we are able to comment on them.

It seems I have a new varmint rifle; one I didn't plan on. But before I tell about it, readers of this column in past issues may recall that our results with 30-06 and 30-30 Accelerator cartridges were decidedly spotty. If judged by deer rifle standards, their accuracy was probably adequate, but these *aren't* big game cartridges. For varmints—which is what they're intended for—the necessary accuracy just

wasn't there in most of the rifles we tried them in.

Consequently, when it came to test firing the 308 member of the family, my expectations weren't very high. But what a surprise we received. These Accelerators really shoot! The very first five-shot group out of our 308 Winchester Model 70 Target rifle went into 1½", which was surprising, but to the writer's utter amazement groups got better as we went along, and a best group measuring just ⅝" shot in gusty wind bordered on the unbelievable. With that sort of consistent accuracy, my 308 has qualified as a first class varmint rifle.

As for velocity those 55-grain pointed soft points in their sabots are traveling an average 3678 fps as they leave the 24" barrel of this rifle. Right then is when I got into trouble! Let me warn all you chronographers what can happen when these Accelerators are fired over Skyscreens. Twice, to my consternation, the plastic sabots hit and penetrated the Stop screen box leaving star-shaped holes I had to stop and patch. It's a tribute to the ruggedness of Dr. Oehler's Skyscreens that despite this punishment they never once ceased to register. Only those handsome groups stifled my cussing.

R-P's 180-grain high velocity loading of the 44 Magnum was also put through its paces, using Ruger's new "Redhawk" double-action revolver. Rated as having a muzzle velocity of 1610 fps, the Oehler Chronotach gave out readings of 1613, 1625, 1629, 1656 and 1689 for an average of 1652 fps from the 7½" barrel. This is some 235 fps faster than the standard 240-gr. R-P load from the same gun, and recoil is noticeably less. My guess is that 44 Magnum shooters are going to like this new Remington round.

Super Vel

That old familiar name, Super Vel, is with us again, I'm pleased to report, but from a new location. The H&H Cartridge Corporation, makers of that effective line of revolver and pistol ammunition, has relocated to Hamilton Road, Route 2, Fond du Lac, WI 54935.

Their 1981 brochure lists eighteen handgun cartridges in calibers from 380 ACP to 45 ACP, and some of the quoted velocities are indeed heady numbers. For example, take their 90-gr. JHP loading for the 9mm Luger rated at 1370 fps from a Browning High Power, and a 357 Magnum round with 110-gr. JSP at 1470 fps, or 150-gr. JHP at 1300 from a 6" barrel Colt Python.

Especially impressive is a 180-gr. JHP loading in 44 Magnum said to develop 1760 fps from a 7½" Ruger Super Blackhawk.

Left—Norma's 38 Special Magnum cartridges have been redesignated as +P loads. Right—Two 38 caliber cartridges from PMC, at left a 158-grain semi-wadcutter and at right a 148-grain wadcutter, they compliment a previously introduced 158-grain round nose.

We're practically certain to hear more from this outfit in coming months.

Norma

Probably the Norma news of interest to the largest number of U.S. shooters concerns the on-going discussions and testing of their 38 Special Norma Magnum cartridge introduced in 1980, which has resulted in its re-designation as a +P round in the United States.

Norma rated this ammunition, identified as Stock No. 19119, "Magnum" based on its superior ballistic performance, said to develop 20% higher muzzle velocity with 45% more kinetic energy than standard 38 Special rounds. Loaded with 110-grain jacketed hollow-point bullets, an MV of 1225 fps and energy of 367 ft. lbs. from a 4″ test barrel was claimed. In 6″ test barrels, the comparable figures were 1542 fps and 580 f.p.

Despite these impressive ballistics however, Norma originally didn't identify these cartridges as being "+P;" in fact, early boxes bore a label stating they were "not +P." That decision appears to have been based upon repeated tests in European laboratories, including one or more not connected with the Norma firm, all of which reaffirmed the contention that pressures were at standard rather than +P levels.

Controversy and doubts continued to persist in this country, stemming from American lab results reported as showing average pressures between 18,500 and slightly over 19,500 CUP (Copper Units of Pressure). If so, this would indeed call for a +P rating under U.S. commercial standards which classify as +P 38 Special loads developing between 17,000 and 20,000 CUP, as compared to a limit of 17,000 CUP for standard 38 Special ammunition.

Naturally, the question arrives as to why pressure readings taken from the same ammunition in American and European labs should differ? Several possible answers come to mind, including a European predilection towards free-boring barrels to reduce pressures, but I'm reminded also of something once told me by a noted Scandinavian ballistician. He explained that whereas American pressure barrels are loaded with cartridges having standard brass cases through which a hole may be blown opposite the pressure reading copper (or lead) piston upon firing, European practice calls for the use of pre-drilled cases; that is, with a hole provided in case walls at the piston location.

Apparently this system eliminates any variables due to brass strength, thereby giving a truer picture of actual pressures from the Continental point of view. Whether or not one subscribes to this theory, it is obvious that somewhat different pressure readings can be expected, depending upon which method is used. Any appreciable difference in the throating of test barrels could likewise produce significant variations in pressure readings.

Finally, it should be noted also that where the difference between a +P and standard 38 Special loads may be as little as 1500 to 2000 CUP, a rather fine line is being drawn. Cartridges from the same lot, or even the same box, might conceivably vary by that much in their individual pressure readings.

Norma's solution has been to re-designate these high velocity 38 Special cartridges as +P in observation of U.S. industry standards, simultaneously affirming that although 38 Special Norma Magnum cartridges will henceforth bear a +P headstamp, their ballistics will remain unchanged. This seems an admirable arrangement in that owners of guns approved for use with +P loads will continue to be able to obtain these high performance cartridges, while those with older, light or alloy frame guns are fore-warned against their use.

For 1981, Norma's new offering is in the category of metric rifle calibers, for which they are world famous. Designated the 7.62x39 Short Russian, this is the sporting or commercial version of the Russian military assault cartridge known as the M-43 from its adoption in 1943 as an answer to the German 7.92mm Kurz cartridge.

In recent years, semi-automatic rifles of Finnish manufacture, appearing much like their Russian military counterparts but lacking a full-automatic capability have been sold on the American market. It was necessary either to use imported military Ball ammo with Berdan primers, or to form cases for reloading from 6.5 Mannlicher or 7.35mm Carcano brass in such arms.

That won't be necessary now that Norma has made available a commercial loading in Boxer-primed cases with 125-grain soft point bullet having a rated muzzle velocity of 2385 fps and muzzle energy of 1580 ft. pounds. With ballistics approaching those of a 30-30, this is an effective round for its size. After observing a Valmet semi-auto of this caliber in action on a police range, I'm impressed by its capabilities. From this point on, reloading of the little cartridge will be a whole lot easier.

PMC

A couple of years ago an outfit calling themselves the Poongsan Metal Corporation of South Korea began exporting newly manufactured military ball ammunition to the

U.S. in 30 M-1 Carbine and 5.56mm M-193 (223 Remington) calibers. We tested some rounds in both calibers from an early shipment, finding it somewhat less accurate than American ammo but developing higher velocities and selling for about one-third less. I suspect the exceedingly high velocities of the 5.56mm cartridges may have been at least partly responsible for their lesser accuracy.

Now under the trademark PMC—which also stands for Patton and Morgan Corporation, New York importers of this ammunition—other calibers have been added to the line, including a 147-grain loading for the 308 Winchester with FMC-BT (full metal clad boat-tail) bullet designated M-80, and 150-grain FMC (M-2) issue in 30-06 Springfield caliber.

Additionally, PMC now offers a sporting line with soft point bullets in calibers 223, 308 and 30-06, plus centerfire handgun ammunition in calibers 9mm Luger and 38 Special. Seven American distributors in as many states across the country are equipped to supply local dealers with this ammo, all of which is put up in new brass cases with non-mercuric non-corrosive Boxer (anvil) primers and progressive burning powders.

Smith & Wesson

Last year we told readers about Smith & Wesson's Nyclad ammunition in 38 Special and 357 Magnum calibers. Since then they've added a Nyclad load for the 9mm with 125-gr. SWCHP bullet registering 1102 fps with 339 f.p. muzzle energy from a 4″ barrel S&W Model 39.

The one I particularly want to tell you about though is their new load which they call the "Chief's Special." Specifically designed for use in 2″ barrel snubbies with alloy frames that aren't up to handling +P ammunition, these cartridges are loaded with 125-grain semi-wadcutter hollow-point Nyclad bullets to a muzzle velocity of 825 fps, which is roughly 90% as fast as a +P load with same bullet also from 2″ barrels.

What's more, S&W claims it does this with the low pressure and mild recoil of a conventional wadcutter target load. Add to that bullet expansion to 60-caliber or greater on impact and we have what appears to be an ideal cartridge for plainclothesmen and others dependent upon the little short barrel guns.

The regular line of S&W factory ammo for 380, 9mm, 38 Special, 357 Magnum, 44 Magnum and 45 Auto are, I expect, too well known to require further comment here except to note a point of which readers may or may not be aware, namely that Smith & Wesson make their own bullets to meet rigid requirements and insure desired bullet penetration and expansion performance. I've been seeing increasing numbers of S&W blue boxes on firing ranges the past year or so.

Dynamit Nobel

Good news for owners and handloaders of rifles in the Continental calibers: The big Dynamit Nobel combine of RWS, Rottweil and Geco are actively seeking American business, as a result of which they have established their own jobber's outlet in this country. Now retailers can order directly from Dynamit Nobel of America, Inc., at 105 Stonehurst Court, Northvale, NJ 07647.

First there are RWS centerfire rifle cartridges in thirty-two different calibers from 22 Hornet to the 10.75x73, including such interesting numbers as the 5.6x50 Magnum, 6.5x68, 7x65R, 8x60S, 8x68, 8.15x46R, 9.3x64, 9.3x72R and 9.3x74R. Many are loaded with the world famous Brenneke TIG and TUG bullets, including (believe it or not), a 30-06 loading with 181-gr. Brenneke TUG bullets.

Expensive yes, but really top quality ammunition.

Then there's the Geco line of pistol and revolver cartridges—a total of seventeen different rounds, most interesting of which are a 32 S&W Long target cartridge with 100-grain wadcutter bullet, and a round listed as the 9mm Police or 9mm Ultra with 94-gr. FMJ bullet. The 30 Luger is there also with a 93-gr. FMJ bullet.

Next comes the Rottweil line of Brenneke rifled slugs, and RWS rimfire cartridges which we'll leave for others to tell about. As a confirmed handloader, I found myself engrossed in the listings of RWS bullets for centerfire rifles, unprimed RWS cases, and RWS primers. Of the latter there are six types of anvil (Boxer) primers, and a selection of *nine* Berdan primers. This especially should arouse the interest of a sizeable passel of American handloaders.

For big bore rifle shooters/handloaders, 9.3mm and 10.75mm bullets are sure to attract attention, but there are also excellent selections of 7mm and 8mm bullets. Somewhat disappointing are the 6.5mm bullets, diameters of which are given as .264″. I know I'm not alone in wishing someone would produce a good 160-grain jacketed soft point bullet with a diameter of .267″ for a properly tight fit in 6.5 Mannlicher barrels, most of those I've measured as having .267″ groove diameter. Then the little carbines should show the accuracy of which I've long believed them to be capable.

The RWS unprimed cases in several calibers should also prove popular, especially the 9.3x72R, 9.3x74R and 7x57R. In those calibers with which I've worked, RWS brass has been shown to be of excellent quality with expert annealing.

B.E.L.L.

Speaking of cases for some of the less commonly encountered calibers, here's another outstanding product: cases for English and obsolete rifles from Jim Bell's Brass Extrusion Laboratories. Since we last wrote of BELL cases, Jim has added a pair of additional ones, badly needed like their predecessors.

Now there are gleaming brass hulls for the 425 Westley Richards and that most often seen big British caliber, the 450-3¼″ Express. The latter is being made with two different rim thicknesses—the thin or Standard .040″ rim as used in Purdey double rifles, and a .065″-thick Jeffery rim. While it's possibly coincidence, most all the rifles I've tried them in other than Jefferys, require the thin .040″ rim.

These cases can also be re-formed to fit a pretty fair number of other chambers, including the 450/400, 369 Purdey, 360 No. 2, 333 Rimmed Jeffery, 40-110 Winchester, and several of the old European military rifles such as the 11mm Gras.

Perhaps best of all, they're all pocketed for standard American Large Rifle primers, and have been giving us excellent service in a 450 Purdey double rifle. I'm looking forward to when Jim Bell brings out his indispensable cases for the 405 Winchester and 280 Ross. They will be as warmly received as was his 11mm Mauser brass.

Sierra

Again, as last year, Sierra added five new bullets to their lineup for 1981. In the Game King series of hunting bullets for the longer ranges there is a new .224″ 55-grain FMJ boat-tail with ballistic coefficient of .285.

Competition shooters/handloaders will welcome the addition of a 150-grain 7mm (.284″) hollow-point boat-tail and a similarly contoured 30-caliber HPBT likewise of 150-grain. These should prove especially useful for 200-yard and 300-meter four-position contestants.

And finally for handgun competition shooters, a 220-

grain flat-nose FMJ for 41 Magnums similar to the 44 flat-nose of same weight introduced in 1980, plus a 125-grain round-nose FMJ of .357″ diameter. The new 41 Magnum bullet should find much use on the silhouette ranges.

Other Sierra developments worthy of note are:

(1) Their employment of a system of quality control that requires precision drawing of bullet jackets to tough tolerances: .0006″ for hunting bullets and .0003″ for match bullets, plus weight parameters of ± .3-grain. Much of Sierra's fine reputation for accuracy stems from this exactitude.

(2) Sierra has a new Second Edition of their Reloader's Manual off the press. It's more than just a compendium of load data, having a large Exterior Ballistics section including wind deflection plus explanations on such topics as angular shooting and the effects of altitude. Every serious handloader should have a copy of this book.

(3) Sierra has established a ballistics service to assist shooters with special computations. For a basic price of ten dollars they will also provide complete ballistic data for three different sets of shooting conditions. Sounds like a real service.

CCI-Speer

Comparing 1981 listings with those of 1980, the Speer bullet line doesn't appear to have changed much. Rifle bullet No. 1039, their 22-caliber 52-grain Gold Match hollow-point has disappeared from the catalog, and a new 22-caliber 55-grain spitzer soft point with a cannelure—bullet No. 1049—has been added, I suspect to allow crimping for use in autoloading rifles.

What continues to impress this writer however, is Speer's unique "Lawman" series of centerfire handgun cartridges. Because there are now 23 different cartridges in six calibers comprising this line of factory loaded ammo, its entirely logical that I haven't tested all of them. But those I have tried have proven excellent indeed.

Take Lawman cartridge No. 3965, for instance. It's a 200-grain jacketed hollow-point load for 45 Automatics. In our Colt Gold Cup auto it will group five shots in ¾″ at 50 feet and 4½″ at 50 yards while exiting the muzzle at 908 fps, a fine combination of accuracy, velocity and power. Other favorites are the 357 Magnum and 38 Special with jacketed 140-grain hollow-points.

Emphasis is placed on controlling bullet base upset with this ammo as a means of improving accuracy with what I would judge to be considerable success.

And with police use in mind, Speer ballisticians have selected powders for this series of cartridges which reduce muzzle flash to a minimum. It's easy to see why they're so proud of the Lawman line.

Hornady

Before commenting on the year's doings at Hornady, this writer wishes to express deepest regrets at the passing of Joyce Hornady, talented founder of Hornady Manufacturing Company. Beyond his professional competence, he was a gentleman and our friend. He will be missed.

In May, 1980, Hornady announced that their Frontier Ammunition division had been chosen as the supplier of ammunition for the 1980 International Practical Shooting Confederation U.S. Championships. This honor conferred by the IPSC Match Committee involved the use of Frontier 45 ACP and 9mm cartridges, and optionally 357 Magnum ammo, all of which was loaded with full metal jacket flat-point bullets.

In line with current thinking, Hornady has introduced a 55-grain 22-caliber full metal jacket boat-tail bullet for military shooters as well as hunters of fur bearing animals,

Left—Hornady's newly-introduced 25 caliber, 50-grain full metal jacket round nose bullet. Below —Their new 22 caliber 55-grain full metal jacket boat-tail.

observing that its boat-tail base added to the typical Hornady secant ogive shape increases the ballistic coefficient.

Also in step with what appears to be somewhat of a trend, they've added a new 50-grain FMJ bullet for 25 Automatic pistols. With recent imports of the little pistols and increasing ammunition costs, shooters of this tiny round must be taking up handloading. Join the fraternity.

Certain to meet with wide acceptance are a pair of new boat-tail bullets for 6mm rifles—an 87-grain hollow-point and a 100-grain soft point, increasing the ranging powers of the already flat-shooting Sixes.

A bullet I particularly look forward to taking afield is Hornady's 140-grain BTSP in 270-caliber. This one may be the means of settling all those old disputes about whether a 130- or 150-grain is better. Could be the new 140-grain will out-do both of 'em?

Continuing their expanding list of boat-tail spire point bullets with improved medium-to-long range performance in mind, two of Hornady's most recent developments have been a 7mm 162-gr. BTSP and a 190-gr. BTSP, both beautifully streamlined bullets that will help defy the law of gravity while their special Interlock construction takes care of things on impact. Should be great hunting bullets for the wide-open spaces.

Last but surely not least from the competitive target rifleman's outlook is a new 190-grain hollow-point boat-tail Match bullet in 30-caliber for use clear out to a thousand yards. With a match bullet, consistent accuracy is the whole show, and no effort has been spared to incorporate proven accuracy features. These include a longer bearing surface for better alignment with the bore, a shorter point section to reduce free-bore effect and place the bullet closer to the rifling origin, combined in a shorter over-all length for better stability in flight.

It does seem that handloading components as well as factory loaded metallic cartridges get better every year, both in performance and selection. Let's hope it continues.

●

CENTERFIRE RIFLE CARTRIDGES—BALLISTICS AND PRICES

(R)= REMINGTON; (W) = WINCHESTER-WESTERN); (F) = FEDERAL; (H) = HORNADY-FRONTIER; (PMC) = Patton & Morgan Corp.

Cartridge	— BULLET — Wt. Grs.	Type	Bbl. (in.)	— VELOCITY (fps) — Muzzle	100 yds.	200 yds.	300 yds.	— ENERGY (ft. lbs.) — Muzzle	100 yds.	200 yds.	300 yds.	— BULLET PATH† — 100 yds.	200 yds.	300 yds.	Price Per Box
17 Remington (R)	25	HPPL	24	4040	3284	2644	2086	906	599	388	242	+0.5	-1.5	-8.5	$10.80
22 Hornet (R) (W)	45	PSP	24	2690	2042	1502	1128	723	417	225	127	0.0	-7.7	-31.3	*19.90
22 Hornet (R)	45	HP	24	2690	2042	1502	1128	723	417	225	127	0.0	-7.7	-31.3	*19.90
22 Hornet (W)	46	OPE (HP)	24	2690	2042	1502	1128	739	426	230	130	0.0	-7.7	-31.3	*19.90
218 Bee (W)	46	OPE (HP)	24	2760	2102	1550	1155	778	451	245	136	0.0	-7.2	-29.4	*29.40
222 Remington (R) (W) (F) (H)	50	PSP, SX	24	3140	2602	2123	1700	1094	752	500	321	+2.2	0.0	-10.0	8.50
222 Remington (R)	50	HPPL	24	3140	2635	2182	1777	1094	771	529	351	+2.1	0.0	-9.5	9.25
222 Remington (R)	55	MC	24	3000	2544	2130	1759	1099	790	554	378	+2.3	0.0	-10.0	8.50
222 Remington (W)	55	FMC	24	3020	2675	2355	2057	1114	874	677	517	+2.0	0.0	-8.3	8.50
222 Remington (F)	55	MC BT	24	3020	2740	2480	2230	1115	915	750	610	+1.9	0.0	-7.7	8.50
222 Remington Magnum (R)	55	PSP	24	3240	2748	2305	1906	1282	922	649	444	+1.9	0.0	-8.5	9.65
222 Remington Magnum (R)	55	HPPL	24	3240	2773	2352	1969	1282	939	675	473	+1.8	0.0	-8.5	10.30
223 Remington (R) (W) (F) (H)	55	PSP	24	3240	2747	2304	1905	1282	921	648	443	+1.9	0.0	-8.5	9.30
223 Remington (R)	55	HPPL	24	3240	2773	2352	1969	1282	939	675	473	+1.8	0.0	-8.2	10.00
223 Remington (R) (H)	55	MC	24	3240	2759	2326	1933	1282	929	660	456	+1.9	0.0	-8.4	9.30
223 Remington (W) (F) (PMC)	55	FMC, MC BT	24	3240	2877	2543	2232	1282	1011	790	608	+1.7	0.0	-7.1	9.30
225 Winchester (W)	55	PSP	24	3570	3066	2616	2208	1556	1148	836	595	+1.2	0.0	-6.2	10.15
22-250 Remington (R) (W) (F) (H)	55	PSP	24	3730	3180	2695	2257	1699	1235	887	622	+1.0	0.0	-5.7	9.30
22-250 Remington (R)	55	HPCL	24	3730	3253	2826	2436	1699	1292	975	725	+0.9	0.0	-5.2	10.00
22-250 Remington (F) — Premium	55	BTHP	24	3730	3330	2960	2630	1700	1350	1070	840	+0.8	0.0	-4.8	10.10
220 Swift (H)	55	SP	24	3630	3176	2755	2370	1609	1229	927	686	+1.0	0.0	-5.6	12.95
220 Swift (H)	60	HP	24	3530	3134	2763	2420	1657	1305	1016	780	+1.1	0.0	-5.7	12.95
243 (W) (R) (F) (H)	80	PSP, HPPL, FMJ	24	3350	2955	2593	2259	1993	1551	1194	906	+1.6	0.0	-7.0	11.60
243 Winchester (F) — Premium	85	BTHP	24	3320	3070	2830	2600	2080	1770	1510	1280	+1.5	0.0	-6.8	12.45
243 Winchester (W) (R) (F) (H)	100	PPSP, PSPCL, SP	24	2960	2697	2449	2215	1945	1615	1332	1089	+1.9	0.0	-7.8	11.60
243 Winchester (F) — Premium	100	BTSP	24	2960	2760	2570	2380	1950	1690	1460	1260	+1.4	0.0	-5.8	12.45
6mm Remington (R) (W) (Also, .244)	80	PSP, HPPL	24	3470	3064	2694	2352	2139	1667	1289	982	+1.2	0.0	-6.0	11.60
6mm Remington (R) (Also, .244)	90	PSPCL	24	3190	2863	2558	2273	2033	1638	1307	1032	+1.7	0.0	-7.0	11.60
6mm Remington (R) (W) (F)	100	PSPCL, PPSP	24	3130	2857	2600	2357	2175	1812	1501	1233	+1.7	0.0	-6.8	11.60
25-20 Winchester (W) (R)	86	SP, LEAD	24	1460	1194	1030	931	407	272	203	165	0.0	-23.5	-79.6	*18.85
256 Winchester (W)	60	OPE (HP)	24	2760	2097	1542	1149	1015	586	317	176	0.0	-7.3	-29.6	*23.75
25-35 Winchester (W)	117	SP	24	2230	1866	1545	1282	1292	904	620	427	0.0	-9.2	-33.1	12.90
250 Savage (W)	87	PSP	24	3030	2673	2342	2036	1773	1380	1059	801	+2.0	0.0	-8.4	11.80
250 Savage (W)	100	ST	24	2820	2467	2140	1839	1765	1351	1017	751	+2.4	0.0	-10.1	12.45
250 Savage (R)	100	PSP	24	2820	2504	2210	1936	1765	1392	1084	832	+2.3	0.0	-9.5	11.80
257 Roberts (W)	87	PSP	24	3170	2802	2462	2147	1941	1516	1171	890	+1.8	0.0	-7.5	10.50
257 Roberts (W)	100	ST	24	2900	2541	2210	1904	1867	1433	1084	805	+2.3	0.0	-9.4	13.70
257 Roberts (W) (R)	117	PPSP, SPCL	24	2650	2291	1961	1663	1824	1363	999	718	+2.9	0.0	-12.0	13.00
25-06 Remington (R)	87	HPPL	24	3440	2995	2591	2222	2286	1733	1297	954	+1.2	0.0	-6.3	12.60
25-06 Remington (W) (F)	90	PEP, HP	24	3440	3043	2680	2344	2364	1850	1435	1098	+1.2	0.0	-6.1	12.60
25-06 Remington (R)	100	PSPCL	24	3230	2893	2580	2287	2316	1858	1478	1161	+1.6	0.0	-6.9	12.60
25-06 Remington (F)	117	SP	24	3060	2790	2530	2280	2430	2020	1660	1360	+1.8	0.0	-7.3	12.60
25-06 Remington (R) (W)	120	PSPCL, PEP	24	3010	2749	2502	2269	2414	2013	1668	1372	+1.9	0.0	-7.4	12.60
6.5mm Remington Magnum (R)	120	PSPCL	24	3210	2905	2621	2353	2745	2248	1830	1475	+1.3	0.0	-6.6	18.85
264 Winchester Magnum (W) (R)	100	PSP, PSPCL	24	3320	2926	2565	2231	2447	1901	1461	1105	+1.3	0.0	-6.7	16.25
264 Winchester Magnum (W) (R)	140	PPSP, PSPCL	24	3030	2782	2548	2326	2854	2406	2018	1682	+1.8	0.0	-7.2	16.25
270 Winchester (W) (R)	100	PSP	24	3480	3067	2690	2343	2689	2088	1606	1219	+1.2	0.0	-6.2	12.60
270 Winchester (W) (R) (F)	130	PPSP, BP, SP	24	3110	2849	2604	2371	2791	2343	1957	1622	+1.7	0.0	-6.8	13.30
270 Winchester (W) (R) (H)	130	ST, PSPCL	24	3110	2823	2554	2300	2791	2300	1883	1527	+1.7	0.0	-7.1	12.60
270 Winchester (F) — Premium	130	BTSP	24	3110	2880	2670	2460	2790	2400	2050	1740	+1.6	0.0	-6.5	13.55
270 Winchester (W) (H)	150	PPSP	24	2900	2632	2380	2142	2801	2307	1886	1528	+2.1	0.0	-8.2	12.60
270 Winchester (F) — Premium	150	BTSP	24	2900	2710	2520	2350	2800	2440	2120	1830	+1.6	0.0	-7.0	13.55
270 Winchester (R) (F)	150	SPCL, SP	24	2900	2550	2225	1926	2801	2165	1649	1235	+2.2	0.0	-9.3	12.60
270 Winchester (F) — Premium	150	NP	24	2900	2630	2380	2140	2800	2310	1890	1530	+2.1	0.0	-8.2	16.60
7mm Mauser (R) (W)	175	SP	24	2440	2137	1857	1603	2313	1774	1340	998	0.0	-6.8	-23.7	12.85
7mm Mauser (F)	175	SP	24	2470	2170	1880	1630	2370	1820	1380	1030	0.0	-6.6	-23.0	12.85
7mm-08 Remington (R)	140	PSPCL	24	2860	2625	2402	2189	2542	2142	1793	1490	+2.1	0.0	-8.1	12.60
7mm Express Remington (R)	150	SPCL	24	2970	2699	2444	2203	2937	2426	1989	1616	+1.9	0.0	-7.8	12.60
280 Remington (R)	165	SPCL	24	2820	2510	2220	1950	2913	2308	1805	1393	+2.3	0.0	-9.4	12.60
284 Winchester (W)	125	PPSP	24	3140	2829	2538	2265	2736	2221	1788	1424	+1.7	0.0	-7.2	13.15
284 Winchester (W)	150	PPSP	24	2860	2595	2344	2108	2724	2243	1830	1480	+2.1	0.0	-8.5	14.60
7mm Remington Magnum (W)	125	PPSP	24	3310	2976	2666	2376	3040	2458	1972	1567	+1.2	0.0	-6.5	15.65
7mm Remington Magnum (R) (W) (F)	150	PSPCL, PPSP, SP	24	3110	2830	2568	2320	3221	2667	2196	1792	+1.7	0.0	-7.0	15.60
7mm Remington Magnum (F)	150	BTSP-Prem.	24	3110	2920	2750	2580	3220	2850	2510	2210	+1.6	0.0	-6.2	16.60
7mm Remington Magnum (F)	165	BTSP-Prem.	24	2860	2710	2560	2420	3000	2690	2410	2150	+1.6	0.0	-6.9	16.60
7mm Remington Magnum (R) (W) (F) (H)	175	PSPCL, PPSP	24	2860	2645	2440	2244	3178	2718	2313	1956	+2.0	0.0	-7.9	15.60
7mm Remington Magnum (F)	160	NP	24	2950	2730	2520	2320	3090	2650	2250	1910	+1.8	0.0	-7.7	19.55
30 Carbine (R) (W) (F) (H)	110	SP, HSP, SP, RN	20	1990	1567	1236	1035	967	600	373	262	0.0	-13.5	-49.9	*20.25
30 Carbine (W) (F) (H) (PMC)	110	FMC, MC, FMJ, FMC	20	1990	1596	1278	1070	967	622	399	280	0.0	-13.0	-47.4	8.10
30 Remington (R) (W)	170	SPCL, ST	24	2120	1822	1555	1328	1696	1253	913	666	0.0	-9.7	-33.8	12.75
30-30 Accelerator (R)	55	SP	24	3400	2693	2085	1570	1412	886	521	301	+2.0	0.0	-10.2	11.00
30-30 Winchester (F)	125	HP	24	2570	2090	1660	1320	1830	1210	770	480	0.0	-7.3	-28.1	9.90
30-30 Winchester (W) (F)	150	OPE, PPSP, ST, SP	24	2390	2018	1684	1398	1902	1356	944	651	0.0	-7.7	-27.9	9.90
30-30 Winchester (R) (H)	150	SPCL	24	2390	1973	1605	1303	1902	1296	858	565	0.0	-8.2	-30.0	9.90
30-30 Winchester (W) (R) (F)	170	PPSP, ST, SPCL, SP, HPCL	24	2200	1895	1619	1381	1827	1355	989	720	0.0	-8.9	-31.1	9.90
300 Savage (R)	150	SPCL	24	2630	2247	1897	1585	2303	1681	1198	837	0.0	-6.1	-21.9	12.70
300 Savage (W)	150	PPSP	24	2630	2311	2015	1743	2303	1779	1352	1012	+2.8	0.0	-11.5	12.75
300 Savage (W) (F) (R)	150	ST, SP, PSPCL	24	2630	2354	2095	1853	2303	1845	1462	1143	+2.7	0.0	-10.7	12.70
300 Savage (R) (W)	180	SPCL, PPSP	24	2350	2025	1728	1467	2207	1639	1193	860	0.0	-7.7	-27.1	12.70
300 Savage (R) (W)	180	PSPCL, ST	24	2350	2137	1935	1745	2207	1825	1496	1217	0.0	-6.7	-22.8	12.70
30-40 Krag (R) (W)	180	SPCL, PPSP	24	2430	2098	1795	1525	2360	1761	1288	929	0.0	-7.1	-25.0	13.25
30-40 Krag (R) (W)	180	PSPCL, ST	24	2430	2213	2007	1813	2360	1957	1610	1314	0.0	-6.2	-21.1	13.25
303 Savage (W)	190	ST	24	1940	1657	1410	1211	1588	1158	839	619	0.0	-11.9	-41.4	15.00
308 Accelerator (R)	55	PSP	24	3770	3215	2726	2286	1735	1262	907	638	+1.0	0.0	-5.6	14.00
308 Winchester (W)	110	PSP	24	3180	2666	2206	1795	2470	1736	1188	787	+2.0	0.0	-9.3	12.60
308 Winchester (W)	125	PSP	24	3050	2697	2370	2067	2582	2019	1559	1186	+2.0	0.0	-8.2	12.60
308 Winchester (W)	150	PPSP	24	2820	2488	2179	1893	2648	2061	1581	1193	+2.4	0.0	-9.8	12.60
308 Winchester (W) (R) (F) (H) (PMC)	150	ST, PSPCL, SP	24	2820	2533	2263	2009	2648	2137	1705	1344	+2.3	0.0	-9.1	12.60
308 Winchester (PMC)	147	FMC-BT	24	2750	2473	2257	2052	2428	2037	1697	1403	+2.3	0.0	-9.1	8.00
308 Winchester (F) (H)	165	BTSP, SPBT	24	2700	2520	2330	2160	2670	2310	1990	1700	+2.0	0.0	-8.4	12.60
308 Winchester (W) (R)	180	PPSP, SPCL	24	2620	2274	1955	1666	2743	2086	1527	1109	+2.9	0.0	-12.1	12.60
308 Winchester (W) (R) (F) (PMC)	180	ST, PSPCL, SP	24	2620	2393	2178	1974	2743	2288	1896	1557	+2.6	0.0	-9.9	12.60
308 Winchester (W)	200	ST	24	2450	2208	1980	1767	2665	2165	1741	1386	0.0	-6.3	-21.4	13.30
30-06 Springfield (W)	110	PSP	24	3380	2843	2365	1936	2790	1974	1366	915	+1.7	0.0	-8.0	12.60
30-06 Springfield (W) (R) (F)	125	PSP, PSP, SP	24	3140	2780	2447	2138	2736	2145	1662	1269	+1.8	0.0	-7.7	12.60
30-16 Springfield (W)	150	PPSP	24	2920	2580	2265	1972	2839	2217	1708	1295	+2.2	0.0	-9.0	12.00
30-06 Springfield (W) (R) (F) (H) (PMC)	150	ST, PSPCL, SP, SP	24	2910	2617	2342	2083	2820	2281	1827	1445	+2.1	0.0	-8.5	12.60
30-06 Springfield (R)	150	BP	24	2910	2656	2416	2189	2820	2349	1944	1596	+2.0	0.0	-8.0	13.30
30-06 Springfield (PMC)	150	FMC (M-2)	24	2810	2555	2310	2080	2630	2170	1780	1440	+2.2	0.0	-8.8	8.00
30-06 Accelerator	55	PSP	24	4080	3485	2965	2502	2033	1483	1074	764	+1.0	0.0	-5.0	14.00
30-06 Springfield (R)	165	PSPCL	24	2800	2534	2283	2047	2872	2352	1909	1534	+2.3	0.0	-9.0	12.60
30-06 Springfield (F) (H)	165	BTSP	24	2800	2610	2420	2240	2870	2490	2150	1840	+2.1	0.0	-8.0	13.15

CENTERFIRE RIFLE CARTRIDGES—BALLISTICS AND PRICES (continued)

Cartridge	Bullet Wt. Grs.	Bullet Type	Bbl. (in.)	Velocity (fps) Muzzle	Velocity 100 yds.	Velocity 200 yds.	Velocity 300 yds.	Energy (ft. lbs.) Muzzle	Energy 100 yds.	Energy 200 yds.	Energy 300 yds.	Bullet Path† 100 yds.	Bullet Path 200 yds.	Bullet Path 300 yds.	Price Per Box
30-06 Springfield (R) (W)	180	SPCL, PPSP	24	2700	2348	2023	1727	2913	2203	1635	1192	+2.7	0.0	– 11.3	**12.60**
30-06 Springfield (R) (W) (F) (H) (PMC)	180	PSPCL, ST, NOSLER	24	2700	2469	2250	2042	2913	2436	2023	1666	+2.4	0.0	– 9.3	**12.60**
30-06 Springfield (R)	180	BP	24	2700	2485	2280	2084	2913	2468	2077	1736	+2.4	0.0	– 9.1	**13.30**
30-06 Springfield (F)	200	BTSP	24	2550	2400	2260	2120	2890	2560	2270	2000	+2.3	0.0	– 9.0	**13.15**
30-06 Springfield (W) (R)	220	PPSP, SPCL	24	2410	2130	1870	1632	2837	2216	1708	1301	0.0	– 6.8	– 23.6	**12.60**
30-06 Springfield (W)	220	ST	24	2410	2192	1985	1791	2837	2347	1924	1567	0.0	– 6.4	– 21.6	**13.30**
300 H & H Magnum (W)	150	ST	24	3130	2822	2534	2264	3262	2652	2138	1707	+1.7	0.0	– 7.2	**13.30**
300 H & H Magnum (W) (R)	180	ST, PSPCL	24	2880	2640	2412	2196	3315	2785	2325	1927	+2.1	0.0	– 8.0	**16.90**
300 H & H Magnum (W)	220	ST	24	2580	2341	2114	1901	3251	2677	2183	1765	+2.7	0.0	– 10.5	**16.05**
300 Winchester Magnum (W) (R)	150	PPSP, PSPCL	24	3290	2951	2636	2342	3605	2900	2314	1827	+1.3	0.0	– 6.6	**16.45**
300 Winchester Mgnum (W) (R) (F) (H)	180	PPSP, PSPCL, SP	24	2960	2745	2540	2344	3501	3011	2578	2196	+1.9	0.0	– 7.3	**16.45**
300 Winchester Magnum (F) Premium	200	BTSP	24	2830	2680	2530	2380	3560	3180	2830	2520	+1.7	0.0	– 7.1	**13.55**
303 British (R)	180	SPCL	24	2460	2124	1817	1542	2418	1803	1319	950	0.0	– 6.9	– 24.4	**12.95**
303 British (W)	180	PPSP	24	2460	2233	2018	1816	2418	1993	1627	1318	0.0	– 6.1	– 20.8	**12.95**
32-20 Winchester (W) (R)	100	SP	24	1210	1021	913	834	325	231	185	154	0.0	–32.3	–106.3	***18.95**
32-20 Winchester (W) (R)	100	L	24	1210	1021	913	834	325	231	185	154	0.0	–32.3	–106.3	***15.35**
.32 Winchester Special (W)	170	PPSP, ST	24	2250	1870	1537	1267	1911	1320	892	606	0.0	– 9.2	– 33.2	**11.15**
32 Winchester Special (F) (R)	170	SP	24	2250	1920	1630	1370	1911	1390	1000	710	0.0	– 8.6	– 30.5	**10.55**
8mm Mauser (R) (W)	170	SPCL, PPSP	24	2360	1969	1622	1333	2102	1463	993	671	0.0	– 8.2	– 29.8	**13.00**
8mm Mauser (F)	170	SP	24	2510	2110	1740	1430	2380	1670	1140	770	0.0	– 7.0	– 25.7	**13.00**
8mm Remington Magnum (R)	185	PSPCL	24	3080	2761	2464	2186	3896	3131	2494	1963	+1.8	0.0	– 7.6	**18.45**
8mm Remington Magnum (R)	220	PSPCL	24	2830	2581	2346	2123	3912	3254	2688	2201	+2.2	0.0	– 8.5	**18.45**
338 Winchester Magnum (W)	200	PPSP	24	2960	2658	2375	2110	3890	3137	2505	1977	+2.0	0.0	– 8.2	**19.80**
338 Winchester Magnum (W)	250	ST	24	2660	2395	2145	1910	3927	3184	2554	2025	+2.6	0.0	– 10.2	**18.75**
348 Winchester (W)	200	ST	24	2520	2215	1931	1672	2820	2178	1656	1241	0.0	– 6.2	– 21.9	**24.00**
351 Winchester S.L. (W)	180	SP	**20**	1850	1556	1310	1128	1368	968	686	508	0.0	–13.6	– 47.5	***32.25**
35 Remington (R)	150	PSPCL	24	2300	1874	1506	1218	1762	1169	755	494	0.0	– 9.2	– 33.0	**11.65**
35 Remington (R) (F)	200	SPCL, SP	24	2080	1698	1376	1140	1921	1280	841	577	0.0	–11.3	– 41.2	**11.65**
35 Remington (W)	200	PPSP, ST	24	2020	1646	1335	1114	1812	1203	791	551	0.0	–12.1	– 43.9	**11.65**
358 Winchester (W)	200	ST	24	2490	2171	1876	1610	2753	2093	1563	1151	0.0	– 6.5	– 23.0	**18.40**
350 Remington Magnum (R)	200	PSPCL	**20**	2710	2410	2130	1870	3261	2579	2014	1553	+2.6	0.0	– 10.3	**18.15**
375 Winchester (W)	200	PPSP	24	2200	1841	1526	1268	2150	1506	1034	714	0.0	– 9.5	– 33.8	**15.05**
375 Winchester (W)	250	PPSP	24	1900	1647	1424	1239	2005	1506	1126	852	0.0	–12.0	– 40.9	**15.05**
38-55 Winchester (W)	255	SP	24	1320	1190	1091	1018	987	802	674	587	0.0	–23.4	– 75.2	**14.00**
375 H & H Magnum (R) (W)	270	SP, PPSP	24	2690	2420	2166	1928	4337	3510	2812	2228	+2.5	0.0	– 10.0	**19.55**
375 H & H Magnum (W)	300	ST	24	2530	2268	2022	1793	4263	3426	2723	2141	+2.9	0.0	– 11.5	**20.65**
375 H & H Magnum (W) (R)	300	FMC, MC	24	2530	2171	1843	1551	4263	3139	2262	1602	0.0	– 6.5	– 23.4	**19.55**
38-40 Winchester (W)	180	SP	24	1160	999	901	827	538	399	324	273	0.0	–33.9	–110.6	***24.05**
44-40 Winchester (W) (R)	200	SP, SP	24	1190	1006	900	822	629	449	360	300	0.0	–33.3	–109.5	***25.40**
44 Remington Magnum (R)	240	SP, SJHP	**20**	1760	1380	1114	970	1650	1015	661	501	0.0	–17.6	– 63.1	**9.60**
44 Remington Magnum (F) (W)	240	HSP	**20**	1760	1380	1090	950	1650	1015	640	485	0.0	–18.1	– 65.1	**9.60**
444 Marlin (R)	240	SP	24	2350	1815	1377	1087	2942	1755	1010	630	0.0	– 9.9	– 38.5	**14.05**
444 Marlin (R)	265	SP	24	2120	1733	1405	1160	2644	1768	1162	791	0.0	–10.8	– 39.5	**14.25**
45-70 Government (F)	300	HSP	24	1810	1410	1120	970	2180	1320	840	630	0.0	–17.0	– 61.4	**14.35**
45-70 Government (W)	300	JHP	24	1880	1559	1294	1105	2355	1619	1116	814	0.0	–13.5	– 47.1	**14.35**
45-70 Government (W) (R)	405	SP	24	1330	1168	1055	977	1590	1227	1001	858	0.0	–24.6	– 80.3	**14.35**
458 Winchester Magnum (W) (R)	500	FMC, MC	24	2040	1823	1623	1442	4620	3689	2924	2308	0.0	– 9.6	– 32.5	**40.05**
458 Winchester Magnum (W) (R)	510	SP, SP	24	2040	1770	1527	1319	4712	3547	2640	1970	0.0	–10.3	– 35.6	**26.40**

*Price for 50. †Bullet Path based on line-of-sight 0.9" above center of bore. Bullet type abbreviations: BP—Bronze Point; BT—Boat Tail; CL—Core Lokt; FN—Flat Nose; FMC—Full Metal Case; FMJ—Full Metal Jacket; HP—Hollow Point; HSP—Hollow Soft Point; JHP—Jacketed Hollow Point; L—Lead; Lu—Lubaloy; MAT—Match; MC—Metal Case; NP—Nosler Partition; OPE—Open Point Expanding; PCL—Pointed Core Lokt; PEP—Pointed Expanding Point; PL—Power-Lokt; PP—Power Point; Prem.—Premium; PSP—Pointed Soft Point; SJHP—Semi-Jacketed Hollow Point; SJMP—Semi-Jacketed Metal Point; SP—Soft Point; ST—Silvertip; SX—Super Explosive.

WEATHERBY MAGNUM CARTRIDGES—BALLISTICS AND PRICES

Cartridge	Bullet Wt. Grs.	Bullet Type	Bbl. (in.)	Velocity (fps) Muzzle	Velocity 100 Yds.	Velocity 200 Yds.	Velocity 300 Yds.	Energy (ft. lbs.) Muzzle	Energy 100 Yds.	Energy 200 Yds.	Energy 300 Yds.	Bullet Path† 100 Yds.	Bullet Path 200 Yds.	Bullet Path 300 Yds.	Price Per Box
224 Weatherby Magnum	50	PE	26	3750	3263	2814	2402	1562	1182	879	640	+2.6	+3.6	0.0	**$21.95**
224 Weatherby Magnum	55	PE	26	3650	3214	2808	2433	1627	1262	963	723	+2.8	+3.6	0.0	**21.95**
240 Weatherby Magnum	70	PE	26	3850	3424	3025	2654	2305	1823	1423	1095	+2.2	+3.0	0.0	**21.95**
240 Weatherby Magnum	87	PE	26	3500	3165	2848	2550	2367	1935	1567	1256	+2.8	+3.6	0.0	**21.95**
240 Weatherby Magnum	100	PE	26	3395	3115	2848	2594	2560	2155	1802	1495	+2.8	+3.5	0.0	**21.95**
240 Weatherby Magnum	100	NP	26	3395	3068	2758	2468	2560	2090	1690	1353	+1.1	0.0	– 5.7	**29.95**
257 Weatherby Magnum	87	PE	26	3825	3470	3135	2818	2827	2327	1900	1535	+2.1	+2.9	0.0	**22.95**
257 Weatherby Magnum	100	PE	26	3555	3256	2971	2700	2807	2355	1960	1619	+2.5	+3.2	0.0	**22.95**
257 Weatherby Magnum	100	NP	26	3555	3242	2945	2663	2807	2335	1926	1575	+0.9	0.0	– 4.7	**31.95**
257 Weatherby Magnum	117	SPE	26	3300	2853	2443	2074	2830	2115	1551	1118	+3.8	+4.9	0.0	**22.95**
257 Weatherby Magnum	117	NP	26	3300	3027	2767	2520	2830	2381	1990	1650	+1.2	0.0	– 5.9	**31.95**
270 Weatherby Magnum	100	PE	26	3760	3341	2949	2585	3140	2479	1932	1484	+2.4	+3.2	0.0	**22.95**
270 Weatherby Magnum	130	PE	26	3375	3110	2856	2615	3289	2793	2355	1974	+2.8	+3.5	0.0	**22.95**
270 Weatherby Magnum	130	NP	26	3375	3113	2862	2624	3289	2798	2365	1988	+1.0	0.0	– 5.2	**31.95**
270 Weatherby Magnum	150	PE	26	3245	3012	2789	2575	3508	3022	2592	2209	+3.1	+3.8	0.0	**22.95**
270 Weatherby Magnum	150	NP	26	3245	3022	2809	2604	3508	3043	2629	2259	+1.2	0.0	– 5.4	**22.95**
7mm Weatherby Magnum	139	PE	26	3300	3037	2786	2546	3362	2848	2396	2001	+3.0	+3.7	0.0	**22.95**
7mm Weatherby Magnum	140	NP	26	3300	3047	2806	2575	3386	2887	2448	2062	+1.1	0.0	– 5.4	**31.95**
7mm Weatherby Magnum	154	PE	26	3160	2928	2706	2494	3415	2932	2504	2127	+3.3	+4.1	0.0	**22.95**
7mm Weatherby Magnum	160	NP	26	3150	2935	2727	2528	3526	3061	2643	2271	+1.3	0.0	– 5.8	**31.95**
7mm Weatherby Magnum	175	RN	26	3070	2714	2383	2082	3663	2863	2207	1685	+1.6	0.0	– 7.5	**22.95**
300 Weatherby Magnum	110	PE	26	3900	3465	3057	2677	3716	2933	2283	1750	+2.2	+3.0	0.0	**22.95**
300 Weatherby Magnum	150	PE	26	3545	3248	2965	2696	4187	3515	2929	2422	+2.5	+3.2	0.0	**22.95**
300 Weatherby Magnum	150	NP	26	3545	3191	2857	2544	4187	3392	2719	2156	+1.0	0.0	– 5.3	**32.95**
300 Weatherby Magnum	180	PE	26	3245	3010	2785	2569	4210	3622	3100	2639	+3.1	+3.8	0.0	**22.95**
300 Weatherby Magnum	180	NP	26	3245	2964	2696	2444	4210	3512	2906	2388	+1.3	0.0	– 6.0	**22.95**
300 Weatherby Magnum	200	NP	26	3000	2740	2494	2262	3998	3335	2763	2273	+1.6	0.0	– 7.3	**32.95**
300 Weatherby Magnum	220	SPE	26	2905	2578	2276	2000	4123	3248	2531	1955	+1.9	0.0	– 8.6	**22.95**
340 Weatherby Magnum	200	PE	26	3210	2947	2696	2458	4577	3857	3228	2683	+3.2	+4.0	0.0	**24.20**
340 Weatherby Magnum	210	NP	26	3180	2927	2686	2457	4717	3996	3365	2816	+1.3	0.0	– 6.2	**38.95**
340 Weatherby Magnum	250	SPE	26	2850	2516	2209	1929	4510	3515	2710	2066	+2.0	0.0	– 9.2	**24.20**
340 Weatherby Magnum	250	NP	26	2850	2563	2296	2049	4510	3648	2927	2331	+1.8	0.0	– 8.2	**24.20**
378 Weatherby Magnum	270	SPE	26	3180	2796	2440	2117	6064	4688	3570	2688	+1.5	0.0	– 7.3	**44.95**
378 Weatherby Magnum	270	NP	26	3180	2840	2515	2220	6064	4837	3793	2955	+3.9	+4.9	0.0	**44.95**
378 Weatherby Magnum	300	SPE	26	2925	2564	2234	1935	5700	4380	3325	2495	+1.9	0.0	– 9.0	**44.95**
378 Weatherby Magnum	300	NP	26	2925	2620	2340	2080	5700	4574	3649	2883	+4.9	+6.0	0.0	**44.95**
460 Weatherby Magnum	500	RN	26	2700	2395	2115	1858	8095	6370	4968	3834	+2.3	0.0	–10.3	**42.95**
460 Weatherby Magnum	500	FMJ	26	2700	2416	2154	1912	8095	6482	5153	4060	+2.2	0.0	– 9.8	**49.95**

Note: 26" barrels used to obtain Weatherby ballistic data. †Bullet Path based on line of sight 1.5" above center of bore. Bullet type abbreviations: FMJ—Full Metal Jacket; NP—Nosler Partition; PE—Pointed Expanding; RN—Round Nose; SPE—Semi-Pointed Expanding.

NORMA C.F. RIFLE CARTRIDGES—BALLISTICS AND PRICES

Cartridge	Wt. Grs.	Bullet Type	Bbl. (in.)	Velocity (fps) Muzzle	100 Yds.	200 Yds.	300 Yds.	Energy(ft. lbs.) Muzzle	100 Yds.	200 Yds.	300 Yds.	Bullet Path† 100 Yds.	200 Yds.	300 Yds.	Price Per Box
222 Remington	50	SP	24	3200	2650	2170	1750	1137	780	520	340	+1.6	0.0	− 8.2	$9.60
222 Remington	50	FJ	24	3200	2610	2080	1630	1137	756	480	295	+1.9	0.0	−10.1	11.70
222 Remington	53	SpPSP	24	3117	2670	2267	1901	1142	838	604	425	+1.7	0.0	− 8.7	9.60
22-250 Remington	53	SpPSP	24	3707	3192	2741	2332	1616	1198	883	639	+1.0	0.0	− 5.7	9.70
220 Swift	50	SP	24	4110	3611	3133	2681	1877	1448	1090	799	+0.6	0.0	− 4.1	18.00
22 Savage Hi-Power (5.6 x 52R)	71	SP	24	2790	2296	1886	1558	1226	831	561	383	+2.4	0.0	−11.4	21.70
22 Savage Hi-Power (5.6 x 52R)	71	FJ	24	2790	2296	1886	1558	1226	831	561	383	+2.4	0.0	−11.4	21.70
243 Winchester	100	SP, FJ	24	3070	2790	2540	2320	2090	1730	1430	1190	+1.4	0.0	− 6.3	13.00
6.5mm Carcano	139	PPDC	24	2576	2379	2192	2012	2046	1745	1481	1249	+2.3	0.0	− 9.6	21.95
6.5mm Carcano	156	SP	24	2430	2208	2000	1800	2046	1689	1386	1123	+2.9	0.0	−11.7	21.00
6.5mm JAP	139	SPBT	24	2430	2280	2130	1990	1820	1605	1401	1223	+2.7	0.0	−10.8	21.00
6.5mm JAP	156	SP	24	2065	1871	1692	1529	1481	1213	992	810	+4.3	0.0	−16.4	21.00
6.5mm Norma (6.5 x 55)	77	SP	29	2725	2362	2030	1811	1271	956	706	562	+2.4	0.0	−10.9	21.00
6.5mm Norma (6.5 x 55)	139	PPDC	29	2790	2630	2470	2320	2402	2136	1883	1662	+1.8	0.0	− 7.8	21.00
6.5mm Norma (6.5 x 55)	156	SP	29	2495	2271	2062	1867	2153	1787	1473	1208	+2.6	0.0	−10.9	21.00
270 Winchester	130	SPBT	24	3140	2884	2639	2404	2847	2401	2011	1669	+1.4	0.0	− 6.6	14.20
270 Winchester	150	SPBT	24	2800	2616	2436	2262	2616	2280	1977	1705	+1.8	0.0	− 7.7	14.20
7mm Mauser (7 x 57)	150	SPBT	24	2755	2539	2331	2133	2530	2148	1810	1516	+2.0	0.0	− 8.4	15.00
7 x 57 R	150	SPBT, FJ BT	24	2690	2476	2270	2077	2411	2042	1717	1437	+2.1	0.0	− 8.9	22.50
7 x 64	150	SPBT	24	2890	2598	2329	2113	2779	2249	1807	1487	+1.7	0.0	− 7.5	22.50
7mm Rem. Express (.280 Rem.)	150	SPBT	24	2900	2683	2475	2277	2802	2398	2041	1727	+1.7	0.0	− 7.4	14.75
7mm Remington Magnum	150	SPBT	26	3250	2960	2638	2440	3519	2919	2318	1983	+1.2	0.0	− 5.8	18.30
30 Carbine U.S.	110	SP	18	1970	1595	1300	1090	948	622	413	290	0.0	−12.4	−45.7	12.60
30-30 Winchester	150	SPFN	20	2410	2075	1790	1550	1934	1433	1066	799	0.0	− 7.0	−26.1	13.30
30-30 Winchester	170	SPFN	20	2220	1890	1630	1410	1860	1350	1000	750	0.0	− 8.1	−29.2	13.30
7.5 x 55 Swiss	180	SPBT	24	2650	2441	2248	2056	2792	2380	2020	1690	+2.1	0.0	− 8.9	22.00
7.62 x 39 Short Russian	125	SP		2385				1580							17.00
7.62 Russian	180	SPBT	24	2625	2415	2222	2030	2749	2326	1970	1644	+2.2	0.0	− 9.1	22.35
308 Winchester	130	SPBT	24	2900	2590	2300	2030	2428	1937	1527	1190	+1.9	0.0	− 8.6	14.15
308 Winchester	150	SPBT	24	2860	2570	2300	2050	2725	2200	1760	1400	+1.9	0.0	− 8.5	14.70
308 Winchester	180	PPDC	24	2610	2400	2210	2020	2725	2303	1952	1631	+2.3	0.0	− 9.4	16.35
30-06	130	SPBT	24	3205	2876	2561	2263	2966	2388	1894	1479	+1.4	0.0	− 6.7	14.15
30-06	150	SPBT	24	2970	2680	2402	2141	2943	2393	1922	1527	+1.7	0.0	− 7.8	14.15
30-06	180	SP	24	2700	2477	2261	2070	2914	2430	2025	1713	+2.1	0.0	− 8.7	14.15
30-06	180	PPDC	24	2700	2494	2296	2109	2914	2487	2107	1778	+2.0	0.0	− 8.6	14.15
303 British	150	SP	24	2720	2440	2170	1930	2465	1983	1569	1241	+2.0	0.0	− 8.6	15.70
303 British	180	SPBT	24	2540	2340	2147	1965	2579	2189	1843	1544	+2.4	0.0	−10.0	15.70
308 Norma Magnum	180	PPDC	26	3020	2798	2585	2382	3646	3130	2671	2268	+1.3	0.0	− 6.1	27.90
7.65mm Argentine	150	SP	24	2920	2630	2355	2105	2841	2304	1848	1476	+1.7	0.0	− 7.8	21.95
7.7mm JAP	130	SP	24	2950	2635	2340	2065	2513	2004	1581	1231	+1.8	0.0	− 8.2	22.50
7.7mm JAP	180	SPBT	24	2495	2292	2101	1922	2484	2100	1765	1477	+2.6	0.0	−10.4	22.50
8 x 57J (.318)	196	SP	24	2525	2195	1894	1627	2778	2097	1562	1152	+2.9	0.0	−12.7	23.00
8mm Mauser (8 x 57JS)	196	SP	24	2525	2195	1894	1627	2778	2097	1562	1152	+2.9	0.0	−12.7	15.50
358 Norma Magnum	250	SP	26	2800	2493	2231	2001	4322	3451	2764	2223	+2.0	0.0	− 8.3	27.95
9.3 x 57 mm	286	PPDC	24	2065	1818	1595	1404	2714	2099	1616	1252	0.0	− 9.1	−32.0	19.75
9.3 x 62 mm	286	PPDC	24	2360	2088	1815	1592	3544	2769	2092	1700	+3.3	0.0	−13.7	19.75

†Bullet Path based on line of sight 1.5″ above center of bore. Bullet type abbreviations: BT—Boat Tail; DC—Dual Core; FJ—Full Jacket; FJBT—Full Jacket Boat Tail; FP—Flat Point; HP—Hollow Point; MC—Metal Case; P—Pointed; PP—Plastic Point; RN—Round Nose; SP—Soft Point; SPFN—Soft Point Flat Nose; SPSBT—Soft Point Semi-Pointed Boat Tail; SPSP—Soft Point Semi-Point; SpPSP—Spire point Soft Point.

RIMFIRE CARTRIDGES—BALLISTICS AND PRICES

Remington-Peters, Winchester-Western, Federal, Omark/CCI

All loads available from all manufacturers except as indicated: R-P (a); W-W (b); Fed. (c); CCI (d). **All prices are approximate.**

CARTRIDGE	WT. GRS.	BULLET TYPE	VELOCITY FT. PER SEC. MUZZLE	100 YDS.	ENERGY FT. LBS. MUZZLE	100 YDS.	MID-RANGE TRAJECTORY 100 YDS	HANDGUN BARREL LENGTH	BALLISTICS M.V. F.P.S	M.E. F.P	PRICE PER BOX
22 Short T22 (b)	29	C, L*	1045	810	70	42	5.6	6″	865	48	$1.88
22 Short Hi-Vel. (c)	29	C, L	1125	920	81	54	4.3	6″	1035	69	1.88
22 Short HP-Hi-Vel. (a, b, c)	27	C, L	1155	920	80	51	4.2		—	—	2.00
22 Short Std. Vel. (a, b, c)	29	L*	1045	870	70	49	8.7	—	1045	870	1.88
22 Short Target (a)	29	L	1045	872	70	49	4.8	—	—	—	1.88
22 Stinger	32	C, HP	1686	1047	202	78	−2.61	—	—	—	2.85
22 Long Rifle Yellow Jacket	33	HVTCHP	1500	1075	185	85	2.8	—	1500	165	2.63
22 Long Rifle Target (a)	40	L	1150	976	117	85	4.0	—	—	—	2.15
22 Long Rifle Match Rifle (a)	40	L	—	—	—	—	—	—	—	—	7.18
22 Long Rifle Match Pistol (a)	40	L	—	—	—	—	—	—	—	—	7.18
22 Long Hi-Vel. (c)	29	C, L	1045	870	70	49	8.7	—	1045	70	4.30
22 Long Rifle T22 (a, b)†[1]	40	L*	1145	975	116	84	4.0	6″	950	80	2.15
22 Long Rifle (b)†[2]	40	L*	1120	950	111	80	4.2	—	—	—	4.30
22 Long Rifle (b)†[3]	40	L*	—	—	—	—	—	6¾″	1060	100	4.30
22 Long Rifle (d)†[4]	40	C	1165	980	121	84	4.0	—	—	—	2.15
22 Long Rifle Hi-Vel.	40	C, L	1285	1025	147	93	3.4	6″	1125	112	2.15
22 Long Rifle HP Hi-Vel. (b, d)	37	C, L	131	1020	142	85	3.4	—	1255	140	2.37
22 Long Rifle HP Hi-Vel. (a, c)	38	C, HP	1280	1020	138	88	6.1	—	1280	138	2.37
22 Long Rifle (b, c)		No. 12 Shot	—	—	—	—	—	—	—	—	4.36
22 WMR Mini-Mag Shotshell (d)		No. 11 Shot	1000	—	—	—	—	6″	—	—	2.22
22 LR Mini-Mag Shotshell (d)		No. 12 Shot	950	—	—	—	—	6″	—	—	2.22
22 WMR Mag.	40	HP	2000	1390	355	170	1.6	6½″	1550	213	5.90
22 WMR Mag.	40	MC	2000	1390	355	170	1.6	6½″	1550	213	5.90
5mm Rem. RFM (a)	38	PLHP	2100	1605	372	217		Not Available			13.52

†Target loads of these ballistics available in: (1) Rem. Match; (2) W-W, Super Match Mark III; (3) Super Match Mark IV Pistol Match; (4) CCI MiniGroup.
C—Copper plated L—Lead (Wax Coated) L*—Lead, lubricated D—Disintegrating MC—Metal Case HP—Hollow Point JHP—Jacket Hollow Point
PLHP—Power-Lokt Hollow Point HVTCHP—Hyper Velocity Truncated Cone Hollow Point.

CENTER FIRE HANDGUN CARTRIDGES BALLISTICS AND PRICES
Win.-Western, Rem.-Peters, Norma, PMC, and Federal

Most loads are available from W-W and R-P. All available Norma loads are listed. Federal cartridges are marked with an asterisk. Other loads supplied by only one source are indicated by a letter, thus: Norma (a); R-P (b); W-W (c); PMC (d); CCI (e). Prices are approximate.

Cartridge	Gr.	Bullet Style	Muzzle Velocity	Muzzle Energy	Barrel Inches	Price Per Box
22 Jet (b)	40	SP	2100	390	8⅜	$21.00
221 Fireball (b)	50	SP	2650	780	10½	9.70
25 (6.35mm) Auto*	50	MC	810	73	2	12.25
25 ACP (c)	45	Exp. Pt.	835	70	2	12.90
256 Winchester Magnum (c)	60	HP	2350	735	8½	23.75
30 (7.65mm) Luger Auto*	93	MC	1220	307	4½	19.70
32 S&W Blank (b, c)	No bullet		—	—	—	11.70
32 S&W Blank, BP (c)	No bullet		—	—	—	11.70
32 Short Colt	80	Lead	745	100	4	11.75
32 Long Colt IL (c)	82	Lub.	755	104	4	12.25
32 Auto (c)	60	STHP	970	125	4	15.15
32 (7.65mm) Auto*	71	MC	905	129	4	14.00
32 (7.65mm) Auto Pistol (a)	77	MC	900	162	4	15.15
32 S&W	88	Lead	680	90	3	11.85
32 S&W Long	98	Lead	705	115	4	12.25
32-20 Winchester	100	Lead	1030	271	6	15.35
32-20 Winchester	100	SP	1030	271	6	19.00
357 Magnum	110	JHP	1295	410	4	18.40
357 Magnum	110	SJHP	1295	410	4	18.45
357 Magnum	125	JHP	1450	583	4	18.40
357 Magnum (d)	125	JHC	1450	583	4	—
357 Magnum (e)	125	JSP	1900	1001	—	18.43
357 Magnum (e)	140	JHP	1775	979	—	18.43
357 Magnum (e)	150	FMJ	1600	852	—	18.43
357 Magnum*	158	SWC	1235	535	4	15.60
357 Magnum (b) (e)	158	JSP	1550	845	8⅜	18.40
357 Magnum	158	MP	1410	695	8⅜	18.15
357 Magnum	158	Lead	1410	696	8⅜	15.60
357 Magnum	158	Lead	1450	735	8⅜	18.40
9mm Luger (c)	95	JSP	1355	387	4	17.45
9mm Luger (c)	115	FMC	1155	341	4	17.40
9mm Luger (c)	115	STHP	1255	383	4	18.30
9mm Luger*	115	JHP	1165	349	4	17.40
9mm Luger*	125	MC	1120	345	4	17.40
9mm Luger (e)	125	JSP	1100	335	—	17.43
9mm Winchester Magnum (c)	115	FMC	1475	556	5	18.65
38 S&W Blank	No bullet		—	—	—	14.15
38 Smith & Wesson	145	Lead	685	150	4	13.15
38 S&W	146	Lead	730	172	4	13.15
38 Special Blank	No bullet		—	—	—	14.25
38 Special (e)	110	JHP	1200	351	—	16.82
38 Special, IL +P (c)	150	Lub.	1060	375	6	14.70
38 Special IL +P (c)	150	MP	1060	375	6	16.80
38 Special	158	Lead	855	256	6	13.25
38 Special	200	Lead	730	236	6	14.15
38 Special	158	MP	855	256	6	16.80
38 Special (b)	125	SJHP		Not available		16.80
38 Special WC (b)	148	Lead	770	195	6	13.80
38 Special Match, IL	148	Lead	770	195	6	13.80
38 Special Match, IL (b)	158	Lead	855	256	6	13.80
38 Special*	158	LRN	755	200	4	13.25
38 Special	158	RN	900	320	6	14.85
38 Special	158	SWC	755	200	4	13.55
38 Special Match*	148	WC	710	166	4	13.80
38 Special +P (c)	95	STHP	1100	255	4	17.65
38 Special +P	95	SJHP				16.80
38 Special +P (b)	110	SJHP	1020	254	4	16.80
38 Special +P	125	JSP	945	248	4	16.80
38 Special +P	158	LRN	915	294	4	14.70
38 Special +P (b)	158	LHP	915	294	4	14.40
38 Special +P*	158	SWC	915	294	4	13.55
38 Special +P*	158	SWCHP	915	294	4	14.40
38 Special +P*	158	LSWC	915	294	4	13.55
38 Special +P (e)	140	JHP	1275	504	—	16.82
38 Special +P (e)	150	FMJ	1175	461	—	16.82
38 Special +P*	110	JHP	1020	254	4	16.80
38 Special +P*	125	JHP	945	248	4	16.80
38 Special Norma +P (a)	110	JHP	1542	580	6	29.20
38 Short Colt	125	Lead	730	150	6	12.90
38 Short Colt, Greased	130	Lub.	730	155	6	12.95
38 Long Colt	150	Lead	730	175	6	19.45
38 Super Auto +P (b)	130	MC	1280	475	5	15.15
38 Super Auto +P (b)	115	JHP	1300	431	5	15.75
38 Auto, for Colt 38 Super (c)	125	JHP	1280	475	5	15.75
38 Auto	130	MC	1040	312	4½	15.65
38 Auto +P	130	FMC	1280	475	5	15.15
380 Auto (c)	85	STHP	1000	189	3¾	14.35
380 Auto*	95	MC	955	190	3¾	10.90
380 Auto	95	MC	955	192	3¾	14.35
380 Auto	88	JHP	990	191	4	14.35
380 Auto*	90	JHP	1000	200	3¾	14.35
38-40 Winchester	180	SP	975	380	5	24.05
41 Remington Magnum	210	Lead	1050	515	8¾	20.70
41 Remington Magnum	210	SP	1500	1050	8¾	24.20
44 S&W Spec.*	200	LSW	960	410	7½	18.25
44 S&W Special	246	Lead	755	311	6½	18.55
44 Remington Magnum*	180	JHP	1610	1045	4	21.80
44 Remington Magnum (e)	200	JHP	1650	1208	—	12.02
44 Remington Magnum (e)	240	JSP	1625	1406	—	12.02
44 Remington Magnum (b)	240	SP	1470	1150	6½	9.60
44 Remington Magnum	240	Lead	1470	1150	6½	23.50
44 Remington Magnum	240	SJHP	1180	741	4	9.60
44 Remington Magnum (a)	240	JPC	1533	1253	8½	14.35
44 Auto Mag (a)	240	JPC	1350	976	6½	45.00
44-40 Winchester	200	SP	975	420	7½	25.40
45 Colt*	225	SWCHP	900	405	5½	17.75
45 Colt	250	Lead	860	410	5½	17.80
45 Colt, IL (c)	255	Lub., L	860	410	5½	18.85
45 Auto (c)	185	STHP	1000	411	5	8.05
45 Auto (e)	200	JHP	1025	466	—	9.93

Cartridge	Gr.	Bullet Style	Muzzle Velocity	Muzzle Energy	Barrel Inches	Price Per Box
45 Auto	230	MC	850	369	5	19.20
45 ACP	230	JHP	850	370	5	19.20
45 Auto WC*	185	MC	775	245	5	19.85
45 Auto*	185	JHP	950	370	5	19.85
45 Auto MC	230	MC	850	369	5	19.85
45 Auto Match (c)	185		775	247	5	19.85
45 Auto Match*	230	MC	850	370	5	19.20
45 Winchester Magnum (c)	230	FMC	1400	1001	5	20.55
45 Auto Rim (b)	230	Lead	810	335	5½	20.50

IL—Inside Lub.   JSP—Jacketed Soft Point   WC—Wad Cutter
RN—Round Nose   HP—Hollow Point   Lub—Lubricated
MC—Metal Case   SP—Soft Point   MP—Metal Point
LGC—Lead, Gas Check   JHP—Jacketed Hollow Point
SWC—Semi Wad Cutter   SJHP—Semi Jacketed Hollow Point

SHOTSHELL LOADS AND PRICES
Winchester-Western, Remington-Peters, Federal

In certain loadings one manufacturer may offer fewer or more shot sizes than another, but in general all makers offer equivalent loadings. Sources are indicated by letters, thus: W-W (a); R-P (b); Fed. (c). Prices are approximate, list is a random sampling of offerings.

GAUGE	Length Shell Ins.	Powder Equiv. Drams	Shot Ozs.	Shot Size	PRICE PER BOX
MAGNUM LOADS					
10 (a)	3½	4½	2¼	BB, 2, 4	$24.65
10 (a¹, b)	3½	Max	2	BB, 2, 4	22.95
12 (a, b, c)	3	Max	1⅞	BB, 2, 4	15.35
12 (a, b, c)	3	4	1⅝	2, 4, 6	14.20
12 (a¹, b)	2¾	Max	1½	2, 4, 5, 6	12.85
16 (a, b, c)	2¾	Max	1¼	2, 4, 6	12.65
20 (a, b, c)	3	Max	1¼	2, 4, 6, 7½	11.90
20 (a¹)	3	3	1¼	4, 6, 7½	9.03
20 (a¹, b, c)	2¾	2¾	1⅛	4, 6, 7½	10.55
LONG RANGE LOADS					
10 (a)	2⅞	4¾	1⅝	4	14.15
12 (a¹, b, c)	2¾	3¾	1¼	BB, 2, 4, 5, 6, 7½, 8, 9	9.90
16 (a, b, c)	2¾	3¼	1⅛	4, 5, 6, 7½, 8, 9	9.50
20 (a¹, b, c)	2¾	2¾	1	4, 5, 6, 7½, 9	8.70
28 (a, b)	2¾	2¼	¾	6, 7½, 8	8.75
410 (b)	2½	Max	½	6, 7½	6.90
410 (b)	3	Max	11/16	4, 5, 6, 7½, 8	8.15
FIELD LOADS					
12 (a, b, c)	2¾	3¼	1¼	7½, 8, 9	8.75
12 (a, b, c)	2¾	3¼	1⅛	4, 5, 6, 7½, 8, 9	8.45
12 (a, b, c)	2¾	3¼	1⅛	4, 5, 6, 7½, 8	8.45
12 (a)	3	4	1⅞	BB, 2, 4, 6	16.45
16 (a, b, c)	2¾	2¾	1⅛	4, 5, 6, 7½, 8	8.45
16 (a, b, c)	2¾	2¾	1⅛	4, 6, 7½, 8	8.45
20 (a, b, c)	2¾	2½	1	4, 5, 6, 7½, 8, 9	7.65
20 (a, b, c)	2¾	2½	1	4, 5, 6, 7½, 8, 9	7.65
SCATTER LOADS					
12 (b)	2¾	3	1⅛	8	9.00
TARGET LOADS					
12 (a)	2¾	3	1⅛	7½, 8	8.10
12 (a, b, c)	2¾	2¾	1⅛	7½, 8	8.10
20 (a, b, c)	2¾	2½	⅞	9	7.05
28 (a, b, c)	2¾	2	¾	9	8.55
410 (a, b, c)	2½	Max	½	9	6.95
SKEET & TRAP					
12 (a, b, c)	2¾	3	1⅛	7½, 8	8.10
12 (a, b, c)	2¾	2¾	1⅛	7½, 8, 9	7.85
20 (a, b, c)	2¾	2½	⅞	9	7.05
20 (a)	2¾	2½	⅞	9	7.05
28 (a)	2¾	2	¾	9	8.55
410 (a, b, c)	2½	Max	½	9	6.95
BUCKSHOT					
10 (c)	3½	Sup. Mag.	—	4 Buck—54 pellets	4.70
12 (a, b, c)	3 Mag.	4½	—	00 Buck—15 pellets	3.55
12 (a, b, c)	3 Mag.	4½	—	4 Buck—41 pellets	3.55
12 (b)	2¾ Mag.	4	—	1 Buck—20 pellets	3.10
12 (a, b, c)	2¾ Mag.	4	—	00 Buck—12 pellets	3.10
12 (a, b, c)	2¾	Max	—	00 Buck— 9 pellets	3.10
12 (a, b, c)	2¾	3¾	—	0 Buck—12 pellets	2.80
12 (a, b, c)	2¾	Max	—	1 Buck—16 pellets	2.80
12 (a, b, c)	2¾	Max	—	4 Buck—27 pellets	2.80
12 (a)	2¾ Mag.	—	—	000 Buck— 8 pellets	2.80
12 (a)	3 Mag.	—	—	000 Buck—10 pellets	3.55
16 (a, b, c)	2¾	3	—	1 Buck—12 pellets	2.80
20 (a, b, c)	2¾	Max	—	3 Buck—20 pellets	2.80
RIFLED SLUGS					
12 (a, b, c)	2¾	Max	1	Slug 5-pack	3.20
16 (a, b, c,)	2¾	Max	⅘	Slug	3.20
20 (a, b, c)	2¾	Max	⅝	Slug	2.65
20 (a)	2¾	Max	¾	Slug	2.95
410 (a, b, c)	2½	Max	⅕	Slug	2.80
STEEL SHOT LOADS					
10 (c)	3½	Max	1⅝	BB, 2	20.85
12 (c)	2¾	3¾	1⅛	1, 2, 4	9.43
12 (a, c)	2¾	Max	1¼	BB, 1, 2, 4	14.90
12 (b)	3	Max	1¼	1, 2, 4	16.10
12 (b)	2¾	Max	1⅛	1, 2, 4	12.40
20 (c)	3	3¼	1	4	11.90

W-W 410, 28 and 10-ga. Magnum shells available in paper cases only, as are their scatter and target loads; their Skeet and trap loads come in both plastic and paper.

R-P shells are all of plastic with Power Piston wads except; 12 ga. scatter loads have Post Wad: all 10 ga., 410-3" and rifled slug loads have standard wad columns.

Federal magnum, range, buckshot, slug and all 410 loads are made in plastic only. Field loads are available in both paper and plastic.

¹—These loads available from W-W with Lubaloy shot at higher price.

The Handloader's Catalog

Welcome to the catalog section of the 9th edition of HANDLOADER'S DIGEST. This is the place where all the nuts and bolts come together and you, the reader, get to exercise your freedom of choice. No one brand of press, dies or reloading component is necessarily the best—that's what competition is all about. As a result, you'll find a wide variety of quality gear to choose from.

The prices? Well, like everything else, they're approximate, suggested retail only. When it comes to finding the "best price," we'd suggest you shop around for the best deal—prices for reloading gear have always been, and will continue to be, *highly* competitive.

If you've got more questions than our catalog section has answers for, then be sure to check our trade directory for the manufacturers addresses you may need.

Most importantly we want you, the reader, to enjoy our catalog. Good luck and safe reloading!

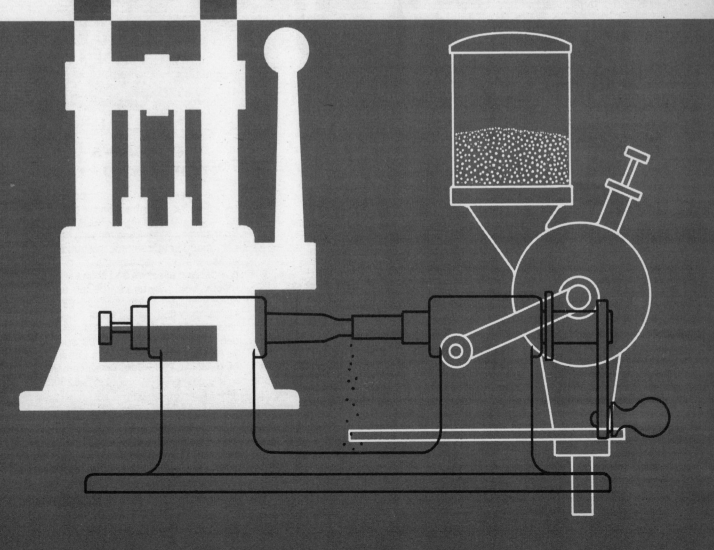

9th EDITION — PART 1

TOOLS AND ACCESSORIES FOR
METALLIC CARTRIDGES

Notes on Presses . . .

Presses, like other pieces of machinery are designed to work within certain limits. The largest and strongest presses will handle any job, from neck sizing the 22 Hornet up to swaging 375 caliber bullets. Before buying a press the novice should keep in mind that, as his knowledge of handloading increases, so will his desire to reload additional cartridges He should try to anticipate his future requirements—it will save him money in the end.

The handgun shooter, loading for himself only, cannot go wrong buying a Pacific, Lyman, C-H "C" type or some similar press. All handle handgun ammunition

with ease, of course, as well as rifle cartridges. The Lyman #310 tool, the old reliable, also handles both types of ammunition. These are sturdy but not fast tools. After a few months though, suppose our handgunner decides to handload ammo for several friends. In that case his original choice of a press may not be adequate for a larger volume of business handloading.

Or, let's assume instead that he moves on to bullet swaging. Can his original press handle bullet-swaging pressures?

All these things should be carefully thought out before buying any handload-

ing press It will save time, breakage and money. In any case, it is better to buy just a little stronger press than your present needs call for.

On the other hand, the shooter who travels, who moves and lives, perhaps, in a confined space or the man who does not do much shooting would be wise to purchase a small, light tool—say the Lee (rifle or shotgun), the Lyman 310 or the Pak-Tool Hand Loader, one of the finest small portable tools. Using this tool a man can sit in his car, canoe or on a log in the woods and reload cartridges with accuracy and dependability.

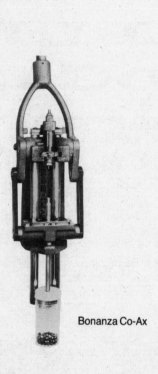

Bonanza Co-Ax

Bonanza 68

C-H 444-X

BONANZA CO-AX Press

Coaxial design for powerful leverage and true alignment. Dies quickly snap-in, handle moves 180 degrees. Floating guide rods reduce friction and wear. Takes standard ⅞-14 dies and Bonanza BSI-MU shell holders for priming station.

Model B-1, as shown with spent primer catcher, self-acting shell holder and overhead priming assembly. . . **$113.15**

BONANZA 68

Press is O-type offering ample power for loading and case forming. Frame and lever are castings; linkage pins are hardened and ground. Uses Bonanza BSI-MU shell holders and any ⅞-14 dies. Press operates on downstroke only, but handle stops in up or down position. Co-Ax priming device moves on a common axis within the ram, seats to a uniform depth and punch can be changed without tools. Spent primers can be collected behind the ram. Packaged with ram, priming device with large and small punches. Price, less shell holder and dies. **$60.60**

C-H 444-X Pistol Champ Press

This three station, semi-progressive reloading tool is highly suitable for loading large quantities of pistol ammunition: Tungsten carbide sizing die with decapper, Speed Seater seating die, button operated powder measure that dispenses powder and expands and bells the case mouth, fixed powder charge bar (available for different charges). Three strokes of the operating handle produces a finished round. Up to 200 rounds per hour can be loaded. Available in 38 Special/357 Mag., 30 Carbine, 9mm Luger, 44 Mag., 45 ACP, 45 Colt. Press complete with accessories **$269.50**

444-X Conversion Kits:
38/357, 44 Mag., 45 ACP, Colt, carbide **$64.00**
As above, steel **$49.60**
9mm Luger, carbide **$68.40**
As above, steel **$49.60**
30 Carbine, carbide **$81.40**
As above, steel **$49.60**

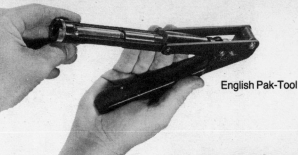

English Pak-Tool

C-H Mark V

W. H. ENGLISH Pak-Tool

Designed for the handloader who lacks room or facilities for a bench tool, it's ideal for the bench-rest shooter, the varmint hunter, the man back in the bush or the rifleman who likes to load at the shooting range.

The leverage of the Pak-Tool makes full length sizing of such cartridges as the 357 and 44 Magnums possible. For rifle, cartridges the Pak-Tool neck sizes only. The Pak-Tool is 100% straight line in all operations. Price complete for one standard rifle caliber **$49.50**
Handgun calibers **$54.50**

CAMDEX JS-63 Loader

Choice of either hand or motorized operation. Tube case feeder, takes standard 7/8-14 sizing dies. Spring loaded primer slide is adjustable for pick-up location and seating location. Powder station uses standard Pacific powder bushings. Crimp station uses standard 7/8-14 die. This 8-station press comes completely assembled and ready to go.

Hand operated with tooling for one caliber **$1,100.00**
Automatic (motorized), complete **$2,350.00**
Caliber conversion kits **$375.00**

C-H 444 H Press

New press offers four-station versatility—2, 3, or 4-piece die sets can be used. Or, a powder measure can be used with 2- or 3-piece die sets. Improved casting design offers increased strength and there is room for the longest magnum cases. Press comes complete with four rams, four shell holders, small or large primer area, and primer catcher **$158.00**
As above, with one standard caliber die set **$174.00**
Extra primer arm **$2.40**

C-H MARK V Auto Champion Press

A heavy duty H-type progressive loading machine that gives one completed round with each pull of the handle. Powder is dropped through a special "Flow-Through" belling and expanding die. Tungsten carbide sizing die. Fixed powder bars. Automatic case advancing makes double charging impossible. Seating stems are available for any type bullet.

Operating stations are in a straight line at the front of the machine. The three stations are clearly visible with no blind spots. Available only in 38 Special/357 Mag., 9mm Luger, 44 Mag., 45 ACP. Bullet seating stems are available for semi-wadcutter, wad cutter or round nose. Many improved features.

Press, complete (includes 1 primer tube, 2 cases tubes) **$699.00**
Extra case tubes (holding 15 cases each), 2 for **$3.60**
Extra powder bushings (specify type and weight) **$2.40**
Bullet seating stems **$1.80**

C-H "Champion" Heavy-Weight

A very heavy-duty O-type press with a ram 1.185" in diameter. Press is drilled to allow spent primers and debris fall through. Takes universal shell holders and is threaded 7/8-14 for standard dies. Well suited for case forming and bullet swaging operations. Solid steel handle. Toggle is designed so that it "breaks" slightly over top dead center for extreme leverage.

Price, including universal primer arm and shell holder head **$199.00**
Price complete with one set of standard dies **$217.00**

CAMDEX Reloading Machine

This electrically operated loading machine can produce 4400 completed rounds per hour. It is a cam operated index loader that comes with a T-C resizing die, a "Fail Safe" primer control system including a primer pocket probe. Controls monitor and shut down machine automatically if any of five functions are not satisfied. Machine comes ready to operate with conversion kits available to load any center fire pistol caliber and several rifle calibers. Price of machine one caliber **$5,650.00**
Auto primer filler **$525.00**
Conversions **$1,440.00** to **$1,500.00**

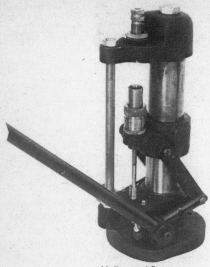

Hollywood Senior

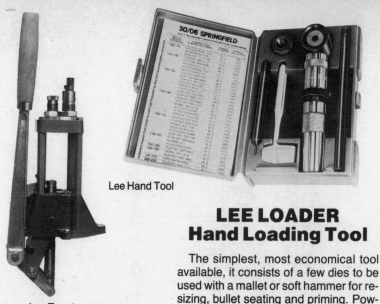

Lee Hand Tool

Lee Turret

LEE LOADER
Hand Loading Tool

The simplest, most economical tool available, it consists of a few dies to be used with a mallet or soft hammer for resizing, bullet seating and priming. Powder charges are measured with a charge cup. All parts of the Lee Loader are fully guaranteed and will be replaced free of charge if they break or prove defective in normal usage. Available for most popular rifle and pistol cartridges. From Lee Precision, Inc. $13.98

HOLLYWOOD
"Senior" Reloading
Tool

A massive (43 lbs. stripped) tool with leverage and bearing surfaces ample for the most efficient operation in reloading cartridges or swaging bullets. The castings are heat treated Meehanite. Precision ground 2½" pillar, in one-piece construction with base. Operating handle of ¾" steel 15" long gives tremendous leverage and ease of operation with a downward stroke for case sizing or bullet swaging. ⅝" steel tie-down rod furnished for added strength when swaging bullets.

Heavy steel toggle and camming ams held by ½" steel pins in reamed holes. Extra holes are drilled for greater leverage in bullet swaging.

The 1½" steel die bushing takes standard ⅞-14 dies; when bushing is removed it allows the tool to accept Hollywood shotshell dies $229.00

HOLLYWOOD
"Senior" Turret Tool

Same superb quality and features as the regular "Senior" except has 3-position turret head. Holes in turret may be had tapped 1½" or ⅞" or with 4 of each. Height 15", weight 47 lbs. stripped. Comes complete with one ½" die shell holder bushing, turret indexing handle, and one ⅝" tiedown rod for swaging $290.00
    Primer rods, small or large . . . $10.00
    Shell holders $7.00

HOLLYWOOD
Automatic Press

This is basically the Senior Turret tool but with improvements to make it completely automatic, except for power. Automatic indexing shell plate, auto wad feed. Capacity to reload up to 1,800 rifle, pistol or shotshells per hour. From Whitney Sales.
    Price, complete $2,250.00

LEE
Turret Press

"O" frame strength with a quick replaceable turret. Entire turret with dies can be replaced in 10 seconds—rotate the turret 30° to lift out. To change primer size, lift out the primer arm and rotate 180°. Accepts all standard ⅞-14 dies and universal shell holders. Built-in primer catcher. Compound leverage and accessory mounting holes.

Press can be easily changed for left-hand use. Handle is adjustable for the most convenient angle at the end of the stroke.

Available with a hard maple storage box and lock. Box serves as a bench for completely portable loading. Because of the compound leverage, forces required are so modest that when the loader is box mounted, it can be used on a card table. From Lee Precision, Inc.
    Press only $59.88
    Press with box $84.98
    Extra turret $9.98

Lyman T-Mag

LYMAN
T-Mag Press

This new press allows the reloader to mount six different reloading dies and two primer feed that can be left in place, ready for reloading at all times. Uses standard ⅞-14 dies, and has a ¾" steel stud and extra heavy support post holding the turret. Base has three holes for greater leverage and solid mounting. Uses O-Mag primer feed and primer catcher. Press comes with one standard AA pistol or rifle die set and shell-holder $149.95

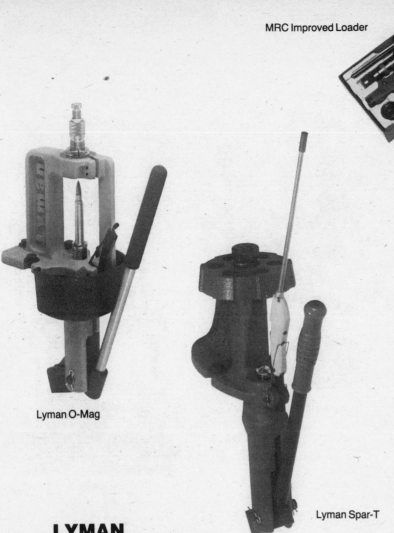

MRC Improved Loader

Lyman O-Mag

Lyman Spar-T

MRC LOADER Improved Hand Loading Tool

A simple, economical tool, it consists of a few dies to be used with a mallet or soft hammer for resizing, bullet seating and priming. Powder charges are measured with a charge cup. All parts of the MRC Loader have a limited warranty and will be replaced free of charge if they break or prove defective in two years of normal usage. Available for most popular rifle and pistol cartridges. From Mequon Reloading Corp............... **$17.98**

MRC Target Model Loader

Designed with the bench rest shooter in mind, this simple, economical tool loads target-quality ammunition at less than the cost of a conventional loading press. The loader features neck line reaming, positive straightline bullet seating, micrometer depth bullet seating. Set includes primer pocket cleaner, chamfer tool, case trimmer, MRC priming tool, neck reamer, bullet seater. All that's needed are the components. All parts have limited warranty and unit is available for most popular rifle calibers. From Mequon Reloading Corp. Price, complete........................ **$59.98**

LYMAN O-Mag Press

This new press has a 4½″ opening to handle the largest rifle cartridges. Sturdy construction and three mounting holes for extra leverage. The heavy duty handle has a long, non-slip gripping surface. Uses standard ⅞-14 dies. Comes with Universal Primer Arm. Weighs 17 lbs. stripped..................... **$79.95**

O-Mag set includes O-Mag press, primer catcher, primer arm, detachable shell holder, one complete set of standard Lyman AA dies.......... **$99.95**

LYMAN No. 310 Tool

Reloads pistol or rifle cartridges. A low-cost portable tool for smaller-quantity reloaders and those who want a compact and handy reloading outfit. An adjustable extractor hook and the Adapter Die let many rimmed or rimless cases be processed in the same handles. Price includes dies, etc............... **$47.45**

LYMAN Spar-T Turret Press

Combines fast "turret-loading" with the strength and simplicity of the popular "C" press. Frame and 6-station turret are high-silicon iron castings. Verti-Lock Turret secured to frame by heavy duty ¾″ steel stud provides positive stop, audible click indexing.

Turret locks rigidly for swaging; powerful leverage (25 to 1); up- or downstroke operation. Alignment ramp positions shell holder at top of stroke. Price, with ram and priming arm **$94.95**

All-American dies (specify caliber): Standard: **$24.50**; Deluxe: **$46.95**

Optional equipment: Spart-T auto. primer feed (as shown) **$12.95**

Lyman 55 powder measure (not shown)..................... **$48.95**

Optional primer catcher (fits either Spartan or Spar-T) **$3.95**

PACIFIC 0-7 Reloading Press

This O-frame press is angled to give better access to the working area. Frame is cast of a special new alloy to resist springing and alignment problems. Uses the PPS Priming System, new auto primer feed, and offset handle. Takes ⅞-14 dies **$65.95**

0-7 Automatic primer feed.... **$11.00**

With one set of dies, primer catcher, shell holder, and PPS priming system........................ **$93.50**

Pacific 00-7

Ponsness-Warren P-200

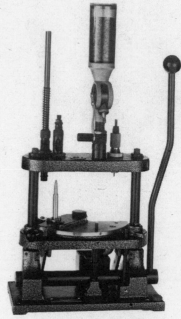

Ponsness-Warren M-II

PACIFIC
00-7 Reloading Press

Follows the 0-7 design in providing an O-type frame which is angled 30° to one side, but uses special handle-to-ram linkage for extra power in case resizing and bullet swaging. The "Power-Pac" linkage greatly multiplies the force applied to the ram through the lever designed to be at a maximum during the final ½-inch of lever stroke. Also includes Pacific's PPS priming system for fully automatic priming **$93.95**
00-7 auto primer feed **$11.00**
00-7 with die package (includes PPS, primer catcher, shell holder, and one set of Durachrome dies) **$116.50**

PACIFIC
Multi-Power "C" Press

This heavy-duty O-type press of high-density annealed iron is suitable for all reloading and case forming operations. Swinging toggle multiplies leverage. All bearing surfaces are hardened and ground—links are of steel for maximum strength. Takes standard ⅞-14 dies and snap-in shell holder heads (not included). Comes with priming arm . . . **$92.50**
Multi-Power "C" package includes press, primer catcher, set of dies and shell holder head (specify caliber) **$115.00**

PONSNESS/
WARREN
Metal-Matic
P-200 Press

This loader is designed to load straight-wall metallic cases at the rate of about 200-300 per hour. The 10-hole die head is tapped for standard ⅞-14 dies, and is designed to hold two calibers at one time. Once the case is inserted into the shellholder, it is not removed until all loading operations have been completed. A spring-loaded ball check precisely indexes the shellholder arm as it moves under the die head. The P-200 uses twin guide posts for durability, and comes with a removable spent primer box, large and small priming tools. Made of heavy die cast aluminum. The P-200 comes without dies, powder measure, shellholder, or primer feed (optional).

Metal-Matic P-200 . . . . **$275.00**
Primer feed **$38.50**

PONSNESS/
WARREN
Metallic M-II Press

This H-type press is capable of loading 150 rounds or more of rifle or handgun ammunition. The die head has four ⅞-14 holes to accept standard dies, powder measure, and other accessories. Conversion from one caliber to another is accomplished in less than five minutes. Once the case is inserted into the shellholder, it is not removed until it has been resized, reprimed, charged with powder, a bullet seated and crimped. Case is moved to each station on a side-swinging carrier. Press comes with an automatic primer feed. The Metallic M-II comes without dies, powder measure, or shellholder. Optional features include additional die heads, powder measure extension, and the P/W CAL-die bullet seater.

Metallic M-II press and primer feed **$440.00**

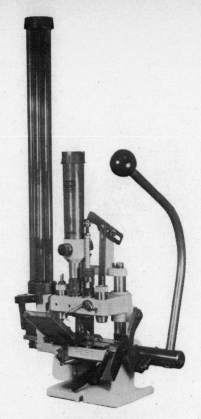

RCBS Green Machine

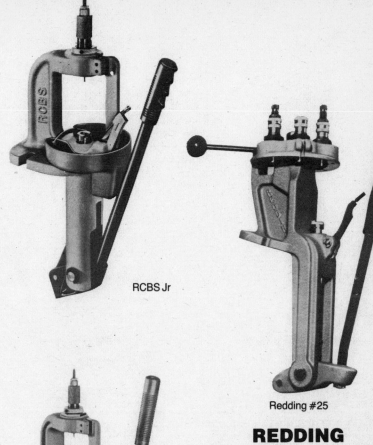

RCBS Jr

Redding #25

RCBS Rockchucker

RCBS
Green Machine

This four station, progressive, hand-operated tool can load 38/357 Mag. at a rate of 600 rounds per hour. Uses standard crimper and carbide sizer dies, specially designed expander and seater dies. The seater die is the "window" type. Powder is automatically measured from the Little Dandy powder measure. Comes with automatic case feed magazine, primer feed and magazine, dies, powder measure, and dust cover. Machine is pre-adjusted for target loads at the factory. Each pull of the operating handle produces a loaded round.

Price, complete, about **$500.00**

RCBS
Model "Jr" Press

Rugged "O"-frame design resists springing. Changes to up- or down-stroke in minutes—nothing extra to buy. Standard ⅞-14 dies. Ample leverage to do all reloading and case forming **$65.00**

Reloader Special—includes: RCBS "Jr" Press, primer catcher, removable head type shell holder, universal primer arm and one set of RCBS dies. Available in most popular calibers. Specify caliber.. . . . . **$89.50**

RCBS
Rock Chucker Press

Using the familiar RCBS Block "O" frame design to reduce springing and allow plenty of room to process cartridges up to the magnums, the Rock Chucker, with down-stroke compound leverage system, eases reloading chores. This 20 lb. press comes with removable "snap-action" shell holder head. **$92.50**

Rock Chucker Combo includes rifle or pistol dies (specify caliber) primer arm and primer catcher. **$115.50**

REDDING
No. 25 Turret Press

Machined ferrous alloy castings and toggle leverage system combine with a 6-station turret head for increased ease and speed in reloading metallic cases. Extremely rugged frame weighs 24 lbs. Progressive linkage develops 50-to-1 leverage. Ram uses standard shell holders. Turret accepts ⅞-14 dies. Complete with 6-hole turret **$164.95**

Kit form includes press, shell holder, and one No. 10 die. **$186.50**

Extra turrets (6 station) **$38.00**

REDDING
No. 7 "C" Press

New improvements include a stronger frame for the heaviest reloading tasks, an extremely shallow throat that eliminates deflection and a stronger alloy steel lower linkage. The added rear mounting lug prevents springing and bench splitting. Snap-in shell holder may be rotated to any position. Press accepts all standard ⅞-14 threaded dies and all universal shell holders. Includes handle, linkage, ram, frame and primer arm **$64.00**

Kit form includes press, shell holder, and one set of dies. **$86.00**

Shell holders, universal **$4.75**

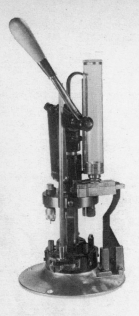

Star Progressive

Texan T-II

Texan 301-H3

STAR Universal Progressive Reloader

Handles all popular handgun calibers (38 Spl. and 45 ACP parts in stock), including 30 Carb., 357 and 44 Magnums; 44 Spl., 45 Auto Rim, 45 Colt. Same otherwise as the regular Star.

When ordering, specify powder charge and type, primer make, and send sample bullet. If no bullet is available, give complete description or catalog number. (Not illus.)

With Lifetyme Carbide Die .$1,110.00
Extra tool head for one caliber with Lifetyme Carbide Die $425.00
Additional charge for 30 Carbine and 9mm.

STAR Progressive Reloader

Designed for fast, efficient reloading of 38 Special cartridges, this tool is unsurpassed in stability of continuous operation by any loader in the field. The non-adjustable powder carrier will throw as accurate a charge as can be metered, and all tools and dies are adjustably mounted in the tool head, performing their operations simultaneously. With each stroke of the operating lever, a loaded round is accurately completed. Drilled and tapped for quick installation of the Hulme Automatic Case Feeder (described elsewhere).

Complete for 38 Special with Lifetyme Carbide Dies. $510.00

TEXAN 256 Double "C" Press

Broached ASTM #30 ferrous alloy casting of double "C" design for strength without adding weight or bulk. One-piece offset handle and toggle system gives more working room. Accepts standard ⅞-14 dies and snap-in shell holder heads. Comes complete with universal ram and primer arm $62.95

TEXAN 301-H3 Press

Heavy duty H-type press has wide access area for easy case handling. Strong 3-column design reduces springing to a minimum. Powerful leverage makes this press suitable for all reloading, case forming and bullet swaging operations. A complete ⅞-14 three-die set may be set up simultaneously—uses H-type rams and universal shell holders. Base is drilled for bench mounting. Price is for stripped tool except for universal priming arm and 3 rams $134.95

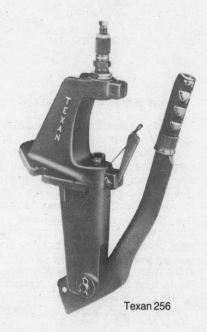

Texan 256

TEXAN Loadmaster Model 101 T-II

7-station turret can take dies for 3 different calibers plus powder measure. Rugged 2-column press, long stroke. Reloads the big magnums, swages bullets $210.00

Model T-II complete with auto primer feed, universal ram and one shell holder head $235.00
Auto primer feed separately . . $34.95

Notes on Dies for Metallic Cartridges . . .

Rifle dies usually come in sets of two. The first deprimes and resizes. The second die seats the bullet and in some types also crimps the case mouth into the cannelure ring in the bullet. An example of this is the 30-30 Winchester. This cartridge is usually carried in a tubular magazine so that pressure is constantly exerted against the nose of the bullet. As a result, the bullet must be solidly crimped to keep it from pushing back into the case. Recoil can also cause the bullet to be pushed back into the case in some instances.

There are also handgun dies in sets of two that work the same as rifle dies. The seater die of these sets is invariably a crimping die also. Nowadays, for improved load quality, many handgun die sets consist of 3 or 4 dies. In these the first die simply resizes the case. The second die deprimes and expands (bells) the mouth of the case. The third die seats and crimps the bullet. In the four-die set the third die merely seats the bullet and the fourth die crimps the case mouth into the bullet. For the best and most accurate ammunition, it is always advisable to seat the bullet in one operation, then crimp the bullet in a second operation.

For the man who reloads thousands of cases a year, a sizing die with a carbide insert is the type he needs. This ring of extremely hard tungsten carbide will resize a half-million cases before any wear shows! Ordinary steel dies won't, generally, process a third this many. Furthermore, cases don't have to be cleaned when using carbide dies. Dirty cases won't scratch these dies nor will the dies scratch the cases. Instead, the cases come out highly polished.

Some manufacturers offer presses that will use only their dies. When buying replacement dies always be certain that you specify the press in which the dies are to be used. Lyman and SAECO were two firms that offered special-size dies in the past.

Some dies are chrome-plated, some are not. If proper case lubrication is used there is little difference between the life of these two types of dies.

Bonanza Bench Rest

Bonanza Blue Ribbon

Bonanza Pistol Dies

BONANZA "Blue Ribbon" Carbide Pistol Dies

Made of the finest tungsten carbide, machined to exacting tolerances, with a polished mirror finish, these dies will give years of service.

Carbide sizer only, 38/357, 44 Spcl./44 Mag., 45ACP, 32 S&W Long . . . **$31.90**

Sizer only, 9mm Luger, 30 Carbine **$36.50**

Carbide 3-die sets, 38/357, 44 Spcl./44 Mag., 45 ACP, 32 S&W Long **$49.95**

As above, 9mm Luger, 30 Carbine **$54.55**

BONANZA Pistol Dies

Bonanza Pistol Dies are 3-die sets made of hardened and polished steel. The first die is for sizing, second is the expander and the third is for seating the bullets. The seater crimps the bullet (except cartridges for auto pistols) and seats it to a pre-determined depth. The 38 Spec./357 Mag. and 44 Spec./44 Mag. dies can be used to load two calibers. Special taper crimp die is available for 45 ACP, 38 and 357.

3-die set **$25.98**
Taper crimp die **$12.65**

BONANZA Co-Ax Bench Rest Dies

Case is supported full length in seating die. Inner sleeve holds case and bullet concentric, while outer sleeve seats bullet. Coaxial design simulates hand-seater efficiency but functions in a press. Seating die is not hardened and does not crimp. Sizing die same as Co-Ax Die. Usable in most presses, these dies are available in 52 popular calibers . **$31.15**

Bonanza Co-Ax

Hollywood

Lyman AA Dies

C-H
2-Die Rifle Set

Made of chrome-plated steel with a super-hard finish, C-H dies are available for all popular cartridges. They fit all tools having a ⅞-14 thread......... **$21.50**
3-die rifle set (includes the C-H neck sizing die) **$27.00**

BONANZA
Co-Ax Dies

Made of hardened and polished steel. Expander button is located high on the decapping stem, thus it expands the neck while the latter is still partly in the sizing position. Much less effort is needed, another feature. Seating die features optional crimp. All dies ⅞-14 with split locking ring. Available for most popular rifle calibers **$24.85**

C-H
Taper Crimp Die

Each die is precision honed, hardened and polished to a mirror finish on the inside; the outside has a non-glare satin finish. The taper crimp die allows a uniform tapered crimp, especially useful for autoloaders that headspace off the case mouth. Available in 38/357, 9mm Luger, 45 ACP, 30 Carbine **$11.00**

C-H
3-Die Pistol Set

3-die pistol sets eliminate many of the problems resulting from non-uniform cases or instances of varying wall thickness. These sets are available for all straight walled pistol cases. All C-H dies are made of steel, heat treated and satin finished **$21.50**

HART
Sizing Die

Made of hardened steel, this die for the precision loader/shooter, is of the drive-in/drive-out type and is available in 222 Rem., 222 Mag., 6×47, 308, 25-06 and 6mm Rem. The knock-out rod decaps the case at the same time **$46.00**

HART
Bullet Seater

Designed with the precision handloader/shooter in mind, this straight line bullet seater is adjustable for depth and is available for 222 Rem., 222 Magnum, 6×47, 308, 25-06 and 6mm Rem. The body, base and head are all made of stainless steel. **$34.95**

HOLLYWOOD
2-Die Sets

Precision made and finished. Standard ⅞-14 thread. Seating dies are hardened like the sizing dies, important when loading crimped shells, as the crimping section of the die receives the most wear. Lock rings are 1½" in diameter. . **$25.00**
Special dies (1½" threads to fit Hollywood Senior and Turret tools) made for such loads as 50-cal. MG, 416 Rigby, 500 Jeffery, 505 Gibbs, 577, 600 Nitro Express, etc. .... **$58.00** to **$80.00**
Special shell holders are available (specify caliber) **$10.00**

HOLLYWOOD
CENTURY
Tungsten Carbide
Dies

Made in most calibers. Standard thread body. All are made to SAAMI specs, but special dies can be ordered. T-C dies for the Star and Ammoload reloading tools are available.
Sizer die only **$29.00**
Die sets **$45.00**
Die sets with full length sizer in T-C:
9mm Luger **$55.00**
30 Carbine **$63.00**
44 Auto Mag **$114.00**

LYMAN T-C Pistol Die

Tungsten carbide resizing and decapping die for 38 S&W (fits 38 ACP and 38 Super); 38 Spl. (fits 357 Mag.); 41 Mag.; 44 Spl. (fits 44 Mag.); 45 ACP, 45 Colt.
Price **$31.50**

Lyman AA Dies

A standard 2-die set for loading jacketed bullets in bottlenecked rifle cases. Available for most calibers. A 3-die set is available for straight-wall cases for loading both cast and jacketed bullets.
3-die Multi-Deluxe pistol set (includes Tungsten Carbide sizer, 2-step neck expander and seater). **$46.95**
Standard 2-die rifle set **$24.50**
Standard 3-die rifle set, from . **$25.50**
Standard 3-die pistol set, from **$25.50**
Two-step "M" neck expanding die for cast rifle bullets............. **$10.95**

Ponsness-Warren CAL-Die

Pacific Durachrome

LYMAN AA
Bench Rest Dies

A precision made and finished 2-die set that has a neck-size-only die and a micrometer-head adjustable seating die for precise seating depth and alignment. The head gives .001″ click adjustments, .025″ per rotation. Seats with or without crimping. Available for 14 varmint and target calibers.

Complete set $49.95
Micrometer Seating Die only . $39.95
Neck Sizing Die only $16.50

Lyman Bench Rest

LYMAN AA
Taper Crimp Dies

This die applies the proper taper crimp to auto pistol cases. Available for 38 Super Auto, 380 ACP, 9mm Luger, 45 ACP $11.95

LYMAN
Small Base Dies

This 2-die set is for loading jacketed bullets when the finished cartridge should be sized to minimum dimensions, especially in auto, pump, and lever actions. Available for 223, 243, 270, 30-06, or 308. . . . . $24.50

LYMAN
Die Adaptor

This threaded steel adaptor is used to mount smaller diameter 310 and obsolete Tru-Line dies to modern ⅞-14 presses $2.00

LYMAN Ideal Dies

For #310 tong tool, either rifle or handgun. Neck sizes only, 6-piece set. Available for all popular calibers. Usable in ⅞-14 threaded presses with adaptor.
Price $27.50

PACIFIC
Durachrome Dies

Guaranteed for life. Heavy duty solid steel spindles with collet-type hex nuts to insure accurate alignment. Standard ⅞-14 thread with steel lock rings. Adjustable crimper. Chrome plated finish. Cavities are polished after heat treating. Packed in plastic compartmented box with sizing lube and spare decapping pin.
2-die rifle set . . . . . . $24.50 to $28.00
3-die pistol set . . . . . $25.50 to $28.00
3-die set with carbide sizer . . . $44.95
Carbide pistol sizing die only . $31.95

PONSNESS/
WARREN
CAL-die Bullet
Seater

Designed for the P/W Metallic M-II loader, the CAL-die requires only one die body for all bullet diameters from .224″ to .358″. To change calibers, only a different bullet retaining sleeve is required, which slips easily into the die body. The retaining sleeve holds the bullet until the case is pushed into the die and seated. The bullet is simply dropped through the side port of the die body.

The CAL-die comes with a large bullet seating pin for 30-cal. and larger, a small pin for under 30-cal., and a .308″ bullet retaining sleeve. Die body is threaded ⅞-14. Bullet retaining sleeve diameters offered: .224″, .243″, .257″, .264″, .270″, .284″, .308″, .32″, .338″, .358″.
CAL-die (with 308 sleeve) $33.00
Additional retaining sleeves . . . $6.50

RCBS
Case Forming Dies

RCBS has long produced dies for forming hard-to-get cases from available brass. Prices vary, depending on the job to be done and the number of dies required. Making 22-250 cases from 30-06 brass, for instance, requires 4 dies, a reamer and an expander. Dies not cataloged will be furnished on special order.

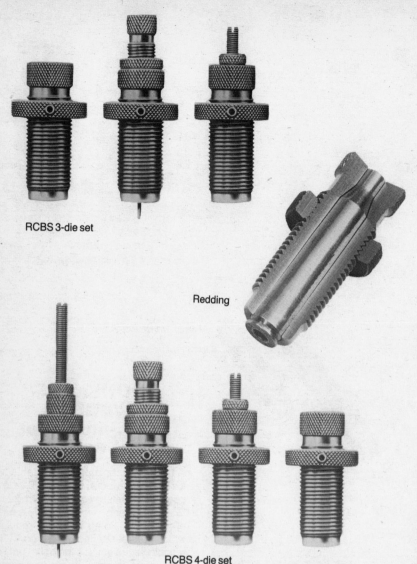

RCBS 3-die set

Redding

RCBS 4-die set

Redding #10 set

REDDING
Combination Dies

These special die sets are provided for the shooter who wants the convenience of one die set to load more than one caliber. Available in 38 Spl./357 Mag. and 44 Spl./44 Mag. Other calibers on request $29.50

REDDING
Form & Trim Dies

The Redding file trim dies are different from others. The internal dimensions are to chamber size and, therefore, do not full length resize the brass unnecessarily. Those accuracy buffs and varmint shooters who neck size their brass only will find this feature a great advantage. For case forming, these dies perform the perfect intermediate step before final sizing in the proper full-length sizing die.

Most calibers $12.95
Specials $18.00

RCBS
Competition Dies

Designed with the competition shooter in mind. The sizing die has a hardened ball that is mounted further up on the decapping rod for easier neck expansion. Seater die is fitted with micrometer head with click adjustments in .001" increments. Die also has a "window" with sliding guide for correct bullet alignment before and during seating. Both dies are made to extremely close tolerances and are finished in black oxide with white numerals. When necessary an extended shell holder is included for shorter rounds. Each die set comes with a set-screw wrench, hexagonal lock rings, and packed in a fitted hardwood box. Available for: 222, 223, 22-250, 243, 270, 7mm-08, 7mm Rem. Mag., 30-06, 308. . . . . $52.00

RCBS
2-, 3-, 4-Die Sets

RCBS dies are manufactured to close tolerances on turret lathes (not on screw machines) and hand polished before and after heat treating. Threaded 7/8-14. Decapping stems in calibers above 264 (6.5mm) are heavy-duty type. Seating dies have a built-in crimper which can be used at the operator's discretion. Special dies are available for semi-automatic rifles which require minimum-dimension cartridges for reliable functioning.

Four types of die sets are available: standard 2-die for bottle-neck rifle and handgun calibers, 3- and 4-die for handgun calibers, and a somewhat different 3-die set for straight-side rifle calibers, such as the old black powder numbers. . . . . $25.00 to $49.95

3-die set with RCBS tungsten carbide sizer. $49.95

REDDING
Model #10 Die Sets

Made from alloy steels, heat treated and hand polished. All Redding dies are lifetime guaranteed and use no aluminum or plating. Standard 7/8-14 thread. Available in 2- or 3-die rifle sets, 3- or 4-die pistol sets with taper crimp.

Series A $24.50
Series B $29.50
Series C $34.50

Neck sizing dies are available in most bottleneck calibers. Prices will vary from $16.50 to $19.50 for the neck die only. Sets are from $24.50 with standard seater to $44.00 with the new straight line benchrest seating die.

Custom-made dies available on special order. Priced from $29.00 to $48.00.

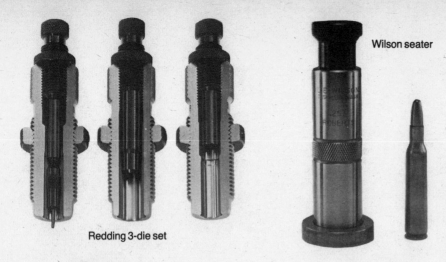

Wilson seater

Redding 3-die set

Wilson sizer

Redding Titanium

WEATHERBY "Universal" Loading Dies

Bullet is introduced into the sliding bullet guide in the cut-away at the side of the die. This insures alignment of the bullet and cartridge case during the bullet seating operation. Visual observation also simplifies bullet seating to the proper depth. ⅞-14 thread.

3-piece set (includes neck sizing sleeve) in 270, 30-06 and all Weatherby Magnum cals. except 224, 378 and 460.......................**$46.95**

2-piece set, in 270, 30-06 and all Weatherby cals **$42.95**

To neck size, a neck sizing sleeve is inserted into the bullet seating die. Not available for 224, 378 or 460 Weatherby Magnum **$11.25**

Extra seating inserts, Weatherby calibers **$6.75**

Universal bullet seating die, complete.......................**$21.50**

REDDING Straight Line Benchrest Seater Die

These dies are made exactly like benchrest seating dies, but can be used in most conventional presses (⅞-14 threaded body). The case is fully supported in the chamber section of the die before the bullet is seated, assuring concentric bullet seating. There are no internal sliding parts to add to concentricity problems. Available in most benchrest and popular varmint calibers.... **$32.00**

REDDING Titanium Carbide Pistol Dies

Titanium carbide has the highest hardness of any readily available carbides, yet is not brittle. The smooth micrograins present a slippery, non-galling surface not attainable with other carbides. Available in most popular handgun calibers.

Sizing die only.............**$45.00**
Complete set **$59.00**

TEXAN Micro-Bore Dies

Precision bored special alloy steel dies are hardened and lapped and Armoloy coated for longer wear and better performance. Double hex-nut permits die adjustment to be secured with wrench. Standard ⅞-14 thread to fit most presses. Available as 2-die rifle and 3-die pistol sets for most calibers..... **$28.95**

REDDING Taper Crimp Dies

Made to the same high standards as all other Redding dies, then carefully heat treated and hand polished.

Taper Crimp dies are available in most popular handgun calibers for those who prefer the uniformity of a tapered crimp to the conventional roll crimp. It is especially useful for those autoloaders that headspace off the end of the case. Standard ⅞-14 thread fits most presses.

Most calibers **$12.95**
Specials **$18.00**

WILSON Straight Line Full Length Resizing Dies

These dies place no strain on case rim, and correct headspace is assured at all times.

As regularly furnished, dies are adjusted to produce a resized case correct for rifles of normal headspace. A die for a rifle having less or more than normal headspace can be made ($3.00 extra) if the customer will mail in several fired cases from his rifle.

Available in all popular calibers, including wildcats **$13.75**

WILSON Chamber Type Bullet Seaters

The case is aligned and supported by the chamber section from start to finish of seating, while the bullet is aligned and seated by the close-fitting plunger in the bore section. With this chamber type seater, the case is all the way "home" before any movement of the bullet takes place.

Seaters are available in all popular calibers **$27.50**

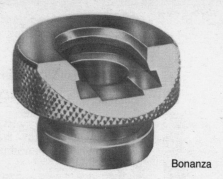

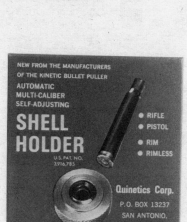

Quinetics

Bonanza

Hollywood

RCBS

Shell Holders and Rams*

Make	Holder C	Holder H	Ram C	Ram H	Tools Fitted	Notes	Holder C	Holder H	Ram C	Ram H
Bonanza	x		x		Most C	Snap-in action.	$ 4.00			
C-H	x	x	x	x	Most H & C	Held by spring clip, relieved for primer clearance. Floating shell holder action.	4.00	$ 4.00	$ 5.25	$5.25
Hollywood	Special				H'wood only	Order by caliber. Fit H'wood turret and standard presses. Same as C-H.		7.00 to 10.00		
Lyman	x	x	x	x	See notes	Solid H type (J) fits Lyman Turret and Tru-Line; C-type fits Spartan, Spar-T, Pacific, etc.	4.50		6.95	
McLean	Special				Most all	Universal cartridge holder.	8.00			
Pacific	x		x		Most C types	One-piece holder/ram also available for C tools, $5.75.	4.50			
Quinetics	x	x			Most all	Universal cartridge holder.	12.75			
RCBS	x	x	x	x	Most H & C	Heavy duty style for bullet making, A2 or C press, $4.50. Special ram required for A2, $3.60. Head extension for all rams, $3.00.	4.40	4.40	8.50	8.50
Redding	x		x		Most C types	Snap-in spring action holder. Ram price includes upper and lower links.	4.75		21.50	
Texan	x	x	x	x	Most H & C	Universal cartridge holder.	5.00	5.00	9.00	9.00

*All holders are detachable-head type except as mentioned in notes.

Notes on Powder Scales...

Powder scales are probably the single most important tool in the handloader's kit. So many cartriges are today loaded to near-maximum that it is important to know precisely what the powder charge is. A few grains over may cause severe damage to the firearm and to the shooter.

Powder scales vary greatly in both price and quality. Generally, you get what you pay for, but some quite inexpensive models do an adequate job. The critical parts of a scale are the knife edges and the bearing surfaces that these knife edges rest upon. They must be hardened and ground correctly, then polished. Keep them clean and free of rust, but don't use an ordinary oil. A siliconized fluid will work fine, in most cases.

It's always a good idea to keep the scale covered when it's not being used to minimize dirt and dust accumulation. Many manufacturers sell dust covers made especially for their scales.

Powder scales that have graduated beams with sliding adjustments must have these beams properly machined, calibrated and checked, otherwise incorrect readings will result. Notches should be deep enough that the sliding weights will not easily be moved by accident.

Precision weights are available so that any scale can be checked to make certain the marked weights are correct. Once this zero is known, the scales may be used with complete confidence. Many scales have one or more built-in levels and/or leveling screws. Most scales must be level or they won't give the correct reading.

BONANZA "Blue Ribbon" Scale

This new scale has 511 grain capacity and three poises for better accuracy. Diamond polished agate "V" bearings. Base is moulded from Cycolac, beam and pan from Lexan. Base has 3-point suspension with wide-stance auxiliary leg. The minimum weight poise is located near the beam pointer so that the eyes need not be shifted during final adjustments. Center poise measurement is 10 grains; right poise 1 grain; left poise 1/10 grain. Beam is dampened in three seconds. Guaranteed accurate to 1/10-grain; sensitivity to 1/20-grain **$42.95**
Metric model **$46.95**

Bonanza "Blue Ribbon"

BONANZA Model C

This scale features a beam of "Marlon-Lexan," a nonconductive, non-magnetic material, allowing the beam to be free from static electricity. Scale is accurate to 1/10 grain and sensitivity is guaranteed to 1/20 grain with a capacity of 330 grains. For weighing both powder and bullets. This scale does not have an oil or magnetic damping device. Has a leveling screw for convenient zeroing. Price, complete **$28.60**

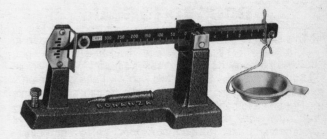
Bonanza Model M

BONANZA Model M

Scale has a big 505 grain capacity for weighing powder, shot and bullets. Ounces to grains conversion scale cast into the base. Tempered stainless steel poise. The agate "V" bearings minimize friction for more accurate readings. Beam and pan are made from "Lexan" while base is moulded from Cycolac. Three point suspension, guaranteed accurate to 1/10-grain. Magnetically damped for quick, true readings **$35.85**

C-H Powder and Bullet Scale

This scale features a chrome plated brass beam, graduated in 10 grain and 1/10-grain increments. The pan has a convenient pouring spout and there is a leveling screw on the base. All metal construction. Scale has a maximum capacity of 360 grains **$33.95**

Bonanza Model C

LYMAN D-7

This scale has a large 505 grain capacity with a white beam marked in black. Magnetically damped for fast readings. Unique beam lifter assures less wear and tear on the beam when the scale is not in use. Precision ground knife edge agate bearings. Accuracy to within 1/10 grain. **$42.95**

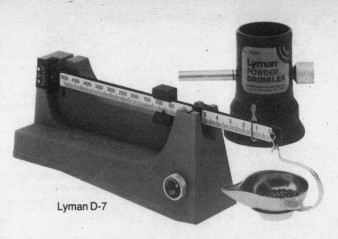

Lyman D-7

PACIFIC Deluxe Powder Scale

A single beam balance with three counterpoises and built-in oil reservoir for damping if desired. A 1/10-grain over-under scale is fitted at the pointer end of the beam to simplify sorting bullets, etc. Capacity, 500 grains. Adjustable leg for leveling. Magnetic damping system **$42.00**

RCBS 5-0-5 Scale

This scale features a three poise system. Calibrations on the left side of the beam are in full 10 grain increments with widely spaced deep beam notches. Two small poises on the right side of the beam adjust from 0.1 to 10 grains. Scale is magnetically damped; self-aligning agate bearings support the hardened steel beam pivots with a guaranteed sensitivity of 1/10 grain. Maximum capacity is 511 grains and the scale has an improved leveling leg for perfect zero **$39.90**
Vinyl dust cover **$3.50**

Pacific Deluxe

RCBS 10-10 Scale

This scale features a micrometer poise and approach to weight system for accuracy and speed. An attachment weight, stored in the leveling screw, increases capacity to 1010 grains. Pan is anti-tip design. Sensitivity is 1/10 grain. Left side of beam is graduated in 10 grain increments, while the right side consists of 1 grain increments. The micrometer poise, which can be locked into place, divides these into 10ths. Approach to weight system alerts user to beam movement before the pointer reaches zero, thus preventing overloading. When not in use, all components can be stored in the die cast base. A hard plastic dust cover is included. An ounce to grain conversion chart for shotgun reloaders is affixed to the scale. **$67.20**

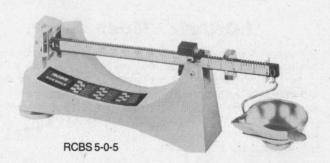

RCBS 5-0-5

RCBS 5-10 Powder Scale

This 510-grain capacity scale features both a micrometer poise (1/10-grain to 10 grains) and approach to weight system for speed and accuracy. When the attachment weight is added to the beam, the capacity increases to 1,010 grains. Die cast base holds the scale components and converts into a dust proof carrying case. Anti-tip pan and large leveling leg. Magnetically damped and utilizes self-aligning agate bearings **$56.70**
With metric reading scale **$64.90**
Vinyl dust cover **$3.50**

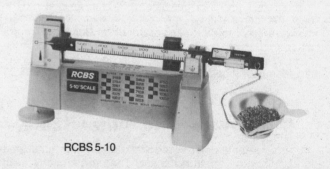

RCBS 5-10

RCBS 304

RCBS 304 Dial-O-Grain

A laboratory quality scale designed for the serious reloader. Scale has a 1,110 grain capacity and its features include hardened steel knives and polished agate bearings, magnetic damping, oversized pan, extra-stable die cast base, and powder trickler. As in fine laboratory instruments, the dial is engraved with easy to read increment values from $\frac{1}{10}$ grain to 10 grains **$166.50**

REDDING Standard No. RS-1

Gunmetal Blue-black beam is clearly graduated, has a total capacity of 380 grains. $\frac{1}{10}$-grain over-under scale allows checking of variations without re-adjustment of counterpoises.

Self-aligning bearings hardened and honed to eliminate rubbing and side friction, built-in leveling screw. Guaranteed accurate to less than $\frac{1}{10}$-grain **$32.95**

Redding No. 2

REDDING No. 2
Master Powder Scale

Guaranteed accurate to less than $\frac{1}{10}$-grain, scale has magnetic damping for fast readings. Over/under scale permits checking charge variations without moving counterpoises. Capacity is 505 grains. Blue-black beam with white graduations. Pour spout pan, stable cast base and large convenient leveling screw. Scale has hardened and honed self-aligning beam bearings for lifetime accuracy **$42.00**

TEXAN No. 304

The beam of this scale, graduated to read from $\frac{1}{10}$ to 500 grains, has hardened knife-edge fulcrum points, permanent counterpoises and is magnetically damped. The large-capacity pan has a spout which permits pouring powder into cases without using a funnel. Price complete **$34.95**

Texan 304

WEBSTER Model MB-5

This magnetic dampened scale has a capacity of 510 grains in divisions of $\frac{1}{10}$-grain. The aluminum alloy beam has large, deep notches with white numbers for easy relading and three permanently attached weights. The large weight on the inside is graduated to 10 grains per notch; outside weight is for $\frac{1}{10}$-grain and 1 grain. Aluminum frame and parts **$35.50**

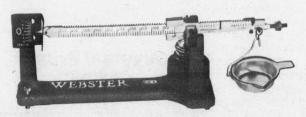

Webster RW-5

WEBSTER Model RW-5

Has 510-grain capacity in divisions of $\frac{1}{10}$-grain, three permanently attached weights, each having a graduated and notched portion of the beam.

Aluminum alloy beam has large, deep notches which retain the weights at their proper setting with reasonable care when weighing. Should a weight jump a notch it is much more quickly detected. This model is oil dampened with a removeable oil bottle and comes complete with oil **$35.50**

Notes on Priming and Priming Tools...

Often great care is exercised in selecting uniform cases and weighing charges and bullets, but priming is done by many without much thought. Yet uniform seating of primers is essential for best accuracy. Poor alignment with the pocket can result in the pellet of priming compound being cracked as the primer is forced into place. Excessive seating pressure can produce the same result. Variation in seating depth can induce ignition and velocity errors that result in less accuracy.

All these factors can be controlled if one takes the time to do so. Priming as a separate step after resizing allows more attention to the "feel" of the primer going into the pocket. Cases in which primers enter with too much or too little pressure can then be segregated and used for plinking or other not-so-important shooting. The heavy, powerful linkages on many presses prevent one from sensitively feeling the primer enter its pocket. Use of separate priming tools, such as the Hart, Lee, RCBS, or Bonanza, is desirable for that reason.

Many priming arms and punches are said to be adjustable for seating depth. In a sense they are, but the case is supported by the front face of its rim during priming. This means that seating depth will vary as much from case to case as does the rim thickness. In rimmed cases, this dimension will vary as much as .006" to .008", and even more in some rimless and belted cartridges. Unless primer seating depth is controlled by the rear face of the case head, adjustment of the priming punch itself really doesn't accomplish much toward uniformity. A case with a thin rim will usually have a shallowly seated primer, while a thick rim will produce a deeply seated one.

We now have a sensitive priming tool that locks the case firmly, allowing uniform primer seating if primer pockets are of equal depth.

Bonanza "Blue Ribbon"

Bonanza Co-Ax

BONANZA "Blue Ribbon" Co-Ax Primer Seater

This newly-designed automatic primer seater has its own built-in primer flipper and loading tray. Primers are seated flat and coaxially with the cartridge case. Primer tube hold 40 primers. Tool's jaws grip the case extractor groove with zero tolerance for precise primer sealing. Jaws will work on most Boxer-primed rifle and pistol cases having a rim thickness of .050" to .072". They will not work on 45 Auto Rim. For large or small primers **$33.45**

BONANZA "Blue Ribbon" Co-Ax Priming Device

A new shellholder for the Co-Ax press is available and is now standard on the Bonanza Co-Ax Automatic Priming Tool. Primers are seated flat and coaxially. To accommodate variables in different brands of cases, the tool jaws are set against the extraction groove with zero tolerance, thereby maintaining perfect concentricity. The jaws will work on most Boxer-primed rifle and pistol cartridges having a rim thickness of .050" to .072". They will not accommodate the 45 Auto Rim.

Price .... **NA**

C-H Auto Primer Feed

This Automatic Primer Feeder will fit all C-HH-type presses with the priming post at the left-hand station. Will not fit the C-H Magnum "H" press. Easy to install and makes primer feeding a snap. For large or small primers **$29.95**
Extra primer stud **$2.65**
Extra primer tube **$3.90**
Extra primer slide **$6.00**

C-H Universal Primer Arms

Furnished with 4 seating punches, springs, etc., everything needed to seat all metallic case primers. For most C-type presses **$3.50**
For Model 444 press **$2.40**

Lee Auto-Prime

MRC Unitized

Lee Improved

Ponsness P-200

LYMAN
Auto Primer Feed

For all current Lyman presses. Does away with individual handling of primers. Comes with tubes for large and small primers.

O-Mag	$12.95
Spar-T	$12.95
Spartan	$12.95

For AA turret press. Push Button primer feed to eliminate handling of primers and increase speed $34.95

EFEMES
Power-Punch
Berdan Primer
Decapper

This tool decaps Berdan-primed brass efficiently—a Boxer primer is detonated *inside* the cartridge case, forcing the spent primer out instantly. Virtually any caliber tool can be furnished. The tool is made of steel and light alloys and comes postpaid, complete with instructions. From Efemes Enterprises...... $23.95

LEE
Auto-Prime

A fast, safe and accurate priming tool that automatically feeds and installs primers as fast as you can place shells in the holder. Thumb pressure allows the reloader to feel primers being seated. Built-in primer flipper turns them right side up. Dump primers in the tray, shake, and replace the cover and it's ready to work. Interchangeable shellholders available for most popular calibers. From Lee Precision, Inc. $11.98
  Shellholders $1.98

MRC
Unitized Priming
Tool

Made of strong flex nylon, this hand-operated tool is made with an integral shell holder. The low cost makes it practical for each caliber to be loaded. Available for most popular calibers. From Mequon Reloading Corp. $5.98

HART
Primer Seater

Intended primarily for the benchrest shooters/reloaders, this tool is a compact, short-lever primer seater that handles both large and small primers through the use of an adaptor. Seating depth is fixed and primers cannot be crushed by this tool. Price complete....................... $70.00

LEE
Improved Priming
Tool

Thumb pressure seats the primer with a "feel." Small enough to be pocketable, yet delivers primer seating qualities sought by precision shooters. Same tool as the Auto-Prime except without the automatic feed. From Lee Precision, Inc............................ $5.98
  Additional shell holders $1.98

PONSNESS/
WARREN
P-200 Primer Feed

Designed for the P/W Metal-Matic straight-wall case loader, this primer feed will fit the ⅞-14 threads of the die head. Handles both large and small primers, and has a shielded tube protector. Fits all existing P-200s........ $38.50

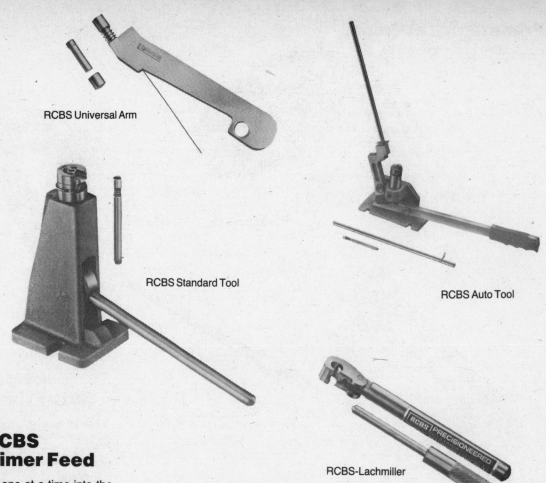

RCBS Universal Arm

RCBS Standard Tool

RCBS Auto Tool

RCBS-Lachmiller

RCBS Auto Primer Feed

Feeds primers one at a time into the sleeve of the primer arm. Designed for use with RCBS Jr press but will work on most C-type presses. Furnished with tubes for both large and small size primers.......................... **$12.25**

RCBS UNIVERSAL Primer Arm

Designed for use with RCBS Jr and most "C" type presses. Interchangeable primer plugs and sleeves fit all sizes of primers **$5.50**
Primer plug and sleeve **$1.90**

RCBS Standard Priming Tool

This low-cost tool is cam operated for sensitive "feel." Tells you when primers are properly seated to the bottom of the pocket. Two Primer Rod assemblies are furnished to handle all American-made Boxer-type primers. Will accept most popular shell holders. Tool attaches to bench with bolts or a C clamp.

Tool, less shell holder **$23.30**

RCBS Auto Priming Tool

The single stage leverage system gives user plenty of "feel" when seating primers. Tool permits a visual check of each primer pocket before seating the primer. Primers are fed through the RCBS automatic primer feed. Primer rod assemblies furnished with tool all use large and small rifle and pistol primers. Tool, less shell holder **$39.60**

RCBS LACHMILLER Berdan Depriming Tool

Handles a wide range of Berdan primed cases, such as the 8mm Rimless, 6.5mm Mannlicher-Schoenauer, and 11.7mm Rimmed. Offers a dry method of removing about 200 Berdan primers per hour. Comes with instructions. Available from RCBS **$22.00**

REDDING Auto Primer Feed

Speeds loading, eliminates handling of primers during sizing operation. Comes complete with tubes for both large and small primers. Capacity is approximately 75 primers.
No. 19 (for No. 7 press) **$12.00**
No. 19T Primer Feed (for Nos. 24 and 25 presses only).............. **$14.00**

REDDING #26 Primer Arm Assembly

Universal design, fits *all* Redding presses. Complete with all necessary parts for proper seating of both large and small primers **$7.00**

Primer Pocket Tools for G.I. Brass

All G.I. brass, even newly manufactured, is made with the primers heavily crimped-in. Because ordinary decapping pins may bend or break under the strain of removing such primers, extra sturdy "punch and base" sets are available from several tool makers.

Because these G.I.-brass tools are fast and handy, many shooters use them in preference to other decapping means. Primer pockets, for one thing, are easily inspected, cleaned or gauged.

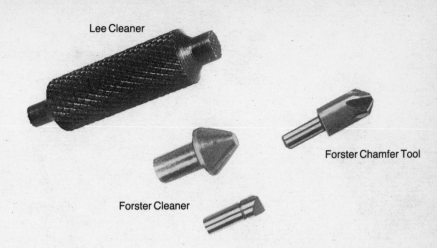

Lee Cleaner

Forster Chamfer Tool

Forster Cleaner

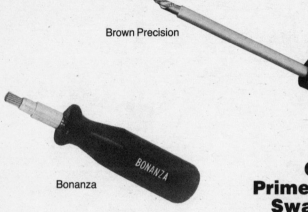

Brown Precision

Bonanza

BONANZA Primer Pocket Cleaner

Suitable for large or small primer pockets, this tool will clean out powder residue with a quick twist. Comes complete with both large and small interchangeable brushes $6.10

BROWN PRECISION Flash Hole Uniformer

A necessary tool for benchrest shooters, it is designed to chamfer the inside flash hole of match cases for round-to-round uniformity. The tool is quick and easy to use. All you need are the tool and fired cases with the spent primer still in place. Simply insert the pointed end through the case neck until it goes into the flash hole, then rotate it until it stops cutting.

Small Flash Hole Uniformer (22-cal. and larger)................... $8.50
Large Uniformer (7mm and up) . $8.50

C-H Primer Pocket Swage Die

Removes the crimp from any military case. Use with any reloading tool and standard shell holder to swage large and small primer pockets. Comes complete for large and small pockets $16.95
Shell holder................. $4.00
Extra swage punch.......... $4.50
Shell holder clip .... $ .40

C-H G.I. Decapper/ Swager

Does good job of decapping and primer pocket swaging of G.I. cases. Two positions; one for decapping and the other for swaging the crimp from the primer pocket. Large primer size only ... $7.00

C-H Primer Pocket Reamer

Quickly and easily removes the crimp from military cases. A slight twist on the top edge of the pocket is all that is necessary. Available in either small or large size (specify). Price, each $4.50

J. DEWEY "Baby Crocogator"

This primer pocket cleaner cleans both large and small pockets by using either end of the tool. The ends are radiused to conform to pocket contours. Small diamond-shaped teeth assure proper cleaning. Made from hardened steel $3.00

FORSTER Primer Pocket Cleaner

A scraper-type tool that mounts on the cutter bar of the Precision Case Trimmer to remove powder residue quickly and easily without removing any metal. Available in .210 or .175 size, with center $5.30
Extra cleaner................ $3.00

FORSTER Chamfering/ Primer Pocket Tool

Will remove most, if not all, of the crimp in military brass, making it easy to seat new primers. Can be used with either Forster case trimmer. Price includes center $11.10
Chamfering tool only $8.80

KUHARSKY BROS. Pedestal Crank

Designed especially for use with the Kuharsky wire brush cleaner, it fastens easily to a bench, taking the place of costly power equipment. Crank only. From Modern Industries $4.95

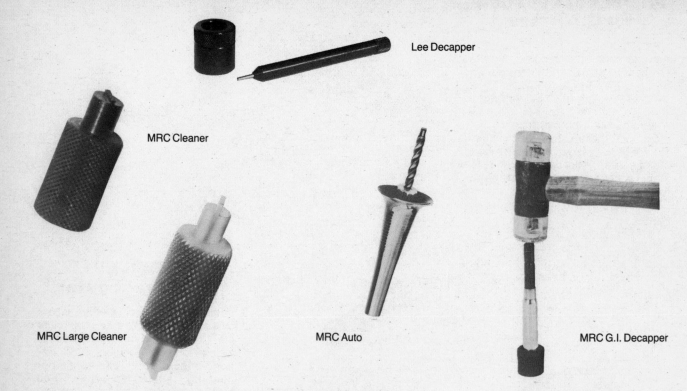

Lee Decapper

MRC Cleaner

MRC Large Cleaner

MRC Auto

MRC G.I. Decapper

KUHARSKY BROS. Primer Pocket Cleaner

Fine steel wire brush scrubs pockets quickly, leaves them clean and bright. For use in any motor or hand driven chuck. Specify large or small primer size. From Modern Industries **$1.50**

LEE Decapper and Base

For removing crimped-in primers from G.I. brass, this tool is guaranteed unbreakable. A simple yet efficient unit that is necessary for working with this type of brass. From Lee Precision, Inc. . . **$2.48**

Lee Primer Pocket Cleaner

Hand held tool for scraping residue from the primer pocket without damaging the pocket or flash hole. Available for either large or small primers. From Lee Precision, Inc. .... **98¢**

LYMAN Primer Pocket Cleaner

Cleans fouling out of the primer pocket bottom with a scraping action. Available in large and small sizes. Wooden handle **$4.95**

LYMAN Primer Pocket Reamer

Hand-held with a wooden handle that removes crimp burr and carbon deposits from G.I. 45, 38 or 30-cal. cases. Specify large or small primer **$6.95**

MRC G.I. Decapper and Base

A two-piece tool used for removing crimped primers from G.I. brass. Carries a two year limited warranty. This basic tool will prevent breaking conventional decapping pins. From Mequon Reloading Corp. **$3.98**

MRC Primer Pocket Cleaner

This small, hand held tool is for scraping residue from the primer pocket without damaging the pocket or flash hole. Available for either large or small primers. From Mequon Reloading Corp. **$1.48**

MRC Automatic Primer Pocket Cleaner

A fast and easy method of cleaning the primer pocket and flash hole without damaging them. One quick push does the job in the same fashion as a "Yankee" screwdriver. Available for large and small primers (specify). From Mequon Reloading Corp. **$3.98**

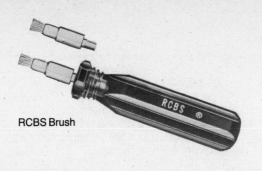

RCBS Brush

RCBS Swager

Pacific Universal

Wilson Reamer

Wilson Punch and Base

PACIFIC
Universal Handle

A new tool for Pacific is their Universal Accessory Handle, made of polished, knurled aluminum and threaded to accept Pacific's case neck brushes, primer pocket cleaners, and primer pocket reamers. Brushes are available in calibers from 17 through 45.

Handle alone. **$1.75**
Handle and primer pocket cleaner brush **$4.75**
Handle and primer pocket reamer tip **$6.50**
Case neck brushes, each **$1.10**

RCBS
Primer Pocket Brush

A twist of this tool thoroughly cleans residue out of primer pockets. Interchangeable stainless steel brushes, for large and small primer pockets. Attaches easily to accessory handle.

Complete, Combo **$7.70**
Brush only, Large or Small **$3.65**

RCBS
Primer Pocket
Swager

Designed for use in presses accepting ⅞-14 dies and removable shell holder heads. Removes the crimp found in G.I. brass; for either large or small primers **$13.25**
A-2 case stripper washer (extra) **$1.10**

WILSON
Primer Pocket
Reamer

Designed for use in the Wilson Case Trimmer, the trimmer acts as a jig for obtaining correct alignment between cartridge case and reamer, and provides firm support during reaming.

By the time the reamer contacts the bottom of the pocket, the outside corner is rounded for easy insertion of the new primer. Since the reamer stops cutting when it hits the bottom of the pocket (no pounding or forcing is used), the flash hole is undamaged and the smooth, neat, properly shaped primer hole insures corrct seating of primers. Case trimmer is not included. Reamer and handle only. **$11.00**
Reaming device complete for most rifle calibers. **$23.25**
Pistol calibers **$23.75**

WILSON
Punch and Base Sets

The punch, an insert with spherical end, is made of SAE 50100 steel heat treated to Rc 60-64 for maximum strength. The case hardened base, recessed at the top to support the case head, is counterbored at the bottom to collect the driven-out primers. Punches and bases available in nearly all popular calibers **$5.00**
Punch only **$3.50**
Base only. **$1.50**

Notes on Chamfering Tools...

A case after trimming often shows a burred or roughened mouth, both inside and out. Chamfering tools remove these burrs and also cone the inside of the mouth, making for easier bullet seating. Many handloaders chamfer the inside of their untrimmed cases for the latter reason.

The tools mentioned here are all of hardened steel, precision ground to give clean cutting without chattering. They are knurled or relieved for easy gripping and most have a center pin to keep the case aligned during outside deburring. All sporting caliber cases can be processed with these tools. For best results, apply only light pressure; these are not designed to shorten cases materially, but to smooth them.

Some tools have tungsten carbide cutting surfaces for lifetime use, accounting for a higher price. However, it's unlikely that the average reloader will ever wear out any of these tools, no matter how inexpensive.

CHAMFERING TOOLS

Bonanza Cricket	$3.10
Forster	$6.50
Lee	$1.98
Lyman	$6.95
Pacific Gun Sight	$6.75
RCBS	$7.75
Texan	$9.75
Wilson (17-45 cal.)	$6.50

Bonanza Cricket

MRC Chamfer Tool

Easy to use hand-held tool used to chamfer the case mouth. Replaceable cutter blades. Comes with one blade. From Mequon Reloading Corp. . . **$3.48**
Replacement blades, each **$1.48**

Lee Chamfer

WILSON Burring Tool

This burring tool is knurled to allow a good grip and has a locator pin that keeps the case in position while the outside is burred. (Other end chamfers the case mouth.) It services cases from 17 to 45 cal. **$6.50**

RCBS Deburring Tool

For beveling and removing burrs from case mouths of new factory cases or newly formed and trimmed cases. To bevel, insert pointed end of tool into case mouth and twist slightly. To remove burrs, place other end of tool over case mouth and twist. Precision machined and hardened. For 17 to 45 calibers **$7.75**

Notes on Case and Die Lubricants...

It is practically impossible to resize fired cases full length without proper lubrication. Some of the smaller handgun calibers may work all right that way, but even there you are courting a stuck case and short die life unless you use carbide dies—these will handle even dirty cases! To do the job properly, the lubricant must have a high film strength under pressure. Ordinary oils and greases do not work well. More than one stuck case has resulted from the use of the family can of oil.

Many commercial sizing lubricants do a fine job. Today, virtually all reloading tool manufacturers offer one under their own trade names at a reasonable price. There are also dry lubes, such as Motor Mica anti-friction compound. Probably oldest in use and still one of the best is common anhydrous lanolin, available from many local drugstores. Green soap also works well, as do most soaps, colored or not!

Whatever lube is used, it must be applied sparingly. Any excess is forced to collect between case and die, and it may form unsightly dents in the case. Harmless unless very large, the dents are a sign of sloppy work.

BONANZA Case Sizing Lube

A high pressure lubricant to adhere to cases when forced into the sizing die. Makes resizing easier and saves equipment. Comes in 2-oz plastic bottle **$1.30**

C-H Die Lube

A liquid designed for lubricating dies and full length case sizing. 2-oz. poly bottle **$1.35**

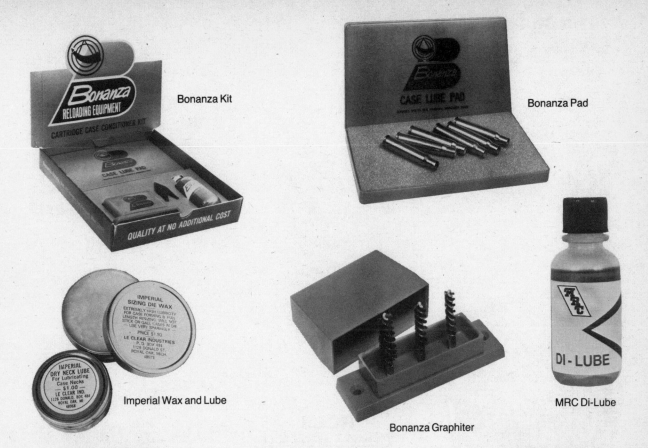

Bonanza Kit

Bonanza Pad

Imperial Wax and Lube

Bonanza Graphiter

MRC Di-Lube

BONANZA
Case Conditioner Kit

Kit contains all the necessary equipment and lubricant to properly lubricate metallic cases before resizing. Contains pad, Bonanza Case Graphiter, Bonanza Case Sizing Lubricant, neck cleaning tool with 22 and 30-cal. brushes, and the Bonanza Cricket combination tool for deburring and cleaning primer pockets. Kit complete **$12.15**

BONANZA
Case Lube Pad

This Bonanza pad applies just the right amount of lube to the cases. Too much lube causes dents and malformations to the cases. A quick roll over the foam pad puts on a thin layer of lubricant . . . **$4.05**

BONANZA
Case Graphiter

Made of impact resistant plastic, this unit has three brushes to lubricate the mouth of any case from 22 to 35 cal. (other brushes 50¢). Cover is supplied to keep graphite in and dust and grit out. **$6.10**

CLENZOIL

Metallic cartridge cases and jackets for swaging may be lubricated with a tiny amount of this formula. Prevents rust and may be used as a superior gun oil also. One pint **$3.25**

HODGDON
Miracle Lube

This is a pure, non-toxic, non-sticky resizing and reforming case lube. Resists oxidation, corrosion and rust, and has a cleaning effect on brass.
2 oz. bottle **$2.50**

IMPERIAL
Sizing Die Wax

This is an extremely high lubricity wax designed to ease case forming and resizing operations. Only a very light coat of wax is needed and one tin will last for several thousand cases. Eliminates puckered or dented shoulders. From LeClear Industries. Price less postage, per 1-oz. tin **$1.75**
Price, per 2-oz. tin **$3.00**

IMPERIAL
Dry Neck Lube

A dry, graphite-like powder of special ingredients that doesn't "pack" like graphite. Dipping the case mouth into the tin lubes the neck without danger of contaminating powder charge. From LeClear Industries. Price, less postage, per 1-oz. tin **$1.35**

LYMAN
Case Lube Kit

A complete kit for efficient case lubrication. Includes Lyman's improved resizing lubricant, a case lubricating pad, and a handle with three interchangeable brushes covering every caliber for inside neck lubrication **$9.95**
Resizing lube only **$1.95**
Lube pad only **$5.95**

MRC
Di-Lube

A dry film lubricant that is applied to the interior of the resizing die. Prevents contamination of the case mouth and eliminates the need to clean cases after resizing. One-ounce bottle. From Mequon Reloading Corp. **$3.48**

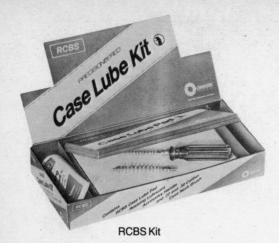

RCBS Kit

RCBS Lube

Redding #12 Kit

Pacific Lube

Redding Lube

RCBS
Case Lube Kit

Contains everything needed for cleaning and lubricating cases inside and out. Includes: RCBS Case Lube Pad, 2-oz. tube of RCBS Resizing Lubricant, and Accessory Handle with interchangeable 22 and 30-cal. case neck brushes **$9.30**

MOTOR MICA
Compound

A clean, white, dry lubricant, long used by industry for deep drawing. A small amount eases resizing, reduces die wear. 1 lb. (postpaid) **$3.55**

RCBS
Resizing Lubricant

Easily applied with the RCBS Case Lube Pad or with the fingers. Comes in 1-oz. tube **$1.25**

REDDING #12
Case Lube Kit

New case lube tongs simplify and speed up lubrication process. They conform to all cases and insure proper case neck lubrication. Includes a 2 oz. bottle of Redding case lube **$7.50**

PACIFIC
Case Sizing Lube

A clean, clear liquid lubricant that stays on the case during the entire sizing operation. 2 oz. plastic bottle **$2.25**

RCBS
Case Lube Pad

For lubricating cases or bullet jackets before sizing or forming. A thin coating of lubricant is applied to the pad and cases are then rolled across it to pick up lubricant **$4.50**

TEXAN
Case Lube Pad

A fast, easy way to lubricate cases and get the right amount of lube for easy operations **$6.95**

PONSNESS-
WARREN S.T.O.S.

A grease-type lubricant recommended for reloading equipment, as a case sizing lubricant, and for use on firearms. Has a tackiness to it which creates a self-coating friction-free surface. A clear, completely safe grease. 2-oz. jars **$3.25**

REDDING
#21 Case Lube

Compounded to eliminate stuck cases and pulled rims. Prolongs life of the dies and makes reforming easier. 2-oz. plastic bottle **$2.50**

TEXAN Die Lube

Specially formulated lubricant to make sizing easier and more efficient. Exacting companion to Texan Micro-Bore dies. 2-oz. bottle **$2.00**

Notes on Case Mouth Trimmers . . .

Repeated firings cause brass to flow forward—more pronounced in some calibers than others—and this excess length must be trimmed periodically. Unless such cases are trimmed, chambering effort may be increased, case mouths may wedge into throats and higher pressures result because of lessened neck clearance.

Case trimmers run from hand-held types for minimum in-the-field brass cutting to "file-type" dies, to miniature lathe-style devices.

Bonanza Co-Ax

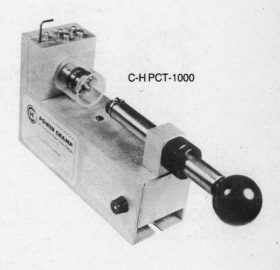

C-H PCT-1000

Bonanza 66

BONANZA Co-Ax Case Trimmer

This new tool from Bonanza has a cutter shaft that rides within a honed bearing for easy turning. Hardened and ground cutter teeth remove excess brass easily. Case locks in a collet holder. An adjustable collar stop is provided on the shaft for proper trim length settings. State calibers desired.

Case trimmer complete with 1 collet, 1 pilot **$30.60**
Trimmer less pilot and collet . **$26.60**
Pilot **$1.40**
Collet **$4.35**
17-cal. shaft **$8.65**
17-cal. pilot **$1.40**

BONANZA "66" Case Trimmer

Using a pilot and mandrel system, this tool trims cases to size without chattering. Four-bladed cutter can be resharpened at the factory. Mandrel for the primer pocket reverses so that all Boxer-primed cases can be trimmed. Two screw holes provided for mounting **$20.75**
Extra pilots (state caliber) **$1.40**
Cutter sharpening (exchange) . **$2.30**

C-H Trim Die

For shortening case neck length, these dies are hardened so they will not be affected by filing or a fine tooth hack saw used in the operation. Available for most popular rifle calibers **$10.00**

C-H Model PCT-1000 Power Case Trimmer

This motorized tool trims and deburrs the outside of the case neck in one operation. It will accept any case length and has a tough tungsten carbide cutter. Easily adjusted for precise trimming. Comes complete with one shell holder and pilot of your choice **$179.00**
Extra shell holders, each **$4.00**
Extra pilots, each **$2.50**

C-H MODEL 301 Case Trimmer

A clamp locks case holder in position, eliminates danger of cutting fingers. Insures uniformity from 22 cal. through 45 cal., either rifle or handgun cases. Price includes one case holder **$21.95**
Extra case holders **$3.50**

Forster DBT Base

Forster Power Trimmer

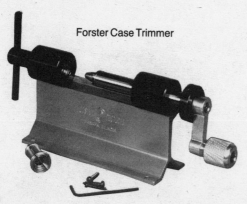

Forster Case Trimmer

Forster DBT Adapter

Forster Neck Reamer

J. DEWEY "Little Shaver"

This is a fully adjustable neck turning tool that will accurately turn cartridges from 17 to 30 caliber with the changing of a properly sized mandrel to fit the case neck. Four fired cases needed when ordering. Case clamp also available for belted magnums. Price, with one mandrel **$27.00**
Case holding clamp **$6.50**
Extra mandrel **$6.50**

FORSTER DBT Adapter Base

Allows you to turn the standard Forster Case Trimmer into a deburring tool holder. The Adapter mounts on the end of the cutter shaft and is used with the Case Trimmer collet housing removed. **$11.00**

FORSTER Power Case Trimmer

Permits use of electric drill press for trimming cases. Accurately lined up by means of a furnished line-up bar. Non-chattering cutter comes with choice of ¼" or ⅜" shank. Price includes one collet and pilot **$29.00**

Check Chart of Forster Collets

Forster collets have three steps and each collet will handle the popular cartridge cases shown in the following tabulation:

#1 COLLET—17, 30-06, 6.5mm 243, 264, 270, 308, 338, 358, 401 & 458 Win.; 250 & 300 Sav.; 222, 222 Mag., 244, 35 & 44 Mag. Rem.; 22 Var.; 22-250, 220 Swift, 22 Lovell; 6mm; 243 RCBS; 257 Roberts; 250-3000; 25 Souper; 25-06; 6.5mm Dutch; 6.5×57 Mauser; 6.5mm Jap; 6.5 Mannlicher; 256 Newton; 270 Gibbs; 250, 270, 300 & 375 Weatherby; 7×57 Mauser; 7mm Gradle; 7mm Ackley; 7mm Mashburn; 7×61 S&H, 7×64; 276; 30 & 35 Newton; 300 & 375 Mag.; 303 British; 32 S&W Long; 8×57 & 8×57 JR; 8×60; 35 Whelen; 375-06; 375 Barnes; 38-40; 395-400; 41 Colt; 44 S&W Spec.; 45 ACP; 45 Long Colt; 450 Watts.

#2 COLLET—22 Hornet; 22K-H, 218 Bee & M-Bee; 219 Zipper & Wasp; 22 Sav.; 22/30-30; 6mm/30-30; 25-20; 25-35; 25 Rem.; 30-30; 30 Rem.; 303 Sav.; 32-20; 7.7mm Jap; 9mm Luger; 38 Colt Super; 41 Rem. Mag.; 45 Long Colt.

#3 COLLET—22 Hornet; 22K Hornet; and Krag case; 30 Carbine; 38 Spec.; 357 Magnum; 35 Win.

In addition, Forster has a special collet to take 33 Win., 348 Win., 38-50, 45-70, 45-90.

FORSTER Neck Reamer

Mounted in the Forster case trimmer, this tool removes excess brass from inside case necks. Available in: 17 (requires 17 cal. cutter shaft), 220, 223, 224, 243, 257, 263, 277, 284, 308, 311, 323, 338, 348, 358, 375, 410, 432, 452, 458, and .239" plus .4275". The staggered teeth cut smoothly, and are ground to .002"-.003" over max. bullet diameter. Give cartridge and caliber **$10.00**

FORSTER Precision Case Trimmer

Hardened and ground cutter shaft has four staggered cutting teeth for smooth, chatterless cutting. Collet holds case without any end movement. All cases cut to same length even if head diameter varies. Stop collar features a fine adjustment screw **$33.50**
Extra pilots (state cal.) **$1.50**
Extra collets (state cal.) **$4.00**
Extra cutters **$8.00**

I.S.W. Neck Turner

Lyman Universal

Lee Improved

MRC Case Trimmer

FORSTER
Outside Neck Turner

The necessary clearance of .002" to .003" cannot be maintained between case and chamber neck when repeated firing thickens brass, or when cases are formed from heavier brass. This tool removes the excess metal from the outside of the necks by passing the neck between a hardened pilot and a carbide cutter. The operation is identical in principle to that of lathe-turning on a mandrel. The process produces very uniform neck thickness. Must be used on the frame of the basic Forster case trimmer. Only a new pilot is needed to change caliber. Available in diameters .224", .243", .257", .263", .277", .284", .308", .311", .323", .333", .338", .358", .375". Price does not include Case Trimmer . **$20.50**
Extra pilots **$3.50**

HART
Neck Turning Tool

This tool is designed to turn the outside of the case neck to any desired wall thickness and depth. The mandrel has an end stop so that all cases are turned to the same length. Requires a mandrel and expansion plug for each caliber from 22 through 30. Tool will hold a wall thickness of .0003". Cutter is high speed steel and mandrels are hardened. Additional handles are required for each individual caliber and are available for most calibers to 30-338 . . . . **$42.50**
Extra handles **$5.95**
Extra mandrel and button **$9.95**

I.S.W.
Case Neck Turner

This hand-operated case neck turning tool comes with a "universal" hand vise and the turner. The cartridge case is held in the vise and inserted into the cutter and rotated. Comes with a pilot of a single diameter but others are available for standard calibers **$35.00**
Extra pilots **$4.00**

LEE
Improved Case
Trimmer

A simple hand tool that automatically trims cases to proper length. Price is complete for one caliber. Shank fits ¼ inch drill chucks. Spins cases for trimming, chamfering and polishing. All operations can be done without removing the shell or stopping the tool. Lee Precision, Inc. **$3.48**
Extra pilot and shell holder to change caliber **$3.48**

LYMAN Universal
Drill Press Trimmer

The universal chuck head bolts to your drill press. By mounting the cutter head and case head pilot to your drill chuck, you can process large quantities of cases accurately. State caliber.. . . . . . . **$34.95**

LYMAN
Universal Case
Trimmer

This simple, yet efficient, trimmer has a chuck head that accepts all metallic rifle or pistol cases, regardless of rim thickness. To change calibers, simply change the inexpensive case head pilot. Cutter has coarse and fine cutting adjustments and rides on an oil impregnated bronze bearing. Cast base can be mounted to bench. Complete trimmer less pilot **$43.95**
Multi-Pak Trimmer (Trimmer with five pilots) **$45.95**
Extra pilots (specify) **$1.95**
Replacement cutter head **$2.50**

MRC
New Case Trimmer

This trimmer is factory adjusted to trim cases to the maximum length. Case mouth is "trued" during trimming, as well as sized. Available for most popular calibers. From Mequon Reloading Corp.
Sizing case holder **$4.98**
Cutter and knockout rod **$3.98**

Marquart

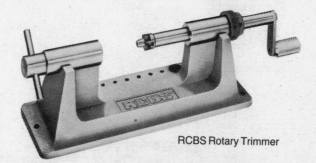

RCBS Rotary Trimmer

Pacific Trimmer

RCBS File Trimmer

MARQUART PRECISION Case Neck Turning Tool

A very compact and precision device for taking a shaving cut on metallic cartridge case necks. The case holder is held in the jaws of a bench vise; a case is inserted and the jaws tightened. The cutter is then pushed onto the arbor and rotated. The cutter is adjustable in the frame to control the depth of the cut. Tool is accurate to within .0001″. Complete tool with one pilot and case holder. **$42.00**

Additional holders. (222 through 378 W. M.) **$7.00**

Additional adjustable pilots (17 through 30 cal.). **$7.00**

PACIFIC Case Trimmer

Uses regular removable shell holder heads instead of collets, and is adjustable for any length case. Also attaches to a ¼″ drill for use as a power trimmer. Extra shell holder heads ($4.50) and pilots ($2.25) are quickly installed **$35.00**

PACIFIC File Trimmer and Case Former

For trimming and case forming. A fine grade file will not scratch the hardened surfaces. Available in most calibers. Fits ⅞-14 presses **$11.95**

RCBS File Type Trimmer

Quickly trims cases to exact length by filing off any portion of the case above the die. Hardened to withstand the roughest use. Standard ⅞″-14 thread. Available in all calibers with over-all case length of 0.875″ or more. Cases measuring shorter than 1.70″ require an extension on shell holder. See RCBS catalog for die group references.

Die group A, B. **$13.50**

RCBS Rotary Case Trimmer

Working just like a lathe, this unit trims a brass case to the desired length—quickly, easily and accurately. Interchangeable quick-release pilots are available for all popular calibers (17 to 45). **$29.70**

Collets **$5.00**

Pilots **$1.65**

RCBS Extension for File Type Case Trimmer

Extension is used to gain the extra length necessary when using the RCBS File Type Case Trimmer for cases with over-all length of 0.875″ to 1.700″. **$5.50**

Redding Master

Sandia "Autotrim"

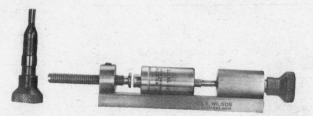

Wilson Neck Reamer

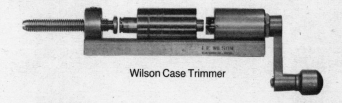

Wilson Case Trimmer

REDDING
Master Case
Trimmer

This unit features a universal collet that accepts *all* rifle and pistol cases. Frame is solid cast iron with storage holes in the base for extra pilots. Both coarse and fine adjustments are provided for case length. Shipped with two pilots (22 and 30 cals.), universal collet, two neck cleaning brushes (22 through 30), and two primer pocket cleaners (large and small).

    Model 1400 . . . . $42.50
    Model 1500 pilots $1.75

SANDIA
Power Adaptor

This unit adapts to a ¼-inch or larger hand drill or directly on a ½-inch motor shaft. It is suitable for inside and outside deburring, and for primer pocket reaming on military cases. It will accommodate most deburring tools and Wilson large or small primer pocket reamers. Enables the user to deburr several thousand cases per hour.

    Power Adaptor $14.95
    With polishing attachment. . . . $17.45

SANDIA
"Autotrim"

This air operated automatic cartridge case trimmer processes 3500-plus cases per hour. Available for 223, 30 Carbine, 308 and 30-06. Tube or hand fed. Has micrometer-type head adjustment for raising or lowering the head. Adjustable speed control. Also available to ream primer pockets.

    Complete for one caliber . $4,860.00
    Additional caliber plates $216.00

WILSON
Inside Neck Reamer

Used with the Wilson case trimmer, and made in popular calibers from 17 to 458. The case trimmer keeps the case correctly aligned while this reamer is run into the neck to remove excess metal, reducing wall thickness. Price, reamer and handle only $12.75
    Complete with trimmer base . $25.00
    Special size reamer (only) made to order $16.00
    Complete reaming device with special reamer. $28.25

WILSON
Universal Case
Trimmer

This simple, rugged tool is one of the oldest trimmers on the market, and it does excellent work. Cases are held by the body, not the rim, producing truly square mouths; needs no pilots. Pistol holders only are hardened. Case holders are available in most popular calibers, will accept more than one caliber where body diameter and taper are similar. Because of slow taper and case expansion, holders for lever action, some bolt and slide action rifle calibers are furnished in 2 sizes—fired and unfired cases (write to Wilson for details). Fired case size will be furnished unless otherwise specified. This trimmer is used as the basis for other Wilson accessories. Instructions and a table of cartridge case lengths accompany each trimmer. For rifle calibers $25.75
    Pistol calibers $26.25
    Extra shellholder; rifle, $3.50; special rifle, $6.00; pistol $4.00

Notes on Powder Measures . . .

The powder measure is a distinct help in speeding up the reloading operation. Throwing loads accurate enough for most hunting purposes, they should not, however, be relied on when loading near-maximum or maximum charges. In any case, the powder measure must always be used in conjunction with an accurate powder scale, using the scale to check the accuracy of the first charge thrown and spot checking subsequent charges as the reloading operation continues. It's a good idea to weigh every tenth charge thrown. An inexpensive set of *gram* weights will check your grain scale for inherent accuracy.

Variations in charges thrown will depend on several factors, among them amount of powder in the hopper, size of powder grains and ability of the operator. Many measures have built-in baffles in the hopper to maintain a more even pressure on the powder going into the charge tube, but even with these it is wise not to let the powder level get too low, causing a decrease in pressure on the powder. In any powder measure there is a slicing action on the powder as it is metered into the charge tube. In cutting the coarser powders the attendant slight jarring of the measure may result in a charge variance of 3 to 4 tenths of a grain. A precise, consistent operator will get less of a variation of powder charges—he will work the handle with the same speed and force, drop the knocker (if measure is so equipped) or gently rap the charge tube to settle the powder down into the metering chamber.

Belding & Mull

Bonanza Bulls-Eye

Bonanza Bench Rest

BELDING & MULL
Visible Powder Measure

The B&M measure feeds powder from the main hopper into a secondary reservoir as needed. Movement of the operating handle then fills the separate charge tube. With this method, powder density in the lower reservoir is near constant; this is believed to aid loading uniformity. **$48.10**

With micrometer charge tube	**$53.30**
Extra charge tubes, standard	**$6.05**
Extra magnum charge tubes	**$7.20**
Micrometer charge tubes	**$11.25**
Micrometer magnum tubes	**$13.25**

BONANZA
"Bulls-Eye" Pistol Powder Measure

Body of this measure is machined from steel. Rotors are machined from hard brass, drilled for charges of Hercules Bullseye Pistol Powder. Large capacity reservoir; contour of the measure will accept all pistol case sizes. Measure may be mounted to the bench and easily removed for operation with a reloading block. Comes complete with attaching bracket and choice of rotor. Also included is a comprehensive table of equivalents of various brands of powders adapted to most popular pistol cartridges. Each rotor number is listed and cross-referenced for the charge thrown. Price, with one rotor. **$27.45**
Extra charge rotors in following grain weights: 2.5, 2.7, 3, 3.5, 4, 4.5, 5.3, 5.5, 6.0, 6.5, 7.0, 7.5, 8.4 (for Hercules Bullseye Powder) **$4.60**
Extra rotor (blank with pilot hole) **$4.60**
Measure stand **$18.50**

BONANZA
Bench Rest Measure

The large plastic hopper may also be used as powder and shot funnel, and the lid is a primer turner. Easily read vernier on handle can be set by pouring a weighed charge into hopper. Adjustable for charges from 2½ grains of Bullseye to 95 grains of 4350. Minimal powder shearing. Hopper is quickly emptied by removing the charge bar. Two drop-tubes are supplied **$38.70**

Long drop tube	**$3.45**
Measure stand	**$18.50**

Hollywood

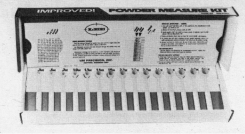

Lee Measure Kit

Lyman #55

Pacific Deluxe

Pacific Pistol

C-H Pushbutton Powder Measure

The same measure used on the C-H Pistol Champ press. Can be used with any conventional single station press or turret-type press. Dispenses powder and bells the case mouth as well. Seventeen different bushings available for over 215 powder/load combinations **$37.50**

As above, without Hollow Expander **$28.50**

Extra bushings **$2.40**

HOLLYWOOD Powder Measure

Adjustable from 2½ grains of Bullseye to 93 grains of 4350. Disc baffle helps assure constant powder pressure on metering chamber. Hard-coated conical bearing surfaces for precise powder cutoff. Threaded ⅞-14 to fit many presses; large lock ring secures measure to tool. Integral thumbscrew bracket for bench mounting. One drop tube (22-270 or 7mm-45) supplied **$70.00**

Extra drop tubes, **$8.00,** special long shotshell drop tube **$8.00**

LEE Powder Measure Kit

Contains 15 individual powder dippers and a slide rule chart listing 69 different powders. These are the simplest of the measuring devices; not recommended for maximum loads. Over 1300 loads listed with the kit. From Lee Precision, Inc. **$4.98**

LYMAN No. 55 Measure

Calibrated slides and micrometer screws offer precise adjustments. Threaded drop tubes (large and small), and integral knocker are included. Stem is threaded for Lyman (and other) press mounting convenience **$48.95**

1-lb. reservoir, extra **$7.95**

Adapter for turret mounting **$2.00**

Measure stand **$12.95**

MRC Powder Measure Kit

This kit contains 13 individual powder dippers and a slide rule chart listing 86 different powders. These are the simplest of the measuring devices; not recommended for maximum loads. Over 1115 loads listed with the kit. From Mequon Reloading Corp. **$5.48**

PACIFIC Pistol Powder Measure

This measure is designed primarily for pistol powders. The charge bar has interchangeable bushings that provide a wide range of charges. Price includes measure stand **$25.00**

Extra bushings **$2.00**

PACIFIC Deluxe Measure

Throws up to 100 grains per charge. All parts are precision finished. Equipped with large capacity powder hopper and micrometer adjusting screw for recording settings. Two plastic drop tubes included (22-30 cal. and 30-45 cal.) Available for either rifle or pistol **$55.00**

Extra drum (rifle or pistol) **$11.00**

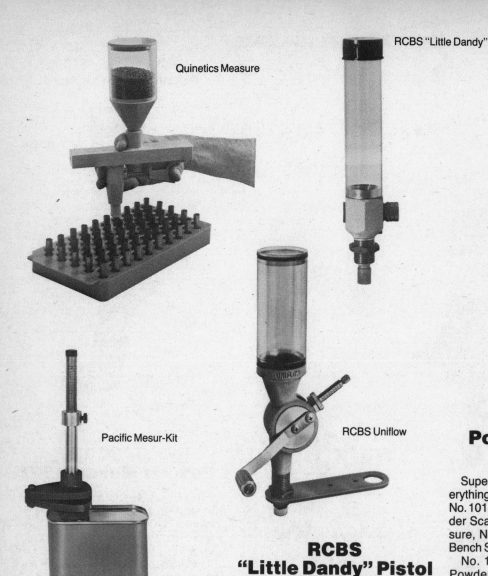

Quinetics Measure

RCBS "Little Dandy"

Redding #3

Pacific Mesur-Kit

RCBS Uniflow

REDDING
Powder Measure Kits

Supercharger powder kit contains everything needed for accurate charges. No. 101 Kit includes: No 1 Standard Powder Scale, No. 3 Master Powder Measure, No. 5 Powder Trickler and No. 6 Bench Stand $98.00
No. 102 Kit contains: No. 2 Master Powder Scale, No. 3 Master Powder Measure, No. 5 Powder Trickler and No. 6 Bench Stand $106.00

PACIFIC
Mesur-Kit

This simple measure screws onto powder can. Adjustable tube has graduations for easy set-up. Springloaded charge arm drops powder instantly—no bridging or clogging problems. Chart to set tube for more than 1000 loads included $13.25

RCBS
"Little Dandy" Pistol Measure

Designed specifically for pistol shooters and small-caliber rifle shooters, this measure is intended to be hand held but can be used with a powder measure stand. With 26 interchangeable, fixed charge powder rotors available you can load most any popular powder and make up any of 250 or more load combinations.
"Little Dandy" measure $22.00
Extra charge rotors, each $4.50

RCBS
Uniflow Measure

Big acrylic hopper. Measuring cylinders are ground and honed, have calibrated screw to record settings. Big cylinder holds to 110 grains of 4350; small one up to 60 grs. 4350 (specify which). Shank has 7/8-14 thread. Stand plate, 2 drop tubes, and 1 cylinder included . . $39.50
With both cylinders $47.50
Stand (extra) $12.95

REDDING
#3 Master Powder Measure

Has a micrometer-type metering chamber with lock screw right in front for easy setting and reading. The micrometer graduations allow the user to repeat exactly the same setting at a later date. Handles charges up to 100 grains and is supplied with a chart for normal settings. Features a large transparent reservoir and see-thru drop tube (22 to 60 cal.). Critical areas are honed for precise fit to avoid jamming of fine powders. No aluminum parts are used.
Model #3 with Universal or pistol chamber $52.00
Model #3K includes both metering chambers $62.00
Model #3-12 Universal or pistol chamber $12.00

QUINETICS
Powder Measure

This adjustable, hand-held powder measure is able to throw charges with a high degree of accuracy. For use with rifle or pistol powders. Special design of the spring-action mechanism eliminates shearing of powder grains. Made of plastic. Complete. $19.95

SAECO
Tru Speed
Pistol Measure

For use with pistol powders from 1.5 gr. Bullseye to 19 gr. of 2400. Screwdriver adjustable. Uses same cast iron body as Micro Setting Powder Measure. Honed to accept ground steel pistol drum. 8″ powder hopper. Drum assembly is available separately and is interchangeable with Micro Setting Powder Measure. Cast iron bench stand available. **$44.50**

Tru Speed drum assembly, with handle **$24.50**
Bench stand **$11.00**

Saeco M-S

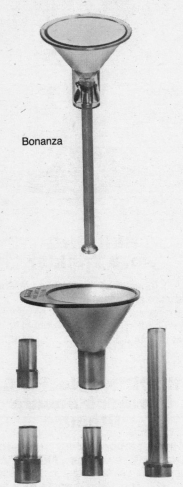
Bonanza

MTM Adapto

MTM
Adapto Powder
Funnel

A unique five-in-one funnel with interchangeable adapter tube to provide an exact fit for all cartridge sizes and to make loading easier. Four different tubes are supplied to fit cartridges ranging from 17 cal. to 45 cal. Eliminates powder build-up around case necks **$2.95**

Notes on
Powder Funnels . . .

A handy, almost indispensable, accessory for the reloader, the powder funnel provides a means of easy transfer of powder from the scale pan. These universal funnels have tapered shell feed tubes that accommodate all cases from the 22's through 45-70.

Bonanza Clear plastic **$2.05**
With long drop tube **$3.45**

Bonanza Powder and shot funnel, large size, clear plastic **$3.50**

C-H Clear, anti-static plastic **$1.50**

Flambeau Anti-static treated to eliminate clinging powder grains. Large flange serves as handle **$1.20**

Fitz Amm-O-Cone—Fluorscent red plastic **$1.50**

Lyman Black opaque plastic **$1.95**

MTM Funnel Kit (Illus.) **$2.39**

MTM Clear, transparent plastic . . **$1.36**

Pacific Aluminum; Spill-proof spout 17-cal., 22-270, 28-45 cals **$2.25**

RCBS Fluorescent green tenite, antistatic treated. Square lips prevent rolling **$1.90**

RCBS 17 Caliber **$1.90**

Redding Anti-static plastic, 22 thru 50 cal. **$1.98**

Texan Bright yellow luminescent plastic in two sizes—264 and under, 270 and over. Each **$1.50**

SAECO
Micro Setting
Powder Measure

Micro setting adjustment for rifle and heavy pistol loads. Will accurately measure 3.0 gr. of Bullseye to 95 gr. of 4350. Cast iron body honed to accept ground steel drum. A heavy duty precision measure. 8″ powder hopper 22 and 30 to 45 drop tubes furnished. Drum assembly is available separately to convert Tru-Speed pistol measure for use with rifle powders **$62.50**
Micro Setting drum assembly . **$39.50**

Redding

Bonanza

MTM

MTM
Benchrest Funnel

Color-coded ABS funnels designed specifically for the benchrest shooter. One fits 222 and 243 cases only, the other 7mm and 308 cases. Both can be used with pharmaceutical vials popular with benchrest shooters for storage of pre-weighed charges **$2.39**

Bonanza

Redding #5

RCBS Trickler

Bonanza "Big Red"

Saeco

BONANZA "Big Red" Trickler

Companion tool for the Bonanza powder and bullet scale, this handy item brings underweight charges up to proper reading by adding a few granules of powder at a time. Two piece construction. Ballast may be added for stability. **$6.10**

BONANZA Powder Measure Stand

This cast aluminum-alloy stand is painted in the familiar Bonanza red wrinkle-finish. Can be bolted to the loading bench or a separate block. Will fit either the Bonanza Bench Rest or Bulls-Eye powder measures **$18.50**

C-H Powder Measure Stand

Stand can be bolted to the bench or secured with "C" clamps. Will accommodate any measure with ⅞-14 threads. It is made at a convenient height for charging cases **$6.95**

C-H Powder Dripper

For use with most scales, a twist of the knob will dispense one kernel at a time to bring charge weights up to specifications. Has an extra large square base to minimize tipping. Base insert furnished allowing ballast to be added for additional stability **$5.25**

LYMAN Powder Dribbler

Allows exactness with a minimum of effort. Features a large reservoir, ideal height and an over-sized base to reduce the chances of tipping **$7.50**

RCBS Powder Measure Stand

Bolted to your loading bench edge or a wooden platform, this stand provides plenty of room for loading block or powder scale. Made of aluminum alloy, in RCBS green, for powder measures with standard ⅞-14 threaded drop-tube **$12.95**

RCBS Powder Trickler

Very useful when weighing charges. Simply set measure to throw an underweight charge, then feed just enough powder to balance the scale with this handy device.................... **$6.75**

REDDING No. 5 Trickler

A companion to the Redding powder measure and scale, this trickler will add the necessary few kernels of powder when loading maximum or highest accuracy ammunition............... **$9.95**

REDDING No. RS-6 Powder Measure Stand

Provides convenient bench-top mounting for the Redding Master Powder Measure or other measures threaded ⅞-14. This stand is *not* threaded—measure is secured with a lock ring allowing the reservoir to be quickly dumped..................... **$13.95**

SAECO Powder Measure Stand

This cast iron bench stand accepts the Saeco Micro Setting powder measure or the Saeco TruSpeed pistol measure. Base is drilled for easy mounting . **$11.00**

Notes on Case Gauges..

Few beginners realize it, but one of the most important tools a reloader can have is an accurate case length gauge. Made in various designs, many of these are simply measuring devices of the Go-No Go type. Their purpose is to tell the reloader if the over-all length of a fired case exceeds the allowable maximum. If it does, it must be trimmed, for chambering a too-long case jams it into the rear of the lands, crimping it on the bullet's ogive and leaving no clearance for expansion on firing—therefore boosting the pressure to dangerous levels.

Some combination gauges, such as the Wilson and Forster, also measure head to shoulder length, thus indicate headspace condition and show whether a case has been altered by a sizing die. All in all, these are very useful and important items, and well worth their cost.

B-Square Thickness Gauge

B-Square Cartridge Spinner

B-Square Bullet Spinner

B-Square Length Gauge

B-SQUARE Case Length Gauge

A precision comparator that will measure cases just as fast as you can slip them under the large, easy-to-read dial indicator. Measures 1.7" to 2.9" lengths without adjustment. Has a lifter to make measuring easier. The heavy base is precision ground. The 2" diameter indicator accurate to .001". Complete with dial indicator **$49.95**
  2.00000 gauge standard **$7.95**

B-SQUARE Cartridge Spinner Gauge

This tool measures either bullet or case neck run-out, relative to case body. An adjustable stop allows any part of the bullet or case neck to be checked. Gauge comes complete with precision .0001" dial indicator **$104.95**
  Without dial indicator **$49.95**

B-SQUARE Case Thickness Gauge

Precision, all machined, with heat treated ground steel arbor. The mar proof hold downs keep the case against the arbor for measuring by the .0001" dial indicator.
  Price, with indicator **$104.95**
  Without dial indicator **$49.95**

B-SQUARE Bullet Spinner Gauge

All machined rigid frame with cup-centers. Centers may be adjusted to check bullet run-out at any location. Tool is furnished with .0001" dial indicator.
  Price, complete **$104.95**
  Without dial indicator **$49.95**

B-SQUARE Ratchet Micrometer

Measures to .0001". Has a positive locking clamp to stay on measurement. Cast iron frame, satin chrome thimble. Spindle and anvil are fully hardened, precision ground and have carbide faces. Comes in fitted case with spanner wrench.
  Range 0" to 1" **$31.00**
  Range 0" to 2" **$37.00**
  Range 2" to 3" **$42.00**

B-SQUARE Gauge Set

This set includes the B-Square Case Thickness, Bullet Spinner, and Cartridge Spinner gauges with one interchangeable indicator. Add $3.00 postage. From B-Square Co. **$199.50**

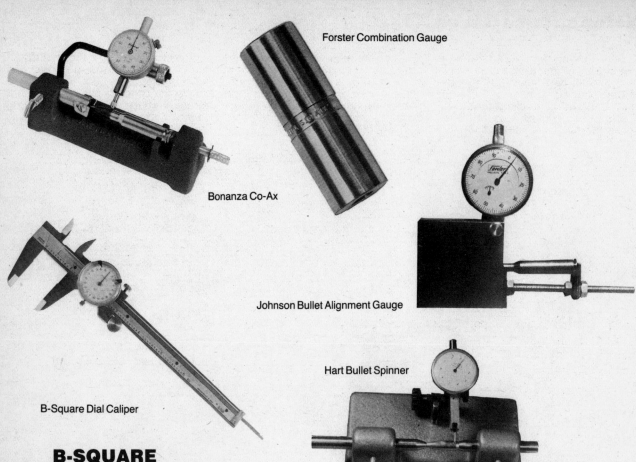

Forster Combination Gauge

Bonanza Co-Ax

Johnson Bullet Alignment Gauge

Hart Bullet Spinner

B-Square Dial Caliper

B-Square Primer Gauge

B-SQUARE
Primer Depth Gauge

Reads to .001″ above or below the case surface. Also, since primers are seated against the bottom of the pocket, a stylus is included for measuring primer pocket depth. Eliminates primer depth variations, case-to-case.
Complete **$49.95**

B-SQUARE
Dial Caliper

Fast, accurate, direct-reading dial caliper made of satin chrome-plated stainless steel. Inside and outside measuring jaws measure to a full 6″, plus 6″ depth gauge. Dial reads directly to .001″ **$69.00**

BONANZA
Co-Ax Indicator

Designed to show the degree of concentricity between case and bullet, this device can show misalignment of .0005″. The cartridge is held against a recessed adjustable rod by a spring loaded plunger; the case head, held in a "V" block, is rotated by finger pressure. Price less dial indicator **$21.35**
Dial indicator only **$31.35**

FORSTER
Combination Case and Headspace Gauge

Measures head to shoulder length (headspace) as well as over- all length. Available in most popular calibers, including many popular wildcats and belted magnums **$9.60**

HART
Bullet Spinner

Designed to reveal runout of as little as .0001″ on bullets, flat-base or boat-tail— from 22 through 30 cal. Heavy base is made of fine-grained cast iron. Price includes precision dial indicator . **$119.75**

JOHNSON
Bullet Alignment Gauge

This gauge accurately measures the alignment (concentricity) of completed cartridges. It is designed to be used with the same dial indicator as used on the Johnson case neck gauge. Price, including precision dial indicator **$59.00**
Price without dial indicator . . . **$24.00**

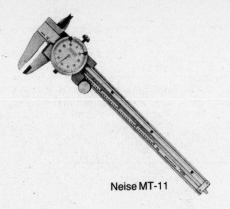

Neise MT-11

Wilson Case Gauge

McKillen & Heyer

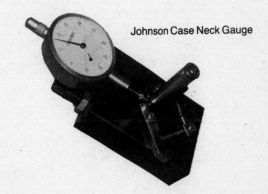

Johnson Case Neck Gauge

JOHNSON
Case-Neck Gauge

Two spring-loaded stabilizer arms press neck tightly against a hardened steel spindle. As case is rotated, dial indicator shows variation of wall thickness to .001" or less. Price, including the precision dial indicator gauge **$64.00**
Without dial indicator. **$29.00**

LOCK'S
Combination Gauge

Two-step gauge to measure maximum case length and over-all cartridge length. Each gauge is cut for a specific caliber and is non-adjustable. Made of ⅛" flat ground steel. Specify cartridge when ordering this gauge **$5.00**

McKILLEN & HEYER
Case Length Gauge

A multiple-case gauge, hard chrome plated, for measuring fired and sized cartridge cases.
Calibers are marked in raised letters for ease of reading. Shows most popular calibers **$6.50**

KARL A. NEISE
MT-11 Caliper

An adjustable dial caliper with a maximum capacity of 6". Indicator is divided into .001" increments with a red dot accurately spotted between each division—each dot showing .0005"— variations to .00025" may be discerned. An ideal tool for measuring jacketed bullets—faster than a mike. 6" caliper **$61.70**
Other sizes available: 8" **$80.65**
12" **$123.00**

RCBS
Dial Caliper
Case Length
Gauge

This dial caliper accurately measures over-all lengths of cases and other things. Includes instructions. Gauge is made of tough, durable plastic. Comes with hard storage case **$19.95**

WILSON
Cartridge Case
Gauge

An invaluable gauge for checking case cone-to-head and over-all length. Each end has both steps milled at one pass for greater accuracy. They are also useful in setting the case trimmer or—it's most important function—in setting up any adjustable resizing die. All popular calibers, including many wildcats **$12.00**
Adjustable Case Gauge for all belted magnums **$16.25**
Case length gauge for cases having no neck and a straight taper **$6.75**

ZENITH
Primer Mike

A dependable micrometer depth gauge that takes all the guess work out of primer seating. Eliminates improperly seated or high primers. Graduated in thousandths of an inch, with primer depth indicated by a plus (high) or minus (low) reading. Compares primer pocket depth case-to-case. **$10.00**

Notes on Bullet Pullers . .

An efficient means of pulling a quantity of bullets from loaded ammunition can often produce quite a saving in one's shooting. Most often, surplus military ammunition is the target for pulling. Bullets can easily be pulled and replaced with hunting types. This practice is ordinarily safe so long as bullets of equal or less weight than the originals are used. If heavier bullets are desired, then powder charges most be reduced or another powder used.

One may also acquire a windfall of cheap or free ammunition which is of no use in its original loading. Pulling the bullets and salvaging the other components can save money.

Most pullers use a simple screw actuated collet to hold the bullet while the case is drawn off it. This type does not mark bullets and is probably the best choice for general use, even though separate collets are required for each caliber. Semi-automatic types are very fast, but do mark or indent the bullet, making them of little use for reloading. For only occasional use the inertia type is the best choice.

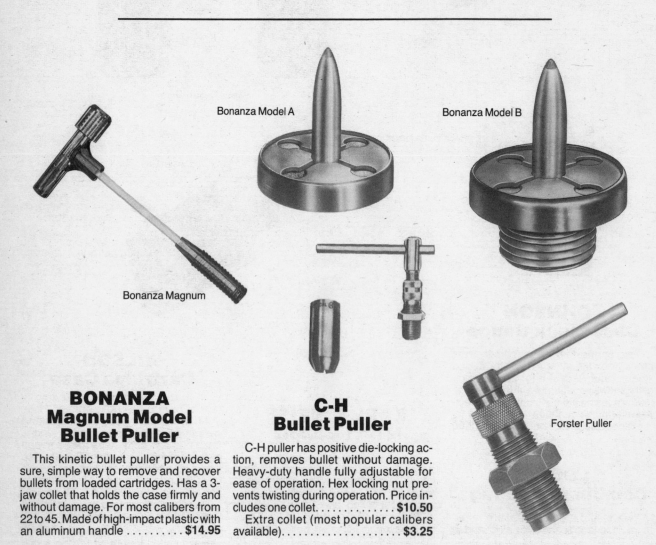

Bonanza Model A

Bonanza Model B

Bonanza Magnum

Forster Puller

BONANZA
Magnum Model
Bullet Puller

This kinetic bullet puller provides a sure, simple way to remove and recover bullets from loaded cartridges. Has a 3-jaw collet that holds the case firmly and without damage. For most calibers from 22 to 45. Made of high-impact plastic with an aluminum handle **$14.95**

C-H
Bullet Puller

C-H puller has positive die-locking action, removes bullet without damage. Heavy-duty handle fully adjustable for ease of operation. Hex locking nut prevents twisting during operation. Price includes one collet. **$10.50**
Extra collet (most popular calibers available). **$3.25**

BONANZA
"A" Bullet Puller

Designed specifically for the Co-Ax press, this tool has flexible jaws which close on the bullet automatically. Bullets do not become egg-shaped and are reusable. Available in 22, 243, 25, 264, 270, 284, 30 and 32 caliber **$3.45**
Model B. Same as Model A, but for use in presses with ⅞-14 threads **$4.60**

FORSTER
Bullet Puller

Has standard ⅞-14 threads to fit most reloading tools. Made of steel throughout and designed to tighten the grip on the bullet as pulling pressure is increased. Collets available for 22, 6mm (243-244), 25, 6.5mm, 270, 7mm (280 Rem.), 30, 303, 8mm (32), 358, 357, 45 ACP. Comes with one collet (specify) . **$11.00**
Extra collets 17, 333, 338, 348, 375, 410, 432 (44 Mag.), 458 . . . . **$4.50**

HOLLYWOOD
Collet
Bullet Puller

Standard collet design exerts even pressure on the bullet, yet doesn't mar the surface. From Whitney Sales.
With one collet **$13.00**
Extra collets, 22-375 cal. **$6.00**
For larger calibers such as 450-50, plus 20mm **$50.00**
Extra collets **$23.00**

Quinetics Magnum Puller

Pacific Bullet Puller

RCBS Puller

Lac-Cum Puller

RCBS Intertia

KEXPLORE
Bullet Puller

This inertia bullet puller removes bullets without distorting cases. Does not damage soft lead bullets or lose any powder. Handles cartridges from the Hornet through the 45-70 and most magnums. *For use with centerfire cartridges only* **$9.95**

LAC-CUM
Bullet Puller

This inexpensive tool is designed to pull bullets using all popular presses—Lyman, Tru-Line, Junior, Pacific, Dunbar, Hollywood, RCBS or any reloading press that lifts the case up through the die holder. It will pull all sporting and military crimped or non-crimped bullets as long as there is any reasonable amount of the cylindrical part of the bullet extending beyond the case neck. Requires only a slight firm grip of the hand. Does not damage or mar the bullets and is available in sizes from 22 through 375 Mag. Comes complete with one collet and wrench...................... **$9.49**
Interchangable collets........ **$3.25**

LYMAN
Intertia Bullet
Puller

Removes bullets from 22 to 45 cal. centerfire cases without damaging case or bullet, even those made of soft lead. This hammer type tool is quick and simple to use and all salvaged components are reusable **$19.95**

PACIFIC
Bullet Puller

This new bullet puller uses a threaded body in conjunction with a threaded handle assembly. The collet drops in from the top and is available in 13 sizes from 17 caliber to 458. After the collet is installed, a handle is inserted into the puller body. As the handle assembly is screwed in, the collet is pushed down over the bullet and locked into place.
Puller body (no collet) **$9.00**
Collets (specify caliber)....... **$4.75**

QUINETICS
Magnum Bullet
Puller

This intertia-type puller features a three-jawed chuck assembly that grips the cartridge quickly and efficiently, allowing speed in operation. User pushes round into the chuck, twist-tightens the cap and raps unit to pull bullet. Handles most cartridges from 22 to 458 Win. Mag., centerfire only **$15.95**

RCBS
Inertia Bullet
Puller

Made of unbreakable plastic with a rugged aluminum handle, this kinetic puller can be used for cartridges from 22 Hornet through 458 Win. Mag. A three-jaw chuck grips the cartridge affording strength and reliability. The hollow head traps components after extraction, leaving case and bullet unmarked... **$17.50**

RCBS
Bullet Puller

Usable in all presses with 7/8-14 thread. Working like a draw-in collet chuck on a lathe, the internally machined collets pull any length bullets quickly and easily without damage to them... **$8.50**
Extra collets **$5.00**

TEXAN
Bullet Puller

Collet design produces even pressure on circumference of bullet, releases bullet promptly when tension is off. Will not mar or scratch bullets. Standard 7/8-14 thread. All popular calibers **$13.95**
Extra collets **$6.00**

Miscellany for Handloaders . .

Gadgets to lure the reloader are numerous indeed! Just about as many, if not more, have appeared and then disappeared. Some of the accessories available are worthwhile, even—to those ammo makers who load in quantity or who are concerned with ultra-precision cartridges—a real necessity. At the other extreme, of course, are items you can well do without, maybe but you will have to decide that for yourself. In between there are small tools of real utility, products which can be helpful to you or not, as your personal needs—or fancied needs— demand.

Further on, in various other divisions, you'll find additional notes.

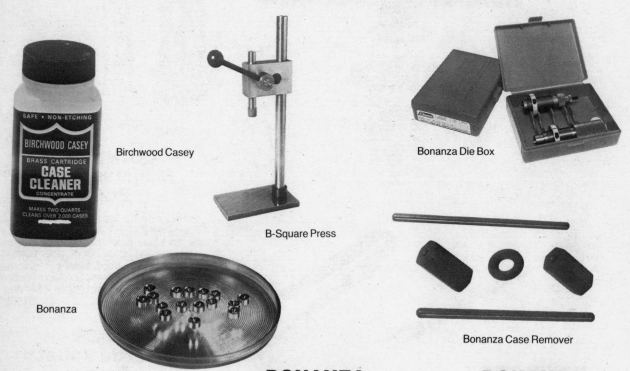

Birchwood Casey

B-Square Press

Bonanza Die Box

Bonanza

Bonanza Case Remover

BONANZA
Primer Turner

The cover of the Bonanza powder measure serves as a primer turning plate. Made of unbreakable plastic, it is helpful in loading automatic primer tubes. May be had separately . . . **$1.75**

BONANZA
Case Neck Cleaner

This one-step tool quickly cleans residue from case necks. Handle uses 8-32 thread and can be used with the primer pocket brushes.
Handle only **$1.75**
Brush. **$1.10**

BONANZA
Stuck Case Remover

This five-piece kit will easily remove cartridge cases stuck in either a Bonanza or RCBS sizing die. No drilling or tapping required with this kit. **$6.55**

BONANZA
Die Box

Box provides a safe, dust-free and dry storage for your dies while not in use. Each box has a moisture absorbent disc to prevent rust and the inside lid provides tips and suggestions to questions or problems regarding reloading. Made of high impact plastic. **$1.75**

C-H
Case Cluster

An accessory for the Mk I, Mk II, Mk III and Mk IV Auto Champs, as well as for other makes of progressive loading tools, including the Star (assuming that it has a Hulme feeder). This is a spring loaded indexer accommodating six case tubes, and will hold 90 38 Spec. cases, 120 45 ACP, or 138 9mm Luger cases. When one tube is empty, a twist of the unit will index another full tube into position and lock.
Complete with two threaded inserts for all calibers. **$39.95**
As above except for the Star machine **$44.95**

B-SQUARE
Arbor Press

Designed primarily for the benchrest shooter, this press is used for in-line seating and for pushing cases into neck-sizing dies, then for driving them out again. Adjustable for left- or right-hand use and for all benchrest tools up to 10″ high. Base is removeable for storage. Measures 12″ high, base is 3″×5″, weighs 3 lbs. **$59.95**
Magnum model **$79.95**

BIRCHWOOD CASEY
Case Cleaner

A liquid chemical formula for cleaning and restoring the brass to the original natural finish. Does not etch the metal and is easy to use. No harmful fumes or offending odors and will not stain hands or clothing. 3-oz. bottle. **$2.00**

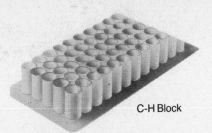
C-H Block

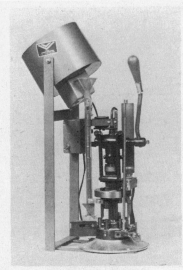
Chevron Case Master

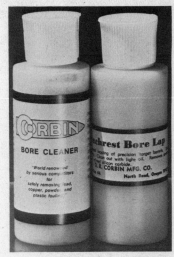
Corbin Cleaner and Lap

C-H Loading Block

Holds 60 cartridges for easy reloading. Comes in black, white, red and blue—handy for the reloader who works up cases for different loads, etc. Holes are $^{15}/_{16}$" deep. Not large enough for 45-70 or 348, but holds all sizes up to 375 Holland & Holland **$1.65**

C-H Stuck Case Puller

This tool kit removes cases stuck in reloading dies. It consists of the drill bit, tip, washer, allen-type screw and wrench. Easy to use and efficient. **$5.95**

CATCO Land Grabber Bullet Patches

Intended only for lead bullets cast and/or sized to reduced diameters, these paper patches have printed instructions and proper trimming marks on each patch. Paper is 16 lb. bond, 25% cotton. Price, per packet of 50 patches (postpaid). **$1.00**

CHEVRON Case Master

The Chevron Case Master is an automatic pistol case feeder that's designed to be used with production ammo loading machines which use a shell case feeding system, such as the Star, Phelps, C&H Model 375, etc. It may also be adapted for filling tubes for use on other machines.

The Chevron Case Master automatically orients and feeds to a constant level, the following pistol cartridges: 38 Spec., 357 Mag., 44 Spec., 44 Mag., 45 ACP, 45 Auto Rim and 45 Colt. To load 9mm, 38 Super and smaller cases, the company recommends that you purchase their "shell-plate." When ordering this unit specify the caliber(s) needed. No alterations to your loading machine are necessary. **$189.00**

CORBIN Vibrator Motor Kit

Complete vibrator motor and mounting kit to make a high efficiency case polisher out of any flat-bottomed pail. Motor is mounted to the bottom of the pail, and pail is suspended by a rope. Powerful vibrations churn the contents (regular polishing medium such as walnut shells and rouge). For 115 volt AC operation. **$19.50**

CORBIN Bore Cleaner

Safe cleaner for fine target barrels, contains no corrosives or harsh abrasives. Removes lead, copper, and powder fouling from pistol, rifle, and shotgun bores. Also removes plastic wad fouling. 2 oz. jar **$2.98**

CORBIN Bore Lap

Compound for lapping rough or badly fouled gun barrels, smoothing minor chatter marks, restoring rusted surfaces. Used on tight cloth patch or lead lap. 2 oz. jar **$4.50**

FITZ Flipper

Made of high-impact Fitz Duramite in brilliant red color. Flips all sizes of rifle or pistol primers base up or base down **$1.50**

FLAMBEAU Twin-60 Loading Block

One side holds 60 cases from 30-06 through belted H&H head size. When flipped over, the same block accommodates the smaller head sizes. Bright yellow plastic **$2.35**

Forster Case Kit

Forster Hollow Pointer

Forster Gauge

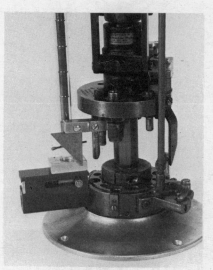

Hulme Case Feeder

FLAMBEAU
Primer Arranger

An easy-to-use, necessary tool for the active reloader. For use with non-automatic primer posts and automatic primer arms. Easily flips all primers base up or base down. Green plastic **$1.50**

FORSTER
Headspace Gauges

These Forster gauges are made to ± .0002" tolerance to insure accurate testing. Gauges are available in "Go," "No Go," and "Field." Most popular calibers.
Rimless **$9.60**
Rimmed, with pilot **$9.60**
Rimmed, less pilot **$7.20**

FORSTER
Case Conditioning
Kit

A complete selection of all the Forster tools. Kit includes: Forster Case Trimmer with collet and pilot, deburring tool, DBT Adapter, case length gauge, neck reamer, primer pocket cleaner, primer pocket center, and the outside neck turner. Kit is available in the following calibers: 38 Special, 357 Magnum, 219 Donaldson, 222 Rem., 222 Rem. Mag., 223 Rem., 22-250, 243 Win., 30-06, 8×57 Mauser, 257 Roberts, 244 Rem., 7×57 Mauser, 280 Rem., and 284 Win. Complete **$75.00**

FORSTER
Hollow Pointer

An accessory for the Forster Power Case Trimmer. Available in either 1/16" or 1/8" drill size. Complete with guide bushing and drill for any caliber rifle or pistol cartridge **$7.20**
Extra drills (state size wanted) . **$3.00**

FORSTER
Hollow Pointer
for Pistol Cartridges

Used on the Forster Precision Case Trimmer, this tool hollow-points factory or handloaded pistol cartridges only—assembled rounds with lead bullet in case. Available for 38 Spl., 357 Magnum, 44 Spl., 45 Long Colt or 45 ACP. Only the guide bushing is changed to handle a different cartridge **$7.20**
Guide bushings only **$4.80**
Extra drill only **$3.00**

HODGDON
Case Cleaner

A mild, acidic solution is diluted with water for soaking or tumbling dirty cases. Cleans brass bright and shiny without etching. Four-ounce bottle cleans hundreds of cases **$2.00**

HULME
Automatic Case
Feeder

Installed on the Star reloader it expedites the feeding of empty cases, eliminating the individual handling of the case during the reloading cycle.

Mark III available for any Star loader and made in two models.

Mark III, complete for 38 ACP, 38 Spl., 44 Spl., 45 Auto Rim and the 45 ACP, ... **$126.50**

Mark IIIA, complete for 38 ACP, 357 Mag., 41 Mag., 44 Mag., 45 Colt, 45 Auto Rim, 45 ACP and 30 Carbine . . **$129.00**
Extra magazine tube **$4.57**
Extra selector plates **$20.35**
Extra cam and bracket. **$20.35**
Magazine guide spring **$1.95**

Note: Star tools made before 1959 require drilling and tapping for installation of the Hulme Case Feeder. If your tool is not already tapped, Hulme will include a drill jig ($2.50). Tap and drill set available at **$11.50**

Pacific Sure-Loc Rings

Pacific Case Remover

Pacific Primer Turner

RCBS Brush

RCBS Scale Cover

I-DENT-A Re-Load Marker

This tool marks the primer of freshly loaded ammunition with an identification number to indicate the load used and corresponds to data in your log book. Since only the primer is marked with the fast-drying ink, the number is automatically disposed of when the case is reloaded. Can be used on all centerfire ammunition. Tool has interchangeable rubber stamp numbers from 00 through 9. From Edmisten Co. **$25.95**

LYMAN Die Box

New orange-colored box is made of tough plastic with a hinged, lifetime, snap-lock cover. Holds each die firmly. Impervious to moisture, bore cleaner or oil.. . . . . **$1.95**

LYMAN Primer Catcher

Made of heavy duty plastic, this catcher locks securely to the press, yet is easily removable for emptying or cleaning. For O-Mag, T-Mag or Spar-T presses. **$3.95**

MTM Primer-Flipper

An indispensable time saver for the busy reloader. Especially useful if automatic feed priming tool is used . . . **$1.36**

MTM CASE-GARD 150 Loading Tray

Holds all cartridges for reloading. Front side has large and small openings (50 each) for cartridges from 17 cal. to 458 Win. Reverse side has holes for 45 and 9mm pistol cases. Made of durable polypropylene. **$2.49**

PACIFIC Primer Catcher

Deep-welled and wide-faced to catch all primers and prevent them from bouncing out. Made of durable plastic . . **$3.75**

PACIFIC Case Cleaner

Each Like-Nu 6 oz. bottle will clean and bleach 200 30-06 size cases if used full strength. When used in the Pacific Tumbler this 6 oz. bottle will handle 600 30-06 size cases **$3.75**

PACIFIC Primer Turner

Made of plastic, it permits easy primer handling. After picking up all of the base down primers, merely replace lid and flip over **$2.00**

PACIFIC Stuck Case Remover

A new 3-piece tool that consists of a #7 drill, 1/4-20 tap and a remover body designed to fit the universal shell holder on any standard press. Easy and fast to use. No wrenches needed. **$8.00**

PACIFIC Sure-Loc Die Rings

The Sure-Loc lock ring comes with an allen wrench and has a unique locking screw which pulls the collar tight around the threaded die body. As it tightens, it applies even pressure around the die. This feature prevents seizing but allows the lock ring to be easily loosened. Made of blued steel. Price, each **$1.75**

RCBS Universal Scale Cover

Made of durable vinyl, this cover was designed for the RCBS 5-0-5 scale, but it may be used with other popular models. Protects the scale from dirt and foreign matter **$3.50**

RCBS Case Neck Brush

For lubricating inside of case neck before sizing. Nylon bristles withstand years of service. 22, 6mm, 270, 30, 35 and 45 calibers. Handle. **$2.00**
Brushes. **$1.25**

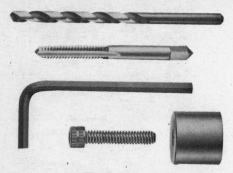

RCBS Case Remover

RCBS Accessory Kit

RCBS Primer Tray

RCBS Wrenches

RCBS Ammo-Crafter

RCBS
Loading Block

Made of unbreakable moulded plastic, this block fits all metallic cartridge cases. Flip over design allows for a full range of hole variations. 80 cavities on one side, 40 on the other, of 3 different depths and diameters are used to accommodate all cases $3.00

RCBS
Setscrew Wrenches

A handy item for every reloading bench. The convenient hexagonal plastic handle will not roll off the bench and is easy on the hands. Wrench size is stamped in large easy-to-read numbers for quick identification. Available in two sizes to fit all popular RCBS products. Combination $4.00

RCBS
Stuck Case Remover

This Williams-type device removes stuck cases from sizing dies quickly and efficiently. Case head is drilled and tapped, stuck case remover is placed over die and hex head screw is turned with wrench until case pulls free. Comes complete with drill, tap and wrench. $8.00

RCBS
Primer Tray

Designed to position primers anvil side up for fast, easy handling and insertion into the primer arm sleeve. Also can be used to load the automatic primer feed tubes by positioning primers with anvil side down. Tray holds 100 primers. Sturdy plastic $1.60

RCBS
Primer Catcher

Attaches quickly without screws. Will fit RCBS Jr and Pacific Super Presses $3.65

RCBS
Die Box

Made of durable, green impact plastic this box will store any 2- or 3-die set and protect it from dust and dirt. Label on end of box for identification, another inside the lid to list pet loads for the dies. $2.00

RCBS
Accessory Kit II

Kit contains the following accessories that simplify and speed-up reloading: powder measure stand, powder trickler, automatic primer feed, primer tray, primer pocket brush combo, case loading block, and setscrew wrench combo. A handy package, especially for the beginner.

Kit, complete $45.60

RCBS
Rifle-Pistol
Ammo Crafter Kit

Contains everything needed to prepare cases for reloading and handling powder charges in one easy purchase. Kit includes Speer #10 Manual, case loading block, deburring tool, powder funnel, case lube kit, 5-10 powder and bullet scale, Uni-flow powder measure combo $127.50

Redding Die Box

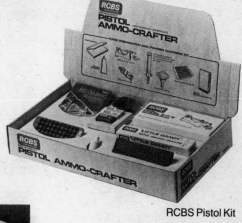

RCBS Pistol Kit

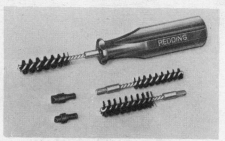

Redding #18 Kit

RIG 2

RIG 3

RCBS
Pistol Ammo Crafter

This kit has everything needed to prepare handgun cases for the reloading process. Included are: Speer #10 Manual, case loading block, resizing lubricant, case lube pad, 5-0-5 powder and bullet scale, powder funnel, Little Dandy Pistol Powder Measure and two rotors. Complete kit $93.50

REDDING
Model #18
Case Preparation Kit

Contains all the necessary tools you need for removing the dirt and powder residue from the inside of case neck and primer pockets. This all-in-one kit comes complete with accessory handle, both large and small primer pocket cleaners and three nylon case neck brushes which handle all cartridges from 22 thru 45 caliber $7.95

REDDING
Primer Catcher

Designed for the Redding Standard No. 7 "C" press. Eliminates the dropping of spent primers to the floor $6.00

REDDING
Combination Die
Box/Loading Block

Unbreakable polypropylene box provides a convenient storage for dies when not in use and, also, has a provision for the storage of shellholders. Will accept any brand of dies regardless of lockring diameter. Doubles as a loading block—top has provision for 20 cartridges with base size up to 30-06. Bottom has provision for 20 cartridges of Magnum base size up to 458 Win. or for large pistol cartridges. Included with all Redding Dies and available separately $4.50

RIG
RIG 2 and RIG 3

RIG 3 degreaser is an excellent die and brass cleaner for the handloader. One bath of RIG 3 removes both sizing and bullet lube from your favorite rifle or pistol dies. Once they have been thoroughly cleaned, spraying the dies with RIG 2 aerosol lubricant prior to storing them is an effective rust and corrosion preventative. This is a simple 2-step operation that extends die life and eliminates replacing ruined dies.

Another use for RIG 3 is in the area of brass cleaning. Once you've sized and/or polished the brass, spray them clean with RIG 3—it removes sizing lube and polishing rouge, instantly. Price per 8-ounce can of either RIG 2 or RIG 3, from RIG Products $2.50

Shassere Caddy

Vibra-Tek Polisher

Vibra-Tek Media

RIG Grease

RIG Universal Grease

RIG is an excellent preservative for long-term storage of reloading dies and firearms. A thin film of RIG, inside and out, keeps your dies like new until they're used again. Three sizes of RIG are available: 1-oz. ($1.25), 3¾-oz. ($2.50), and 15-oz. ($5.00). From RIG Products.

SANDIA Cartridge Cut-Off Machine

This tool attaches to a drill press and enables the operator to cut to length (not including final trim) about 700 cases per hour. Especially useful for cutting down military brass and such cases as 38 Special to 38 S&W or 308 Win. cases to 44 Auto Mag. $125.00

SHASSERE Cartridge Case Caddy

This handy bench accessory holds six cartridge blocks (up to 300 rounds) and has adjustable spacing to accommodate different case sizes. The Caddy is made of solid hardwood with satin varnish. Holds both rifle and handgun cases. Unit measures 5″ × 8½″ × 10⅞″ and comes with three blocks. A useful, well-made item. From Shassere $25.00

SHASSERE Caddy Blocks

These solid hardwood blocks are intended to be used in the Case Caddy, but can be used separately. Each holds 50 cases and can be had in eight different hole sizes. From Shassere, each. **$2.75**

SIL'S GUN PRODUCTS K-Spinner Mk-II

Used to clean cartridge cases, the K-Spinner is a caliber-size mandrel used in an electric drill chuck. To use, a cleaning pad is held against the resized spinning case. Removes all foreign material and polishes. Cases can be slipped on and off with drill running. Specify caliber when ordering. $2.00

TSI 400 Ammo Brass Cleaner

A safe non-polluting, non-flammable ammo cleaner that is instant-acting. No rubbing or wire-brushing necessary. A dip process that leaves brass shining and reduces the need for future cleaning. Comes in pint, quart and gallon containers. Pint $2.98

VIBRA-TEK Brass Polisher

This polisher holds up to 300 pistol cases. It works at a very high vibrating speed and cleans and polishes the exterior, interior and primer pockets. Has an adjustable vibrating action to suit different needs. Works fast, no mess, and is relatively quiet. Can also be used with a cleaning solvent to clean gun parts. Comes with a full supply of polishing compound. $59.95

Magnum model holds 5 lbs. of polishing media and can process 2500 rounds of 30-06 brass per day. $135.00

Vibra-Bright media re-charging liquid, 2 oz. bottle. $2.00

VIBRA-TEK Polishing Media

This shell media is designed to be used in the Vibra-Tek brass polisher. It is made of finely ground black walnut shells impregnated with iron oxide. Small enough so it won't lodge in the brass. Can also be used in case tumblers. Comes in 1- to 2-lb. plastic bags and shipped in ½-gallon plastic tubs. From TES Products.

1-lb. bag. $2.50
2-lb. bag. $4.99

TOOLS AND ACCESSORIES FOR

SHOTSHELLS

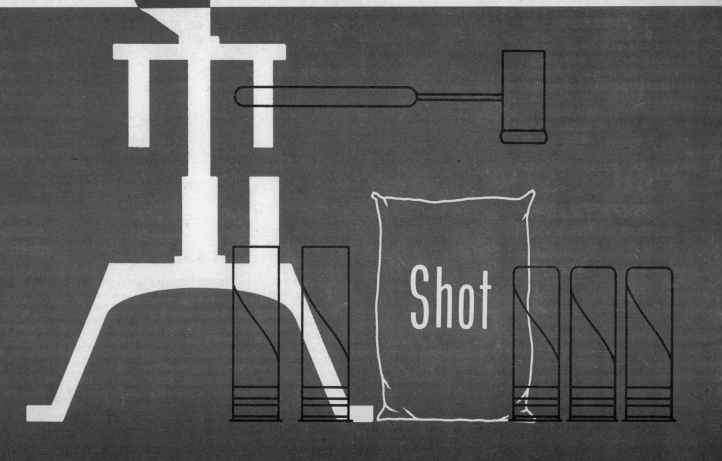

Shot

Notes on Shotshell Presses . . .

In the selection of a shotshell press the handloader may choose a tool that will produce handloads at rates from 10-20 per hours to 500 or more per hour, that range in price from just over $10 to $500 and more. He can make adequate match grade target loads or whatever suits his fancy.

Simpler types of shotshell tools—like the Lee—offer the occasional shotgun shooter the opportunity to reload his cases with little outlay of cash. It takes a bit more time and effort with these tools as compared to the Skeet or trap shooter using the latest progressive tool, and the finished shells may not have the fine look of a commercially loaded shell, but his loads will do the job that he wants done.

The careful operator of a modern progressive tool can be assured of reloads second to none. His shells will be consistent performers at the traps or in the field and will have the clean crimp and smooth body of commercial loads; best of all, he'll have made them with little more than the up and down stroke of the operating handle of his tool.

There are the multi-station tools that range in efficiency—as well as price—from those using dippers for shot and powder measuring to the near-progressive types which charge the cases from shot and powder hoppers with a flick of the charge bar.

Select a press in the price bracket you can afford that has features that you want. Don't expect a lower price press to do things beyond its capabilities, and don't buy a $300 automatic loader unless you want to reload hundreds of shells. In the majority of the presses, the quality of the finished shell is inherent in the press, and is only varied by the competence of the operator.

CAMDEX
Rotofloat Loader

This hand operated machine features resizing and depriming operations with "floating dies" to reduce operator force. Station indexing and lever arm operation are ball bearing assisted. Clockwise rotation of shot and powder canisters allows fast bushing changes. Slide bar can be specified to accommodate MEC or Pacific bushings. The adjustable taper crimp design returns the same amount of hull material, eliminating the need to separate hulls of various manufacture. Contact Camdex for full details..... **$640.00**

HOLLYWOOD
Center-X Automatic

A manually operated automatic loading machine. Comes complete for one gauge (10, 12, 16, or 20), with powder and shot measures, primer feed and case feed. Custom made and requires 25% deposit when ordering. **$2,250.00**

HOLLYWOOD
Senior Turret

Loads 200 shotshells or more per hour, and is rugged enough for metallic case full-length resizing and bullet swaging in any caliber. Turret head has 8 stations, tapped for 1½" die sets or in combination of 1½" and ⅞" for both metallic and shot-shell dies. Shotshell dies, powder and shot measures, shell holder, etc......................... **$290.00**
Hollywood Shotshell set **$115.00**
Change over die set, with shell holder for another gauge............. **$87.00**

Lee Load-All

Lee Load-All Jr.

LEE
Load-All

This is a low cost but durable shotshell press that will load plastic or paper shells in 6 or 8 segment crimps, with trap, field and magnum loads in 2¾" or 3" lengths. Dies are made of nylon. Built-in shot and powder baffles. Each step of the loading process ends at a positive stop. No wad pressure adjustments. Full length sizes the entire head and rim. Press comes with a new charge bar with 24 replaceable shot and powder bushings (may be bought separately to update older models, $5.00). Comes complete with load data, 12, 16 and 20 gauge...... **$38.98**

LEE
Load-All Junior

A complete reloading press for 12 gauge shotgun shells. Loads all types of shells including plastic 6 or 8 segment crimp, high or low brass, trap, field or Magnum loads. Full length sizes, adjustable shot measure, nylon dies, load data and complete instructions. Easily adjusted to load 2¾" or 3" shells. Everything you need to start loading including the screws for mounting........... **$14.98**

Hydramec Super 650

Versamec 700

MEC 600 Jr.

MEC Super 650

HYDRAMEC SUPER 650 Hydraulic Shotshell Loader

This is essentially the MEC 650 adapted to hydraulic power operation. The Hydramec is installed on a special base containing a hydraulic actuating cylinder connected to a foot-pedal-operated electrically driven gear pump. Up to 800 rounds per hour can be loaded with this tool. Not available in 10 ga. Operates on 110V household current **$770.19**

MEC Versamec 700

Updated version of the MEC 600 Jr. but has a Platform Cam which provides a longer ejection stroke at the resize station, and the Pro-Check which programs the charge bar and wad guide. No adjustments or part changes are required for different brass length. Quickly changes from 6 to 8 point plastic crimp spinner to the smooth cone for fired paper shells. Available in 10, 12, 16, 20, 28 gauge **$132.45**

MEC Hustler 76

The "Hustler 76" utilizes all of the features of the Grabber 76 and adds the benefits of hydraulic power. It features a toe-touch control that allows continuous action or stops anywhere in the cycle, as desired by the operator. The hydraulic 110 volt unit attaches with a single hose. **$855.83**
To replace 650 HydraMEC order Hustler less cylinder **$372.53**
Press, minus complete hydraulic system. **$406.59**

MEC 600 JR All Standard Gauges

A single stage tool that has many features of the automated MEC 650, including the 650's cam-actuated crimper. Produces loads equal in quality to the 600, but at a slower rate. Press is fitted with Spindex Crimp Head. Available in 10, 12, 16, 20, 28 or 410 ga. **$115.71**

MEC SUPER 650 All Standard Gauges

A progressive tool which can turn out 400 to 600 plastics—even more paper shells—per hour. Uses a circular 6-station shell plate, indexed manually. A completed shell with each stroke. Takes 2¾" or 3" shells. Primer feed is automatic, as is charging with powder and shot. Crimp is formed by a 2-stage cam-operated die. With Auto Cycle charge bar feature. Not available in 10 ga. **$232.45**

MEC Size Master 77

Pacific 266

MRC Loader

Pacific 366

MEC Size Master 77

Available in 10, 12, 16, 20, 28 and 410 gauges, the Size Master handles both brass or steel heads, high or low base. Auto primer feed and charge bar window are standard equipment. The Spindex Crimper changes heads in seconds from six to eight point or smooth cone.

Price includes primer feed. . **$177.27**
77 Die Set 12, 16, 20, 28 and 410 . . . . **$66.74**
77-10 10 ga. Die Set **$78.34**

MEC Grabber 76

MEC's "Grabber 76" combines the operations of six stations with every pull of the handle—a finished shell is produced with each stroke. Resizing, primer feed and cycle charge bar are all automatic. Crimping is cam actuated for uniformity and the Spindex Crimper Head changes inserts in seconds. All units include a powder and shot measure, large powder container and Magnum shot container. Press comes complete for all gauges except 10. . . . . **$318.52**

MRC Loader

Wads, sizes and crimps in one continuous operation. Set includes powder and shot measures, decapper, capper, wadding tool, resizer, crimper and instructions. Tool carries a limited two year warranty. From Mequon Reloading Corp. **$12.98**

PACIFIC Model 266 Loader

Over 250 uniform rounds can be reloaded per hour. All operations end on a complete stop. Charge bar is of the positive action type. Available in 12, 12 Mag., 20, 20 Mag **$208.00**
Die set (12 or 20) **$49.00**
Die set (16, 28, 410) **$49.00**
Press, 16, 28, or 410 . . . . . . **$214.00**
Charge bar bushing (not included with die set) **$2.00**

PACIFIC 366 Auto Loader

A progressive tool that has an automatic turntable and swingout wad guide in addition to the regular features of the DL-366. Eight shells move around the turntable and eight different operations are performed automatically with each stroke of the operating lever. After loading, the finished shell is ejected. Operator simply sets an empty hull on the shell plate and inserts a wad in the machine. The new tool also has a shot and powder shutoff. Available in 12, 16, 20 or 28 gauge. The older standard 366 can be updated to automatic operation by returning the tool to the Pacific factory.

Model 336 Auto **$399.95**
Conversion Kit, 12 & 20 ga. . . . **$77.00**
Conversion Kit, 16 & 28 ga. . . . **$82.50**

P-W 375 Du-O-Matic

P-W Magn-O-Matic

PONSNESS-WARREN M375 Du-O-Matic

A single stage tool requiring only 4 moves to produce a loaded shell. Change gauges in 5 minutes. No crimp starter needed for paper cases. Price complete for one gauge **$275.00**
   Conversion unit (12, 16, 20, 28, 410 gauge)..................... **$105.00**
   Crimp starter (6 or 8 point).... **$19.00**
   Bushing (shot or powder) **$3.25**
   Conversion unit to change to 3½" 10 ga..................... **$154.00**
   Conversion unit for 3" 12, 20, 410........................ **$16.00**

PONSNESS-WARREN Magn-O-Matic 10

Essentially a redesigned Du-O-Matic press, the Magn-O-Matic has all the same features with the exception of being convertible to other gauges. This press is exclusively for 10 gauge 3½" shells. An extra-large shot drop tube allows up to #2 shot to be loaded easily while a special bushing access plug allows direct shot drop for even larger sizes. Shells are held in a sizing die throughout the five station loading process. Press, complete with 6-point crimp starter **$305.00**
   Magn-O-Matic crimp starter (6-point) **$22.50**

PONSNESS-WARREN ST-800C Loader

This is P/W's newest silver-vein painted shotshell loader incorporating the taper crimp in the loading procedure while retaining full length sizing of the case. This is essentially the 800B updated with the taper crimp and new silver coating. Reloads are resized, taper-crimped, and look "new, out-of-the-box." **$950.00**

PACIFIC Model 105

A simplified version of the DL-155. All operations are the same as more expensive loaders, but this model is designed and constructed to lower costs for the beginner. Not available with auto primer feed. Comes in 12, 16 or 20 gauge only (specify) **$95.00**
   Extra die set.............. **$30.00**

Pacific 155 APF

PACIFIC 155/155APF Loader

This loader sizes head and rim of cases before loading and the rest of the case after. Loads over 200 shells per hour and turns out a shell that functions in all types of actions. Model 155APF comes with automatic primer feed, 12 or 20........................ **$161.00**
   M155APF, 16, 28 or 410 .... **$166.00**
   Die set (12 or 20 gauge) **$45.00**
   Die set (16, 28, 410)........ **$45.00**
   Charge bar bushings **$2.00**
   10 gauge loader (no APF)... **$161.00**
   M155, 12 or 20 .... **$139.95**
   M155, 16, 28 or 410....... **$144.95**

P-W 800B Size-O-Matic

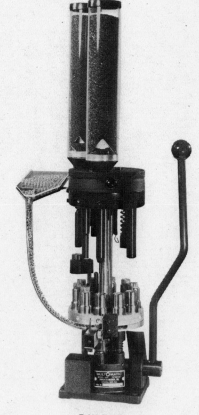

P-W 600B

Redding Super 32

PONSNESS-WARREN Model 800-B Size-O-Matic Loader

A semi-automatic progressive loading tool; handles both paper and plastic shells, new or fired. Cases are resized full length and remain in the sizing die through all operations. Eight such dies are permanently assembled to the die cylinder which indexes automatically to position shells for each operation. A cam-operated carrier receives and positions wads for seating. Wad pressure is adjustable from 10 to 130 pounds. Powder and shot measures can be shut off or emptied at any time without disassembly. Operating handle can be positioned on either side.

With a helper available to keep components moving, up to 700 rounds per hour can be loaded.

12, 20, 28 or 410 gauge..... **$840.00**

PONSNESS-WARREN Mult-O-Matic 600B

Designed for the trap and Skeet shooters, this is an improved version of the original Mult-O-Matic. It gives high production rate and versatility. Each shell is contained in its own full length resizing die through the entire reloading operation. One operator can load up to 500 rounds per hour. Additional tooling sets available in all standard gauges and can be installed in 10 minutes. Complete in 12, 16 or 20, 28 or 410 gauge with 8 or 6 point crimp starter (specify) ... **$525.00**

Additional tool sets (12, 16, or 20, 28 or 410 gauge, specify)......... **$185.00**
Conv. kit for 3″ 12 or 20 ga. ... **$185.00**

REDDING SUPER 32 Shotshell Loader

This is a turret-type shotshell press capable of producing 300 reloads per hour. All reloading operations are performed at one station to eliminate shell handling. Resizes high and low brass shells without adjustments. Fully adjustable wad pressure, fool-proof charge bar and a tilt-top for the easy change of powder and shot. The quick-release die head assembly allows a complete gauge change in seconds. Price complete, 12 or 20 gauge....... **$164.95**
16, 28 or 410 gauge....... **$172.95**

Texan GT

Texan FW

Texan M IV

TEXAN
Model RT

A six-station progressive press. Adjustable wad pressure. Shot drops while wad pressure is being applied and the press has a self-aligning nylon crimp starter. Has powerful double-link leverage, swivel-top easy drain of powder or shot from reservoirs. Indexing turret, convenient primer catcher box on front of press. Has high speed production capabilities and is ideally suited to competition shooters. Price, 12 or 20 gauge, complete **$259.95**

TEXAN
Model GT

A sturdy and economical shotshell press available in all popular gauges. Features include four station design, complete case resizing and depriming with cam ejection, self lowering wad guide. Loads 2¾″ or 3″ shells with minor adjustments. All steel frame and dual post construction for long life and positive alignment. Powerful leverage conserves operator energy.

Available in 12, 16, 20, 28 or 410 gauge (specify) **$99.95**

TEXAN
Model FW

Available in 12, 16, 20, 28 or 410, the FW resizes for high or low brass without adjustment. Wad guide automatically lowers and raises for easy and fast insertion of wads. Crimp starter seeks out original fold for perfect crimps. Nylon wad guide fingers, double column design for rigidity and strength and accuracy. Quick changing of powder and shot without bar changes plus easy conversion to other gauges.

12, 16 or 20 gauge **$129.95**
28 or 410 gauge **$129.95**

TEXAN
Model MIV

A 10-station automatic turret tool, massive and heavy, that reloads 200 shells without refilling, delivers a loaded shell with every pull of the handle. Available in 12, 16, 20, 28 and 410 gauge. Price, complete **$499.00**

Model M-V with new brass resizing station, complete **$599.00**

Notes on Shotshell Loading Dies . . .

Shotshell dies are designed to perform the following operations: decapping and recapping; seating wads under proper pressure; sizing and crimping. Provisions for inserting powder and shot charges must also be made, but this is not a function of the die set. Sequence of the operations may vary somewhat, depending upon the dies and press used. All shotshell presses as such in this volume perform the above operations with dies designed specifically for the individual presses. Their dies will not usually interchange.

MEC Spindex Head

MRC Star Crimper

MRC Shell Sizer

HOLLYWOOD
Shotshell Dies

Intended for use only in the various Hollywood presses; standard equipment in the big Hollywood automatic tool. A complete die is furnished for each operation so that no changing of parts is required. The complete set can be installed in the Hollywood Senior Turret tool. Well finished and polished, available in gauges 410 through 10 for paper, plastic or metal shells.

Price **$115.00**
Change-over kit to convert to another gauge **$87.00**

MEC
Spindex Crimp Head

An 8-point crimp starter which rotates as it adjusts itself to the original creases in the case mouth. No indexing is required, yet a neat tight crimp is assured every time. Can be installed on all MEC presses (specify gauge) **$7.19**
Smooth cone insert **$1.10**

MRC
Shotshell Sizer

A simple hand tool comprised of the support tube and sizing ring that is slipped over the fired case to resize it. From Mequon Reloading Corp.

Support Tube **$2.98**
Sizing Ring (10, 12, 16, 20, 28, 410, standard and magnums) **$2.98**

MRC
Wad Guide

Moulded of a new polycarbonate material that makes wad starting easy in all types of shells. Guaranteed for two years. In 12, 16 and 20 gauge. Mequon Reloading Corp.

Price. **$2.98**

MRC
Star Crimper

This starting die is made of unbreakable nylon, and can be used on all plastic or unfired paper shells. Available for 8-point crimping of 10, 12, 16, or 20 gauge; 6-point, 10, 12, 16, 20, 28, or 410 gauge shells, specify. From Mequon Reloading Corp. **$1.98**

MRC
Wad Guide Fingers

These replacement wad guide fingers are designed for all presses using the MEC type guides. Available in 10, 12, 16, 20, 28 and 410 gauge. The fingers come packed two per package. From Mequon Reloading Corp. **$1.48**

MRC
Deluxe Wad Guides

New aluminum full length wad guide with replaceable MRC Wad Fingers. A convenient and easy to use wad starting tool. Available in 10, 10 magnum, 12, 12 magnum, 16, 20, 20 magnum, 28 and 410 (2½" and 3"). Complete with an extra set of wad fingers. From Mequon Reloading Corp.. . . . . **$3.98**

Redding #33 Dies

Texan Starter

Redding #23 Starter

Ponsness-Warren Wad Guides

PONSNESS-WARREN
Taper Crimp Kit

The P/W Taper Crimp Kit converts all models of P/W loaders to the "new, out-of-the-box" taper crimp. The Taper Crimp Kit enables you to round the crimp of all shotshell cases while retaining the full-length sizing.
Prices:
For 800B — 8 new sizing dies + tooling **$135.00**
Convert your dies + tooling . . **$95.00**
For 600B — 10 new sizing dies + tooling **$145.00**
Convert your dies + tooling . **$105.00**
For 375 — new sizing die + tooling **$50.00**
Convert your die + tooling . . . **$40.00**
The Taper Crimp kit is available now in 12 gauge; other gauges will be introduced in 1982.

PONSNESS-WARREN
Crimp Starters

Six and eight point crimp starters are ball bearing lined and have an automatic pick-up to assure perfect crimp alignment.
Crimp starter complete (8 or 6 point) specify **$19.00**
Crimp Starter Head (8 or 6 point) specify **$10.00**

PONSNESS-WARREN
Paper Crimp Assembly

This conversion kit is intended for shooters who reload paper shells predominately. The standard crimp assembly on Ponsness-Warren tools is primarily for plastic shells. This assembly can be installed in a matter of minutes. Specify gauge **$16.00**

PONSNESS-WARREN
Wad Guide Fingers

Replacement wad guide fingers adaptable to most reloading tools and available in 10, 12, 16, 20, 28, and 410 gauge. These fingers accommodate all wads and assure exact wad seating. Specify gauge **$1.85**

REDDING
MODEL 33
Shotshell Dies

Available in 12, 16, 20, 28 and 410 gauges, these dies consist of a decap rod, resize sleeve, rammer tube, wad guide assembly, crimp starter, crimp die assembly, and shell holder. For use with Model 32 and Super 32 reloaders.
12 or 20 gauge **$36.00**
16, 28 or 410 gauge **$44.00**

REDDING
MODEL 23
Star Crimp Starter

This is a self-indexing, ball bearing crimp starter that fits all Redding shotshell loaders and many others ($5/16$-24 stem). Available in 6 or 8 point. Specify gauge and points. **$9.50**

REDDING
MODEL 34
Conversion Kit

For use with the Redding Super 32 press only. Available in 12, 16, 20, 28 or 410 gauge. Consists of complete die head assembly, dies, crimp starter, shell holder, bushings and quick release pin. All that is necessary to convert the Super 32 from one gauge to another in seconds.
12 or 20 gauge **$58.00**
16, 28 or 410 gauge **$66.00**

TEXAN
Crimp Starters

These crimp starters are for crimping both paper and plastic shells and are available in both 6 or 8 point versions, for all Texan shotshell presses. Specify gauge and number of points **$6.95**

Miscellany for Handloaders . . .

Gadgets to lure the reloader are numerous indeed! Just about as many, if not more, have appeared and then disappeared. Some of the accessories available are worthwhile, even—to those ammo makers who load in quantity or who are concerned with ultra-precision cartridges—a real necessity. At the other extreme, of course, are items you can well do without, maybe, but you will have to decide that for yourself. In between there are small tools of real utility, products which can be helpful to you or not, as your personal needs—or fancied needs—demand.

Further on, in various other divisions, you'll find additional notes.

Cont. Dev. Co.

Jasco Shell Caddy

MTM Tray

Griffin Auto Drive

BRENNEKE
Rifled Shotgun Slug Loaded Shells

Designed for shotgun hunting of big game, the Brenneke loads can be used in any shotgun regardless of choking. Wad and slug are joined together forming a long projectile for improved ballistic performance. Weight is comparable to a standard field load of shot. Available from Ballistic Research Ind. in 12 gauge only.

Per 10, 12 ga. (pack) $7.50
Loaded rounds, per 5 . . . . $7.50

CONTAINER DEV. CO.
Handi-Bin

Modified polypropylene hopper front assembly and storage bins. One-piece construction in various colors and sizes. Won't rust; resists oil, water and many chemicals. Stackable. Racks, rotary assemblies, bench mounts, floor stands and trucks. Write for prices.

GRIFFIN
Auto Drive For Ponsness-Warren 800B Press

An electrically operated, non-hydraulic, non-pneumatic drive mechanism for the Ponsness-Warren 800B shotshell reloader. Once the reloader is installed on top of the drive mechanism, no alterations are necessary—the two components are then adjusted to function as an integral unit. The operator has total control over the loading. An Emergency Reverse button can stop potential jams before they start. On/Off power is keylock controlled for safety. All loading operations are via pushbutton. Price, complete Auto drive, less press. . . $375.00

FLAMBEAU
Twin-50 Loading Block

Bright yellow polyethylene block holds 50 shotshells on each side. One side is for 12 or 16 gauge, the other for 20 or 28 gauge $3.25

JASCO
Shell Caddy

A 50-shell, 1-piece, molded block that holds shotgun shell sizes from 10 to 410. Made of durable, oil-resistant, high-impact plastic, in natural white color.

Price, postpaid $2.85

MTM
Shotshell Loading Tray

Precision molded tray holds 50 shells during the reloading process. Trays fit the MTM Case-Gard 100 shotshell case. Perfect for storing reloads. Available for 12, 16 or 20 gauge shells. $2.79

Multi-Scale Ltd.

MEC Super Sizer

P-W Scale Cover

MEC E-Z Pak

MULTI-SCALE CHARGE Universal Charge Bars

This replacement charge bar is fully adjustable for shot and powder charges. Shot capacity (with #4 low antimony shot) is from ½ oz. to 2 oz.; powder capacity from 12 to 55 grains. A powder and shot chart with 420 settings is included. All metal construction, with bottom guides for powder and shot valves, highly simplified method for reading and adjusting scales. Two models are available—Model D for the MEC 650 and Grabber, Model C for MEC 600 Jr., 700 Versamec, Sizemaster 77, MEC 600, 400, 250 and 250 Super, Texan LT, GT and FW models.
Price **$19.95**

MEC Super-Sizer

The Super-Sizer accommodates 12-gauge shells only; however, the company advised that other gauges are to follow in the near future. One pull forces eight steel fingers against the brass. Sizing pressure is spread out evenly over the entire surface of base metal. MEC says that the metal is actually drawn back to factory specifications creating a resized shell that will work freely in any magazine tube and will chamber properly.
Price **$66.47**

MEC E-Z Pak

The easy way to pack shotshells. As each shell is reloaded, they're placed in this device as if they were being placed in the box. After each 25 shells, the original box is slipped over E-Z Pak which is then turned upside down and removed. Available in all gauges............... **$4.95**

MEC E-Z Prime "5"

MEC's E-Z Prime "5" model auto primer feed is designed for the MEC Super 600 and 650 series of shotshell reloaders. Primers transfer directly from carton to reloader eliminating tubes and tube fillers. Adapts to all domestic and most foreign primers with adjustment of the cover **$29.02**
E-Z Prime "V" for Model 600 Jr. and Versamec 700 presses **$29.02**

PACIFIC Primer Tube Filler

A fast and simple way to load primer tubes for shotshell presses—just turn the dial of this plastic device and the tube is filled. Will not drop primer with base inverted **$9.50**

PONSNESS-WARREN Canvas Dust Cover

This rugged and handsome cover provides a practical way to keep dust and dirt off the press when not in use.
Cover for Size-O-Matic **$18.50**
Cover for other P-W presses **$15.00**

Redding #28 Bushings

Ponsness-Warren Bushings

Vitt/Boos Slug

Texan Conditioner

PONSNESS-WARREN Shot, Powder Bushings

For use with the Ponsness-Warren presses, these bushings are made with extreme care to assure accuracy. Shot and powder bushings are of different diameters to eliminate any possibility of their being reversed. Powder bushings are of aluminum. Each........ **$3.25**

REDDING MODEL 28 Shotshell Bushing

For use with Redding Model 32, Super 32 and Model 16 shotshell reloaders. Bushings facilitate changing powder and/or shot charge from one load to another. Clearly marked, foolproof design prevents shot bushing being used for powder and vice-versa........................ **$3.00**

TEXAN Shotshell Conditioner

Plastic or paper shotshell cases can be completely reconditioned with this tool. One pull of the handle resizes both the body and brass head. Optional heating element ($5.95 extra). Complete for 12, 16, 20, 28 or 410 gauge ... **$49.95**

WHIT'S Rotary Shotshell Ironer

Hardened tool steel device, carrying a ¼" shaft for motor or drill press mounting, quickly restores shells to usefulness. Also for cleaning or re-paraffining case mouths. All gauges except 410........................... **$6.95**

VITT/BOOS Aerodynamic Shotgun Slug

Modified and improved from the old reliable Brenneke slug. The high, thin, helical ribs tightly fit the bore for accuracy, but because they are thin and soft they pass through the tightest choke with complete safety. Maker says the ribs induce rotation to improve accuracy.

For complete descriptive literature and prices, write to Raymond Boos.

Box of 25, 12 ga. only **$9.00**

T & T HOLLOW POINT Shotgun Slug

T&T's hollow point shotgun slugs come with three segmented grooves that are designed specifically to ensure slug breakup once it gets inside the intended target. According to the manufacturer, the slug actually breaks up into three distinct projectiles; and, it isn't affected by shooting in, or through, normal brush cover. Slug made of pure virgin lead.

12, 16 & 20 ga., per 25 .... **$3.99**

Loaded Ammo (12 ga. only, per 5-round pack).................. **$2.99**

Notes on Powder and Shot Measuring . . .

One of the most important phases of shotshell reloading is the complete understanding of shot and powder measurement. Shot loading is simple if the handloader will follow the recommended charges in the various manuals.

In the case of powder charges, there is some misunderstanding about the meaning of "drams equivalent" and "bulk" and "dense" powders.

Bulk powders were smokeless powders of a chemical composition which allowed them to be loaded "bulk for bulk"—that is, volumetrically equal—with black powder. This simplified reloading during the transition period between the black powder and smokeless powder eras. The last of these is Du Pont Bulk, but it is *not* a 100% bulk powder. According to the manufacturer, *it produces about twice the chamber pressure of an equal amount of black powder.* This should be kept in mind.

Dense powders, simply, are those (smokeless powders) which, because of their chemical makeup, have a higher specific gravity and deliver a greater amount of energy than an equal weight of bulk or black powder. They *dare not* be loaded "bulk for bulk" with black powder as they create much higher pressures.

Drams equivalent. As explained by Du Pont, "a dram is a measure used for black powder and is normally used as a volume measure (although strictly speaking it is a weight measure equivalent to 1⁄16 oz. or 1/256 lb.) A certain dram charge of black powder imparts a certain velocity to a given weight of shot. For example, three drams of black powder with 1⅛ oz. of shot in 12 gauge gives about 1200 fps muzzle velocity. When the change to smokeless power was made, the dram equivalent designation was used as a measure of the approximate power of the load *regardless of the actual powder charge.* For example, in 12 gauge, a 3 dram equivalent load with 1⅛ oz. shot gives a muzzle velocity of about 1200 fps. A method was devised to relate velocity and shot weight of commercial loads to the dram equivalent system, but modern loadings depart from the system in a number of instances."

"Some shooters mistakenly believe a low dram equivalent is synonymous with low pressure. This is not so, as all modern shotshells regardless of dram equivalent marking, gauge, brand, powder or shot charge are loaded to approximately the same pressure level. Therefore, those who attach significance to the term 'dram equivalent' in respect to chamber pressure are in error."

Many people—particularly owners of damascus-barrel guns—think that Skeet and trap loads are low pressure shells because of their relatively light shot charges, but the reverse is true; these are among the highest pressure loads available and should not be used in guns of questionable strength.—Ed.

"The main problem is that people still confuse a 'dram equivalent' designation with a 'dram measure' of powder and this may be serious in the case of modern fast shotshell powders. Taking the density of black and smokeless powders into account, a volumetric 3-dram measure of such modern fast powders is approximately 40 grains (where a grain equals 1/7000 lb.) *or about a double charge.*"

With this understood, any of the powder and shot measures, be they the simple dippers or mechanical measures, will do a good accurate job.

Courtesy Of Speer, Inc.

BULLET ENERGY TABLES

Following are factors computed by Homer Powley which, when multiplied by the bullet's weight, determines the amount of energy produced at a given velocity. The left hand column of figures is velocity in hundreds of feet; the figures across the top of the tables is velocity in tens of feet. To illustrate the use of the tables let's imagine that we have a 150 grain bullet with a velocity of 2500 fps. You would then locate the 2500 figure in the left hand column. Since the velocity is in exact hundreds of fps the factor will be found in the column immediately to the right numbered 00. By multiplying this factor, 13.88, by the weight of the bullet, 150 grains, we find that we have 2082 foot pounds of energy. Now suppose that the same 150 grain bullet has a velocity of 2540 fps. To determine this factor it is necessary to locate the 2500 figure in the left hand column and the 40 figure at the top of the tables. By scanning down the 40 column and across the 2500 row of figures we find the factor number which intersects the two columns, 14.32. Multiplying this factor by 150 grains we find the bullet energy to be 2148 foot pounds.

Vel., f.p.s.	00	10	20	30	40	50	60	70	80	90
2600	15.01	15.13	15.24	15.36	15.48	15.59	15.71	15.83	15.96	16.07
2700	16.19	16.31	16.43	16.55	16.67	16.79	16.91	17.04	17.16	17.28
2800	17.41	17.53	17.66	17.78	17.91	18.04	18.16	18.29	18.42	18.55
2900	18.67	18.80	18.93	19.06	19.19	19.32	19.45	19.59	19.72	19.85
3000	20.00	20.12	20.25	20.39	20.52	20.66	20.79	20.93	21.07	21.16
3100	21.29	21.43	21.57	21.71	21.85	21.99	22.12	22.26	22.41	22.55
3200	22.69	22.83	22.97	23.12	23.26	23.41	23.55	23.70	23.84	23.99
3300	24.14	24.28	24.43	24.58	24.73	24.87	25.02	25.17	25.32	25.47
3400	25.62	25.77	25.93	26.08	26.23	26.38	26.54	26.69	26.85	27.00
3500	27.16	27.31	27.47	27.62	27.78	27.94	28.10	28.25	28.41	28.57
3600	28.73	28.94	29.10	29.26	29.42	29.58	29.75	29.91	30.07	30.24
3700	30.40	30.56	30.73	30.90	31.06	31.23	31.40	31.56	31.73	31.90
3800	32.07	32.24	32.41	32.58	32.75	32.92	33.09	33.26	33.45	33.62
3900	33.78	33.95	34.12	34.30	34.48	34.65	34.82	35.00	35.18	35.36
4000	35.53	35.71	35.89	36.07	36.25	36.43	36.61	36.79	36.97	37.15
4100	37.33	37.51	37.70	37.88	38.06	38.25	38.43	38.62	38.80	38.99
4200	39.18	39.36	39.55	39.74	39.92	40.11	40.30	40.49	40.68	40.87
4300	41.06	41.25	41.45	41.64	41.83	42.02	42.22	42.41	42.61	42.80
4400	43.00	43.19	43.39	43.58	43.78	43.98	44.18	44.38	44.58	44.77
4500	44.97	45.17	45.37	45.58	45.78	45.98	46.18	46.38	46.59	46.79
4600	46.98	47.18	47.39	47.60	47.80	48.00	48.21	48.41	48.62	48.83
4700	49.04	49.25	49.46	49.67	49.88	50.10	50.31	50.51	50.72	50.94
4800	51.15	51.37	51.58	51.80	52.01	52.21	52.43	52.65	52.87	53.09
4900	53.30	53.52	53.74	53.96	54.18	54.40	54.61	54.83	55.06	55.28
5000	55.50	55.73	55.95	56.17	56.40	56.63	56.84	57.06	57.29	57.52
5100	57.75	57.97	58.20	58.43	58.66	58.89	59.10	59.34	59.57	59.80
5200	60.03	60.26	60.50	60.73	60.96	61.18	61.42	61.65	61.89	62.13
5300	62.36	62.60	62.83	63.08	63.31	63.55	63.78	64.02	64.23	64.50
5400	64.74	64.98	65.22	65.46	65.70	65.93	66.18	66.43	66.67	66.91
5500	67.16	67.40	67.65	67.90	68.15	68.39	68.62	68.87	69.12	69.37
5600	69.62	69.87	70.12	70.37	70.63	70.86	71.11	71.37	71.62	71.88
5700	72.13	72.39	72.64	72.90	73.15	73.41	73.65	73.91	74.17	74.42
5800	74.68	74.94	75.20	75.46	75.72	75.97	76.23	76.49	76.75	77.02
5900	77.28	77.55	77.81	78.07	78.34	78.61	78.85	79.12	79.39	79.66
6000	79.92	80.19	80.46	80.73	81.00	81.25	81.52	81.79	82.06	82.34

ENERGY PER GRAIN OF BULLET WEIGHT

Vel., f.p.s.	00	10	20	30	40	50	60	70	80	90
600	.80	.82	.85	.88	.91	.94	.96	.99	1.02	1.05
700	1.08	1.11	1.15	1.18	1.21	1.24	1.28	1.31	1.34	1.38
800	1.42	1.45	1.49	1.53	1.56	1.60	1.64	1.68	1.72	1.76
900	1.79	1.83	1.87	1.92	1.96	2.00	2.04	2.08	2.13	2.17
1000	2.22	2.26	2.31	2.35	2.40	2.45	2.49	2.54	2.59	2.63
1100	2.68	2.73	2.78	2.83	2.88	2.93	2.99	3.04	3.09	3.14
1200	3.19	3.25	3.30	3.36	3.41	3.47	3.52	3.58	3.63	3.69
1300	3.75	3.81	3.86	3.92	3.98	4.04	4.10	4.16	4.22	4.29
1400	4.35	4.41	4.47	4.54	4.60	4.66	4.73	4.79	4.86	4.93
1500	5.00	5.06	5.13	5.19	5.26	5.33	5.40	5.47	5.54	5.61
1600	5.68	5.75	5.82	5.90	5.97	6.04	6.12	6.19	6.26	6.34
1700	6.41	6.49	6.57	6.64	6.72	6.80	6.88	6.95	7.03	7.11
1800	7.19	7.27	7.35	7.43	7.51	7.60	7.68	7.76	7.84	7.93
1900	8.01	8.10	8.18	8.27	8.35	8.44	8.53	8.61	8.70	8.79
2000	8.88	8.97	9.06	9.15	9.24	9.33	9.42	9.50	9.60	9.70
2100	9.80	9.90	9.98	10.07	10.17	10.26	10.36	10.45	10.55	10.65
2200	10.74	10.84	10.94	11.04	11.14	11.24	11.34	11.44	11.54	11.64
2300	11.74	11.83	11.95	12.05	12.16	12.26	12.37	12.47	12.58	12.68
2400	12.78	12.90	13.00	13.11	13.22	13.33	13.44	13.55	13.66	13.77
2500	13.88	13.99	14.10	14.20	14.32	14.44	14.55	14.67	14.78	14.89

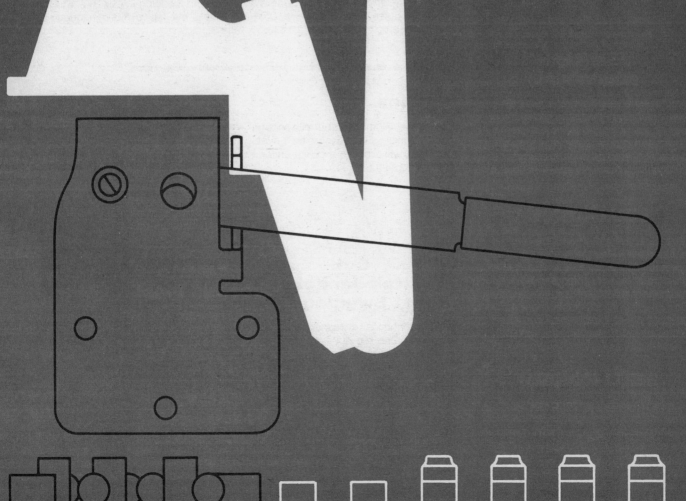

9th EDITION — PART 3

TOOLS AND ACCESSORIES FOR

BULLET SWAGING

Notes on Bullet Swaging Presses . . .

Swaging lead cores or slugs into bullets requires tremendous pressure, therefore presses for such use must be rigid, sturdy and with sufficient leverage to adequately cold form the lead.

Many of the more substantial presses available are adequate for swaging half-jacket pistol and rifle bullets, but only the more solid tools designed for heavy-duty work should be used for the swaging of *full jacket* rifle bullets because of the force required.

The handloader who now owns a press of sturdy construction may purchase bullet swaging dies for use in his press. Those who don't own a strong enough press, or who don't want to disturb their dies, should get a separate press for bullet swaging. The big advantage of the presses shown here, designed for bullet swaging only, is that they may be set up and used whenever the need arises without the bothersome task of removing the reloading dies, inserting the swaging dies, etc.

Obviously, because of the forces involved here, the need for a strong loading bench is of prime importance, too. Be sure to have your press properly anchored to a sturdy bench-top before doing any bullet swaging.

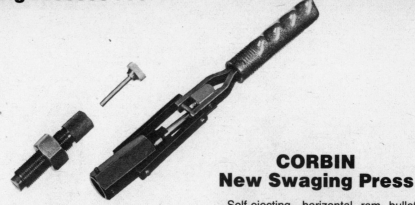

Corbin Power Ejector

CORBIN
Power Ejector

Powerful compound leverage unit slips over the top of Corbin bullet swage dies, gently pushes bullets from die cavity without hammering. Fits many standard 7⁄8″ diameter dies. Has adjustable ram so that maximum power can be obtained at the start of the stroke. Unit is a miniature press without the head, complete with ejector rod **$39.50**

CORBIN
New Swaging Press

Self-ejecting, horizontal ram bullet swaging press with floating alignment punch holder uses the special Mity Mite swage dies and punches made by Corbin. Extremely high precision for bench-rest work, coupled with a wide range of special drawing dies and availability in any standard or custom caliber, style or weight of bullet. Built to custom order. Each order is a hand-built system for making a specific kind of bullet. Write for quote on the bullet swage system to suit individual purpose. Prices shown are typical examples only.

Corbin Swaging Press **$129.50**
Press with typical rifle or handgun die set **$338.00**

Notes on Bullet Swaging Dies . . .

Bullet swaging dies are the keystone to the successful production of lead core, cold formed bullets. In selecting the correct dies the handloader should first decide what type of bullets he wants to make, and for what purpose. It would be foolish to buy expensive dies if the bullets were to be used only for plinking, but it would also be foolish for the perfectionist, the competitive target shooter or the person who wants to produce great quantities of bullets to expect lower priced dies to perform to his expectations.

All of the dies on the following pages will produce quite uniform half-jacket pistol or rifle bullets. The quality and degree of uniformity of the bullets made will depend on the workmanship, design and manufacturing tolerances of the press and dies in use. These qualities cannot be as high in mass-produced dies as in hand-honed and fitted ones; after all, they sell for a fraction of the cost of the others.

The operator is also important in the final quality of the finished bullet. A properly adjusted die that bleeds off just enough lead to assure you of a dense, completely filled bullet, but not enough to cause excessive pressure on the tool and dies, will produce a clean, uniform bullet, properly formed.

C-H
Half Jacket
Bullet Swaging Dies

An economical swaging die for the beginner. One die does the complete operation—forms and swages the bullet, automatically bleeds off excess lead. One tap on the ejector ejects the finished bullet, ready to load in the case. Available in .308″, .355″, .357″, .429″ and .451″ diameters with either round nose or SWC nose punches. Can be used in any loading tool which accepts snap-in shell holder and 7⁄8 x 14 die threads.

Swaging die **$19.75**
Nose punch **$5.50**

C-H Swaging Dies

Corbin Swage Dies

22RF jackets from Corbin dies

Corbin Draw Dies

C-H Swage Dies

C-H Bullet Swaging Dies

These dies are for making ¾-jacket bullets for pistols. Available in: 38, 41, 44 and 45 calibers. Any bullet weight desired is possible.

Dies, complete............. **$38.95**
Solid nose punches **$3.65**
Hollow point punches **$4.20**

CORBIN Rimfire Jacket Maker

Turns fired 22 Long Rifle cases into either .224" or 6mm rifle bullet jackets. Typical jacket length is 0.705". Makes a 52 grain open tip or 65 grain lead tip 224-cal. bullet capable of varmint shooting accuracy at speeds up to 3,500 fps. Works in regular ⅞x14 reloading press, produces virtually free bullet jackets.

224 jacket maker **$29.50**
243 jacket maker **$34.50**

CORBIN BULLET SWAGING DIES

Corbin Bullet Swaging Dies are made in all calibers from 17 to 458, in all styles from lead pistol wadcutters to copper tubing, multiple jacket African game bullets. Partitioned bullets, boattails, nylon tip bullets. . .even bullets made from fired 22 cases

Shown are two of the basic kinds of Corbin dies. . .the reloading press (⅞-14) type which Corbin makes in all handgun calibers up to 357, in all styles including full jacket and partitioned designs, and in both the 224 and 243 rifle calibers; and the Corbin System dies which fit the Corbin Swaging Press, a powerful horizontal stroke O-frame press brought out to replace the old Mity Mite C-frame. Every kind of bullet can be made on the Corbin press, using the Corbin self-alignment and automatic ejecting system. Press and dies to make:

Semi-wadcutter bullets **$258.50**
Flat base open tip bullets ... **$338.00**
Rebated boattail bullets **$432.50**
Lead tip flat base bullets **$397.50**
Flat or rebated, open or lead tip (all above)..................... **$551.50**
Corbin swaging press alone **$129.50**
Corbin system die sets alone:
1-die lead bullet pistol set **$79.50**
2-die semi-wadcutter pistol set **$129.00**
3-die rifle or FMJ pistol set .. **$208.50**
4-die RBT rifle set **$303.00**
5-die flat and RBT rifle set ... **$362.50**

CORBIN Bullet Jacket Draw Dies

Die and punch sets for regular reloading presses to draw standard jackets to smaller calibers, to increase jacket lengths and thin walls, and to make oversized jackets smaller for proper fit in custom dies. Custom sizes made to order. All dies, write for details. All calibers available.

Jacket Draw Die to reduce a jacket one caliber size. **$49.50**
Die set to turn regular 38 cal. jackets into 30 carbine jackets **$49.50**
Die set to make 17 and 20 caliber jackets from 224 jackets (two steps including trim) **$59.50**

HOLLYWOOD Bullet Swaging Dies

Guaranteed to swag uniform, precision bullets in the Hollywood press, these 2-piece dies will produce thousands of accurate bullets.

The nose forming piece is top-vented to carry away the bleed-off from pistol bullets and permit the escape of air trapped in the point of the rifle nose-die. Extra parts are available to change nose style. Write for prices on all popular calibers.

Pistol dies.................. **$55.00**
Rifle dies.................. **$75.00**

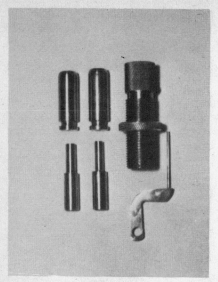

L.L.F. Swage Dies

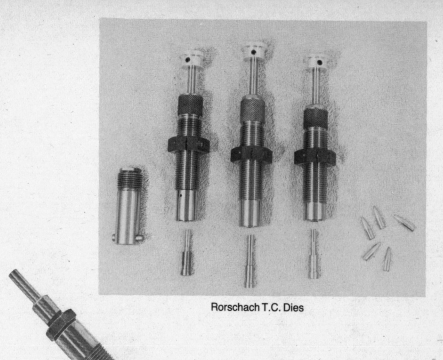

Rorschach T.C. Dies

Sport Flite

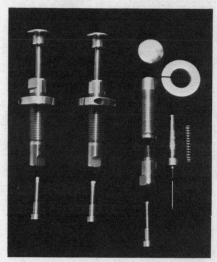

Simonson Swage Dies

L.L.F.
Die Shop

These dies fit nearly all presses suitable for bullet swaging. Adjustable for desired bullet weight, bullets are automatically ejected after forming. Dies are available in 17, 20, 22, 227, 228, 230, 234, 6mm, 25, 6.5mm, 270, 7mm, 7.35mm and 30 calibers. When ordering, give make and model of press, brand of jackets to be used and caliber.

Complete set of rifle dies .. **$125.00**
Automatic pistol dies
Solid nose................**$87.50**
Complete set Universal Dies
Solid nose................**$67.50**

RORSCHACH
PRECISION
Tungsten Carbide
Bullet
Making Dies

Ultra-precision 3-die set available in extra-hard grade of tungsten carbide insuring more than a million bullets without wear, or in a premium-grade steel. Available in .224" or .243" with 7S ogive and .308" with 8S ogive. A comprehensive 5 page brochure is available (50¢) that details the dies, manufacturing process and ordering instructions. Complete set for presses threaded ⅞-14, approximately:

Tungsten Carbide........**$750.00**
Premium Steel...........**$480.00**

SIMONSON
Bullet Swaging Dies

Made to order only. B&A type 3-die sets in .224", .243" and .308" may be had in 6, 7 or 8 caliber ogives. An ejector frame with ram adaptor for the RCBS A-2 Rock Chucker press included. Available in flat base only........**$437.50**

SPORT FLITE
Swaging Dies

Dies are threaded ⅞-14 for standard presses and heat treated to 52 Rockwell "C", then honed to a micro finish. Available in 30 cal. (.308-.309), 38/357, 9mm, 44, 45 caliber pistol solid nose punch styles, semi-wad cutter, round nose and conical. Additional punches are available. Adjustable for a wide range of bullet weights. From Sport Flite. Complete.....................**$14.95**
Nose punches..............**$5.95**
Extra base punch, zinc or jacketed **$3.95**

WOOD
Swaging Dies

These self ejecting dies will work only in the RCBS Rock Chucker press. Any weight bullet can be made. For half and three-quarter jackets. Any nose shape desired (specify). Formerly Bahler Dies.

Die set for solid nose......**$100.00**
Die set for hollow points ...**$100.00**
17 caliber dies, from.......**$350.00**
Boat-tails from............**$700.00**

Notes on Jackets and Gas Checks . . .

Ballistic performance with lead rifle bullets is limited. If an attempt is made to drive them fast, they often leave lead deposits in the bore—an inconvenience. Sometimes the base itself melts because of high powder combustion temperature. Both affect accuracy to a very noticeable extent.

To avoid these and other faults, a copper or alloy envelope called a jacket is added to part or most of the lead bullet. Being of harder, more durable material, this eliminates the barrel leading problem, as it prevents lead-to-bore contact. These jackets permit driving the bullet to the highest velocity practicable.

Jacketed rifle bullets have been factory manufactured for at least a century, but only since WWII have they been commonly made by handloaders using home-shop swaging tools. Several companies offer bullet-making dies for use in heavy-duty loading presses, while others sell jackets and lead wire for cores. Commercial jacket material is usually gilding metal (a zinc-copper alloy), rather than pure copper, which sometimes causes fouling. Uniformity in length, weight, mouth concentricity, wall thickness, etc. are necessary for top results. Cores are normally of pure lead; occasionally a small amount of antimony is permitted.

A desire for high velocity and the success of the swaging dies for rifle bullets caused a similar interest in handgun bullet swaging. The addition of ½- and ¾-jackets—in effect, lengthened gas checks—gives them benefits similar to the rifle versions although the possibility of leading is not completely eliminated so long as any lead touches the bore.

CORBIN
Bullet Jackets

Corbin supplies not only jackets but dies and tooling to make jackets from copper tubing, fired 22 cases, fired shotgun primers, and other scrap materials.

Caliber	Length	Quantity	Price
224	.600"	500	$15
224	.650"	500	15
224	.705"	500	15
243	.750"	500	18
243	.825"	500	18
257	.625"	500	24
257	.850"	500	24
264	.850"	500	24
264	.950"	500	24
270	.825"	500	24
270	.900"	500	24
270	1.00"	500	24
284	.850"	500	24
284	.950"	500	24
284	1.00"	500	24
284	1.30"	500	24
308	.375"	250	10
308	.925"	250	12
308	1.00"	250	12
308	1.10"	250	12
308	1.25"	250	12
323	1.00"	250	12
357	.25"	500	15
357	.44"	500	18
357	.50"	500	18
429	.54"	250	12
452	.54"	250	12

Jackets other than those listed can be made from larger jackets with Corbin drawing dies, $49.50 each. Big bore jackets can be made from ordinary copper tubing (plumbing pipe) with Corbin Tubing Jacket Maker kits at $125 each.

C-H TOOL & DIE
Copper Jacket Cups

22 cal. (.705") Copper Jackets	$37.00/M
6mm cal. (.825") Copper Jackets	43.88/M
30 cal. 1/2 Jackets	37.00/M
38 cal. 1/2 Jackets	38.38/M
38 cal. 3/4 Jackets	39.75/M
38 cal. (extra long) 3/4 Jackets	41.13/M
41 cal. 3/4 Jackets	43.88/M
44 cal. 3/4 Jackets	50.50/M
45 cal. 3/4 Jackets	50.50/M

Corbin Jackets

HORNADY
Crimp-On
Gas Checks

Made with open edge thicker than the sidewall so that sizing die crimps them permanently to bullets. Price per 1000 in calibers 22, 25, 35, 6mm, 6.5 . . . **$8.80**

In 270, 7mm, 30, 32, 338, 348, 375. . . . . **$10.00**

In 44, 45 . . . . **$12.75**

LYMAN
Gas Checks

Protect bullet base from hot powder gases, permit higher velocities with cast bullets. Seated during sizing operation.

22 through 35, per M	$13.50
375 through 45	$15.50

SPORT FLITE
Copper Half Jackets

Caliber	Quantity	Price
30	1,000	$28.60
38	1,000	29.70
44	1,000	45.00
45	1,000	49.50

From Sport Flite Mfg. Co.

SPORT FLITE
Zinc Bases

Zinc-based swaged bullets can be fired at the same velocity as half-copper-jacketed bullets. The price is about ½th of copper jackets. The zinc base remains with the bullet, even after impact.

Caliber	Quantity	Price
9mm/38/357	1,000	$6.00
44	1,000	6.70
45	1,000	7.00

Notes on Lead Wire . . .

The lead wire used in bullet swaging should be, usually, of the highest quality pure soft lead. Alloys are generally too hard for the average swaging operation, but there are some that will swage satisfactorily in heavy duty presses. For all practical purposes, pure soft lead is the best and easiest to use.

Pure lead will flow and yet stay in one piece, whereas harder lead alloys tend to shatter or disintegrate. Pure lead bullets have unsurpassed shocking power, and when combined with copper jackets to permit high velocities, make deadly missiles.

The following companies offer lead wire in the following standard sizes for bullet swaging: ⅛″ for the 17 cal., 3/16″, ¼″, .290″, .305″, 5/16″, .365″ and .390″. This wire is generally available in 20, 25, 100 and 250-lbs. spools, and in some instances in straight cut lengths.

Lead prices fluctuate quite often, and for that reason we cannot show retail prices. Contact your local dealer or write direct for current price sheet. Because of the high shipping cost we suggest you order from the company nearest you.

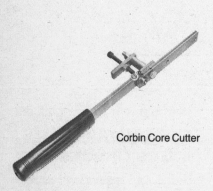

Corbin Core Cutter

Coats Core Cutter

C-H Core Cutter

LESTER COATS
Core Cutter

This lead wire cutter has six apertures drilled and reamed to accept wire sizes normally used in swaging bullets. All cutting surfaces are finely machined. Each aperture is fully adjustable for any desired bullet weight. Tension on the two cutting surfaces is adjustable.

Cutter, complete $25.00

CORBIN
Precision Core Cutter

A die-type cutter that uses two hardened tool steel dies in a steel frame with a fine thread stop screw to cut lead wire into precise lengths. Accuracy on the order of 0.1 grains in .224 is possible with this hand made cutter. Four dies cover a full range of lead diameters. Comes with one set of dies.

Corbin Core Cutter $29.50
Additional sets of dies $5.00

C-H
Core Cutter

A scissors-type cutter of all steel construction with a rubber handle to eliminate hand fatigue. Drilled for bench mounting and fully adjustable for weight of cores cut.

Complete $19.75

C-H Tool & Die
Box L
Owen, WI 54460

Corbin Mfg. & Supply
P.O. Box 758
Phoenix, OR 97535

Division Lead Co.
7742 W. 61st Place
Summit, Illinois

National Lead Co.
111 Broadway
New York 6, N.Y.

Precise Alloys, Inc.
69 Kinkel St.
Westbury, NY 11590

Rochester Lead Works
76 Anderson Ave.
Rochester, N.Y. 14607

HOLLYWOOD
Lead Core Cutter

An improved lead core cutter for use on the Hollywood Senior or Super tool, with ample power to cut alloy wire. Handles all sizes from 22 caliber to 45 caliber. Adjustable for core length.

Available with micrometer adjustment in place of standard stop screw. Lengths and weights of cut cores may be recorded for future use.

Standard $40.00
Micrometer $52.00

L.L.F.
Lead Wire Cutter

A well-made tool for all sizes of lead wire. Adjustable stop to control length of cut core $24.00

SPORT FLITE
Lead Wire Cutter

A scissors-type cutter that cuts lead wire: .250″, .300 and .365″ diameters. Length is regulated by an adjustable stop. Body and shear are of hardened steel. Adjustable for weights. A sturdy, economical tool.

Price $14.95

TOOLS AND
ACCESSORIES FOR
BULLET
CASTING

Notes on Furnaces & Pots . . .

Satisfactory bullet casting may be done with gas-heated lead pots, but electric furnaces will not only save time and labor, but also will improve the quality of the bullets cast.

It is important that the molten lead be stirred frequently, otherwise the tin and antimony (if any) will separate. If you are using a dipper, insert it into the bottom of the pot and bring it up from the bottom with the opening up. This not only keeps the mixture stirred, but gives you a ladle of clean metal without scum.

Lead and tin alloys require a temperature of about 600 degrees F., while an alloy containing antimony needs about 750 degrees F.

Beeswax or tallow is used to flux the alloy. A small ball (about the size of a marble) of either should be added to the heated alloy, mixed in, and if it does not ignite by itself, it should be lit with a match. This will help mix the metals and cause any slag or impurities to rise to the surface where they can be skimmed off.

Some of the aids to bullet casting are available around the home. A blanket or soft pad should be used to catch the bullets dropped from the mould, and it is wise to use gloves when casting to prevent burns.

Lee Bullet Caster

Lee Production Pot IV

Lyman Mould Master XX

LEE
Bullet Caster

The perfect melter for the casual bullet caster. Holds over 4 pounds of lead. Drawn steel pot with an extruded aluminum jacket. Large stable base. Maintains adequate heat for all bullet alloys without thermostat. Has a 275-watt tubular heater. Two year guarantee.

Price $19.98

LEE
Precision Melter

A high-speed melter with infinite heat control. Takes less than 15 minutes to melt 4 pounds of lead. Designed for continuous duty industrial soldering. Basically the same as the Bullet Caster model except has thermostat. 500 watts AC only. Guaranteed for 2 years. 220 volt 3-wire cord models for export are $3.00 extra.

Price complete. $25.98

LEE
Production Pot

This large, deep pot holds about 10 pounds of lead. Melting time is under 20 minutes. The bottom-pour spout is in the front where it can be seen. Uses 500 watts during initial heat-up, less later on to maintain temperature. Pot also has the infinite heat control thermostat mounted away from the high heat of the bowl. Well suited for commercial casting, clubs, etc. 220 volt 3-wire cord for export use, $3.00 extra. Pot guaranteed for 2 years.

Price, complete $43.98

Production Pot IV gives four inches of clearance under the spout instead of the standard two inches. This is high enough to accept all brands of bullet moulds and most sinker moulds. Same specs as standard Production Pot.

Price $46.98

LYMAN
Mould Master XX

An electric furnace equal to the needs of the most demanding bullet caster. 115 volts, AC-DC, 1000 watts, 11 lbs. capacity. Thermostatic control calibrated from 450° to 850°F. Pours from the bottom; flow adjustable. One ingot mould is included with the unit $129.95

Ingot mould, casts 4 pigs. $6.50

LYMAN
Mould Master XX

A thermostatically-controlled electric casting furnace with 20-lb. capacity. The thermostat housing has been relocated to one side allowing the caster a better view of the bottom pour spout. Access to the pot for ladle casting has been improved over the other Lyman models. This furnace is compatible with Lyman's Mould Guide, Ingot Mould and other Lyman casting products. Operates on 115 VAC.

Furnace with Mould Guide . $149.95

Ingot mould casts 4 pigs $6.50

Merit Pot

Saeco Model 32

RCBS Pro-Melt

Saeco Model 24

SAECO Model 24 Electric Furnace

Bottom pour, 11 lb. capacity with calibrated thermostat maintains temperature at plus or minus 20°F over a 450°F to 850°F temperature range. Flow rate adjustable, cool operating handle, large heavy base for stability, 1000 watt 110-120 volt AC/DC 9 Amp heating element brings full furnace to casting temperature in 20 minutes. Insulated to minimize heat loss. Ingot mould included, 220 volt available.

Model 24 furnace $119.50
Extra ingot mould $6.10

MAGMA Bullet Master Model 2400 MK3

This automated bullet casting machine can produce bullets of any caliber in the small arms field in excess of 2,000 rounds per hour. Uses most standard cavities and bullet styles can be changed quickly. Machine weighs 200 lbs., operated by 220 volt current. Lead reservoir holds 100 lbs. of lead.
Complete $2,995.00

SAECO Model 32 Electric Casting Pot

20 lb. capacity casting pot with calibrated thermostat maintains temperature at plus or minus 20° F over operating range of 450° F to 850° F. 1000 watt 110-120 volt AC/DC amp heating element brings full furnace to casting temperature in 20 minutes. Insulated to minimize heat loss. Ingot mould included, 220 volt model available.

Model 32 furnace $93.50
Extra ingot mould $6.10

RCBS PRO-MELT 10-Kilo Casting Pot

The Pro-Melt 10 Kilo (22-lb.) pot has temperature control of 450 to 850 degrees controlled by an industrial thermostat. The pot is made of steel and has a bottom pour valve. Pot liner is of stainless steel. A fully adjustable mould guide is standard, as is an "on-off" switch with indicator light. 800 watts, 120 volts AC. From RCBS . . . $159.50

MERIT Melting Pot

A 20-lb. capacity furnace with a controlled-flow downspout for slag-free mould filling. 2-piece design permits ready adjustment for bigger, multi-cavity moulds. Pot is used over a gas burner (not included).
Price (F.O.B.) $72.50

Lee Mould.

Lee Dipper

Lee Pot

Lyman Master Kit

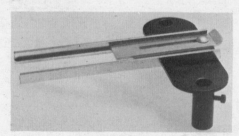

Lyman Pot

Lyman Mould Guide

LEE
Ingot Mould

A clever improvement on the standard 4-pig ingot mould, this new Lee unit is cast of an aluminum alloy and has a wooden handle that allows the mould to be flipped and emptied, and stays cool. There are four cavities — two for 1-lb. ingots, two for ½-lb. ingots. Perfect for alloying and storage **$5.98**

LEE
Lead Ladle

A convenient size ladle for bullet casting. Works equally well for right or left handers. Handy for skimming and stirring the metal **$2.24**

LEE
Lead Pot

This drawn steel pot holds four pounds of lead. The flat bottom makes it quite stable and provides good contact with the heat supply **$2.24**

LYMAN
Casting Mallet

A hardwood mallet expressly designed to open and close sprue cutters. Stuck bullets are quickly freed by the mallet with a light tap on the mould handle hinge **$4.50**

LYMAN
Lead Pot

This Ideal unit is still the simplest and cheapest way of melting bullet metal. The pot can be used on almost any gas range or liquid fuel burner, or on an electric range if a high heat burner is available **$6.50**
Dipper **$6.50**

LYMAN
Master Bullet
Casting Kit

Everything needed for casting bullets except the lead. Kit includes the Mould Master XX furnace, No. 450 lubrisizer, a Lyman mould with handles, Ideal bullet lube, Lyman User's Guide, top punch and sizing dies, and an ingot mould **$234.95**

LYMAN
Mould Guide

Installs on bottom pouring electric casting furnaces. Makes precise positioning of mould beneath pouring spout easy. Usable with all moulds up to and including 4-cavity size. Guide is fully adjustable for easy positioning ... **$13.95**

Marmel Thermometer

Lyman Custom Kit

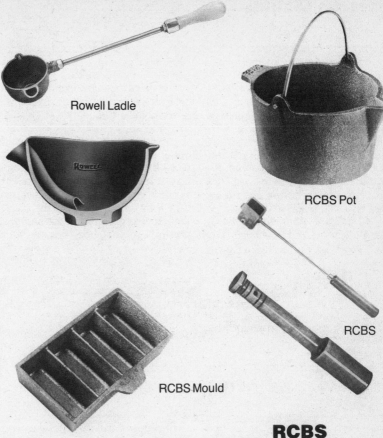
Rowell Ladle

RCBS Pot

RCBS

RCBS Mould

LYMAN
Custom Bullet
Casting Kit

This kit contains the No. 450 lubrisizer, ingot mould, top punch and sizing dies, Lyman User's Guide, Ideal lubricant, Lyman mould with handles, and a lead pot and dipper.................. **$124.95**

The Basic Bullet Casting Kit includes a Lyman mould with handles, lead pot and dipper, sizing die and punch, lube cutter, 4" lube pan, Ideal lubricant, and Lyman User's Guide................. **$54.95**

MARMEL
Marvelux

This lead-alloy flux is non-corrosive to iron and steel and the manufacturer advises that its regular use will keep your lead pot free of rust. Marvelux reduces dross formation and increases fluidity of bullet alloys thereby making it easier to obtain a well-filled bullet. Marvelux is nonsmoking, flameless and has no odor.

½ lb. **$2.75**
1 lb. **$5.00**
4 lbs. **$11.00**
8 lbs. **$17.50**

MARMEL
Lead Thermometer

This thermometer is calibrated to show lead-mix temperatures on a highly legible dial from 200° to 1000° F. The 8½" stem is inserted into the heated alloy to get the reading. The upper dial portion remains cool enough to handle during melting/pouring operations.

Price **$39.00**

RCBS
Lead Dipper

This tool features an extra long handle and an ovaled spout contoured exactly to the sprue opening. The cup-shaped open top of the dipper allows for easy scooping and stirring of the bullet alloy **$6.75**

RCBS
Ingot Mould

A heavy duty iron mould which forms four easy-to-use ingots. Excellent for preparing alloys for future use and easy handling..................... **$6.75**

RCBS
Lead Pot

This pot holds approximately 10 pounds of bullet alloy and is ideal for casting or blending metals. Flat, anti-tip bottom, pouring spout, bale handle lifter.

Price....................... **$6.60**

RCBS
Mould Mallet

This mallet is recommended for use when opening and closing the mould blocks and cutting sprues. The dense hardwood mallet is contoured for maximum efficiency and convenience **$6.00**

ROWELL
Bottom Pour Ladle

This bottom-pouring ladle delivers clean lead from the dipper via a spout that goes to the base of the bowl. Ten sizes are offered but only the numbers 1 and 2 are suitable for bullet casting. No. 2 ladle has a 3-inch bowl and 14-inch handle. From Advance Car Mover Co.

No. 1, 1 lb. lead capacity..... **$6.85**
No. 2, 2 lb. lead capacity..... **$7.95**

Notes on Moulds . . .

Cast bullets that do not perform accurately may have some internal defect that causes instability in flight. These defects may not be noticeable when weighing and sorting the bullets after casting, so every precaution should be taken to prevent them while casting.

The alignment of the two blocks is a critical factor in proper bullet casting. Extreme care should be taken that the mould is not dropped or hit with any force. The sprue cutter should be rapped only with a plastic or wood mallet — never steel! All moulds must be properly broken-in to do the best job of casting. After 100 or so bullets are cast, your mould will be putting out better buttlets — or it should!

The first 10 or 12 bullets cast from a cold mould should be discarded — it takes at least that length of time for a mould to reach the proper temperature for accurate casting. If the bullet comes out of the mould with wrinkles or open spaces, the mould (or the lead) is too cold. Frosted bullets mean too hot a temperature, though the effect is harmless. Wait long enough for the bullet to harden before cutting off the sprue; cutting the sprue too soon results in a deformed base.

Lead should be poured into the mould slowly to permit the air in the mould cavity to escape, thus preventing air pockets.

The oil or grease on a new mould will not permit good bullets to be cast until the lube is burned away. Solvent or thinner can be helpful in removing this grease, and the newer mould-release fluids are good.

When you are through casting, leave a bullet in the cavity — this will help prevent rusting, thus eliminating the need to regrease the cavity.

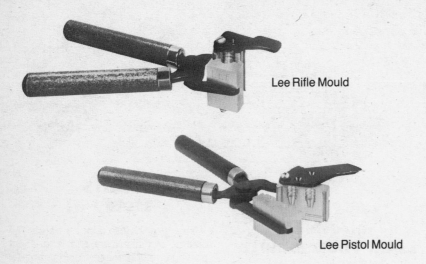

Lee Rifle Mould

Lee Pistol Mould

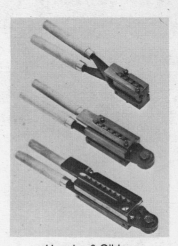

Hensley & Gibbs

CORBIN
Core Moulds

Four-cavity style, these moulds mount to the bench, require no handles or mallets, and eject their fully-adjustable weight cores from precision honed cavities in tool steel dies. All calibers are available. Write for information on matching cores to jackets and caliber.
Four Cavity Mould......... $49.50

HENSLEY & GIBBS
Handgun
Bullet Moulds

Made to give years of service. Many styles and weights available in 38, 44 and 45; any popular bullet weight and style made to order. Specify sized diameter of bullet and make of sizer when ordering. Moulds come complete with handles. Prices are approximate.

4-cavity	$93.50
6-cavity	$137.50
10-cavity (8 in 44 or 45)	$231.00

LEE
Pistol Bullet Moulds

These moulds have aluminum blocks that heat up faster and cool quicker. Moulds are substantially lighter than conventional steel types and can be preheated in molten lead without damage. Blocks are well vented reducing voids and, since lead won't stick to the aluminum, there is no "soldering" the blocks. Steel mould clamps with wood handles are light and the handles stay cool during casting operations. Available in 44 popular pistol sizes. Can be had with either single or double cavity blocks. Many hollow point styles are offered but only with single cavity mould.

Single cavity mould, complete with handles $14.98

Single cavity mould, complete with handles and automatic core pin for hollow points $19.98

Double cavity mould, complete with handles $19.98

LEE
Rifle Bullet Moulds

Same design and construction as the pistol bullet moulds except offered in 18 popular bullet styles in 6 calibers. Blocks are aluminum for rapid heating, come complete with handles.

Single cavity	$14.98
Hollow point	$19.98
Double cavity	$19.98

DEAN LINCOLN
Core Mould

This 5-cavity mould casts lead cores for bullet swaging. It is bottom vented and has a base and sprue cutter 1/4" thick. Offered in 3 sizes — .277" diameter for 30-cal. bullets; .311" for 38 and 357, and .375" for 44-45s — all cores are cast 3" long, allowing them to be cut to the required swaging length. Designed to accept Lyman *large* size mould handles. $54.00

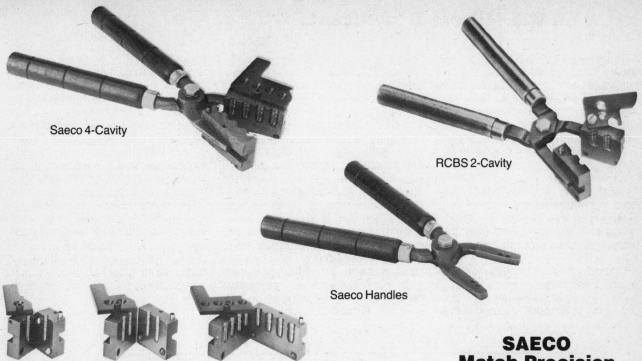

Saeco 4-Cavity

RCBS 2-Cavity

Saeco Handles

Saeco Mould Blocks

LYMAN
Ideal Moulds

Made in single, double and 4-cavity types; available in over 800 bullet and ball styles. Precision machined and finished. Write to Lyman for their catalog for detailed descriptions.

Double cavity pistol, from **$27.50**
Double cavity, rifle **$29.50**
Four cavity **$59.50**
Hollow base or hollow point . **$34.50**
Handles (not interchangeable), specify single or double cavity mould . **$10.95**
Handles, four cavity **$14.95**

LYMAN
Mould Rebuild
Kits

These kits provide replacement parts for worn moulds. Kits include sprue cutter, sprue cutter washer, screw and lock screw, and handle screws.

Single and double cavity kits . **$4.95**
Four cavity kit **$6.95**

RCBS
Bullet Moulds

Mould blocks are made of malleable iron allowing the sprue cutter to be hardened and sharpened. Tungsten carbide tooling is used to cut the cavity. Blocks are vented over the entire bullet surface to release trapped air. Alignment pins are hardened for durability. Most handgun and some rifle calibers available. Handles have extra long wood sheaths and are completely interchangeable between RCBS blocks.

Single cavity mould, Minnie ball, less handles **$32.50**
Single cavity mould, round ball, less handles **$27.50**
Double cavity, plain or gas check, less handles **$27.50**
Handles **$11.50**

LYMAN
Shotgun Slug Mould

Casts unrifled, hollow base slugs in 12 or 20. Lyman recommends these be shot as cast, as extensive tests indicate slugs are not rotated by rifling grooves but travel head-on in the manner of a shuttle-cock because the greater mass is in the front of the projectile. Slug mould block only **$34.50**
Handles **$10.95**

SAECO
Match Precision
Bullet Moulds

Designed with accuracy, consistency and speed in mind. Made from specially formulated steel to provide smooth bullets, rapid cavity filling and a high resistance to mould tining. Heavy mould blocks retain even temperatures. Long heavy-duty handles remain cool in use. One handle fits 1, 2 and 4 cavity moulds. Over 150 popular styles of bullets available: handgun, target, combat and silhouette, rifle, precision and target, roundballs and maxi balls and a wide selection of classic bullets for obsolete and turn of the century rifles.

Moulds without handles:
1 cavity **$34.50**
2 cavity **$34.50**
4 cavity **$52.50**
Hardwood handles **$12.80**
Moulds with handles:
1 cavity with handles **$43.80**
2 cavity with handles **$46.80**
4 cavity with handles **$64.80**

SPORT FLITE
Adjustable Core
Mould

This is an economical means of casting slugs for swaged bullets. This mould is adjustable to give the length and weight desired. When the core is cast, cut the sprue and bump the spring-loaded ejector pin on the bench, popping the core out of the mould. Available in 30, 38 and 44/45 calibers. Complete **$10.00**

Notes on Lubri-Sizers & Lubricants . . .

To be truly accurate, cast bullets are usually sized (forced through a die to bring diameter down to correct measurement), though some bullets shoot well "as cast." The combination tools shown on the following pages do this easily and quickly, and at the same time force a lubricant into the grooves of the bullet.

All lead alloy unjacketed bullets must be lubricated to prevent leading of the bore. Bullet lubricants should not only be able to lubricate properly at high temperatures, they should maintain this property in storage and must not melt in hot climates.

Operated properly, that is, maintaining the proper pressure on the lubricant and hesitating for a moment at the bottom of the downstroke to permit the lubricant to flow into all of the bullet grooves, these tools will help make your bullets more accurate, and they will also insure a minimum of bore leading.

Your sizing die-cast bullet combination should, ideally, be one in which a minimum amount of lead is removed. In other words, let your lube-sizer remove only a thousandth or two from the bullet diameter. When you size away too much lead you decrease the lube capacity of the grooves, make the lead area in contact with the bore greater, and you'll have to exert more effort, too, in doing the sizing-lubing. Regardless of the tool type used, care must be exercised in selecting dies. Bullet concentricity must be maintained. If all, or most of, the diameter reduction is on one side, the bullet's balance will be impaired, reducing its accuracy. Correctly designed dies contain a cylindrical cavity large enough to accept the as-cast bullet. A gradual, highly polished taper connects this portion to another cylinder of the diameter to which the bullet is to be sized. Both cylinders must be concentric. In this type of die the bullet is smoothly swaged to the correct diameter without loss of weight or concentricity.

Some older dies have a very short taper, or even an abrupt shoulder, connecting the two diameters. They simply shear excess metal off the bullet, usually more on one side than the other, producing a poorly balanced, inaccurate bullet. Casting is hot work — don't waste it by poor lubricating and sizing.

CAMDEX Luber-Sizer

A mass production unit that sizes and lubes cast or swaged bullets at 4400 per hour. It feeds vertically and dispenses horizontally for bulk or tube packaging. Bullet lube is heated with a cartridge type element in an aluminum block. Lube pressure is held constant by a ratchet and spring assembly inside the reservoir. Powered by a ⅓-hp. electric motor. Comes with the cartridge heater, foot pedal and forward/reverse switch
Price **$2,050.00**

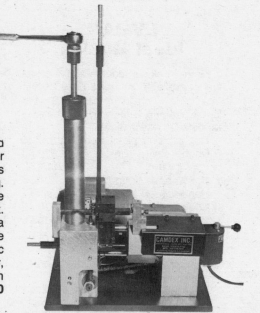

Camdex Luber-Sizer

Lyman 450

MAGMA Lube Master

This is a high-output machine that automatically sizes and lubricates cast lead bullets at the rate of 4300 per hour. Both bullet and lube feeds are vertical with bullet delivery coming through the bottom of the base plate. Powered by a 110VAC ½-hp. electric motor. Comes complete with one size of die and one bullet feed tube. From Magma Engineering.
Price **$1,495.00**
Conversion kit for caliber change.
Price **$45.00**

LYMAN 450 Lubricator and Sizer

The short stroke, power link leverage of this tool sizes, lubes and seats gas checks with little effort. Large C-type iron-steel cast frame is line bored for best die alignment. Adaptable to all bullets by changing sizing dies. Price less dies **$74.95**

LYMAN Lubricating & Sizing Die Sets

These current "G", "H" and "I" dies feature a precisely controlled entering taper, a smooth concentric bore, and dimensions held to minimum tolerances, and a grease-sealing O-ring that means clean bullet bases. Made in over 80 sizes from .222" to .580". "G" top punch **$3.95**
"H" and "I" assembly (state bullet diameter) **$10.95**

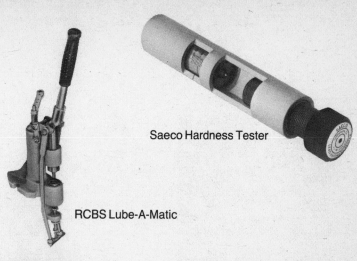

Saeco Hardness Tester

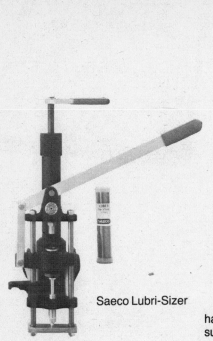

Saeco Lubri-Sizer

RCBS Lube-A-Matic

SAECO
Lead Hardness
Tester

A precision instrument to determine hardness of bullet casting alloy by measuring penetration of a hardened steel penetrator into a bullet. Hardness is read from a Vernier scale — reads in arbitrary units running from 0 (Brinell 5) for pure lead to 10 for linotype (Brinell 22). Wheels weight vary from 7 to 9 (Brinell 10-13). A hardness of at least 6 is required for medium handgun velocities, over 8 for magnum handgun and gas checked rifle bullets. Conversion to Brinell included. Use for quality control or sorting scrap to provide usable casting alloy. Should pay for itself many times over by allowing use of scrap lead **$91.50**

Sandia "Lubricator"

RCBS
Lube-A-Matic

This lubricator-sizer automatically controls lubricant pressure and feeds grease into the bullet grooves. Pressure is controlled with each stroke of the operating handle. Unit has finger tip adjustments for controlling depth of sizing for various bullets. Uses either Lube-A-Matic or Lyman dies. Price without dies **$78.00**
Lube-A-Matic dies available in most popular sizes **$11.00**
Top punches **$3.85**

SAECO
Lubri-Sizer

Heavy duty cast bullet sizer and lubricating press with integral gas check seater. Features a spring loaded lubricant reservoir which lubricates 20-40 bullets between turns of the pressurizing screw. Parallel guide rods maximize top punch and die alignment. Double "C" clamp available for bench attachment.

Dies are hardened and ground to .0002″ accuracy. Tapered lead on die minimizes bullet distortion. Dies available in most popular sizes.

SAECO Lubri-Sizer **$79.50**
Lubri-Sizer dies **$12.00**
Top Punches **$5.00**
Double "C" Clamp **$9.50**

SANDIA
"The Lubricator"

A high-output lubricator/sizer for cast or swaged lead rifle and pistol bullets. Variable speed up through 15,000 pieces per hour through use of adjustable pulleys. A precise lube flow adjustment eliminates over or under lubrication. Cam-operated lube piston. Thermostatically controlled heater located under lube reservoir which holds enough lube for 6,000 to 8,000 38-cal. wadcutter bullets. Machine comes complete for one caliber, including counter, wrenches and tools necessary for maintenance, plus 10 bullet tubes holding 78 bullets each, and a ½-hp. 110 VAC motor. From Sandia Die and Cartridge
Price **$3,700.00**
Caliber change (30, 9mm, 38/357, 41, 44, 45), per caliber **$350.00**
Steel machine stand (for two machines) **$212.00**
Extra bullet tubes, each **$3.50**

STAR
Automatic
Lubricator &
Resizer

This lubricator, substantially and carefully built, is accurate and positive in its operations. A storage pressure system is used in the grease reservoir, which feeds the grease to a high-pressure pump. This forces the lubricant into the grooves of the bullet. The bullet is then forced through the die by the entering of the next one. One setting of the pressure screw greases from 100 to 200 bullets. The bullets are forced through the die, and are processed about three times as fast as in the ordinary lubricator.

This item is equipped with hardened dies and is adaptable to any caliber.

Give bullet number (Lyman, SAECO or Hensley & Gibbs) and size of die wanted, or send sample bullet and state size of die wanted **$90.00**

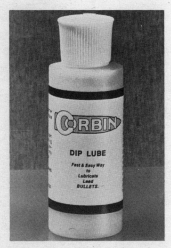

Lee "Lub Cutter"

Lee Kit

Lee Punch

Corbin Dip Lube

Javelina Super Lube

CORBIN
Dip Lube

Dip-type lubricant for cast or swaged lead bullets. Bullets are placed in a pan and lube is poured over them. Upon drying, a thin film of lubricant remains in the pores and on surface of the bullet. No lubricator-sizer machine required. Also makes pre-lubricated patches for muzzle loaders and paper patching bullets. 2 oz. dispenser $2.50

JAVELINA
Super Bullet Lube

A blend of Alox 2138F and pure beeswax (50/50). Warm weather will cause sticks to soften but mix will not separate. Available as solid or hollow sticks. $1.50

LEE
Resizer and Punch

A quick and easy way of accurately resizing the bullets after lubricating. Generous taper leading to resize portion permits resizing without lead shaving. Order by bullet diameter . . . $4.98

COOPER-
WOODWARD
Perfect Lube

Made in hollow or solid sticks, this lube works in any lubricating machine. Performs equally well in cold or hot weather because of its minimum contraction and high melting point. $1.50

LEE
"Lub Cutter"

Aluminum cutter neatly wedges the lubricant away from the bullets, leaving holes in the lubricant for placement of the next batch of bullets and eliminating the need to re-melt the lubricant. $2.98

LYMAN
Ideal Lubricant

This cast bullet lubricant increases accuracy and eliminates barrel leading. Sticks of this lube are moulded to fit the Lyman 450 sizer/lubricator $2.50

HODGDON
Bullet Lube (Alox)

This high quality bullet lube gives increased accuracy and higher lead bullet velocity without leading. A mixture of pure beeswax and Alox 2138F. Available in hollow sticks only. Price per 1¾-oz. stick $2.25

LEE
Lubricating &
Resizing Kit

Everything needed for lubricating and resizing bullets. Kit includes 2 oz. Alox bullet lubricant, Lub Cutter, convenient sized lube pan, resizer die and punch and complete instructions. Complete $8.98

LYMAN
Alox Bullet
Lubricant

The oldest such lubricant on the market and an excellent all-purpose formula. Available in solid or hollow sticks $2.50

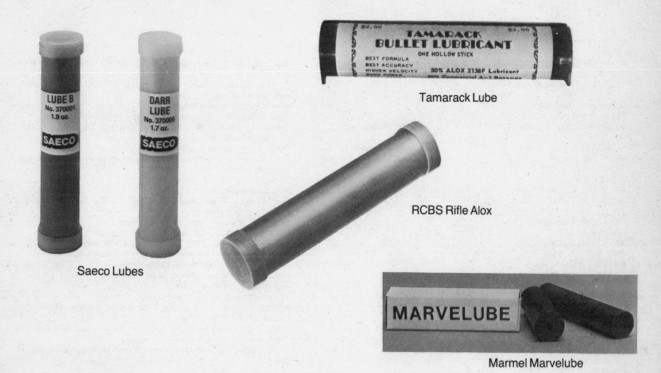

Saeco Lubes

Tamarack Lube

RCBS Rifle Alox

Marmel Marvelube

MARMEL
Marvelube

Marvelube is available in either hollow- or solid-core configuration for use in most cast bullet lubricator/sizers. This lubricant eliminates cast-bullet barrel leading and is intended for both rifle and pistol use. Price per stick....... **$2.50**

MICRO-LUBE

Formulated for both rifles and handguns, this lube is not sticky, will not gum or separate in your tools. Long storage life, heat and cold resistant. Complete satisfaction guaranteed by the maker, Micro Ammunition Co.

Solid or Hollow sticks........ **$1.00**
X500, super refined **$1.50**

MIRROR-LUBE

A patented formula bullet lubricant. Eliminates loading jams and reduces leading. Works equally well with rifle or pistol bullets. Its lubricating qualities are unaffected by weather conditions and it can be stored indefinitely. Keeps bore mirror clean. Solid or hollow sticks. Each........................... **$1.25**

RCBS
Rifle Bullet Lube

A special blend of Alox and beeswax formulated to NRA recommendations. Made primarily to withstand the higher velocity of rifle bullets, but works well for pistol bullets. Hollow stick. Comes in plastic storage tube........... **$1.85**

RCBS
Bullet Lubricant

Designed to fit the RCBS Lube-A-Matic sizer-lubricator and others requiring a hollow stick lubricant. Alox free, heat and cold resistant. Long storage life. Per stick................. **$1.85**

SAECO DARR
Bullet Lubricant

A proven match winning lubricant. Formulated to provide excellent results over a wide temperature and velocity range. 100% petroleum product will not deteriorate with age. White in color and clean to use.

Hollow, 1.7 oz stick......... **$2.00**
Solid, 1.9 oz stick **$2.00**
Bulk, 1 lb. **$8.00**

SAECO
"B" Lubricant

SAECO "B" Lubricant is low in residue, will not separate under heat or pressure and keeps barrels bright and lead free. This lube also makes an excellent fluxing agent.

Hollow, 1.7 oz stick.......... **$2.00**
Solid, 1.9 oz stick **$2.00**
Bulk, 1.7 lb. **$16.00**

TAMARACK
Bullet Lubricant

This bullet lube is the same as that developed by the National Rifle Association. It consists of 50% Alox 2138-F and 50% commercial A-1 beeswax. Alox-based bullet lube raises the potential power limit of cast bullets and generally improves the performance of cast-bullet loads of all kinds. Sticks of Tamarack lube are available in either hollow or solid-core configuration.

Price per stick **$2.00**

OBSOLETE POWDERS

Make and name	Type	Remarks
DU PONT		
No. 1 Rifle Smokeless (1894-1926)	Irregular grains	Bulk type for low pressures (20,000-25,000 psi). For cartridges like .45-90.
Smokeless Rifle No. 2 (1894-1926)	"	Like No. 1 above, but for interchangeable rifle-revolver cartridges such as .44-40, etc.
Schuetzen (1908-1923)	"	Like Rifle Smokeless No. 1.
Schultz Shotgun (1900-1926)	"	Also light gallery charges in metallic cases.
Gallery Rifle No. 75 (1904-1928)	Irregular, smoothed	Previously called "Marksman," and widely used for reloading military rifle cartridges.
SR 80 (1913-1939)	Irregular grains	Bulk type for black powder cartridges.
MR 19 (1908-1909)	Tube	A double base type for full to medium loads in large to medium capacity cases.
MR 10 (1910-1915)	Tube	Designed for the .280 Ross.
MR 21 (1913-1926)	"	Full charges in medium cases.
IMR 15 (1914-1917)	"	For full loads with metal-jacketed bullets. The first IMR (progressive burning) powder.
IMR 13 (1917-1918)	"	IMR type. Made for special government use.
IMR 16 (1916-1927)	"	30,000-55,000-lb. pressures; a very flexible powder.
IMR 17 (1915-1925)	"	Military powder for .303 Lee-Enfield, .30-06, too.
IMR 18 (1915-1930)	"	Small to full rifle charges; a very flexible powder.
IMR 15½ (1919-1934)	"	For full loads in .30-06 size cartridges.
IMR 17½ (1923-1933)	"	Full and mid-range loads in large cartridges.
IMR 1147 (1923-1935)	Short tube	Full loads in military cases.
IMR 1204 (1925-1935)	Tube	For small capacity rifle cartridges.
Pyro Cal. .30, DG (1909-1927)	"	Military powder for the .30-06 not commercially offered. Also called MR 20 at one time.
IMR 1185 (1926-1938)	"	For 173-gr. Mark I bullet in .30-06. Never commercially available.
RSQ (Resque) (1909-1911)	Smooth, egg shaped	Pistol powder of bulk type.
Pistol No. 1 (1914-1915)	Disc	A nitroglycerine powder, never offered commercially, and like Bullseye.
Pistol No. 3 (1913-1921)	"	A dense gov't. pistol powder.
Pistol No. 5 (1920-1940)	Flake	Full and medium handgun charges.
Pistol No. 6 (1932-1953)	"	Reduced to medium handgun charges.
Ballistite (1909-1926)	"	A dense shotgun type, still a popular form in Europe.
MX Shotgun (1933-1953)	"	Designed for standard loads.
Oval Shotgun (1921-1942)	Disc	Maximum load shotshells.
HERCULES		
** E.C. Powder (1894-1931)	Irregular grains	Designed for shotguns, but useful also in light rifle loads.
308 (1915-1930)	Tube	Military powder for the .30-06 and like Pyro DG.
300 (1916-1932)	"	For full lodas with metal-jacketed bullets. A single base powder quite like Du Pont IMR 15.
Sharpshooter (No. 1 1897-1953; No. 2 1902-†)	Disc	Full or reduced loads in black powder cartridges. Fastest of the old double base powders.
W.A. .30 cal. (1898-1930)	"	Military powder for .30-40 Krag.
Lighting (No. 1 1899-1950; No. 2 1903-1917)	"	Full and reduced loads in medium to .30-06 size cartridges.
Pyro Pistol (1922-1928)	"	Dense .45 ACP (gov't.) powder.
HiVel No. 1 (1908-1915)	Tube	Military powder for .30-06.
HiVel No. 2 (1908-1964)	"	Full to medium loads in large to medium capacity cases.
HiVel No. 3 (1926-1940)	"	Full loads in medium capacity cases.
HiVel No. 5 (1929-1934)	"	Special for .30-06.
HiVel No. 6 (1933-1941)	"	High velocities with heavy bullets. Was not available to the public.
HiVel No. 6.5 (1937-1939)	"	High velocity .30-06.
1908 Bear (1908-†)	"	Not generally available to handloaders, this was intended for medium capacity cases.
1908 Stag (1908-1914)	"	Like 1908 Bear.
KINGS Semi-smokeless	Grain	Any and all black powder cartridges.

**Also manufactured by Du Pont previous to formation of Hercules.

†Still available to loading companies.

Most of the above powders were discontinued in the late 30's and early 40's. Kings Semi-smokeless powder, a bulk type, was manufactured and used from 1899 to about 1936. It was pouplar in small-bore match cartridges as it gave les smoke and fouling than black powder. Granulation range was similar to black powder, but there was also a size made called "Cg," for musket use, that was larger than Fg.

MR = Military Rifle   IMR = Improved Military Rifle

COMPONENTS

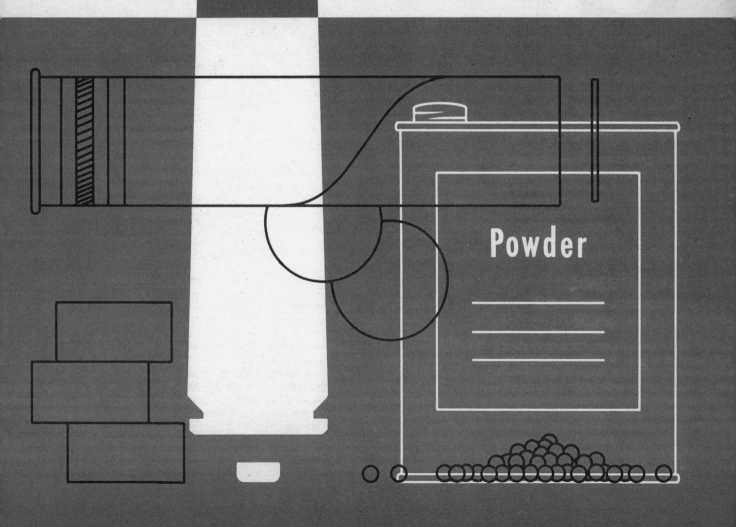

Powder

Notes on Powder . . .

Powders, generally, may be divided into three groups, depending on their use—pistol, rifle and shotgun. Some powders can be loaded for more than one use: Hercules 2400, basically a rifle powder, can be used for high velocity loads in some revolvers, or for 410 shotshells.

The manufacturers' suggested loads should be adhered to completely for accurate safe loads (let the "max" loads go for awhile) and only those powders specified should be loaded. "Wildcatting" of shotshells, too, is unnecessary and dangerous!

Leave the experimenting to experienced reloaders.

Rifle Powders

Hercules offers only Unique and 2400. The RelodeR powders were discontinued in 1971, but in late 1977 RelodeR 7 was brought back. Both are double base types, containing both nitrocellulose and nitroglycerine in percentages calculated to produce the desired performance. Du Pont makes an extensive line of rifle powders—IMR (Improved Military Rifle) numbers 4198, 4320, 4227, 3031, 4064, 4350 and 4831. Recently 4895, long available only as a surplus military powder, was released in standard canister lots. These powders are all single-base types containing no nitroglycerin. Their formulas are essentially the same; they differ primarily in granulation and coating required to vary their burning rates. Du Pont SR (Sporting Rifle) 4759 is especially useful in loading for obsolete cartridges at relatively low pressures. Hodgdon continues to offer many surplus powders, all excellent values.

Shotgun Powders

Shotgun powders are made only in dense form today, now that Du Pont's Bulk Shotgun Smokeless has been obsoleted. Du Pont's dense powders are PB (porous base) for high velocity and magnum loads, and Hi-Skor for target loads. Hercules Unique is used primarily for medium loads, Red Dot is used for light target loads, Green Dot for medium loads and Blue Dot and Herco, a coarse-grained powder, are used in the heavier loads. 2400 should be used only in low velocity 410 shells.

Pistol Powders

Smokeless pistol powders are relatively fast burning. The short barrels of pistols demand this quality to achieve best results. Hercules' Bullseye, the oldest smokeless pistol powder made, has a nitroglycerin content and is finely granulated. This permits it to burn freely and ignite easily under all conditions. It is used successfully in large capacity cases made originally for black powder; in 38 Spl. and 45 ACP target loads, and is the powder most used for factory cartridges. Hercules' Unique for medium and heavy loads and 2400 magnum loads have been consistently used, in their proper place, by handloaders for many years. The Winchester-Western Ball powder for standard loads, 231 (formerly 230P and 230), has been rapidly gaining in popularity since its introduction in 1960. W-W 295 HP, a ball powder for magnum loads, was discontinued shortly after its introduction. Hodgdon's H-4227 is a surplus military powder repacked into convenient size canisters. Norma has recently introduced two new pistol powders, R-1, for 38 Spl., and R-123 for 357 and 44 Magnum loads. Hodgdon's new Pyrodex CTG is for black powder cartridges.

SMOKELESS SPORTING POWDERS FOR RELOADING

Hercules is offering seven double-base powders for the reloader. They discontinued their RelodeR powders, 7, 11 and 21 in 1971, although the ReloadeR 7 has been reintroduced. Until recently Hercules was the only U.S. maker of double-base sporting powders (Du Pont's 700-X has a nitroglycerin component). Blue Dot is their latest addition to the line, intended for magnum shotshells. **Prices are approximate.**

2400 Powder A fine-grained powder intended for small-capacity rifle cartridges and for reduced loads, or light projectiles in larger capacity rifle cartridges, 410-gauge shotshells, and high-velocity loads in some revolvers.

1-lb. canister **$10.70**

RelodeR 7 Rifle Fastest burning of Hercules' rifle powders, it is adapted to the smaller size cases, from 222 Remington up through 30-30 for full charge loads. Performs well in some larger cases for reduced loads.

1-lb. canister **$10.92**

Bullseye Pistol A high-energy, quick-burning powder designed for pistol and revolver ammunition; available in 16-ounce canisters, 3-pound kegs, and 15-pound kegs.

1-lb. canister **$11.34**

Unique Powder An all-round powder, designed for large-caliber and for medium-gauge shotshells. It can also be used for gallery loads in rifle cartridges.

1-lb. canister **$9.98**

Red Dot Shotgun The powder preferred by many for light and standard shotshell loads.

1-lb. canister **$9.98**

Green Dot Shotgun Developed for light and medium 12-gauge shotshell loads. Uniform ignition and performance; minimum blast and residue, nonhygroscopic.

1-lb. canister **$9.98**

Blue Dot Shotgun The most recent addition to the Hercules line, Blue Dot is specifically designed for magnum waterfowl shotshells.

1-lb. canister **$10.26**

Herco Shotgun A coarse grained powder for use in heavy hunting loads.

1-lb. canister **$9.98**

Note: Prices listed are for smallest containers.

HODGDON
MODERN SMOKELESS POWDERS

H4227, H4198 Fastest burning of the IMR series. Well adapted to Hornet, light bullets in 222 and all bullets in 357 and 44 mag. 1 lb. can **$11.75**

HS6 A spherical magnum shotshell powder. Leaves ample space for wad column. 1 lb. can **$8.95**

H110 A spherical powder designed for the M1 carbine. Adaptable to heavy pistol and 410 shotshell. 1 lb. can . **$8.95**

Spherical BL-C 2 A favorite of the benchrest shooters. Best performance is in the 222, and in other cases smaller than 30-06. 1 lb. can **$10.95**

H4895 May well be the most versatile of all rifle propellants. It gives desirable performance in almost all cases from the 222 to the 458. Reduced loads, as little as ⅗ of maximum, still give target accuracy. 1 lb. can **$11.75**

Spherical H380 Excellent in the 22/250, 220 Swift, the 6mm's, 257 and 30-06; can be used in moderate charges in the 25-06 and bigger cases. 1 lb. can **$10.95**

H4831 The most popular of all powders for the bigger magnums. Outstanding performance with medium and heavy bullets in the 6mm's, 25-06 and 270. Comes in 1 lb. can **$11.75**

Spherical H335 Best adapted to 222 and 308 Winchester. 1 lb. can . **$10.95**

H322 This extruded powder fills the gap between H4198 and BL-C (2), and performs best in small to medium capacity cases. Excellent in 22 and 308 benchrest guns. 1 lb. can **$11.75**

Spherical H450 A good powder for maximum loads in most cartridges; gives excellent performance in 30-06 and larger calibers, including magnums. Comes in 1 lb. can **$10.25**

H870 has a very slow burning rate adaptable to overbore capacity magnum cases such as 257, 264, 270 and 300 Mag. with heavy bullets. 1 lb. can **$5.95**

Spherical H414 In many popular medium to medium-large calibers, pressure velocity relationship is better with this new spherical powder. 1 lb. can . **$10.25**

HP 38 A fast pistol powder for most pistol loading, especially recommended for 38 Special. 12 oz. can **$7.50**

Trap 100 A spherical trap and light field load powder, also excellent for target loads in centerfire pistols. Mild recoil. 8 oz. can **$4.75**

HS-7 For magnum field loads, HS-7 does not pack in the measure. Delivers uniform charges and is dense to allow sufficient wad column for best patterns. Comes in 1 lb. can **$8.95**

Pyrodex CTG For black powder cartridges, CTG will duplicate black powder loads in rifle, pistol, and shotshell cartridges. 1 lb. can **$6.50**

Prices are approximate

DU PONT Smokeless Powders

For many reloaders, Du Pont powders have long been considered the standard of excellence in quality and performance. Commercial loaders and the military services, as well, have confidence in Du Pont's consistently high quality.

Du Pont laboratories are constantly at work, not only developing new, improved products, but also performing endless checks to maintain the high standards of their current powders.

IMR-4227 Rifle Designed for relatively small capacity cartridges. It is too quick in burning to function to the best adavantage in relatively large capacity cartridges, except in reduced loads.

IMR-4198 Rifle Developed especially for use in medium capacity cartridges and for reduced loads. An extremely popular powder for handloading.

IMR-4895 Rifle Used in billions of rounds of 30-cal. military ammunition and proved an excellent performer in cases from the 222 to the 458, now available in canister lots. Slightly faster than 4320.

IMR-4064 Rifle A powder for large capacity cartridges that has exceptional burning qualities. Consistent accuracy is easily achieved with this powder when it is loaded properly.

IMR-4320 Rifle Intended specifically for use in military cartridges, but is equally satisfactory in all ordinary high-velocity cartridges.

SR-4759 Single Base Powder. Ideally suited for cast bullet rifle loads. Long time favorite for single-shot rifles.

IMR-4350 Rifle An excellent powder designed especially for magnum cartridges. When properly loaded this powder will give very uniform results.

IMR-4831 Rifle Made for the first time by Du Pont as a canister-grade hand-loading powder. It is the slowest burning powder in the Du Pont line. Suitable for rifle calibers such as the 17 Rem. and 220 Swift up through the 375 H & H Mag. and 458 Win. Mag.

SR 7625 For use in 12-gauge high velocity shotshell loads; also suitable for a wide variety of centerfire handgun cartridges.

IMR-3031 Rifle Particularly recommended for medium capacity and mid-range loads. For the purpose indicated the reloader will find this one of the most satisfactory powders on the market.

PB Shotgun This powder replaces the old Du Pont MX. It is a dense powder for use in high base shells for high-velocity and magnum loads. Single base type.

SR 4756 Shotgun For magnum shotshells. Produces excellent 410-bore target ammunition when loaded per manufacturer's instructions. Useful in heavy centerfire handgun ammunition.

Hi-Skor 700X Shotgun Double Base. Developed for 12-gauge components, gives optimum ballistics at minimum charge weight. Wad pressures not critical.

NORMA Smokeless Powders

Norma offers reloaders 5 nitrocellulose (single-base) rifle powders, designed to cover cartridges from 222 Remington to the large magnums. These make up the Norma "200" series; their relative burning rates are indicated by their numbers, the lowest being the fastest burning, the highest the slowest burning.

There are two handgun powders available to reloaders. These are non-hygroscopic and their special composition is claimed to reduce combustion temperature and therefore decrease barrel erosion. Write for their latest prices.

N-200 Rifle Medium-fast burning, especially adapted to the 222 but good with light bullets and/or light loads in larger cases. 400-gram canister**$18.30**

N201 Rifle Recommended for light bullets in medium size cases, or with some big caliber cartridges having a large bore volume which must be quickly filled by expanding gases. Comes in 500-gram canister **$22.50**

N-202 Rifle Medium burning rate; the most widely used powder in Norma factory ammunition. Excellent with cartridges of 30-06 class. 500-gram canister **$22.50**

N-204 Rifle Slow burning. Adapted to cartridges of large capacity or those using heavy bullets in relation to their caliber (270/150-gr. bullet and similar capacity necked-down wildcats). Comes in 500- gram canister **$22.50**

MRP Rifle Very slow burning. Developed for high velocity with large volume cases. Do not load below recommended *minimum* with this powder. Comes in 400-gram canister **$18.30**

R-1 Handgun Powder A fast burning powder especially adapted for revolver cartridges with lead bullets such as the 38 Special in a target load. It is exceptionally clean burning and the granules are of such size and shape that they flow easily in the powder measure. 275 gram canister **$21.95**

R-123 Handgun Powder A slow burning handgun powder for heavy loads in cartridges such as 357 or 44 Magnum, especially when using jacketed bullets. Gives a low breech pressure and the charge weight can therefore be increased for higher bullet velocities. 400-gram canister **$33.35**

WINCHESTER- WESTERN
Ball Powders

Ball powder, used for years by Winchester-Western in the loading of commercial and military ammunition, is offered to handloaders in five shotshell grades, two centerfire pistol types and four centerfire rifle types. It is highly suited to handloading because of its stability and clean burning. The smooth, round, graphited grains flow easily through powder measures, resulting in accurate charges.

452AA For 12 gauge trap, Skeet and field loads. Available in 1 lb. canisters, 3 lb. quarter kegs, 6 lb. drums and 10 lb. kegs. 1 lb. **$9.59**

473AA For 20 gauge Skeet and field, the same as used in factory 20 gauge AA but can also be used for 12 and 16 gauge. Same packaging as 452AA. 1 lb. **$9.22**

571 For 12 gauge 3″ magnum shotshells. Will also give superior performance in 20 and 28 gauge. Comes in 1 lb. canisters, 3 lb. quarter kegs, 8 lb. drums and 12 lb. kegs. 1 lb. **$9.60**

296 For 410 bore, magnum pistol and 30 Carbine. In magnum pistol cartridges, it requires heavy bullets and heavy crimps. Comes in 1 lb. canisters, 3 lb. quarter kegs and 8 lb. drums. 1 lb. **$9.22**

540 For heavy shot charges in 12 and 20 gauge. Excellent for 28 gauge. Higher density permits easier crimping of heavy loads. Comes in 1 lb. canisters, 3 lb. quarter kegs, 8 lb. drums and 12 lb. kegs. 1 lb. **$9.59**

231 Exceptionally fast, high energy, clean burning powder for target and standard velocity loads in handguns. 1 lb. **$9.95**

680 For small rifle cases. A very fast powder for small capacity rifle cases such as the 22 Hornet and 256 Winchester. 1 lb. canisters only ... **$10.38**

748 For centerfire rifles. Excellent for a variety of cartridges including 222 Remington and 458 Win. Mag. Popular with bench rest shooters. 1 lb. canisters, 8 lb. drums. 1 lb. **$10.36**

760 For medium to large cartridges. Broad range of proven application in medium to large cases. 1 lb. canisters, 8 lb. drums. 1 lb. **$10.36**

785 Slow burning rifle powder for large capacity cases and some belted magnum cases. 1 lb. **$10.36**

Courtesy Winchester-Western

Small arms ammunition manufactured in the U.S. and Canada utilizes a single flash hole and Boxer primers. They consist of a brass cup into which is pressed a pellet of priming compound and a 2- or 3-legged anvil. Generally speaking, the rest of the world uses Berdan primers. They are similar except that the anvil is an integral part of the bottom of the primer pocket and 2 or more flash holes are used.

Boxer primers used in sporting and most military ammunition come in two basic sizes—.175″ and .210″ diameter — and two strengths. Those for handgun use contain less priming compound and have thinner and softer cups than primers for rifle use. Handgun cartridges contain less powder, thus require less flash for ignition, and pistols do not have the heavy firing pin blow necessary to properly indent the heavy rifle cups. Consequently, there are four basic primer types — large rifle, small rifle, large pistol and small pistol. In addition, Federal offers a special rifle primer for use in large capacity magnum-type cases with heavy powder charges. Also, CCI produces a "Magnum" primer in each of the four types for essentially the same reason. The magnum types reportedly produce a larger flash of longer duration, intended to give more uniform ignition of large charges than standard primers impart.

Remington introduced three new primers a few years back, the 9½M, 5½ and 7½. The 9½M is for magnum belted rifle cases, particularly those using very heavy charges. The 5½ and 7½, in general, supplement the older 6½ and replace it in several instances. For years the 6½ was used in such revolver cartridges as the 357 Magnum and in small rifle loads like the 222. However, on occasion it proved too hard and/or thick for the 357, yet at the same time too soft or thin for the 222. The 5½ is specifically designed for the 357 and the 7½ for small rifle cartridges from the 221 Fireball to the 222 Magnum.

Oil and grease kill primers. Do not handle them with greasy fingers or allow oil on any part of the reloading tool with which they come in contact. This applies especially to automatic primer feeds where only dry lubricants can safely be used.

So far as can be determined all commercial primers available today are noncorrosive and nonmercuric. This means, simply, that their residues will neither cause the bore to rust nor the cases to be weakened — problems that

	CCI	Federal	Rem.-Pet.	Win.-West
Large Rifle	200	210	9½	8½-120
	250M	215M	9½M	
Small Rifle	400	200	6½	6½-116
	450M	205	7½	
		205M		
Large Pistol	300	150	2½	7-111
	350M			7M-111F
Small Pistol	500	100	1½	1½-108
	550M		5½	1½M-108
Shotshell Caps	209B			
	PC57			
Shotshell[a]	109	209[c]		209
Shotshell[b]	157	399	57	
		410	97[d]	
			97-4	
			209	
Percussion Caps			10 (.162″)	
			11 (.167″)	
			12 (.172″)	

NOTE: Large rifle and large pistol primers measure .210″; small rifle and small pistol measure .175″.

(a) For Winchester-Western, Monarch, J. C. Higgins, Revelation and Canuck cases.

(b) For Remington-Peters paper cases.

(c) Long battery cup type for Winchester-Western or Federal plastic shells.

(d) Battery cup; used in 12-ga. plastic trap and Skeet loads.

existed in the past. Careful cleaning prevented the rusting, even then, but nothing could be done to salvage cases once they were contaminated by mercuric primers. They became brittle and unsafe. Now handloaders don't have that worry.

U.S.-made shotshells and some imports use battery cup primers. Reloading is normally done by replacing the complete primer; however, the battery cup and anvil can be re-used at a considerable saving if one cares to go to extra trouble. The battery cup is made of copper, open at one end and pierced by a flash hole at the other. First, a pointed anvil is pressed down into the cup, then a cap containing the priming compound is pressed into place. The cap looks much like a standard large pistol primer

without its anvil.

Primers for Winchester-Western shotshells will not interchange with some of Remington-Peters make. Independent makers produce primers for both makes and those for W-W cases have the number 209 in their designation. When intended for use in R-P paper cases (or 28 gauge plastic), primers have 57 in the designation. In addition, R-P uses a special size battery cup in 28 and 410 gauge paper cases.

Remington-Peters No. 97 primer, introduced a number of years ago, has the same dimensions as other standard shotshell primers, and is interchangeable with them. Today most battery cup primers have the flash hole closed with a waterproof seal which also keeps powder granules from entering the cup.

Cases, Metallic and Shotshell:

The average case can be reloaded many times, and it is not unusual to find handloaders who have reloaded a metallic case 20 or more times. Handgun cases, and those rifle cases that must be crimped every time they are reloaded, will have a somewhat shorter life span. Maximum loads shorten case life, too. Shotshell cases won't take as many reloadings, of course—particularly those of paper—for the mouth soon frays.

When a cartridge is fired, the case expands to the size of the chamber, then springs back slightly if the brass is correctly annealed. If such cases are to be fired again in the same rifle, only neck sizing is usually needed; full length sizing is generally required if cases will be used in a rifle other than the one they came out of. Standard 7/8-14 dies can do both jobs—for neck sizing only position the die 1/8" or so away from contact with the shell holder. Full length sizing of paper and plastic shotshell cases is virtually a must, and all tools are made to do so.

Cases should be carefully examined before and during reloading, and any defective cases discarded. Watch for split necks and bodies; incipient head separations; swelling of head and primer pocket, torn or frayed mouths of paper cases.

You'll get better results from your handloads if you keep your cases segregated by make and lot. Mixed cases

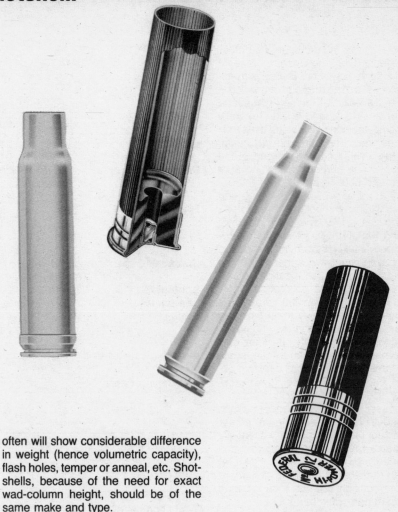

often will show considerable difference in weight (hence volumetric capacity), flash holes, temper or anneal, etc. Shotshells, because of the need for exact wad-column height, should be of the same make and type.

Centerfire Primer/Cartridge Reference Chart

Large Rifle	270 Winchester	7.62x39	358 Norma Mag.	6x47	32 S&W
219 Zipper	284 Winchester	7.62mm Russian	9.3x57	25-20 Winchester	32 S&W Long
22 Savage Hi-Power	7mm Mauser	303 Savage	9.3x62	256 Win. Magnum	32 Short Colt
220 Swift	7x57R	303 British	375 Winchester	30 Carbine	32 Long Colt
22-250	280 Remington	7.7 Japanese	375 H&H Magnum	32-20 Winchester	32 Colt New Police
224 Weatherby	7mm Exp. Rem.	32 Win. Special	38-55 Winchester		9mm Luger
225 Winchester	7mm Rem. Magnum	32 Remington	444 Marlin	Large (Reg.) Pistol	38 S&W
240 Weatherby	7mm Weatherby	32-40 Winchester	45-70 Gov't.	357 Auto Mag	38 Special
243 Winchester	7x61 S&H	8mm Mauser	458 Win. Magnum	38-40 Winchester	38 Short Colt
6mm Remington	7x64	8x57J	460 Weatherby	44 W&W Special	38 Long Colt
25-35 Winchester	7.5x55 Swiss	8x57 JS	50-70 Gov't.	44 Auto Mag	38 Colt New Police
250 Savage	30-30 Winchester	8mm Rem. Mag		44-40 Winchester	38 Super Auto
25-06 Remington	30 Remington	8mm/06	Small Rifle	45 Auto Rim	38 Automatic
257 Roberts	30-06 Springfield	8mm/338	17 Remington	45 Colt	380 ACP
257 Weatherby	30-40 Krag	33 Winchester	218 Bee	45 ACP	
6.5 Carcano	300 Win. Magnum	338 Win. Magnum	22 Hornet		Large (Mag.) Pistol
6.5 Japanese	300 H&H Magnum	340 Weatherby	22 PPC	Small (Reg.) Pistol	41 Rem. Magnum
6.5x54	300 Savage	348 Winchester	221 Rem. F'ball	22 Rem. Jet	44 Rem. Magnum
6.5x55	308 Winchester	350 Rem. Magnum	222 Remington	25 ACP	
6.5x57	30 Herrett	35 Remington	222 Rem. Magnum	30 Luger	Small (Mag.) Pistol
6.5 Rem. Magnum	300 Weatherby	357 Herrett	223 Remington	30 Mauser	357 Magnum
264 Win. Magnum	308 Norma Mag.	358 Winchester	6mm PPC	32 ACP	

Brass Extrusion Laboratories Ltd. (B.E.L.L.) New "Old" Brass

Brass Extrusion Laboratories Limited was started for the sole purpose of manufacturing obsolete "hard-to-get" brass cartridge cases. Shooting enthusiasts with classic or obsolete guns now have a source for many of those impossible or hard-to-get cases. In the near future B.E.L.L. will be offering the following cartridges: 416 Rigby, 280 Ross, 475 & 450 #2, 505 Gibbs, 500 Jeffrey and others as demand warrants. Those cases currently in production are listed below. Prices are per 20 cases.

Base Case	May Be Formed To	Per 20
577 N.E. Base 3"	577 2¾" & 3" 577/450 Martini Henry 577 Snider, etc.	$29.95
500 N.E. Base 3¼"	500 3 & 3¼, 476 N.E., 470 N.E., 500/465 N.E., 500/450 3¼" and others.	24.95
500/465 N.E. 3¼"	Formed and trimmed.	29.95
50 Sharps Base 3¼"	50-140 3¼" Sharps, 50-90 Sharps, 50-70 Gov't. and others.	24.95
450 Straight 3¼" N.E. Base	333 Rimmed Jeffrey, 360 No. 2, 11mm Murata, 11mm Gras, 10.3x60R Swiss, and many others	24.95
45 RCBS Base 3¼"	45-100 Ballard, 40-75 Bullard, 40-60 Marlin, 44-70 Maynard, 40-50, 40-70 & 40-90 Sharps BN, and many others.	15.95
11mm (.43) Mauser Mauser "A" Base	9.5 Turkish Mauser, 9.5x47R, 7.7x50R	14.95
Rem. Spanish Base	44-60 & 44-77 Sharps/Rem., 44-90 & 44-100 Sharps, 11.7 Danish Rem., 11.15 Spanish Rem.	14.95
470 N.E.	Formed and trimmed.	29.95
425 Westley Richards (rebated rim case)		24.95
404 Jeffrey (FFL required)	280 Jeffrey, 333 Jeffrey, 460 Guns & Ammo Magnum	24.95
375 H&H Magnum Flanged Base	275 Flanged Magnum, Super 30 Flanged Magnum	19.95

HARDIN 7.62 Tokarev/30-Cal. Mauser Cases 44 Auto Mag Cases

These custom-made cases for 7.62mm Tokarev and 30-cal. Mauser Broomhandle pistols are turned out from government surplus 223 brass. They are fully formed, sized and ready for loading. Cases are shipped, unprimed. Cost is about **$8.50** per hundred. Load data is also available from the maker. 44 Auto Mag cases made from 308 brass are also available for about **$10.50** per hundred. Include FFL when ordering. Hardin Specialty Distributors.

RUSSELL L. CAMPBELL Formed Cases

Cases formed for most obsolete, foreign or hard-to-get calibers, made from new brass and trimmed to correct length. Write for latest list or state your needs. Also loaded ammunition available in hundreds of calibers, modern and obsolete.

FEDERAL Match Cases

In addition to their regular line of empty rifle cases, Federal is also offering unprimed, nickel-plated Match cases in calibers 222 Remington and 308 Winchester. The cases are packed 20 per box.

Price: 222 Rem. Match **$3.90**
Price: 308 Win. Match **$5.30**

ROBERT POMEROY Formed Cases

Custom forming of obsolete cases, all made from new 45-70 and 30-40 Krag cases. 45-90, 40-82, 40-70, 38-70, 35 WCF, 40-72 and 38-72 are just a few of the sizes available. Pomeroy also offers custom bullets: .365", .375", .318", 9.3. Write about your needs.

REMINGTON-PETERS Empty Primed Shotshells

Either field or target style, in 10, 12, 16, 20, 28 and 410 gauge, 2¾", plastic. Primed, not mailable. Prices are approximate.

Gauge	F-Field T-Target	Price Per M
10	3 F	$379.20
12	2¾ T-F	128.70
16	2¾ F	125.10
20	2¾ F	123.80
	2¾ T	158.20
28	2¾ T-F	159.20
410	2½ T-F	143.90
	3 T-F	147.50

NORMA
Cartridge Cases

EMPTY CARTRIDGE CASES
Remington, Federal and Winchester Rifle and Handgun Cases

Remington, Federal and Winchester offer the most extensive lines of metallic cases available to handloaders in the U.S. Since they are for the most part identical, data are combined here to save space. Those cases available from only one source are marked thus: (R) Remington; (W) Winchester; (F) Federal.

All rifle cases are packed 20 per box except those marked with an asterisk (*) which are 50 per box. All handgun cases are packed 50 per box except the 221 Rem., which is 20. **Prices are for unprimed (mailable) cases and are approximate.** Primed cases cannot be mailed.

Handgun Cases

Caliber	Primer	Per C
221 Rem. Fireball	S	$19.90
22 Rem. Jet (R)	S	13.14
25 Auto	S	11.20
256 Win. Mag. (W)	S	18.30
30 Luger (R)	S	17.30
32 S&W	S	9.75
32 S&W Long	S	9.75
32 Short Colt (R)	S	9.75
32 Long Colt (R)	S	9.75
32 Colt NP (W)	S	9.75
32 Auto	S	10.90
357 Mag.	S	12.50
9mm Luger	S	16.05
380 Auto	S	10.90
38 Auto	S	13.15
38 Super (Nickel)	S	13.14
38 S&W	S	10.90
38 Special	S	11.35
38 Short Colt	S	10.92
38 Long Colt	S	11.88
41 Mag.	L	16.85
44 Rem. Mag.	L	17.00
44 Special	L	14.15
45 Colt	L	17.00
45 ACP	L	16.05

Rifle Cases

Caliber	Primer	Per C
Rem. Base Case (R)	S	$22.95
17 Rem.	S	27.45
218 Bee*	S	16.00
22 Hornet*	S	16.00
220 Swift	L	27.45
222 Rem.	S	19.20
222 Rem. Match (F)	S	19.50
222 Rem. Mag. (R)	S	21.80
22-250	L	27.45
223 Rem.	S	23.75
225 Win. (W)	L	23.75

Caliber	Primer	Per C
6mm Rem.	L	27.45
243 Win.	L	27.45
25-06	L	28.95
25-20 Win.*	S	18.30
257 Roberts	L	29.55
250 Savage	L	29.55
6.5 Rem. Mag. (R)	L	38.30
264 Win. Mag.	L	36.05
270 Win.	L	28.95
280 Rem. (R)	L	31.20
284 Win. (W)	L	31.20
7mm Rem. Mag.	L	36.05
7x57mm Mauser	L	31.20
30-30 Win.	L	24.90
30 Carbine*	S	16.65
30 Rem.	L	26.75
30-40 Krag	L	31.20
30-06	L	28.95
300 Savage	L	29.55
300 H&H Mag.	L	39.7-
300 Win. Mag.	L	36.05
303 Sav.	L	26.75
303 Br.	L	31.20
308 Win.	L	27.45
308 Win. Match (F)	L	26.50
8mm Rem. Mag. (R)	L	38.05
8mm Mauser	L	31.20
32-20 Win.*	L	18.30
32-40 Win.	L	35.25
32 Win. Spl.	L	26.75
338 Win. Mag. (W)	L	36.05
348 Win.	L	38.30
350 Rem. Mag.	L	38.30
35 Rem.	L	29.55
358 Win. (W)	L	31.20
375 Win.	L	36.05
375 H&H Mag.	L	42.40
38-40 Win.*	S	18.30
38-55 Win.	L	35.25
44-40 Win.	S	18.30
444 Marlin	L	35.25
45-70	L	26.75
458 Win. Mag.	L	42.40

Standard Rifle Cals.	Price, per 20
222 Rem.	$5.40
22-250 Rem.	7.45
243 Win.	7.45
270 Win.	8.35
7mm Mauser (7x57)	8.35
7mm Rem. Mag.	9.65
7mm Rem. Exp. (280 Rem.)	8.20
30 Carbine	4.15
308 Win.	7.45
30-30 Win.	6.60
30-06	7.80
303 British	7.80
8mm Mauser (8x57JS)	8.25

Handgun Cases	Price, per 50
9mm Luger	$12.35
38 Special	8.15
357 Mag.	12.85
44 Mag.	14.85
44 Auto Mag.	17.50

Unique Cals.	Price, per 20
220 Swift	$7.05
22 Sav. Hi Power (5.6x52R)	8.65
6.5 Jap.	8.60
6.5 Carcano	8.60
6.5x55	8.60
7x57R	9.25
7x64	9.25
308 Norma Mag.	11.25
7.5x55 Swiss	9.05
7.62 Russian	9.60
7.65 Argentine Mauser	8.95
7.7 Jap.	8.95
8x57J (.318")	8.95
358 Norma Mag.	11.60
9.3x57	10.65
9.3x62	10.65

Prices are approximate.

WEATHERBY
Unprimed Cartridge Cases

Caliber	Per 20
224 Weatherby Mag.	$13.25
240 Weatherby Mag.	13.25
257 Weatherby Mag.	13.25
270 Weatherby Mag.	13.25
7mm Weatherby Mag.	13.25
300 Weatherby Mag.	13.25
340 Weatherby Mag.	13.25
378 Weatherby Mag.	22.95
460 Weatherby Mag.	25.95

Notes on Rifle Bullets . . .

A basic rule for best rifle accuracy is to match the barrel twist to the bullet weight and length. As an example, a 30-06 barrel with a 1-in-10 twist will handle 150- to 220-grain bullets better than those of 90- to 150-grains, with some exceptions. If only lightweight, high velocity bullets are to be fired in a 30-06, then a twist of either 1-in-12 or 1-in-14 is generally preferable.

There are many types and classes of rifle bullets, each designed to do more or less specific jobs. Light, high velocity varmint bullets should not be used on big game, nor ought long range target bullets be used for varmint shooting. Try to choose the correct bullet for the job to be done.

It is just as imperative to select a load that will utilize the full potential of the bullet. A heavy hunting bullet must be driven at the velocity for which it was designed to obtain correct expansion, shocking power and penetration. For example, a 30-30 bullet, designed for the lower velocities, must not be driven too fast or it will tend to explode on contact and fail to give good performance.

Today virtually all bullet makers make good bullets. Choose one suitable for the job at hand, give it the right velocity and it will do that job — but only if you do your part!

One of the finest hunting bullets is the Nosler Partition bullet. It is designed to provide satisfactory expansion plus maximum penetration, while retaining approximately two-thirds of its original weight when recovered from game. It is also highly accurate.

Hornady, Speer, Sierra, Remington and others, also make a full line of fine hunting bullets.

Match bullets are another thing. Many of the best match bullets are handmade and hand-inspected. The fine Sierra 30 cal. 168-grain, soft-swaged bullets are superbly accurate. In this class it is usually a question of matching the barrel to the bullet, or vice versa. Several smaller makers (you'll find them listed in our Directory) offer excellent match bullets, particularly in the 22 to 6mm range.

Notes on Handgun Bullets . . .

There are today three classes of handgun bullets. The cast lead bullet, relatively hard and lubricated, has been with us many years. It is excellent for target work and hunting at lower velocities.

The swaged lead, lubricated bullet is a relative newcomer. These bullets are just about as perfect as a lead bullet can be. They have no cavities, holes or off-balance hollows. They also make good target and low velocity game bullets.

The newest bullet today is the jacketed or half-jacketed handgun bullet. Some manufacturers use pure lead, others use lead alloys. The softer the lead the greater the shocking power on game. Jackets are swaged right onto the lead cores, permitting a high velocity bullet. For hunting it has no superior.

Some manufacturers not only swage the jacket right onto the lead core, they go further and crimp it on so that the jacket cannot come off in the barrel, in flight or on impact. This also reduces the bearing surface, thus increasing velocity with no increase in pressures. Unless the jacket completely covers all of the bearing surface, this type bullet leads the bore badly. Best are those in which the jacket is turned down at least to some extent over the ogive.

ALBERTS BULLETS

This new name in the bullet field offers a fairly complete line of swaged handgun bullets in calibers 380, 9mm, 38, 41, 44 and 45. Styles available are RN, HBWC, DEWC, and SWC. No grease grooves are used. Instead, a unique dry-film lubricant is applied that is said to virtually eliminated leading in the gun's bore. Two black powder pistol bullets are also available in 36 and 44 calibers. **Prices are approximate.**

Caliber	Grs.	Type	Per 500
380	90	RN	$18.73
9mm	125	RN	18.73
38	148	HBWC	21.47
	148	DEWC*	21.47
	158	SWC	22.89
	158	RN	22.89
	158	SWCHP	24.07
	146	Hydra-Shok	28.01
41	210	SWC	31.43
44	230	SWCHP	34.99
	240	SWC	33.93
45	200	SWC	28.04
	210	SWC	29.88
	225	SWCHP	33.72
	230	RN	32.75
	250	SWC	34.67
Black Powder Pistol Bullets			
36	80	Belted Conical	18.01
44	135	Belted Conical	21.81

*Double End Wad Cutter

224 CLARK BULLETS

The 224 Clark cartridge is a varmint type designed for flat trajectory at long ranges. Clark offers an 80 grain hollow point varmint bullet priced at $8.00 per hundred postpaid. These are hand swaged especially for the 224 Clark.

Also offered is the 85 grain H.P. game bullet priced at $9.00 per hundred, $42.00 per 500, postpaid.

BARNES BULLETS

Formerly Colorado Custom Bullets, this is a complete line of custom bullets for those who want accuracy and efficiency. Jackets are of pure copper tubing, which doesn't shatter on impact; cores are pure lead. Available in over 25 calibers from the 17/25-gr. to the 620/900-gr., including fairly scarce diameters such as .406″, .411″, .416″ and .423″. These are favorites of large-caliber devotees who hunt dangerous game.

To control expansion in the larger calibers, a choice is offered for jacket thicknesses — .032″ and .049″. Only selected samples are listed here. **Prices are approximate.**

Caliber	Grs.	Type	Per C
17 (.172)	25	SPS	$10.00
22 (.224)	60	SPS	9.60
6mm (.243)	110	SPS	10.20
6.5mm (.264)	165	SPS	11.40
270 (.277)	180	RN	11.40
7mm (.284)	195	SPS	12.00
30 (.308)	250	RN	13.80
	250	FJ	19.20
8mm (.323)	250	SPS	13.80
33 WCF	200	FNSP	13.80
333 (.333)	300	RNSP	15.00
338 (.338)	300	RNSP	15.00
348 (.348)	250	FNSP	13.80
35 (.358)	300	RNSP	19.80
375 (.375)	350	RN	22.40
38-55 (.375)	255	FNSP	13.80
404 (423)	400	RNSP	21.60
45 (.458)	600	RNSP	34.80
475 (.488)	500	RNSP	34.20
458	400	RNSP	27.60

SPS — Spitzer S.P. FJ — Full Jacket
RN — Round Nose RNSP — Rnd. Nose S.P.
FN — Flat Nose

B.E.L.L. Solid Bullets

Brass Extrusion Laboratories, Ltd. is now offering high quality steel jacketed solid bullets for the reloader. Three calibers are available — 416 Rigby (410 grain solid), 465 (480 grain), 470 (500 grain). Bullets are packaged 50 per box. Either caliber, per box **$49.95**

BITTERROOT BULLETS

Heavy pure copper jackets are bonded to the core by an exclusive process, one which prevents these bullets from disintegrating when fired at magnum velocities, yet they expand reliably at ranges out to 600 yards and beyond. Prices plus postage.

Caliber	Grs.	Per 20
270	130	$28.00
	150	28.00
7mm	140	28.00
	160	30.00
	175	30.00
30 (.308)	165	30.00
	180	30.00
	200	32.00
338	200	32.00
	225	34.00
	250	36.00
358	225	34.00
	250	36.00
	275	38.00
375	250	36.00
	275	38.00
	300	40.00

CBH BULLETS

Precision designed CBH bullets are cast of specially prepared alloys to assure uniformity of hardness and weight. They are sized and lubricated on automatic machines and are lubricated with a specially formulated bullet lubricant guaranteed not to crack or separate under heat or extreme pressure, giving a minimum of lead fouling. Cast pistol bullets are sized as follows: 9mm — .355″, 38 — .358″, 44 — .429″, and 45 — .452″ and .454″. Wholesale dealers write Sandia Die & Cartridge for pricing.

Caliber	Grs.	Type
9mm	125	RN
38	148	WC
38	150	SWC
38	158	RN
41	210	SERVICE
44	255	SWCGC
44	250	SWC
45	185	WC
45	200	WC
45	230	RN
45(.454″)	250	SERVICE

WC — WADCUTTER
GC — GAS CHECK
SWC — SEMI-WADCUTTER
RN — ROUND NOSE

GREEN BAY BULLETS
Cast, Sized and Lubed

An excellent line of rifle and handgun bullets, produced under rigidly controlled conditions for high uniformity and accuracy. All bullets packed 100 per box except 30 caliber, which are packed in 50s. There are also ½ jacketed swaged bullets available in 30, 38, and 9mm caliber in various weights. **Prices are approximate.**

Cal.	No.	Type/Grs.	Per 100
22	438	RNGC 45	$4.55
	462	RNGC 55	4.55
	367	PGC 59	4.55
6mm	496	RNGC 85	4.80
25	464	RNGC 90	4.80
	312	FPGC 90	4.80
	325	RNGC 115	4.95
6.5mm	469	RNGC 125	5.15
	455	RNGC 140	5.30
7mm	346	RNGC 140	5.30
7.35mm	136	RNGC 145	5.30
32/20	252	RN 75	3.75
	419	FPGC 85	4.80
	445	SWC 95	3.80
30	18	FP 120	4.10
	316	FPGC 115	4.95
	359	PGC 115	4.95
	410	RN 130	4.20
	466	RNGC 155	5.45
	291	RNGC 170	5.80
	41	FPGC 180	5.90
303	334	PGC 190	6.05
32	297	FPGC 180	5.90
	247	FP 165	4.50
25 Auto	420	FPGC 65	3.75
8mm Nambu	116	RN 100	4.00
380 Auto	2423	RN 90	3.90
9mm	404	FP 95	4.00
	402	PFP 125	4.20
	242	RN 125	4.20
	384	PBB 125	4.20
357	1561	SWC 160	4.45
	446	SWC 160	4.45
	156	SWCGC 160	6.60
38	2422	RN 90	3.90
	2421	RN 125	4.20
	87	WC 127	4.20
	871	WC 140	4.35
	50	WC 148	4.35
	91	BBWC 148	4.35
	219	WC 148	4.35
	73	SWC 148	4.35
	311	RN 158	4.45
	430	RN 158	4.45
	446	SWC 160	4.45
	4301	RN 195	5.00

Cal.	No.	Type/Grs.	Per 100
8mm	817	RNGC 170	5.80
	980	RNGC 220	6.05
33	320	FPGC 200	6.05
348	447	FPGC 185	5.90
	457	FPGC 250	6.15
	319	RNGC 170	5.80
	315	RNGC 200	6.05
	248	FP 250	5.50
	43	FP 175	4.80
	169	FP 245	6.25
	98	FP 210	5.45

Cal.	No.	Type/Grs.	Price per 50
405 Win.	263	RN 290	6.30
43 Span.	910	RN 335	7.00
45/70	191	FP 305	6.60
	192	FP 345	7.00
	124	RN 395	7.80
	405	RN 505	9.10
50/70	141	FP 450	9.70
	911	RN 505	10.50
	42	SWC 200	5.00
41	41 L.C.	Heel 195	4.95
	26	WC 200	5.05
	256	SWC 210	5.05
	610	SWCGC 210	7.50
44	215	SWCGC 225	7.85
	383	RN245	5.70
	244	SWCGC 245	8.05
	352	WC 250	5.80
	421	SWC 250	5.80
45 Auto	389	SWC 185	5.15
	130	SWC 185	5.15
	460	SWC 200	5.25
	78	SWC 220	5.40
	374	RN 225	5.50
	400	RN 240	5.65
	225	SWC 240	5.65
45 Colt	424	SWC 225	5.80
	190	SWC 260	5.95

P—Pointed
RN—Round Nose
WC—Wadcutter
BB—Bevel Base
GC—Gas Check
FP—Flat Point
SWC—Semi-Wadcutter

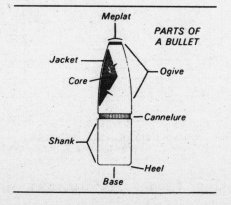

PARTS OF A BULLET

Meplat — Jacket — Core — Ogive — Cannelure — Shank — Heel — Base

FORSTER
Wax Loading Kit

A complete kit for reloading wax bullets: shell holder, primer punch, primer seater, special wax bullet compound, and a supply of modified (enlarged flash hole), unfired cases. Made in 38 Spl., 45 ACP and 45 Colt. Kit, complete **$14.00**

MILLER TRADING CO.
Cast Bullets

This firm offers cast bullets for rifles and handguns in over 40 types and calibers, and seven diameters of round balls. These may be had as cast or sized and lubed. All bullets shipped postpaid and insured in wooden boxes. Write to them for their latest list.

C.H. STOCKING
17 Caliber Bullets

All bullets are hand swaged, of hollow-point form and may be had in 22-, 25-, or 28-grain weights. Stocking also has 20-cal. and 25-cal. bullets. Write to Stocking for more information.

WOOD DIE SHOP

This well-known maker of bullet swage dies produces a line of precision 17-caliber bullets. Swaged by the "expanded-up" method, these bullets are available in 18-, 20-, 22-, 25-, and 28-gr. weights at **$5.00** per hundred.

17-caliber jackets (per M) . . . **$20.00**

ZERO BULLETS

Zero is offering a fine line of swaged bullets in 38, 9mm, and 45 in different styles and weights for all applications. These bullets are high quality due to the quality control measures taken by the makers. They are available in 500 round lots up to 25,000 round lots and are priced accordingly. Write to Zero for the latest price sheet giving styles and weights. Zero is also offering loaded 38 special ammunition in five styles. Minimum 15,000 round order for best prices.

FEDERAL®
AMMUNITION

CENTERFIRE PISTOL CARTRIDGES

Load No.	Cartridge	Bullet	Bullet Weight Grains
25AP	25 Auto Pistol (6.35mm)	MC	50
32AP	32 Auto Pistol (7.65mm)	MC	71
380AP	380 Auto Pistol	MC	95
380BP	380 Auto Pistol	JHP	90
9AP	9mm Luger Auto Pistol	MC	123
9BP	9mm Luger Auto Pistol	JHP	115
38A	38 Special Match	Lead WC	148
38B	38 Special	Lead RN	158
38C	38 Special	Lead SWC	158
‡38D	38 Special (+P)	Lead RN	158
‡38E	38 Special (+P)	JHP	125
‡38F	38 Special (+P)	JHP	110
‡38G	38 Special (+P)	Lead SWC HP	158

Load No.	Cartridge	Bullet	Bullet Weight Grains
‡38H	38 Special (+P)	Lead SWC	158
‡38J	38 Special (+P)	JSP	125
357A	357 Magnum	JSP	158
357B	357 Magnum	JHP	125
357C	357 Magnum	Lead SWC	158
357D	357 Magnum	JHP	110
357E	357 Magnum	JHP	158
†44B	44 Remington Magnum	JHP	180
44SA	44 S&W Special	Lead SWC HP	200
45LCA	45 Colt	Lead SWC HP	225
45A	45 Auto Match	MC	230
45B	45 Auto Match	MC SWC	185
45C	45 Auto	JHP	185

Retail sales records must be kept for all above items per Gun Control Act of 1968.

‡ This ammunition is loaded to a higher pressure, as indicated by the "+P" marking on the case headstamp, to achieve higher velocity. Use only in firearms especially designed for this cartridge and so recommended by the manufacturer.

† For Rifle or Pistol

CENTERFIRE RIFLE CARTRIDGES

Load No.	Cartridge	Bullet	Bullet Weight Grains
●222A	222 Remington	SP	50
●222B	222 Remington	BT MC	55
22250A	22-250 Remington	SP	55
●223A	223 Rem. (5.56mm)	SP	55
●223B	223 Rem. (5.56mm)	BT MC	55
243A	243 Winchester	SP	80
243B	243 Winchester	HI-S SP	100
6A	6mm Remington	SP	80
6B	6mm Remington	HI-S SP	100
2506A	25-06 Remington	HP	90
2506B	25-06 Remington	HI-S SP	117
270A	270 Winchester	HI-S SP	130
270B	270 Winchester	HI-S SP	150
7A	7mm Mauser	HI-S SP	175
7RA	7mm Rem. Magnum	HI-S SP	150
7RB	7mm Rem. Magnum	HI-S SP	175
●30CA	30 Carbine	SP	110
●30CB	30 Carbine	MC	110

Load No.	Cartridge	Bullet	Bullet Weight Grains
●3030A	30-30 Winchester	HI-S SP	150
●3030B	30-30 Winchester	HI-S SP	170
●3030C	30-30 Winchester	HP	125
3006A	30-06 Springfield	HI-S SP	150
3006B	30-06 Springfield	HI-S SP	180
3006C	30-06 Springfield	SP	125
3006D	30-06 Springfield	BT SP	165
3006E	30-06 Springfield	BT SP	200
300A	300 Savage	HI-S SP	150
300B	300 Savage	HI-S SP	180
300WB	300 Win. Magnum	HI-S SP	180
308A	308 Winchester	HI-S SP	150
308B	308 Winchester	HI-S SP	180
8A	8mm Mauser	HI-S SP	170
32A	32 Win. Special	HI-S SP	170
35A	35 Remington	HI-S SP	200
†●44A	44 Rem. Magnum	HSP	240
4570A	45-70 Government	HSP	300

● Retail sales records must be kept for these items per the Gun Control Act of 1968.

MC — Metal Case, JHP — Jacketed Hollow Point, WC — Wadcutter, RN — Round Nose, SWC — Semi-Wadcutter
HP — Hollow Point, JSP — Jacketed Soft Point, SP — Soft Point, HI-S — HI-Shok®, BT — Boat-Tail, HSP — Hollow Soft Point

† For Rifle or Pistol

Federal Cartridge Corporation   2700 Foshay Tower   Minneapolis, MN. 55402

FEDERAL® AMMUNITION

SHOTGUN SHELLS

HI-POWER® SUPER MAGNUM LOADS

Gauge	Load No.	Shell Length Inches	Powder Drams Equiv.	Ounces Shot	Shot Sizes
▲10	F103	3½	4¼	2	BB 2 4
▲12	F131	3	4	1⅞	BB 2 4
▲12	F129	3	4	1⅝	2 4 6
▲12	F130	2¾	3¾	1½	BB 2 4 5 6
▲16	F165	2¾	3¼	1¼	2 4 6
▲20	F207	3	3	1¼	2 4 6 7½
▲20	F205	2¾	2¾	1⅛	4 6 7½

HI-POWER® LOADS

Gauge	Load No.	Shell Length Inches	Powder Drams Equiv.	Ounces Shot	Shot Sizes
12	F127	2¾	3¾	1¼	BB 2 4 5 6 7½ 8 9
16	F164	2¾	3¼	1⅛	4 5 6 7½
20	F203	2¾	2¾	1	4 5 6 7½ 8 9
28	F283	2¾	2¼	¾	6 7½ 8
410	F413	3	Max.	¹¹⁄₁₆	4 5 6 7½ 8
410	F412	2½	Max.	½	6 7½

STEEL SHOT LOADS

Gauge	Load No.	Shell Length Inches	Powder Drams Equiv.	Ounces Shot	Shot Sizes
▲10	W104	3½	Max.	1⅝	BB 2
▲12	W149	3	Max.	1⅜	BB 1 2 4
▲12	W148	2¾	Max.	1¼	BB 1 2 4
12	W147	2¾	3¾	1⅛	1 2 4
▲20	W209	3	3¼	1	4

FIELD LOADS

Gauge	Load No.	Shell Length Inches	Powder Drams Equiv.	Ounces Shot	Shot Sizes
12	F125	2¾	3¼	1¼	7½ 8
12	F124	2¾	3¼	1¼	7½ 8 9
12	F123	2¾	3¼	1⅛	4 5 6 7½ 8 9
16	F162	2¾	2¾	1⅛	4 6 7½ 8
20	F202	2¾	2½	1	4 5 6 7½ 8 9

TARGET LOADS

Gauge	Load No.	Shell Length Inches	Powder Drams Equiv.	Ounces Shot	Shot Sizes
12	F115	2¾	2¾	1⅛	7½ 8 9
12	F116	2¾	3	1⅛	7½ 8 9
12	C117	2¾	2¾	1⅛	7½ 8 8½ 9
12	C118	2¾	3	1⅛	7½ 8 9
12	T122	2¾	3	1⅛	9
20	F206	2¾	2½	⅞	8 9
20	S206	2¾	2½	⅞	9
28	F280	2¾	2	¾	9
410	F412	2½	Max.	½	9

HI-POWER® BUCKSHOT LOADS

Gauge	Load No.	Shell Length Inches	Powder Drams Equiv.	Shot Sizes
10	G108	3½	Mag.	4 Buck — 54 Pellets
12	F131	3	Mag.	000 Buck — 10 Pellets
12	F131	3	Mag.	00 Buck — 15 Pellets
12	F131	3	Mag.	1 Buck — 24 Pellets
12	F131	3	Mag.	4 Buck — 41 Pellets
▲12	A131	3	Mag.	4 Buck — 41 Pellets
12	F130	2¾	Mag.	00 Buck — 12 Pellets
12	F130	2¾	Mag.	1 Buck — 20 Pellets
12	F130	2¾	Mag.	4 Buck — 34 Pellets
▲12	A130	2¾	Mag.	4 Buck — 34 Pellets
12	F127	2¾	Max.	000 Buck — 8 Pellets
12	G127	2¾	Max.	00 Buck — 9 Pellets
12	F127	2¾	Max.	00 Buck — 9 Pellets
12	F127	2¾	Max.	0 Buck — 12 Pellets
12	F127	2¾	Max.	1 Buck — 16 Pellets
12	F127	2¾	Max.	4 Buck — 27 Pellets
▲12	A127	2¾	Max.	4 Buck — 27 Pellets
16	F164	2¾	Max.	1 Buck — 12 Pellets
20	F207	3	Mag.	2 Buck — 18 Pellets
20	F203	2¾	Max.	3 Buck — 20 Pellets

HI-POWER® RIFLED SLUG LOADS

Gauge	Load No.	Shell Length Inches	Powder Drams Equiv.	Shot Sizes
12	F127	2¾	Max.	1 oz. Rifled Slug
▲12	A127	2¾	Max.	1 oz. Rifled Slug
16	F164	2¾	Max.	⅘ oz. Rifled Slug
20	F203	2¾	Max.	⅝ oz. Rifled Slug
410	F412	2½	Max.	⅕ oz. Rifled Slug

22 RIMFIRE CARTRIDGES

Load No.	50 rounds per box, 100 boxes per case except where noted*	Bullet Weight Grains
	HI-POWER® HIGH VELOCITY	
701	22 Short Copper Plated	29
703	22 Short Copper Plated Hollow Point	29
706	22 Long Copper Plated	29
710	22 Long Rifle Copper Plated	40
712	22 Long Rifle Copper Plated Hollow Point	38
716	22 Long Rifle #12 Shot	#12 Shot
*810	22 Long Rifle Copper Plated	40
*812	22 Long Rifle Copper Plated Hollow Point	38
	CHAMPION™ STANDARD VELOCITY	
702	22 Short Lead Lubricated	29
711	22 Long Rifle Lead Lubricated	40
*811	22 Long Rifle Lead Lubricated	40

* 100 rounds per box, 50 boxes per case

Buckshot and Rifled Slugs packed 5 rounds per box, 50 boxes per case except ▲ 25 rounds per box, 10 boxes per case.
All other shotshells packed 25 rounds per box, 20 boxes per case.

FRONTIER
The preferred ammunition for accurate performance

RIFLE AMMUNITION

			PER BOX Retail	

■ 222 REM.

			PER BOX Retail	
50 gr. SX	#8010	$ 8.40	_____
55 gr. SX	#8015	8.40	_____

■ 223 REM.

55 gr. SP	#8025	$ 9.25	_____
55 gr. FMJ	#8027	9.25	_____

■ 22-250 REM.

53 gr. HP	#8030	$ 9.25	_____
55 gr. SP	#8035	9.25	_____
55 gr. FMJ	#8037	9.25	_____

■ 220 SWIFT

55 gr. SP	#8120	$12.95	_____
60 gr. HP	#8122	12.95	_____

■ 243 WIN.

75 gr. HP	#8040	$11.50	_____
80 gr. FMJ	#8043	11.50	_____
100 gr. SP	#8045	11.50	_____

■ 270 WIN.

110 gr. HP	#8050	$12.50	_____
130 gr. SP	#8055	12.50	_____
140 gr. BTSP	#8056	12.65	_____
150 gr. SP	#8058	12.50	_____

■ 7mm REM. MAG.

154 gr. SP	#8060	$15.50	_____
175 gr. SP	#8065	15.50	_____

■ 30 M1 CARBINE

*110 gr. RN	#8070	$20.10	_____
*110 gr. FM	#8077	20.10	_____

■ 30-30 WIN.

150 gr. RN	#8080	$ 9.80	_____
170 gr. FP	#8085	9.80	_____

■ 308 WIN.

150 gr. SP	#8090	$12.50	_____
165 gr. SP	#8095	12.50	_____
165 gr. BTSP	#8098	12.95	_____
168 gr. BTHP (Match)	#8097	14.60	_____

■ 30-06 SPRINGFIELD

			PER BOX Retail	
150 gr. SP	#8110	$12.50	_____
165 gr. BTSP	#8115	12.95	_____
168 gr. BTHP (Match)	#8117	14.60	_____
180 gr. SP	#8118	12.50	_____

■ 300 WIN. MAG.

180 gr. SP	#8200	$16.35	_____

PISTOL AMMUNITION

■ 25 AUTO

*50 gr. FMJ-RN	#9000	$12.15	_____

■ 380 AUTO

*90 gr. JHP	#9010	$14.20	_____
*100 gr. FMJ	#9015	14.20	_____

■ 9MM LUGER

*90 gr. JHP	#9020	$17.25	_____
*100 gr. FMJ	#9023	17.25	_____
*115 gr. JHP	#9025	17.25	_____
*124 gr. FMJ-FP	#9027	17.25	_____

■ 38 SPECIAL

*110 gr. JHP	#9030	$16.35	_____
*125 gr. JHP	#9032	16.35	_____
*125 gr. JFP	#9033	16.35	_____
*148 gr. HBWC (Match)	#9043	14.05	_____
*158 gr. JHP	#9036	16.35	_____
*158 gr. JFP	#9038	16.35	_____
*158 gr. LRN	#9045	13.40	_____
*158 gr. SWC	#9046	13.40	_____

■ 357 MAG.

*125 gr. JHP	#9050	$18.25	_____
*125 gr. JFP	#9053	18.25	_____
*158 gr. JHP	#9056	18.25	_____
*158 gr. JFP	#9058	18.25	_____
*158 gr. SWC	#9065	15.45	_____

■ 44 REM. MAG.

200 gr. JHP	#9080	$ 9.50	_____
240 gr. JHP	#9085	9.50	_____
240 gr. SWC	#9087	8.05	_____

■ 45 ACP

185 gr. JHP	#9090	$ 8.05	_____
185 gr. Target SWC	#9095	8.70	_____
200 gr. SWC	#9110	7.45	_____
230 gr. FMJ-RN	#9097	8.05	_____
230 gr. FMJ-FP	#9098	8.05	_____

*Packed 50 per box. All others packed 20 per box.

Hornady Bullets... A complete selection for every shooting purpose.

RIFLE BULLETS
"I" denotes interlock bullets.

■ 17 CALIBER (.172)

	Price Per 100 Retail
25 gr. HP............#1710	$ 7.55 _____

■ 22 CALIBER (.222)

40 gr. Jet............#2210	$ 6.55 _____

■ 22 CALIBER (.223)

45 gr. Hornet.........#2220	$ 6.55 _____

■ 22 CALIBER (.224)

45 gr. Hornet.........#2230	$ 6.55 _____
50 gr. SPSX............#2240	$ 6.65 _____
50 gr. SP............#2245	$ 6.65 _____

■ 22 CALIBER MATCH

52 gr. BTHP..........#2249	$ 8.00 _____

■ 22 CALIBER MATCH

53 gr. HP............#2250	$ 8.00 _____
55 gr. SPSX..........#2260	$ 6.80 _____
55 gr. SP............#2265	$ 6.80 _____
55 gr. SP w/c........#2266	$ 7.25 _____
55 gr. FMJ-BT w/c..#2267	$ 7.25 _____
60 gr. SP............#2270	$ 7.25 _____
60 gr. HP............#2275	$ 8.00 _____

■ 22 CALIBER (.227)

70 gr. SP............#2280	$ 8.90 _____

■ 6MM CALIBER (.243)

70 gr. SP............#2410	$ 8.45 _____
75 gr. HP............#2420	$ 8.55 _____

6MM Caliber (.243) continued

	Price Per 100 Retail
80 gr. FMJ............#2430	$ 9.25 _____
87 gr. SP............#2440	$ 8.90 _____
87 gr. BTHP..........#2442	$ 9.90 _____
I 100 gr. SP............#2450	$ 9.25 _____
100 gr. BTSP........#2453	$ 9.55 _____
I 100 gr. RN............#2455	$ 9.25 _____

■ 25 CALIBER (.257)

60 gr. FP............#2510	$ 8.45 _____
75 gr. HP............#2520	$ 8.90 _____
87 gr. SP............#2530	$ 9.20 _____
I 100 gr. SP............#2540	$ 9.45 _____
I 117 gr. RN............#2550	$10.10 _____
I 120 gr. HP............#2560	$10.25 _____

■ 6.5MM CALIBER (.264)

100 gr. SP............#2610	$10.10 _____
I 129 gr. SP............#2620	$10.90 _____
I 140 gr. SP............#2630	$11.10 _____
I 160 gr. RN............#2640	$12.25 _____

■ 270 CALIBER (.277)

100 gr. SP............#2710	$ 9.80 _____

270 Caliber (.277) continued

	Price Per 100 Retail
110 gr. HP............#2720	$10.00 _____
I 130 gr. SP............#2730	$10.55 _____
I 140 gr. BTSP........#2735	$11.20 _____
I 150 gr. SP............#2740	$11.10 _____
I 150 gr. RN............#2745	$11.10 _____

■ 7MM CALIBER (.284)

120 gr. SP............#2810	$10.20 _____
120 gr. HP............#2815	$10.20 _____
I 139 gr. SP............#2820	$10.65 _____
I 154 gr. SP............#2830	$11.35 _____
I 154 gr. RN............#2835	$11.55 _____

■ 7MM MATCH

162 gr. BTHP........#2840	$13.65 _____
162 gr. BTSP........#2845	$12.75 _____
I 175 gr. SP............#2850	$12.55 _____
I 175 gr. RN............#2855	$12.55 _____

■ 30 CALIBER (.308)

100 gr. SJ............#3005	$ 6.55 _____
110 gr. SP............#3010	$ 9.25 _____
110 gr. RN............#3015	$ 8.45 _____

Prices effective January 15, 1981 (All prices subject to change without notice.)

30 Caliber (.308) continued

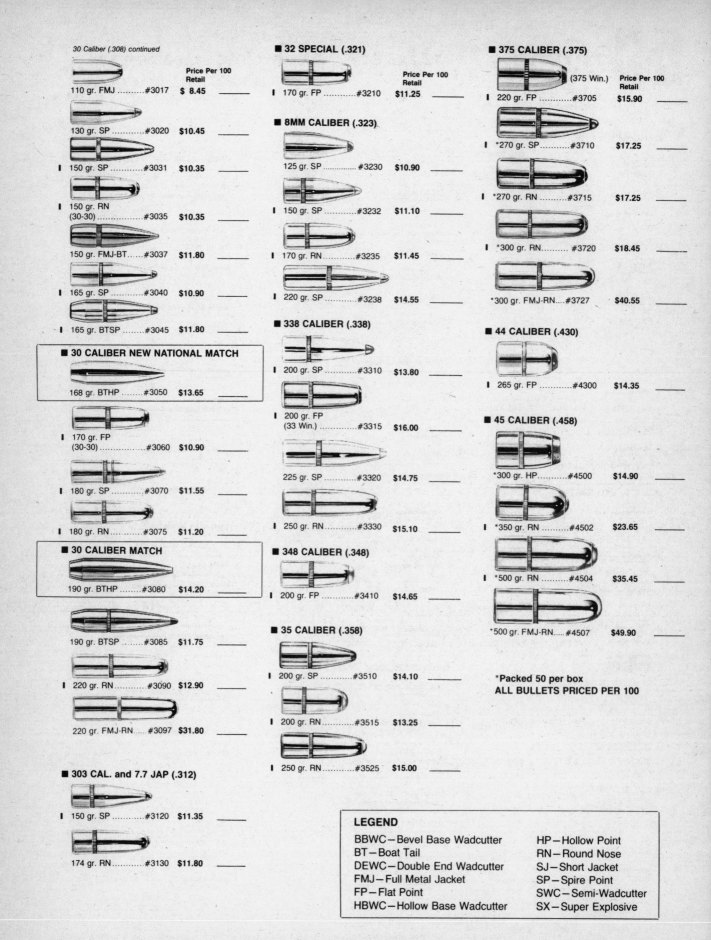

	Price Per 100 Retail
110 gr. FMJ ....#3017	$ 8.45
130 gr. SP ....#3020	$10.45
150 gr. SP ....#3031	$10.35
150 gr. RN (30-30) ....#3035	$10.35
150 gr. FMJ-BT ....#3037	$11.80
165 gr. SP ....#3040	$10.90
165 gr. BTSP ....#3045	$11.80

■ **30 CALIBER NEW NATIONAL MATCH**

168 gr. BTHP ....#3050	$13.65

170 gr. FP (30-30) ....#3060	$10.90
180 gr. SP ....#3070	$11.55
180 gr. RN ....#3075	$11.20

■ **30 CALIBER MATCH**

190 gr. BTHP ....#3080	$14.20

190 gr. BTSP ....#3085	$11.75
220 gr. RN ....#3090	$12.90
220 gr. FMJ-RN .....#3097	$31.80

■ **303 CAL. and 7.7 JAP (.312)**

150 gr. SP ....#3120	$11.35
174 gr. RN ....#3130	$11.80

■ **32 SPECIAL (.321)**

	Price Per 100 Retail
170 gr. FP ....#3210	$11.25

■ **8MM CALIBER (.323)**

125 gr. SP ....#3230	$10.90
150 gr. SP ....#3232	$11.10
170 gr. RN ....#3235	$11.45
220 gr. SP ....#3238	$14.55

■ **338 CALIBER (.338)**

200 gr. SP ....#3310	$13.80
200 gr. FP (33 Win.) ....#3315	$16.00
225 gr. SP ....#3320	$14.75
250 gr. RN ....#3330	$15.10

■ **348 CALIBER (.348)**

200 gr. FP ....#3410	$14.65

■ **35 CALIBER (.358)**

200 gr. SP ....#3510	$14.10
200 gr. RN ....#3515	$13.25
250 gr. RN ....#3525	$15.00

■ **375 CALIBER (.375)**

(375 Win.)

	Price Per 100 Retail
220 gr. FP ....#3705	$15.90
*270 gr. SP ....#3710	$17.25
*270 gr. RN ....#3715	$17.25
*300 gr. RN ....#3720	$18.45
*300 gr. FMJ-RN....#3727	$40.55

■ **44 CALIBER (.430)**

265 gr. FP ....#4300	$14.35

■ **45 CALIBER (.458)**

*300 gr. HP...........#4500	$14.90
*350 gr. RN ....#4502	$23.65
*500 gr. RN ....#4504	$35.45
*500 gr. FMJ-RN.....#4507	$49.90

*Packed 50 per box
ALL BULLETS PRICED PER 100

LEGEND

BBWC—Bevel Base Wadcutter	HP—Hollow Point
BT—Boat Tail	RN—Round Nose
DEWC—Double End Wadcutter	SJ—Short Jacket
FMJ—Full Metal Jacket	SP—Spire Point
FP—Flat Point	SWC—Semi-Wadcutter
HBWC—Hollow Base Wadcutter	SX—Super Explosive

JACKETED PISTOL BULLETS

■ 25 CALIBER (.251)

Price Per 100 Retail

50 gr. FMJ-RN.......#3545 $ 7.20 _____

■ 9MM CALIBER (.355)

90 gr. HP.............#3550 $ 7.45 _____

100 gr. FMJ ....#3552 $ 7.65 _____

115 gr. HP ....#3554 $ 7.75 _____

124 gr. FMJ-FP......#3556 $ 8.20 _____

■ 38 CALIBER (.357)

110 gr. HP ....#3570 $ 7.75 _____

125 gr. HP ....#3571 $ 7.90 _____

125 gr. FP ....#3573 $ 7.90 _____

38 Caliber (.357) continued

Price Per 100 Retail

158 gr. HP...........#3575 $ 8.25 _____

158 gr. FP ....#3578 $ 8.25 _____

160 gr. FMJ ....#3579 $ 9.55 _____

■ 41 CALIBER (.410)

210 gr. HP ....#4100 $10.00 _____

■ 44 CALIBER (.430)

200 gr. HP ....#4410 $10.00 _____

240 gr. HP ....#4420 $10.90 _____

240 gr. FMJ-FP......#4427 $11.65 _____

■ 45 CALIBER (.451)

Price Per 100 Retail

185 gr. HP, ACP ....#4510 $10.35 _____

185 gr. Target SWC, ACP............#4513 $10.65 _____

230 gr. FMJ-RN .....#4517 $10.90 _____

NEW

230 gr. FMJ-FP......#4518 $10.90 _____

■ 45 CALIBER (.452)

250 gr. Long Colt HP ....#4520 $11.10 _____

LEGEND

BBWC—Bevel Base Wadcutter	HP—Hollow Point
BT—Boat Tail	RN—Round Nose
DEWC—Double End Wadcutter	SJ—Short Jacket
FMJ—Full Metal Jacket	SP—Spire Point
FP—Flat Point	SWC—Semi-Wadcutter
HBWC—Hollow Base Wadcutter	SX—Super Explosive

Packed 50 per box. All others packed 20 per box.

LEAD PISTOL BULLETS   *Bulk Price Per 1000

Bulk lead bullets must be ordered in increments of carton quantities per bullet. 5000 bullets per carton except 44 caliber is 4000 per carton.

38 cal. (.358)

148 gr. ....#3580 $ 5.35 _____
BBWC..................* #1010 $42.00 _____

38 cal. (.358)

148 gr. ....#3582 $ 5.35 _____
HBWC ....* #1020 $42.00 _____

38 cal. (.358)

148 gr.   (Bulk only)
DEWC ....* #1030 $42.00 _____

38 cal. (.358)

                              #3586 $ 5.55 _____
158 gr. RN ....* #1050 $45.00 _____

38 cal. (.358)

                              #3588 $ 5.55 _____
158 gr. SWC.............* #1040 $45.00 _____

44 cal. (.430)

                              #4430 $ 8.00 _____
240 gr. SWC.............* #1110 $66.00 _____

45 cal. (.452)

                              #4526 $ 7.00 _____
200 gr. SWC.............* #1210 $60.55 _____

*500 Per Box except 44 cal. (400 Per Box)

ROUND LEAD BALLS

Here is an item for Black Powder shooters. Round Lead Balls in 12 sizes, from .350 through .570.

Price Per 100 Retail

.350..............#6010	$ 4.10	_____
.375..............#6020	4.35	_____
.433..............#6030	5.00	_____
.440..............#6040	5.10	_____
.445..............#6050	5.20	_____
.451..............#6060	5.35	_____
.454..............#6070	5.45	_____
.457..............#6080	5.55	_____
.490..............#6090	6.10	_____
.530..............#6100	6.90	_____
.535..............#6110	7.10	_____
*.570..............#6120	7.90	_____

*Packed 50 per box—all others packed 100 per box.

BARNES BULLETS
P.O. Box 215
American Fork, Utah 84003

CALIBER			Jacket Thickness	Retail
				PER 50
17 Caliber				
.172	25 Gr.	Semi-Spitzer S.P.	030"	$8.00
22 Caliber				
.224	60 Gr.	Semi-Spitzer S.P.	030"	$7.50
.224	60 Gr.	Semi-Spitzer F.M.J.	030"	7.90
.224	70 Gr.	Semi-Spitzer S.P.	030"	7.60
.224	83 Gr.	Semi-Spitzer S.P.	030"	7.80
		.228/.230 diameter $1.00 extra		
6 mm. Caliber				
.243	90 Gr.	Semi-Spitzer S.P.	030"	$8.00
.243	110 Gr.	Semi-Spitzer S.P.	030"	8.20
.243	120 Gr.	Round Nose S.P.	030"	8.40
25 Caliber				
.257	90 Gr.	Semi-Spitzer S.P.	032"	$8.00
.257	90 Gr.	Semi Spitzer F.M.J.	032"	8.40
.257	125 Gr.	Semi-Spitzer S.P.	032"	8.70
6.5 mm. Caliber				
.264	130 Gr.	Semi-Spitzer S.P.	032"	$8.40
.264	150 Gr.	Semi-Spitzer S.P.	032"	8.55
.264	165 Gr.	Semi-Spitzer S.P.	032"	8.90
270 Caliber				
.277	130 Gr.	Semi-Spitzer S.P.	032"	$8.40
.277	130 Gr.	Semi-Spitzer F.M.J.	032"	8.75
.277	150 Gr.	Semi-Spitzer S.P.	032"	8.70
.277	160 Gr.	Semi-Spitzer S.P.	032"	8.85
.277	180 Gr.	Round Nose S.P.	032"	9.25
.277	180 Gr.	Round Nose F.M.J.	032"	10.90
7 mm. Caliber				
.284	125 Gr.	Semi-Spitzer S.P.	032"	$8.40
.284	140 Gr.	Semi-Spitzer S.P.	032"	8.85
.284	160 Gr.	Semi-Spitzer S.P.	032"	9.05
.284	180 Gr.	Semi-Spitzer S.P.	032"	9.25
.284	195 Gr.	Semi-Spitzer S.P.	032"	9.45
.284	200 Gr.	Round Nose F.M.J.	035"	11.05
		.288 diameter $1.00 extra		
30 Caliber				
.308	150 Gr.	Semi-Spitzer S.P.	032"	$9.05
.308	180 Gr.	Semi-Spitzer S.P.	032"	9.25
.308	200 Gr.	Semi-Spitzer S.P.	032"	9.35
.308	225 Gr.	Semi-Spitzer S.P.	032"	9.60
.308	250 Gr.	Round Nose S.P.	032"	9.90
.308	250 Gr.	Round Nose F.M.J.	035"	12.10
8 mm. Caliber				
.323	150 Gr.	Semi-Spitzer S.P.	032"	$9.25
.323	180 Gr.	Semi-Spitzer S.P.	032"	9.40
.323	200 Gr.	Semi-Spitzer S.P.	032"	9.75
.323	225 Gr.	Semi-Spitzer S.P.	049"	14.10
.323	250 Gr.	Semi-Spitzer S.P.	032"	10.10
		.318 diameter $1.00 extra		

CALIBER			Jacket Thickness	Retail
				PER 50
338 Caliber				
.338	200 Gr.	Semi-Spitzer S.P.	032"	$9.85
.338	250 Gr.	Semi-Spitzer S.P.	032"	10.20
.338	250 Gr.	Semi-Spitzer S.P.	049"	14.10
.338	300 Gr.	Round Nose S.P.	049"	15.05
.338	300 Gr.	Round Nose F.M.J.	049"	16.75
		.333/.330 diameter $1.00 extra		
348 Winchester				
.348	250 Gr.	Flat Nose S.P. Cannelured	032"	$9.45
35 Caliber				
.358	200 Gr.	Semi-Spitzer S.P.	032"	$9.90
.358	250 Gr.	Semi-Spitzer S.P.	032"	10.25
.358	275 Gr.	Semi-Spitzer S.P.	049"	14.60
.358	300 Gr.	Round Nose S.P.	032"	10.80
.358	300 Gr.	Round Nose S.P.	049"	15.30
.358	300 Gr.	Round Nose F.M.J.	049"	16.90
9.3 Caliber				
.366	250 Gr.	Semi-Spitzer S.P.	032"	$9.50
.366	300 Gr.	Semi-Spitzer S.P.	032"	10.80
38/55 -375 Winchester				
.375	255 Gr.	Flat Nose S.P.	032"	$9.55
.377	255 Gr.	Flat Nose S.P.	032"	9.55
375 Caliber				
.375	250 Gr.	Semi-Spitzer S.P.	032"	$9.60
.375	300 Gr.	Semi-Spitzer S.P.	032"	10.90
.375	300 Gr.	Semi-Spitzer S.P.	049"	14.80
.375	350 Gr.	Round Nose S.P.	032"	13.50
.375	350 Gr.	Round Nose S.P.	049"	16.20
.375	350 Gr.	Round Nose F.M.J.	049"	17.75
401 Winchester S.L.				
.406	250 Gr.	Round Nose S.P.	032"	$9.55
411 Caliber				
.411	300 Gr.	Semi-Spitzer S.P.	032"	$10.50
.411	400 Gr.	Semi-Spitzer S.P.	032"	13.95
.411	400 Gr.	Round Nose S.P.	049"	17.40
.411	400 Gr.	Round Nose F.M.J.	049"	19.10
		.408 diameter $1.00 extra		
416 Caliber				
.416	300 Gr.	Semi-Spitzer S.P.	032"	$10.60
.416	400 Gr.	Round Nose S.P.	032"	14.10
.416	400 Gr.	Round Nose S.P.	049"	17.70
.416	400 Gr.	Round Nose F.M.J.	049"	19.30
404 Jeffrey				
.423	400 Gr.	Round Nose S.P.	032"	$14.40
.423	400 Gr.	Round Nose S.P.	049"	17.90
.423	400 Gr.	Round Nose F.M.J.	049"	19.70
444 Marlin				
.430	250 Gr.	Flat Nose S.P.	032"	$9.55
.430	300 Gr.	Flat Nose S.P.	032"	9.90

CALIBER			Jacket Thickness	Retail
				PER 50
425 Westley Richards				
.435	410 Gr.	Round Nose S.P.	049"	$18.70
.435	410 Gr.	Round Nose F.M.J.	049"	20.15
45/70 Caliber				
.458	300 Gr.	Semi-Spitzer S.P.	032"	$9.90
.458	300 Gr.	Round Nose S.P.	032"	9.90
.458	400 Gr.	Semi-Spitzer S.P.	032"	12.90
.458	400 Gr.	Round Nose S.P.	032"	12.90
.458	500 Gr.	Semi-Spitzer S.P.	032"	15.30
.458	500 Gr.	Round Nose S.P.	032"	15.30
458 Magnum Caliber				
.458	400 Gr.	Semi-Spitzer S.P.	049"	$17.90
.458	400 Gr.	Round Nose S.P.	049"	17.90
.458	500 Gr.	Semi-Spitzer S.P.	049"	19.70
.458	500 Gr.	Round Nose S.P.	049"	19.70
.458	500 Gr.	Round Nose F.M.J.	049"	22.75
.458	600 Gr.	Semi-Spitzer S.P.	049"	22.55
.458	600 Gr.	Round Nose S.P.	049"	22.56
.458	600 Gr.	Round Nose F.M.J.	049"	25.90
		.455 diameter $1.00 extra		
465 Nitro				
.468	500 Gr.	Round Nose S.P.	049"	$19.80
.468	500 Gr.	Round Nose F.M.J.	049"	23.20
470 Nitro - 475 A&M				
.475	500 Gr.	Round Nose S.P.	049"	$19.80
.475	500 Gr.	Round Nose F.M.J	049"	23.20
.475	600 Gr.	Round Nose S.P.	049"	23.00
.475	600 Gr.	Round Nose F.M.J.	049"	26.60
475 No. 2 Jeffrey				
.488	500 Gr.	Round Nose S.P.	049"	$21.95
.488	500 Gr.	Round Nose F.M.J.	049"	25.50
		.483 diameter $1.00 extra		
505 Gibbs				
.505	600 Gr.	Round Nose S.P.	049"	$27.50
.505	600 Gr.	Round Nose F.M.J.	049"	33.70
.505	700 Gr.	Round Nose S.P.	049"	35.00
.505	700 Gr.	Round Nose F.M.J.	049"	41.90
		.510 Diameter $1.00 extra		
50/110 Winchester				
.510	300 Gr.	Flat Nose S.P.	032"	$10.45
.510	450 Gr.	Flat Nose S.P.	032"	13.20
577 Nitro				**PER 20**
.585	750 Gr.	Round Nose S.P.	049"	$18.00
.585	750 Gr.	Round Nose F.M.J.	049"	23.40
600 Nitro				
.620	900 Gr.	Round Nose S.P.	049"	$24.00
.620	900 Gr.	Round Nose F.M.J.	049"	31.20

A current F.F.L. is required with bullet purchases. If not a license holder order through your local dealer. Dealer prices available. (Outside United States license not required).
Special caliber/weights not listed made to order. Call or write for price quote. Small orders welcome.

Nosler Trophy Grade Bullets

Whether your trophy is a bull elk of Boone and Crockett proportions or an engraved cup awarded in competitive shooting, the performance of every bullet you shoot has to measure up to the job at hand. Nosler designs and manufactures every bullet it makes, both Partition and Solid Base, to perform every time as if your target were a trophy. Because Nosler believes *every* shot you take is important, *every* Nosler bullet has trophy performance built in…in accuracy, in flight characteristics, in striking power. That is why Nosler bullets can truly be called "Trophy Grade" bullets.

Caliber	Diameter	Partition	Bullet Weight and Style	50 PER BOX
6mm	.243″		95 Gr. Spitzer	
	.243″		100 Gr. Semi Spitzer	
.25	.257″		100 Gr. Spitzer	
	.257″		115 Gr. Spitzer	
	.257″		117 Gr. Semi Spitzer	
6.5mm	.264″		125 Gr. Spitzer	
	.264″		140 Gr. Spitzer	
.270	.277″		130 Gr. Spitzer	
	.277″		150 Gr. Spitzer	
	.277″		160 Gr. Semi Spitzer	
7mm	.284″		140 Gr. Spitzer	
	.284″		150 Gr. Spitzer	
	.284″		160 Gr. Spitzer	
	.284″		175 Gr. Semi Spitzer	
.30	.308″		150 Gr. Spitzer	
	.308″		165 Gr. Spitzer	
	.308″		180 Gr. Spitzer	
	.308″		180 Gr. Protected Point	
	.308″		200 Gr. Round Nose	
.338	.338″		210 Gr. Spitzer	
	.338″		250 Gr. Round Nose	

Caliber	Diameter	Solid Base	Bullet Weight and Style
.22	.224″		50 Gr. Spitzer
	.224″		50 Gr. Hollow Point
	.224″		50 Gr. Hollow Pt. Match
	.224″		52 Gr. Hollow Point
	.224″		52 Gr. Hollow Pt. Match
	.224″		55 Gr. Spitzer
	.224″		60 Gr. Spitzer
6mm	.243″		70 Gr. Hollow Point
	.243″		70 Gr. Hollow Pt. Match
	.243″		85 Gr. Spitzer
	.243″		100 Gr. Spitzer
.25	.257″		100 Gr. Spitzer
	.257″		120 Gr. Spitzer
6.5mm	.264″		120 Gr. Spitzer
.270	.277″		100 Gr. Spitzer
	.277″		130 Gr. Spitzer
	.277″		150 Gr. Spitzer
7mm	.284″		120 Gr. Spitzer
	.284″		140 Gr. Spitzer
	.284″		150 Gr. Spitzer
.30	.308″		150 Gr. Flat Point
	.308″		150 Gr. Spitzer
	.308″		150 Gr. Hollow Point
	.308″		150 Gr. Hollow Pt. Match
	.308″		165 Gr. Spitzer
	.308″		168 Gr. Hollow Point
	.308″		168 Gr. Hollow Pt. Match
	.308″		170 Gr. Flat Point
	.308″		180 Gr. Spitzer

REMINGTON RELOADING ZONE

"Core-Lokt® Bullets

The "Number One Mushroom"—a name given by hunters everywhere to the Remington center fire cartridges with "Core-Lokt" bullets.

Superior mushrooming and one-shot stopping power are the results of the advanced design of "Core-Lokt" bullets: metal jacket and lead core are locked together by the jacket's heavy mid-section. "Core-Lokt" bullets are available in a wide variety of types and weights.

Bronze Point Expanding Bullet

A top performing all-around bullet of a unique design for extra long range accuracy and controlled expansion. Travels in a flat trajectory and has great wind bucking qualities.

"Power-Lokt"® Bullets

Remington "Power-Lokt" bullets are uniquely designed with the core and jacket electrolytically bonded into a one-piece unit. This exclusive process produces a better balance and more concentric bullet of uniformly high performance, rapid expansion and amazing accuracy.

ABBREVIATIONS

BrPt—Bronze Point	PL—Power-Lokt
CL—Core-Lokt	PSP—Pointed Soft Point
GC—Gas Check	SJ—Semi-Jacketed
HP—Hollow Point	SP—Soft Point
J—Jacketed	WC—Wadcutter
LD—Lead	SWC—Semi-Wadcutter
MC—Metal Case	

NEW ORDER NO.	OLD ORDER NO.		DESCRIPTION	WT. (LBS.) PER 100
17 cal. (.172)				
B1705	B22936		25 gr. PLHP	0.3
22 cal. (.224)				
B2210	B22704		45 gr. SP	0.7
B2220	B27710		50 gr. PSP	0.7
B2230	B22708		50 gr. MC	0.7
B2240	B22950		50 gr. PLHP	0.7
B2250	B22956		50 gr. PL Match	0.7
B2260	B22948		52 gr. HPBR	0.8
B2270	B22924		55 gr. PSP	0.8
B2280	B22952		55 gr. PLHP	0.8
B2290	B22958		55 gr. PL Match	0.8
B2265	B23558		55 gr. MC WO/C	0.8
6mm (.243)				
B2420	B22966		80 gr. PSP	1.2
B2430	B22954		80 gr. PLHP	1.2
B2440	B22960		80 gr. PL Match	1.2
B2460	B22920		100 gr. PSPCL	1.5
25 cal. (.257)				
B2510	B22752		87 gr. PLHP	1.4
B2520	B22730		100 gr. PSPCL (25-06)	1.5
B2540	B22736		120 gr. PSPCL (25-06)	1.8
6.5mm (.264)				
B2610	B22926		120 gr. PSPCL	1.8
270 cal. (.277)				
B2710	B23744		100 gr. PSP	1.5
B2720	B22746		130 gr. PSPCL	1.9
B2730	B22748		130 gr. BrPt	1.9
B2740	B22750		150 gr. SPCL	2.2
7mm (.284)				
B2830	B22756		150 gr. PSPCL	2.2
B2850	B22918		175 gr. PSPCL 7mm Rem.	2.6
30 cal. (.308)				
B3010	B22796		110 gr. SP Carbine	1.6
B3020	B22770		150 gr. BrPt (30-06)	2.2
B3025	B22774		150 gr. SPCL (30-30)	2.2
B3030	B22776		150 gr. PSPCL	2.2
B3040	B23594		165 gr. PSPCL	2.4
B3050	B22782		170 gr. SPCL	2.5
B3060	B22784		180 gr. BrPt	2.6
B3070	B22786		180 gr. SPCL	2.6

NEW ORDER NO.	OLD ORDER NO.		DESCRIPTION	WT. (LBS.) PER 100
30 Cal. (.308) Cont'd				
B3080	B22788		180 gr. PSPCL	2.6
B3090	B22792		220 gr. SPCL	3.2
32 cal. (.320)				
B3250	B22828		170 gr. SPCL	2.5
8mm (.323)				
B3270	B22984		185 gr. PSPCL	2.8
B3280	B22986		220 gr. PSPCL	3.3
35 cal. (.358)				
B3510	B22868		200 gr. SPCL	2.9
9mm (.354)				
B3550	B22942		115 gr. JHP	1.8
B3552	B22842		124 gr. MC	1.9
38 cal.				
B3810	B22944		95 gr. SJHP	1.4
357/38 cal. (.357)				
B3570	B23586		110 gr. SJHP	1.6
B3572	B22866		125 gr. SJHP	1.9
B3574	B22846		158 gr. SP	2.3
B3576	B22938		158 gr. SJHP	2.3
357 cal. (.358)				
B3578	B22856		158 gr. LEAD SWC†	2.3
38 cal. (.360)*				
B3830	B22850		148 gr. LD WC†	2.2
38 cal. (.358)				
B3840	B22854		158 gr. LEAD†	2.3
B3850	B23568		158 gr. LEAD HP	2.3
41 mag. (.310)				
B4110	B22888		210 gr. SP	3.1
41 mag. (.411)				
B4120	B22922		210 gr. LEAD	3.1
44 cal. (.430)				
B4405	B23588		180 gr. SJHP	2.8
B4410	B22906		240 gr. SP	3.5
B4420	B22940		240 gr. SJHP	3.5
44 cal. (.432)				
B4430	B22884		240 gr. LEAD GC	3.5
B4440	B22768		240 gr. LEAD	3.5
45 cal. (.451)				
B4530	B22892		230 gr. MC†	3.4
B4510	B22890		185 gr. MCWC†	2.7
B4520	B22586		185 gr. JHP	2.7

* .360 dia. for best accuracy.   † Also available in bulk pack.

REMINGTON RELOADING ZONE

Remington brass cases with 5% more brass for extra strength in head section—annealed neck section for longer reloading life—primer pocket dimension controlled to .0005 inch to assure precise primer fit—heavier bridge and sidewalls—formed and machined to exacting tolerances for consistent powder capacity—choice of seventy-one center fire rifle, pistol and revolver cases—

Rifle Cases (Unprimed)

	QTY. PER BOX	"KLEANBORE" PRIMER NO.	PRICE PER BOX
17 REMINGTON • U17REM ✶	20	7½	$6.11
22 HORNET • U22HRN	50	6½	8.89
222 REMINGTON • U222R	20	7½	4.27
222 REMINGTON MAGNUM • U222MG	20	7½	4.83
22-250 REMINGTON • U22250	20	9½	6.11
★ 223 REMINGTON • U223	20	7½	5.28
6mm REMINGTON • U6MM	20	9½	6.11
243 WINCHESTER • U243	20	9½	6.11
25-06 REMINGTON • U2506	20	9½	6.44
270 WINCHESTER • U270	20	9½	6.44
7mm-08 REMINGTON • U7MM08	20	9½	6.11
7mm EXPRESS REMINGTON • U7MM06 ‡	20	9½	6.44
7mm REMINGTON MAGNUM • U7MMAG	20	9½M	8.00
30 CARBINE • U30CAR	50	6½	9.26
30-06 SPRINGFIELD • U3006	20	9½	6.44
30-30 WINCHESTER • U3030	20	9½	5.53
300 WINCHESTER MAGNUM • U300W	20	9½M	8.00
8mm REMINGTON MAGNUM • U8MMAG	20	9½M	8.45
308 WINCHESTER • U308	20	9½	6.11
45-70 GOVERNMENT • U4570	20	9½	5.94

Pistol and Revolver Cases

	QTY. PER BOX	"KLEANBORE" PRIMER NO.	PRICE PER BOX
357 MAGNUM (BRASS) • U357B	50	5½	6.95
9mm LUGER AUTO PISTOL • U9MLUG	50	1½	8.89
38 SPECIAL (BRASS) • U38SPB	50	1½	6.30
41 REMINGTON MAGNUM • U41MAG	50	2½	9.36
44 REMINGTON MAGNUM • U44MAG	50	2½	9.44
45 COLT • U45CLT	50	2½	9.44
45 AUTO • U45AP	50	2½	8.89

* Designed for Remington No. 7½ primer only. Substitutions not recommended. U number is unprimed.

‡ Interchangeable with 280 Rem.

★ NEW

Bench Rest Cases

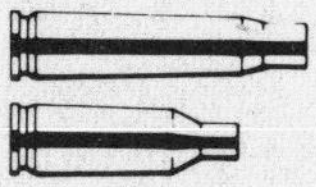

	QTY. PER BOX	"KLEANBORE" PRIMER NO.	PRICE PER BOX
	20	7½	$6.20

Order No. URBR Remington .308 BR case ready for sizing, shortened and necked down to .224, 6mm, or 7mm.

Remington "Kleanbore" CENTER FIRE PRIMERS

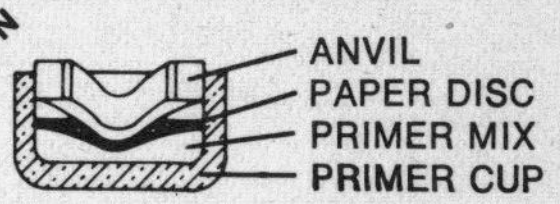

Diagram labels: ANVIL, PAPER DISC, PRIMER MIX, PRIMER CUP

PRIMER NO.	ORDER NO.	DESCRIPTION
Small Pistol 1½	X 22600	Brass. Nickel-plated. For small revolver and pistol cartridges.
Large Pistol 2½	X 22604	Brass. Nickel-plated. For large revolver and pistol cartridges.
Small Pistol 5½	X 22626	Brass. Nickel-plated. Specially designed for 32 S & W and 357 Magnum cartridges.
Small Rifle 6½	X 22606	Brass. Nickel-plated. For small rifle cartridges other than those noted under Primer No. 7½.
Small Rifle Bench Rest 7½	X 22628	Brass. Copper-plated. Specially designed for 17 Rem., 221 Rem., "Fire Ball," 222 Rem., 222 Rem. Mag., 22 Rem. BR and 223 Rem. cartridges.
Large Rifle 9½	X 22608	Brass. For large rifle cartridges.
Magnum Rifle 9½M	X 22622	Brass. For use in belted magnum cartridges, 264 Win., 6.5mm Rem. Magnum., 7mm Rem. Magnum, 300 Win. Magnum, 300 H&H Magnum, 8mm Rem. Magnum, 350 Rem. Magnum, 375 H&H Magnum, 458 Win. Magnum cartridges.

PERCUSSION CAPS

SIZE	INSIDE DIA.	ORDER NO.	DESCRIPTION
10	.162"	X 22616	A hotter primer mix to assure more reliable ignition of both black powder and substitutes. Uniform, dependable performance. F.C. trimmed edge, foil-lined, center fire. Identical in length, priming mixture, weight of charge.
11	.167"	X 22618	
12	.172"	X 22620	

All Remington Center Fire Primers and Percussion Caps packed 100 per box (PC caps—tin), 1,000 per carton, 5,000 per case.

Sierra Bullets

10532 South Painter Avenue
Santa Fe Springs, California 90670

Stock No.	Description	
.22 Caliber .223" Diameter Hornet		
1100	40 gr. Hornet	
1110	45 gr. Hornet	
.22 Caliber .224" Diameter Hornet		
1200	40 gr. Hornet	
1210	45 gr. Hornet	
.22 Caliber .224" Diameter High Velocity		
1300	45 gr. SMP	
1310	45 gr. SPT	
1320	50 gr. SMP	
1330	50 gr. SPT	
1340	50 gr. Blitz	
1350	55 gr. SMP	
1355	55 gr. FMJBT	NEW
1360	55 gr. SPT	
1365	55 gr. SBT	
1370	63 gr. SMP	
.22 Caliber .224" Diameter MatchKing		
1400	53 gr. HP	
1410	52 gr. HPBT	
6MM .243" Diameter		
1500	60 gr. HP	
1505	70 gr. HPBT MatchKing	
1510	75 gr. HP	
1520	85 gr. SPT	
1530	85 gr. HPBT	
1540	100 gr. SPT	
1550	100 gr. SMP	
1560	100 gr. SBT	

Stock No.	Description	
.25 Caliber .257" Diameter		
1600	75 gr. HP	
1610	87 gr. SPT	
1615	90 gr. HPBT	
1620	100 gr. SPT	
1630	117 gr. SBT	
1640	117 gr. SPT	
1650	120 gr. HPBT	
6.5MM .264" Diameter		
1700	85 gr. HP	
1710	100 gr. HP	
1720	120 gr. SPT	
1730	140 gr. SBT	
1740	140 gr. HPBT MatchKing	
.270 Caliber .277" Diameter		
1800	90 gr. HP	
1810	110 gr. SPT	
1820	130 gr. SBT	
1830	130 gr. SPT	
1840	150 gr. SBT	
1850	150 gr. RN	
7MM .284" Diameter		
1900	120 gr. SPT	
1910	140 gr. SPT	
1915	150 gr. HPBT MatchKing	NEW
1920	160 gr. SBT	
1930	168 gr. HPBT MatchKing	
1940	175 gr. SBT	
1950	170 gr. RN	

Stock No.	Description	
.30 Caliber .307" Diameter		
2000	150gr. FN	
2010	170gr. FN	
2020	125gr. HP	
.30 Caliber .308" Diameter		
2100	110gr. RN	
2105	110gr. FMJ	
2110	110gr. HP	
2120	125gr. SPT	
2125	150gr. SBT	
2130	150gr. SPT	
2135	150gr. RN	
2140	165gr. HPBT	
2145	165gr. SBT	
2150	180gr. SPT	
2160	180gr. SBT	
2165	200gr. SBT	
2170	180gr. RN	
2180	220gr. RN	
.30 Caliber .308" Diameter MatchKing		
2190	150gr. HPBT	NEW
2200	168gr. HPBT	
2210	190gr. HPBT	
2220	180gr. HPBT	
2230	200gr. HPBT	
2240	220gr. HPBT	
.303 Caliber .311" Diameter		
2300	150gr. SPT	
2310	180gr. SPT	
8MM .323" Diameter		
2400	150gr. SPT	
2410	175gr. SPT	
2420	220gr. SBT	
.338 Caliber .338" Diameter		
2600	250gr. SBT	
.35 Caliber .358" Diameter		
2800	200gr. RN	

Stock No.	Description	
.375 Caliber .375" Diameter		
3000	300gr. SBT	
.45-70 Caliber .458" Diameter		
8900	300gr. HP	
9MM .355" Diameter		
8100	90gr. JHP	
8110	115gr. JHP	
8120	125gr. FMJ	NEW
.38 Caliber .357" Diameter		
8300	110gr. JHC	
8310	125gr. JSP	
8320	125gr. JHC	
8330	150gr. JHC	
8340	158gr. JSP	
8350	170gr. FMJ Match	
.41 Caliber .410" Diameter		
8500	170gr. JHC	
8520	210gr. JHC	
8530	220gr. FMJ	NEW
.44 Magnum .429" Diameter		
8600	180gr. JHC	
8605	220gr. FMJ Match	
8610	240gr. JHC	
.45 Caliber .451" Diameter		
8800	185gr. JHP	
8810	185gr. FMJ Match	
8815	230gr. FMJ Match	
8820	240gr. JHP	
Accessories		
Sierra Bullet Board With Real Redwood Frame		
Sierra Reloading Manual (700 pgs.)		
Sierra Bullet Patch		
Sierra Bullet Patch, Pin and Decal Set		
Sierra Marksman Cap		
Sierra Bullet Keychain		
Sierra Solid Brass Belt Buckle		
Sierra Bullet Paperweight		

SPEER
OMARK INDUSTRIES

BULLETS

22 CALIBER (.223)

1005 40 Gr. Spire Point

1011 45 Gr. Spitzer

22 CALIBER (.224)

1017 40 Gr. Spire

1023 45 Gr. Spitzer

1029 50 Gr. Spitzer

1035 52 Gr. Hollow Point

1045 55 Gr. F M J

1047 55 Gr. Spitzer

1049 55 Gr. Spitzer

1053 70 Gr. Smi-Spitzer

6mm CALIBER (.243)

1205 75 Gr. Hollow Point

1211 80 Gr. Spitzer

1213 85 Gr. Boat Tail

1215 90 Gr. F M J

1217 90 Gr. Spitzer

1223 105 Gr. Round Nose

1229 105 Gr. Spitzer

25 CALIBER (.257)

1241 87 Gr. Spitzer

1405 100 Gr. spitzer

1407 100 Gr. Hollow Point

1410 120 Gr. Boat Tail

1411 120 Gr. Spitzer

6.5mm CALIBER (.263)

1435 120 Gr. Spitzer

1441 140 Gr. Spitzer

270 CALIBER (.277)

1447 100 Gr. Hollow Point

1453 100 Gr. Spitzer

1458 130 Gr. Boat Tail

1459 130 Gr. Spitzer

1465 130 Gr. Grand Slam

1604 150 Gr. Boat Tail

1605 150 Gr. Spitzer

1608 150 Gr. Grand Slam

7mm CALIBER (.284)

1617 155 Gr. Hollow Point

1623 130 Gr. Spitzer

1628 145 Gr. Boat Tail

1629 145 Gr. Spitzer

1634 160 Gr. Boat Tail

1635 160 Gr. Spitzer

1637 160 Gr. Magnum Mag-Tip

1638 175 Gr. Grand Slam

1641 175 Gr. Magnum Mag.-Tip

1643 175 Gr. Grand Slam

30 CALIBER (.308)

1805 100 Gr. Pinker ®

1835 110 Gr. Hollow Point

1845 110 Gr. Round Nose

1855 110 Gr. Spire Point

2005 130 Gr. Hollow Point

2007 130 Gr. Flat Point

2011 150 Gr. Flat Point

2017 150 Gr. Round Nose

2022 150 Gr. Boat Tail

2023 150 Gr. Spitzer

2025 150 Gr. Magnum Mag.-Tip

2029 160 Gr. Round Nose

2034 165 Gr. Boat Tail

2035 165 Gr. Spitzer

2038 165 Gr. Grand Slam

2041 170 Gr. Flat Point

2047 180 Gr. Round Nose

2052 180 Gr. Boat Tail

2053 180 Gr. Spitzer

2059 180 Gr. Mag.-Tip

2063 180 Gr. Grand Slam

2211 200 Gr. Spitzer

BULLETS

OMARK INDUSTRIES

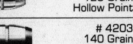

303 CALIBER (.311)

2217
150 Grain
Spitzer

2223
180 Grain
Round Nose

32 CALIBER (.321)

2259
170 Grain
Flat Nose

8mm CALIBER (.323)

2277
150 Grain
Spitzer

2283
170
Semi-Spitzer

2285
200 Grain
Spitzer

338 CALIBER (.338)

2405
200 Grain
Spitzer

2408
250 Grain
Grand Slam

2411
275 Grain
Semi-Spitzer

35 CALIBER (.358)

2435
180 Grain
Flat Nose

2453
250 Grain
Spitzer

375 CALIBER (.375)

2471
235 Grain
Semi-Spitzer

2473
285 Grain
Grand Slam

45 CALIBER (.458)

2479
400 Grain
Flat Nose

9mm CALIBER (.355)

4000
88 Grain
Hollow Point

3983
100 Grain
Hollow Point

4005
125 Grain
Soft Point

38 CALIBER (.357)

4007
110 Grain
Hollow Point

4011
125 Grain
Soft Point

4013
125 Grain
Hollow Point

4203
140 Grain
Hollow Point

4205
146 Grain
Hollow Point

4211
158 Grain
J H P

4217
158 Grain
Soft Point

4223
160 Grain
Soft Point

41 CALIBER (.410)

4405
200 Grain
Soft Point

4417
220 Grain
Soft Point

44 CALIBER (.429)

4425
200 Grain
Mag Hollow Point

4435
225 Grain
Hollow Point

4447
240 Grain
Soft Point

4453
240 Grain
Mag
Hollow Point

4457
240 Grain
Mag Soft Point

45 CALIBER (.451)

4477
200 Grain
Hollow Point

4479
225 Grain
Mag Hollow Point

4481
260 Gr.
Hollow Point

(Lead)

9mm CALIBER (.356)

4601
125 Grain
Round Nose

38 CALIBER (.358)

4605
148 Grain
BBWC

4617
148 Grain
HBWC

4623
158 Grain
SWC

4647
158 Grain
Round Nose

44 CALIBER (.430)

4660
240 Grain
SWC

45 CALIBER (.452)

4677
200 Grain
SWC

4690
230 Grain
Round Nose

4683
250 Grain
SWC

ROUND BALL

#5113 .375	#5135 .454"
#5127 .433"	#5137 .457"
#5129 .440"	#5139 .490"
#5131 .445"	#5142 .530"
#5133 .451"	#5180 .570"

AMMUNITION

22 RIMFIRE

Mini-Mag   Long Rifle   # 0030

Mini-Mag Long Rifle
50 pack paper   # 0034

Mini-Mag Long Rifle
Hollow Point   # 0031

Mini-Group Long Rifle   # 0032

Mini-Mag Long   # 0029

Mini-Mag Short   # 0027

Mini-Mag Short
Hollow Point   # 0028

Mini-Group Short Target   # 0037

Mini-Mag CB Long   # 0038

Mini-Cap CB   # 0026

Mini-Mag Shotshell   # 0039
                                     20/Box

Stinger, Long Rifle
Hollow Point   50/Box   # 0050

Maxi-Mag WMR   # 0023
Solid   50/Box

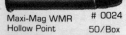
Maxi-Mag WMR   # 0024
Hollow Point   50/Box

Maxi-Mag WMR   # 0025
Shotshell   20/Box

380 AUTO

                                     #3605
380 88JHP
MV1000Ft/Sec.   ME-195 Ft. Lbs.

9mm LUGER

                                     # 3610
9mm Luger,100 JHP   Brass
MV-1315 Ft/Sec. ME-384 Ft. Lbs.

                                     # 3620
9mm Luger, 125 JSP   Brass
MV-1120Ft/Sec. ME-348 Ft. Lbs.

38 SPECIAL

                                     # 3710
38 Special, 110 JHP   Nickel
MV-1245 Ft/Sec., ME-378 Ft. Lbs.

                                     # 3720
38 Special, 125 JHP   Nickel +P
MV-1425 Ft/Sec., ME-563 Ft. Lbs.

                                     # 3725
38 Special, 125 JSP   Nickel +P
MV-1425 Ft/Sec.,ME-563 Ft. Lbs.

                                     # 3740
38 Special, 140 JHP   Nickel +P
MV-1200 Ft/Sec., ME-447 Ft.Lbs.

                                     # 3748
38 Special,148 HBWC   Brass
MV-825 Ft/Sec.,ME-223 Ft. Lbs.

                                     # 3752
38 Special, 158 SWC   Nickel
MV—975 Ft/Sec.,ME-333 Ft. Lbs.

                                     # 3758
38 Special, 158 RN   Nickel
MV-975 Ft/Sec.,ME-333 Ft. Lbs.

                                     # 3759
38 Special, 158 JSP   Nickel +P
MV-1025 Ft/Sec., ME-368 Ft. Lbs.

                                     # 3760
38 Special, 158 JHP   Nickel+P
MV-1025 Ft/Sec.,ME-368 Ft. Lbs.

                                     # 3708
38/357 Shotshell   Neckel
#9 Shot 50/Box
                                     # 3709
38/357 Shotshell   Nickel
#9 shot 10/Box
MV-1150 Ft/Sec.,ME-308 Ft. Lbs.

357 MAGNUM

                                     # 3910
357 Magnum, 110 JHP   Nickel
MV-1700 Ft/Sec., ME-705 Ft. Lbs.

                                     # 3920
357 Magnum, 125 JHP   Nickel
MV-1900 Ft/Sec. ME-1001 Ft. Lbs.

                                     # 3925
357 Magnum, 125 JSP   Nickel
MV-1900 Ft/Sec.,ME-1001 Ft. Lbs.

                                     # 3940
357 Magnum, 140 JHP   Nickel
MV-1780 Ft/Sec. ME-984 Ft. Lbs.

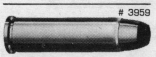
                                     # 3959
357 Magnum, 158 JSP   Nickel
MV-1625 Ft/Sec.,ME-926 Ft. Lbs.

                                     # 3960
357 Magnum, JHP   Nickel
MV-1625 Ft/Sec., ME-926 Ft. Lbs.

44 MAGNUM

                                     # 3972
                          Brass
44 Magnum, 200 JHP   25/Box
MV-1675 Ft/Sec.,ME-1246 Ft. Lbs.

                                     # 3974
                          Brass
44 Magnum, 240 JSP   25/Box
MV-1650 Ft/Sec. ME-1450 Ft. Lbs.

44 Magnum Shotshell   # 3978
#9 shot 25/Box   Brass

44 Magnum Shotshell   # 3979
#9 Shot 10/Box   Brass
MV-1200 Ft/Sec., ME-494 Ft. Lbs.

45 AUTO

                                     # 3965

45 Auto, 200 JHP   Brass
MV-1025 Ft/Sec.,ME-466 Ft.Lbs.

Notes on Wads . . .

There are three basic wad types: over-powder, filler and overshot. The over-powder wads are available in card form (made of compressed paper), or as plastic wads. The over-powder wad separates the powder from the softer filler wads and effects a gas seal ahead of the powder. Filler wads are resilient to cushion the initial shock, and are available in a variety of thicknesses to give the proper wad column height for perfect crimps and correct pressure. Since the majority of shotshells loaded today are star crimped, they need no overshot wad. Only the older roll crimp shells require a wad which is held by the crimp to contain the shot.

Over-shot wads are made of compressed paper, similar to the over-powder type.

Federal

Ljutic Mono

ACTION LB Spin Wad

One wad fits all 12-ga. shells. Gives spiral or circular collapse and has reverse rifled shot flanges, said to give dense and consistent shot patterns.

Price per thousand, postpaid . **$8.00**

LAGE UNIWAD

This universal wad allows a change of powder charge for different cases and still stacks the proper height for a good crimp. Designed for 1⅛ oz. trap and Skeet loads, but it can be used for hunting loads too. Available in 12 and 20 gauge only. From Lage Uniwad Co.

Per M about **$12.95**

Federal

LJUTIC
Plastic Mono Wad

Made in 12 gauge only, this wad features serrated runners the length of the wad to give less drag on the barrel. One piece design eliminates other wads and gives more consistent loads, greater speed with a reduction in powder charge. For use in Winchester AA plastic hulls and Federal plastic and paper shells.

Per M **$12.99**

FEDERAL CARTRIDGE CORP.
Shotshell Wads

Plastic Wad Columns

Type	Gauge	Number	Price/M
Champion	12	12C1	$24.70
Super-Plus	12	12S3	22.70
Super-Plus	12	12S4	22.70
Super-Plus	20	20S1	22.70
Super-Plus	28	28S1	22.70
2½"	410	410SC	22.70

Packed 250 per bag, 20 bags per case of 5,000.

Card Wads

Type	Gauge	Number	Price/M
20 Ga., .135"	20	20-135	$6.30

Packed 1,000 per bag, 20 bags per case of 10,000.

American Wad

Pacific Versalite

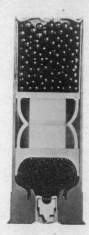

LJUTIC
Fiber Mono Wad

A 1-piece wad for general use that eliminates the 2-piece, 2- or 3-stage wad column. Ljutic Mono-Wads give less recoil and make possible the use of less powder for the same muzzle velocity and pattern. Available in all standard gauges, including 410.

Per M...................$7.99

P & P TOOL CO.
American Wad

This new wad is, so far, available only in 12 gauge. It has a thin-walled powder cup for better gas seal, a newly designed "X" mid-section for even pressure on the shot column. Wad material will not crack or brittle in cold weather. With 1⅛-oz. of shot, wad will fit any standard shell such as Win. AA (red), Win. AA Handicap (black), Rem. (black), Rem RXP and Federal. Quantity discounts available. Price per thousand...................$8.25

PACIFIC
Versalite Wads

A compressible center section in this wad will adjust to the correct wad column length. Available in 12 and 10 gauge, the Versalite provides an excellent gas seal and shot protection. Shot cup is slightly flared to slip easily over the wad seating punch. From Pacific Tool Co.

12 or 20 ga., per M........$18.00
10 ga., per M.............$23.00

PACIFIC
Verelite Wads

The Verelite wad is made in two colors — green for 1⅛ oz. target loads in RP plastic target or WW paper target cases, and blue for 1¼ oz. loads in the WW, AA or Federal paper hulls. 12 ga. only.

Per M...................$18.00

REMINGTON

Power Piston Wads
For Plastic Trap & Skeet Loads

Gauge	Wad No.	Per M
12	RXP12	$20.96
20	RXP20	20.96
20	RP20	20.96
28	SP28	20.96
410	SP410	20.96
410	SP4103	20.96

RXP20 wad replaces R20 wad.

Power Piston Wads
For Plastic Field Loads

Gauge	Wad No.	Per M
10 (1⅝ or 2 oz.)	SP10	$25.84
12 (1 oz. load)	R12L	20.96
12 (1⅛ oz. load)	R12H	20.96
12 (3¼x1¼ oz.)	RP12	20.96
12 (3¾x1¼ oz.)	SP12	20.96
16 (1 oz. load)	R16	20.96
16 (1⅛ oz. load)	SP16	20.96
20 (1 oz. load)	SP20	20.96

Prices are approximate.

TRICO
Precision Wads

These wads are available in 12, 20, 28 and 410 gauge. The 12 and 20 ga. are two-piece construction. They are designed with the MEC press in mind and the Precision 2 wads will fit all 20-ga. shells. Three different color-coded 410 wads are available, each for a different load. All are priced at **$9.00** per thousand. From Trico Products.

WINCHESTER WADS

Type	Gauge	Per M
WAA12	12	$22.70
WAA12R	12	22.70
WAA12XW	12	22.70
WAA12F114	12	22.70
WAA20	20	22.70
WAA20F1	20	22.70
WAA28	28	22.70
WAA41	410	22.70

The Double A is designed to give straight line compression — no tipped wad. The vented skirt at the base allows trapped air to escape when seating the wad during reloading. When fired, hinged posts progressively collapse to absorb recoil.
Courtesy Winchester-Western

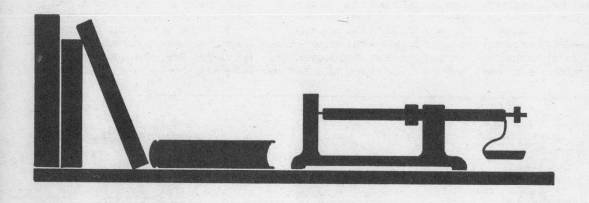

MISCELLANEOUS

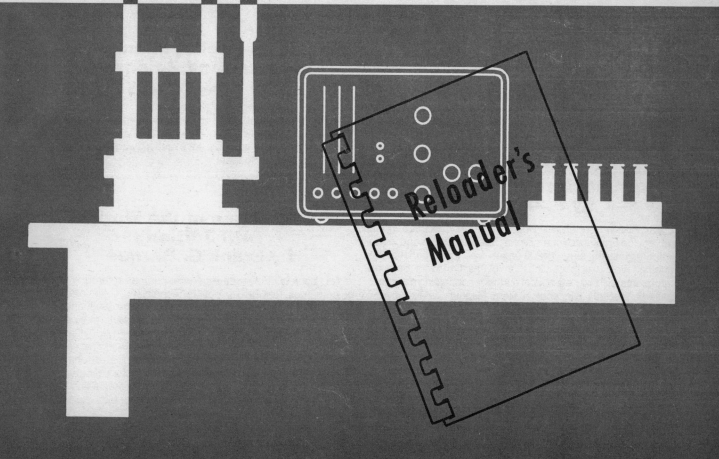

Reloader's Manual

Notes on Books & Manuals . . . .

The reloading bench without a choice selection of books and/or manuals is by no means complete. No case should be charged or bullet seated until the reloader is sure that the load and bullet he is using is the correct one to do the job he wants to have done. Whether you are new to reloading or a veteran of many years, a good selection of written material is a must if you are to produce safe, accurate ammunition each time you reload.

The man who wants to enjoy handloading will read as much material on the subject as he can, he'll go beyond the point of looking at the pictures, captions and bold face type and read and heed the cautions and warnings he'll find in all reloading literature. He'll use only the powder type recommended, approach maximum loads with extreme caution and double check the manuals along every step of his operation. He'll be safe, not sorry—slower, of course, but surer.

Best of all, he'll be able to take advantage of years of testing and experimentation by men who have devoted their lives to handloading. It is a sorry sight indeed to see a man buy a loading press, dies, components, etc., and walk out of the store without a manual of some sort.

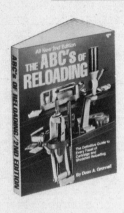 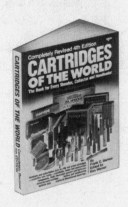 

ABC's of Reloading 2nd Edition
by Dean Grennell

A wealth of new information is included in this new edition. Step-by-step instruction on reloading techniques, basic info on powders, cases, shot, etc. Everything about bullets from casting, sizing and lubrication to swaging. New ballistic information, testing reloads, mathematics and the reloader, shopping for components and equipment, building a reloading library—all facets of the hobby are covered. Complete with a directory of manufacturers of reloading equipment. From DBI Books. **$8.95**

Ackley's Revised Handbook for Shooters and Reloaders
by P. O. Ackley

The excellent reference work of this title described in the 4th Edition of HANDLOADER'S DIGEST has been expanded to two volumes totalling almost 1200 pages. Vol. 1 is a reprint of the original; Vol. 2 is a continuation of the first, with data on approximately 100 new wildcat cartridges, including a number based on the 284 Win. and 350 Rem. Magnum cases. All new factory cartridges are covered, new loading information on old designs is given, a shotgun load section has been added and, because of demand, Ackley's article on action blow-ups has been reprinted. The results of these tests should surprise a number of the newer guncranks who have accepted too much opinion and too little fact. From P. O. Ackley, 2235 Arbor Lane, Salt Lake City, Utah 84117. Separately, **$9.95** each.
Both **$19.50**

Ackley's Pocket Manual for Shooters and Reloaders
by P. O. Ackley

A durable handbook-size volume containing selected data from Ackley's bigger book. Many factory and wildcat cartridges are covered in detail. An excellent working reference for shooters and reloaders.
Price **$4.95**

Cartridges of the World 4th Edition
by Frank C. Barnes

This book is the standard general-purpose reference work on cartridges, for which scientists, technicians, collectors, and laymen alike reach first for answers to cartridge questions. It's a basic book, setting down the dimensions, performance parameters and physical characteristics for over 1,000 different cartridges. This is an encyclopedic reference work that covers rifle and pistol cartridges—rimfire and centerfire—shotshells, loads and components. Both general and historical notes are given for each cartridge, with factory and handloading data and dimensional drawings. From DBI Books, Inc. **$9.95**

The Complete Book of Practical Handloading by John Wooters

This up-to-date book covers reloading rifle, pistol, and shotgun ammunition and takes the reader through all the basic concepts and steps of shooting and handloading. Chapters are devoted to loading for hunting, wildcatting, and for benchrest accuracy. Cast-bullet shooting and loading for black powder cartridge guns are also covered in detail. 320 pages, soft covers. Stoeger Publishing Co. $6.95

Corbin Bullet Swaging Books

Corbin publishes and sells all the bullet swaging books in print. These include the hardcover textbook, *Discover Swaging*, 283 pages, published by Stackpole, and written by Dave Corbin. Price $16.95

The Corbin Handbook & Catalog, Volume V, is the guide to available swaging equipment, how to specify equipment and design bullets, and an introduction to bullet swaging technique. Price $3.00

The Corbin Technical Bulletins, Volume I, is a 66 page soft cover book full of questions and answers about swaging, problems and dealer questions, comparisons with casting, cost figures for making bullets, and other detailed information. Price $5.00

The Corbin Technical Bulletins, Volume II, is a 113 page metallic cover book with the history of swaging, future directions, chapters on each caliber range and how to make specific kinds of bullets for each group of calibers from the sub-cals to the nitro express. Full of photos and practical data. Price $5.00

The Bullet Swage Manual, T. Smith, is the old manuscript by famous pioneer die-maker Smith, published by Corbin in 1976, and is an interesting historical reference for students of bullet swaging. Price $3.50

Complete Guide to Handloading by Philip B. Sharpe

A comprehensive, authoritative coverage, but somewhat dated today. This revised 3rd edition (1953) of the "handloader's bible" gives much information on tools and techniques, old and semi-new, and on every phase of handloading. Containing over 8000 individual loads for rifle, revolver and pistol cartridges, it discusses practically every variety of shell and primer, bullet and bullet mould, for rifle and revolver. Funk & Wagnalls, New York. Fully illustrated, 734 pages. Although out of print and difficult to obtain, some copies are available from arms books dealers.

Du Pont Handloader's Guide

The Du Pont Company has published an updated edition of it's "Handloader's Guide for Smokeless Powders." This 43-page guide lists more than 2,300 loads for shotgun, rifle and handgun ammunition using the 13 Du Pont smokeless powders. Many new loads using recently introduced components were developed for this edition, and several new rifle calibers are included. The new guide is available free at stores carrying Du Pont powders.

Elk Mountain Reloading Manual for Advanced Handloaders Vol. #1, 30-06

A new type of "reloading" manual claiming to contain more loading data than all other manuals. This is the first of a projected series of manuals—one for each cartridge to cover 243, 308, 270, 30-06 and 300 Win. Mag. Data presentation is graphical instead of tabular and both velocity and maximum peak pressure data are presented for all pressures from 20,000 psi to 60,000 psi, using an absolute pressure system with common crusher values noted. Bullet weights for the 30-06 range from 50 to 300 grains. Data for the 150-gr. bullet includes over 60 powders available from the six major distributors. Black powder loads are included but not lead bullets. From Elk Mountain Shooters Supply. $11.95

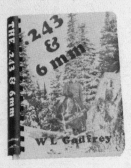

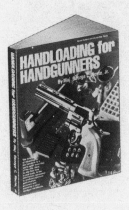

Elk Mountain Reloading Manual Vol. #2, "The 243 & 6mm"

Similar coverage of the two subject cartridges as in Volume 1. Bullet weights from 60 to 155 grains and over 70 powders are covered. From Elk Mountain Shooters Supply... **$11.95**

The 577/450 Martini Henry of 1871

This 18-page booklet deals with a short history, general information and complete, up-to-date reloading information for this cartridge. Full details are given on cases, dies, primers, bullets, powders, bullet lubes, etc. It is written in a narrative style and is more like a feature magazine article than a "loading manual." Two pages of tables are included with all facts about each load. Available from the author, Jim Jukes (2501 Corinth Ave., Los Angeles, CA 90064) for **$2.00**, postpaid.

Handloading For Handgunners by George C. Nonte, Jr.

With shooting costs escalating, more and more handgunners are learning to load their own. Nonte covers the subject in detail, including the many benefits of handloading, basic tools needed and loading bench layouts. Chapters cover selection of bullets, powder and primers. Tells how to cast and prepare bullets, how to swage, how to produce ultralight and powderless loads, how to correct misfires, neck splits, primer leaks and bulged cases. Also includes dimensional ballistics, case capacity and basic loading data tables. From DBI Books, Inc. **$8.95**

Hodgdon's Reloading Data Manual #24

Contains a great deal of loading data (rifle, handgun and shotshell) featuring Hodgdon's many powders, including data on their latest powders, Spherical BL-C(2), and newly manufactured 4831. In most instances it lists specific pressure data collected during Hodgdon's tests. Few other references list actual pressures, so this manual is particularly valuable. Weatherby calibers are also included. This edition also has new data on Pyrodex and black powder, a new section on reloading basics for the beginner, and information on rifle and pistol cast (lead) bullet loads. Hodgdon also publishes a Black Powder Manual and a Shotshell Data Manual for those who enjoy their sport only and do not need the volume of rifle and pistol loads given in this book. Price .... **NA**

Hornady Handbook of Cartridge Reloading — Third Edition

First published in 1967 as a 360-page volume, the handbook has grown to 688 hardbound pages. Expansion of the new third edition provides a wealth of useful information. Details are provided on more than a hundred Hornady bullets for use in 117 different cartridges. This includes information on many popular European cartridges as well as a special section on wildcat and obsolete loads. There is also a special section covering both rifle and pistol calibers for silhouette shooting. Profusely illustrated and comprehensive in its scope. **$11.95**

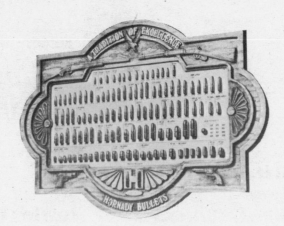

Hornady Bullet Board

A new bullet display board showing the complete line of Hornady rifle and pistol bullets features actual samples of 118 Hornady rifle and pistol bullets and a representative sample of round balls for muzzle loading. It is the seventh in the series of bullet boards produced by Hornady and follows the firm's tradition of producing functional, decorative designs which have been highly popular with collectors and reloaders alike.

Designed in the form of a turn-of-the-century wall carving, the new Hornady bullet display reproduces detailed hand carvings of rifles and pistols and is topped by a soaring American eagle. It measures 16″ by 23″ and is designed for easy mounting in den, office or reloading room. **$63.50**

Home Guide to Cartridge Conversions
by George C. Nonte, Jr.

The single reference book for handloaders who want to convert commercially available cartridge cases for use in shootable but obsolete arms. Tools and materials needed for case reforming are covered as well as step-by-step instructions on the procedures. Over 300 cartridge data sheets are included, giving complete information on adaptable cases, forming operations required and loading data. 404 pp. illustrated. From Rutgers Book Center. **$15.00**

I-DENT-A
Handloader's Data Log

A three-ring vinyl binder with woodgrain finish, the Data-Log comes with 50 data sheets for 1,000 load records. Sheets have columns for the following information: Date, yards, group size, case, number of shots, primer, bullet, powder/grains, powder measure, over-all length, I-Dent-A number, comments, gun, serial number, caliber and barrel. Extra data sheets $4.25 per 50. Data Log from Edmisten Co. **$8.95**

Lazy-X Handloaders Notebook

This is a big hardbound looseleaf notebook for recording data on handloads. It measures 10″x10½″ and has 8 plastic dividers to separate the data as to caliber, powders, etc. The book comes with 72 pages printed on heavy stock, each with spaces for load, powder, bullet, primer, case used and range data. Each page has room for 25 loads. The binder is covered with heavy duty vinyl and is easily cleaned of oil and dirt. Price, postpaid **$8.95**

LYMAN
Shotshell Reloading Basics

Here are 64 pages of basic reloading information for the beginning shotshell reloader. The well illustrated book covers components, chokes, patterns, sighting-in, slug-gun tips, and basic loading data. **$2.95**

LYMAN
Data Log

This handy, vinyl, three-ring binder contains a selection of three different types of data sheets to get the reloader started (12 each for metallic, shotshell and black powder) to record load testing results, favorite loads and other pertinent information. Price is **$8.95.** Refills for any of the three sections come in 50 page packages. **$5.95**

LYMAN
Cast Bullet Handbook
3rd Edition

This handbook contains load data on nearly every popular rifle and pistol cartridge incorporating the most popular cast bullet designs and weights, plus a complete "how-to" section, pictorial listing of cast bullet designs, and a comprehensive black powder section. **$14.95**

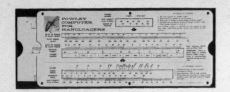

Lyman Shotshell Handbook 2nd Edition

This reloading handbook covers every aspect of shotshell reloading. It includes over 1000 tested loads covering all gauges 10, 12, 16, 20, 28, and 410. Complete "How to Reload" section on choosing a load, factory velocities, assembling shotshells, etc. Finger tabbed and color coded for speed and ease of reference. The large reference section covers up-to-date pressure information, full color case identification chapter, plus chapters on wads, patterns, powder and primers. An indispensable guide for the shotshell reloader. **$10.95**

LYMAN Pistol and Revolver Handbook

This book features 2,065 fresh handgun loads as well as complete trajectory and wind-drift tables. There are 74 pages of data covering new bullets, powders, primers, and cases, plus a section on loading and shooting black powder revolvers. The 280-page book also describes Lyman's composite bullet system. 8½" x 11". Price **$10.95**

Lyman Reloader's Handbook 45th Edition

A standard reloading reference for shooters the world over. Its easy-to-follow instructions will make the novice an expert in no time. The Handbook covers the entire field, including step-by-step instructions on the use of Lyman reloading equipment, complete information on reloading for rifles, pistols, shotguns, and muzzle-loaders. It is a mine of valuable data, including up-to-date information on new loads, pet loads, bullets and techniques. **$10.95**

MTM Handloaders Log

Designed to provide the handloader/shooter with a concise, written, easy-to-use scientific approach to load record keeping. The 3-ring looseleaf binder is vinyl covered and comes with 50 printed pages — enough for 1,000 entries. Log headings and spaces for: rifle model, serial number, date, yards, group size or score, number of shots, powder/grains, bullet weight, primer, case, conditions and notes **$8.59**

50 additional pages **$4.89**

Powley High Velocity Trajectory Chart

This 36" x 24" horizontal chart shows the bullet path to 500 yards for Ingalls' Ballistic Coefficients from 0.15 to 0.50 and 2600 to 5000 f/s muzzle velocities. Fast and easy to use. From Marian Powley. **$27.00**

Powley Computer for Handloaders

This handy 4" x 9" slide chart computes quickly and accurately the following data for handloaders: Most efficient powder for guns using Military Rifle powders. Best powder for combination of bullet weight and case. Powder charge. Estimated velocity. Foreign orders add **$2.00**. From Marian Powley **$7.00**

Combination price for Computer and Calculator .. **$12.50**

Powley PSI Calculator

Used in conjunction with the Powley Computer and a counter chronograph, this 3" x 8½" slide chart supplies pounds-per-square inch chamber pressures. A very useful tool for handloaders. Available from Hutton Rifle Ranch. **$6.00**

Combination price for Computer and Calculator, includes a special powder selection chart, available only from Hutton, postpaid **$12.50**; foreign orders................... **$14.50**

RELOADER'S GUIDE 3rd Edition By R. A. Steindler

This practical book has been newly updated and revised to reflect the changes in this economical and rewarding adjunct to shooting and hunting. Contains the latest technical data, expanded loading tables, tips on solving handloading problems, bullet casting, swaging, and cartridge case conversions. Profusely illustrated with diagrams and photographs of the latest techniques and equipment. 244 pages, soft covers. Stoeger Publishing Co. **$7.95**

Reloading For Shotgunners
Ed. by Robert S. L. Anderson

Sound and savvy articles on "shorty" shells, wildcatting, slug reloading, patterning, skeet and trap loads. Shotshells for the small bores, the 10-gauge magnum and the 12-gauge. Tips and tricks to make reloading easier; how to recognize bad hulls and improperly loaded shotshells, how to avoid component spills and mixups, what wads for what hulls, proper storing of components. Complete listings for all available loading data from powder, press and shot manufacturers. Photos and descriptions of presses in operation and a separate catalog section on presses, components and prices. From DBI Books Inc. $7.95

SIERRA
Reloader's Manual
Second Edition

The Second Edition Sierra Reloader's Manual is designed for the novice and advanced reloader alike. In the sections on Rifle and Handgun Loading Data, numerous loads for all commonly available powders are listed, along with muzzle velocities for each bullet and powder charge. In the large section on Exterior Ballistics are tables for every Sierra bullet, giving velocity ranges, remaining energy, various zero range selections, and wind deflection. The manual comes in a heavy duty 3-ring binder cover that lays flat on the loading bench. There are 700 pages of data and shooting information. $14.95

SIERRA
Bullet Board

Sierra's sixth bullet board in a series is now available. Each frame is made of hand carved California redwood. Examples of each of Sierra's 95 different bullets are mounted on the black simulated leather center and labeled with gold lettering. The bullets are urethane coated to prevent discoloration. The board measures about 18″ x 24″ and weighs about 12 lbs. Price, about $75.00

SPEER
Bullet Board

Speer has just released the latest in their series of bullet boards. Like earlier editions, this new board features another outstanding color painting by noted historical artist, Jack Woodson.

The theme of the board is "The Potlatch," a social event peculiar to several Indian tribes in the Pacific Northwest. The board measures 24″ × 14″ and contains one of all Speer bullets currently in production.
Price $60.00

Speer Reloading Manual No. 10

This latest reloading manual shows the latest, most correct data on rifle and handgun loads, with very comprehensive sections on both. It includes many professional photographs and illustrations. All cartridge drawings have been revised to show both English and metric dimensions and new tables furnish detailed metric and English equivalents. All ballistic data has been retested, confirmed or updated and 200 yard hold-over and energy is shown for all rifle loads. The glossary contains new definitions and is supplemented with detailed illustrations. Has 560 pages, 8,000 powder loads, bullet data, special techniques, etc. The book is hardbound and has plastic coated and soil proof covers to withstand constant use. $10.50

Notes on Chronographs . . .

The chronograph, at one time only for the advanced experimenter, is fast becoming a tool within the reach of more handloaders. Modern production methods and new, improved designs have aroused the interest in this instrument of more and more handloaders. Now many can purchase well-made, dependable instruments capable of accurate readings previously available only to the owners of expensive cumbersome machines. This, of course, is only the beginning. It is not difficult to foresee smaller, less expensive chronographs. Compact transistor types are already here that allow the shooter excellent mobility.

While not yet inexpensive enough for many shooters, the present prices offer an opportunity for clubs or groups to have the facilities available for accurate evaluation of members' loads.

B-Square 75-B

Custom Model 600 Screens

Custom Model 500

Custom Model 900

B-SQUARE Model 75-B Chronograph

An economical unit that is battery operated and can be recharged. It is crystal controlled, and like others, counts time elapsing between the breaking of the start and stop screens. Count numbers are added and velocity is taken from provided chart. There is no "reset" necessary before shooting again. Uses any type screens, checks all velocities from 250 fps to 6000 fps. Comes complete with battery, test screens, screen cables, holders, brackets and instructions. **$189.95**

Extra screens, per hundred **$10.95**

CUSTOM CHRONOGRAPH MODEL 500

A low-cost yet accurate chronograph, this unit is battery powered and compact. Size is 3½" x 6" x 2" and it takes a 6 volt battery giving a minimum life of 150 hours. Standard screen spacing is 2 feet, although it can be ordered with 4 foot spacing for a slight gain in accuracy. Screens are printed breaking-type that must be replaced after each shot. Velocity range is 490 to 5200 fps. Readout is via rotary switch scan and tables for velocity. Time base for the Model 500 is 500 Kc crystal controlled oscillator (250 Kc in 4-foot units). Comes with 50 printed screens, holders, cables and tables. From Custom Chronograph Co. **$79.95**

Extra screens, per hundred **$8.95**

CUSTOM CHRONOGRAPH MODEL 600 Ambient Light Screens

This accessory directly replaces the printed screen holders supplied with the Model 500 chronograph. Automatic gain control in the detectors assures optimum bullet detection whether sky is bright or overcast. Screens are powered by a 9 volt transistor battery with 50-hour life. Sensitive area is oval-shaped 8" x 6".

Price, per pair **$79.95**

CUSTOM CHRONOGRAPH MODEL 900

The Model 900 Ballistic Chronograph reads out velocity directly in feet per second. A single bright number displays the four velocity digits in sequence. For example, the velocity 3192 fps appears as 3, 1, 9, then 2 . . . repeating the sequence until reset. The Model 900 Chronograph also features an instant choice of 2' or 4' screen spacing, and an extended velcocity range of 245 to 5200 fps. This allows the instrument to measure the velocity of pellets and arrows, as well as rifles, handguns, and shotguns. Accuracy assured by a stable ±0.01% quartz crystal. Display reads out screen condition before shooting. Battery powered and very compact. Runs on 6 volt lantern battery. Can be used with printed (standard) or light screens (optional). Price includes 50 screens, screen holders, cables, and complete instructions. **$129.95**

Extra printed screens, per 100 . . . . **$8.95**

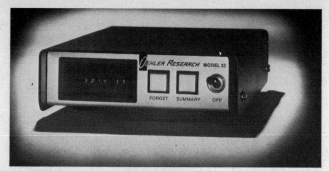

Oehler Model 33

Oehler Model 12

OEHLER Model 33 Chronotach

This new system provides many features not expected in a portable chronograph. Automatic display of both velocity and round number, automatic reset, and an automatic statistical summary of velocity test results are standard features. The statistical summary of up to 255 rounds includes minimum, maximum, extreme variation, average, and standard deviation. Computes velocity for any screen spacing from 1 to 99 feet, or will display time in micro-seconds. It will operate for near 60 hours on the set of flashlight batteries included in the 2″ x 6″ x 10″ aluminum case. Price includes a pair of Skyscreen II detectors, batteries, instructions, and a three-year warranty **$299.95**

OEHLER Model 55 Ballistic Screens

These screens provide a large shooting aperture of 28″ x 16″ with a rectangular sensitive area of approximately 24″ x 14″. Each screen is 36″ high, 18¼″ wide and approximately 3½″ deep. The units are built of steel and can be joined to provide even larger apertures. The output (via BNC connector) is a 12 volt pulse with duration adjustable from 2 to 8 milliseconds. A sensitivity adjustment is provided. Price, per pair **$550.00**

OEHLER Model 34 Chronotach

The Model 34 differs from the Model 33 only in the respect that it is designed for operation with laboratory type screens or other sensors with a +12 volt pulse output signal and that it operates from 120 VAC power instead of batteries.
Price **$400.00**

OEHLER Model 12 Chronograph

The Model 12 is designed for use with the Skyscreen II detectors. It uses a 400,000 Hz oscillator and will measure velocities from 500 to 7,800 fps with the suggested screen spacing of five feet. The unit is exceptionally light and compact measuring only 6½″ x 4″ x 2½″. It operates for approximately 40 hours on a single 9-volt calculator battery. Includes a pair of Skyscreen II detectors, battery, instructions, and three-year warranty **$99.95**

Telepacific TPS-03-E

OEHLER Skyscreen II Detectors

A bullet passing between these detectors and the sky (or other brightly illuminated ceiling) provides the electrical trigger signals required for the Oehler Model 12 or Model 33 chronographs. The detector is roughly the size of a pack of cigarettes and is made of bright orange plastic for visibility. Requires no batteries. These detectors will not work with other chronographs. The price includes 25 foot cable with plug. Price, each **$10.00**

TELEPACIFIC Model TPS-03-E Chronograph

This instrument reads directly in feet-per-second, no velocity tables are required. The shadow cast by the bullet in its passage over two miniature photo-detectors operates both start and stop circuits — no screens to replace. The velocity computer automatically corrects for velocity loss between the muzzle and point of instrumentation. The unit is powered by two self-contained dry batteries. Weight is 6½ lbs., it measures 9″ x 7½″ x 6″. Screen spacing is 4 feet and velocity range is 600 to 4999 fps. Over-all accuracy is ± 1 fps. Comes complete with electroscreen detectors and instructions. Three year warranty. Comes complete with case and screens **$355.00**

Cartridge Boxes and Labels

Cartridge boxes, be they plastic or cardboard, are a great convenience to the handloader, as they provide dust-free storage and a means to keep loads separated. The bottoms of the large-caliber plastic pistol boxes make excellent loading blocks for rifle cartridges.

Labels and record sheets, especially made for handloaders, provide a concise, uniform means of permanently recording all pertinent load data.

MTM Case-Gard 50

MTM Silhouette 100

MTM Rifle Wallet

MTM Case-Gard 100

Fitz Amm-O-Safe. Soft, quiet, polyethylene cartridge boxes. Thumb cut-out. Two rifle, two handgun sizes. High-visibility Hunter Red color. Each . . . **$1.50**

FLAMBEAU Shell and cartridge boxes for popular gauges, calibers. Polyethylene, with snug-fitting tops. Shotgun sizes, **$1.50**; rifle and handgun . **$1.25**

MTM CASE-GARD 20 This 20-round rifle ammo case rides on the belt or slips into the pocket and has a flip-open top for easy access. Comes in 3 sizes for small, medium or large case lengths. Has partitioned wells and the cover keeps out rain and dust. **$1.98**

MTM CASE-GARD Unique ammo boxes made of Polypropylene hold 50 rounds. Hinge is guaranteed for 1 million openings. Positive latch locks top. Load and sight data label inside top. Five sizes available, two for pistol cases and three for rifles. Pistol sizes **$1.49**, rifle-size boxes are. **$3.19**
Same, 60 round capacity. **$3.69**

MTM CASE-GARD 100 This 100-round shotshell case features two loading trays holding 50 rounds each in 12, 16 or 20 gauge. "Tacklebox" latch and stainless steel hinge pin. Measures 7" x 9" x 11". Can also be used to hold factory load boxes, empties, etc. **$11.69**

MTM CASE-GARD MAG 100 Each box holds 100 rounds of handgun ammo. Snap-lok latch, integral hinge. For 38 Spec., 357 Mag., 45 ACP, 41 Mag., 44 Mag. Available in MTM Green or Light Brown **$2.95**

MTM CASE-GARD SILHOUETTE 100 Holds 100 rifle rounds securely. Originally designed for silhouette shooters, it is also excellent for serious ballistic experimenters, varmint hunters (especially prairie dog shooters), big bore competitors, etc. For any caliber from 22-250 to 375 H & H Magnum. Same tough polypropylene as the other MTM boxes. Snap-lok latch, handy folding carrying handle which lies flat for easy storage. Available in MTM Green or Light Brown **$5.10**

MTM CASE-GARD H50 Similar to the Silhouette 100 box except holds 50 rifle rounds. Four sizes available for most calibers from 17 Rem. to 470 Kynoch. There is no #50 case for 378 Wea. Mag., 500 Nitro or 600 Nitro. Available in MTM Green or Light Brown . . **$4.39**

MTM CASE-GARD 9 RIFLE AMMO WALLET Similar to the handgun ammo wallet except these hold 3, 6, or 9 rounds of rifle ammunition. For 22-250 to 8mm Mauser. Available in Dark Brown only.
Three round wallet **$2.49**
Six round wallet **$2.69**
Nine round wallet **$2.99**
Nine round wallet, 22-250 to 375
H & H **$3.10**

MTM CASE-GARD AMMO-WALLET
Slips into hip or coat pocket and flips open for 6, 12 or 18 back-up rounds. Rounds snap into individual compartments and are pressed downward to release. Weighs 2 ozs. empty. Five sizes are available for all pistol ammo.

Six round	**$2.49**
Twelve round	**$2.69**
Eighteen round	**$2.99**

MTM CASE-GARD SHOTSHELL CARRIERS
Made to carry 5, 10, or 25 shotshells. Snap-lok latch, integral hinge. Red color only. For 12 gauge 2¾" and 3" Mag.

Five round	**$2.69**
Ten round	**$2.79**
Twenty-five round, 12 or 20 ga.	**$2.49**

SANDIA
Two-piece non-partitioned fiberboard boxes for most popular bullets and ammunition. Available for centerfire rifle (20 rounds, 30 Carbine 50 rounds) and handgun (50 round capacity). Bullet boxes hold 100 bullets. One-piece units

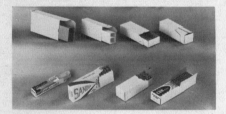

available for 30 Carbine and 45 ACP also. Shotshell boxes for 12, 16, 20 and 410. Two-piece, unprinted boxes **$15.00** per 100 (**$85.00** per 1000), one-piece **$12.20** per 100 (**$56.00** per 1000). Quantity discounts are available.

BRYNIN
Ammo-Info Labels
Self-adhering 2"x3" labels with peel-off backing. Stick permanently to any cartridge container. Space for all pertinent loading data, plus notes. Price per roll of 500 .... **$8.00**

JASCO
Reloader's Labels
Gummed shotshell box labels are printed in red. Space for 14 items of information. Per 40, postpaid ... **$1.25**
Pressure sensitive metallic ammo-box labels adhere firmly—even on plastic. Space for 14 items of information. Printed in red, per 27, postpaid. **$1.25**

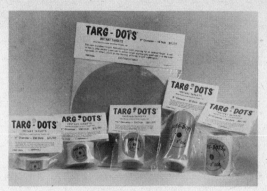

Peterson Targ-Dots

Peterson Labels

PETERSON
Targ-Dots
Targ-Dots come in ½", 1", 1½", 2", 3", and 6" diameters. These fluorescent red, self-sticking aiming points help eliminate fuzzy cross-hairs and blurred iron sights. Size and number of dots per roll follow: ½"/110, 1"/100, 1½"/70, 2"/45, 3"/25, 6"/15—all sell for **$2.15** per package.

Peterson also has self-sticking target pasters in black or white, 200 per box **$2.15**

Slow fire, and timed and rapid fire target centers for 50-foot shooting are available, 3" diameter, 80 targets **$2.15**

Self-sticking 100 and 200-yd. bench-rest squares on 75 and 60 rolls (respectively) are great for making your own targets. Per roll **$2.15**

All items shipped post paid; minimum order **$10.00**

MTM Slip-Top

MTM
Slip-Top Boxes
Standard-type storage boxes made of tough plastic. Each holds 20 rounds of rifle ammo. Red or yellow color.

22-250 to 308 Win.	**$1.29**
270 to 375 Mag.	**$1.29**

Same type of box for handgun calibers is available with either round or square compartments. Red or yellow, 38/357 or 45 Auto sizes.

Square cavity	**$1.29**
Round cavity	**$1.49**

PETERSON
Handload Labels
Pressure sensitive labels that allow you to record pertinent reloading data. Self-sticking to plastic, cardboard and metal cartridge boxes. They come rolled to feed through a typewriter.

2"x2½" (Size C), per 100 ...... **$4.30**
1"x2" (Size B), to fit the end of a cartridge box, 250 per roll **$4.30**

Cartridge Box Size Chart

20 Rounds Rifle 222—30-06	20 Rounds 300 H&H—375 Weatherby	50 Rounds 38 Spl., 22 H., etc.	50 Rounds 44 & 45 pistol
Fitz R. Flambeau 5210, Williams SR-20 or SR-30 Sandia	Fitz M, Flambeau 5211	Fitz 3, Flambeau 5212, Williams SP38WC Sandia	Fitz 4, Flambeau 5213, Sandia

TABLE OF BUCKSHOT SIZES

U.S. designation	Dia. (inches)	No. pellets per lb.	British	Canadian	Belgian	Dutch	French	German
000	0.36	98	LG	—	—	—	—	Posten II
00	0.33	115	SG	SSG	B8	B8	—	Posten III
0	0.32	140	—	—	—	—	—	—
1 Buck	0.30	173	Spec. LG	SG	B6	B6	—	—
2 Buck	0.27	232	—	—	B5	B5	—	Posten IV
3 Buck	0.25	284	SSG	AAAA	—	—	—	—
4 Buck	0.24	344	—	—	—	—	—	—
* FF	0.23	400	—	—	—	—	—	—
* F	0.22	464	—	—	—	—	—	—
* TT	0.21	560	—	—	—	—	—	—
* T	0.20	672	AAA	AAA	OV9	OV9	5/0	5/0

*Obsolete in the U.S. for many years.

SHOTGUN SHELL DIMENSIONAL DATA

Shotgun gauge	Normal bore dia.	Dia. shell body	Dia. rim	Shell length[1]	Type Case[2]							Shot sizes available							
					Paper	Plastic	Brass	Alum.	Buck	R-slug	BB	2	4	5	6	7½	8	9	10
4	0.930	1.025	1.201	4	X							X	X	X			Eley-Kynoch Load		
8	0.835	0.910	1.030	3, 3⅛, 3¼	X							X	X	X			Eley-Kynoch Load		
10	0.775	0.840	0.918	2⅝, 2⅞, 3, 3½	X	X					X	X	X						
12	0.729	0.883	0.876	2, 2⅝, 2¾, 2⅞ and 3	X	X	X	X	X	X	X	X	X	X	X	X	X	X	
14	0.693	0.762	0.820	2-9/16	X		X		Obsolete, no longer U.S. loaded										
16	0.662	0.735	0.810	2¾, 2-9/16	X	X	X		X	X	X	X	X	X	X	X	X	X	
20	0.615	0.681	0.757	2½, 2¾, 2⅞, 3	X	X	X		X	X	X	X	X	X	X	X	X	X	
24	0.579	0.618	0.697	2½	X		X		Obsolete, no longer U.S. loaded										
28	0.550	0.602	0.684	2½	X	X	X		X			X		X	X		X		
32	0.526	0.571	0.653	2½	X		X		Obsolete, no longer U.S. loaded										
410	0.410	0.446	0.528	2, 2½, 3	X	X	X		X			X	X	X	X		X		
9mm	0.309	0.314	0.402	1⅛, 1-9/16	X		X		Loaded by R.W.S. and Alcanz									X	

[1]Some lengths given are obsolete, and all lengths are in opened or fired condition.

[2]Paper and plastic used for modern loaded ammunition. Empty paper, brass and aluminum cases available for handloading. Alcan furnishes paper or brass cases for some obsolete gauges.

TABLE OF SHOT SIZES

U.S. designation	Dia. (inches)	No. pellets per oz.[1]	British	Canadian	Belgian	Dutch	French	German
* BBB	0.19	50	—	—	—	—	—	—
BB	0.18	58	—	—	—	—	—	—
B (Air Rifle)	0.175	65	BB	Air Rifle	OV3	OV3	1	1
* 1	0.16	73	—	—	—	—	—	—
2	0.15	88	—	—	—	—	—	—
* 3	0.14	109	1	2	1	1	3	3
4	0.13	136	3	4	3	3	4	4
5	0.12	172	4	5	4	4	5	5
6	0.11	223	5	6	5	5	6	6
* 7	0.10	299	6	—	6	6	—	—
7½	0.095	345	7	7½	7	7	7	7
8	0.09	409	8	8	8	8	8	8
9	0.08	585	9	9	9	9	9	9
10	0.07	868	—	—	—	—	—	—
* 11	0.06	1380	—	—	—	—	—	—
* 12	0.05	2835	—	—	—	—	—	—
* Dust	0.04	4565	—	—	—	—	—	—

*Obsolete in factory loads in the U.S., however shot sizes below No. 10 are used in rimfire shot cartridges and others.

[1]Chilled shot.

HANDLOADER'S TRADE DIRECTORY

A

Advance Car Mover Co., Inc., P.O. Box 1181, Appleton, WI 54911
Alcan (see Smith & Wesson Ammunition Co.)
American Wad (see: P&P Tool Co.)
Anderson Mfg. Co., Royal, IA 52357
Aurand's, 229 E. 3rd St., Lewistown, PA 17044
Austin Powder Co. (See Red Diamond Distr. Co.)

B

BRI (Ballistic Research Industries), see: Heppler's Gun Shop
B-Square Co., Box 11281, Ft. Worth, TX 76110
Ballard, Bill, 830 Miles Ave., Billings, MT 59101
Ballistek, Weapon Systems Div., 3450 Antelope Dr., Lake Havasu City, AZ 86403
Ballistic Prods., P.O. Box 488, 2105 Shaughnessy Circle, Long Lake, MN 55356
Bear Reloaders Inc., 2110 1st National Tower, Akron, OH 44308
Belding & Mull, 100 N. 4th St., Philipsburg, PA 16866
B.E.L.L. (see Brass Extrusion Labs.)
Berdon Machine Co., Box 483, Hobart, WA 98025
Birchwood-Casey, 7900 Fuller Rd., Eden Prairie, MN 55344
Blackhawk SAA Mtn., Richard Miller, 1337 Delmar Parkway, Aurora, CO 80010
Blackhawk Small Arms Ammunition East, C2274 POB, Loves Park, IL 61131
Blackhawk Small Arms Ammunication West, Box 285, Hiawatha, KS 66434
Bonanza Sports Inc., 412 Western Ave., Faribault, MN 55021
Boos, Richard, 2178 Nichols Ave., Stratford, CT 06497
Bowlin, Gene, Rt. 1, Box 90, Snyder, TX 79549
Brass Extrusion Laboratories, Ltd., 800 W. Maple Lane, Bensenville, IL 60106
Brown Precision Inc., 7786 Molinos Ave., P.O. Box 270, W. Los Molinos, CA 96055
Bryant, A.V., 72 Whiting Rd., E. Hartford, CT 06118
Brynin, Milton, 214 E. Third St., Mt. Vernon, NY 10710

C

C'Arco, P.O. Box 2043, San Bernardino, CA 92406 (Ransom Rest)
CCI (see Omark)
C-H Tool & Die Corp., 106 N. Harding St., Owen, WI 54461
Camdex, Inc., 2228 Fourteen Mile Rd., Warren, MI 48092
Campbell, Russell, 219 Leisure Dr., San Antonio, TX 78201
Carbide Die & Mfg. Co., P.O. Box 226, Covina, CA 91724 (Lifetyme Dies)
Carter Gun Works, 2211 Jefferson Park Ave., Charlottesville, VA 22903
Cascade Cartridge, Inc. (see Omark CCI, Inc.)
Catco-Ambush, Inc.; P.O. Box 300, Corte Madera, CA 94926
Central Products f. Shooters (CPS), 435 Rt. 18, East Brunswick, NJ 08816
Chevron Case Master, R.R. 1, Ottawa, IL 61350
Chopie Mfg. Inc., 531 Copeland, La Crosse, WI 54601
Clenzoil, Box 1226, Sta. C, Canton, OH 44708
Clymer (See Sport Flite Mfg.)
Coats, Lester, 416 Simpson Ave., No. Bend, OR 97459

Container Dev'pt. Corp. (See Lewisystem)
Continental Kite & Key Co., Box 40, Broomall, PA 19008
Cooper-Woodward, Box 972, Riverside, CA 92502
Corbin Mfg. & Supply, Inc., P.O. Box 758, PhoenixR 97535
Custom Chronograph Co., Box 1061, Brewster, WA 98812
Custom Products, 686 Baldwin St., Meadville, PA 16335

D-E

DWM (see Dynamit Nobel)
Dewey, J., Mfg. Co., 186 Skyview Dr., Southbury, CT 06488
Dillon Precision Prods., Inc., 7755 E. Gelding Dr., Suite 106, Scottsdale, AZ 85260
Diverter Arms Inc., P.O. Box 22084, Houston, TX 77036
Division Lead Co., 7742 W. 61st Place, Summit, IL 60502
DuPont Sales Div., Wilmington, DE 19898
Dynamit Nobel of America, Inc., 105 Stonehurst Ct., Northvale, NJ 07647 (DWM, RWS)
Eagle Products Co., 1520 Adelia Ave., So. El Monte, CA 91733
Edmisten Co. Inc., P.O. Box 1293, Boone, NC 28607
Efemes Enterprises, P.O. Box 122M, Bay Shore, NY 11706
Elk Mountain Shooters Supply, 1719 Marie, Pasco, WA 99301
EMCO-Lux, 2050 Fairwood Ave., Columbus, OH 43207 (Unimat 3)
English, W.H., 4411 So. W. 100th, Seattle, WA 98146 (Pak-Tool)
Epps, Ellwood (Orillia), Ltd., Hwy 11 North, Orillia, Ont. L3V6H3, Canada

F

Farmer Bros., 1616-15th St., Eldora, IA 50627
Federal Cartridge Corp., 2700 Foshay Tower, Minneapolis, MN 55402
Fitz, 653 N. Hagar St., San Fernando, CA 91340
Flambeau Products Corp., Middlefield, OH 44062
Forster Products, 82 E. Lanark Ave., Lanark, IL 61046
Frontier Cartridge Co., Inc., Box 1848, Grand Island, NE 68801
Fullmer, Geo. M., 2499 Mavis St., Oakland, CA 94601

G

Gene's Gun Shop, Rt. 1, Box 890, Snyder, TX 79549
Godfrey Reloading Supply, R.R. #1, Box 668, Brighton, IL 62012
Gopher Shooter's Supply, Box 278, Faribault, MN 55021
Green Bay Bullets, 233 N. Ashland, Green Bay, WI 54303 (Cast)
Gun Clinic, 81 Kale St., Mahtomedi, MN 55115
The Gun Shop, 62778 Spring Creek Rd., Montrose, CO 81401
Gussert Bullet & Cartridge Co., Inc., P.O. Box 3945, Green Bay, WI 54303

H

Hardin Specialty Distr., P.O. Box 338, Radcliff, KY 40160
Hart, Robert & Son, 401 Montgomery St., Nescopeck, PA 18635
Henriksen Tool Co., Inc., P.O. Box 668, Phoenix, OR 97535
Hensley & Gibbs, Box 10, Murphy, OR 97533
Heppler's Gun Shop, 6000-B Soquel Ave., Santa Cruz, CA 95062
Hercules Inc., 910 Market St., Wilmington, DE 19899
Hewitt, John C., P.O. Box 007, La Crescenta, CA 91214 (Lazy-X Notebook)
Hoch, Richard, 62778 Spring Creek Rd., Montrose, CO 81401
Hodgdon Powder Co., 7710 W. 63rd St., Shawnee-Mission, KS 66202
Hoffman Prods., P.O. Box 853, Lake Forest, IL 60045
Hollywood Reloading (see Whitney Sales Co.)
Hornady Mfg. Co., Box 1848, Grand Island, NE 68801
House, N.E., 195 West High St., E. Hampton, CT 06424 (Zinc bases)
Hulme Firearm Service, Box 83, Millbrae, CA 94030
Huntington's Die Specialties, P.O. Box 991, Oroville, CA 95965
Hutton Rifle Ranch, 1802 S. Oak Park Dr., Rolling Hills, Tucson, AZ 85710
Hy-Score, 200 Tillary St., Brooklyn, NY 11201 (RWS blank cartridges/air gun pellets)

I-J-K

I.S.W., 106 E. Cairo Dr., Tempe, AZ 85282
Independent Mach. & Gun Shop, 1416 N. Hayes, Pocatello, ID 83201
Ivy Armament, P.O. Box 10, Greendale, WI 53129
J & G Rifle Ranch, Box S80, Turner, MT 59542
JASCO, Box 49751, Los Angeles, CA 90049
Javelina Prod., Box 337, San Bernadino, CA 92402
Jet-Aer Corp., 100 Sixth Ave., Paterson, NJ 07524
Johnson, Norman, Rt. 1, Box 29A, Plum City, WI 54761
Jones, Neil, 686 Baldwin St., Meadville, PA 16335
Kexplore, Box 22084, Houston, TX 77027
Kuharsky Bros., Inc. (see Modern Industries)

L

L.L.F. Die Shop, 1281 Highway 99 N., Eugene, OR 97402
Lac-Cum Bullet Puller, Star Route, Box 242, Apollo, PA 15613
Lachmiller Eng. Co. (see RCBS)
Lage Uniwad Co., 1102 N. Washington St., Eldora, IA 50627
Laszlo, S.E., 200 Tillary St., Brooklyn, NY 11201
Lazy-X Notebook (see John C. Hewitt)
LeClear Industries, P.O. Box 484, Royal Oak, MI 48068
Lee Precision, Inc., 4275 Hwy U, Hartford, WI 53027
Lenz Products Co., Box 1226, Sta. C., Canton, OH 44708
Lewisystems, Menasha Corp., 426 Montgomery St., Watertown, WI 53094
Lifetyme Dies (see Carbide Die & Mfg.)
Lincoln, Dean, Box 1886, Farmington, NM 87401
Liquid Wrench (see Radiator Specialties)
Ljutic Industries, P.O. Box 2117, Yakima, WA 98902 (Mono-wads)
Lock's Philadelphia Gun Exch., 6700 Rowland Ave., Philadelphia, PA 19149
Lyman Products, Rte. 147, Middlefield, CT 06455

M

M&N Bullet Lube, Box 495, Jefferson St., Madras, OR 97741
MTM Molded Prod., 5680 Webster St., Dayton, OH 45414
Magma Eng. Co., Box 881, Chandler, AZ 85224
Marble Arms, 420 Industrial Park, Gladstone, MI 49837
Mariotti, Judson E., Beauty Hill Rd., Barrington, NH 03825
Marmel Prods., P.O. Box 97, Utica, MI 48087 (Marvelube, Marvelux)
Marquart Precision Co., Box 1740, Prescott, AZ 86302
Mayville Eng. Co., 715 South St., Mayville, WI 53050 (MEC)
McKillen & Heyer, Inc., 37603 Arlington Dr., Box 627, Willoughby, OH 44094
McLean, Paul, 2670 Lakeshore Blvd. W., Toronto, Ont. M8V 1G8, Canada
Mequon Reloading Corp., 46 E. Jackson, Hartford, WI 53027
Merit Gun Sight Co., P.O. Box 995, Sequim, WA 98382
Michael's Antique, Box 233, Copiague, L.I., NY 11726 (Balle Blondeau)
Micro Ammunition Co., P.O. Box 117, Mesilla Park, NM 88047 (Micro-Lube)

Mirror-Lube, P.O. Box 693, San Juan Capistrano, CA 92675
Moderntools, 1617 W. McNab Rd., Ft. Lauderdale, FL 33309
Modern Industries, Inc., 613 W 11, Erie, PA 16501
Molykote, 65 Harvard, Stamford, CT 06904
Multi-Scale Charge Ltd., 3269 Niagara Falls Blvd., No. Tonawanda, NY 14120

N

National Lead Co., Box 831, Perth Amboy, NJ 08861
Navy Arms Co., 689 Bergen Blvd., Ridgefield, NJ 07657
Neise, Karl A., Inc., 1671 W. McNab Rd., Ft. Lauderdale, FL 33309
Norma-Precision, 798 Cascadilla St., Ithaca, NY 14850
Northeast Industrial, Inc. (NEI), 2516 Wyoming, El Paso, TX 79903

O-P

Oehler Research, Inc., P.O. Box 9135, Austin, TX 78766
Ohaus (write RCBS)
Omark-CCI, Inc., Box 856, Lewiston, ID 83501
The Oster Group, 50 Sims Ave., Providence, RI 02909 (alloys f. casting bull.)
Outers Laboratories, Inc., P.O. Box 37, Onalaska, WI 54650
PMC, Patton and Morgan Corp., 6 E. 45th St., 4th Floor, New York, 10017
P & P Tool Co., 125 W. Market St., Morrison, IL 61270
Pacific Tool Co., P.O. Drawer 2048, Ordnance Plant Rd., Grand Island, NE 68801
Pak-Tool Co., 4411 S.W. 100th, Seattle, WA 98146
Peterson Labels, P.O. Box 186, Redding Ridge, CT 06876
Pindell, Ferris, R.R. 3, Box 205, Connersville, IN 47337
Plum City Ball. Range, Rt. 1, Box 29A, Plum City, WI 54761
Pomeroy, Robert, Morison Ave, Corinth, ME 04227
Ponsness-Warren, Inc., P.O. Box 8, Rathdrum, ID 83858
Powley, Marian, Petra Lane, R.R. 1, Eldridge, IA 52748
Precise Alloys Inc., 69 Kinkel St., Westbury, NY 11590
Precision Ammunition & Rel., 122 Hildenboro Square, Agincourt, Ont. M1W 1Y3, Canada

Q

Quinetics Corp., Box 29007, San Antonio, TX 78229

R

RCBS, P.O. Box 1919, Oroville, CA 95965
Radiator Specialties, Box 10628, Charlotte, NC 28201
Rainel de P.R., 1353 Boston Post Rd., Madison, CT 06443
Reardon Prod., 103 W. Market St., Morrison, IL 61270
Red Diamond Distributing Co., 1304 Snowdon Dr., Knoxville, TN 37912 (black powder)
Redding Inc., 114 Starr Rd., Cortland, NY 13045
Reloaders Equipment Co., 4680 High St., Ecorse, MI 48229
Remington Arms Co., Bridgeport, CT 06602
RIG Products Co., 21320 Deering Ct., Canoga Park, CA 91304
Rochester Lead Works, 76 Anderson Ave., Rochester, NY 14607
Rorschach Prec. Prods., Box 1613, Irving, TX 75060

S

SAECO, P.O. Box 778, Carpenteria, CA 93013
Sandia Die & Cartridge Co., Rte. 5, Box 5400, Albuquerque, NM 87123
Santa Anita Eng. Co. (see SAECO)
Savage Arms, Springdale Rd., Westfield, MA 01085
Shassere, P.O. Box 35865, Houston, TX 77096
Shiloh Products, 37 Potter St., Farmingdale, NY 11735
Sil's Gun Products, 490 Sylvan Dr., Washington, PA 15301
Simmons, Jerry, 715 Middlebury St., Goshen, IN 46526
Smith & Wesson Ammunition Co., 2399 Forman Rd., Rock Creek, OH 44084
Somers, J.A. Co., P.O. Box 49751, Los Angeles, CA 90049
Speer, Inc., Box 896, Lewiston, ID 83501
Sport Flite Mfg. Co., 2520 Industrial Row, Troy, MI 48084
SSK Industries, Rt. 1, Della Dr., Bloomingdale, OH 43910

Stanley, D.E., Box 323, Arvin, CA 93203
Star Machine Works, 418 10th Ave., San Diego, CA 92101
Sundtek Co., P.O. Box 744, Springfield, OR 97477
Super Vel, Hamilton Rd., Rt. 2, Fond du Lac, WI 54935

T-U-V

T.E.S., Inc., 2200 Bott St., Colorado Springs, CO 80904
TNT (see Independent Machine & Sun Shop)
TSI (see Testing Systems, Inc.)
T&T Products, Inc., 630 Hwy. 14 East, Rochester MN 55901 (Meyer shotgun slug)
Tamarack Prods., Inc., Box 224, Barrington, IL 60010
Taracorp Industries, 16th & Cleveland Blvd., Granite City, IL 62040 (Lawrence Brand lead shot)
Telepacific Electronics Co., Inc., P.O. Box 1329, San Marcos, CA 92069
Tepeco, P.O. Box 502, Moss Point, MS 39563 (Tepeco Speed-Meter)
Testing Systems, Inc., 220 Pegasus Ave., Northvale, NJ 07647
Texan Reloaders, Inc., 444 Cip St., Watseka, IL 60970
Time Electro Systems, Inc., 2200 Bott St., Colorado Springs, CO 80904
Trico Plastics, 590 S. Vincent Ave., Azusa, CA 91702
United Cartridge Co., P.O. Box 604, Valley Industrial Park, Casa Grande, AR 85222 (P.C. wads)
Vibra-Tek, 2200 Bott St., Colorado Springs, CO 80904
Vitt/Boos, Raymond Boos, 2178 Nichols Ave., Stratford, CT 06497

W-X-Y-Z

Walker Mfg. Inc., 8296 S. Channel, Harsen's Island, MI 48028 (Berdan decapper)
Wammes Guns Inc., 236 N. Hayes St., Bellefontaine, OH 43311 (Jim's powder baffles)
Weatherby Inc., 2781 Firestone Blvd., South Gate, CA 90280
Webster Scale Co., Box 188, Sebring, FL 33870
White, H.P., Laboratory, 3114 Scarboro Rd., Street, MD 21154
Whitney Sales Co., Box 875, Reseda, CA 91335 (Hollywood)
Whits Shooting Stuff, Box 1340, Cody, WY 82414
Williams Gun Sight Co., Davison, MI 48423
Wilson, L.E., Box 324, Cashmere, WA 98815
Winchester-Western Div., Olin, New Haven, CT 06504
Xelex Ltd., Box 543, Renfrew, Ont. K7V 4B1, Canada
York, M., 5508 Griffith Rd., Gaithersburg, MD 20760 (pressure tool)
Zenith Enterprises, 361 Flagler Rd., Nordland, WA 98358

CUSTOM AMMUNITION MAKERS

Some of the firms below offer custom loads for pistol, rifle and shotgun, while others may load only one type or the other. Write to them for their list or state your needs.

American Pistol Bullet, 133 Blue Bell Rd., Greensboro, NC 27406
Ballard, Bill, P.O. Box 656, Billings, MT 59103 (ctgl. 25c)
Beal's Bullets, 170 W. Marshall Rd., Lansdowne, PA 19050 (Auto Mag specialists)
Bell's Gun & Sport Shop, 3309-19 Mannheim Rd., Franklin Park, IL 60131
Brass Extrusion Labs. Ltd., 800 W. Maple Lane, Bensenville, IL 60106
Campbell, Russell, 219 Leisure Dr., San Antonio, TX 78201
C. W. Cartridge Co., 71 Hackensack St., Wood-Ridge, NJ 07075

Collectors Shotshell Arsenal, E. Tichy, 365 S. Moore, Lakewood, CO 80226
Crown City Arms, P.O. Box 1126, Courtland, NY 13045
Cumberland Arms, Rt. 1, Shafer Rd., Blantons Chapel, Manchester, TN 37355
Ellis, E.W., RFD 1, Box 139, Corinth, NY 12822
Epps, Ellwood, Hiway 11 North, Orillia, Ont. L3V 6H3, Canada
Gonzalez, Roman B., P.O. Box 370, Monticello, NY 12701
Gussert Bullet & Cartridge Co., P.O. Box 3945, Green Bay, WI 54303
Jensen's Custom Ammunition, 5146 E. Pima, Tucson, AZ 85716
KTW Inc., 710 Foster Pk. Rd., Lorain, OH 44053
Keeler, R.H., 817 "N" St., Port Angeles, WA 98362
Kennon, TC., 5408 Biffle Rd., Stone Mtn., GA 30082
Lincoln, Dean, P.O. Box 1886, Farmington, NM 87401
Lindsley Arms Cartridge Co., P.O. Box 1287, 408 Northeast Third St., Boynton Beach, FL 33435
Mansfield, Paul G., Box 83, New Boston, NH 03070
Numrich Arms Corp., 203 Broadway, W. Hurley, NY 12491
Pomeroy, Robert, Morison Ave., East Corinth, ME 04427
Precision Ammunition & Reloading, 122 Hildenboro Sq., Agincourt, Ont. M1W 1Y3, Canada
Precision Prods. of Wash., Inc., N. 311 Walnut Rd., Spokane, WA 99206 (Exammo)
Sailer, Anthony, 707 W. Third St., P.O. Box L, Owen, WI 54460
Sanders, Bob, 2358 Tyler Lane, Louisville, KY 40205
Spence, George, P.O. Box 222, Steele, MO 63877 (boxer-primed cartridges)
The 3-D Company, Box 142, Doniphan, NE 68832 (reloaded police ammo)

BULLET MAKERS

Some of the manufacturers below make bullets for both rifle and handgun, while others supply only one type or the other. Write them for complete lists.

The Alberts Corp., P.O. Box 157, Franklin Lake, NJ 07417
Amm-O-Mart, P.O. Box 125, Hawkesbury, Ont. K6A 2R8, Canada (Curry Bullets)
Barnes Bullets, P.O. Box 215, American Fork, UT 84003
Bitterroot Bullet Co., Box 412, Lewiston, ID 83501
Clark, Kenneth E., 18738 Highway 99, Madera, CA 93637
Cumberland Arms, Rt. 1, Shafer Rd., Blantons Chapel, Manchester, TN 37355
Curry Bullets (see Amm-O-Mart, Canada)
Elk Mountain Shooters Supply, 1719 Marie, Pasco, WA 99301
Forty-Five Ranch Ent., 119 So. Main St., Miami, OK 74534
Godfrey, Lynn (see Elk Mountain)
Godfrey Rel. Supply, R.R. 1, Box 668, Brighton, IL 52012 (cast bullets)
Gussert Bullet & Cartride Co., Inc., P.O. Box 3945, Green Bay, WI 54303
Hornady Mfg. Co., Box 1848, Grand Island, NE 68801
House, N.E. Co., 195 West High St., E. Hampton, CT 024 (Zinc bases only)
J-4, Inc., 1700 Via Burton, Anaheim, CA 92806
Jaro Bullet Co., P.O. Box 6125, Padadena, TX 77506
KTW Inc., 710 Foster Park Rd., Lorain, OH 44053
L.L.F. Die Shop, 1281 Hwy. 99 North, Eugene, OR 97402
Lomont Precision Bullets, 4421 S. Wayne Ave., Ft. Wayne, IN 46807
Lyman Prods., Route 147, Middlefield, CT 06455
Markell, Inc., 4115 Judah St., San Francisco, CA 94122
Miller Trading Co., 20 S. Front St., Wilmington, NC 28401
Norma-Precision, 798 Cascadilla St., Ithaca, NY 14850
Nosler Bullets, P.O. Box 688, Beaverton, OR 97005
Pomeroy, Robert, Morison Ave., East Corinth, ME 04427
Remington Arms Co., 939 Barnum Ave., Bridgeport, CT 06602
Sandia Die & Cartridge Co., Rte. 5, Box 5400, Albuquerque, NM 87123
Sierra Bullets, 10532 Painter Ave., Santa Fe Springs, CA 90670
Speer Products, Box 896, Lewiston, ID 83501
Stocking, C.H., Rte. 3, Box 195, Hutchinson, MN 55350
Taylor Bullets, 327 E. Hutchins Pl., San Antonio, TX 78221 (cast bullets)
Winchester-Western, 275 Winchester Ave., New Haven, CT 06504
Zero Bullet Co., P.O. Box 1188, Cullman, AL 35055

INDEX